business 7e

O.C. Ferrell
Auburn University

Geoffrey A. Hirt
DePaul University

Linda Ferrell
Auburn University

McGraw Hill

business

EXECUTIVE PORTFOLIO MANAGER: **MEREDITH FOSSEL**

PRODUCT DEVELOPER: **HALEY BURMEISTER**

EXECUTIVE MARKETING MANAGER: **NICOLE YOUNG**

SENIOR PROJECT MANAGER, CORE CONTENT: **KATHRYN D. WRIGHT**

SENIOR PROJECT MANAGER, ASSESSMENT & MEDIA CONTENT: **BRUCE GIN**

SENIOR BUYER: **LAURA FULLER**

SENIOR DESIGNER: **MATT DIAMOND**

LEAD CONTENT LICENSING SPECIALIST: **JACOB SULLIVAN**

COVER IMAGE: **MAXIPHOTO/GETTY IMAGES**

COMPOSITOR: **SPI GLOBAL**

M: BUSINESS, SEVENTH EDITION

1 2 3 4 5 6 7 8 9 LMN 24 23 22 21

ISBN 978-1-260-26256-8 (bound edition)
MHID 1-260-26256-1 (bound edition)

ISBN 978-1-264-12621-7 (loose-leaf edition)
MHID 1-264-12621-2 (loose-leaf edition)

Library of Congress Control Number: 2020920310

mheducation.com/highered

authors

O.C. FERRELL

O.C. Ferrell is the James T. Pursell Sr. Eminent Scholar in Ethics and Director of the Center for Ethical Organizational Cultures in the Raymond J. Harbert College of Business, Auburn University. He was formerly Distinguished Professor of Leadership and Business Ethics at Belmont University and University Distinguished Professor at the University of New Mexico. He has also been on the faculties of the University of Wyoming, Colorado State University, University of Memphis, Texas A&M University, Illinois State University, and Southern Illinois University. He received his PhD in marketing from Louisiana State University.

Dr. Ferrell is past president of the Academy of Marketing Science. He is past president of the Academic Council of the American Marketing Association and chaired the American Marketing Association Ethics Committee. Under his leadership, the committee developed the AMA Code of Ethics and the AMA Code of Ethics for Marketing on the Internet. In addition, he is a former member of the Academy of Marketing Science Board of Governors and is a Society of Marketing Advances and Southwestern Marketing Association Fellow and an Academy of Marketing Science Distinguished Fellow. He served for nine years as the vice president of publications for the Academy of Marketing Science. In 2010, he received a Lifetime Achievement Award from the Macromarketing Society and a special award for service to doctoral students from the Southeast Doctoral Consortium. He received the Harold Berkman Lifetime Service Award from the Academy of Marketing Science and the Cutco Vector Distinguished Marketing Educator Award from the Academy of Marketing Science.

Dr. Ferrell has been involved in entrepreneurial engagements, co-founding Print Avenue in 1981, providing a solution-based printing company. He has been a consultant and served as an expert witness in legal cases related to marketing and business ethics litigation. He has conducted training for a number of global firms, including General Motors. His involvement with direct selling companies includes serving on the Academic Advisory Committee and as a fellow for the Direct Selling Education Foundation.

Dr. Ferrell is the co-author of 20 books and more than 100 published articles and papers. His articles have been published in the *Journal of Marketing Research*, *Journal of Marketing*, *Journal of Business Ethics*, *Journal of Business Research*, *Journal of the Academy of Marketing Science*, *AMS Review*, and the *Journal of Public Policy & Marketing*, as well as other journals.

GEOFFREY A. HIRT

Geoffrey A. Hirt of DePaul University previously taught at Texas Christian University and Illinois State University, where he was chairman of the Department of Finance and Law. At DePaul, he was chairman of the Finance Department from 1987 to 1997 and held the title of Mesirow Financial Fellow. He developed the MBA program in Hong Kong and served as director of international initiatives for the College of Business, supervising overseas programs in Hong Kong, Prague, and Bahrain, and was awarded the Spirit of St. Vincent DePaul award for his contributions to the university. Dr. Hirt directed the Chartered Financial Analysts (CFA) study program for the Investment Analysts Society of Chicago from 1987 to 2003. He has been a visiting professor at the University of Urbino in Italy, where he still maintains a relationship with the economics department. He received his PhD in finance from the University of Illinois at Champaign-Urbana, his MBA at Miami University of Ohio, and his BA from Ohio Wesleyan University.

Dr. Hirt is currently on the Dean's Advisory Board and Executive Committee of DePaul's School of Music. He served on the James C. Tyree Foundation Board and Grant Committee from 2012 to 2016. Dr. Hirt is past president and a current member of the Midwest Finance Association and a former editor of the *Journal of Financial Education*. He belongs to the Pacific Pension Institute, an organization of public pension funds, private equity firms, and international organizations such as the Asian Development Bank, the IMF, and the European Bank for Reconstruction and Development.

Dr. Hirt is widely known for his textbook *Foundations of Financial Management*, published by McGraw-Hill/Irwin. This book, in its seventeenth edition, has been used in more than 31 countries and translated into more than 14 different languages. Additionally, Dr. Hirt is well known for his textbook *Fundamentals of Investment Management*, also published by McGraw-Hill/Irwin and now in its tenth edition. Dr. Hirt enjoys golf, swimming, music, and traveling with his wife, who is a pianist and opera coach.

LINDA FERRELL

Linda Ferrell is Chair and Professor of the Marketing Department in the Raymond J. Harbert College of Business, Auburn University. She was formerly Distinguished Professor of Leadership and Business Ethics at Belmont University. She completed her PhD in business administration, with a concentration in management, at the University of Memphis. She has taught at the University of Tampa, Colorado State University, University of Northern Colorado, University of Memphis, University of Wyoming, and the University of New Mexico. She has also team-taught classes at Thammasat University in Bangkok, Thailand.

Her work experience as an account executive for McDonald's and Pizza Hut's advertising agencies supports her teaching of advertising, marketing strategy, marketing ethics, and marketing principles. She has published in the *Journal of Public Policy & Marketing*, *Journal of Business Research*, *Journal of the Academy of Marketing Science*, *Journal of Business Ethics*, *AMS Review*, *Journal of Academic Ethics*, *Journal of Marketing Education*, *Marketing Education Review*, *Journal of Teaching Business Ethics*, *Marketing Management Journal*, and *Case Research Journal*, and she is co-author of *Business Ethics: Ethical Decision Making and Cases* (thirteenth edition), *Management* (fourth edition), and *Business and Society* (seventh edition).

Dr. Ferrell is the past president of the Academy of Marketing Science and a past president for the Marketing Management Association. She is a member of the NASBA Center for the Public Trust Board, on the Mannatech Board of Directors, and on the college advisory board for Cutco/Vector. She is also on the Board, Executive Committee, and Academic Advisory Committee of the Direct Selling Education Foundation. She has served as an expert witness in cases related to advertising, business ethics, and consumer protection.

Focused, Exciting, Applicable, Happening

M: Business, seventh edition, offers faculty and students a **focused** resource that is **exciting, applicable,** and **happening!** What sets this learning program apart from the competition? An unrivaled mixture of exciting content and resources blended with application focused text and activities, and fresh topics and examples that show students what is happening in the world of business today!

Our product contains all of the essentials that most students should learn in a semester. *M: Business* has, since its inception, delivered a focused presentation of the essential material needed to teach introduction to business. An unrivaled mixture of exciting content and resources, application-focused content and activities, and fresh topics and examples that show students what is happening in the world of business today set this text apart!

FOCUSED!

It's easy for students taking their first steps into business to become overwhelmed. Longer products try to solve this problem by chopping out examples or topics to make ad hoc shorter editions. *M: Business* carefully builds just the right mix of coverage and applications to give your students a firm grounding in business principles. Where other products have you sprinting through the semester to get everything in, Ferrell/Hirt/Ferrell allows you the breathing space to explore topics and incorporate other activities that are important to you and your students. The exceptional resources and the *Active Classroom Resource Manual* support you in this effort every step of the way.

EXCITING

It's exciting to see students succeed! It's exciting to see more As and Bs in a course without grade inflation. Ferrell/Hirt/ Ferrell makes these results possible for your course with its integrated learning package that is proven effective, tailored to each individual student, and easy to use.

APPLICABLE

When students see how content applies to them, their life, their career, and the world around them, they are more engaged in the course. *M: Business* helps students maximize their learning efforts by setting clear objectives; delivering interesting cases and examples; focusing on core issues; and providing engaging activities to apply concepts, build skills, and solve problems.

HAPPENING!

Because it isn't tied to the revision cycle of a larger book, *M: Business* inherits no outdated or irrelevant examples or coverage. Everything in the seventh edition reflects the very latest developments in the business world—such as the COVID-19 (coronavirus) pandemic which resulted in high unemployment, stress on small businesses, and disruption in supply chains. In addition, ethics and social responsibility have become much more important as firms are being rewarded for having a social conscience and addressing unrest and conflicts in society.

Instructors: Student Success Starts with You

Tools to enhance your unique voice

Want to build your own course? No problem. Prefer to use our turnkey, prebuilt course? Easy. Want to make changes throughout the semester? Sure. And you'll save time with Connect's auto-grading too.

65%
Less Time Grading

Laptop: McGraw Hill; Woman/dog: George Doyle/Getty Images

Study made personal

Incorporate adaptive study resources like SmartBook® 2.0 into your course and help your students be better prepared in less time. Learn more about the powerful personalized learning experience available in SmartBook 2.0 at **www.mheducation.com/highered/connect/smartbook**

Affordable solutions, added value

Make technology work for you with LMS integration for single sign-on access, mobile access to the digital textbook, and reports to quickly show you how each of your students is doing. And with our Inclusive Access program you can provide all these tools at a discount to your students. Ask your McGraw Hill representative for more information.

Padlock: Jobalou/Getty Images

Solutions for your challenges

A product isn't a solution. Real solutions are affordable, reliable, and come with training and ongoing support when you need it and how you want it. Visit **www. supportateverystep.com** for videos and resources both you and your students can use throughout the semester.

Checkmark: Jobalou/Getty Images

Students: Get Learning that Fits You

Effective tools for efficient studying

Connect is designed to make you more productive with simple, flexible, intuitive tools that maximize your study time and meet your individual learning needs. Get learning that works for you with Connect.

Study anytime, anywhere

Download the free ReadAnywhere app and access your online eBook or SmartBook 2.0 assignments when it's convenient, even if you're offline. And since the app automatically syncs with your eBook and SmartBook 2.0 assignments in Connect, all of your work is available every time you open it. Find out more at **www.mheducation.com/readanywhere**

> *"I really liked this app—it made it easy to study when you don't have your text-book in front of you."*
>
> - Jordan Cunningham,
>   Eastern Washington University

Calendar: owattaphotos/Getty Images

Everything you need in one place

Your Connect course has everything you need—whether reading on your digital eBook or completing assignments for class, Connect makes it easy to get your work done.

Learning for everyone

McGraw Hill works directly with Accessibility Services Departments and faculty to meet the learning needs of all students. Please contact your Accessibility Services Office and ask them to email accessibility@mheducation.com, or visit **www.mheducation.com/about/accessibility** for more information.

New to This Edition

As always, when revising this material for the current edition, all examples, figures, and statistics have been updated to incorporate any recent developments that affect the world of business. Additionally, content was updated to ensure the most pertinent topical coverage is provided.

Here are the highlights for each chapter:

Chapter one

THE DYNAMICS OF BUSINESS AND ECONOMICS

- New boxed features describing real-world business issues
- Updated unemployment and GDP data
- New stats on inflation
- New stats on women in the workforce
- New section on technology and the economy
- New examples related to the COVID-19 (coronavirus) pandemic
- New figure depicting artificial intelligence in relation to its enablers

Chapter two

BUSINESS ETHICS AND SOCIAL RESPONSIBILITY

- New boxed features describing issues in business ethics and social responsibility
- New data on global trust in different industries
- New examples about ethical issues in the sharing economy
- New content about aggressive financial or business objectives
- New example of a bribery scandal
- Expanded timeline of ethical and socially responsible activities

Chapter two appendix:

THE LEGAL AND REGULATORY ENVIRONMENT

- New boxed feature describing issues in the legal and regulatory environment
- New examples of ethical issues facing today's businesses
- New content about data privacy laws

Chapter three

BUSINESS IN A BORDERLESS WORLD

- New boxed features describing issues in international business
- Updated list of top 10 countries with which the United States has trade deficits/surpluses
- New content on the United States–China trade war
- Updated Euro Zone details
- New details on the EU's General Data Protection Regulation (GDPR)
- New content about the United States–Mexico–Canada Agreement (USMCA)
- New table of U.S. top trading partners

Chapter four

OPTIONS FOR ORGANIZING BUSINESS

- New boxed features describing real-world business issues
- New table of world's biggest dividend payers
- Updated table of America's largest private companies

Chapter five

SMALL BUSINESS, ENTREPRENEURSHIP, AND FRANCHISING

- New boxed features describing current business issues
- Examples of innovative small businesses
- New information on artificial intelligence
- Updated table of the fastest growing franchises
- Updated table of the most business-friendly states
- New stats on small business
- New data on Gen Z in the workforce
- New data on minority-owned businesses

Chapter six

THE NATURE OF MANAGEMENT

- New boxed features describing current business issues
- New content about business models
- New table of compensation packages of CEOs
- New content on gender equality

Chapter seven

ORGANIZATION, TEAMWORK, AND COMMUNICATION

- New boxed features describing current business issues
- New examples of organizational culture
- New content on artificial intelligence
- New content on email and video conferencing usage in the workplace

Chapter eight

MANAGING OPERATIONS AND SUPPLY CHAINS

- New boxed features describing current business operational issues
- New content on marketing research and artificial intelligence
- New section on blockchain technology
- New content on drone technology
- Extensive overhaul of Managing the Supply Chain section
- Updated airline scorecard table
- New examples related to the COVID-19 pandemic and supply chains

Chapter nine

MOTIVATING THE WORKFORCE

- New boxed features describing current business issues
- New examples of organizational culture
- New table of best places for businesses and careers

Chapter ten

MANAGING HUMAN RESOURCES

- New boxed features describing current HR issues
- Updated common job interview questions
- New content on wage gap
- New example of how soft benefits inspire loyalty
- New section on employee relations and sexual harrassment

Chapter eleven

CUSTOMER-DRIVEN MARKETING

- New boxed features describing current marketing issues
- New content on marketing orientation
- New content on supply chain management
- New content on marketing analytics dashboards
- New data on the buying power by race/ethnicity
- New table of companies with the best customer service

Chapter twelve

DIMENSIONS OF MARKETING STRATEGY

- New boxed features describing current marketing issues
- Logistics added as key term
- New definition for physical distribution key term
- Updated figure depicting a company's product mix
- Updated personal care and cleaning products customer satisfaction ratings
- New examples related to the impact of the COVID-19 pandemic on marketing strategy

Chapter thirteen

DIGITAL MARKETING AND SOCIAL MEDIA

- New boxed features describing current digital marketing issues
- New stats on social media use by platform
- New stats on mobile app activities
- New data on the main sources of identity theft
- New section on TikTok

Chapter fourteen

ACCOUNTING AND FINANCIAL STATEMENTS

- New boxed features describing current accounting issues
- Updated rankings of accounting firms in the United States
- New financial information for NVIDIA
- New content on net income and corporate tax rate

Chapter fifteen

MONEY AND THE FINANCIAL SYSTEM

- New boxed features describing current financial issues
- Updated life expectancy of money
- Updated cost to produce coins
- New content on cryptocurrency
- New content on interest rates
- New content on exchange-traded funds (ETFs)

Chapter sixteen

FINANCIAL MANAGEMENT AND SECURITIES MARKETS

- New boxed features describing current financial issues
- Updated short-term investment possibilities
- Updated U.S. corporate bond quotes
- New content on electronic markets
- Updated estimated common stock price-earnings, ratios, and dividends for selected companies
- New table of S&P 500 corrections
- New content on the impacts of the COVID-19 pandemic on financial management

brief contents

Sean Pavone/Shutterstock

contents

ArtisticPhoto/Shutterstock

Part two STARTING AND GROWING A BUSINESS 76

Richard Drew/AP/Shutterstock

Monkey Business Images/Shutterstock

Part four CREATING THE HUMAN RESOURCE ADVANTAGE 172

CHAPTER 9 MOTIVATING THE WORKFORCE 172

Tony Tallec/Alamy Stock Photo

CHAPTER 10 MANAGING HUMAN RESOURCES 188

Part five MARKETING: DEVELOPING RELATIONSHIPS 208

CHAPTER 11 CUSTOMER-DRIVEN MARKETING 208

13_Phunkod/Shutterstock

Chrispictures/Shutterstock

business 7e

the dynamics of
business and economics

Sean Pavone/Shutterstock

LEARNING OBJECTIVES

After reading this chapter, you will be able to:

LO 1-1 Define basic concepts such as business, product, profit, and economics.

LO 1-2 Identify the main participants and activities of business.

LO 1-3 Explain why studying business is important.

LO 1-4 Compare the four types of economic systems.

LO 1-5 Describe the role of supply, demand, and competition in a free-enterprise system.

LO 1-6 Specify why and how the health of the economy is measured.

LO 1-7 Outline the evolution of the American economy.

LO 1-8 Explain the role of the entrepreneur in the economy.

We begin our study of business in this chapter by examining the fundamentals of business and economics. First, we introduce the nature of business, including its goals, activities, and participants. Next, we describe the basics of economics and apply them to the U.S. economy. Finally, we establish a framework for studying business in this text. ∎

LO 1-1 Define basic concepts such as business, product, profit, and economics.

THE NATURE OF BUSINESS

A **business** tries to earn a profit by providing products that satisfy people's needs. The outcomes of its efforts are **products** that have both tangible and intangible characteristics that provide satisfaction and benefits. When you purchase a product, you are buying the benefits and satisfaction you think the product will provide. A Subway sandwich, for example, may be purchased to satisfy hunger, while a Honda Accord may be purchased to satisfy the need for transportation and the desire to present a certain image.

Most people associate the word *product* with tangible goods—an automobile, smartphone, jeans, or some other tangible item. However, a product can also be a service, which occurs when people or machines provide or process something of value to customers. Dry cleaning, a telemedicine visit, a movie or sports event—these are examples of services. An Uber ride satisfies the need for transportation and is therefore a service. A product can also be an idea. Accountants and attorneys, for example, provide ideas for solving problems.

The Goal of Business

The primary goal of all businesses is to earn a **profit**, the difference between what it costs to make and sell a product and what a customer pays for it. In addition, a business has to pay for all expenses necessary to operate. If a company spends $8 to produce, finance, promote, and distribute a product that it sells for $10, the business earns a profit of $2 on each product sold. Businesses have the right to keep and use their profits as they choose—within legal limits—because profit is the reward for their efforts and for the risks they take in providing products. Earning profits contributes to society by creating resources that support our social institutions and government. Businesses that create profits, pay taxes, and create jobs are the foundation of our economy. In addition, profits must be earned in a responsible manner. Most businesses give back to the community to support social and economic causes. Not all organizations are businesses, however. **Nonprofit organizations**—such as National Public Radio (NPR), Habitat for Humanity, and other charities and social causes—do not have the fundamental purpose of earning profits, although they may provide goods or services and engage in fund-raising. They also utilize skills related to management, marketing, and finance. Profits earned by businesses support nonprofit organizations through donations from employees.

To earn a profit, a person or organization needs management skills to plan, organize, and control the activities of the business and to find and develop employees so that it can make products consumers will buy. A business also needs marketing expertise to learn what products consumers need and want and to develop, manufacture, price, promote, and distribute those products. Additionally, a business needs financial resources and skills to fund, maintain, and expand its operations. A business must cover the cost of labor, operate facilities, pay taxes, and provide management. Other challenges for businesspeople include abiding by laws and government regulations, and adapting to economic, technological, political, and social changes. Even nonprofit organizations engage in management, marketing, and finance activities to help reach their goals. Nonprofits need employees with the same skills as businesses do.

To achieve and maintain profitability, businesses have found that they must produce quality products, operate efficiently, and be socially responsible and ethical in dealing with customers, employees, investors, government regulators, and the community. Because these groups have a stake in the success and outcomes of a business, they are sometimes called **stakeholders**. Many businesses, for example, are concerned about how the production and distribution of their products affect the environment. Automakers, for example, are working toward taking a bigger slice of the electric vehicle (EV) market. General Motors and Ford are fighting to catch up with Tesla, the leader in EVs, but it could take many years to achieve that goal.[1] Other businesses are concerned with

business individuals or organizations who try to earn a profit by providing products that satisfy people's needs.

product a good or service with tangible and intangible characteristics that provide satisfaction and benefits.

profit the difference between what it costs to make and sell a product and what a customer pays for it.

nonprofit organizations organizations that may provide goods or services but do not have the fundamental purpose of earning profits.

stakeholders groups that have a stake in the success and outcomes of a business.

Alex's Lemonade Stand Foundation is a nonprofit organization that raises funds and awareness for childhood cancer.

Rebecca Sapp/Getty Images for L.A. Loves Alex's Lemonade

promoting science, engineering, and mathematics careers among women. Traditionally, these careers have been male dominated. According to Bloomberg, when the number of men and women on a team are evenly matched, the companies have a higher return on equity.[2]

LO 1-2   Identify the main participants and activities of business.

The People and Activities of Business

Figure 1.1 shows the people and activities involved in business. At the center of the figure are owners, employees, and customers; the outer circle includes the primary business activities—management, marketing, and finance. Owners have to put up resources—money or credit—to start a business. Employees are responsible for the work that goes on within a business. Owners can manage the business themselves or hire employees to accomplish this task. The president and chief executive officer (CEO) of Procter & Gamble, David S. Taylor, does not own P&G but is an employee who is responsible for managing all the other employees in a way that earns a profit for investors, who are the real owners. Finally, and most importantly, a business's major role is to satisfy the customers who buy its goods or services. Note also that forces beyond an organization's control—such as legal and regulatory forces, the economy, competition, technology, the political environment, and ethical and social concerns—all have an impact on the

daily operations of businesses. You will learn more about these participants in business activities throughout this book. Next, we will examine the major activities of business.

Management. Notice that in Figure 1.1, management and employees are in the same segment of the circle. This is because management involves developing plans, coordinating employees' actions to achieve the firm's goals, organizing people to work efficiently, and motivating them to achieve the business's goals. Management involves the functions of planning, organizing, leading, and controlling. Effective managers who are skilled in these functions display effective leadership, decision making, and delegation of work tasks. Management is also concerned with acquiring, developing, and using resources (including people) effectively and efficiently.

Management involves organization, teamwork, and communication. Operations and supply chain management are also important. Motivating the workforce and managing human resources are necessary for success. Managers at the Ritz-Carlton, for instance, are concerned with transforming resources such as employee actions and hotel amenities into a quality customer service experience. In essence, managers plan, organize, staff, and control the tasks required to carry out the work of the company or nonprofit organization. We take a closer look at management activities in Parts 3 and 4 of this text.

Marketing. Marketing and customers are in the same segment of Figure 1.1 because the focus of all marketing activities is satisfying customers. Marketing includes all the activities designed to provide goods and services that satisfy consumers' needs and wants. Marketers gather information

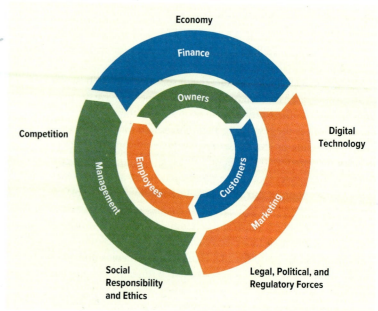

▼**FIGURE 1.1** Overview of the Business World

and conduct research to determine what customers want. Using information gathered from marketing research, marketers plan and develop products and make decisions about how much to charge for their products and when and where to make them available. They also analyze the marketing environment to understand changes in competition and consumers. The retail environment is changing based on competition from online retailing such as Amazon. This has caused many retail stores and malls to close.[3] Marketing focuses on the four P's—product, price, place (or distribution), and promotion—also known as the marketing mix. Product management involves such key management decisions as product adoption, development, branding, and product positioning. Selecting the right price for the product is essential to the organization as it relates directly to profitability. Distribution is an important management concern because it involves making sure products are available to consumers in the right place at the right time. For example, Stevia in the Raw uses advertising as part of its promotion mix to appeal to consumers who enjoy sweets but want a healthier alternative to sugar. In the advertisement, Stevia in the Raw communicates that its product, a zero-calorie sweetener, reduces sugar and calories for a more healthful recipe. Marketers use promotion—advertising, personal selling, sales promotion (coupons, games, sweepstakes, movie tie-ins), and publicity—to communicate the benefits and advantages of their products to consumers and to increase sales. We will examine marketing activities in Part 5 of this text.

Finance. Owners and finance are in the same part of Figure 1.1 because, although management and marketing have to deal with financial considerations, it is the primary responsibility of the owners to provide financial resources for the operation of the business. Accounting, money, and the financial system, as well as understanding the securities market, are important for business success. People who work as accountants, stockbrokers, investment advisors, or bankers are all part of the financial world. Owners sometimes have to borrow money from banks to get started or attract additional investors who become partners or stockholders. Owners of small businesses in particular often rely on bank loans for funding. Part 6 of this text discusses financial management.

Why Study Business?

Studying business can help you develop skills and acquire knowledge to prepare for your future career, regardless of whether you plan to work for a multinational *Fortune* 500 firm, start your own business, work for a government agency, or manage or volunteer

Advertising is one method for marketers to promote benefits and advantages of their products. This advertisement features Stevia in the Raw, a sugar alternative, and instructs consumers on how to make cake with half the sugar and calories.

Source: Stevia in the Raw

at a nonprofit organization. The field of business offers a variety of interesting and challenging career opportunities throughout the world, such as marketing, human resources management, information technology, finance, production, accounting, data analytics, and many more.

The Home Depot Foundation's Veteran Housing Grants Program awards grants to assist in the construction of housing and facilities for veterans.

Jill Braaten/McGraw-Hill Education

economics the study of how resources are distributed for the production of goods and services within a social system.

natural resources land, forests, minerals, water, and other things that are not made by people.

human resources (labor) the physical and mental abilities that people use to produce goods and services.

financial resources (capital) the funds used to acquire the natural and human resources needed to provide products.

economic system a description of how a particular society distributes its resources to produce goods and services.

Studying business can also help you better understand the many business activities that are necessary to provide satisfying goods and services. Most businesses charge a reasonable price for their products to ensure that they cover their production costs, pay their employees, provide their owners with a return on their investment, and perhaps give something back to their local communities and societies. The Home Depot Foundation has provided grants to remodel and renovate homes of U.S. military veterans.[4] Thus, learning about business can help you become a well-informed consumer and member of society.

Business activities help generate the profits that are essential not only to individual businesses and local economies but also to the health of the global economy. Understanding how our free-enterprise economic system allocates resources and provides incentives for industry and the workplace is important to everyone.

LO 1-4 Compare the four types of economic systems.

THE ECONOMIC FOUNDATIONS OF BUSINESS

It is useful to explore the economic environment in which business is conducted. In this section, we examine economic systems, the free-enterprise system, the concepts of supply and demand, and the role of competition. These concepts play important roles in determining how businesses operate in a particular society.

Economics is the study of how resources are distributed for the production of goods and services within a social system. You are already familiar with the types of resources available. Land, forests, minerals, water, and other things that are not made by people are **natural resources**. **Human resources**, or **labor**, refer to the physical and mental abilities that people use to produce goods and services. **Financial resources**, or **capital**, are the funds used to acquire the natural and human resources needed to provide products. These resources are related to the *factors of production*, consisting of land, labor, capital, and enterprise used to produce goods and services. The firm can also have intangible resources such as a good reputation for quality

products or being socially responsible. The goal is to turn the factors of production and intangible resources into a competitive advantage.

Economic Systems

An **economic system** describes how a particular society distributes its resources to produce goods and services. A central issue of economics is how to fulfill an unlimited demand for goods and services in a world with a limited supply of resources. Different economic systems attempt to resolve this central issue in numerous ways, as we shall see.

Although economic systems handle the distribution of resources in different ways, all economic systems must address three important issues:

1. What goods and services, and how much of each, will satisfy consumers' needs?

2. How will goods and services be produced, who will produce them, and with what resources will they be produced?

3. How are the goods and services to be distributed to consumers?

Communism, socialism, and capitalism, the basic economic systems found in the world today (Table 1.1), have fundamental differences in the way they address these issues. The factors of production in command economies are controlled by government planning. In many cases, the government owns or controls the production of goods and services. Communism and socialism are, therefore, considered command economies.

Communism. Karl Marx (1818–1883) first described **communism** as a society in which the people, without regard to class, own all the nation's resources. In his ideal political-economic system, everyone contributes according to ability and receives benefits according to need. In a communist economy, the people (through the government) own and operate all businesses and factors of production. Central government planning determines what goods and services satisfy citizens' needs, how the goods and services are produced, and how they are distributed. However, no true communist economy exists today that satisfies Marx's ideal.

On paper, communism appears to be efficient and equitable, producing less of a gap between rich and poor. In practice, however, communist economies have been marked by low standards of living, critical shortages of consumer goods, high prices, corruption, and little freedom. Russia, Poland, Hungary, and other eastern European nations have turned away from communism and toward economic systems governed by supply and demand rather than by central planning. However, their experiments with alternative economic systems have been fraught with difficulty and hardship. Countries such as Venezuela have tried to incorporate communist economic principles without success. Even Cuba is experiencing changes to its predominately communist system. Similarly, China was the first communist country to make strong economic gains by adopting capitalist approaches to business. Economic prosperity has advanced in China with the government claiming to ensure market openness, equality, and fairness through state capitalism.[5] As a result of economic challenges, communism is declining and its future as an economic system is uncertain.

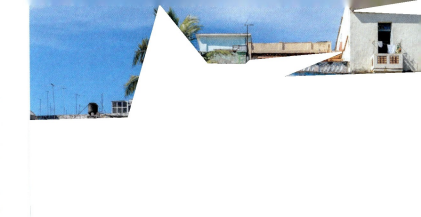

Cuba's new constitution promotes socialism rather than communism.

Anton_Ivanov/Shutterstock

Socialism.
Socialism is an economic system in which the government owns and operates basic industries—postal service, telephone, utilities, transportation, health care, banking, and some manufacturing—but individuals own most businesses. For example, in France the postal service industry La Poste is fully owned by the French government and makes a profit. Central planning determines what basic goods and services are produced, how they are produced, and how they are distributed. Individuals and small businesses provide other goods and services based on consumer demand and the availability of resources. Citizens are dependent on the government for many goods and services.

Most socialist nations, such as Norway, India, and Israel, are democratic and recognize basic individual freedoms. Citizens can vote for political offices, but central government planners usually make many decisions about what is best for the nation. For example, based on government policies and incentives, 60 percent of the new cars purchased in Norway are electric.[6] People are free to go into the occupation of their choice, but they often work in government-operated organizations. Socialists believe their system permits a higher standard of living than other economic systems, but the difference often applies to the nation as a whole rather than to its individual citizens. Socialist economies profess egalitarianism—equal distribution of income and social services. They believe their economies are more stable than those of other nations. Although this may be true, taxes and unemployment are generally higher in socialist countries. However, countries like Denmark have a high standard of living and they rate high in being happy.

Capitalism.
Capitalism, or **free enterprise**, is an economic system in which individuals own and operate the majority of businesses that provide goods and services. Competition, supply, and demand determine which goods and services are produced, how

communism first described by Karl Marx as a society in which the people, without regard to class, own all the nation's resources.

socialism an economic system in which the government owns and operates basic industries but individuals own most businesses.

capitalism (free enterprise) an economic system in which individuals own and operate the majority of businesses that provide goods and services.

▼ **TABLE 1.1** Comparison of Communism, Socialism, and Capitalism

	Communism	Socialism	Capitalism
Business ownership	Most businesses are owned and operated by the government.	The government owns and operates some basic industries; individuals also own businesses.	Individuals own and operate all businesses.
Competition	Government controls competition and the economy.	Restricted in basic industries; encouraged in other businesses.	Encouraged by market forces and government regulations.
Profits	Excess income goes to the government. The government supports social and economic institutions.	Profits earned by businesses may be reinvested in the business; profits from government-owned industries go to the government.	Individuals and businesses are free to keep profits after paying taxes.
Product availability and price	Consumers have a limited choice of goods and services; prices are usually high.	Consumers have a choice of goods and services; prices are determined by supply and demand.	Consumers have a wide choice of goods and services; prices are determined by supply and demand.
Employment options	Little choice in choosing a career; most people work for government-owned industries or farms.	More choice of careers; many people work in government jobs.	Unlimited choice of careers.

free-market system
pure capitalism, in which all economic decisions are made without government intervention.

mixed economies
economies made up of elements from more than one economic system.

they are produced, and how they are distributed. The United States, Canada, Japan, and Australia are examples of economic systems based on capitalism.

There are two forms of capitalism: pure capitalism and modified capitalism. In pure capitalism, also called a **free-market system**, all economic decisions are made without government intervention. This economic system was first described by Adam Smith in *The Wealth of Nations* (1776). Smith, often called the father of capitalism, believed that the "invisible hand of competition" best regulates the economy. He argued that competition should determine what goods and services people need. Smith's system is also called *laissez-faire* ("let it be") *capitalism* because the government does not interfere in business.

Modified capitalism differs from pure capitalism in that the government intervenes and regulates business to some extent. One of the ways in which the United States and Canadian governments regulate business is through laws. Laws such as the Federal Trade Commission Act, which created the Federal Trade Commission to enforce antitrust laws, illustrate the importance of the government's role in the economy. In the United States, states have leeway to regulate business. For example, the state of California requires public companies to have at least one woman on the board of directors, and a number of states have legalized cannabis.[7]

the government but uses capitalistic tools such as listing state-owned companies on the stock market and embracing globalization.[8] State capitalism includes some of the world's largest companies such as Russia's Gazprom, which has the largest reserves of natural gas. China's ability to make huge investments to the point of creating entirely new industries puts many private industries at a disadvantage.[9]

The Free-Enterprise System

Many economies—including those of the United States, Canada, and Japan—are based on free enterprise, and many communist and socialist countries, such as China and Russia, are applying more principles of free enterprise to their own economic systems. Free enterprise provides an opportunity for a business to succeed or fail on the basis of market demand. In a free-enterprise system, companies that can efficiently manufacture and sell products that consumers desire will probably succeed. Inefficient businesses and those that sell products that do not offer needed benefits will likely fail as consumers take their business to firms that have more competitive products.

A number of basic individual and business rights must exist for free enterprise to work. These rights are the goals of many countries that have recently embraced free enterprise.

1. Individuals must have the right to own property and to pass this property on to their heirs. This right motivates people to work hard and save to buy property.

2. Individuals and businesses must have the right to earn profits and to use the profits as they wish, within the constraints of their society's laws, principles, and values.

> ## "No country practices a pure form of communism, socialism, or capitalism, although most tend to favor one system over the others."

Mixed Economies. No country practices a pure form of communism, socialism, or capitalism, although most tend to favor one system over the others. Most nations operate as **mixed economies**, which have elements from more than one economic system. In socialist Sweden, most businesses are owned and operated by private individuals. In capitalist United States, an independent federal agency operates the postal service and another independent agency operates the Tennessee Valley Authority, an electric utility. In Germany, the Deutsche Post is privatized and trades on the stock market. In once-communist Russia, Hungary, Poland, and other eastern European nations, capitalist ideas have been implemented, including private ownership of businesses.

Countries such as China and Russia have used state capitalism to advance the economy. State capitalism tries to integrate the powers of the state with the advantages of capitalism. It is led by

3. Individuals and businesses must have the right to make decisions that determine the way the business operates. Although there is government regulation, the philosophy in countries like the United States and Australia is to permit maximum freedom within a set of rules of fairness.

4. Individuals must have the right to choose what career to pursue, where to live, what goods and services to purchase, and more. Businesses must have the right to choose where to locate, what goods and services to produce, what resources to use in the production process, and so on.

Without these rights, businesses cannot function effectively because they are not motivated to succeed. Thus, these rights make possible the open exchange of goods and services. In the countries that favor free enterprise, such as the United States, citizens have the freedom to make many decisions about the employment they choose and create their own productivity systems.

Many entrepreneurs are more productive in free-enterprise societies because personal and financial incentives are available that can aid in entrepreneurial success. For many entrepreneurs, their work becomes a part of their system of goals, values, and lifestyle. Consider the panelists ("sharks") on the ABC program *Shark Tank* who give entrepreneurs a chance to receive funding to realize their dreams by deciding whether to invest in their projects. They include Barbara Corcoran, who built one of New York's largest real estate companies; Mark Cuban, founder of MicroSolutions and Broadcast.com; and Daymond John, founder of clothing company FUBU, as well as others.[10]

demand the number of goods and services that consumers are willing to buy at different prices at a specific time.

supply the number of products—goods and services—that businesses are willing to sell at different prices at a specific time.

equilibrium price the price at which the number of products that businesses are willing to supply equals the amount of products that consumers are willing to buy at a specific point in time.

LO 1-5   Describe the role of supply, demand, and competition in a free-enterprise system.

The Forces of Supply and Demand

In the United States and in other free-enterprise systems, the distribution of resources and products is determined by supply and demand. **Demand** is the number of goods and services that consumers are willing to buy at different prices at a specific time. From your own experience, you probably recognize that consumers are usually willing to buy more of an item as its price falls because they want to save money. Consider handmade rugs, for example. Consumers may be willing to buy six rugs at $350 each, four at $500 each, but only two at $650 each. The relationship between the price and the number of rugs consumers are willing to buy can be shown graphically with a *demand curve* (see Figure 1.2).

Supply is the number of products that businesses are willing to sell at different prices at a specific time. In general, because the

potential for profits is higher, businesses are willing to supply more of a good or service at higher prices. For example, a company that sells rugs may be willing to sell six at $650 each, four at $500 each, but just two at $350 each. The relationship between the price of rugs and the quantity the company is willing to supply can be shown graphically with a *supply curve* (see Figure 1.2).

In Figure 1.2, the supply and demand curves intersect at the point where supply and demand are equal. The price at which the number of products that businesses are willing to supply equals the amount of products that consumers are willing to buy at a specific point in time is the **equilibrium price**. In our rug example, the company is willing to supply four rugs at $500 each, and consumers are willing to buy four rugs at $500 each. Therefore, $500 is the equilibrium price for a rug at that point in time, and most rug companies will price their rugs at $500. As you might imagine, a business that charges more than $500 (or whatever the current equilibrium price is) for its rugs will not sell as many and might not earn a profit. On the other hand, a business that charges less than $500 accepts a lower profit per rug than could be made at the equilibrium price.

If the cost of making rugs goes up, businesses will not offer as many at the old price. Changing the price alters the supply curve, and a new equilibrium price results. This is an ongoing process, with supply and demand constantly changing in response to changes in economic conditions, availability of resources, and degree of competition. For example, the price of oil can change rapidly and has been between $0 and $113 a barrel over the last 10 years. Oil prices dropped below $0 when demand went down rapidly and supply

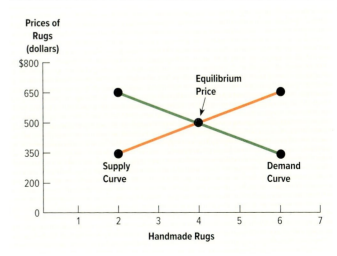

Oprah Winfrey, with a net worth of more than $3 billion, is one of the world's most famous entrepreneurs. Entrepreneurs are more productive in free-enterprise systems.

Frederic J. Brown/AFP/Getty Images

▼**FIGURE 1.2**
Equilibrium Price of Handmade Rugs

Prices of Rugs (dollars)

Equilibrium Price

Supply Curve

Demand Curve

Handmade Rugs

TAYLOR SWIFT FIGHTS SCALPERS

For fans of popular singers like Taylor Swift, the demand for concert tickets is high. Fans must often hurry to purchase tickets before they are sold out. Because there are a limited number of seats, when demand is high the equilibrium price is high as well. While this is profitable for the performer, it also creates opportunities for ticket scalpers.

Because of high demand for certain performers and a limited supply of seats, scalpers know there is a market of fans willing to pay much more than the original price online. This gives them opportunities to purchase large numbers of ticket and sell at a premium on sites like Stub Hub. It is estimated that ticket scalping cost Taylor Swift $85 million during one tour.

Two scalpers in the United Kingdom used bot software and multiple identities to illegally buy and sell tickets, making more than £10.8 million ($14 million). The duo received a collective jail sentence of six and half years from a U.K. court. It was a landmark ruling as it was the first prosecution of its kind in the United Kingdom. As technology advances, it becomes increasingly difficult to fend off cybercriminals.

To fight against scalpers, Swift joined with Ticketmaster to use its Verified Fan system to locate fans less likely to resell their tickets. Fans register and—if they are identified by Ticketmaster's Verified Fan system—they are sent a link that gives them early access to tickets. Swift also added boosters to the system, giving

fans a better chance of being selected if they buy albums, watch music videos, or post about her on social media. The system offers a solution to reward fans and fight against a practice that takes advantage of high demand and limited supply.[a]

Critical Thinking Questions

1. Describe how the supply-demand problem is offering opportunities for scalpers.

2. Scalpers raise the equilibrium price once they control the supply. How do you think this Ticketmaster Verified Fan System will affect this ability?

3. As a service provider, do you think performers like Taylor Swift should take an active role in fighting against scalpers? Why or why not?

---

competition the rivalry among businesses for consumers' dollars.

pure competition the market structure that exists when there are many small businesses selling one standardized product.

monopolistic competition the market structure that exists when there are fewer businesses than in a pure-competition environment and the differences among the goods they sell are small.

> " Competition allows for open markets and provides opportunities for both individuals and businesses to successfully compete. "

The Nature of Competition

Competition, the rivalry among businesses for consumers' dollars, is another vital element in free enterprise. According to Adam Smith, competition fosters efficiency and low prices by forcing producers to offer the best products at the most reasonable price; those who fail to do so are not able to stay in business. Thus, competition should improve the quality of the goods and services available and reduce prices. Competition allows for open markets and provides opportunities for both individuals and businesses to successfully compete. Entrepreneurs can discover new technology, ways to lower prices, as well as methods for providing better distribution or services. Founder Jeff Bezos of Amazon is a prime example. Amazon is able to offer products online at competitive prices. Today, Amazon competes against such retail giants as Walmart and Target in a number of industries, including cloud computing, entertainment, food, and most consumer products found in retail stores. Bezos's Blue Origin rocket company along with Elon Musk's SpaceX and Richard Branson's Virgin Galactic have turned space tourism into a reality.[11]

Within a free-enterprise system, there are four types of competitive environments: pure competition, monopolistic competition, oligopoly, and monopoly.

Pure competition exists when there are many small businesses selling one standardized product, such as agricultural commodities like wheat, corn, and cotton. No one business sells enough of the product to influence the product's price. And, because there is no difference in the products, prices are determined solely by the forces of supply and demand.

Monopolistic competition exists when there are fewer businesses than in a pure-competition environment and the

increased during the COVID-19 pandemic. Oil prices returned to more than $30 a barrel about a month later when supply and demand were more balanced. Prices for goods and services vary according to these changes in supply and demand. Supply and demand is the force that drives the distribution of resources (goods and services, labor, and money) in a free-enterprise economy.

Critics of supply and demand say the system does not distribute resources equally. The forces of supply and demand prevent sellers who have to sell at higher prices (because their costs are high) and buyers who cannot afford to buy goods at the equilibrium price from participating in the market. According to critics, the wealthy can afford to buy more than they need, but the poor may be unable to buy enough of what they need to survive.

differences among the goods they sell are small. Aspirin, soft drinks, and jeans are examples of such goods. These products differ slightly in packaging, warranty, name, and other characteristics, but all satisfy the same consumer need. Businesses have some power over the price they charge in monopolistic competition because they can make consumers aware of product differences through advertising. Consumers value some features more than others and are often willing to pay higher prices for a product with the features they want. For example, many consumers are willing to pay a higher price for organic fruits and vegetables rather than receive a bargain on nonorganic foods. The same holds true for non-genetically modified foods.

An **oligopoly** exists when there are very few businesses selling a product. In an oligopoly, individual businesses have control over their products' price because each business supplies a large portion of the products sold in the marketplace. Nonetheless, the prices charged by different firms stay fairly close because a price cut or increase by one company will trigger a similar response from another company. In the airline industry, for example, when one airline cuts fares to boost sales, other airlines quickly follow with rate decreases to remain competitive. On the other hand, airlines often raise prices at the same time. Oligopolies exist when it is expensive for new firms to enter the marketplace. Not just anyone can acquire enough financial capital to build an automobile production facility or purchase enough airplanes and related resources to build an airline.

When there is one business providing a product in a given market, a **monopoly** exists. Utility companies that supply electricity, natural gas, and water are monopolies. The government permits such monopolies because the cost of creating the good or supplying the service is so great that new producers cannot compete for sales. Government-granted monopolies are subject to government-regulated prices. Some monopolies exist because of technological developments that are protected by patent laws. This monopoly allows the developer to recover research, development, and production expenses and to earn a reasonable profit. A drug can receive a 17-year patent from the time it is discovered or the chemical is identified. For example, Tamiflu lost its patent, and now the generic version can be made by other firms.

Economic Cycles and Productivity

Expansion and Contraction. Economies are not stagnant; they expand and contract. **Economic expansion** occurs when an economy is growing and people are spending more money. Their purchases stimulate the production of goods and services, which in turn stimulates employment. The standard of living rises because more people are employed and have money to spend. Rapid expansions of the economy, however, may

oligopoly the market structure that exists when there are very few businesses selling a product.

monopoly the market structure that exists when there is only one business providing a product in a given market.

economic expansion the situation that occurs when an economy is growing and people are spending more money; their purchases stimulate the production of goods and services, which in turn stimulates employment.

COMPETITION IS BREWING IN KOMBUCHA MARKET

Kombucha might be fizzy like a soft drink, but it has health benefits that soft drinks lack. Kombucha is made by brewing tea, then adding sugar. Afterward the mixture is fermented with a blend of yeast and bacteria called scoby. The bacteria the drink contains makes kombucha a probiotic that helps digestion and gut health. Scoby cultures can produce an endless supply of kombucha, reducing waste and enabling consumers to brew kombucha in their homes.

Kombucha manufacturers operate in a monopolistic competitive industry. Because kombucha is relatively easy to produce, manufacturers take steps to differentiate their products, such as developing drinks in a variety of unique, fruity flavors. With consumer interest in the beverage skyrocketing, the demand is encouraging the entrance of new competitors.

PepsiCo spent around $200 million to acquire KeVita, and Coca-Cola has a stake in Health-Ade. Starbucks has its own line of kombucha under its Evolution Fresh brand. These steps are prompting traditional kombucha manufacturers to become more competitive. For instance, Brew Dr., one of the leading kombucha brands, has advertised its drinks with Portland's soccer teams to increase awareness.

Analysts have compared kombucha to yogurt not only for its probiotic qualities, but for its market qualities. The industry is expected to grow and diversify in the future. The competition between smaller kombucha manufacturers and more established rivals is heating up.[b]

Critical Thinking Questions

1. Why is the competition in the kombucha industry an example of monopolistic competition?

2. How are the forces of supply and demand convincing more established brands like PepsiCo to enter the industry?

3. If more and more entrants enter the industry, what do you think will happen to the price of kombucha?

inflation a condition characterized by a continuing rise in prices

economic contraction a slowdown of the economy characterized by a decline in spending and during which businesses cut back on production and lay off workers.

recession a decline in production, employment, and income.

unemployment the condition in which a percentage of the population wants to work but is unable to find jobs.

depression a condition of the economy in which unemployment is very high, consumer spending is low, and business output is sharply reduced.

result in **inflation**, a continuing rise in prices. Inflation can be harmful if individuals' incomes do not increase at the same pace as rising prices, reducing their buying power. Venezuela inflation reached 10 million percent in 2019.[12]

Economic contraction occurs when spending declines. Businesses cut back on production and lay off workers, and the economy as a whole slows down. Contractions of the economy lead to **recession**—a decline in production, employment, and income. Recessions are often characterized by rising levels of **unemployment**, which is measured as the percentage of the population that wants to work but is unable to find jobs. Figure 1.3 shows the overall unemployment rate in the civilian labor force over the past 75 years. Rising unemployment levels tend to stifle demand for goods and services, which can have the effect of forcing prices downward, a condition known as *deflation*. Deflation poses a serious economic problem because price decreases could result in consumers delaying purchases. If consumers wait for lower prices, the economy could fall into a recession.

The United States has experienced numerous recessions, the most recent ones occurring in 1990–1991, 2002–2003, 2008–2011, and 2020. The Great Recession of 2008–2011 was caused by the collapse in housing prices and consumers' inability to stay current on their mortgage and credit card payments. This caused a crisis in the banking industry, with the government bailing out banks to keep them from failing. This in turn caused a slowdown in spending on consumer goods and a decrease in employment. Unemployment reached 10 percent of the labor force. Ten years later, unemployment was nearing a 50-year low, but during the COVID-19 (coronavirus) pandemic, the unemployment rate skyrocketed to a record 14.7 percent in 2020, the worst since the Great Depression.[13] As Americans were urged to stay home to prevent the spread of the virus, nonessential businesses—such as clothing stores, gyms, and salons—shuttered and many were forced to layoff employees. Even restaurants, many of which remained open for pickup and delivery, suffered greatly. Though online and non-store sales were up 21.2 percent year over year, overall retail sales were down 21.6 percent, according to the U.S. Census Bureau.[14] Don't forget that personal consumption makes up almost 70 percent of gross domestic product, so consumer engagement is extremely important for economic activity. A severe recession may turn into a **depression**, in which unemployment is very high, consumer spending is low, and business output is sharply reduced, such as what occurred in the United States in the early 1930s.

Economies expand and contract in response to changes in consumer, business, and government spending. War also can affect an economy, sometimes stimulating it (as in the United States during World Wars I and II) and sometimes stifling it (as during the Vietnam, Persian Gulf, and Iraq wars). Although fluctuations in the economy are inevitable and to a certain extent predictable, their effects—inflation and unemployment—disrupt lives and thus governments try to minimize them.

▼ **FIGURE 1.3** Annual Average Unemployment Rate, Civilian Labor Force, 16 Years and Over

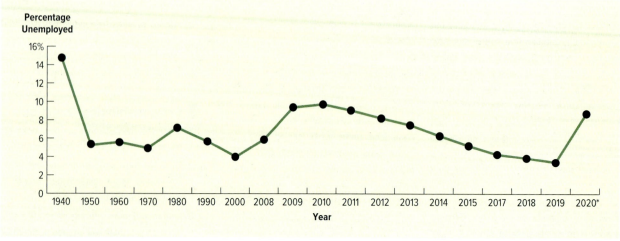

Sources: *Bureau of Labor Statistics,* "Labor Force Statistics from the Current Population Survey," http://data.bls.gov/timeseries/LNS14000000 (accessed May 14, 2020).

*Average based on data available from January–July, 2020.

FIGURE 1.4
Change in U.S.
Gross Domestic
Product

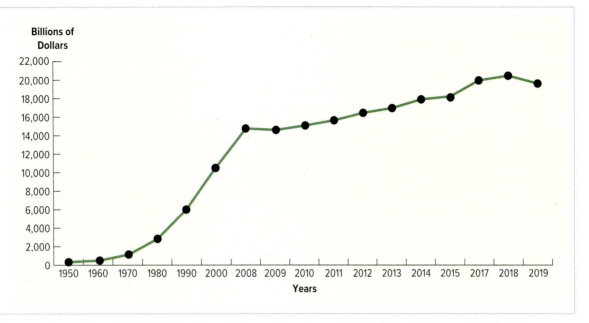

Source: *U.S. Department of Commerce Bureau of Economic Analysis,* "National Economic Accounts," www.bea.gov/national/index.htm#gdp (accessed May 14, 2020).

LO 1-6 Specify why and how the health of the economy is measured.

Measuring the Economy. Countries measure the state of their economies to determine whether they are expanding or contracting and whether corrective action is necessary to minimize the fluctuations. One commonly used measure is **gross domestic product (GDP)**—the sum of all goods and services produced in a country during a year. GDP measures only those goods and services made within a country and therefore does not include profits from companies' overseas operations; it does include profits earned by foreign companies within the country being measured. However, it does not take into account the concept of GDP in relation to population (GDP per capita). Figure 1.4 shows the increase in U.S. GDP over several years.

Another important indicator of a nation's economic health is the relationship between its spending and income (from taxes). When a nation spends more than it takes in from taxes, it has a **budget deficit**. In the 1990s, the U.S. government eliminated its long-standing budget deficit by balancing the money spent for social, defense, and other programs with the amount of money taken in from taxes.

In recent years, however, the budget deficit has reemerged and grown to record levels. Because many Americans do not want their taxes increased and Congress has difficulty agreeing on appropriate tax rates, it is difficult to increase taxes and reduce the deficit. Like consumers and businesses, when the government needs money, it borrows from the public, banks, and even foreign investors. The national debt is more than $25 trillion.[15] This figure is especially worrisome because to reduce the debt to a manageable level, the government either has to increase its revenues (raise taxes) or reduce spending on social, defense, and legal programs, neither of which is politically popular. The national debt figure changes daily and can be seen at the Department of the Treasury, Bureau of the Public Debt, website. Table 1.2 describes some of the other ways we evaluate our nation's economy.

gross domestic product (GDP) the sum of all goods and services produced in a country during a year.

budget deficit the condition in which a nation spends more than it takes in from taxes.

▼ **TABLE 1.2** How Do We Evaluate Our Nation's Economy?

Unit of Measure	Description
Trade balance	The difference between our exports and our imports. If the balance is negative, as it has been since the mid-1980s, it is called a trade deficit and is generally viewed as unhealthy for our economy.
Consumer Price Index	Measures changes in prices of goods and services purchased for consumption by typical urban households.
Per capita income	Indicates the income level of "average" Americans. Useful in determining how much "average" consumers spend and how much money Americans are earning.
Unemployment rate	Indicates how many working-age Americans are not working who otherwise want to work.
Inflation	Monitors price increases in consumer goods and services over specified periods of time. Used to determine if costs of goods and services are exceeding worker compensation over time.
Worker productivity	The amount of goods and services produced for each hour worked.

LO 1-7 Outline the evolution of the American economy.

THE AMERICAN ECONOMY

As we said previously, the United States is a mixed economy with a foundation based on capitalism. The answers to the three basic economic issues are determined primarily by competition and the forces of supply and demand, although the federal government does intervene in economic decisions to a certain extent. For instance, the federal government exerts oversight over the airline industry to make sure airlines remain economically viable as well as for safety and security purposes.

Standard of living refers to the level of wealth and material comfort that people have available to them. The United States, Germany, Australia, and Norway all have a high standard of living, meaning that most of their citizens are able to afford basic necessities and some degree of comfort. These nations are often characterized by a high GDP per capita. However, a higher GDP per capita does not automatically translate into a higher standard of living. Costs of goods and services are also factors. The European Union and Japan, for instance, tend to have higher costs of living than in the United States. Higher prices mean that it costs more to obtain a certain level of comfort than it does in other countries. Countries with low standards of living are usually characterized by poverty, higher unemployment, and lower education rates. To understand the current state of the American economy and its effect on business practices, it is helpful to examine its history and the roles of the entrepreneur and the government.

The Importance of the American Economy

The American economy is an **open economy**, or an economy in which economic activities occur between the country and the international community. As an open economy, the United States is a major player in international trade. Open economies tend to grow faster than economies that do not engage in international trade. This is because international trade is positively related to efficiency and productivity. Companies in the United States have greater access to a wider range of resources and knowledge, including technology. In today's global environment, the ability to harness technology is critical toward increased innovation.[16] In contrast, research indicates a negative relationship between regulatory actions and innovation in firms, suggesting that too much regulation hinders business activities and their contribution to the American economy.[17]

When looking at the American economy, growth in GDP and jobs are the two primary factors economists consider. A positive relationship exists between a country's employment rate and economic growth. A nation's output depends on the amount of labor used in the production process, so there is also a positive correlation between output and employment. In general, as the labor force and productivity increase, so does GDP. Profitable companies tend to hire more workers than those that are unprofitable. Therefore, companies that hire employees not only improve their profitability but also drive the economic well-being of the American economy.[18]

Government public policy often moves quickly to protect the economy. For example, during the COVID-19 pandemic, Congress passed the Coronavirus Aid, Relief, and Economic Security (CARES) Act to provide financial assistance to small business, state and local governments, as well as some larger firms. For individuals, each adult with an income of less than $99,000 received a direct payment of up to $1,200 and $500 per child or up to $3,400 for a family of four. This historic action was designed to protect the economy while many businesses had to close to prevent the spread of the virus.[19]

Government public policy also drives the economy through job creation. In order for any nation to ensure the social and economic health of the country, there must be a tax base to provide for the public interest. The vast majority of taxes come from individuals. It is estimated that the U.S. government obtains $2.6 trillion in individual income taxes annually.[20] Individuals who earn more than $510,300 pay 37 percent of individual income taxes.[21]

Businesses are also an important form of tax revenue. Those that are classified as sole proprietorships, partnerships, and S corporations (discussed further in the chapter titled "Options for Organizing Business") pay taxes according to the individual income tax code. Corporations are taxed differently. Approximately 4.4 percent of the government's total revenues comes from corporate income taxes.[22] In 2017, the largest tax reform in the U.S. tax rate in over 30 years changed the corporate tax rate from 35 percent to 21 percent.[23] The average global corporate tax rate is 24 percent, while some countries such as Ireland have a corporate tax rate as low as 12.5 percent. The U.S. tax reform lowered the highest individual tax rate from 39.6 percent to 37 percent, but the reform capped the deduction of state and local taxes at $10,000.[24]

A Brief History of the American Economy

The Early Economy. Before the colonization of North America, Native Americans lived as hunter/gatherers and farmers, with some trade among tribes. The colonists who came later operated primarily as an *agricultural economy*. People were self-sufficient and produced everything they needed at home, including food, clothing, and furniture. Abundant natural resources and a moderate climate nourished industries such as farming, fishing, shipping, and fur trading. A few manufactured goods and money for the colonies' burgeoning industries came from England and other countries.

As the nation expanded slowly toward the West, people found natural resources such as coal, copper, and iron ore and used them to produce goods such as horseshoes, farm implements, and kitchen utensils. Farm families who produced surplus goods sold or traded them for things they could not produce themselves, such as coffee, salt, and farm equipment. Some families also spent time turning raw materials into clothes and household goods. Because these goods were produced at home, this system was called the domestic system.

The Industrial Revolution.
The 19th century and the Industrial Revolution brought the development of new technology and factories. The factory brought together all the resources needed to make a product—materials, machines, and workers. Work in factories became specialized as workers focused on one or two tasks. As work became more efficient, productivity increased, making more goods available at lower prices. Railroads brought major changes, allowing farmers to send their agricultural products all over the nation to markets.

Factories began to spring up along the railways to manufacture farm equipment and products such as textiles, clothing, and household items to be shipped by rail. Eli Whitney revolutionized the cotton industry with his cotton gin. John Deere's farm equipment increased farm production and reduced the number of farmers required to feed the young nation. Farmers began to move to cities to find jobs in factories and a higher standard of living. Henry Ford developed the assembly-line system to produce automobiles. Workers focused on one part of an automobile and then pushed it to the next stage until it rolled off the assembly line as a finished automobile. Ford's assembly line could manufacture many automobiles efficiently, and the price of his cars was $200, making them affordable to many Americans.

The Manufacturing and Marketing Economies.
Industrialization brought increased prosperity, and the United States gradually became a *manufacturing economy*—one devoted to manufacturing goods and providing services rather than producing agricultural products. Businesses became more concerned with the needs of the consumer and entered the *marketing economy*. Marketing advanced when Alexander Turney Stewart built one of the first department stores in the 1860s. Aaron Montgomery Ward developed a catalog with 10,000 items that could be shipped by train in 1872. The development of retail institutions created the demand for more manufactured products. Companies conducted research to find out what products consumers needed and wanted. Advertising

DID YOU KNOW?

Approximately 70 percent of women with children under the age of 18 are involved in the workforce.[c]

made consumers aware of products and important information about features, prices, and other competitive advantages.

Because these developments occurred in a free-enterprise system, consumers determined what goods and services were produced. They did this by purchasing the products they liked at prices they were willing to pay. The United States prospered, and American citizens had one of the highest standards of living in the world.

The Service and New Digital Economy.
After World War II, with the increased standard of living, Americans had more money and more time. They began to pay others to perform services that made their lives easier. Beginning in the 1960s, more and more women entered the workforce. The United States began experiencing major shifts in the population. The U.S. population experienced the slowest pace of growth since the Great Depression, with the South leading the population gains. While the birth rate in the United States is declining, new immigrants help with population gains.[25] The profile of the family is also changing: Today there are more single-parent families and individuals living alone, and in two-parent families, both parents often work.

One result of this trend is that time-pressed Americans are increasingly paying others to do tasks they used to do at home, like cooking, laundry, landscaping, and child care. These trends have gradually changed the United States to a *service economy*—one devoted to the production of services that make life easier for busy consumers. Businesses increased their demand for services, especially in the areas of finance and information technology. Service industries such as restaurants, banking, health care, child care, auto repair, leisure-related industries, and even education are growing rapidly and may account for as much as 80 percent of the U.S. economy. These trends continue with advanced technology contributing to new service products based on technology and digital media that provide smartphones, social networking, and virtual worlds. This has led to the growth of e-commerce, or transactions involving goods and services over the Internet. E-commerce has led to firms that would have been unheard of a few decades ago, such as eBay, Shopify, Etsy, and Amazon. More about the digital world, business, and new online social media can be found in the chapter titled "Digital Marketing and Social Media."

The economy experienced a major shift in 2020 as a result of the COVID-19 pandemic. Travel bans were issued, people across the globe were ordered to stay at home, nonessential businesses were closed, students attended school online, major events were canceled, and many people began to work remotely. Even as businesses began to reopen, the world experienced a new normal. As working from home became mainstream, many companies reevaluated their real estate needs and permanently shuttered offices in major cities, impacting the commercial real-estate market.[26] Online grocery ordering gained popularity, telemedicine became widespread, and shopping shifted online. In fact, roughly 100,000 stores are estimated to close before 2025, according to UBS, an investment banking company.[27] Additionally, the virus accelerated the adoption of certain technologies in business such as cloud technology, cybersecurity, and artificial intelligence.[28]

Technology and the Economy

Technology is rapidly accelerating and is changing the environment of business. **Technology** includes the methods and processes creating applications to solve problems, perform tasks and make decisions. New technology associated with artificial intelligence enabled by big data and advanced computing systems are changing the way work is accomplished. The result is disruptive technology such as smart buildings, digital wallets, and drones, robotics, and machines that can communicate and make decisions like humans. This creates opportunities for new business models and job opportunities.

Artificial intelligence (AI) relates to machine (computer) learning that is able to perform activities and tasks that usually require human intelligence such as decisions, visual perception, and speech recognition. In short, it makes computers act like humans. Although it's estimated AI will disrupt

25 percent of U.S. jobs, the timeline is uncertain. However, the World Economic Forum predicts that AI will create more jobs than it takes, including new roles that do not exist today. Because of this, education institutions and business will need to keep employment dynamic by providing individuals with the soft skills need to work alongside AI and its enablers.[29] AI's enablers, as seen in Figure 1.5, include big data, blockchain, drones, robotics, and more.

AI is moving rapidly across business functions because it can resolve predictable business activities. For example, using machine technology to analyze thousands of emails with customer service concerns can create a response that is faster and more accurate than using humans to respond. Delta uses an AI-powered business chat tool to supplement its customer service team, allowing its agents to handle more complex tasks while responding to a higher volume of inquiries.[30] Approximately 40 percent of Americans that use the internet indicate they would rather use digital customer services than speak to a service provider on the phone.[31] Additionally, AI has the potential to make the world more efficient in predictable, physical work such as assembly lines, food preparation, packaging, welding, and other repetitive tasks.

While it has the potential to provide greater productivity and higher quality service, it also creates new challenges.[32] For instance, AI has the potential to be just as biased as humans since it can adopt pre-existing human biases and engage in unintentional discrimination.[33] Surveillance is another sensitive issue that is related to privacy. Facial recognition has been found to falsely identify Asian and African American faces 10 to 100 times more often than Caucasian faces, according to the National Institute of Standards and Technology.[34] Tracking communication, profiles, and other searchable information will accelerate with AI.

Business have an unprecedented amount of data at their fingertips. **Big data** refers to large volumes of structured and unstructured data this is transmitted at very fast speeds. AI systems learn from big data, such as consumer shopping habits, web browsing history, and social media activity. Insights from big data can improve decision making and inform business strategies. For example, Johnson & Johnson uses big data to determine the likelihood of success for new drugs.[35] However, the amount of data available to businesses creates consumer privacy concerns. Half of business ethics violations are related to the improper use of big data analytics, according to Gartner.[36] It's important for businesses to consider the best ways to collect, store, and share consumer data.

Blockchain will enable AI with the development of databases that can be used in AI learning. **Blockchain** is a decentralized

▼FIGURE 1.5 AI in Relation to Its Enablers

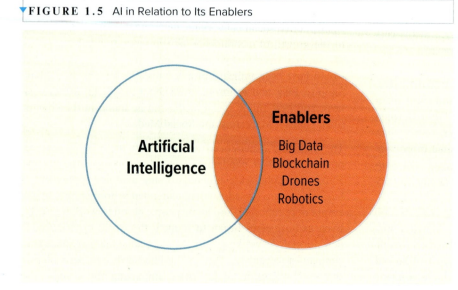

Enablers

Big Data
Blockchain
Drones
Robotics

Artificial Intelligence

record-keeping technology that stores linked block of ordered transactions over time. The distinguishing feature of a blockchain are the ordered rules of how the data goes into the database. The data is locked into a system without a central person controlling it. The key is no single authority can make changes to fit their needs. The finance industry, supply chain, marketing, human resource management, and most other areas of business will become more efficient in developing and tracking information.[37]

Blockchain has the potential to make databases and the digital infrastructures more secure and trustworthy. For example, scanning data in a blockchain database and tracking products from a point of production to consumption. For this reason, blockchain is especially important in managing the supply chain. It can track product history, generate invoices, detect counterfeit products, manage returned products, and help find and reuse materials rather than new resources. It can enable firms to trace deliveries, verify transactions, and handle payments. It is transforming the supply side of business.[38] This means that the movement of agricultural products, for instance, can be tracked from the farm to the table. Walmart uses the technology to track their products through the entire supply chain to the store. According to Walmart, the time it takes to trace the origin of an item decreased from seven days to 2.2 seconds.[39]

Drones, unmanned aerial devices, can be programmed with AI to perform human tasks such as delivering products or collecting environmental data and imagery. Drones can be beneficial in a variety of industries such as construction, farming, defense, insurance, outdoor entertainment, and retail. During the COVID-19 pandemic, UPS used drones to deliver prescription medication from CVS to retirees in Florida.[40] As of now, adoption of this technology is limited because few companies have permission to fly drones beyond visual line of sight from the Federal Aviation Administration (FAA).[41] Drones pose a challenge not only to airspace but privacy as well. Though businesses may not intentionally surveil on the population, drones with cameras have the potential to take photos and videos of people without their consent.

In addition to drones, robots can be programmed with AI to perform human-like actions by learning, reasoning, and using language through machine learning. Lowe's, for instance, has a customer service robot called OSHbot which can speak with customers in multiple languages and help locate items in the store. Robots used in this type of application can efficiently and effectively assist customers. As with AI's other enablers, privacy is a concern with robots because they have the potential to collect sensitive data that could violate an individual's privacy.[42]

AI and its enablers are rapidly changing the world of business. Big data can be combined with AI machine learning to provide important information and help leaders make decisions on key issues. Blockchain combined with AI can enable new business models. For example, cryptocurrency such as bitcoin is based on blockchain technology. Drones can help extend the reach of businesses, and robots can create a personalized shopping experience. These advanced technologies will make it possible to create entrepreneurs that will develop new business.

LO 1-8 Explain the role of the entrepreneur in the economy.

The Role of the Entrepreneur

An **entrepreneur** is an individual who risks his or her wealth, time, and effort to develop for profit an innovative product or way of doing something. Heidi Ganahl is a true American entrepreneur. She took the unusual concept of a day care center for dogs and turned it into a successful $85 million franchise operation with Camp Bow Wow which offers boarding, playtime, grooming, and other services for dogs. Additionally, Ganahl founded a startup incubator called Fight Back Foundation to support social entrepreneurs.[43]

The free-enterprise system provides the conditions necessary for entrepreneurs like Ganahl to succeed. In the past, entrepreneurs

Ripe.io aims to use blockchain technology to address issues like food fraud and food safety in the restaurant industry. The agritech startup has worked with restaurants like Sweetgreen to track produce from farm to restaurant.

Jeffrey MacMillan/Getty Images

Apple Pay is a mobile payment system that allows users to store credit card or debit card information on their phones. When checking out at stores, users can bring up their credit card with two taps and use the information to pay for their purchases.

How Hwee Young/Epa/REX/Shutterstock

were often inventors who brought all the factors of production together to produce a new product. Thomas Edison, whose inventions include the record player and light bulb, was an early American entrepreneur. Henry Ford was one of the first persons to develop mass assembly methods in the automobile industry. Other entrepreneurs, so-called captains of industry, invested in the country's growth. John D. Rockefeller built Standard Oil out of the fledgling oil industry, and Andrew Carnegie invested in railroads and founded the United States Steel Corporation. Andrew Mellon built the Aluminum Company of America and Gulf Oil. J. P. Morgan started financial institutions to fund the business activities of other entrepreneurs. Although these entrepreneurs were born in another century, their legacy to the American economy lives on in the companies they started, many of which still operate today. Consider the history of Eli

Lilly. Colonel Eli Lilly in Indianapolis, Indiana, was continually frustrated with the quality of pharmaceutical products sold at the time. As a pharmaceutical chemist, he decided to start his own firm that would offer the highest-quality medicines. His firm, Eli Lilly and Company, would go on to make landmark achievements, including being one of the first pharmaceutical firms to mass-produce penicillin. Today, Eli Lilly is one of the largest pharmaceutical firms in the world.[44]

Entrepreneurs are constantly changing American business practices with new technology and innovative management techniques. Bill Gates, for example, built Microsoft, a software company whose products include Word and Windows, into a multibillion-dollar enterprise. Frederick Smith had an idea to deliver packages overnight, and now his FedEx Company plays an important role in getting documents and packages delivered all over the world for businesses and individuals. Steve Jobs co-founded Apple and turned the company into a successful consumer electronics firm that revolutionized many different industries, with products such as the iPod. Entrepreneurs have been associated with such uniquely American concepts as Walt Disney, Spanx, Tesla, McDonald's, SpaceX, Google, Facebook, and Walmart. We will examine the importance of entrepreneurship further in the chapter "Small Business, Entrepreneurship, and Franchising."

The Role of Government in the American Economy

The American economic system is best described as modified capitalism because the government regulates business to preserve competition and protect consumers and employees.

UP IN THE AIR: DRONES AND AIR TRAFFIC CONTROL

The U.S. practices modified capitalism, where free enterprise is encouraged, but the government intervenes and regulates business to some extent. Air traffic control, for instance, is run by the government to regulate and manage air space. While this type of government control works for airplanes, the rise of a new type of product taking to the skies calls for a more autonomous type of control.

As drones increase in popularity, the need for a new air traffic control system has increased. As many as 7 million drones could be in the sky at once, according to the Federal Aviation Administration (FAA). Drones are used to take pictures, deliver packages, inspect infrastructure, and more.

Companies like Amazon, Airbus, and Google are leading the charge for a private, nationwide drone air traffic control system. Unlike the air traffic control system for airplanes, this drone system is private. Eight companies, including T-Mobile and Intel, have been selected to develop the technology that will enable remote drone identification. The FAA will define a drone traffic management framework that commercial operators will follow.

Drones would use sensors to scan their surroundings and broadcast that information to other drones around them. This proposed system could lead to an overhaul of the air traffic control system, which has remained largely

unchanged since the 1940s, because the same infrastructure could be applied to airplanes. Technology is evolving fast, and a future where the skies are filled with drones is not far away.[d]

Critical Thinking Questions

1. How does this situation demonstrate a modified capitalist economic system?

2. What is the difference between the current air traffic control system and the proposed air traffic control system for drones?

3. Why would it be harder for the government to maintain as much control over drones as it does for airplanes?

Federal, state, and local governments intervene in the economy with laws and regulations designed to promote competition and to protect consumers, employees, and the environment. Many of these laws are discussed in the Chapter 2 Appendix.

Additionally, government agencies such as the U.S. Department of Commerce measure the health of the economy (GDP, productivity, etc.) and, when necessary, take steps to minimize the disruptive effects of economic fluctuations and reduce unemployment. When the economy is contracting and unemployment is rising, the federal government through the Federal Reserve Board (see chapter titled "Money and the Financial System") tries to spur growth so that consumers will spend more money and businesses will hire more employees. To accomplish this, it may reduce interest rates or increase its own spending for goods and services. When the economy expands so fast that inflation results, the government may intervene to reduce inflation by slowing down economic growth. This can be accomplished by raising interest rates to discourage spending by businesses and consumers. Techniques used to control the economy are discussed in "Money and the Financial System."

The Role of Ethics and Social Responsibility in Business

In the past few years, there have been a number of scandals at well-known corporations, including Fifth Third Bank, Airbus, and the University of Phoenix. In many cases, misconduct by individuals within these firms had an adverse effect on employees, investors, and others associated with these firms. These scandals undermined public confidence in corporate America and sparked a new debate about ethics in business. *Business ethics* generally refers to the standards and principles used by society to define appropriate and inappropriate conduct in the workplace. In many cases, these standards have been codified as laws prohibiting actions deemed unacceptable.

Society is increasingly demanding that businesspeople behave socially responsibly toward their stakeholders, including customers, employees, investors, government regulators, communities, and the natural environment. Diversity in the workforce is not only socially responsible, but also highly beneficial to the financial performance of companies. According to a McKinsey consulting firm study, organizations that have diverse leadership are more likely to report higher financial returns. This study defined diversity as women and minorities. Diversity creates increased employee satisfaction and improved decision making.[45] When actions are heavily criticized, a balance is usually required to support and protect various stakeholders.

While one view is that ethics and social responsibility are a good supplement to business activities, there is an alternative viewpoint. Ethical behavior can not only enhance a company's reputation, but can also drive profits.[46] The ethical and socially responsible conduct of companies such as Microsoft, Patagonia, and Ben & Jerry's provides evidence that good ethics is good business. There is growing recognition that

the long-term value of conducting business in an ethical and socially responsible manner that considers the interests of all stakeholders creates superior financial performance.[47]

To promote socially responsible and ethical behavior while achieving organizational goals, businesses can monitor changes and trends in society's values. Businesses should determine what society wants and attempt to predict the long-term effects of their decisions. While it requires an effort to address the interests of all stakeholders, businesses can prioritize and attempt to balance conflicting demands. The goal is to develop a solid reputation of trust and avoid misconduct to develop effective workplace ethics.

CAN YOU LEARN BUSINESS IN A CLASSROOM?

Obviously, the answer is yes, or there would be no purpose for this textbook or course! To be successful in business, you need knowledge, skills, experience, and good judgment. The topics covered in this chapter and throughout this book provide some of the knowledge you need to understand the world of business. In addition, the "Building Your Soft Skills" exercise will help you develop skills that may be useful in your future career. However, good judgment is based on knowledge and experience plus personal insight and understanding. Therefore, you need more courses in business, along with some practical experience in the business world, to help you develop the special insight necessary to put your personal stamp on knowledge as you apply it. The challenge in business is in the area of judgment, and judgment does not develop from memorizing an introductory business textbook. If you are observant in your daily experiences as an employee, as a student, and as a consumer, you will improve your ability to make good business judgments.

BUILDING YOUR SOFT SKILLS

BY SETTING GOALS

Employers today want employees with strong soft skills—skills such as communication, leadership, teamwork, self-management, critical thinking, and people skills. You learned in this chapter that all businesses have goals. Consider your own goals for taking this course. What do you hope to learn or gain? Next, set a *specific* goal for yourself related to this course. For example, your goal might be to earn a grade of B or higher or to determine which particular field of business you are most interested in pursuing. Finally, list three *specific* steps you can take to ensure you meet your goal by the end of the course.

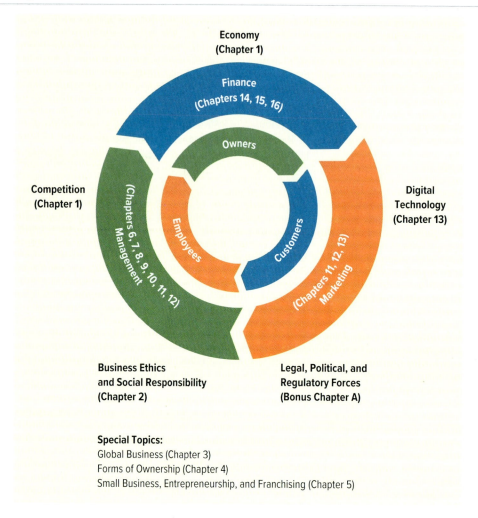

Special Topics:
Global Business (Chapter 3)
Forms of Ownership (Chapter 4)
Small Business, Entrepreneurship, and Franchising (Chapter 5)

Whether you choose to work at an organization or become an entrepreneur, you will be required to know the basic concepts and principles in this book. You need to be prepared for changes in the way business will be conducted in the future. New business models or ways businesses create value will emerge based on the Internet, connected technologies, drones, driverless cars, and artificial intelligence. It should be exciting to think about your opportunities and the challenges of creating a successful career. Our society needs a strong economic foundation to help people develop a desired standard of living.

Team Exercise

Major economic systems, including capitalism, socialism, and communism, as well as mixed economic systems were discussed in this chapter. Assuming that you want an economic system that is best for the majority, not just a few members of society, defend one of the economic systems as the best system. Form groups and try to reach an agreement on one economic system. Defend why you support the system that you advance.

Our world economy is becoming more digital and competitive, requiring new skills and job positions. Individuals like you can become leaders in business, nonprofits, and government to create a better life.

Figure 1.6 is an overview of how the chapters in this book are linked together and how the chapters relate to the participants, the activities, and the environmental factors found in the business world. The topics presented in the chapters that follow are those that will give you the best opportunity to begin the process of understanding the world of business. ■

ARE YOU PREPARED // to Take Advantage of Emerging Job Opportunities? /

When most people think of a career in business, they see themselves entering the door to large companies and multinationals that they read about in the news and that are discussed in class. In a national survey, students indicated they would like to work for Google, Ernst & Young, and PricewaterhouseCoopers. In fact, most jobs are not with large corporations, but are in small companies, nonprofit organizations, government, and even as self-employed individuals. There will continue to be an increase in independent workers. With more than 77 percent of the economy based on services, there are many jobs available in industries such as health care, finance, education, hospitality, and entertainment. E-commerce has led to the evolution of supply chain jobs related to purchasing, transportation, and operations. The world is changing quickly and large corporations replace the equivalent of their entire workforce every four years.

The fast pace of technology today means that you have to be prepared to take advantage of emerging job opportunities and markets. You must also become adaptive and recognize that business is becoming more global, with job opportunities around the world. If you want to obtain such a job, you shouldn't miss a chance to spend some time overseas. To get you started on the path to thinking about job opportunities, consider all of the changes in business today that might affect your possible long-term track and that could bring you lots of success. Companies are looking for employees with skills that can be used to address the changing business environment. For example, the demand for graduates that are good at analyzing data is on the rise.

You're on the road to learning the key knowledge, skills, and trends that you can use to be a star in business. Business's impact on our society, especially in the area of sustainability and improvement of the environment, is a growing challenge and opportunity. Green businesses and green jobs in the business world are provided to give you a glimpse at the possibilities. Along the way, we will introduce you to some specific careers and offer advice on developing your own job opportunities. Research indicates that you won't be that happy with your job unless you enjoy your work and feel that it has a purpose. Because you spend most of your waking hours every day at work, you need to seriously think about what is important to you in a job.[e]

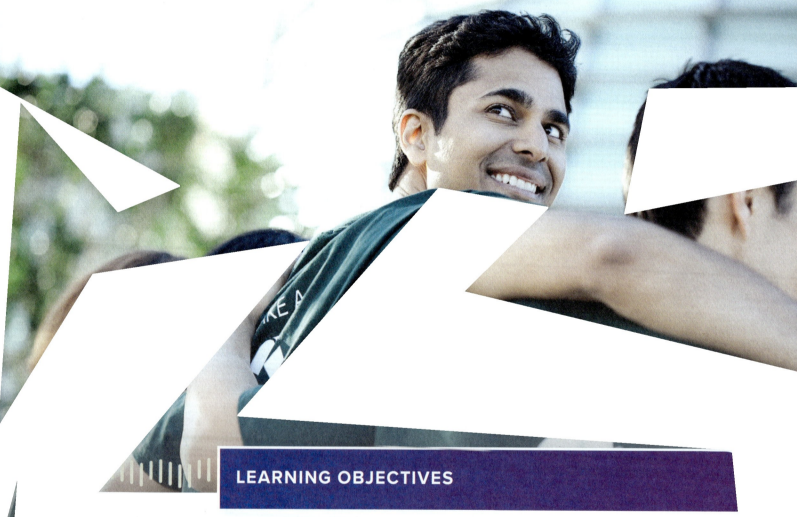

business ethics and
social responsibility

Simon Jarratt/Corbis/VCG/Getty Images

LEARNING OBJECTIVES

After reading this chapter, you will be able to:

LO 2-1 Describe the importance of business ethics and social responsibility.

LO 2-2 Detect some of the ethical issues that may arise in business.

LO 2-3 Specify how businesses can promote ethical behavior.

LO 2-4 Explain the four dimensions of social responsibility.

LO 2-5 Evaluate an organization's social responsibilities to owners, employees, consumers, the environment, and the community.

Any organization, including nonprofits, has to manage the ethical behavior of employees and participants in the overall operations of the organization. Firms that are highly ethical tend to be more profitable with more satisfied employees and customers.[1] Therefore, there are no conflicts between profits and ethics—in fact, unethical conduct is more likely to lower profits than raise them. For instance, Volkswagen pleaded guilty to criminal charges for cheating on U.S. emissions tests, and the company faced $25 billion in the United States for fines, vehicle buybacks, and repairs.[2] Wrongdoing by some businesses has focused public attention and government involvement on encouraging more acceptable business conduct. Any organizational decision may be judged as right or wrong, ethical or unethical, legal or illegal.

In this chapter, we take a look at the role of ethics and social responsibility in business decision making. First, we define *business ethics* and examine why it is important to understand ethics' role in business. Next, we explore a number of business ethics issues to help you learn to recognize such issues when they arise. Finally, we consider steps businesses can take to improve ethical behavior in their organizations. The second half of the chapter focuses on social responsibility and unemployment. We describe some important issues and detail how companies have responded to them. ■

LO 2-1   Describe the importance of business ethics and social responsibility.

BUSINESS ETHICS AND SOCIAL RESPONSIBILITY

In this chapter, we define **business ethics** as the principles and standards that determine acceptable conduct in business organizations. Personal ethics, on the other hand, relates to an individual's values, principles, and standards of conduct. The acceptability of behavior in business is determined by not only the organization but also stakeholders such as customers, competitors, government regulators, interest groups, and the public, as well as each individual's personal principles and values. The publicity and debate surrounding highly visible legal and ethical issues at a number of well-known firms, including Wells Fargo and Volkswagen, highlight the need for businesses to integrate ethics and responsibility into all business decisions. For instance, Wells Fargo provided incentives to its sales department that resulted in opening 3.5 million accounts without customer knowledge. This resulted in lowering customers' credit ratings and additional expenses for customers. Most unethical activities within organizations are supported by an organizational culture that encourages employees to bend the rules. On the other hand, trust in business is the glue that holds relationships together. In Figure 2.1, you can see that trust in financial services is lower than in other industries. While the majority of the population trusts business, a significant portion does not.

Organizations that exhibit a high ethical culture encourage employees to act with integrity and adhere to business values. For example, Illycaffè, an Italian family business, has been recognized as an ethical leader in quality, sustainability, and supply chain practices. The company is a leader in the science and technology of coffee and the world's most global coffee brand.[3] Many experts agree that ethical leadership, ethical values, and

business ethics
principles and standards that determine acceptable conduct in business.

Wells Fargo opened 3.5 million fake accounts that hurt customers credit ratings.

Kristi Blokhin/Shutterstock

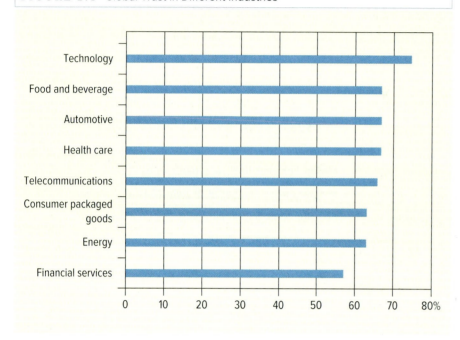

Source: Edelman, *2020 Edelman Trust Barometer Global Report,* https://www.edelman.com/sites/g/files/aatuss191/files/2020-01/2020%20Edelman%20Trust%20Barometer%20Global%20Report_LIVE.pdf (accessed May 22, 2020).

social responsibility
a business's obligation to maximize its positive impact and minimize its negative impact on society.

negative impact on society. Although many people use the terms *social responsibility* and *ethics* interchangeably, they do not mean the same thing. Business ethics relates to an *individual's* or a *work group's* decisions that society evaluates as right or wrong, whereas social responsibility is a broader concept that concerns the impact of the *entire business's* activities on society. From an ethical perspective, for example, we may be concerned about a health care organization overcharging the government for Medicare services. From a social responsibility perspective, we might be concerned about the impact that this overcharging will have on the ability of the health care system to provide adequate services for all citizens.[6]

The most basic ethical and social responsibility concerns have been codified by laws and regulations that encourage businesses to conform to society's standards, values, and attitudes. Laws and regulations attempt to institutionalize ethical conduct and prevent harm to customers, the environment, and other stakeholders. Accounting, finance, and marketing professionals have to understand laws and regulations that apply to their work. For example, the Dodd-Frank Act was passed to reform the financial industry and offer consumers protection against complex and/or deceptive financial products. At a minimum, managers are expected to obey all laws and regulations. Most legal issues arise as choices that society deems unethical, irresponsible, or otherwise unacceptable. However, all actions deemed unethical by society are not necessarily illegal, and both legal and ethical concerns change over time (see Table 2.1). More recently, identity theft has become the number-one consumer complaint with the Federal Trade Commission, and companies have an ethical responsibility to protect customer data. *Business law* refers to the laws and

compliance are important in creating good business ethics. To truly create an ethical culture, however, managers must show a strong commitment to ethics and compliance. This "tone at the top" requires top managers to acknowledge their own role in supporting ethics and compliance, clearly communicate company expectations for ethical behavior to all employees, educate all managers and supervisors in the business about the company's ethics policies, and train managers and employees on what to do if an ethics crisis occurs.[4]

> ## "Businesses should not only make a profit, but also consider the social implications of their activities."

Businesses should not only make a profit, but also consider the social implications of their activities. For instance, Walmart to date has donated more than 1.5 billion pounds of food and $2 billion to fight hunger.[5] However, profits permit businesses to contribute to society. The firms that are more well known for their strong social contributions tend to be those that are more profitable. We define **social responsibility** as a business's obligation to maximize its positive impact and minimize its

regulations that govern the conduct of business. Many problems and conflicts in business could be avoided if owners, managers, and employees knew more about business law and the legal system. Business ethics, social responsibility, and laws together act as a compliance system, requiring that businesses and employees act responsibly in society. In this chapter, we explore ethics and social responsibility. Chapter 2 Appendix provides an overview of the legal and regulatory environment.

▼ TABLE 2.1 Timeline of Ethical and Socially Responsible Activities

1960s	1970s	1980s
• Social issues • Consumer Bill of Rights • Disadvantaged consumer • Environmental issues • Product safety	• Business ethics • Social responsibility • Diversity • Bribery • Discrimination • Identifying ethical issues	• Standards for ethical conduct • Financial misconduct • Self-regulation • Codes of conduct • Ethics training
1990s	**2000s**	**2010s**
• Corporate ethics programs • Regulation to support business ethics • Health issues • Safe working conditions • Detecting misconduct	• Transparency in financial markets • Cyber security • Intellectual property • Regulation of accounting and finance • Executive compensation • Identity theft	• Sustainability • Supply chain transparency • Sexual misconduct • Data protection • Disruptive technologies

THE ROLE OF ETHICS IN BUSINESS

You have only to pick up *The Wall Street Journal* or *USA Today* to see examples of the growing concern about legal and ethical issues in business. For example, Apple CEO Tim Cook has called for stronger U.S. data protection regulation to help prevent the sharing of personal information. Many other tech firms have joined the call for stronger U.S. legislation that creates comprehensive laws similar to the European Union's General Data Protection Regulation which created several laws preventing companies from collecting and sharing personal data.[7] Regardless of what an individual believes about a particular action, if society judges it to be unethical or wrong, whether correctly or not, that judgment directly affects the organization's ability to achieve its business goals.[8]

Many firms are recognized for their ethical conduct. 3M is consistently placed on the World's Most Ethical Companies list. Furthermore, 3M's chief compliance officer states, "it is not enough to just win in business—it matters how you do it." 3M sees ethics as a competitive advantage.[9] The mass media frequently report about firms that engage in misconduct related to bribery, fraud, and unsafe products. However, the good ethical conduct of the vast majority of firms is not reported as often. Therefore, the public often gets the impression that misconduct is more widespread than it is in reality.

Often, misconduct starts as ethical conflicts but evolves into legal disputes when cooperative conflict resolution cannot be accomplished. This is because individuals may have different ethical beliefs and resort to legal activities to resolve issues. Also, there are many ethical gray areas, which occur when a new, undetermined or ambiguous situation arises. There may be no values, codes, or laws that answer the question about appropriate action. The sharing economy with peer-to-peer relationships like Uber, Lyft, and Airbnb provide new business models where existing regulations were inadequate, ambiguous, or in some cases blocking progress. For example, Uber has been accused of price gouging, endangering riders' safety, sexual harassment, stealing secret information on self-driving cars from Google, and violating local regulations on public transportation in some countries, states, and cities.[10]

However, it is important to understand that business ethics goes beyond legal issues. Ethical conduct builds trust among individuals and in business relationships, which validates and promotes confidence in business relationships. Establishing trust and confidence is much more difficult in organizations that have reputations for acting unethically. If you were to discover, for example, that a manager had misled you about company benefits when you were hired, your trust and confidence in that company would probably diminish. And if you learned that a colleague had lied to you about something, you probably would not trust or rely on that person in the future.

Ethical issues are not limited to for-profit organizations either. Ethical issues include all areas of organizational activities. In government, politicians and some high-ranking officials have faced disciplinary actions over ethical indiscretions. There has been ethical misconduct in sports, and even ethical lapses in well-known nonprofits, such as the American Red Cross. Whether made in science, politics, sports, or business, most decisions are judged as right or wrong, ethical or unethical. Negative judgments can affect an organization's ability to build relationships with customers and suppliers, attract investors, and retain employees.[11]

Although we will not tell you in this chapter what you ought to do, others—your superiors, co-workers, and family—will make judgments about the ethics of your actions and decisions. Learning how to recognize and resolve ethical issues is a key step in evaluating ethical decisions in business.

Recognizing Ethical Issues in Business

Recognizing ethical issues is the most important step in understanding business ethics. An **ethical issue** is an identifiable problem, situation, or opportunity that requires a person to choose from among several actions that may be evaluated as right or wrong, ethical or unethical. Learning how to choose from alternatives and make a decision requires not only good personal values, but also knowledge competence in the business area of concern. Employees also need to know when to rely on their organizations' policies and codes of ethics or have discussions with co-workers or managers on appropriate conduct. Ethical decision making is not always easy because there are always gray areas that create dilemmas, no matter how decisions are made. For instance, should an employee report on a co-worker engaging in time theft? Or should you report a friend cheating on a test? Should a salesperson omit facts about a product's poor safety record in his presentation to a customer? Such questions require the decision maker to evaluate the ethics of his or her choice and decide whether to ask for guidance.

ethical issue an identifiable problem, situation, or opportunity that requires a person to choose from among several actions that may be evaluated as right or wrong, ethical or unethical.

bribes payments, gifts, or special favors intended to influence the outcome of a decision.

One of the principal causes of unethical behavior in organizations is rewards for overly aggressive financial or business objectives. It is not possible to discuss every issue, of course. However, a discussion of a few issues can help you begin to recognize the ethical problems with which businesspersons must deal. Many ethical issues in business can be categorized in the context of their relation with abusive and intimidating behavior, conflicts of interest, fairness and honesty, communications, misuse of company resources, and business associations. The Global Business Ethics Survey found that workers witness many instances of ethical misconduct in their organizations and sometimes feel pressured to compromise standards (see Table 2.2). Overall, 47 percent of employees surveyed observed misconduct. Many observed multiple issues including abusive behavior (26 percent), lying (22 percent), and conflict of interest (15 percent). During the COVID-19 (coronavirus) pandemic in 2020, many companies shifted to remote workforces. While the increased number of people working from home likely reduced incidences of bullying and sexual harassment, many companies were unable to effectively

▼ **TABLE 2.2** Organizational Misconduct in the United States

Misconduct Facts	Percentage
Observed misconduct	47
Abusive behavior	26
Lying to stakeholders	22
Conflict of interest	15
Internet abuse	16
Health violations	15
Pressure to compromise standards	16
Report observed misconduct	69
Experience retaliation for reporting	44

Source: Ethics and Compliance Initiative, 2018 Global Business Ethics Survey™: The State of Ethics and Compliance in the Workplace (Arlington, VA: Ethics and Compliance Initiative, 2018).

monitor employees to identify misconduct. As working from home becomes increasingly mainstream, companies will have to adjust their monitoring programs to better identify potential compliance violations.[12]

To help you understand ethical issues that perplex business-people today, we will take a brief look at some of them in this section. Ethical issues can be more complex now than in the past. The vast number of news-format investigative programs has increased consumer and employee awareness of organizational misconduct. In addition, the multitude of cable channels and Internet resources has improved the awareness of ethical problems among the general public.

Bribery.   Many business issues seem straightforward and easy to resolve on the surface, but are, in reality, very complex. A person often needs several years of experience in business to understand what is acceptable or ethical. For example, it is considered improper to give or accept **bribes**, which are payments, gifts, or special favors intended to influence the outcome of a decision. A bribe benefits an individual or a company at the expense of other stakeholders. Companies that do business overseas should be aware that bribes are a significant ethical issue and are, in fact, illegal in many countries. In the United States, the Foreign Corrupt Practices Act imposes heavy penalties on companies found guilty of bribing foreign government officials.

Ethics is also related to the culture in which a business operates. In the United States, for example, it would be inappropriate for a businessperson to bring an elaborately wrapped gift to a prospective client on their first meeting—the gift could be viewed as a bribe. In Japan, however, it is considered impolite *not* to bring a gift. Experience with the culture in which a business operates is critical to understanding what is ethical or unethical. On the other hand, firms must also abide by the values and policies of global business.

South Korea's president, Park Geun-hye was removed from office over a bribery scandal. The heir to the Samsung Group

A former Siemens executive plead guilty in a $100 million Argentina bribery case. The engineering firm itself was involved in a decades long legal investigation.

LUKAS BARTH/EPA-EFE/REX/Shutterstock

was sentenced to 25 years in prison for bribery and embezzlement though the sentence was reduced due to a retrial. There was a "donation" of $25 million to the National Pension Fund at the time of a Samsung merger. This case heightens the awareness of the political risks associated with bribery.[13] Such political scandals demonstrate that political ethical behavior must be proactively practiced at all levels of public service.

Misuse of Company Time.

Theft of time is a common area of misconduct observed in the workplace.[14] One example of misusing time in the workplace is by engaging in activities that are not necessary for the job. Some companies have chosen to block certain sites such as Facebook, YouTube, or Pandora from employees. In this case, the employee is misusing not only time, but also company resources by using the company's computer and Internet access for personal use. Time theft costs can be difficult to measure but are estimated to cost companies hundreds of billions of dollars annually. It is widely believed that the average employee "steals" 4.5 hours a week with late arrivals, leaving early, long lunch breaks, inappropriate sick days, excessive socializing, and engaging in personal activities such as online shopping and watching sports while on the job. For example, on Cyber Monday, nearly 25 percent of employees say they shop online while at work.[15] All of these activities add up to lost productivity and profits for the employer—and relate to ethical issues in the area of time theft.

Abusive and Intimidating Behavior.

Abusive or intimidating behavior is the most common ethical problem for employees. These concepts can mean anything from physical threats, false accusations, profanity, insults, yelling, harshness, and unreasonableness to ignoring someone or simply being annoying; and the meaning of these words can differ by person—you probably have some ideas of your own. Abusive behavior can be placed on a continuum from a minor distraction to a disruption of the workplace. For example, what one person may define as yelling might be another's definition of normal speech. Civility in our society is a concern, and the workplace is no exception. The productivity level of many organizations has been diminished by the time spent unraveling abusive relationships.

Abusive behavior is difficult to assess and manage because of diversity in culture and lifestyle. What does it mean to speak profanely? Is profanity only related to specific words or other such terms that are common in today's business world? If you are using words that are normal in your language but that others consider to be profanity, have you just insulted, abused, or disrespected them?

Within the concept of abusive behavior, intent should be a consideration. If the employee was trying to convey a compliment but the comment was considered abusive, then it was probably a mistake. The way a word is said (voice inflection) can be important. Add to this the fact that we now live in a multicultural environment—doing business and working with many different cultural groups—and the businessperson soon realizes the depth of the ethical and legal issues that may arise. There are problems of word meanings by age and within cultures. For example, an expression such as "Did you guys hook up last night?" can have various meanings, including some that could be considered offensive in a work environment.

Bullying is associated with a hostile workplace when a person or group is targeted and is threatened, harassed, belittled, verbally abused, or overly criticized. Bullying may create what some consider a hostile environment, a term generally associated with sexual harassment. Recently there has been an explosion of concern about sexual harassment. Ethical misconduct has been unveiled with exposure of sexual harassment that has been part of the culture of the entertainment and hospitality industries, as well as other areas such as government and many corporations.[16] Google employees staged a walkout over Google's treatment of sexual harassment claims for several senior executives,

> **Bullying is a widespread problem in the United States and can cause psychological damage that can result in health-endangering consequences to the target.**

▼ **TABLE 2.3** Actions Associated with Bullies

1. Spreading rumors to damage others
2. Blocking others' communication in the workplace
3. Flaunting status or authority to take advantage of others
4. Discrediting others' ideas and opinions
5. Using e-mail to demean others
6. Failing to communicate or return communication
7. Insults, yelling, and shouting
8. Using terminology to discriminate by gender, race, or age
9. Using eye or body language to hurt others or their reputation
10. Taking credit for others' work or ideas

Upset by alleged financial aid embezzlement by Howard University employees, students occupied the administration building to protest the misuse of university resources.

Astrid Riecken For The Washington Post/Getty Images

including one who received a $90 million exit package after being accused of sexual misconduct. Employee protestors called for Google to improve transparency for sexual misconduct cases and demanded equal pay and opportunity for employees.[17] Although sexual harassment has legal recourse, bullying has little legal recourse at this time. Bullying is a widespread problem in the United States and can cause psychological damage that can result in health-endangering consequences to the target. Surveys reveal that bullying in the workplace is on the rise.[18] As Table 2.3 indicates, bullying can use a mix of verbal, nonverbal, and manipulative threatening expressions to damage workplace productivity. One may wonder why workers tolerate such activities. The problem is that bullies often outrank their victims.

Misuse of Company Resources. Misuse of company resources has been identified by the Ethics Resource Center as a leading issue in observed misconduct in organizations. Issues might include spending an excessive amount of time on personal e-mails, submitting personal expenses on company expense reports, or using the company copier for personal use. Six Howard University employees were fired after they allegedly stole nearly $1 million via grants and tuition remission from the financial aid department.[19] While serious resource abuse can result in firing, some abuse can have legal repercussions.

Employee internal theft or the misuse of the employer's assets is a major loss of resources for many firms, especially retailers. For example, employees may hide company items in a handbag, backpack, or briefcase. Customers may be overcharged while the employees keep the extra money. Employees may ship personal items using a firm's account number. Contract maintenance personnel may steal materials or office equipment. Food service employees may provide free drinks or food to friends or even customers hoping for an extra tip. Estheticians or hair stylists may pocket money when clients pay with cash. There are many other ways to steal from the company. Firms need a good monitoring system and employee training to prevent the theft of resources.

The most common way that employees abuse resources is by using company computers for personal use. Typical examples of using a computer for personal use include shopping on the Internet, downloading music, doing personal banking, surfing

the Internet for entertainment purposes, or visiting Facebook. Some companies choose to take a flexible approach to addressing this issue. For example, many have instituted policies that allow for some personal computer use as long as the use does not detract significantly from the workday.

No matter what approach a business chooses to take, it must have policies in place to prevent company resource abuse. Because misuse of company resources is such a widespread problem, many companies, like Coca-Cola, have implemented official policies delineating acceptable use of company resources. Coca-Cola's policy states that company assets should not be used for personal gain or outside business or for anything illegal or unethical.[20] This kind of policy is in line with that of many companies, particularly large ones that can easily lose millions of dollars and thousands of hours of productivity to these activities.

Conflict of Interest. A conflict of interest, one of the most common ethical issues identified by employees, exists when an individual must choose whether to advance the individual's own personal interests or those of others. For example, a manager in a corporation is supposed to ensure that the company is profitable so that its stockholder-owners receive a return on their investment. In other words, the manager has a responsibility to investors. If she instead makes decisions that give her more power or money but do not help the company, then she has a conflict of interest—she is acting to benefit herself at the expense of her company and is not fulfilling her responsibilities as an employee. To avoid conflicts of interest, employees must be able to separate their personal financial interests from their business dealings. Adam Neumann, one of the founders of WeWork, is an example of an executive who engaged in self-serving behavior when he was the CEO. Neumann leased buildings to WeWork that he had a personal investment in. This was a conflict of interest because

The Office of Government Ethics decided cryptocurrency, such as bitcoin, should be covered by conflict of interest laws for federal employees who must now report virtual money on their financial disclosure statements.

Omar Marques/SOPA Images/LightRocket/Getty Images

▼ **TABLE 2.4** Least Corrupt Countries

Rank	Country
1	Denmark
1	New Zealand
3	Finland
4	Sweden
4	Singapore
4	Switzerland
7	Norway
8	Netherlands
9	Germany
9	Luxembourg
11	Iceland
12	Austria
12	Australia
12	United Kingdom
12	Canada
16	Hong Kong
17	Belgium
18	Estonia
18	Ireland
20	Japan

Source: Corruption Perceptions Index 2019, Transparency International, https://www.transparency.org/en/cpi/2019/results/table (accessed May 20, 2020).

he stood to profit at the company's expense. Additionally, he reserved the "We" trademark through an entity he owned then sold the rights to WeWork for $5.9 million in stock.[21] Conflict of interest can be particularly problematic in the finance industry because bad decisions can result in significant financial losses.

Insider trading is an example of a conflict of interest. Insider trading is the buying or selling of stocks by insiders who possess material that is still not public. Bribery can also be a conflict of interest. While bribery is an increasing issue in many countries, it is more prevalent in some countries than in others. Transparency International has developed a Corruption Perceptions Index (Table 2.4). Note that the United States, ranked at 23, does not appear in the top 20. The five countries rated by Transparency International as most corrupt include Yemen, Syria, Venezuela, South Sudan, and Somalia.[22]

Fairness and Honesty

Fairness and honesty are at the heart of business ethics and relate to the general values of decision makers. At a minimum, businesspersons are expected to follow all applicable laws and regulations. But beyond obeying the law, they are expected not to harm customers, employees, clients, or competitors knowingly through deception, misrepresentation, coercion, or discrimination. Honesty and fairness can relate to how the employees use the resources of the organization. In contrast, dishonesty is usually associated with a lack of integrity, lack of disclosure, and lying. One common example of dishonesty is theft of office supplies. Although the majority of office supply thefts involve small things such as pencils or Post-it Notes, some workers admit to stealing more expensive items or equipment such as computers or software. Employees should be aware of policies on stealing items and recognize how these decisions relate to ethical behavior.

One aspect of fairness relates to competition. For example, a former Apple employee was charged with stealing secrets related to its autonomous car technology for a Chinese startup, Xiaopeng Motors.[23] Although numerous laws have been passed to foster competition and make monopolistic practices illegal, companies sometimes gain control over markets by using questionable practices that harm competition. For instance, the U.S. Justice Department is filing antitrust charges against Google because of the company's dominance and alleged anticompetitive behavior in the online advertising industry. Because Google holds 90 percent of the search engine market globally, the controversy over how it abuses its dominance to remain ahead of the competition is likely to intensify.[24]

Another aspect of fairness and honesty relates to disclosure of potential harm caused by product use. Health-Ade, a kombucha company based in Los Angeles, paid a $4 million settlement due to discrepancies between the actual sugar and alcohol levels of its drinks and the amounts stated on its packaging. In addition to implementing a formula change to make its product more consistent, the company also agreed to add a disclosure to its product labels.[25]

Dishonesty has become a significant problem in the United States. The Houston Astros were fined $5 million after it was discovered the team used video surveillance to steal catchers' signals to pitchers. Coaches and players could see what pitch was coming next and then beat on a trash can to alert the team's player at bat.[26] In another example, Philip Esformes bribed the University of Pennsylvania's basketball coach to help his son get admitted to the university. This college admissions scandal was part of a large cheating scheme, dubbed Operation Varsity Blues, by more than 50 people across the United States who paid money to William Rick Singer, the organizer. Parents included celebrities Felicity Huffman and Lori Loughlin. Loughlin and husband Mossimo Giannulli plead guilty and received short-term prison sentences. Singer used money to fraudulently inflate college entrance exam scores and bribe college officials. Participants attempted to cheat the admissions system, giving their children an unfair advantage over other applicants.[27]

Communications.

Communications is another area in which ethical concerns may arise. False and misleading advertising, as well as deceptive personal-selling tactics, anger consumers and can lead to the failure of a business. Truthfulness about product

The FDA has strict labeling requirements for tobacco products. American Spirit advertises its cigarettes as being natural with a superior taste but is also required to include a warning that these cigarettes are no safer than other cigarettes.

Source: American Spirit

safety and quality is also important to consumers. Takata, a former automotive parts company, pleaded guilty to fraud and providing false data and agreed to pay $1 billion in a settlement to victims and car manufacturers for exploding airbags.[28]

Another important aspect of communications that may raise ethical concerns relates to product labeling. This becomes an even greater concern with potentially harmful products like cigarettes. The FDA warned three cigarette manufacturers against using "additive-free" or "natural" on their labeling out of concern that consumers would associate these terms as meaning that their products were healthier.[29] In the advertisement, American Spirit labels its cigarettes as "natural" but includes a warning that its product is not safer than other cigarettes. However, labeling of other products raises ethical questions when it threatens basic rights, such as freedom of speech and expression. This is the heart of the controversy surrounding the movement to require warning labels on movies and videogames, rating their content, language, and appropriate audience age. Although people in the entertainment industry claim that such labeling violates their First Amendment right to freedom of expression, other consumers—particularly parents—believe that labeling is needed to protect children from harmful influences. Internet regulation, particularly regulation designed to protect children and the elderly, is on the forefront in consumer protection legislation. Because of the debate surrounding the acceptability of these business activities, they remain major ethical issues.

Business Relationships.

The behavior of businesspersons toward customers, suppliers, and others in their workplace may also generate ethical concerns. Ethical behavior within a business involves keeping company secrets, meeting obligations and responsibilities, and avoiding undue pressure that may force others to act unethically. Managers in particular, because of the authority of their position, have the opportunity to influence employees' actions.

It is the responsibility of managers to create a work environment that helps the organization achieve its objectives and fulfill its responsibilities. However, the methods that managers use to enforce these responsibilities should not compromise employee rights. Organizational pressures may encourage a person to engage in activities that he or she might otherwise view as unethical, such as invading others' privacy or stealing a competitor's secrets. The firm may provide only vague or lax supervision on ethical issues, creating the opportunity for misconduct. Managers who offer no ethical direction to employees create many opportunities for manipulation, dishonesty, and conflicts of interest. This happened to Wells Fargo in creating 3.5 million fake accounts that hurt customers' credit ratings as well as other misconduct that damaged customers. The Federal Reserve restricted the bank's ability to grow until they could provide more oversight and reduce risks.[30]

Plagiarism—taking someone else's work and presenting it as your own without mentioning the source—is another ethical issue. As a student, you may be familiar with plagiarism in school—for example, copying someone else's term paper

▼ **TABLE 2.5** Questions to Consider in Determining
Whether an Action Is Ethical

Are there any potential legal restrictions or violations that could result from the action?
Does your company have a specific code of ethics or policy on the action?
Is this activity customary in your industry? Are there any industry trade groups that provide guidelines or codes of conduct that address this issue?
Would this activity be accepted by your co-workers? Will your decision or action withstand open discussion with co-workers and managers and survive untarnished?
How does this activity fit with your own beliefs and values?

Turnitin is an Internet service that allows teachers to determine if their students have plagiarized content.

Sharaf Maksumov/Shutterstock

or quoting from a published work or Internet source without acknowledging it. In business, an ethical issue arises when employees copy reports or take the work or ideas of others and present it as their own. A manager attempting to take credit for a subordinate's ideas is engaging in another type of plagiarism.

Making Decisions about Ethical Issues

It can be difficult to recognize specific ethical issues in practice. Managers, for example, tend to be more concerned about issues that affect those close to them, as well as issues that have immediate rather than long-term consequences. Thus, the perceived importance of an ethical issue substantially affects choices. However, only a few issues receive scrutiny, and most receive no

attention at all.[31] Managers make intuitive decisions sometimes without recognizing the embedded ethical issue.

Table 2.5 lists some questions you may want to ask yourself and others when trying to determine whether an action is ethical. Open discussion of ethical issues does not eliminate ethical problems, but it does promote both trust and learning in an organization.[32] When people feel that they cannot discuss what they are doing with their co-workers or superiors, there is a good chance that an ethical issue exists. Once a person has recognized an ethical issue and can openly discuss it with others, he or she has begun the process of resolving that issue.

LO 2-3 Specify how businesses can promote ethical behavior.

Improving Ethical Behavior in Business

Understanding how people make ethical choices and what prompts a person to act unethically may result in better ethical decisions. Ethical decisions in an organization are influenced by three key factors: individual moral standards and values, the influence of managers and co-workers, and the opportunity to engage in misconduct (Figure 2.2). While you have great control over your personal ethics outside the workplace, your co-workers and superiors exert significant control over your choices at work through authority and example. In fact, the activities and examples set by co-workers, along with rules and policies established by the firm, are critical in gaining consistent ethical compliance in an organization. If the company fails to provide good examples and direction for appropriate conduct, confusion and conflict will develop and result in the opportunity for misconduct. If your boss or co-workers leave work early, you may be tempted to do so as well. If you see co-workers engaged in personal activities such as shopping online or if they ignore the misconduct of others, then you may be more likely to do so also. Having sound personal values is important because you will be responsible for your own conduct.

Because ethical issues often emerge from conflict, it is useful to examine the causes of ethical conflict. Business managers and employees often experience some tension between their own ethical beliefs and their obligations to the organizations in which

▼ **FIGURE 2.2** Three Factors That Influence Business Ethics

Individual Standards and Values	+	Managers' and Co-workers' Influence	+	Opportunity: Codes and Compliance Requirements	=	Ethical/Unethical Choices in Business

codes of ethics formalized rules and standards that describe what a company expects of its employees.

whistleblowing the act of an employee exposing an employer's wrongdoing to outsiders, such as the media or government regulatory agencies.

they work. Many employees utilize different ethical standards at work than they do at home. This conflict increases when employees feel that their company is encouraging unethical conduct or exerting pressure on them to engage in it.

It is difficult for employees to determine what conduct is acceptable within a company if the firm does not have established ethics policies and standards. And without such policies and standards, employees may base decisions on how their peers and superiors behave. Professional **codes of ethics** are formalized rules and standards that describe what the company expects of its employees. Codes of ethics do not have to be so detailed that they take into account every situation, but they should provide guidelines and principles that can help employees achieve organizational objectives and address risks in an acceptable and ethical way. The development of a code of ethics should include not only a firm's executives and board of directors, but also legal staff and employees from all areas of a firm.[33] Table 2.6 lists why a code of ethics is important.

Codes of ethics, policies on ethics, and ethics training programs advance ethical behavior because they prescribe which activities are acceptable and which are not, and they limit the opportunity for misconduct by providing punishments for violations of the rules and standards. This creates compliance requirements to establish uniform behavior among all employees. Codes and policies on ethics encourage the creation of an ethical culture in the company. According to the Global Business Ethics Survey, employees in organizations that have written codes of conduct and ethics training, ethics offices or hotlines, and systems for reporting are more likely to report misconduct when they observe it. The survey found that a company's ethical culture is the greatest determinant of future misconduct.[34]

The enforcement of ethical codes and policies through rewards and punishments increases the acceptance of ethical standards by employees. One of the most important components of an ethics program is a means through which employees can report observed misconduct anonymously. Although the risk of retaliation is still a major factor in whether an employee will report illegal conduct, the Global Business Ethics Survey found that whistleblowing

Kim Gwang-ho, an automotive engineer, was a whistleblower who exposed Hyundai for allegedly hiding defects in its vehicles from the public.
emirhankaramuk/Shutterstock

has increased in the past few years. Approximately 69 percent of respondents said they reported misconduct when they observed it.[35] **Whistleblowing** occurs when an employee exposes an employer's wrongdoing to outsiders, such as the media or government regulatory agencies. Howard Wilkinson, a trader for a Danske Bank branch in Estonia, discovered massive fraud through his branch after he downloaded a report for a London business that reported that it had no assets. Wilkinson reported his findings to Danske officials, which kicked off the investigation that discovered the money laundering scheme. The internal investigation exonerated top management and shifted blame onto dozens of low-level employees, but CEO Thomas Borgen decided to resign nonetheless.[36] More companies are establishing programs to encourage employees to report illegal or unethical practices internally so that they can take steps to remedy problems before they result in legal action or generate negative publicity. Unfortunately, whistleblowers are often treated negatively in organizations. The government, therefore, tries to encourage employees to report observed misconduct. Congress has also taken steps to close a legislative loophole in whistleblowing legislation that has led to the dismissal of many whistleblowers. Congress passed the Dodd-Frank Act, which includes a "whistleblower bounty program." The Securities and Exchange Commission can now award whistleblowers between 10 and 30 percent of monetary sanctions over $1 million. The hope is that incentives will encourage more people to come forward with information regarding corporate misconduct.

▼ **TABLE 2.6** Why a Code of Ethics Is Important

• Alerts employees about important issues and risks to address.
• Provides values such as integrity, transparency, honesty, and fairness that give the foundation for building an ethical culture.
• Gives guidance to employees when facing gray or ambiguous situations or ethical issues that they have never faced before.
• Alerts employees to systems for reporting or places to go for advice when facing an ethical issue.
• Helps establish uniform ethical conduct and values that provide a shared approach to dealing with ethical decisions.
• Serves as an important document for communicating to the public, suppliers, and regulatory authorities about the company's values and compliance.
• Provides the foundation for evaluation and improvement of ethical decision making.

The current trend is to move away from legally based ethical initiatives in organizations to cultural- or integrity-based initiatives that make ethics a part of core organizational values. Organizations recognize that effective business ethics programs are good for business performance. Firms that develop higher levels of trust function more efficiently and effectively and avoid damaged company reputations and product images. Organizational ethics initiatives have been supportive of many positive and diverse organizational objectives, such as profitability, hiring, employee satisfaction, and customer loyalty.[37] Conversely, lack of organizational ethics initiatives and the absence of workplace values such as honesty, trust, and integrity can have a negative impact on organizational objectives and employee retention. According to one survey, companies with a weak ethical culture experience fewer favorable outcomes.[38]

LO 2-4 Explain the four dimensions of social responsibility.

THE NATURE OF SOCIAL RESPONSIBILITY

For our purposes, we classify four stages of social responsibility: financial, legal compliance, ethics, and philanthropy (Table 2.7). Another way of categorizing these four dimensions of social responsibility include economic, legal, ethical, and voluntary (including philanthropic).[39] Earning profits is the financial or economic foundation, and complying with the law is the next step. However, a business whose *sole* objective is to maximize profits is not likely to consider its social responsibility, although its activities will probably be legal. (We looked at ethical responsibilities in the first half of this chapter.) Voluntary responsibilities are additional activities that may not be required but which promote human welfare or goodwill. Legal and economic concerns have long been acknowledged in business, and voluntary and ethical issues are now being addressed by most firms.

Corporate citizenship is the extent to which businesses meet the legal, ethical, economic, and voluntary responsibilities placed on them by their various stakeholders. It involves the activities and organizational processes adopted by businesses to meet their social responsibilities. A commitment to corporate citizenship by a firm indicates a strategic focus on fulfilling the social responsibilities expected of it by its stakeholders. For example, CVS demonstrated corporate citizenship by eliminating tobacco products from its pharmacies. Although this cost the firm $2 billion in sales, CVS believed it was contradictory to market itself as a health care services business while still selling a dangerous product.[40] Corporate citizenship involves action and measurement of the extent to which a firm embraces the corporate citizenship philosophy and then follows through by implementing citizenship and social responsibility initiatives. One of the major corporate citizenship issues is the focus on preserving the environment. The majority of people agree that climate change is a global emergency, but there is no agreement on how to solve the problem.[41] Another example of a corporate citizenship issue might be animal rights—an issue that is important to many stakeholders. As the organic and local foods movements grow and become more profitable, more and more stakeholders are calling for more humane practices in factory farms as well.[42] Large factory farms are where most Americans get their meat, but some businesses are looking at more animal-friendly options in response to public outcry.

Part of the answer to climate change issues is alternative energy such as solar, wind, biofuels, and hydro applications. The drive for alternative fuels such as ethanol from corn has added new issues such as food price increases and food shortages. A survey revealed that 73 percent of American consumers feel that it is important for the government to invest in renewable energy.[43]

corporate citizenship the extent to which businesses meet the legal, ethical, economic, and voluntary responsibilities placed on them by their stakeholders.

▼ **TABLE 2.7** Social Responsibility Requirements

Stages	Examples
Stage 1: Financial and economic viability	Starbucks offers investors a healthy return on investment, including paying dividends.
Stage 2: Compliance with legal and regulatory requirements	Starbucks specifies in its code of conduct that payments made to foreign government officials must be lawful according to the laws of the United States and the foreign country.
Stage 3: Ethics, principles, and values	Starbucks' mission and values create ethical culture with ethical leaders.
Stage 4: Philanthropic activities	Starbucks created the Starbucks College Achievement Plan that offers eligible employees full tuition to earn a bachelor's degree in partnership with Arizona State University.

" A COMMITMENT TO CORPORATE CITIZENSHIP BY A FIRM INDICATES A STRATEGIC FOCUS ON FULFILLING THE SOCIAL RESPONSIBILITIES EXPECTED OF IT BY ITS STAKEHOLDERS. "

To respond to these developments, most companies are introducing eco-friendly products and marketing efforts. Dell introduced laptops that come in sustainably sourced packaging made from 25 percent recycled ocean-bound plastics and locally recycled plastics. This is part of a greater effort for Dell to increase its use of sustainable packaging from 85 percent to 100 percent by 2030. Since 2012, Dell has used more than 100 million pounds of sustainable materials in its commitment to recycled packaging.[44] Almost 40 percent of consumers have bought a product for the first time due to the brand taking a stance on an important societal or political issue. About 64 percent chose to switch or abandon brands based on the company's stance on an issue. An example of a high-profile company taking a stance is when Audi promoted gender pay equality in a commercial that aired during the Super Bowl.[45] This is because many businesses are promoting themselves as green-conscious and concerned about the environment without actually making the necessary commitments to environmental health.

The Ethisphere Institute selects an annual list of the world's most ethical companies based on the following criteria: corporate citizenship and responsibility; corporate governance; innovation that contributes to the public well-being; industry leadership; executive leadership and tone from the top; legal, regulatory, and reputation track record; and internal systems and ethics/compliance program.[46] Table 2.8 shows 26 from that list.

Although the concept of social responsibility is receiving more and more attention, it is still not universally accepted. Table 2.9 lists some of the arguments for and against social responsibility.

Nike released a series of controversial ads featuring Colin Kaepernick, a former NFL quarterback who kneeled during the national anthem to call attention to racial injustice. The campaign resulted in record-breaking brand engagement.

Angela Weiss/AFP/Getty Images

▼ **TABLE 2.8** A Selection of the World's Most Ethical Companies

L'Oréal	HASBRO Inc.
Sony	Intel
Microsoft	Xcel Energy
3M Company	General Motors
T-Mobile	Cummins Inc.
PepsiCo	John Deere
ManpowerGroup	LinkedIn
Colgate-Palmolive Company	Prudential
International Paper Co.	Thrivent Financial
Visa Inc.	Western Digital
USAA	Kellogg Company
Accenture	Aflac Incorporated
Wyndham Hotels & Resorts	Dell

Source: Ethisphere Institute, "The 2020 World's Most Ethical Companies® Honoree List," http://www.worldsmostethicalcompanies.com/honorees/ (accessed May 20, 2020).

IKEA was founded in Sweden in 1943 by Ingvar Kamprad. A favorite among customers searching for well-designed products at a low price, it has become the largest furniture retailer in the world. The culture of IKEA heavily reflects Swedish cultural values of hard-working, friendly, and helpful people. These values helped create IKEA's vision, which is "to create a better everyday life for the many people."

Corporate social responsibility (CSR) is a large factor in IKEA's company culture. Employees are encouraged to mentor young students, assist senior citizens, and more. By volunteering for these tasks, employees learn valuable skills that can transfer over to their jobs. IKEA has also found that CSR is a powerful recruiting tool. Through CSR, IKEA can help communities while attracting better talent.

In 1982, IKEA opened the IKEA foundation. Initially, the foundation focused on architecture and interior design, but the foundation expanded to fight for children's rights and education. The IKEA Foundation awarded a grant of $2.3 million to the World Resources Institute to help bring clean electricity to a million people in India and East Africa.

Another focus for IKEA is reducing carbon emissions. In fact, IKEA's long-term goal is to become "carbon positive," which means removing more carbon dioxide emissions than it creates. IKEA is already moving toward this goal by switching to electric delivery trucks. The company is committed to completely switching over to electric trucks in every location within the next several years. IKEA has invested around $2 billion in renewable energy and expects to be climate positive—producing more energy than they use—by 2030.[b]

Critical Thinking Questions

1. Describe the strides IKEA is attempting to take in sustainability.

2. How does IKEA display corporate social responsibility? How does this differ from ethical conduct?

3. Why do you think a culture of volunteerism might be helpful in recruiting new employees?

LO 2-5 Evaluate an organization's social responsibilities to owners, employees, consumers, the environment, and the community.

Social Responsibility Issues

Managers consider and make social responsibility decisions on a daily basis. Among the many social issues that managers must consider are their firms' relations with stakeholders, including owners and stockholders, employees, consumers, regulators, communities, and environmental advocates.

Social responsibility is a dynamic area with issues changing constantly in response to society's demands. There is much evidence that social responsibility is associated with improved business performance. Consumers are refusing to buy from businesses that receive publicity about misconduct. A number of studies have found a direct relationship between social responsibility and profitability, as well as a link that exists between employee commitment and customer loyalty—two major concerns of any firm trying to increase profits.[47] This section highlights a few of the many social responsibility issues that managers face; as managers become aware of and work toward the solution of current social problems, new ones will certainly emerge.

▼ **TABLE 2.9** The Arguments For and Against Social Responsibility

For:
1. Social responsibility rests on stakeholder engagement and results in benefits to society and improved firm performance.
2. Businesses are responsible because they have the financial and technical resources to address sustainability, health, and education.
3. As members of society, businesses and their employees should support society through taxes and contributions to social causes.
4. Socially responsible decision making by businesses can prevent increased government regulation.
5. Social responsibility is necessary to ensure economic survival: If businesses want educated and healthy employees, customers with money to spend, and suppliers with quality goods and services in years to come, they must take steps to help solve the social and environmental problems that exist today.

Against:
1. It sidetracks managers from the primary goal of business—earning profit. The responsibility of business to society is to earn profits and create jobs.
2. Participation in social programs gives businesses greater power, perhaps at the expense of concerned stakeholders.
3. Does business have the expertise needed to assess and make decisions about social and economic issues?
4. Social problems are the responsibility of the government agencies and officials, who can be held accountable by voters.
5. Creation of nonprofits and contributions to them are the best ways to implement social responsibility.

Relations with Owners and Stockholders.

Businesses must first be responsible to their owners, who are primarily concerned with earning a profit or a return on their investment in a company. In a small business, this responsibility is fairly easy to fulfill because the owner(s) personally manages the business or knows the managers well. In larger businesses, particularly corporations owned by thousands of stockholders, ensuring responsibility becomes a more difficult task.

A business's obligations to its owners and investors, as well as to the financial community at large, include maintaining proper accounting procedures, providing all relevant information to investors about the current and projected performance of the firm, and protecting the owners' rights and investments. In short, the business must maximize the owners' investments in the firm.

Employee Relations.

Another issue of importance to a business is its responsibilities to employees. Without employees, a business cannot carry out its goals. Employees expect businesses to provide a safe workplace, pay them adequately for their work, and keep them informed of what is happening in their company. They want employers to listen to their grievances and treat them fairly. After increased criticism about pay and benefits for its warehouse workers, Amazon raised the minimum wage paid to U.S. workers to $15 an hour. This pay increase boosted the wage of 250,000 current employees and 100,000 seasonal employees.[48]

OSHA ordered its inspectors to crack down on employers who fail to file the necessary electronic paperwork to document injury reports.

Herdik Herlambang/Shutterstock

Congress has passed several laws regulating safety in the workplace, many of which are enforced by the Occupational Safety and Health Administration (OSHA). Labor unions have also made significant contributions to achieving safety in the workplace and improving wages and benefits. Most organizations now recognize that the safety and satisfaction of their employees are critical ingredients in their success, and many strive to go beyond what is legally expected of them. Healthy, satisfied employees also supply more than just labor to their employers. Employers are beginning to realize the importance of obtaining input from even the lowest-level employees to help the company reach its objectives.

A major social responsibility for business is providing equal opportunities for all employees regardless of their sex, age, race, religion, or nationality. Diversity is also helpful to a firm financially. Corporations that raised the share of female executives to 30 percent saw a 15 percent increase in profitability.[49] Also, it has been found that when men and women managers are evenly matched, there is a better chance of generating stronger profits. Thus, many firms are trying to become more inclusive, embracing diversity.[50] Yet, despite these benefits, women and minorities have been slighted in the past in terms of education, employment, and advancement opportunities; additionally, many of their needs have not been addressed by business. After a U.K. High Court ruling, Lloyds Banking Group was ordered to equalize pension benefits for men and women. This ruling occurred after a dispute was filed by a female employee who pointed out that pensions for women were increasing at a lower rate than male pension plans for the company. The ruling is estimated to cost nearly €150 million and could result in additional costs and liabilities for the bank. Lloyds welcomed the ruling and claimed that the issue occurs industrywide and should be resolved.[51] Women, who continue to bear most child-rearing responsibilities, often experience conflict between those responsibilities and their duties as employees. Consequently, day care has become a major employment issue for women, and more companies are providing day care facilities as part of their effort to recruit and advance women in the workforce. A class-action lawsuit was filed against Avon, alleging the company discriminated against pregnant women.[52] Many Americans today believe business has a social obligation to provide special opportunities for women and minorities to improve their standing in society.

Consumer Relations.

A critical issue in business today is business's responsibility to customers, who look to business to provide them with satisfying, safe products and to respect their rights as consumers. The activities that independent individuals, groups, and organizations undertake to protect their rights as consumers are known as **consumerism**. To achieve their objectives, consumers and their advocates write letters to companies, lobby government agencies, make public service announcements, and boycott companies whose activities they deem irresponsible.

Many of the desires of those involved in the consumer movement have a foundation in John F. Kennedy's 1962 consumer bill of rights, which highlighted four rights. The *right to safety* means that a business must not knowingly sell anything that could result in personal injury or harm to consumers. Defective or dangerous products erode public confidence in the ability of business to serve society. They also result in expensive litigation that ultimately increases the cost of products for all consumers. The right to safety also means businesses must provide a safe place for consumers to shop.

The *right to be informed* gives consumers the freedom to review complete information about a product before they buy it. This means that detailed information about risks and instructions for use are to be printed on labels and packages. The *right to choose* ensures that consumers have access to a variety of goods and services at competitive prices. The assurance of both satisfactory quality and service at a fair price is also a part of the consumer's right to choose. The *right to be heard* assures consumers that their interests will receive full and sympathetic consideration when the government formulates policy. It also ensures the fair treatment of consumers who voice complaints about a purchased product.

The role of the Federal Trade Commission's Bureau of Consumer Protection exists to protect consumers against unfair, deceptive, or fraudulent practices. The bureau, which enforces a variety of consumer protection laws, is divided into five divisions. The Division of Enforcement monitors legal compliance and investigates violations of laws, including unfulfilled holiday delivery promises by online shopping sites, employment opportunities fraud, scholarship scams, misleading advertising for health care products, and more.

Sustainability Issues.

Most people probably associate the term *environment* with nature, including wildlife, trees, oceans, and mountains. Until the 20th century, people generally thought of the environment solely in terms of how these resources could be harnessed to satisfy their needs for food, shelter, transportation, and recreation. As the earth's population swelled throughout the 20th century, however, humans began to use more and more of these resources and, with technological advancements,

The Federal Trade Commission's Bureau of Consumer Protection protects consumers against unfair, deceptive, or fraudulent practices.

Mark Van Scyoc/Shutterstock

to do so with ever-greater efficiency. Although these conditions have resulted in a much-improved standard of living, they come with a cost. Plant and animal species, along with wildlife habitats, are disappearing at an accelerated rate. For example, the bumblebee population has suffered almost 90 percent decline in the past 20 years. Bees are important to pollinating most fruits and vegetables. The bumblebee was placed on the endangered species list and its habitats were protected.[53]

sustainability
conducting activities in a way that allows for the long-term well-being of the natural environment, including all biological entities; involves the assessment and improvement of business strategies, economic sectors, work practices, technologies, and lifestyles so that they maintain the health of the natural environment.

Although the scope of the word *sustainability* is broad, in this book we discuss the term from a strategic business perspective. Thus, we define **sustainability** as conducting activities in such a way as to provide for the long-term well-being of the natural environment, including all biological entities. Sustainability involves the interaction among nature and individuals, organizations, and business strategies and includes the assessment and improvement of business strategies, economic sectors, work practices, technologies, and lifestyles so that they maintain the health of the natural environment. In recent years, business has played a significant role in adapting, using, and maintaining the quality of sustainability.

Environmental protection emerged as a major issue in the 20th century in the face of increasing evidence that pollution, uncontrolled use of natural resources, and population growth were putting increasing pressure on the long-term sustainability of these resources. In recent years, companies have been increasingly incorporating these issues into their overall business strategies. Some nonprofit organizations have stepped forward to provide leadership in gaining the cooperation of diverse groups in responsible environmental activities.

In the following sections, we examine some of the most significant sustainability and environmental health issues facing business and society today, including pollution and alternative energy.

Pollution.

A major issue in the area of environmental responsibility is pollution. Water pollution results from dumping toxic chemicals and raw sewage into rivers and oceans, oil spills, and the burial of industrial waste in the ground where it may filter into underground water supplies. Fertilizers and insecticides used in farming and grounds maintenance also run off into water supplies with each rainfall. Water pollution problems are especially notable in heavily industrialized areas. Society is demanding that water supplies be clean and healthful to reduce the potential danger from these substances.

Air pollution is usually the result of smoke and other pollutants emitted by manufacturing facilities, as well as carbon monoxide and hydrocarbons emitted by motor vehicles. In addition to the health risks posed by air pollution, when some chemical compounds emitted by manufacturing facilities react with air and rain, acid rain results. Acid rain has contributed to the deaths of many forests and lakes in North America as well as in Europe. Air pollution may also contribute to global warming; as carbon dioxide collects in the earth's atmosphere, it traps the sun's heat and prevents the earth's surface from cooling. It is indisputable that the global surface temperature has been increasing over the past 35 years. Worldwide passenger vehicle ownership has been growing due to rapid industrialization and consumer purchasing power in China, India, and other developing countries with large populations. The most important way to contain climate change is to control carbon emissions. For example, some utilities charge more for electricity in peak demand periods, which encourages behavioral changes that reduce consumption.

More and more consumers are recognizing the need to protect the planet. Figure 2.3 shows consumers' likelihood to personally address social responsibility and environmental issues. Although most consumers admit that sustainable products are important and that they bear responsibility for properly using and disposing of the product, many admit that they fail to do this.

Land pollution is tied directly to water pollution because many of the chemicals and toxic wastes that are dumped on the land eventually work their way into the water supply. A study conducted by the Environmental Protection Agency found residues of prescription drugs, soaps, and other contaminants in virtually every waterway in the United States. Effects of these pollutants on humans and wildlife are uncertain, but there is some evidence to suggest that fish and other water-dwellers are starting to suffer serious effects. Land pollution results from the dumping of residential and industrial waste, strip mining, forest fires, and poor forest conservation. The world's forests cover more than 30 percent of the planet, but over the past 25 years, forests shrank by 502,000 square miles. In Brazil, more than 89,000 fires started by humans burned the Amazon in 2019, the most biodiverse rainforest on the planet.[54] During the COVID-19 pandemic in 2020, which prompted lockdowns and job loss in many countries, rainforest deforestation doubled.[55] Scientists fear the Amazon is close to a tipping point where it will enter an irreversible cycle of collapse.[56] Large-scale deforestation also depletes the oxygen supply available to humans and other animals.

Related to the problem of land pollution is the larger issue of how to dispose of waste in an environmentally responsible manner. Americans use approximately 100 billion plastic bags per year.[57] Some states and many other countries are also in the process of phasing out lightweight plastic bags.

Alternative Energy.

With ongoing plans to reduce global carbon emissions, countries and companies alike are looking toward alternative energy sources. Traditional fossil fuels are problematic because of their emissions, but also because stores have been greatly depleted.

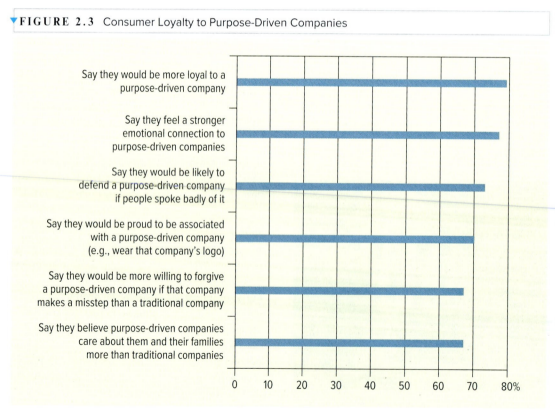

▼ **FIGURE 2.3** Consumer Loyalty to Purpose-Driven Companies

Source: Cone/Porter Novelli, "2018 Cone/Porter Novelli Purpose Study: How to Build Deeper Bonds, Amplify Your Message and Expand Your Consumer Base," http://www.conecomm.com/2018-purpose-study-pdf (accessed May 20, 2020).

Foreign fossil fuels are often imported from politically and economically unstable regions, often making it unsafe to conduct business there. However, the United States is becoming an energy powerhouse with its ability to drill for natural gas in large shale reserves. This is allowing the United States to move forward on its goals to reach energy independence. On the other hand, concerns over how these drilling methods are affecting the environment make this a controversial topic.

The U.S. government has begun to recognize the need to look toward alternative forms of energy as a source of fuel and electricity. There have been many different ideas as to which form of alternative energy would best suit the United States' energy needs. These sources include wind power, solar power, nuclear power, biofuels, electric cars, and hydro- and geothermal power. As of yet, no "best" form of alternative fuel has been selected to replace gasoline. Additionally, there are numerous challenges with the economic viability of alternative energy sources. For instance, wind and solar power cost significantly more than traditional energy. Alternative energy will likely require government subsidies to make any significant strides. However, the news for solar power might be getting brighter. Electric cars are also gaining importance. Most automobile companies such as Tesla, BMW, General Motors, Nissan, and Toyota are introducing electric cars to help with sustainability.

DID YOU KNOW?

About 50 million tons of electronic waste is generated each year, including discarded laptops, mobile phones, and televisions.[c]

Response to Environmental Issues. Many firms are trying to eliminate wasteful practices, the emission of pollutants, and/or the use of harmful chemicals from their manufacturing processes. In response to a plastic straw ban in Seattle, McDonald's began testing plastic straw alternatives, such as paper straws, in its restaurants.[58] Other companies are seeking ways to improve their products. Utility providers, for example, are increasingly supplementing their services with alternative energy sources, including solar, wind, and geothermal power.

Environmentalists are concerned that some companies are merely *greenwashing,* or "creating a positive association with environmental issues for an unsuitable product, service, or practice."

Indeed, a growing number of businesses and consumers are choosing green power sources where available. New Belgium Brewing Company, the fourth-largest craft brewer in the United States, is the first all-wind-powered brewery in the country. Many businesses have turned to *recycling,* the reprocessing of materials—aluminum, paper, glass, and some plastic—for reuse. Such efforts to make products, packaging, and processes more environmentally friendly have been labeled "green" business or marketing by the public and media. For example, lumber products at The Home Depot may carry a seal from the Forest Stewardship Council to indicate that they were harvested from sustainable forests using environmentally friendly methods.[59]

SHERWIN-WILLIAMS PAINTS ITSELF IN A CORNER

Most would agree that companies advertising a dangerous product should be held accountable. However, what if the advertisement was more than a century old? This is the dilemma paint makers like Sherwin-Williams are facing from a California lawsuit seeking damages for the firms' marketing of lead paint in homes.

For nearly two decades, California counties have demanded that paint manufacturers pay more than $1 billion into a state fund for investigating and removing lead paint from as many as 1.6 million homes. The courts initially ruled that Sherwin-Williams, NL Industries, and ConAgra were liable for the cleanup. Later, the damages were limited to paint used in houses prior to 1950, after which paint manufacturers began publicly acknowledging the dangers of

lead paint. Lead paint in homes would not officially become illegal until 1978.

After the ruling, paint manufacturers tried to fund a ballot initiative for taxpayers to fund the cleanup efforts but abandoned it after public outcry. After nearly 20 years of litigation, the final settlement was reduced to $305 million to be paid by Sherwin-Williams, NL Industries, and ConAgra over a period of six years, and the companies were not required to admit any wrongdoing.

A major consideration is how long these companies knew about the dangers. Some maintain Sherwin-Williams knew about the hazards since 1900. Sherwin-Williams denies it knew about the health risks before they were scientifically accepted. This case has important implications for the industry. This case could set a precedent that could increase potential

liability for advertisers, making them liable if their products are found to be hazardous further down the road—even if they are currently legal.[d]

Critical Thinking Questions

1. Describe the ethical issue in this case. Why do you think it has been so difficult to come to a solid verdict?

2. If Sherwin-Williams knew about the dangers of lead paint more than a century ago (it denies this claim), how would this violate the concepts of fairness and honesty? Do you think this should affect the verdict?

3. Recall that lead paint in homes was not made illegal until 1978. Yet knowledge that it was toxic inside the home was accepted since the 1950s. Do you think other stakeholders should be held liable for the cleanup?

With the increasing popularity of electric vehicles, companies like BMW, Volkswagen, and Tesla have introduced new electric car models.

Darren Brode/Shutterstock

It is important to recognize that, with current technology, environmental responsibility requires trade-offs. Society must weigh the huge costs of limiting or eliminating pollution against the health threat posed by the pollution. Environmental responsibility imposes costs on both business and the public. Managers must coordinate environmental goals with other social and economic ones.

Community Relations. A final, yet very significant, issue for businesses concerns their responsibilities to the general welfare of the communities and societies in which they operate. Many businesses simply want to make their communities better places for everyone to live and work. The most common way that businesses exercise their community responsibility is through donations to local and national charitable organizations. For example, companies and their employees hold fundraising efforts to raise money for the United Way.[60] As a highly successful company, Adobe invests heavily in community development and sustainability. It invests 1 percent of its pretax profits in the Adobe Foundation, which partners with teams of employees to use the funds to improve local communities. The company donates software to more than 15,000 nonprofits.[61]

UNEMPLOYMENT

After realizing that the current pool of prospective employees lacks many basic skills necessary to work, many companies have become concerned about the quality of education in the United

Team Exercise

Sam Walton, founder of Walmart, had an early strategy for growing his business related to pricing. The "Opening Price Point" strategy used by Walton involved offering the introductory product in a product line at the lowest point in the market. For example, a minimally equipped microwave oven would sell for less than anyone else in town could sell the same unit. The strategy was that if consumers saw a product, such as the microwave, and saw it as a good value, they would assume that all of the microwaves were good values. Walton also noted that most people don't buy the entry-level product; they want more features and capabilities and often trade up.

Form teams and assign the role of defending this strategy or casting this strategy as an unethical act. Present your thoughts on either side of the issue.

States. Unemployment reached 10 percent during the Great Recession, which began in 2008, but had fallen to 3.5 percent in 2019. However, it reached 14.7 percent during the COVID-19 pandemic in 2020.

Although most would argue that unemployment is an economic issue, it also carries ethical implications. Protests often occur in areas where unemployment is high, particularly when there seems to be a large gap between rich and poor.

Factory closures are another ethical issue because factories usually employ hundreds of workers. Sometimes it is necessary to close a plant due to economic reasons. However, factory closures not only affect individual employees, but their communities as well. After years of withstanding closures, even as other factories around it closed, a factory in the small town of Hanover, Illinois, shuttered its doors and transferred to Mexico. Several of the factory workers felt betrayed, and about 100 lost their jobs. Factory closures also have repercussions on other businesses in the area because more unemployed people mean fewer sales.[62]

Another criticism levied against companies involves hiring standards. Some employers have been accused of having unreasonable hiring standards that most applicants cannot meet, often leaving these jobs unfilled. Critics have accused companies of not wanting to take the time to train employees.[63] Employers, however, believe there is a significant lack of skills needed among job applicants. With more companies requiring specialized knowledge and a strong educational background, jobs are becoming increasingly competitive among those looking for employment.

On the other hand, several businesses are working to reduce unemployment. JPMorgan Chase introduced a public policy agenda, investing more than $7 million to reduce barriers to employment for people with criminal backgrounds.[64] Additionally, businesses are beginning to take more responsibility for the hard-core unemployed. These are people who have never had a job or who have been unemployed for a long period of time. Some are mentally or physically handicapped; some are homeless. Organizations such as the National Alliance of Businessmen fund programs to train the hard-core unemployed so that they can find jobs and support themselves. Such commitment enhances self-esteem and helps people become productive members of society. ■

ARE YOU READY // to Go Green and Think Ethics with Your Career? /

In the words of Kermit the Frog, "It's not easy being green." It may not be easy, but green business opportunities abound. A popular catch phrase, "Green is the new black," indicates how fashionable green business is becoming. Consumers are more in tune with and concerned about green products, policies, and behaviors by companies than ever before. Companies are looking for new hires to help them see their business creatively and bring insights to all aspects of business operations.

The International Renewable Energy Industry estimates that the number of jobs in the renewable energy job market could rise to 24 million by 2030. Green business strategies not only give a firm a commercial advantage in the marketplace, but also help lead the way toward a greener world. The fight to reduce our carbon footprint in an attempt against climate change has opened up opportunities for renewable energy, recycling, conservation, and increasing overall efficiency in the way resources are used. New businesses that focus on hydro, wind, and solar power are on the rise and will need talented businesspeople to

lead them. Carbon emissions' trading is gaining popularity as large corporations and individuals alike seek to lower their footprints. A job in this growing field could be similar to that of a stock trader, or you could lead the search for carbon-efficient companies in which to invest.

In the ethics arena, current trends in business governance strongly support the development of ethics and compliance departments to help guide organizational integrity. This alone is a billion-dollar business, and there are jobs in developing organizational ethics programs, developing company policies, and training employees and management. An entry-level position might be as a communication specialist or trainer for programs in a business ethics department. Eventually there's an opportunity to become an ethics officer that would have typical responsibilities of meeting with employees, the board of directors, and top management to discuss and provide advice about ethics issues in the industry, developing and distributing a code of ethics, creating and maintaining an anonymous, confidential service to answer questions about ethical issues,

taking actions on possible ethics code violations, and reviewing and modifying the code of ethics of the organization.

There are also opportunities to help with initiatives to help companies relate social responsibility to stakeholder interests and needs. These jobs could involve coordinating and implementing philanthropic programs that give back to others important to the organization or developing a community volunteering program for employees. In addition to the human relations function, most companies develop programs to assist employees and their families to improve their quality of life. Companies have found that the healthier and happier employees are, the more productive they will be in the workforce.

Social responsibility, ethics, and sustainable business practices are not a trend; they are good for business and the bottom line. New industries are being created and old ones are adapting to the new market demands, opening up many varied job opportunities that will lead not only to a paycheck, but also to the satisfaction of making the world a better place.[e]

the legal and regulatory environment

Business law refers to the rules and regulations that govern the conduct of business. Problems in this area come from the failure to keep promises, misunderstandings, disagreements about expectations, or, in some cases, attempts to take advantage of others. The regulatory environment offers a framework and enforcement system in order to provide a fair playing field for all businesses. The regulatory environment is created based on inputs from competitors, customers, employees, special interest groups, and the public's elected representatives. Lobbying by pressure groups who try to influence legislation often shapes the legal and regulatory environment.

SOURCES OF LAW

Laws are classified as either criminal or civil. *Criminal law* not only prohibits a specific kind of action, such as unfair competition or mail fraud, but also imposes a fine or imprisonment as punishment for violating the law. A violation of a criminal law is thus called a crime. *Civil law* defines all the laws not classified as criminal, and it specifies the rights and duties of individuals and organizations (including businesses). Violations of civil law may result in fines but not imprisonment. The primary difference between criminal and civil law is that criminal laws are enforced by the state or nation, whereas civil laws are enforced through the court system by individuals or organizations.

Criminal and civil laws are derived from four sources: the Constitution (constitutional law), precedents established by judges (common law), federal and state statutes (statutory law), and federal and state administrative agencies (administrative law). Federal administrative agencies established by Congress control and influence business by enforcing laws and regulations to encourage competition and protect consumers, workers, and the environment. The Supreme Court is the ultimate authority on legal and regulatory decisions for appropriate conduct in business.

COURTS AND THE RESOLUTION OF DISPUTES

The primary method of resolving conflicts and business disputes is through **lawsuits**, where one individual or organization takes another to court using civil laws. The legal system, therefore, provides a forum for businesspeople to resolve disputes based on our legal foundations. The courts may decide when harm or damage results from the actions of others.

[**"Business law refers to the rules and regulations that govern the conduct of business."**]

Because lawsuits are so frequent in the world of business, it is important to understand more about the court system where such disputes are resolved. Both financial restitution and specific actions to undo wrongdoing can result from going before a court to resolve a conflict. All decisions made in the courts are based on criminal and civil laws derived from the legal and regulatory system.

A businessperson may win a lawsuit in court and receive a judgment, or court order, requiring the loser of the suit to pay monetary damages. However, this does not guarantee the victor will be able to collect those damages. If the loser of the suit lacks the financial resources to pay the judgment—for example, if the loser is a bankrupt business—the winner of the suit may not be able to collect the award. Most business lawsuits involve a request for a sum of money, but some lawsuits request that a court specifically order a person or organization to do or to refrain from doing a certain act.

The Court System

Jurisdiction is the legal power of a court, through a judge, to interpret and apply the law and make a binding decision in a particular case. In some instances, other courts will not enforce the decision of a prior court because it lacked jurisdiction. Federal courts are granted jurisdiction by the Constitution or by Congress. State legislatures and constitutions determine which state courts hear certain types of cases. Courts of general jurisdiction hear all types of cases; those of limited jurisdiction hear only specific types of cases. The Federal Bankruptcy Court, for example, hears only cases involving bankruptcy. There is some combination of limited and general jurisdiction courts in every state.

In a **trial court** (whether in a court of general or limited jurisdiction and whether in the state or the federal system), two tasks must be completed. First, the court (acting through the judge or a jury) must determine the facts of the case. In other words, if there is conflicting evidence, the judge or jury must decide who to believe. Second, the judge must decide which law or set of laws is pertinent to the case and must then apply those laws to resolve the dispute.

An **appellate court**, on the other hand, deals solely with appeals relating to the interpretation of law. Thus, when you hear about a case being appealed, it is not retried, but rather reevaluated. Appellate judges do not hear witnesses but instead base their decisions on a written transcript of the original trial. Moreover, appellate courts do not draw factual conclusions; the appellate judge is limited to deciding whether the trial judge made a mistake in interpreting the law that probably affected the outcome of the trial. If the trial judge made no mistake (or if mistakes would not have changed the result of the trial), the appellate court will let the trial court's decision stand. If the appellate court finds a mistake, it usually sends the case back to the trial court so that the mistake can be corrected. Correction may involve the granting of a new trial. On occasion, appellate courts modify the verdict of the trial court without sending the case back to the trial court.

When workers and management cannot come to an agreement, workers may choose to picket and go on strike. Going on strike is usually reserved as a last resort if mediation and arbitration fail.

Tannen Maury/EPA/Shutterstock

Alternative Dispute Resolution Methods

Although the main remedy for business disputes is a lawsuit, other dispute resolution methods are becoming popular. The schedules of state and federal trial courts are often crowded; long delays between the filing of a case and the trial date are common. Further, complex cases can become quite expensive to pursue. As a result, many businesspeople are turning to alternative methods of resolving business arguments: mediation and arbitration, the mini-trial, and litigation in a private court.

Mediation is a form of negotiation to resolve a dispute by bringing in one or more third-party mediators, usually chosen by the disputing parties, to help reach a settlement. The mediator suggests different ways to resolve a dispute between the parties. The mediator's resolution is nonbinding—that is, the parties do not have to accept the mediator's suggestions; they are strictly voluntary.

Arbitration involves submission of a dispute to one or more third-party arbitrators, usually chosen by the disputing parties, whose decision is final. Arbitration differs from mediation in that an arbitrator's decision must be followed, whereas a mediator merely offers

business law the rules and regulations that govern the conduct of business.

lawsuit where one individual or organization takes another to court using civil laws.

jurisdiction the legal power of a court, through a judge, to interpret and apply the law and make a binding decision in a particular case.

trial court when a court (acting through the judge or jury) must determine the facts of the case, decide which law or set of laws is pertinent to the case, and apply those laws to resolve the dispute.

appellate court a court that deals solely with appeals relating to the interpretation of law.

mediation a method of outside resolution of labor and management differences in which the third party's role is to suggest or propose a solution to the problem.

arbitration settlement of a labor/management dispute by a third party whose solution is legally binding and enforceable.

The Federal Trade Commission regulates business activities related to questionable practices in order to protect consumers.

Source: Carol M. Highsmith Archive, Library of Congress, Prints and Photographs Division

mini-trial a situation in which both parties agree to present a summarized version of their case to an independent third party; the third party advises them of his or her impression of the probable outcome if the case were to be tried.

private court system similar to arbitration in that an independent third party resolves the case after hearing both sides of the story.

Federal Trade Commission (FTC) the federal regulatory unit that most influences business activities related to questionable practices that create disputes between businesses and their customers.

suggestions and facilitates negotiations. Cases may be submitted to arbitration because a contract—such as a labor contract—requires it or because the parties agree to do so. Some consumers are barred from taking claims to court by agreements drafted by banks, brokers, health plans, and others. Instead, they are required to take complaints to mandatory arbitration. Arbitration can be an attractive alternative to a lawsuit because it is often cheaper and quicker, and the parties frequently can choose arbitrators who are knowledgeable about the particular area of business at issue.

A method of dispute resolution that may become increasingly important in settling complex disputes is the **mini-trial**, in which both parties agree to present a summarized version of their case to an independent third party. That person then advises them of his or her impression of the probable outcome if the case were to be tried. Representatives of both sides then attempt to negotiate a settlement based on the advisor's recommendations. For example, employees in a large corporation who believe they have muscular or skeletal stress injuries caused by the strain of repetitive motion in using a computer could agree to a mini-trial to address a dispute related to damages. Although the mini-trial itself does not resolve the dispute, it can help the parties

resolve the case before going to court. Because the mini-trial is not subject to formal court rules, it can save companies a great deal of money, allowing them to recognize the weaknesses in a particular case.

In some areas of the country, disputes can be submitted to a private nongovernmental court for resolution. In a sense, a **private court system** is similar to arbitration in that an independent third party resolves the case after hearing both sides of the story. Trials in private courts may be either informal or highly formal, depending on the people involved. Businesses typically agree to have their disputes decided in private courts to save time and money.

REGULATORY ADMINISTRATIVE AGENCIES

Federal and state administrative agencies (listed in Table A.1) also have some judicial powers. Many administrative agencies, such as the Federal Trade Commission, decide disputes that involve their regulations. In such disputes, the resolution process is usually called a "hearing" rather than a trial. In these cases, an administrative law judge decides all issues.

Federal regulatory agencies influence many business activities and cover product liability, safety, and the regulation or deregulation of public utilities. Usually, these bodies have the power to enforce specific laws, such as the Federal Trade Commission Act, and have some discretion in establishing operating rules and regulations to guide certain types of industry practices. Because of this discretion and overlapping areas of responsibility, confusion or conflict regarding which agencies have jurisdiction over which activities is common.

Of all the federal regulatory units, the **Federal Trade Commission (FTC)** most influences business activities related to questionable practices that create disputes between businesses and their customers. Although the FTC regulates a variety of business practices, it allocates a large portion of resources to curbing false advertising, misleading pricing, and deceptive packaging and labeling. When it receives a complaint or otherwise has reason to believe that a firm is violating a law, the FTC issues a complaint stating that the business is in violation.

If a company continues the questionable practice, the FTC can issue a cease-and-desist order, which is an order for the business to stop doing whatever has caused the complaint. In such cases, the charged firm can appeal to the federal courts to have the order rescinded. However, the FTC can seek civil penalties in court—up to a maximum penalty of $10,000 a day for each infraction—if a cease-and-desist order is violated. In its battle against unfair pricing, the FTC has issued consent decrees alleging that corporate attempts to engage in price fixing or invitations to competitors to collude are violations even when

Agency	Major Areas of Responsibility
Federal Trade Commission (FTC)	Enforces laws and guidelines regarding business practices; takes action to stop false and deceptive advertising and labeling.
Food and Drug Administration (FDA)	Enforces laws and regulations to prevent distribution of adulterated or misbranded foods, drugs, medical devices, cosmetics, veterinary products, and particularly hazardous consumer products.
Consumer Product Safety Commission (CPSC)	Ensures compliance with the Consumer Product Safety Act; protects the public from unreasonable risk of injury from any consumer product not covered by other regulatory agencies.
Interstate Commerce Commission (ICC)	Regulates franchises, rates, and finances of interstate rail, bus, truck, and water carriers.
Federal Communications Commission (FCC)	Regulates communication by wire, radio, and television in interstate and foreign commerce.
Environmental Protection Agency (EPA)	Develops and enforces environmental protection standards and conducts research into the adverse effects of pollution.
Federal Energy Regulatory Commission (FERC)	Regulates rates and sales of natural gas products, thereby affecting the supply and price of gas available to consumers; also regulates wholesale rates for electricity and gas, pipeline construction, and U.S. imports and exports of natural gas and electricity.
Equal Employment Opportunity Commission (EEOC)	Investigates and resolves discrimination in employment practices.
Federal Aviation Administration (FAA)	Oversees the policies and regulations of the airline industry.
Federal Highway Administration (FHA)	Regulates vehicle safety requirements.
Occupational Safety and Health Administration (OSHA)	Develops policy to promote worker safety and health and investigates infractions.
Securities and Exchange Commission (SEC)	Regulates corporate securities trading and develops protection from fraud and other abuses; provides an accounting oversight board.
Consumer Financial Protection Bureau (CFPB)	Regulates financial products and institutions to ensure consumer protection.

the competitors in question refuse the invitations. The commission can also require companies to run corrective advertising in response to previous ads considered misleading.

The FTC also assists businesses in complying with laws. New marketing methods are evaluated every year. When general sets of guidelines are needed to improve business practices in a particular industry, the FTC sometimes encourages firms within that industry to establish a set of trade practices voluntarily. The FTC may even sponsor a conference bringing together industry leaders and consumers for the purpose of establishing acceptable trade practices.

Unlike the FTC, other regulatory units are limited to dealing with specific goods, services, or business activities. The Food and Drug Administration (FDA) enforces regulations prohibiting the sale and distribution of adulterated, misbranded, or hazardous food and drug products. For example, the FDA outlawed the sale and distribution of most over-the-counter hair-loss remedies after research indicated that few of the products were effective in restoring hair growth.

The Environmental Protection Agency (EPA) develops and enforces environmental protection standards and conducts research into the adverse effects of pollution. The Consumer Product Safety Commission recalls about 300 products a year, ranging from small, inexpensive toys to major appliances. The Consumer Product Safety Commission's website provides details regarding

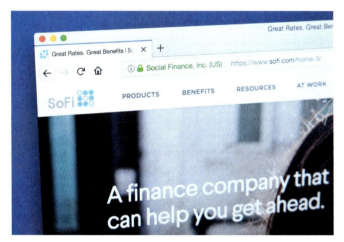

SoFi reached a settlement with the FTC over the financial services company's deceptive advertising about loan refinancing savings.
chrisdorney/Shutterstock

current recalls. The Consumer Product Safety Commission has fallen under increasing scrutiny in the wake of a number of product safety scandals involving children's toys. The most notable of these issues was lead paint discovered in toys produced in China. Some items are not even targeted to children but can be dangerous because children think they are food. Magnetic desk toys and Tide Pods have both been mistaken as candy by children.

IMPORTANT ELEMENTS OF BUSINESS LAW

To avoid violating criminal and civil laws, as well as discouraging lawsuits from consumers, employees, suppliers, and others, businesspeople need to be familiar with laws that address business practices.

The Uniform Commercial Code

At one time, states had their own specific laws governing various business practices, and transacting business across state lines was difficult because of the variation in the laws from state to state. To simplify commerce, every state—except Louisiana—has enacted the Uniform Commercial Code (Louisiana has enacted portions of the code). The **Uniform Commercial Code (UCC)** is a set of statutory laws covering several business law topics. Article II of the Uniform Commercial Code, which is discussed in the following paragraphs, has a significant impact on business.

Sales Agreements.

Article II of the Uniform Commercial Code covers sales agreements for goods and services such as installation but does not cover the sale of stocks and bonds, personal services, or real estate. Among its many provisions, Article II stipulates that a sales agreement can be enforced even though it does not specify the selling price or the time or place of delivery. It also requires that a buyer pay a reasonable price for goods at the time of delivery if the buyer and seller have not reached an agreement on price. Specifically, Article II addresses the rights of buyers and sellers, transfers of ownership, warranties, and the legal placement of risk during manufacture and delivery.

Article II also deals with express and implied warranties. An **express warranty** stipulates the specific terms the seller will honor. Many automobile manufacturers, for example, provide three-year or 36,000-mile warranties on their vehicles, during which period they will fix any and all defects specified in the warranty. An **implied warranty** is imposed on the producer or seller by law, although it may not be a written document provided at the time of sale. Under Article II, a consumer may assume that the product for sale has a clear title (in other words, that it is not stolen) and that the product will serve the purpose for which it was made and sold as well as function as advertised.

The Law of Torts and Fraud

A **tort** is a private or civil wrong other than a breach of contract. For example, a tort can result if the driver of a Domino's

Pizza delivery car loses control of the vehicle and damages property or injures a person. In the case of the delivery car accident, the injured persons might sue the driver and the owner of the company—Domino's in this case—for damages resulting from the accident.

Fraud is a purposefully unlawful act to deceive or manipulate in order to damage others. Thus, in some cases, fraud may also represent a violation of criminal law. Health care fraud has become a major issue in the courts.

An important aspect of tort law involves **product liability**—businesses' legal responsibility for any negligence in the design, production, sale, and consumption of products. Product liability laws have evolved from both common and statutory law. Some states have expanded the concept of product liability to include injuries by products whether or not the producer is proven negligent. Under this strict product liability, a consumer who files suit because of an injury has to prove only that the product was defective, that the defect caused the injury, and that the defect made the product unreasonably dangerous. For example, a carving knife is expected to be sharp and is not considered defective if you cut your finger using it. But an electric knife could be considered defective and unreasonably dangerous if it continued to operate after being switched off.

Reforming tort law, particularly in regard to product liability, has become a hot political issue as businesses look for relief from huge judgments in lawsuits. Although many lawsuits are warranted—few would disagree that a wrong has occurred when a patient dies because of negligence during a medical procedure or when a child is seriously injured by a defective toy and that the families deserve some compensation—many suits are not. Because of multimillion-dollar judgments, companies are trying to minimize their liability, and sometimes they pass on the costs of the damage awards to their customers in the form of higher prices. Some states have passed laws limiting damage awards and some tort reform is occurring at the federal level. Table A.2 lists the state courts systems the U.S. Chamber of Commerce's Institute for Legal Reform has identified as being "friendliest" and "least friendly" to business in terms of juries' fairness, judges' competence and impartiality, and other factors.

The Law of Contracts

Virtually every business transaction is carried out by means of a **contract**, a mutual agreement between two or more parties that can be enforced in a court if one party chooses not to comply with the terms of the contract. If you rent an apartment or house, for example, your lease is a contract. If you have borrowed money under a student loan program, you have a contractual agreement to repay the money. Many aspects of contract law are covered under the Uniform Commercial Code.

A "handshake deal" is, in most cases, as fully and completely binding as a written, signed contract agreement. Indeed, many oil-drilling and construction contractors have for years agreed to take on projects on the basis of such handshake deals. However, individual states require that some contracts be in writing to be enforceable. Most states require that at least some of the following contracts be in writing:

- Contracts involving the sale of land or an interest in land.

- Contracts to pay somebody else's debt.

- Contracts that cannot be fulfilled within one year.

- Contracts for the sale of goods that cost more than $500 (required by the Uniform Commercial Code).

Only those contracts that meet certain requirements—called *elements*—are enforceable by the courts. A person or business seeking to enforce a contract must show that it contains the following elements: voluntary agreement, consideration, contractual capacity of the parties, and legality.

For any agreement to be considered a legal contract, all persons involved must agree to be bound by the terms of the contract. *Voluntary agreement* typically comes about when one party makes an offer and the other accepts. If both the offer and the acceptance are freely, voluntarily, and knowingly made, the acceptance forms the basis for the contract. If, however, either the offer or the acceptance is the result of fraud or force, the individual or organization subject to the fraud or force can void, or invalidate, the resulting agreement or receive compensation for damages.

The second requirement for enforcement of a contract is that it must be supported by *consideration*—that is, money or something of value must be given in return for fulfilling a contract. As a general rule, a person cannot be forced to abide by the terms of a promise unless that person receives a consideration. The "something of value" could be money, goods, services, or even a promise to do or not to do something.

Contractual capacity is the legal ability to enter into a contract. As a general rule, a court cannot enforce a contract if either

▼ **TABLE A.2** State Court Systems' Reputations for Supporting Business

Most Friendly to Business	Least Friendly to Business
Delaware	Georgia
Maine	Alabama
Connecticut	New Jersey
Wyoming	Missouri
Alaska	West Virginia
North Dakota	Florida
Montana	Mississippi
Nebraska	California
Idaho	Louisiana
South Dakota	Illinois

Source: U.S. Chamber Institute for Legal Reform, "States," www.instituteforlegalreform.com/states (accessed May 21, 2020).

party to the agreement lacks contractual capacity. A person's contractual capacity may be limited or nonexistent if he or she is a minor (under the age of 18), mentally unstable, intellectually disabled, insane, or intoxicated.

Legality is the state or condition of being lawful. For an otherwise binding contract to be enforceable, both the purpose of and the consideration for the contract must be legal. A contract in which a bank loans money at a rate of interest prohibited by law, a practice known as usury, would be an illegal contract, for example. The fact that one of the parties may commit an illegal act while performing a contract does not render the contract itself illegal, however.

Breach of contract is the failure or refusal of a party to a contract to live up to his or her promises. In the case of an apartment lease, failure to pay rent would be considered breach of contract. The breaching party—the one who fails to comply—may be liable for monetary damages that he or she causes the other person.

The Law of Agency

An **agency** is a common business relationship created when one person acts on behalf of another and under that person's control. Two parties are involved in an agency relationship: The **principal** is the one who wishes to have a specific task accomplished; the **agent** is the one who acts on behalf of the principal to accomplish the task. Authors, movie stars, and athletes often employ agents to help them obtain the best contract terms.

An agency relationship is created by the mutual agreement of the principal and the agent. It is usually not necessary that such an agreement be in writing, although putting it in writing is certainly advisable. An agency relationship continues as long as both the principal and the agent so desire. It can be terminated by mutual agreement, by fulfillment of the purpose of the agency, by the refusal of either party to continue in the relationship, or by the death of either the principal or the agent. In most cases, a principal grants authority to the agent through a formal *power of attorney*, which is a legal document authorizing a person to act as someone else's agent. The power of attorney can be used for any agency relationship, and its use is not limited to lawyers. For instance, in real estate transactions, often a lawyer or real estate agent is given power of attorney with the authority to purchase real estate for the buyer. Accounting firms often give employees agency relationships in making financial transactions.

inventory, and clothing. *Intangible property* consists of rights and duties; its existence may be represented by a document or by some other tangible item. For example, accounts receivable, stock in a corporation, goodwill, and trademarks are all examples of intangible personal property. **Intellectual property** refers to property, such as musical works, artwork, books, and computer software, that is generated by a person's creative activities.

Copyrights, patents, and trademarks provide protection to the owners of property by giving them the exclusive right to use it. *Copyrights* protect the ownership rights on material (often intellectual property) such as books, music, videos, photos, and computer software. The creators of such works, or their heirs, generally have exclusive rights to the published or unpublished works for the creator's lifetime, plus 50 years. *Patents* give inventors exclusive rights to their invention for 20 years. The most intense competition for patents is in the pharmaceutical industry. Most patents take a minimum of 18 months to secure.

A *trademark* is a brand (name, mark, or symbol) that is registered with the U.S. Patent and Trademark Office and is thus legally protected from use by any other firm. Among the symbols that have been so protected are McDonald's golden arches. It is estimated that large multinational firms may have as many as 15,000 conflicts related to trademarks. Companies are diligent about protecting their trademarks both to avoid confusion in consumers' minds and because a term that becomes part of

> ## " COPYRIGHTS, PATENTS, AND TRADEMARKS PROVIDE PROTECTION TO THE OWNERS OF PROPERTY BY GIVING THEM THE EXCLUSIVE RIGHT TO USE IT. "

Both officers and directors of corporations are fiduciaries, or people of trust, who use due care and loyalty as an agent in making decisions on behalf of the organization. This relationship creates a duty of care, also called duty of diligence, to make informed decisions. These agents of the corporation are not held responsible for negative outcomes if they are informed and diligent in their decisions. The duty of loyalty means that all decisions should be in the interests of the corporation and its stakeholders. After Wells Fargo was found to be engaging in widespread misconduct, a new board chair and several new board members were brought in to improve risk management and oversight.[1]

The Law of Property

Property law is extremely broad in scope because it covers the ownership and transfer of all kinds of real, personal, and intellectual property. **Real property** consists of real estate and everything permanently attached to it; **personal property** basically is everything else. Personal property can be further subdivided into tangible and intangible property. *Tangible property* refers to items that have a physical existence, such as automobiles, business

Christian Louboutin has received intellectual property protection for its signature red sole shoes. This type of protection is known as trade dress.
denisfilm/123RF

David's Bridal filed for Chapter 11 bankruptcy protection to reduce its $500 million in debt.

1000Photography/Shutterstock

everyday language can no longer be trademarked. The names *aspirin* and *nylon*, for example, were once the exclusive property of their creators but became so widely used as product names (rather than brand names) that now anyone can use them. A related term is *trade dress*, which refers to the visual appearance of a product or its packaging. Coca-Cola's contoured bottle and Hershey's 12 rectangular panels for its chocolate bars are examples of visual characteristics protected as intellectual property. In order for these visual characteristics to receive protection, consumers must strongly associate the shape or design with the product itself.[2]

As the trend toward globalization of trade continues, and more and more businesses trade across national boundaries,

protecting property rights, particularly intellectual property such as computer software, has become an increasing challenge. While a company may be able to register a trademark, a brand name, or a symbol in its home country, it may not be able to secure that protection abroad. Some countries have copyright and patent laws that are less strict than those of the United States; some countries will not enforce U.S. laws. China, for example, has often been criticized for permitting U.S. goods to be counterfeited there. Pacific Mall in Markham in Ontario, Canada, has been labeled as one of several notorious markets selling counterfeit products at the same level as the Silk Market in Beijing and open air markets in Mexico City.[3] Such counterfeiting harms not only the sales of U.S. companies, but also their reputations if the knockoffs are of poor quality. Thus, businesses engaging in foreign trade may have to take extra steps to protect their property because local laws may be insufficient to protect them.

The Law of Bankruptcy

Although few businesses and individuals intentionally fail to repay (or default on) their debts, sometimes they cannot fulfill their financial obligations. Individuals may charge goods and services beyond their ability to pay for them. Businesses may take on too much debt in order to finance growth, or business events such as an increase in the cost of commodities can bankrupt a company. An option of last resort in these cases is bankruptcy, or legal insolvency. Some well-known companies that have declared bankruptcy include Hostess, American Apparel, and RadioShack.

Individuals or companies may ask a bankruptcy court to declare them unable to pay their debts and thus release them from the obligation of repaying those debts. The debtor's assets may then be sold to pay off as much of the debt as possible. In the case

OUT OF TUNE: GIBSON FILES FOR BANKRUPTCY

Gibson Brands Inc., the Nashville-based guitar company known for Gibson and Epiphone guitars, filed for bankruptcy in May 2018. As guitar sales began to slip, Gibson's former CEO negotiated to buy an audio and home entertainment company and a Japanese consumer electronics company in an effort to diversify Gibson into a "music lifestyle" company. However, the $135 million investment stretched the company too far, and it faced $500 million in debt before it went bankrupt.

Gibson filed for Chapter 11 bankruptcy protection. Under Chapter 11, the debtor proposes a plan to reorganize the company so it can keep

the business running and pay creditors back over time. The reorganization included the liquidation of its consumer electronics businesses; an agreement with the creditors to hand the company over to funds managed by KKR and Co.; and the selection of a new CEO, James Curleigh. The company hopes these moves will allow it to rebound.

Gibson is trying to get back to the basics. A U.S. bankruptcy court in the state of Delaware signed off on Gibson's reorganization plan, signaling the end of its bankruptcy status after five months. Under the new plan, the company will continue to produce its famous Gibson and Epiphone guitars along with maintaining its

professional audio business. In 2020, Gibson announced plans to expand its guitar selection and focus on its newly-launched nonprofit, Gibson Foundation. The company has a long way to go to restore its former glory.[a]

Critical Thinking Questions

1. Why did Gibson declare Chapter 11 bankruptcy instead of Chapter 7 or Chapter 13?

2. How will the lawsuit likely impact Gibson in its current state?

3. What do you think will happen to Gibson if its attempts at reorganization are unsuccessful?

Chapter 7	Requires that the business be dissolved and its assets liquidated, or sold, to pay off the debts. Individuals declaring Chapter 7 retain a limited amount of exempt assets, the amount of which may be determined by state or federal law, at the debtor's option. Although the type and value of exempt assets vary from state to state, most states' laws allow a bankrupt individual to keep an automobile, some household goods, clothing, furnishings, and at least some of the value of the debtor's residence. All nonexempt assets must be sold to pay debts.
Chapter 11	Temporarily frees a business from its financial obligations while it reorganizes and works out a payment plan with its creditors. The indebted company continues to operate its business during bankruptcy proceedings. Often, the business sells off assets and less-profitable subsidiaries to raise cash to pay off its immediate obligations.
Chapter 13	Similar to Chapter 11 but limited to individuals. This proceeding allows an individual to establish a three- to five-year plan for repaying his or her debt. Under this plan, an individual ultimately may repay as little as 10 percent of his or her debt.

Sherman Antitrust Act passed in 1890 to prevent businesses from restraining trade and monopolizing markets.

Clayton Act prohibits price discrimination, tying and exclusive agreements, and the acquisition of stock in another corporation where the effect may be to substantially lessen competition or tend to create a monopoly.

of a personal bankruptcy, although the individual is released from repaying debts and can start over with a clean slate, obtaining credit after bankruptcy proceedings is very difficult. However, a restrictive allows fewer consumers to use bankruptcy to eliminate their debts. The law makes it harder for consumers to prove that they should be allowed to clear their debts for what is called a "fresh start" or Chapter 7 bankruptcy. Although the person or company in debt usually initiates bankruptcy proceedings, creditors may also initiate them. The subprime mortgage crisis caused a string of bankruptcies among individuals, and Chapter 7 and Chapter 11 bankruptcies among banks and other businesses as well. Table A.3 describes the various levels of bankruptcy protection a business or individual may seek.

LAWS AFFECTING BUSINESS PRACTICES

One of the government's many roles is to act as a watchdog to ensure that businesses behave in accordance with the wishes of society. Congress has enacted a number of laws that affect business practices; some of the most important of these are summarized in Table A.4. Many state legislatures have enacted similar laws governing business within specific states.

The **Sherman Antitrust Act**, passed in 1890 to prevent businesses from restraining trade and monopolizing markets, condemns "every contract, combination, or conspiracy in restraint of trade." For example, a request that a competitor agree to fix prices or divide markets would, if accepted, result in a violation of the Sherman Antitrust Act. The FTC challenged the proposed merger between Staples and Office Depot because it believed the merger could significantly reduce the competition in the "consumable" office supply market.[4] The Sherman Antitrust Act, still highly relevant 100 years after its passage,

is being copied throughout the world as the basis for regulating fair competition.

Because the provisions of the Sherman Antitrust Act are rather vague, courts have not always interpreted it as its creators intended. The Clayton Act was passed in 1914 to limit specific activities that can reduce competition. The **Clayton Act** prohibits price discrimination, tying and exclusive agreements, and the acquisition of stock in another corporation where the effect may be to substantially lessen competition or tend to create a monopoly. In addition, the Clayton Act prohibits members of one company's board of directors from holding seats on the boards of competing corporations. The act also exempts farm cooperatives and labor organizations from antitrust laws.

In spite of these laws regulating business practices, there are still many questions about the regulation of business. For instance, it is difficult to determine what constitutes an acceptable degree of competition and whether a monopoly is harmful to a particular market. Many mergers were permitted that resulted in less competition in the banking, publishing, and automobile industries. In some industries, such as utilities, it is not cost effective to have too many competitors. For this reason, the government permits utility monopolies, although recently, the telephone, electricity, and communications industries have been deregulated. Furthermore, the antitrust laws are often rather vague and require interpretation, which may vary from judge to judge and court to court. Thus, what one judge defines as a monopoly or trust today may be permitted by another judge a few years from now. Businesspeople need to understand what the law says on these issues and try to conduct their affairs within the bounds of these laws.

THE INTERNET: LEGAL AND REGULATORY ISSUES

Our use and dependence on the Internet is increasingly creating a potential legal problem for businesses. With this growing use come questions of maintaining an acceptable level of privacy for consumers and proper competitive use of the medium. Some might consider that tracking individuals who visit or "hit" their website by attaching a "cookie" (identifying you as a website visitor for potential recontact and tracking your movement

Act (Date Enacted)	Purpose
Sherman Antitrust Act (1890)	Prohibits contracts, combinations, or conspiracies to restrain trade; establishes as a misdemeanor monopolizing or attempting to monopolize.
Clayton Act (1914)	Prohibits specific practices such as price discrimination, exclusive dealer arrangements, and stock acquisitions in which the effect may notably lessen competition or tend to create a monopoly.
Federal Trade Commission Act (1914)	Created the Federal Trade Commission; also gives the FTC investigatory powers to be used in preventing unfair methods of competition.
Robinson-Patman Act (1936)	Prohibits price discrimination that lessens competition among wholesalers or retailers; prohibits producers from giving disproportionate services of facilities to large buyers.
Wheeler-Lea Act (1938)	Prohibits unfair and deceptive acts and practices regardless of whether competition is injured; places advertising of foods and drugs under the jurisdiction of the FTC.
Lanham Act (1946)	Provides protections and regulation of brand names, brand marks, trade names, and trademarks.
Celler-Kefauver Act (1950)	Prohibits any corporation engaged in commerce from acquiring the whole or any part of the stock or other share of the capital assets of another corporation when the effect substantially lessens competition or tends to create a monopoly.
Fair Packaging and Labeling Act (1966)	Makes illegal the unfair or deceptive packaging or labeling of consumer products.
Magnuson-Moss Warranty (FTC) Act (1975)	Provides for minimum disclosure standards for written consumer product warranties; defines minimum consent standards for written warranties; allows the FTC to prescribe interpretive rules in policy statements regarding unfair or deceptive practices.
Consumer Goods Pricing Act (1975)	Prohibits the use of price maintenance agreements among manufacturers and resellers in interstate commerce.
Antitrust Improvements Act (1976)	Requires large corporations to inform federal regulators of prospective mergers or acquisitions so that they can be studied for any possible violations of the law.
Trademark Counterfeiting Act (1980)	Provides civil and criminal penalties against those who deal in counterfeit consumer goods or any counterfeit goods that can threaten health or safety.
Trademark Law Revision Act (1988)	Amends the Lanham Act to allow brands not yet introduced to be protected through registration with the Patent and Trademark Office.
Nutrition Labeling and Education Act (1990)	Prohibits exaggerated health claims and requires all processed foods to contain labels with nutritional information.
Telephone Consumer Protection Act (1991)	Establishes procedures to avoid unwanted telephone solicitations; prohibits marketers from using automated telephone dialing system or an artificial or prerecorded voice to certain telephone lines.
Federal Trademark Dilution Act (1995)	Provides trademark owners the right to protect trademarks and requires relinquishment of names that match or parallel existing trademarks.
Digital Millennium Copyright Act (1998)	Refined copyright laws to protect digital versions of copyrighted materials, including music and movies.
Children's Online Privacy Protection Act (2000)	Regulates the collection of personally identifiable information (name, address, e-mail address, hobbies, interests, or information collected through cookies) online from children under age 13.
Sarbanes-Oxley Act (2002)	Made securities fraud a criminal offense; stiffened penalties for corporate fraud; created an accounting oversight board; instituted numerous other provisions designed to increase corporate transparency and compliance.
Do Not Call Implementation Act (2003)	Directs FCC and FTC to coordinate so their rules are consistent regarding telemarketing call practices, including the Do Not Call Registry.
Dodd-Frank Wall Street Reform and Consumer Protection Act (2010)	Increases accountability and transparency in the financial industry; protects consumers from deceptive financial practices; establishes the Consumer Financial Protection Bureau.

throughout the site) is an improper use of the Internet for business purposes. Others may find such practices acceptable and similar to the practices of non-Internet retailers who copy information from checks or ask customers for their name, address, or phone number before they will process a transaction. There are few specific laws that regulate business on the Internet, but the standards for acceptable behavior that are reflected in the basic laws and regulations designed for traditional businesses can be applied to business on the Internet as well. One law aimed specifically at advertising on the Internet is the CAN-SPAM Act. The law restricts unsolicited e-mail advertisements by requiring the consent of the recipient. Furthermore, the CAN-SPAM Act follows the "opt-out" model wherein recipients can elect not to receive further e-mails from a sender simply by clicking on a link.[5]

The central focus for future legislation of business conducted on the Internet is the protection of personal privacy. The present basis of personal privacy protection is the U.S. Constitution, various Supreme Court rulings, and laws such as the 1971 Fair Credit Reporting Act; the 1978 Right to Financial Privacy Act; and the 1974 Privacy Act, which deals with the release of government records. With few regulations on the use of information by businesses, companies legally buy and sell information on customers to gain competitive advantage. The United States currently has no federal data privacy law that is comprehensive compared to the EU's General Data Protection Regulation (GDPR). Following several high-profile privacy violation cases, however, there is growing interest at the federal level to enact more legislation. It is anticipated that many states will follow California by enacting privacy regulations in the next several years. Although the California Consumer Privacy Act (CCPA) was developed in 2018 and passed in 2019, changes to the regulation continued in 2020. The development and evolution of these regulations will continue to advance over the next few years.[6]

Internet use is different from traditional interaction with businesses in that it is readily accessible, and most online businesses are able to develop databases of information on customers. Congress has restricted the development of databases on children

for early adopters. Due to concerns about dishonest advertising, the FTC requires influencers to clearly disclose any connection they have with brands they promote. Neglecting to make a disclosure is viewed as deceptive advertising. Cases have been filed against Lord & Taylor, Warner Bros. Home Entertainment, Machinima, ADT, and more. According to the FTC, any level of compensation much be disclosed, whether a partnership is paid or an influencer strictly receives free product.[8]

LEGAL PRESSURE FOR RESPONSIBLE BUSINESS CONDUCT

To ensure greater compliance with society's desires, both federal and state governments are moving toward increased organizational accountability for misconduct. Before 1991, laws mainly punished those employees directly responsible for an offense. Under new guidelines established by the Federal Sentencing Guidelines for Organizations (FSGO), however, both the responsible employees and the firms that employ them are held accountable for violations of federal law. Thus, the government

> Organizations cannot succeed solely through a legalistic approach to compliance with the sentencing guidelines; top management must cultivate high ethical standards that will serve as barriers to illegal conduct.

using the Internet. The Children's Online Privacy Protection Act (COPPA) of 2000 prohibits website and Internet providers from seeking personal information from children under age 13 without parental consent. Companies are still running afoul of COPPA. Google and YouTube paid a record $170 million settlement after the FTC said YouTube illegally collected personal information from children without parental consent in violation of COPPA. In addition to the financial penalty, YouTube reworked its content system to identify and appropriately handle child-directed content.[7]

The FTC rules for online advertising and marketing are the same as any form of communication or advertising. These rules help maintain the credibility of the Internet as an advertising medium. To avoid deception all online communication must tell the truth and cannot mislead consumers. In addition, all claims must be substantiated. Influencer marketing is relatively new compared with other forms of digital marketing, so it should be no surprise there have been road bumps

now places responsibility for controlling and preventing misconduct squarely on the shoulders of top management. The main objectives of the federal guidelines are to train employees, self-monitor and supervise employee conduct, deter unethical acts, and punish those organizational members who engage in illegal acts.

A 2010 amendment to the FSGO directs ethics officers to report directly to the board of directors rather than simply the general counsel or top officers. This places the responsibility on the shoulders of the firm's leadership, usually the board of directors. The board must ensure that there is a high-ranking manager accountable for the day-to-day operational oversight of the ethics program. The board must provide for adequate authority, resources, and access to the board or an appropriate subcommittee of the board. The board must ensure that there are confidential mechanisms available so that the organization's employees and agents may report or seek guidance about potential or actual misconduct without fear of retaliation.

Sarbanes-Oxley Act
a law that criminalized securities fraud and strengthened penalties for corporate fraud.

Finally, the board is required to oversee the discovery of risks and to design, implement, and modify approaches to deal with those risks.

If an organization's culture and policies reward or provide opportunities to engage in misconduct through lack of managerial concern or failure to comply with the seven minimum requirements of the FSGO (provided in Table A.5), then the organization may incur not only penalties but also the loss of customer trust, public confidence, and other intangible assets. For this reason, organizations cannot succeed solely through a legalistic approach to compliance with the sentencing guidelines; top management must cultivate high ethical standards that will serve as barriers to illegal conduct. The organization must want to be a good citizen and recognize the importance of compliance to successful workplace activities and relationships. In fact, the top concern of corporate lawyers is ethics and compliance. Implementing ethics and compliance ranks higher than any other concern, possibly due to the pressures placed on companies by the passage of Sarbanes-Oxley, the Dodd-Frank Act, and the Federal Sentencing Guidelines.[9]

The federal guidelines also require businesses to develop programs that can detect—and that will deter employees from engaging in—misconduct. To be considered effective, such compliance programs must include disclosure of any wrongdoing, cooperation with the government, and acceptance of responsibility for the misconduct. Codes of ethics, employee ethics training, hotlines (direct 800 phone numbers), compliance directors, newsletters, brochures, and other communication methods are typical components of a compliance program. The ethics component, discussed in the "Business Ethics and Social Responsibility" chapter, acts as a buffer, keeping firms away from the thin line that separates unethical and illegal conduct.

Despite the existing legislation, a number of ethics scandals in the early 2000s led Congress to pass–almost unanimously– the **Sarbanes-Oxley Act**, which criminalized securities fraud and strengthened penalties for corporate fraud. It also created an accounting oversight board that requires corporations to establish codes of ethics for financial reporting and to develop greater transparency in financial reports to investors and other interested parties. Additionally, the law requires top corporate executives to sign off on their firms' financial reports, and they risk fines and jail sentences if they misrepresent their companies' financial position. Table A.6 summarizes the major provisions of the Sarbanes-Oxley Act.

The Sarbanes-Oxley Act has created a number of concerns and is considered burdensome and expensive to corporations. Large corporations report spending more than $1.3 million each year to comply with the act, according to an annual survey by Proviti, a management consulting firm. The act has caused more than 500 public companies a year to report problems in their accounting systems. Additionally, Sarbanes-Oxley failed to prevent and detect the widespread misconduct of financial institutions that led to the financial crisis.

On the other hand, there are many benefits, including greater accountability of top managers and boards of directors, that improve investor confidence and protect employees, especially their retirement plans. It is believed that the law has more benefits than drawbacks—with the greatest benefit being that boards of directors and top managers are better informed. Some companies such as Cisco and Pitney Bowes report improved efficiency and cost savings from better financial information.

In spite of the benefits Sarbanes-Oxley offers, it did not prevent widespread corporate corruption from leading to the most recent recession. The resulting financial crisis prompted the Obama administration to create new regulation to reform Wall Street and the financial industry. In 2010, the Dodd-Frank Wall Street Reform and Consumer Protection Act was passed. In addition to new regulations for financial institutions, the legislation created a Consumer Financial Protection Bureau (CFPB) to protect consumers from complex or deceptive financial products.

The Dodd-Frank Act contains 16 titles meant to increase consumer protection, enhance transparency and accountability in the financial sector, and create new financial agencies. In some ways, Dodd-Frank is attempting to improve upon provisions laid out in the Sarbanes-Oxley Act. For instance, Dodd-Frank takes whistleblower protection a step further by offering additional incentives to whistleblowers for reporting misconduct. If whistleblowers report misconduct that results in penalties of more than

▼ **TABLE A.5** Seven Steps to Compliance

1. Develop standards and procedures to reduce the propensity for criminal conduct.
2. Designate a high-level compliance manager or ethics officer to oversee the compliance program.
3. Avoid delegating authority to people known to have a propensity to engage in misconduct.
4. Communicate standards and procedures to employees, other agents, and independent contractors through training programs and publications.
5. Establish systems to monitor and audit misconduct and to allow employees and agents to report criminal activity.
6. Enforce standards and punishments consistently across all employees in the organization.
7. Respond immediately to misconduct and take reasonable steps to prevent further criminal conduct.

▼ TABLE A.6 Major Provisions of the Sarbanes-Oxley Act

1. Requires the establishment of a Public Company Accounting Oversight Board in charge of regulations administered by the Securities and Exchange Commission.

2. Requires CEOs and CFOs to certify that their companies' financial statements are true and without misleading statements.

3. Requires that corporate boards of directors' audit committees consist of independent members who have no material interests in the company.

4. Prohibits corporations from making or offering loans to officers and board members.

5. Requires codes of ethics for senior financial officers; code must be registered with the SEC.

6. Prohibits accounting firms from providing both auditing and consulting services to the same client without the approval of the client firm's audit committee.

7. Requires company attorneys to report wrongdoing to top managers and, if necessary, to the board of directors; if managers and directors fail to respond to reports of wrongdoing, the attorney should stop representing the company.

8. Mandates "whistleblower protection" for persons who disclose wrongdoing to authorities.

9. Requires financial securities analysts to certify that their recommendations are based on objective reports.

10. Requires mutual fund managers to disclose how they vote shareholder proxies, giving investors information about how their shares influence decisions.

11. Establishes a 10-year penalty for mail/wire fraud.

12. Prohibits the two senior auditors from working on a corporation's account for more than five years; other auditors are prohibited from working on an account for more than seven years. In other words, accounting firms must rotate individual auditors from one account to another from time to time.

Source: Pub. L. 107-204,116 Stat. 745 (2002).

$1 million, the whistleblower will be entitled to a percentage of the settlement.[10] Additionally, complex financial instruments must now be made more transparent so that consumers will have a better understanding of what these instruments involve.

The act also created three new agencies: The Consumer Financial Protection Bureau (CFPB), the Office of Financial Research, and the Financial Stability Oversight Council. While the CFPB was created to protect consumers, the other two agencies work to maintain stability in the financial industry so such a crisis will not recur in the future.[11] Although it is too early to tell whether these regulations will serve to create wide-scale positive financial reform, the Dodd-Frank Act is certainly leading to major changes on Wall Street and in the financial sector.

chapter three

business in a borderless world

ArtisticPhoto/Shutterstock

LEARNING OBJECTIVES

After reading this chapter, you will be able to:

LO 3-1 Explore some of the factors within the international trade environment that influence business.

LO 3-2 Assess some of the economic, legal, political, social, cultural, and technological barriers to international business.

LO 3-3 Specify some of the agreements, alliances, and organizations that may encourage trade across international boundaries.

LO 3-4 Summarize the different levels of organizational involvement in international trade.

LO 3-5 Contrast two basic strategies used in international business.

Consumers around the world can drink Coca-Cola and Pepsi, eat at McDonald's and Pizza Hut, buy an Apple phone made in China, and watch CNN and MTV on Samsung televisions. It may surprise you that German automaker BMW has manufacturing facilities in Mexico and South Africa that export many of their cars to the United States. In fact, BMW has 30 production and assembly facilities in 14 countries.[1] The products you consume today are just as likely to have been made in China, India, or Germany as in the United States.[2] Likewise, consumers in other countries buy Western electrical equipment, clothing, rock music, cosmetics, and toiletries, as well as computers, robots, and household goods. Google's YouTube has more than 1 billion hours of global viewing of videos a day.[3]

Many U.S. firms are finding that international markets provide tremendous opportunities for growth. Accessing these markets can promote innovation, while intensifying global competition spurs companies to market better and less expensive products. Today, more than 7 billion people who inhabit the earth comprise one tremendous marketplace.

In this chapter, we explore business in this exciting global marketplace. First, we look at the nature of international business, including barriers and promoters of trade across international boundaries. Next, we consider the levels of organizational involvement in international business. Finally, we briefly discuss strategies for trading across national borders. ■

THE ROLE OF INTERNATIONAL BUSINESS

International business refers to the buying, selling, and trading of goods and services across national boundaries. Falling political barriers and new technology are making it possible for more and more companies to sell their products overseas as well as at home. And, as differences among nations continue to narrow, the trend toward the globalization of business is becoming increasingly important. Starbucks serves millions of global customers at more than 24,000 locations in 75 markets.[4] The Internet and the ease by which mobile applications can be developed provide many companies with easier entry to access global markets than opening brick-and-mortar stores.[5] Independent record labels are experiencing a surge in revenue from services like Spotify. Now through streaming, foreign markets are accessible and many are drawing almost half their listeners from outside their home country.[6] Amazon, an online retailer, has distribution centers from Nevada to Germany that fill millions of orders a day and ship them to customers in every corner of the world. Outside of the United States, China and Europe are Apple's largest markets.[7] Indeed, most of the world's population and two-thirds of its total

purchasing power are outside the United States.

When McDonald's sells a Big Mac in Moscow, Sony sells a television in Detroit, or a small Swiss medical supply company sells a shipment of orthopedic devices to a hospital in Monterrey, Mexico, the sale affects the economies of the countries involved. The U.S. market, with 328 million consumers, makes up only 4.2 percent of the more than 7.8 billion people in the world to whom global companies must consider

international business the buying, selling, and trading of goods and services across national boundaries.

Subway has more restaurants around the world than any other fast-food chain.

Andrew Resek/McGraw-Hill Education

DID YOU KNOW?

Despite declining sales, Subway has surpassed McDonald's as the largest global restaurant chain, with more than 42,000 restaurants.[a]

Many companies choose to outsource manufacturing to factories in Asia due to lower costs of labor.

Roberto Westbrook/Blend Images

marketing. Global marketing requires balancing a firm's global brand with the needs of local consumers.[8] To begin our study of international business, we must first consider some economic issues: why nations trade, exporting and importing, and the balance of trade.

Why Nations Trade

Nations and businesses engage in international trade to obtain raw materials and goods that are otherwise unavailable to them or are available elsewhere at a lower price than what they can produce. A nation, or individuals and organizations from a nation, sell materials and goods to buy the goods, services, and ideas its people need. Countries like Ethiopia, Cameroon, and Kenya trade with Western nations in order to acquire technology and techniques to advance their economy. Which goods and services a nation sells depends on what resources it has available and its ability to compete in global markets.

Some nations have a monopoly on the production of a particular resource or product. Such a monopoly, or **absolute advantage**, exists when a country is the only source of an item, the only producer of an item, or the most efficient producer of an item. An example would be an African mining company that possesses the only mine where a specialty diamond can be

---

HARLEY-DAVIDSON GETS UP TO SPEED IN INTERNATIONAL MARKETS

Harley-Davidson is one of America's most recognized brands, but its popularity has fallen significantly. The average age of a Harley owner is about 50 years old. Harley-Davidson has about 50 percent of the U.S. market share for motorcycles, but motorcycle sales are decreasing. As a result, Harley-Davidson is looking toward increasing international sales.

Harley-Davidson markets its bike model called LiveWire, a small electric bike designed to compete with electric bike brands like Honda. Europe could be a lucrative market for Harley-Davidson's Livewire because the top 10 most "environmentally conscious" countries are European. Additionally, about 80 percent of households in Indonesia, Thailand, and Vietnam own a motorcycle or scooter. Harley's new design philosophy fits well in Europe and Asia, where people need small, affordable bikes for

transportation. Harley-Davidson faces competition from already-established brands like Royal Enfield, the leading bike brand in Asia.

Though Harley-Davidson has secured a nearly 8 percent share of Europe's heavyweight motorcycle market, global motorcycle business took a hit as a result of the COVID-19 (coronavirus) pandemic beginning in 2019. The crisis led to a new strategic plan for the company referred to as The Rewire. Harley-Davidson's plan is to reduce the complexity of its products and sharpen the strategic focus of its business, investing in markets that will drive profitability and growth.

Tariffs are another challenge. Thailand, India, and China have large tariffs on U.S. goods, making exporting from the United States difficult. Harley is overcoming this challenge by building international plants. Harley-Davidson's

plant in India allows it to avoid a 50 percent tariff that would be levied if exporting from the United States. Harley's Thailand plant services China and 10 other Asian countries while helping it avoid tariffs in those countries. Although Harley-Davidson has a tough road ahead in the United States, it has big plans for building its international presence in Asia and Europe.[b]

Critical Thinking Questions:

1. What barriers does Harley-Davidson face in marketing its motorcycles to countries outside of the United States?

2. What are some ways Harley-Davidson is overcoming these challenges?

3. What opportunities does Harley-Davidson have in other countries that they do not necessarily have in the United States?

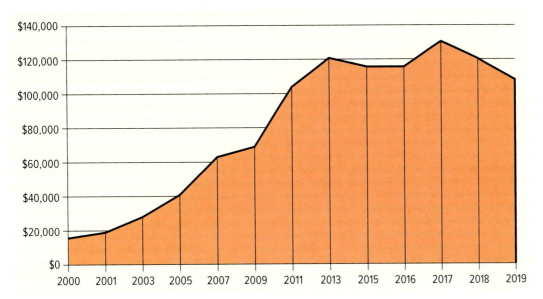

▼ FIGURE 3.1 U.S. Exports to China (millions of U.S. dollars)

Source: U.S. Census Bureau, "Trade in Goods with China," https://www.census.gov/foreign-trade/balance/c5700.html (accessed May 26, 2020).

outsourcing the transferring of manufacturing or other tasks—such as data processing—to countries where labor and supplies are less expensive.

exporting the sale of goods and services to foreign markets.

importing the purchase of goods and services from foreign sources.

balance of trade the difference in value between a nation's exports and its imports.

trade deficit a nation's negative balance of trade, which exists when that country imports more products than it exports.

found. Russia has an absolute advantage in yuksporite, a rare and useful mineral that can be found only in Russia.

Most international trade is based on **comparative advantage**, which occurs when a country specializes in products that it can supply more efficiently or at a lower cost than it can produce other items. France has a comparative advantage in making wine because of its agricultural capabilities, reputation, and the experience of its vintners. The United States, having adopted new technological methods in hydraulic fracturing, has created a comparative advantage in the drilling and exporting of natural gas.[9] Other countries, particularly India and Ireland, are also gaining a comparative advantage over the United States in the provision of some services, such as call-center operations, engineering, and software programming. As a result, U.S. companies are increasingly **outsourcing**, or transferring manufacturing and other tasks to countries where labor and supplies are less expensive. Outsourcing has become a controversial practice in the United States because many jobs have moved overseas where those tasks can be accomplished for lower costs. Ireland has become a destination of choice for U.S. companies because of a well-educated workforce and technological capabilities.

Trade between Countries

To obtain needed goods and services, nations trade by exporting and importing. **Exporting** is the sale of goods and services to foreign markets. The United States exports more than $2.4 trillion in goods and services annually.[10] U.S. businesses export many goods and services, particularly agricultural, entertainment (movies, television shows, etc.), and technological products. **Importing** is the purchase of goods and services from foreign sources. Many of the goods you buy in the United States are likely to be imports or to have some imported components. Sometimes, you may not even realize they are imports. The United States imports more than $3.1 trillion each year.[11]

Balance of Trade

You have probably read or heard about the fact that the United States has a trade deficit, but what is a trade deficit? A nation's **balance of trade** is the difference in value between its exports and imports. Because the United States (and some other nations as well) imports more products than it exports, it has a negative balance of trade, or **trade deficit**. U.S. exports to China rapidly increased, as Figure 3.1 indicates, but not fast enough to offset the imports from China. Table 3.1 shows the

▼ TABLE 3.1 U.S. Trade Deficit (in billions of dollars)

	1990	2000	2010	2011	2012	2013	2014	2015	2016	2017	2018	2019
Exports	535.2	1,075.3	1,853.0	2,125.9	2,218.3	2,294.2	2,376.7	2,266.7	2,215.8	2,352.5	2,508.8	2,498.0
Imports	616.1	1,447.8	2,348.3	2,675.6	2,755.8	2,755.3	2,866.2	2,765.2	2,718.8	2,902.7	3,129.0	3,114.5
Trade surplus/deficit	−80.9	−372.5	−495.2	−549.7	−537.4	−461.1	−489.6	−498.5	−503.0	−550.1	−627.7	−616.4

Source: U.S. Bureau of the Census, Foreign Trade Division, "U.S. Trade in Goods and Services—Balance of Payments (BOP) Basis," March 6, 2020, www.census.gov/foreign-trade/statistics/historical/gands.pdf (accessed May 26, 2020).

balance of payments the difference between the flow of money into and out of a country.

infrastructure the physical facilities that support a country's economic activities, such as railroads, highways, ports, airfields, utilities and power plants, schools, hospitals, communication systems, and commercial distribution systems.

exchange rate the ratio at which one nation's currency can be exchanged for another nation's currency.

overall trade deficit for the United States, which is currently around $616 million.[12] The trade deficit fluctuates according to such factors as the health of the United States and other economies, productivity, perceived quality, and exchange rates. Trade deficits are harmful because they can mean the failure of businesses, the loss of jobs, and a lowered standard of living.

Of course, when a nation exports more goods than it imports, it has a favorable balance of trade, or trade surplus. Until about 1970, the United States had a trade surplus due to an abundance of natural resources and the relative efficiency of its manufacturing systems and distribution systems. Table 3.2 shows the top 10 countries with which the United States has a trade deficit and a trade surplus.

The difference between the flow of money into and out of a country is called its **balance of payments**. A country's balance of trade, foreign investments, foreign aid, loans, military expenditures, and money spent by tourists comprise its balance of payments. As you might expect, a country with a trade surplus generally has a favorable balance of payments because it is receiving more money from trade with foreign countries than it is paying out. When a country has a trade deficit, more money flows out of the country than into it. If more money flows out of the country than into it from tourism and other sources, the country may experience declining production and higher unemployment because there is less money available for spending.

▼ **TABLE 3.2** Top 10 Countries with which the United States Has Trade Deficits/Surpluses

Trade Deficit	Trade Surplus
1. China	Netherlands
2. Mexico	Hong Kong
3. Germany	Brazil
4. Japan	United Arab Emirates
5. Ireland	United Kingdom
6. Vietnam	Australia
7. Switzerland	Belgium
8. Malaysia	Panama
9. Italy	Chile
10. Canada	Colombia

Sources: "Top Trading Partners," March 2020, https://www.census.gov/foreign-trade/statistics/highlights/toppartners.html (accessed May 26, 2020).

LO 3-2 Assess some of the economic, legal, political, social, cultural, and technological barriers to international business.

INTERNATIONAL TRADE BARRIERS

Completely free trade seldom exists. When a company decides to do business outside its own country, it will encounter a number of barriers to international trade. Any firm considering international business must research the other country's economic, legal, political, social, cultural, and technological background. Such research will help the company choose an appropriate level of involvement and operating strategies, as we will see later in this chapter.

Economic Barriers

When looking at doing business in another country, managers must consider a number of basic economic factors, such as economic development, infrastructure, and exchange rates.

Economic Development.
When considering doing business abroad, U.S. businesspeople need to recognize that they cannot take for granted that other countries offer the same things as are found in *industrialized nations*—economically advanced countries such as the United States, Japan, Great Britain, and Canada. Many countries in Africa, Asia, and South America, for example, are in general poorer and less economically advanced than those in North America and Europe; they are often called *less-developed countries* (LDCs). LDCs are characterized by low per-capita income (income generated by the nation's production of goods and services divided by the population), which means that consumers are less likely to purchase nonessential products. Nonetheless, LDCs represent a potentially huge and profitable market for many businesses because they may be buying technology to improve their infrastructures, and much of the population may desire consumer products. For example, automobile manufacturers are looking toward LDCs as a way to expand their customer base. The rising middle class has caused many consumers in India and China to desire their own vehicles. The automobile market in China is now larger than the market in the United States.

A country's level of development is determined in part by its **infrastructure**, the physical facilities that support its economic activities, such as railroads, highways, ports, airfields, utilities and power plants, schools, hospitals, communication systems, and commercial distribution systems. When doing business in LDCs, for example, a business may need to compensate for rudimentary distribution and communication systems, or even a lack of technology.

Exchange Rates.
The ratio at which one nation's currency can be exchanged for another nation's currency is the **exchange rate**. Exchange rates vary daily and can be found in

newspapers and through many sites on the Internet. Familiarity with exchange rates is important because they affect the cost of imports and exports. When the value of the U.S. dollar declines relative to other currencies, such as the euro, the price of imports becomes more economical for U.S. consumers. For example, if the exchange rate for the dollar moves from $1.40 per euro to $1.25 per euro, then imports from Europe will be less expensive. On the other hand, U.S. exports become relatively expensive for international markets—in this example, the European Union (EU). The U.S. dollar is most frequently used in international trade, with 90 percent of trade finance conducted in U.S. dollars.[13]

Occasionally, a government may intentionally alter the value of its currency through fiscal policy. Devaluation decreases the value of currency in relation to other currencies. If the U.S. government were to devalue the dollar, it would lower the cost of American goods abroad and make trips to the United States less expensive for foreign tourists. Thus, devaluation encourages the sale of domestic goods and tourism. On the other hand, when Switzerland's central bank let the value of the Swiss franc rise by 30 percent against the euro, it resulted in increasing the costs of exports. This made everything exported from Switzerland more expensive, including tourism. However, Swiss brands including expensive watches were offered at large discounts if bought using Swiss francs.[14] Revaluation, as in the Swiss example, increases the value of a currency in relation to other currencies, but occurs rarely.

> **Occasionally, a government may intentionally alter the value of its currency through fiscal policy.**

Ethical, Legal, and Political Barriers

A company that decides to enter the international marketplace must contend with potentially complex relationships among the different laws of its own nation, international laws, and the laws of the nation with which it will be trading; various trade restrictions imposed on international trade; changing political climates; and different ethical values. For example, with tension rising between the U.S. and Russia, McDonald's has attempted to put distance between the two countries by sourcing ingredients locally for its restaurants in Russia.[15] Legal and ethical requirements for successful business are increasing globally.

Laws and Regulations.
The United States has a number of laws and regulations that govern the activities of U.S. firms engaged in international trade and has a variety of friendship, commerce, and navigation treaties with other nations. These treaties allow business to be transacted between U.S. companies and citizens of the specified countries. We discuss some of these relationships in this chapter.

Once outside U.S. borders, businesspeople are likely to find that the laws of other nations differ from those of the United States. Many of the legal rights that Americans take for granted do not exist in other countries, and a firm doing business abroad must understand and obey the laws of the host country. Some countries have strict laws limiting the amount of local currency that can be taken out of the country and the amount of currency that can be brought in; others limit how foreign companies can operate within the country. While the United States has been slow to adopt aviation regulations for commercial drones, Australia, Singapore, and Britain have regulations that have allowed drone deliveries to grow quickly.[16]

Some countries have copyright and patent laws that are less strict than those of the United States, and some countries fail to honor U.S. laws. Although countries such as China and Vietnam have and enforce their copyright laws, controlling the amount of counterfeit products sold in their countries is very challenging. China pays $8 billion a year for U.S. intellectual property, only slightly more than South Korea, an economy one-tenth the size of China.[17] Companies are angry because the counterfeits harm not only their sales but also their reputations if the knock-offs are of poor quality. Such counterfeiting is not limited to China or Vietnam. It is estimated that nearly half of all software installed on personal computers worldwide is not properly licensed.[18] In countries where these activities occur, laws against them may not be sufficiently enforced if counterfeiting is deemed illegal. Thus, businesses engaging in foreign trade may have to take extra steps to protect their products because local laws may be insufficient to do so.

Tariffs and Trade Restrictions.
Tariffs and other trade restrictions are part of a country's legal structure but may be established or removed for political reasons. An **import tariff** is a tax levied by a nation on goods imported into the country. A *fixed tariff* is a specific amount of money levied on each unit of a product brought into the country, while an *ad valorem tariff* is based on the value of the item. Most countries allow citizens traveling abroad to bring home a certain amount of merchandise without paying an import tariff. A U.S. citizen may bring $200, $800, or $1,600 worth of merchandise into the United States duty free depending on the country visited. After that, U.S. citizens must pay an ad valorem tariff based on the cost of the item and the country of origin. Thus, identical items purchased in different countries might have different tariffs.

Countries sometimes levy tariffs for political reasons, as when they impose sanctions against other countries to protest their actions. However, import tariffs are more commonly imposed to protect domestic products by raising the price of imported ones. Such protective tariffs have become controversial as Americans become increasingly concerned over the U.S. trade deficit. Protective tariffs allow more expensive domestic goods

> **import tariff** a tax levied by a nation on goods imported into the country.

exchange controls regulations that restrict the amount of currency that can be bought or sold.

quota a restriction on the number of units of a particular product that can be imported into a country.

embargo a prohibition on trade in a particular product.

Exchange controls restrict the amount of currency that can be bought or sold. Some countries control their foreign trade by forcing businesspeople to buy and sell foreign products through a central bank. If John Deere, for example, receives payments for its tractors in a foreign currency, it may be required to sell the currency to that nation's central bank. When foreign currency is in short supply, as it is in many LDCs, the government uses foreign currency to purchase necessities and capital goods and produces other products locally, thus limiting its need for foreign imports.

A **quota** limits the number of units of a particular product that can be imported into a country. A quota may be established by voluntary agreement or by government decree. The United States imposes quotas on certain goods, such as garments produced in Vietnam and China. Quotas are designed to protect the industries and jobs of the country imposing the quota. Quotas help domestic suppliers but will lead to higher prices for consumers.

An **embargo** prohibits trade in a particular product. Embargoes are generally directed at specific goods or countries and may be established for political, economic, health, or religious reasons. The United States currently maintains a trade embargo with Cuba. While the Obama administration reestablished trade and diplomatic relations between Cuba and the United States, the Trump administration tightened the embargo by restricting access to hotels and stores tied to the Cuban military from Americans. It is much easier to travel to Cuba than in previous decades, and U.S. citizens can bring back Cuban cigars and rum. The government also approved the building of a U.S. factory in Cuba, the first time in more than 50 years.[23] It may be surprising to know that U.S. farmers export hundreds of millions of dollars' worth of commodities to Cuba each year, based on a 2000 law that provided permission for some trade to the embargoed country.[24] Health embargoes prevent the importing of various pharmaceuticals, animals, plants, and agricultural products. Muslim nations forbid the importation of alcoholic beverages on religious grounds.

Tariffs on U.S. wine exports to China negatively impacted U.S. sellers.

Nicolas Asfouri/AFP/Getty Images

to compete with foreign ones. For example, the United States has imposed tariffs on steel imported into the United States because imports have caused many local steelworks to crash.[19] Other countries can produce steel more cheaply than the United States. The United States placed tariffs on aluminum and steel imports from all countries but Canada and Mexico in 2008 and expanded the tariffs to include products made of steel and aluminum in 2020. Small manufacturers that fabricate metal into parts for cars, appliances, and other components feared job loss and higher prices.[20] The United States indicated it would drop the 25 percent tariffs on steel and aluminum if other countries would make concessions on other trade issues.[21] In addition, the United States entered into an escalating trade war with China in 2018. After the United States imposed tariffs on some high-tech products, China responded with a 25 percent tariff on U.S. products such as airplanes and soybeans. Retaliation was suspended briefly but resumed in 2019. By 2020, tensions between the countries were at an all-time high as a result of the COVID-19 (coronavirus) pandemic. China's foreign minister, Wang Yi, said political attacks over the coronavirus and global trade were "pushing our two countries to the brink of a new cold war."[22]

The EU levies tariffs on many products, including some seafood imports and fruits. Critics of protective tariffs argue that their use inhibits free trade and competition. Supporters of protective tariffs say they insulate domestic industries, particularly new ones, against well-established foreign competitors. Once an industry matures, however, its advocates may be reluctant to let go of the tariff that protected it. Tariffs also help when, because of low labor costs and other advantages, foreign competitors can afford to sell their products at prices lower than those charged by domestic companies. Some Americans argue that tariffs should be used to keep domestic wages high and unemployment low. Recently, there are fears that a trade war could develop that damages the world economy.

Due to the U.S. embargo against Cuba, many Cubans drive older automobiles.

Horizon Images/Motion/Alamy Stock Photo

Political instability in many nations has led to an influx of refugees. The potential for political turmoil is a substantial risk businesses face when expanding overseas.

Sk Hasan Ali/Shutterstock

One common reason for setting quotas or tariffs is to prohibit **dumping**, which occurs when a country or business sells products at less than what it costs to produce them. For example, China accused the EU and Japan of dumping its stainless-steel tubes, thus harming China's domestic industry.[25] A company may dump its products for several reasons. Dumping permits quick entry into a market. Sometimes, dumping occurs when the domestic market for a firm's product is too small to support an efficient level of production. In other cases, technologically obsolete products that are no longer salable in the country of origin are dumped overseas. Dumping is relatively difficult to prove, but even the suspicion of dumping can lead to the imposition of quotas or tariffs. China instituted anti-dumping duties on EU and Japanese imports.[26] As with other trade restrictions, dumping quotas or tariffs result in higher prices for consumers.

Political Barriers. Unlike legal issues, political considerations are seldom written down and often change rapidly. Nations that have been subject to economic sanctions for political reasons in recent years include Cuba, Iran, Syria, and North Korea. While these were dramatic events, political considerations affect international business daily as governments enact tariffs, embargoes, or other types of trade restrictions in response to political events.

Businesses engaged in international trade must consider the relative instability of countries such as Iraq, Ukraine, and Venezuela. Political unrest in countries such as Pakistan, Somalia, and the Democratic Republic of the Congo may create a hostile or even dangerous environment for foreign businesses. Natural disasters can cripple a country's government, making the region even more unstable. Finally, a sudden change in power can result in a regime that is hostile to foreign investment. Some businesses have been forced out of a country altogether, as when Hugo Chavez conducted a socialist revolution in Venezuela to force out or take over American oil companies. Whether they like it or not, companies are often involved directly or indirectly in international politics. Today, Venezuela has a sinking economy with shortages of products and political unrest.

Political concerns may lead a group of nations to form a **cartel**, a group of firms or nations that agrees to act as a monopoly and not compete with each other, to generate a competitive advantage in world markets. Probably the most famous cartel is OPEC, the Organization of Petroleum Exporting Countries, founded in the 1960s to increase the price of petroleum throughout the world and to maintain high prices. By working to ensure stable oil prices, OPEC hopes to enhance the economies of its member nations. In 2018, OPEC and some non-OPEC members agreed to cut oil production to increase and stabilize prices.

Social and Cultural Barriers

Most businesspeople engaged in international trade underestimate the importance of social and cultural differences, but these differences can derail an important transaction. Tiffany & Co. learned that more attentive customer service was necessary in order to succeed in Japan, and bold marketing and advertising served as the recipe for success in China.[27] And in Europe, Starbucks took the unprecedented step of allowing its locations to be franchised in order to reach smaller markets that are unfamiliar. This way, Starbucks reduced some of the cultural and social risks involved in entering such markets.[28] For example, Starbucks opened its first store in Italy in 2018.[29] Starbucks waited to enter Italy because it needed to understand the coffee culture there. Unfortunately, cultural norms are rarely written down, and what is written down may well be inaccurate.

Cultural differences include differences in spoken and written language. Although it is certainly possible to translate words

dumping the act of a country or business selling products at less than what it costs to produce them.

cartel a group of firms or nations that agrees to act as a monopoly and not compete with each other, in order to generate a competitive advantage in world markets.

> **Most businesspeople engaged in international trade underestimate the importance of social and cultural differences, but these differences can derail an important transaction.**

Sociocultural differences can create challenges for businesses that want to invest in other countries.

LEE SNIDER PHOTO IMAGES/Shutterstock

from one language to another, the true meaning is sometimes misinterpreted or lost. Consider some translations that went awry in foreign markets:

- Scandinavian vacuum manufacturer Electrolux used the following in an American campaign: "Nothing sucks like an Electrolux."

- The Coca-Cola name in China was first read as "Ke-kou-ke-la," meaning "bite the wax tadpole."

- In Italy, a campaign for Schweppes Tonic Water translated the name into Schweppes Toilet Water.[30]

Translators cannot just translate slogans, advertising campaigns, and website language; they must know the cultural differences that could affect a company's success. Netflix, which supports more than 20 languages, developed Hermes, a proficiency test for its caption translators to improve translations and account for the subtleties of different languages. Its focus on international growth has contributed greatly to its success with more than 180 million subscribers globally.[31]

Differences in body language and personal space also affect international trade. Body language is nonverbal, usually unconscious communication through gestures, posture, and facial expression. Personal space is the distance at which one person feels comfortable talking to another. Americans tend to stand a moderate distance away from the person with whom they are speaking. Arab businessmen tend to stand face-to-face with the

object of their conversation. Additionally, gestures vary from culture to culture, and gestures considered acceptable in American society—pointing, for example—may be considered rude in others. Table 3.3 shows some of the behaviors considered rude or unacceptable in other countries. Such cultural differences may generate uncomfortable feelings or misunderstandings when businesspeople of different countries negotiate with each other.

Family roles also influence marketing activities. Many countries do not allow children to be used in advertising, for example. Advertising that features people in nontraditional social roles may or may not be successful either. Companies should also guard against marketing that could be perceived as reinforcing negative stereotypes. Chinese online retailers pulled Dolce & Gabbana products following an ad campaign that featured an Asian model eating Italian food with chopsticks. Critics called the advertisements disrespectful and racist. In response, Dolce & Gabbana pulled the ads and canceled its Shanghai fashion show, which the advertisements promoted.[32]

The people of other nations quite often have a different perception of time as well. Americans value promptness; a business meeting scheduled for a specific time seldom starts more than a few minutes late. In Mexico and Spain, however, it is not unusual for a meeting to be delayed half an hour or more. Such a late start might produce resentment in an American negotiating in Spain for the first time.

Companies engaged in foreign trade must observe the national and religious holidays and local customs of the host country. In many Islamic countries, for example, workers expect to take a break at certain times of the day to observe religious rites. A Tesco supermarket chain a mile away from one of London's biggest mosques was forced to apologize after displaying bacon-flavored Pringles as part of a Ramadan promotion. Muslims are forbidden from eating pork products, and the display was considered offensive due to the high concentration of Muslim customers in the area.[33] Companies also must monitor their advertising to guard against offending customers. In Thailand and many other countries, public displays of affection are unacceptable in advertising messages; in many Middle Eastern nations, it is unacceptable to show the soles of one's feet.[34] In Russia, smiling is considered appropriate only in private settings, not in business.

▼ **TABLE 3.3** Cultural Behavioral Differences

Gestures Viewed as Rude or Unacceptable	
Japan, Hong Kong, Middle East	Summoning with the index finger
Middle and Far East	Pointing with index finger
Thailand, Japan, France	Sitting with soles of shoes showing
Brazil, Germany	Forming a circle with fingers (the "O.K." sign in the United States)
Japan	Winking means "I love you"
Buddhist countries	Patting someone on the head

Source: Adapted from Judie Haynes, "Communicating with Gestures," EverythingESL (n.d.), www.everythingesl.net/inservices/body_language.php (accessed November 24, 2018).

With the exception of the United States, most nations use the metric system. This lack of uniformity creates problems for both buyers and sellers in the international marketplace. American sellers, for instance, must package goods destined for foreign markets in liters or meters, and Japanese sellers must convert to the English system if they plan to sell a product in the United States. Tools also must be calibrated in the correct system if they are to function correctly. Hyundai and

Though U.S. growth of Ireland-based retailer Primark was initially slow, U.S. shoppers warmed to the retailer's store-only shopping strategy.

Helen89/Shutterstock

Honda service technicians need metric tools to make repairs on those cars.

The literature dealing with international business is filled with accounts of sometimes humorous but often costly mistakes that occurred because of a lack of understanding of the social and cultural differences between buyers and sellers. Such problems cannot always be avoided, but they can be minimized through research on the cultural and social differences of the host country.

Technological Barriers

Many countries lack the technological infrastructure found in the United States, and some marketers are viewing such barriers as opportunities. For instance, marketers are targeting many countries such as India and China and some African countries where there are few private phone lines. Citizens of these countries are turning instead to wireless communication through cell phones. Technological advances are creating additional global marketing opportunities. Along with opportunities, changing technologies also create new challenges and competition. The U.S. market share of the personal computer market is dropping as new competitors emerge that are challenging U.S. PC makers. In fact, out of the top five global PC companies—Lenovo, Hewlett-Packard, Dell, Asus, and Acer Group—three are from Asian countries. On the other hand, Apple Inc.'s iPad and other tablet computer makers have significantly eroded the market share of traditional personal computers, placing the industry in the maturity stage of the product life cycle.[35]

LO 3-3 Specify some of the agreements, alliances, and organizations that may encourage trade across international boundaries.

TRADE AGREEMENTS, ALLIANCES, AND ORGANIZATIONS

Although these economic, political, legal, and sociocultural issues may seem like daunting barriers to international trade, there are also organizations and agreements—such as the

CHINESE AIRLINES SOARING TO GREAT HEIGHTS

In 1979, China started economic reforms that have given rise to the growth of Chinese airlines. Previously, flying was seen as a luxury that only the rich could afford. In the early 2000s, as more people could afford to fly, Chinese airlines began growing at a rapid rate. China's three largest airlines emerged: Air China, China Southern Airlines, and China Eastern Airlines. By 2029, China will surpass the U.S. with the world's largest passenger market.

This growth is accompanied by its share of issues. Currently, Chinese airlines do not have the infrastructure to handle all the flights, leading to significant layovers, delays, and cancellations. China also needs more airports. The United States has 330 airports compared to China's 210. China is overcoming this challenge by constructing more airports. The added infrastructure could help Chinese airlines match the profits of U.S. airlines. Air China currently makes one-sixth the profit of American Airlines.

Given these low profits, it is surprising Chinese airlines have been able to grow so quickly. The answer is behind the governmental subsidies. Local Chinese governments are paying so airlines will come to their cities. These subsidies are allowing China's airlines to grab market share, negatively affecting nearby countries. For example, Hong Kong's Cathay Pacific saw its net income drop 82 percent in six months. Other countries are taking notice. In Europe, many companies are proposing sanctions against airlines receiving subsidies. Additionally, Chinese airlines were hard hit by the COVID-19 (coronavirus) pandemic as both local and international travel were stunted in 2019 and 2020. Recovery will be impacted by uncertain changes to business and international travel. Chinese airlines must overcome these obstacles to continue its status as a major player among global airlines.[c]

Critical Thinking Questions

1. What advantages do U.S. airlines have over Chinese airlines? What advantages do Chinese airlines have over U.S. airlines?

2. What barriers are Chinese airlines facing as they rapidly grow as a global player?

3. How do you think China's subsidies of its airlines will impact its relations with airlines in other countries? Explain your answer.

General Agreement on Tariffs and Trade (GATT)
a trade agreement, originally signed by 23 nations in 1947, that provided a forum for tariff negotiations and a place where international trade problems could be discussed and resolved.

World Trade Organization (WTO) international organization dealing with the rules of trade between nations.

United States–Mexico–Canada Agreement (USMCA) agreement that eliminated most tariffs and trade restrictions to encourage trade among the United States, Mexico, and Canada

General Agreement on Tariffs and Trade, the World Bank, and the International Monetary Fund—that foster international trade and can help companies get involved in and succeed in global markets. Various regional trade agreements, such as the North American Free Trade Agreement and the EU, also promote trade among member nations by eliminating tariffs and trade restrictions. In this section, we'll look briefly at these agreements and organizations.

General Agreement on Tariffs and Trade

During the Great Depression of the 1930s, nations established so many protective tariffs covering so many products that international trade became virtually impossible. By the end of World War II, there was considerable international momentum to liberalize trade and minimize the effects of tariffs. The **General Agreement on Tariffs and Trade (GATT)**, originally signed by 23 nations in 1947, provided a forum for tariff negotiations and a place where international trade problems could be discussed and resolved. More than 100 nations abided by its rules. GATT sponsored rounds of negotiations aimed at reducing trade restrictions. The most recent round, the Uruguay Round (1988–1994), further reduced trade barriers for most products and provided new rules to prevent dumping.

The **World Trade Organization (WTO)**, an international organization dealing with the rules of trade between nations, was created in 1995 by the Uruguay Round. Key to the World Trade Organization are the WTO agreements, which are the legal ground rules for international commerce. The agreements were negotiated and signed by most of the world's trading nations and ratified by their parliaments. The goal is to help producers of goods and services and exporters and importers conduct their business. In addition to administering the WTO trade agreements, the WTO presents a forum for trade negotiations, monitors national trade policies, provides technical assistance and training for developing countries, and cooperates with other international organizations. Based in Geneva, Switzerland, the WTO has also adopted a leadership role in negotiating trade disputes among nations.[36] For example, the WTO ruled that China's antidumping measures taken against Japan and the EU violated trade rules because China had not adequately proven

USMCA replaced NAFTA as the trade agreement among Mexico, the United States, and Canada.

Lars Hagberg/AFP/Getty Images

that the imports of the stainless steel tubes had harmed China's domestic industry.[37]

The United States–Mexico–Canada Agreement

The North American Free Trade Agreement (NAFTA), which went into effect on January 1, 1994, effectively merged Canada, the United States, and Mexico into one market of nearly 450 million consumers. NAFTA virtually eliminated all tariffs on goods produced and traded among Canada, Mexico, and the United States to create a free trade area.[38] NAFTA made it easier for U.S. businesses to invest in Mexico and Canada; provided protection for intellectual property (of special interest to high-technology and entertainment industries); expanded trade by requiring equal treatment of U.S. firms in both countries; and simplified country-of-origin rules. NAFTA was replaced by the **United States–Mexico–Canada Agreement (USMCA)** which includes major changes on cars and new policies on labor and environmental standards, intellectual property protections, and some digital trade provisions.

Canada's nearly 38 million consumers are relatively affluent, with a per capita GDP of $51,300.[39] The United States exports more than $290 billion in goods to Canada while importing more than $319 billion.[40] In fact, Canada is the single largest trading partner of the United States. These trade agreements have also increased trade between Canada and Mexico. Mexico is Canada's fifth largest export market and third largest import market.[41]

With a per capita GDP of $18,100, Mexico's 126 million consumers are less affluent than Canadian consumers.[42] However, trade between the United States and Mexico has tripled since NAFTA was initiated. Mexico purchases more than $256 billion in U.S. products annually.[43] Millions of Americans cite their heritage as Mexican, making them the most populous Hispanic group in the country. These individuals often have close ties to relatives in Mexico and assist in Mexican–U.S.

economic development and trade. Mexico is on a course of a market economy, rule of law, respect for human rights, and responsible public policies. There is also a commitment to the environment and sustainable human development. Many U.S. companies have taken advantage of Mexico's low labor costs and proximity to the United States to set up production facilities, sometimes called *maquiladoras.* Mexico is also attracting major technological industries, including electronics, software, and aerospace. Investors see many growth opportunities in Mexico, particularly in light of recent reforms. For instance, Mexico passed legislation to open up its state-controlled oil reserves to foreign companies. Additionally, if the United States does well economically, Mexico—one of its biggest customers—is also likely to do well.[44]

However, there is great disparity within Mexico. The country's southern states cannot seem to catch up with the more affluent northern states on almost any socioeconomic indicator. The disparities are growing, as can be seen comparing the south to the northern industrial capital of Monterrey, which is beginning to seem like south Texas.[45] Drug gang wars threaten the economic stability of Mexico, especially in the northern states close to the U.S. border. However, this situation is improving as the economy is growing and violence is decreasing.

While many Americans feared NAFTA would erase jobs in the United States, Mexicans were disappointed that the agreement failed to create more jobs. USMCA, however, has the goal to have more car and truck parts made in North America. Cars or trucks with 75 percent of its components made in Canada, Mexico, or the U.S. will qualify for zero tariffs. It makes improvements to environmental and labor regulations that will benefit Mexico in particular. Additionally, the agreement created changes for agricultural products, intellectual property, copyrights, and digital trade between the three countries.[46]

The European Union

The **European Union (EU)**, also called the *European Community* or *Common Market*, was established in 1958 to promote trade among its members, which initially included Belgium, France, Italy, West Germany, Luxembourg, and the Netherlands.

East and West Germany united in 1991, and by 1995 the United Kingdom, Spain, Denmark, Greece, Portugal, Ireland, Austria, Finland, and Sweden had joined as well. The Czech Republic, Estonia, Hungary, Latvia, Lithuania, Poland, Slovakia, and Slovenia joined in 2004. In 2007, Bulgaria and Romania also became members, Cyprus and Malta joined in 2008, and Croatia joined in 2013. Today, the Euro Zone (countries that have adopted the euro as their currency) consists of 19 separate countries with varying political landscapes.[47] In 1991, East and West Germany united, and by 2015, the EU included the United Kingdom, Spain, Denmark, Greece, Portugal, Ireland, Austria, Finland, Sweden, Cyprus, Poland, Hungary, the Czech Republic, Slovenia, Estonia, Latvia, Lithuania, Slovakia, Malta, Romania,

Bulgaria, Belgium, France, Germany, Italy, Luxembourg, The Netherlands, and Croatia. The Former Yugoslav Republic of Macedonia, Montenegro, Serbia, and Turkey are candidate countries that hope to join the European Union in the near future.[48] In 2020, the United Kingdom left the EU. Until 1993, each nation functioned as a separate market, but at that time members officially unified into one of the largest single world markets, which today has more than half a billion consumers with a GDP of more than $15 trillion.[49]

To facilitate free trade among members, the EU is working toward standardization of business regulations and requirements, import duties, and value-added taxes; the elimination of customs checks; and the creation of a standardized currency for use by all members. Many European nations (Austria, Belgium, Finland, France, Germany, Greece, Ireland, Italy, Luxembourg, the Netherlands, Portugal, Spain, and Slovenia) link their exchange rates to a common currency, the *euro*; however, some EU members have rejected use of the euro in their countries. Although the common currency requires many marketers to modify their pricing strategies and will subject them to increased competition, the use of a single currency frees companies that sell goods among European countries from the nuisance of dealing with complex exchange rates.[50] The long-term goals are to eliminate all trade barriers within the EU, improve the economic efficiency of the EU nations, and stimulate economic growth, thus making the union's economy more competitive in global markets, particularly against Japan and other Pacific Rim nations, and in North America. However, several disputes and debates still divide the member-nations, and many barriers to completely free trade remain. Consequently, it may take many years before the EU is truly one deregulated market.

The EU has also enacted some of the world's strictest laws concerning antitrust issues, which have had unexpected consequences for some non-European firms. The European Parliament is also encouraging the breakup of Google's search engine business from its other businesses.[51] The EU passed General Data Protection Regulation (GDPR) privacy law after five years of debate. The very complex 2,000-page law attempts to make data privacy clear with one's personal data a fundamental human right.[52] Consent to collect and use personal data now has to be "unambiguous." Individuals have the right to demand to view their data, have their data deleted, and have to give permission to have data transferred to another service.

In 2016, the United Kingdom voted to exit the European Union. This decision to exit, called "Brexit," resulted in the value of the pound falling sharply. Brexit took effect in 2020. There remain many questions about the impact of the exit on trade relationships with other countries.[53] The government's priority appears to

DATA PRIVACY CONCERNS TAKE THE WORLD BY STORM

A privacy law in the EU caused major changes to the way companies like Facebook and Google collected and used user data. The law, called General Data Protection Regulation (GDPR), allows people to request data that has been collected about them and restricts businesses on how they can use that data. It also forces companies to notify users of how data collected about them will be used. If companies don't comply with this new regulation, they could face up to $1 billion in fines.

Not only has this regulation had a major impact on companies doing business in Europe, but Brazil, Japan, and South Korea are following Europe's lead. The EU is encouraging other countries to develop tougher online privacy regulations by making data protection a part of trade deals. Even companies not based in the EU are subject to the regulation if it involves processing personal data of EU citizens. These requirements are making privacy protection a globalized issue. Conversely, the United States continues to have fewer privacy regulations on Internet data collection.

These regulatory barriers could have a profound impact on large companies like Facebook, where data collection used for behavioral advertising is worth billions of dollars annually. Facebook claims that user data are crucial to perform the functions that it contracts with users to do. The battle between what data are necessary and what are not is a battle that could loom for a long time.[d]

Critical Thinking Questions

1. What type of international barriers are companies like Facebook and Google facing in the realm of user privacy?

2. Describe the global implications of the GDPR law.

3. How might tougher regulations make it harder for users in Europe to utilize online services?

Asia-Pacific Economic Cooperation (APEC) an international trade alliance that promotes open trade and economic and technical cooperation among member nations.

Asia-Pacific Economic Cooperation

The **Asia-Pacific Economic Cooperation (APEC)**, established in 1989, promotes open trade and economic and technical cooperation among member economies, which initially included Australia, Brunei Darussalam, Canada, Indonesia, Japan, South Korea, Malaysia, New Zealand, the Philippines, Singapore, Thailand, and the United States. Since then, the alliance has grown to include Chile; China; Hong Kong, China; Mexico; Papua New Guinea; Peru; Russia; Chinese Taipei; and Vietnam. The 21-member alliance represents approximately 38 percent of the world's population, 60 percent of the world's GDP, and nearly 47 percent of global trade.[55] APEC differs from other international trade alliances in its commitment to facilitating business and its practice of allowing the business/private sector to participate in a wide range of APEC activities.[56]

be first reaching trade agreements with EU members and then with America.[54]

Companies of the APEC have become increasingly competitive and sophisticated in global business in the past three decades. The Japanese and South Koreans, in particular, have made tremendous inroads on world markets for automobiles, cameras, and audio and video equipment. Products from Samsung, Sony, Canon, Toyota, Daewoo, Mitsubishi, Suzuki, and Lenovo are sold all over the world and have set standards of quality by which other products are often judged. The People's Republic of China, a country of more than 1.3 billion people, has launched a program of economic reform to stimulate its economy by privatizing many industries, restructuring its banking system, and increasing public spending on infrastructure (including railways and telecommunications). For many years, China was a manufacturing powerhouse with 10 percent growth at its height. However, in recent years, growth has slowed to 6 percent.[57] China's export market has consistently outpaced its import growth in recent years and its GDP represents the world's second-largest economy, behind the United States. In fact, China has overtaken the United States as the world's largest trader.[58] The global Internet retailer Alibaba is one of the world's most valuable companies.[59]

Increased industrialization has also caused China to become the world's largest emitter of greenhouse gases. China has overtaken the United States to become the world's largest oil importer.[60]

> **"Increased industrialization has also caused China to become the world's largest emitter of greenhouse gases."**

On the other hand, China has also begun a quest to become a world leader in green initiatives and renewable energy. This is an increasingly important quest as the country becomes more polluted.

Another risk area for China is the fact that the government owns or has stakes in so many enterprises. On the one hand, China's system of state-directed capitalism has benefited the country because reforms and decisions can be made more quickly. On the other hand, state-backed companies lack many of the competitors that private industries have. Remember that competition often spurs innovation and lowers costs. If China's firms lack sufficient competition, their costs may very likely increase.[61] China's growing debt liabilities have also caused concern among foreign investors.[62] Recently, the U.S.–China trade war has negatively impacted economic growth.

Other visible Pacific Rim regions, such as Thailand, Singapore, Taiwan, Vietnam, and Hong Kong, have also become major manufacturing and financial centers. Vietnam, with one of the world's most open economies, has bypassed its communist government with private firms moving ahead despite bureaucracy, corruption, and poor infrastructure. In a country of 96 million, Vietnamese firms now compete internationally due to an agricultural miracle, making the country one of the world's main providers of farm produce.[63] As China's labor costs continue to grow, more businesses are turning toward Vietnam to open factories.[64] The United States has expressed concern about fair competition in the region.

Association of Southeast Asian Nations

The **Association of Southeast Asian Nations (ASEAN)**, established in 1967, promotes trade and economic integration among member nations in Southeast Asia, including Malaysia, the Philippines, Singapore, Thailand, Brunei Darussalam, Vietnam, Laos, Indonesia, Myanmar, and Cambodia.[65] The 10-member alliance represents 650 million people with a GDP of $2.8 trillion.[66] ASEAN's goals include the promotion of free trade, peace, and collaboration between its members.[67]

However, ASEAN is facing challenges in becoming a unified trade bloc. Unlike members of the EU, the economic systems of ASEAN members are quite different, with political systems including democracies (Philippines and Malaysia), constitutional monarchies (Cambodia), and communism (Vietnam).[68] Major conflicts have also occurred between member-nations. In Thailand the military staged a coup and placed the country under martial law, a change that not only impacted Thailand but also ASEAN as a whole.[69] Unlike the EU, ASEAN will not have a common currency or fully free labor flows between member-nations. In this way, ASEAN plans to avoid some of the pitfalls

that occurred among nations in the EU during the latest worldwide recession.[70]

World Bank

The **World Bank**, more formally known as the International Bank for Reconstruction and Development, was established by the industrialized nations, including the United States, in 1946 to loan money to underdeveloped and developing countries. It loans its own funds or borrows funds from member countries to finance projects ranging from road and factory construction to the building of medical and educational facilities. The World Bank and other multilateral development banks (banks with international support that provide loans to developing countries) are the largest source of advice and assistance for developing nations. The International Development Association and the International Finance Corporation are associated with the World Bank and provide loans to private businesses and member countries.

International Monetary Fund

The **International Monetary Fund (IMF)** was established in 1947 to promote trade among member-nations by eliminating trade barriers and fostering financial cooperation. It also makes short-term loans to member countries that have balance-of-payment deficits and provides foreign currencies to member nations. The IMF tries to avoid financial crises and panics by alerting the international community about countries that will not be able to repay their debts. The IMF's Internet site provides additional information about the organization, including news releases, frequently asked questions, and members.

The IMF is the closest thing the world has to an international central bank. If countries get into financial trouble, they can borrow from the World Bank. However, the global economic crisis created many challenges for the IMF as it was forced to significantly increase its loans to both emerging economies and more developed nations. The usefulness of the IMF for developed countries is limited because these countries use private markets as a major source of capital.[71] Yet the European debt crisis changed this somewhat. Portugal, Ireland, Greece, and Spain (often referred to with the acronym PIGS) required billions of dollars in bailouts from the IMF to keep their economies afloat.

Association of Southeast Asian Nations (ASEAN) a trade alliance that promotes trade and economic integration among member nations in Southeast Asia.

World Bank an organization established by the industrialized nations in 1946 to loan money to underdeveloped and developing countries; formally known as the International Bank for Reconstruction and Development.

International Monetary Fund (IMF) an organization established in 1947 to promote trade among member nations by eliminating trade barriers and fostering financial cooperation.

LO 3-4 Summarize the different levels of organizational involvement in international trade.

GETTING INVOLVED IN INTERNATIONAL BUSINESS

Businesses may get involved in international trade at many levels—from a small Kenyan firm that occasionally exports African crafts to a huge multinational corporation such as Shell Oil that sells products around the globe. The degree of commitment of resources and effort required increases according to the level at which a business involves itself in international trade. This section examines exporting and importing, trading companies, licensing and franchising, contract manufacturing, joint ventures, direct investment, and multinational corporations.

Exporting and Importing

Many companies first get involved in international trade when they import goods from other countries for resale in their own businesses. For example, a grocery store chain may import bananas from Honduras and coffee from Colombia. A business may get involved in exporting when it is called upon to supply a foreign company with a particular product. For example, the U.S. has become a net petroleum exporter.[72] Such exporting enables enterprises of all sizes to participate in international business. Exporting to other countries becomes a necessity for established countries that seek to grow continually. Products

often have higher sales growth potential in foreign countries than they have in the parent country. For instance, General Motors and YUM! Brands sell more of their products in China than in the United States. Cadillac's sales are growing rapidly in China where it has a long heritage and pedigree.[73] Table 3.4 shows the U.S.'s top 10 trading partners.

Exporting sometimes takes place through **countertrade agreements**, which involve bartering products for other products instead of for currency. Such arrangements are fairly common in international trade, especially between Western companies and eastern European nations. An estimated 40 percent or more of all international trade agreements contain countertrade provisions.

Although a company may export its wares overseas directly or import goods directly from their manufacturer, many choose to deal with an intermediary, commonly called an *export agent*. Export agents seldom produce goods themselves; instead, they usually handle international transactions for other firms. Export agents either purchase products outright or take them on consignment. If they purchase them outright, they generally mark up the price they have paid and attempt to sell the product in the international marketplace. They are also responsible for storage and transportation.

An advantage of trading through an agent instead of directly is that the company does not have to deal with foreign currencies or the red tape (paying tariffs and handling paperwork) of international business. A major disadvantage is that, because the export agent must make a profit, either the price of the product must be increased or the domestic company must provide a larger discount than it would in a domestic transaction.

Trading Companies

A **trading company** buys goods in one country and sells them to buyers in another country. Trading companies handle all activities required to move products from one country to another, including consulting, marketing research, advertising, insurance, product research and design, warehousing, and foreign exchange services to companies interested in selling their products in foreign markets. Trading companies are similar to export agents, but their role in international trade is larger. By linking sellers and buyers of goods in different countries, trading companies promote international trade. WTSC offers a 24-hour-per-day online world trade system that connects 20 million companies in 245 countries, offering more than 60 million products.[74]

Licensing and Franchising

Licensing is a trade arrangement in which one company—the *licensor*—allows another company—the *licensee*—to use its company name, products, patents, brands, trademarks, raw materials, and/or production processes in exchange for a fee or royalty.

▼ **TABLE 3.4** U.S. Top Trading Partners

Rank	Country	Exports	Imports	Total Trade	Percent of Total Trade
1	Mexico	256.4	358.1	614.5	14.8%
2	Canada	292.7	319.7	612.4	14.8%
3	China	106.6	452.2	558.9	13.5%
4	Japan	74.7	143.6	218.3	5.3%
5	Germany	60.3	127.5	187.8	4.5%
6	Korea, South	56.9	77.5	134.4	3.2%
7	United Kingdom	69.2	63.2	132.3	3.2%
8	France	37.8	57.4	95.2	2.3%
9	India	34.4	57.7	92.1	2.2%
10	Taiwan	31.2	54.3	85.5	2.1%

Source: United States Census Bureau, "Top Trading Partners—December 2019," https://www.census.gov/foreign-trade/statistics/highlights/top/top1912yr.html (accessed May 26, 2020).

The Coca-Cola Company and PepsiCo frequently use licensing as a means to market their soft drinks, apparel, and other merchandise in other countries. Licensing is an attractive alternative to direct investment when the political stability of a foreign country is in doubt or when resources are unavailable for direct investment. Licensing is especially advantageous for small manufacturers wanting to launch a well-known brand internationally. Yoplait is a French yogurt that is licensed for production in the United States.

Franchising is a form of licensing in which a company—the *franchiser*—agrees to provide a *franchisee* the name, logo, methods of operation, advertising, products, and other elements associated with the franchiser's business, in return for a financial commitment and the agreement to conduct business in accordance with the franchiser's standard of operations. Wendy's, McDonald's, H&R Block, and Holiday Inn are well-known franchisers with international visibility. Table 3.5 lists the top 10 global franchises.

Licensing and franchising enable a company to enter the international marketplace without spending large sums of money abroad or hiring or transferring personnel to handle overseas affairs. They also minimize problems associated with shipping costs, tariffs, and trade restrictions, and they allow the firm to establish goodwill for its products in a foreign market, which will help the company if it decides to produce or market its products directly in the foreign country at some future date. However, if the licensee (or franchisee) does not maintain high standards of quality, the product's image may be hurt; therefore, it is important for the licensor to monitor its products overseas and to enforce its quality standards.

Contract Manufacturing

Contract manufacturing occurs when a company hires a foreign company to produce a specified volume of the firm's product to specification; the final product carries the domestic firm's name. Foxconn Technology Group in Taiwan is the world's largest electronics contract manufacturer and makes products for other companies. Its clients include Sony Corp, Apple Inc., and Nintendo Co. In fact, Foxconn is the largest iPhone assembler.[75]

Outsourcing

Earlier, we defined *outsourcing* as transferring manufacturing or other tasks (such as information technology operations) to companies in countries where labor and supplies are less expensive. Many U.S. firms have outsourced tasks to India, Ireland, Mexico, and the Philippines, where there are many well-educated workers and significantly lower labor costs. Services, such as taxes or customer service, can also be outsourced.

Although outsourcing has become politically controversial in recent years amid concerns over jobs lost to overseas workers, foreign companies transfer tasks and jobs to U.S. companies—sometimes called *insourcing*—far more often than U.S. companies outsource tasks and jobs abroad.[76] However, some firms are bringing their outsourced jobs back after concerns that foreign workers were not adding enough value. Companies such as General Electric and Caterpillar are returning to the United States due to increasing labor costs in places such as China, the expense of shipping products across the ocean, and fears of fraud or intellectual property theft. Companies from other countries have also been moving some of their production to the United States; Caterpillar and Ford brought production of some of their excavators and medium-duty commercial trucks back to the United States.[77]

Offshoring

Offshoring is the relocation of a business process by a company, or a subsidiary, to another country. Offshoring is different than outsourcing: the company retains control of the process because it is not subcontracting to a different company. Companies may choose to offshore for a number of reasons, ranging from lower wages, skilled labor, or taking advantage of time zone differences in order to offer services around the clock. Some banks have chosen not to outsource because of concerns about data security in other countries. These institutions may, instead, engage in offshoring, which allows a company more control over

licensing a trade agreement in which one company—the licensor—allows another company—the licensee—to use its company name, products, patents, brands, trademarks, raw materials, and/or production processes in exchange for a fee or royalty.

franchising a form of licensing in which a company—the franchiser—agrees to provide a franchisee a name, logo, methods of operation, advertising, products, and other elements associated with a franchiser's business in return for a financial commitment and the agreement to conduct business in accordance with the franchiser's standard of operations.

contract manufacturing the hiring of a foreign company to produce a specified volume of the initiating company's product to specification; the final product carries the domestic firm's name.

▼ **TABLE 3.5** Top 10 Global Franchises

Ranking	Franchise
1	McDonald's
2	KFC
3	Marriott International
4	Pizza Hut
5	Burger King
6	Domino's
7	Dunkin'
8	Subway
9	Circle K
10	InterContinental Hotels & Resorts

Source: "Top 100 Franchises 2020," *Franchise Direct*, https://www.franchisedirect.com/top100globalfranchises/rankings/ (accessed May 26, 2020).

IBM has more employees in India than in the United States.

Ramesh Pathania/Mint/Getty Images

offshoring the relocation of business processes by a company or subsidiary to another country; offshoring is different than outsourcing.

joint venture a partnership established for a specific project or for a limited time.

strategic alliance a partnership formed to create competitive advantage on a worldwide basis.

direct investment the ownership of overseas facilities.

multinational corporation (MNC) a corporation that operates on a worldwide scale, without significant ties to any one nation or region.

international operations because the offshore office is an extension of the company. Shell, for example, opened a delivery center in India and moved its global IT jobs to that area.[78] General Motors resumed production of the Chevy Blazer, produced exclusively at the GM plant located in Mexico.[79]

Joint Ventures and Alliances

Many countries, particularly LDCs, do not permit direct investment by foreign companies or individuals. A company may also lack sufficient resources or expertise to operate in another country. In such cases, a company that wants to do business in another country may set up a **joint venture** by finding a local partner (occasionally, the host nation itself) to share the costs and operation of the business. Rival car manufacturers Ford and Toyota formed a joint venture to develop a hybrid system for light trucks. The joint venture helped both companies share the burden of research and development costs while creating technology that benefits the environment.[80]

In some industries, such as automobiles and computers, strategic alliances are becoming the predominant means of competing. A **strategic alliance** is a partnership formed to create competitive advantage on a worldwide basis. In such industries, international competition is so fierce and the costs of competing on a global basis are so high that few firms have the resources to go it alone, so they collaborate with other companies. An

example of a strategic alliance is the partnership between LinkedIn and accounting firm Ernst & Young. The companies hope to use their combined expertise to assist other companies in using technology, social networking, and sales effectively.[81]

Direct Investment

Companies that want more control and are willing to invest considerable resources in international business may consider **direct investment**, the ownership of overseas facilities. Direct investment may involve the development and operation of new facilities—such as when Starbucks opens a new coffee shop in Japan—or the purchase of all or part of an existing operation in a foreign country. General Motor's Cadillac brand was so successful in exporting to China, it opened a $1.2 billion plant in Shanghai to build the CT6 Sedan and XT5 SUV. Cadillac doubled its dealerships and avoided a 25 percent import tariff because the vehicles are locally built.[82]

The highest level of international business involvement is the **multinational corporation (MNC)**, a corporation, such as IBM or ExxonMobil, that operates on a worldwide scale, without significant ties to any one nation or region. Table 3.6 lists 10 well-known multinational corporations. MNCs are more than simple corporations. They often have greater assets than some of the countries in which they do business. Nestlé, with headquarters in Switzerland, operates more than 400 factories around the world and receives revenues from Europe; North, Central, and South America; Africa; and Asia.[83] The Royal Dutch/Shell Group, one of the world's major oil producers, is another MNC. Its main offices are located in The Hague and London. Other MNCs include BASF, British Petroleum, Matsushita, Mitsubishi, Siemens, Toyota, and Unilever. Many MNCs have been targeted by anti-globalization activists at global business forums, and some protests have turned violent. The activists contend that MNCs increase the gap between rich and poor nations, misuse and misallocate scarce resources, exploit the labor markets in LDCs, and harm their natural environments.[84]

Under CEO Marillyn A. Hewson's leadership, Lockheed Martin's global business strategy is aimed at international expansion and strengthening national and economic security.

Aflo/REX/Shutterstock

Company	Country	Description
Royal Dutch Shell	Netherlands	Oil and gas; largest company in the world in terms of revenue
Toyota	Japan	Largest automobile manufacturer in the world
Walmart	United States	Largest retailer in the world; largest private employer in the world
Siemens	Germany	Engineering and electronics; largest engineering company in Europe
Nestlé	Switzerland	Nutritional, snack-food, and health-related consumer goods
Samsung	South Korea	Subsidiaries specializing in electronics, electronic components, telecommunications equipment, medical equipment, and more
Unilever	United Kingdom	Consumer goods including cleaning and personal care, foods, beverages
Boeing	United States	Aerospace and defense; largest U.S. exporter
Lenovo	China	Computer technology; highest share of PC market
Subway	United States	Largest fast-food chain; fastest-growing franchises in 105 countries

LO 3-5 Contrast two basic strategies used in international business.

INTERNATIONAL BUSINESS STRATEGIES

Planning in a global economy requires businesspeople to understand the economic, legal, political, and sociocultural realities of the countries in which they will operate. These factors will affect the strategy a business chooses to use outside its own borders.

Developing Strategies

Companies doing business internationally have traditionally used a **multinational strategy**, customizing their products, promotion, and distribution according to cultural, technological, regional, and national differences. When McDonald's opened its first restaurant in Vietnam, it offered its traditional menu items as well as McPork sandwiches specifically targeted toward Vietnam consumers.[85] Many soap and detergent manufacturers have adapted their products to local water conditions, washing equipment, and washing habits. For customers in some LDCs, Colgate-Palmolive Co. has developed an inexpensive, plastic, hand-powered washing machine for use in households that have no electricity. Even when products are standardized, advertising often has to be modified to adapt to language and cultural differences. For example, Mars has been in the China pet food market for more than two decades with brands like Royal Canin, Whiskies, and Pedigree. U.S.-based Mars has competitive advantage because in China people are concerned about the safety of locally produced pet-food.

More and more companies are moving from this customization strategy to a **global strategy (globalization)**, which involves standardizing products (and, as much as possible, their promotion and distribution) for the whole world, as if it were a single

entity. Examples of globalized products are American clothing, movies, music, and cosmetics. In the advertisement, which appeared in an American magazine, Air France promotes the features and benefits of its mobile app. The tagline "France is in the air" is used

multinational strategy a plan, used by international companies, that involves customizing products, promotion, and distribution according to cultural, technological, regional, and national differences.

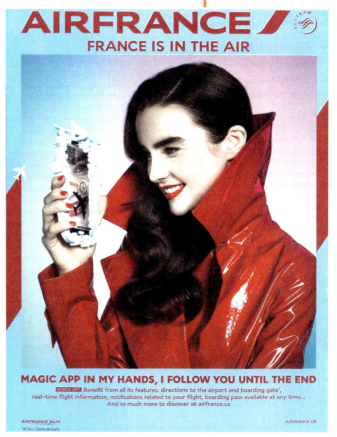

Air France uses the tagline "France is in the air" globally.

Source: Air France

global strategy (globalization) a strategy that involves standardizing products (and, as much as possible, their promotion and distribution) for the whole world, as if it were a single entity.

in its advertisements worldwide. Social media sites are important channels that brands are using to connect with their global customers. According to AdAge, Fashion Nova, Huda Beauty, and Victoria's Secret are the most engaging consumer brands on social media.[86]

Before moving outside their own borders, companies must conduct environmental analyses to evaluate the potential of and problems associated with various markets and to determine what strategy is best for doing business in those markets. Failure to do so may result in losses and even negative publicity. Some companies rely on local managers to gain greater insights and faster response to changes within a country. Astute businesspeople today "think globally, act locally." That is, while constantly being aware of the total picture, they adjust their firms' strategies to conform to local needs and tastes.

Managing the Challenges of Global Business

As we've pointed out in this chapter, many past political barriers to trade have fallen or been minimized,

> **Before moving outside their own borders, companies must conduct environmental analyses to evaluate the potential of and problems associated with various markets and to determine what strategy is best for doing business in those markets.**

expanding and opening new market opportunities. Managers who can meet the challenges of creating and implementing effective and sensitive business strategies for the global marketplace can help lead their companies to success. For example, the Commercial Service is the global business solutions unit of the U.S. Department of Commerce that offers U.S. firms wide and deep practical knowledge of international markets and industries, a unique global network, inventive use of information technology, and a focus on small and mid-sized businesses. Another example is the benchmarking of best international practices that benefits U.S. firms, which is conducted by the network of CIBERs (Centers for International Business Education and Research) at leading business schools in the United States. These CIBERs are funded by the U.S. government to help U.S. firms become more competitive globally. A major element of the assistance that these governmental organizations can provide firms (especially for small and medium-sized firms) is knowledge of the internationalization process.[87]

Small businesses, too, can succeed in foreign markets when their managers have carefully studied those markets and prepared and implemented appropriate strategies. Being globally aware is therefore an important quality for today's managers and will remain a critical attribute for managers of the 21st century. ■

READY TO TAKE // Your Career on a Global Adventure? /

Have you always dreamt of traveling the world? Whether backpacking your way through Central America or sipping espressos at five-star European restaurants is your style, the increasing globalization of business might just give you your chance to see what the world has to offer. Most new jobs will have at least some global component, even if located within the United States, so being globally aware and keeping an open mind to different cultures is vital in today's business world. Think about the billions of consumers in China who have already purchased mobile phones. In the future, some of the largest markets will be in Asia.

Many jobs discussed in chapters throughout this text tend to have strong international components. For example, product management and distribution management are discussed as marketing careers in the chapter "Dimensions of Marketing Strategy." As more and more companies sell products around the globe, their function, design, packaging, and promotions need to be culturally relevant to many different people in many different places. Products very often cross multiple borders before reaching the final consumer, both in their distribution and through the supply chain to produce the products.

Jobs exist in export and import management, product and pricing management, distribution and transportation, and advertising. Many "born global" companies such as Google operate virtually and consider all countries their market. Many companies sell their products through eBay and other Internet sites and never leave the United States. Today, communication and transportation facilitates selling and buying products worldwide with delivery in a few days. You may have sold or purchased a product on eBay outside the United States without thinking about how easy and accessible international markets are to business. If you have, welcome to the world of global business.

To be successful, you must have an idea not only of differing regulations from country to country, but of different language, ethics, and communication styles and varying needs and wants of international markets. From a regulatory side, you may need to be aware of laws related to intellectual property, copyrights, antitrust, advertising, and pricing in every country. Translating is never only about translating the language. Perhaps even more important is ensuring that your message gets through. Whether on a product label or in advertising or promotional materials, the use of images and words varies widely across the globe.

four

options for
organizing business

Richard Drew/AP/Shutterstock

LEARNING OBJECTIVES

After reading this chapter, you will be able to:

LO 4-1 Describe the advantages and disadvantages of the sole proprietorship form of organization.

LO 4-2 Describe the two types of business partnership and their advantages and disadvantages.

LO 4-3 Describe the corporate form of organization and its advantages and disadvantages.

LO 4-4 Assess the advantages and disadvantages of mergers, acquisitions, and leveraged buyouts.

The legal form of ownership taken by a business is seldom of great concern to you as a customer. When you eat at a restaurant, you probably don't care whether the restaurant is owned by one person (a sole proprietorship), has two or more owners who share the business (a partnership), or is an entity owned by many stockholders (a corporation); all you want is good food. If you buy a foreign car, you probably don't care whether the company that made it has laws governing its form of organization that are different from those for businesses in the United States. All businesses must select a form of organization that is most appropriate for their owners and the scope of their business. A business's legal form of ownership affects how it operates, how much it pays in taxes, and how much control its owners have.

This chapter examines three primary forms of business ownership—sole proprietorship, partnership, and corporation—and weighs the advantages and disadvantages of each. These forms are the most often used whether the business is a traditional brick-and-mortar company, an online-only one, or a combination of both. We also take a look at S corporations, limited liability companies, and cooperatives; discuss some trends in business ownership; and touch on one of the most common forms of organizations for nonprofits. You may wish to refer to Table 4.1 to compare the various forms of business ownership mentioned in the chapter. ■

LO 4-1 Describe the advantages and disadvantages of the sole proprietorship form of organization.

SOLE PROPRIETORSHIPS

Sole proprietorships, businesses owned and operated by one individual, are the most common form of business organization in the United States. Common examples include many retailers such as restaurants, hair salons, flower shops, dog kennels, and independent grocery stores. For example, Chris Nolte, a veteran who served in Iraq, started his own electric-assisted bicycle business called Propel Electric Bikes.[1] Sole proprietors also include independent contractors who complete projects or engage in entrepreneurial activities for different organizations but who are not employees. These include those engaged in direct selling for firms such as Mary Kay, Avon, or Cutco. Many sole proprietors focus on services—small retail stores, financial counseling, automobile repair, child care, and the like—rather than on the manufacture of goods, which often requires large sums of money not available to most small businesses. Etsy provides small proprietors the opportunity to set up online shops in the Etsy marketplace. Etsy takes a percentage of the sales and provides online services to 2 million sellers of more than 50 million products. This opens up opportunities for small business owners—particularly women, who make up 87 percent of Etsy sellers.[2] As you can see in Figure 4.1, proprietorships far outnumber corporations. However, they net far fewer sales and less income. Differences

sole proprietorships businesses owned and operated by one individual; the most common form of business organization in the United States.

▼ **TABLE 4.1** Various Forms of Business Ownership

Structure	Ownership	Taxation	Liability	Use
Sole proprietorship	One owner	Individual income taxed	Unlimited	Owned by a single individual and is the easiest way to conduct business
Partnership	Two or more owners	Individual owners' income taxed	Somewhat limited	Easy way for two individuals to conduct business
Corporation	Any number of shareholders	Corporate and shareholder taxed	Limited	A legal entity with shareholders or stockholders
S corporation	Up to 100 shareholders	Taxed as a partnership	Limited	A legal entity with tax advantages for restricted number of shareholders
Limited liability company	Unlimited number of shareholders	Taxed as a partnership	Limited	Avoid personal lawsuits

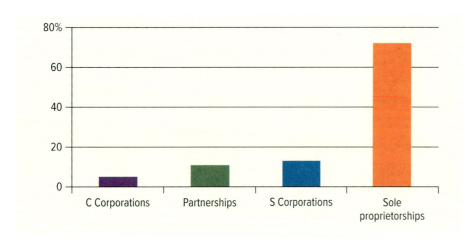

FIGURE 4.1 Comparison of Sole Proprietorships, Partnerships, S Corporations, and C Corporations

Source: Tax Policy Center, "Fiscal Facts: Breakdown of US Businesses," May 11, 2020, https://www.taxpolicycenter.org/fiscal-fact/breakdown-us-businesses-ff-05112020 (accessed May 27, 2020).

between S corporations and C corporations will be discussed later in this text.

Sole proprietorships are typically small businesses employing fewer than 50 people. (We'll look at small businesses in greater detail in the chapter "Small Business, Entrepreneurship, and Franchising.") Sole proprietorships constitute approximately three-fourths of all businesses in the United States. It is interesting to note that women business owners are less likely to get access to credit than their male counterparts.[3] In many areas, small businesses make up the vast majority of the economy.

> **Sole proprietorships make possible the greatest degree of secrecy.**

Advantages of Sole Proprietorships

Sole proprietorships are generally managed by their owners. Because of this simple management structure, the owner/manager can make decisions quickly. This is just one of many advantages of the sole proprietorship form of business.

Ease and Cost of Formation. Forming a sole proprietorship is relatively easy and inexpensive. In some states, creating a sole proprietorship involves merely announcing the new business in the local newspaper. Other proprietorships, such as barber shops and restaurants, may require state and local licenses and permits because of the nature of the business. The cost of these permits may run from $25 to $100. Lawyers are not usually needed to create such enterprises, and the owner can usually take care of the required paperwork without much assistance.

Of course, an entrepreneur starting a new sole proprietorship must find a suitable site from which to operate the business, even if it is an online business. Some sole proprietors look no farther than their garage or a spare bedroom when seeking a workshop or office. Among the more famous businesses that sprang to life in their founders' homes are Amazon, Microsoft, Google, Disney, and Under Armour.[4] Computers, personal copiers, scanners, and websites have been a boon for home-based businesses, permitting them to interact quickly with customers, suppliers, and others. Many independent salespersons and contractors can perform their work using a smartphone or tablet computer as they travel. E-mail and social networks have made it possible for many proprietorships to develop in the services area. Internet connections also allow small businesses to establish websites to promote their products and even to make low-cost long-distance phone calls with voice-over Internet protocol (VoIP) technology. One of the most famous services using VoIP is Skype, which allows people to make free calls over the Internet.

Secrecy. Sole proprietorships make possible the greatest degree of secrecy. The proprietor, unlike the owners of a partnership or corporation, does not have to discuss publicly his or her operating plans, minimizing the possibility that competitors can obtain trade secrets. Financial reports need not be disclosed, as do the financial reports of publicly owned corporations.

Distribution and Use of Profits. All profits from a sole proprietorship belong exclusively to the owner. He or she does not have to share them with any partners or stockholders. The owner decides how to use the funds—for

Sole proprietorships, the most common form of business organization in the United States, commonly include businesses such as florists, restaurants, and hair salons.

Hero Images Inc./Alamy Stock Photo

expansion of the business, for salary increases, for travel to purchase additional inventory, or to find new customers.

Flexibility and Control of the Business.

The sole proprietor has complete control over the business and can make decisions on the spot without anyone else's approval. This control allows the owner to respond quickly to competitive business conditions or to changes in the economy. The ability to quickly change prices or products can provide a competitive advantage for the business.

Government Regulation.

Sole proprietorships have the most freedom from government regulation. Many government regulations—federal, state, and local—apply only to businesses that have a certain number of employees, and securities laws apply only to corporations that issue stock. Nonetheless, sole proprietors must ensure that they follow all laws that do apply to their business. For example, sole proprietorships must be careful to obey employee and consumer protection regulation.

Taxation.

Profits from sole proprietorships are considered personal income and are taxed at individual tax rates. The owner, therefore, pays one income tax that includes the business and individual income. Another tax benefit is that a sole proprietor is allowed to establish a tax-exempt retirement account or a tax-exempt profit-sharing account. Such accounts are exempt from current income tax, but payments taken after retirement are taxed when they are received.

Closing the Business.

A sole proprietorship can be dissolved easily. No approval of co-owners or partners is necessary. The only legal condition is that all financial obligations must be paid or resolved. If a proprietor does a going-out-of-business sale, most states require that the business actually close.

Disadvantages of Sole Proprietorships

What may be seen as an advantage by one person may turn out to be a disadvantage to another. For profitable businesses managed by capable owners, many of the following factors do not cause problems. On the other hand, proprietors starting out with little management experience and little money are likely to encounter many of the disadvantages.

Unlimited Liability.

The sole proprietor has unlimited liability in meeting the debts of the business. In other words, if the business cannot pay its creditors, the owner may be forced to use personal, nonbusiness holdings such as a car or a home to pay off the debts. There are only a few states in which houses and homesteads cannot be taken by creditors, even if the proprietor declares bankruptcy. The more wealth an individual has, the greater is the disadvantage of unlimited liability.

Limited Sources of Funds.

Among the relatively few sources of money available to the sole proprietorship are banks, friends, family, the Small Business Administration, or his or her own funds. The owner's personal financial condition determines his or her credit standing. Additionally, sole proprietorships may have to pay higher interest rates on funds borrowed from banks than do large corporations because they are considered greater risks. More proprietors are using nonbank financial institutions for transactions that charge higher interest rates than banks. Often, the only way a sole proprietor can borrow for business purposes is to pledge a car, a house, other real estate, or other personal assets to guarantee the loan. If the business fails, the owner may lose the personal assets as well as the business. Publicly owned corporations, in contrast, can not only obtain funds from commercial banks but can sell stocks and bonds to the public to raise money. If a public company goes out of business, the owners do not lose personal assets. However, they will lose the value of their stocks or bonds.

Limited Skills.

The sole proprietor must be able to perform many functions and possess skills in diverse fields such as management, marketing, finance, accounting, bookkeeping, and personnel management. Specialized professionals, such as accountants or attorneys, can be hired by businesses for help or advice. Sometimes, sole proprietors need assistance with certain business functions. For instance, Network Solutions offers web services for small- and medium-sized businesses that want to grow their online presence. The company offers website hosting, or storage space and access for websites, as well as tools to help build a website and online marketing services.[5] In the end, however, it is up to the business owner to make the final decision in all areas of the business.

Lack of Continuity.

The life expectancy of a sole proprietorship is directly linked to that of the owner and his or her ability to work. The serious illness of the owner could result in failure of the business if competent help cannot be found. It is difficult to arrange for the sale of a proprietorship and, at the same time, assure customers that the business will continue to meet their needs. For instance, how does one sell a veterinary practice? A veterinarian's major asset is patients. If the vet dies suddenly, the equipment can be sold, but the patients will not necessarily remain loyal to the office. On the other hand, a veterinarian who wants to retire could take in a younger partner and sell the practice to the partner over time. One advantage to the partnership is that some of the customers are likely to stay with the business, even if ownership changes.

Lack of Qualified Employees.

It is sometimes difficult for a small sole proprietorship to match the wages and benefits offered by a large competing corporation because the proprietorship's profits may not be as high. In addition, there may be less room for advancement within a sole proprietorship, so the owner may have difficulty attracting and retaining qualified employees. On the other hand, the trend of large corporations downsizing and outsourcing tasks has created renewed opportunities for small businesses to acquire well-trained employees.

Taxation.

Although we listed taxation as an advantage for sole proprietorships, it can also be a disadvantage, depending on the proprietor's income. Under current tax rates, sole proprietors pay a higher tax rate than do small corporations on income

partnership, each partner has unlimited liability for the debts of the business. Professionals such as lawyers, accountants, and architects often join together in general partnerships.

of less than $75,000. However, sole proprietorships avoid the double taxation of corporate and personal taxes that occurs with corporations. The tax effect often determines whether a sole proprietor chooses to incorporate his or her business.

LO 4-2 Describe the two types of business partnership and their advantages and disadvantages.

PARTNERSHIPS

One way to minimize the disadvantages of a sole proprietorship and maximize its advantages is to have more than one owner. Most states have a model law governing partnerships based on the Uniform Partnership Act. This law defines a **partnership** as "an association of two or more persons who carry on as co-owners of a business for profit." For example, Rebecca Minkoff, a luxury handbag and accessories designer, partnered with her brother, Uri Minkoff, to establish her namesake brand.[6] Partnerships are the least used form of business. They are typically larger than sole proprietorships but smaller than corporations. Partnerships can be a fruitful form of business, as long as some basic keys to success, which are outlined in Table 4.2, are followed.

Types of Partnership

There are two basic types of partnership: general partnership and limited partnership. A **general partnership** involves a complete sharing in the management of a business. In a general

A **limited partnership** has at least one general partner, who assumes unlimited liability, and at least one limited partner, whose liability is limited to his or her investment in the business. Limited partnerships exist for risky investment projects where the chance of loss is great. The general partners accept the risk of loss; the limited partners' losses are limited to their initial investment. Limited partners do not participate in the management of the business but share in the profits in accordance with the terms of a partnership agreement. Usually, the general partner receives a larger share of the profits after the limited partners have received their initial investment back. A *master limited partnership* (MLP) is a limited partnership traded on securities exchanges. MLPs have the tax benefits of a limited partnership but the liquidity (ability to convert assets into cash) of a corporation. Popular examples of MLPs include oil and gas companies and pipeline operators.[7]

Articles of Partnership

Articles of partnership are legal documents that set forth the basic agreement between partners. Most states require articles of partnership, but even if they are not required, it makes good sense for partners to draw them up. Articles of partnership usually list the money or assets that each partner has contributed (called *partnership capital*), state each partner's individual management role or duty, specify how the profits and losses of the partnership will be divided among the partners, and describe how a partner may leave the partnership as well as any other restrictions that might apply to the agreement. Table 4.3 lists some of the issues and provisions that should be included in articles of partnership.

▼ **TABLE 4.2** Keys to Success in Business Partnerships

1. Keep profit sharing equitable based on contributions.
2. Partners should have different skill sets or resource contributions.
3. Ethics and compliance are required.
4. Must maintain effective communication skills.
5. Maintain transparency with stakeholders.
6. Must be realistic in resource and financial management.
7. Previous experience related to business is helpful.
8. Maintain life balance in time spent on business.
9. Focus on customer satisfaction and product quality.
10. Maintain resources in line with sales and growth expectations and planning.

The Blackstone Group L.P., one of the world's leading investment firms, is an example of a limited partnership.

Mark Lennihan/AP/Shutterstock

▼ TABLE 4.3 Issues and Provisions in Articles of Partnership

1. Name, purpose, location
2. Duration of the agreement
3. Authority and responsibility of each partner
4. Character of partners (i.e., general or limited, active or silent)
5. Amount of contribution from each partner
6. Division of profits or losses
7. Salaries of each partner
8. How much each partner is allowed to withdraw
9. Death of partner
10. Sale of partnership interest
11. Arbitration of disputes
12. Required and prohibited actions
13. Absence and disability
14. Restrictive covenants
15. Buying and selling agreements

Advantages of Partnerships

Law firms, accounting firms, and investment firms with several hundred partners have partnership agreements that are quite complicated in comparison with the partnership agreement among two or three people owning a computer repair shop. The advantages must be compared with those offered by other forms of business organization, and not all apply to every partnership.

Ease of Organization.
Starting a partnership requires little more than drawing up articles of partnership. No legal charters have to be granted, but the name of the business should be registered with the state.

Availability of Capital and Credit.
When a business has several partners, it has the benefit of a combination of talents and skills and pooled financial resources. Partnerships tend to be larger than sole proprietorships and, therefore, have greater earning power and better credit ratings. Because many limited partnerships have been formed for tax purposes rather than for economic profits, the combined income of all U.S. partnerships is quite low. Nevertheless, the professional partnerships of many lawyers, accountants, and banking firms make quite large profits. For instance, the partners at the law firm Baker McKenzie in Chicago likely take home large incomes as the firm earns revenues of more than $2.6 billion a year.[8]

Combined Knowledge and Skills.
Partners in the most successful partnerships acknowledge each other's talents and avoid confusion and conflict by specializing in a particular area of expertise such as marketing, production, accounting, or service. The diversity of skills in a partnership makes it possible for the business to be run by a management team of specialists instead of by a generalist sole proprietor. Co-founders Sierra Tishgart and Maddy Moelis credit their diverse professional experience as being a key component to the success of their cookware line, Great Jones. Tishgart is a James Beard Award-winning food editor and Moelis is a former Zola product management consultant. The pair raised more than $3 million to create the company and plan to take on the likes of established brands like Le Creuset.[9] Service-oriented partnerships in fields such as law, financial planning, and accounting may attract customers because clients may think that the service offered by a diverse team is of higher quality than that provided by one person. Larger law firms, for example, often have individual partners who specialize in certain areas of the law–such as family, bankruptcy, corporate, entertainment, and criminal law.

Decision Making.
Small partnerships can react more quickly to changes in the business environment than can large partnerships and corporations. Such fast reactions are possible because the partners are involved in day-to-day operations and can make decisions quickly after consultation. Large partnerships with hundreds of partners in many states are not common. In those that do exist, decision making is likely to be slow. However, some partnerships have been successful despite their large size. The accounting firm Ernst & Young is one of the largest accounting and advisory firms in the United States. In one year, it promoted 1,163 individuals to the rank of partner, 30 percent of whom were women. With global revenues of more than $36 billion, some have attributed Ernst & Young's success to its strong approach to diversity and the innovation of its teams.[10]

Regulatory Controls.
Like a sole proprietorship, a partnership has fewer regulatory controls affecting its activities than does a corporation. A partnership does not have to file public financial statements with government agencies or send out quarterly financial statements to several thousand owners, as do corporations such as Apple and Ford Motor Co. A partnership does, however, have to abide by all laws relevant to the industry or profession in which it operates as well as state and federal laws relating to financial reports, employees, consumer protection, and environmental regulations, just as the sole proprietorship does.

Disadvantages of Partnerships

Partnerships have many advantages compared to sole proprietorships and corporations, but they also have some disadvantages. Limited partners have no voice in the management of the partnership, and they may bear most of the risk of the business, while the general partner reaps a larger share of the benefits. There may be a change in the goals and objectives of one partner but not the other, particularly when the partners are multinational organizations. This can cause friction, giving rise to an enterprise that fails to satisfy both parties or even forcing an end to the partnership. Many partnership disputes wind up in court or require outside mediation. A partnership can be jeopardized when two business partners cannot resolve disputes.

> ## "In general partnerships, the general partners have unlimited liability for the debts incurred by the business, just as the sole proprietor has unlimited liability for his or her business."

For instance, two co-founders of photo-sharing mobile application Snapchat reached a financial settlement with their former fraternity brother, who sued the co-founders because the business was based around his idea.[11] In some cases, the ultimate solution may be dissolving the partnership. Major disadvantages of partnerships include the following.

Unlimited Liability.
In general partnerships, the general partners have unlimited liability for the debts incurred by the business, just as the sole proprietor has unlimited liability for his or her business. Such unlimited liability can be a distinct disadvantage to one partner if his or her personal financial resources are greater than those of the others. A potential partner should check to make sure that all partners have comparable resources to help the business in time of trouble. This disadvantage is eliminated for limited partners, who can lose only their initial investment.

Business Responsibility.
All partners are responsible for the business actions of all others. Partners may have the ability to commit the partnership to a contract without approval of the other partners. A bad decision by one partner may put the other partners' personal resources in jeopardy. Personal problems such as a divorce can eliminate a significant portion of one partner's financial resources and weaken the financial structure of the whole partnership.

Life of the Partnership.
A partnership is terminated when a partner dies or withdraws. In a two-person partnership, if one partner withdraws, the firm's liabilities would be paid off and the assets divided between the partners. Obviously, the partner who wishes to continue in the business would be at a serious disadvantage. The business could be disrupted, financing would be reduced, and the management skills of the departing partner would be lost. The remaining partner would have to find another or reorganize the business as a sole proprietorship. In very large partnerships such as those found in law firms and investment banks, the continuation of the partnership may be provided for in the articles of partnership. The provision may simply state the terms for a new partnership agreement among the remaining partners. In such cases, the disadvantage to the other partners is minimal.

Selling a partnership interest has the same effect as the death or withdrawal of a partner. It is difficult to place a value on a partner's share of the partnership. No public value is placed on the partnership, as there is on publicly owned corporations. What

is a law firm worth? What is the local hardware store worth? Coming up with a fair value that all partners can agree to is not easy. Selling a partnership interest is easier if the articles of partnership specify a method of valuation. Even if there is not a procedure for selling one partner's interest, the old partnership must still be dissolved and a new one created. In contrast, in the corporate form of business, the departure of owners has little effect on the financial resources of the business, and the loss of managers does not cause long-term changes in the structure of the organization.

Distribution of Profits.
Profits earned by the partnership are distributed to the partners in the proportions specified in the articles of partnership. This may be a disadvantage if the division of the profits does not reflect the work each partner puts into the business. You may have encountered this disadvantage while working on a student group project: You may have felt that you did most of the work and that the other students in the group received grades based on your efforts. Even the perception of an unfair profit-sharing agreement may cause tension between the partners, and unhappy partners can have a negative effect on the profitability of the business.

Limited Sources of Funds.
As with a sole proprietorship, the sources of funds available to a partnership are limited. Because no public value is placed on the business (such as the current trading price of a corporation's stock), potential partners do not always know what one partnership share is worth, although third parties can access the value. Moreover, because partnership shares cannot be bought and sold easily in public markets, potential owners may not want to tie up their money in assets that cannot be readily sold on short notice. Accumulating enough funds to operate a national business, especially a business requiring intensive investments in facilities and equipment, can be difficult. Partnerships also may have to pay higher interest rates on funds borrowed from banks than do large corporations because partnerships may be considered greater risks.

Taxation of Partnerships
Partnerships are quasi-taxable organizations. This means that partnerships do not pay taxes when submitting the partnership tax return to the Internal Revenue Service. The tax return simply provides information about the profitability of the organization and the distribution of profits among the partners. Partners must report their share of profits on their individual tax returns

corporation a legal entity, created by the state, whose assets and liabilities are separate from its owners.

stock shares of a corporation that may be bought or sold.

dividends profits of a corporation that are distributed in the form of cash payments to stockholders.

and pay taxes at the income tax rate for individuals. Master limited partnerships require financial reports similar to corporations, which are discussed in the next section.

> **LO 4-3** Describe the corporate form of organization and its advantages and disadvantages.

CORPORATIONS

When you think of a business, you probably think of a huge corporation such as General Electric, Procter & Gamble, or Sony because a large portion of your consumer dollars go to such corporations. A **corporation** is a legal entity, created by the state, whose assets and liabilities are separate from its owners. As a legal entity, a corporation has many of the rights, duties, and powers of a person, such as the right to receive, own, and transfer property. Corporations can enter into contracts with individuals or with other legal entities, and they can sue and be sued in court.

Corporations account for the majority of all U.S. sales and income. Thus, most of the dollars you spend as a consumer probably go to incorporated businesses. Most corporations are not mega-companies like General Mills or Ford Motor Co.; even small businesses can incorporate. As we shall see later in the chapter, many smaller firms elect to incorporate as "S Corporations," which operate under slightly different rules and have greater flexibility than do traditional "C Corporations" like General Mills.

Corporations are typically owned by many individuals and organizations who own shares of the business, called **stock** (thus, corporate owners are often called *shareholders* or *stockholders*). Stockholders can buy, sell, give or receive as gifts, or inherit their shares of stock. As owners, the stockholders are entitled to all profits that are left after all the corporation's other obligations have been paid. These profits may be distributed in the form of cash payments called **dividends**. For example, if a corporation earns $100 million after expenses and taxes and decides to pay the owners $40 million in dividends, the stockholders receive 40 percent of the profits in cash dividends. In recent years, companies in the United States have paid shareholders more than $485 billion per year in dividends. Table 4.4 lists the world's biggest dividend payers. However, not all after-tax profits are paid to stockholders in dividends. Some corporations may retain profits to expand the business. For example, Alphabet (Google's parent company), Amazon, Biogen, and Tesla have not paid dividends in the past because they reinvest their earnings.

Creating a Corporation

A corporation is created, or incorporated, under the laws of the state in which it incorporates. The individuals creating the corporation are known as *incorporators*. Each state has a specific procedure, sometimes called *chartering the corporation*, for incorporating a business. Most states require a minimum of three incorporators; thus, many small businesses can be and are incorporated. Another requirement is that the new corporation's name cannot be similar to that of another business. In most states, a corporation's name must end in "company," "corporation," "incorporated," or "limited" to show that the owners have limited liability. (In this text, however, the word *company* means any organization engaged in a commercial enterprise and can refer to a sole proprietorship, a partnership, or a corporation.)

The incorporators must file legal documents generally referred to as *articles of incorporation* with the appropriate state office (often the secretary of state). The articles of incorporation contain basic information about the business. The following 10 items are found in the Model Business Corporation Act, issued by the American Bar Association, which is followed by most states:

1. Name and address of the corporation.
2. Objectives of the corporation.
3. Classes of stock (common, preferred, voting, nonvoting) and the number of shares for each class of stock to be issued.
4. Expected life of the corporation (corporations are usually created to last forever).
5. Financial capital required at the time of incorporation.
6. Provisions for transferring shares of stock between owners.
7. Provisions for the regulation of internal corporate affairs.
8. Address of the business office registered with the state of incorporation.
9. Names and addresses of the initial board of directors.
10. Names and addresses of the incorporators.

▼ **TABLE 4.4** World's Biggest Dividend Payers

Rank	Company
1.	Rio Tinto
2.	Nestlé SA
3.	Sberbank of Russia
4.	Sanofi
5.	Allianz SE
6.	BNP Paribas
7.	HSBC Holdings
8.	Daimler AG
9.	Intesa Sanpaolo Spa
10.	Total S.A.

Source: *Janus Henderson Global Dividend Index,* Edition 23, August 2019, p. 13.

Based on the information in the articles of incorporation, the state issues a **corporate charter** to the company. After securing this charter, the owners hold an organizational meeting at which they establish the corporation's bylaws and elect a board of directors. The bylaws might set up committees of the board of directors and describe the rules and procedures for their operation.

Types of Corporations

If the corporation does business in the state in which it is chartered, it is known as a *domestic corporation*. In other states where the corporation does business, it is known as a *foreign corporation*. If a corporation does business outside the nation in which it is incorporated, it is called an *alien corporation*. A corporation may be privately or publicly owned.

A **private corporation** is owned by just one or a few people who are closely involved in managing the business. These people, often a family, own all the corporation's stock, and no stock is sold to the public. Many corporations are quite large, yet remain private, including Publix Super Markets. It is the nation's eighth largest privately held corporation, with annual revenues of more than $36 billion. Founded in 1930, today the company is run by the founder's grandson, who is the fourth family member to lead the company.[12] Table 4.5 lists the 10 largest private companies in the United States. Privately owned corporations are not required to disclose financial information publicly, but they must, of course, pay taxes.

A **public corporation** is one whose stock anyone may buy, sell, or trade. A few thousand multinational firms influence what

Chinese e-commerce company Alibaba released the largest IPO globally at $25 billion.

Pieter Beens/Shutterstock

billions of consumers watch, wear, and eat.[13] Companies like IBM, McDonald's, Caterpillar, and Procter & Gamble earn more than half of their revenue outside the United Sates, as Table 4.6 indicates. Thousands of smaller public corporations in the United States have sales under $10 million. In large public corporations such as AT&T, the stockholders are often far removed from the management of the company. In other public corporations, the managers are often the founders and the major shareholders. Facebook CEO Mark Zuckerberg, for example, holds a 53.1 percent voting majority position in the firm.[14] Publicly owned corporations must disclose financial information to the public under specific laws that regulate the trade of stocks and other securities.

A private corporation that needs more money to expand or to take advantage of opportunities may have to obtain financing by "going public" through an **initial public offering (IPO)**—that is, becoming a public corporation by selling stock so that it can be traded in public markets. Digital media companies are leading a surge in initial public offerings. For example, Upwork, an online freelancer marketplace, priced its IPO at $15 per share with 12.5 million shares.[15]

▼ **TABLE 4.5** America's Largest Private Companies

Rank	Company	Industry	Revenue (in billions)	Employees
1.	Cargill	Food, drink, and tobacco	$113.5	160,000
2.	Koch Industries	Multicompany	$110.0	130,000
3.	Albertsons	Food markets	$ 60.5	267,000
4.	Deloitte	Business services and supplies	$ 46.2	310,000
5.	PricewaterhouseCoopers	Business services and supplies	$ 42.4	276,000
6.	Mars	Food, drink, and tobacco	$ 37.0	115,000
7.	Ernst & Young	Business services and supplies	$ 36.4	100,000
8.	Publix Super Markets	Food markets	$ 36.1	202,000
9.	Reyes Holding	Food, drink, and tobacco	$ 30.0	33,000
10.	Pilot Flying J	Convenience stores and gas stations	$ 29.0	26,050

Source: "America's Largest Private Companies," *Forbes,* https://www.forbes.com/largest-private-companies/list/ (accessed May 27, 2020).

Company	Description
Caterpillar Inc.	Designs, manufactures, markets, and sells machinery, engines, and financial products
Dow Chemical	Manufactures chemicals, with products including plastics, oil, and crop technology
General Electric	Operates in the technology infrastructure, energy, capital finance, and consumer and industrial fields, with products including appliances, locomotives, weapons, lighting, and gas
General Motors	Sells automobiles with brands including Chevrolet, Buick, Cadillac, and Isuzu
IBM	Conducts technological research, develops intellectual property including software and hardware, and offers consulting services
Intel	Manufactures and develops semiconductor chips and microprocessors
McDonald's	Operates second-largest chain of fast-food restaurants worldwide after Subway
Nike	Designs, develops, markets, and sells athletic shoes and clothing
Procter & Gamble	Sells consumer goods with brands including Tide, Bounty, Crest, and Iams
Yum! Brands	Operates and licenses restaurants including Taco Bell, Kentucky Fried Chicken, and Pizza Hut

Also, privately owned firms are occasionally forced to go public with stock offerings when a major owner dies and the heirs have large estate taxes to pay. The tax payment may only be possible with the proceeds of the sale of stock. This happened to the brewer Adolph Coors Inc. After Adolph Coors died, the business went public and his family sold shares of stock to the public in order to pay the estate taxes.

On the other hand, public corporations can be "taken private" when one or a few individuals (perhaps the management of the firm) purchase all the firm's stock so that it can no longer be sold publicly. Taking a corporation private may be desirable when owners want to exert more control over the firm or they want the flexibility to make decisions for restructuring operations. For example, Michael Dell took his company private in order to set a

CASCADE ENGINEERING: GO B CORP OR GO HOME

Cascade Engineering based in Grand Rapids, Michigan, makes an unlikely B corporation, in that it manufactures plastic products, operating in an industry that tends to be seen as environmentally unfriendly. B corporations are not your typical corporation. The *B* stands for *beneficial,* and it is a certification awarded by the nonprofit B Lab to signal that member-companies will conform to a set of transparent and comprehensive social and environmental performance standards. These businesses are purpose-driven and are designed to give back to communities, the environment, and employees.

Cascade made the proactive decision to make sustainability the focus of its strategy in product and business development. When evaluating alternatives, sustainability is a primary consideration. To further this goal, the company produces its own alternative energy products. By using thermoplastics and multiple types of molding that cut down on waste, the company is able to produce goods that do not negatively affect the environment.

Most manufacturers would feel constrained by the performance standards of a B corporation.

Fred Keller, Cascade Engineering's founder, saw things differently. He welcomed regulation, using it as a motivation to improve processes. Cascade Engineering looks at decisions based on how they can benefit the community, which often requires managers to make nonprogrammed decisions to develop unique solutions. Taking proactive steps to become a sustainable company has value to both the environment and the company. Rather than waiting for legislation and ethical guidelines to be imposed by the government, Cascade Engineering has taken it upon themselves to adopt ecofriendly business practices.

The company has spent more than a decade helping customers reduce oil use and eliminate waste. It has developed a cradle-to-cradle certified product line based on a design concept that stresses reusable and safe materials, renewable energy, water quality, social fairness, and continuous improvement. Unlike many manufacturers, Cascade supports a switch to renewable energy. While this might be perceived as a risky move, Cascade is aware that this type of energy is at the forefront of innovation. Company

decisions focus on sustainable solutions as the best alternative for the continued success of the company and society.

Cascade Engineering has worked to develop a culture of positive decision-making when addressing the impact of the industry. Although many believe that companies should focus on profits first, Keller believes that businesses should be analyzed not only by how much money they make but also by how they benefit society. His efforts have netted him multiple awards, respect, and the business of like-minded companies.[a]

🔵 Critical Thinking Questions:

1. How does Cascade use B corporation certification as a way to improve both company processes as well as the environment?

2. How does B corporation certification encourage corporations to be socially responsible?

3. Do you think it is possible for a plastics company to make a positive contribution toward sustainability?

new direction as PC sales continue to decline. Becoming a private company again allowed Dell to focus on the needs of the company more fully without having to worry about the stock price for investors.[16] Several years later, Dell became a public company once again.[17] Taking a corporation private is also one technique for avoiding a takeover by another corporation.

Quasi-public corporations and nonprofits are two types of public corporations. **Quasi-public corporations** are owned and operated by the federal, state, or local government. The focus of these entities is to provide a service to citizens, such as mail delivery, rather than earning a profit. Indeed, many quasi-public corporations operate at a loss. Examples of quasi-public corporations include the National Aeronautics and Space Administration (NASA) and the U.S. Postal Service.

Like quasi-public corporations, **nonprofit corporations** focus on providing a service rather than earning a profit, but they are not owned by a government entity. Organizations such as the Sesame Workshop, the Elks Clubs, the American Lung Association, the American Red Cross, museums, and private schools provide services without a profit motive. United Way Worldwide is the largest charity in the United States with total revenue of $3.6 billion.[18] To fund their operations and services, nonprofit organizations solicit donations from individuals and companies, apply for grants from the government and other charitable foundations, and charge for their services. Habitat for Humanity, a nonprofit that builds affordable homes using volunteer labor for families in need, operates hundreds of Habitat for Humanity ReStore locations, outlets for discount furniture, appliances, building materials, and more. All of the profits from its stores benefit its home-building program.[19] Nonprofits do not have shareholders, and most are organized as 501(c)(3) organizations. A 501(c)(3) organization receives certain tax exemptions, and donors contributing to these organizations may reduce their tax deductibility for their donations. Organizations that have 501(c)(3) status include public charities (e.g., the Leukemia & Lymphoma Society), private foundations (e.g., the Daniels Fund), and private operating foundations that sponsor and fund their own programs (e.g., day camp for underprivileged children).[20]

Elements of a Corporation

The Board of Directors.
A **board of directors**, elected by the stockholders to oversee the general operation of the corporation, sets the long-range objectives of the corporation. It is the board's responsibility to ensure that the objectives are achieved on schedule. Board members have a duty of care and loyalty to oversee the management of the firm or for any misuse of funds. An important duty of the board of directors is to hire corporate officers, such as the president and the chief executive officer (CEO), who are responsible to the directors for the management and daily operations of the firm. The role and expectations of the board of directors took on greater significance after the accounting scandals of the early 2000s and the passage of the Sarbanes-Oxley Act.[21] As a result, most corporations have restructured how they compensate board directors for their time and expertise.

However, some experts now speculate that Sarbanes-Oxley did little to motivate directors to increase company oversight. At the same time, the pay rate of directors is rising. On average, corporate directors are paid around $245,000, with compensation ranging from $0 to more than $1 million. Over the past several years, the trend of increasing directors' pay has continued, resulting in higher and higher pay levels. Although such pay is meant to attract top-quality directors, concerns exist over whether excessive pay will have unintended consequences. Some believe that this trend is contributing to the declining effectiveness in corporate governance.[22]

Directors can be employees of the company (*inside directors*) or people unaffiliated with the company (*outside directors*). Inside directors are usually the officers responsible for running the company. Outside directors are often top executives from other companies, lawyers, bankers, even professors. Directors today are increasingly chosen for their expertise, competence, and ability to bring diverse perspectives to strategic discussions. Outside directors are also thought to bring more independence to the monitoring function because they are not bound by past allegiances, friendships, a current role in the company, or some other issue that may create a conflict of interest. Many of the corporate scandals uncovered in recent years might have been prevented if each of the companies' boards of directors had been better qualified, more knowledgeable, and more independent.

There is a growing shortage of available and qualified board members. Boards are increasingly telling their own CEOs that they should be focused on serving their company, not serving on outside boards. Because of this, the average CEO sits on less than one outside board. This represents a decline from a decade ago when the average was two. Because many CEOs are turning down

> **"There is a growing shortage of available and qualified board members."**

outside positions, many companies have taken steps to ensure that boards have experienced directors. They have increased the mandatory retirement age to 72 or older, and some have raised it to 75 or even older. Minimizing the amount of overlap between directors sitting on different boards helps to limit conflicts of interest and provides for independence in decision making.

Stock Ownership. Corporations issue two types of stock: preferred and common. Owners of **preferred stock** are a special class of owners because, although they generally do not have any say in running the company, they have a claim to profits before any other stockholders. Other stockholders do not receive any dividends unless the preferred stockholders have already been paid. Dividend payments on preferred stock are usually a fixed percentage of the initial issuing price (set by the board of directors). For example, if a share of preferred stock originally cost $100 and the dividend rate was stated at 7.5 percent, the dividend payment will be $7.50 per share per year. Dividends are usually paid quarterly. Most preferred stock carries a cumulative claim to dividends. This means that if the company does not pay preferred-stock dividends in one year because of losses, the dividends accumulate to the next year. Such dividends unpaid from previous years must also be paid to preferred stockholders before other stockholders can receive any dividends.

Although owners of **common stock** do not get such preferential treatment with regard to dividends, they do get some say in the operation of the corporation. Their ownership gives them the right to vote for members of the board of directors and on other important issues. Common stock dividends may vary according to the profitability of the business, and some corporations do not issue dividends at all, but instead plow their profits back into the company to fund expansion.

Common stockholders are the voting owners of a corporation. They are usually entitled to one vote per share of common stock. During an annual stockholders' meeting, common stockholders elect a board of directors. Some boards find it easier than others to attract high-profile individuals. For example, in 2020 the board of Procter & Gamble consisted of Francis S. Blake, former CEO of Home Depot; Angela F. Braly, former CEO of Anthem; Amy L. Chang, CEO of Accompany Inc.; and others.[23] Because they can choose the board of directors, common stockholders have some say in how the company will operate. Common stockholders may vote by *proxy*, which is a written authorization by which stockholders assign their voting privilege to someone else, who then votes for his or her choice at the stockholders' meeting. It is a normal practice for management to request proxy statements from shareholders who are not planning to attend the annual meeting. Most owners do not attend annual meetings of the very large companies, such as Westinghouse or Boeing, unless they live in the city where the meeting is held.

Common stockholders have another advantage over preferred shareholders. In most states, when the corporation decides to sell new shares of common stock in the marketplace, common stockholders have the first right, called a *preemptive right*, to purchase new shares of the stock from the corporation. A preemptive right is often included in the articles of incorporation. This right is important because it allows stockholders to purchase new shares to maintain their original positions. For example, if a stockholder owns 10 percent of a corporation that decides to issue new shares, that stockholder has the right to buy enough of the new shares to retain the 10 percent ownership.

Advantages of Corporations

Because a corporation is a separate legal entity, it has some very specific advantages over other forms of ownership. The biggest advantage may be the limited liability of the owners.

Limited Liability. Because the corporation's assets (money and resources) and liabilities (debts and other obligations) are separate from its owners', in most cases the stockholders are not held responsible for the firm's debts if it fails. Their liability or potential loss is limited to the amount of their original investment. Although a creditor can sue a corporation for not paying its debts, even forcing the corporation into bankruptcy, it cannot make the stockholders pay the corporation's debts out of their personal assets. Occasionally, the owners of a

Airbnb's board of directors includes Kenneth I. Chenault, former CEO of American Express.

lev radin/Shutterstock

Caterpillar pays foreign taxes as well as U.S. taxes when profits are brought back into the country.

pabrady63/123RF

private corporation may pledge personal assets to secure a loan for the corporation; this would be most unusual for a public corporation.

Ease of Transfer of Ownership.
Stockholders can sell or trade shares of stock to other people without causing the termination of the corporation, and they can do this without the prior approval of other shareholders. The transfer of ownership (unless it is a majority position) does not affect the daily or long-term operations of the corporation.

Perpetual Life.
A corporation usually is chartered to last forever unless its articles of incorporation stipulate otherwise. The existence of the corporation is unaffected by the death or withdrawal of any of its stockholders. It survives until the owners sell it or liquidate its assets. However, in some cases, bankruptcy ends a corporation's life. Bankruptcies occur when companies are unable to operate and earn profits. Eventually, uncompetitive businesses must close or seek protection from creditors in bankruptcy court while the business tries to reorganize.

External Sources of Funds.
Of all the forms of business organization, the public corporation finds it easiest to raise money. When a large or public corporation needs to raise more money, it can sell more stock shares or issue bonds (corporate "IOUs," which pledge to repay debt), attracting funds from anywhere in the United States and even overseas. The larger a corporation becomes, the more sources of financing are available to it. We take a closer look at some of these in the chapter "Money and the Financial System."

Expansion Potential.
Because large public corporations can find long-term financing

readily, they can easily expand into national and international markets. And, as a legal entity, a corporation can enter into contracts without as much difficulty as a partnership.

Disadvantages of Corporations
Corporations have some distinct disadvantages resulting from tax laws and government regulation.

Double Taxation.
As a legal entity, the corporation must pay taxes on its income just like you do. The United States has a tax rate of 21 percent. The global average is 24 percent.[24] Global companies such as Apple and Caterpillar have to pay foreign taxes as well as U.S. taxes when profits are brought back into the country. When after-tax corporate profits are paid out as dividends to the stockholders, the dividends are taxed a second time as part of the individual owner's income. This process creates double taxation for the stockholders of dividend-paying corporations. Double taxation does not occur with the other forms of business organization.

Forming a Corporation.
The formation of a corporation can be costly. A charter must be obtained, and this usually requires the services of an attorney and payment of legal fees. Filing fees ranging from $25 to $150 must be paid to the state that awards the corporate charter, and certain states require that an annual fee be paid to maintain the charter. Today, a number of Internet services such as LegalZoom.com and Business.com make it easier, quicker, and less costly to form a corporation. However, in making it easier for people to form businesses without expert consultation, these services have increased the risk that people will not choose the kind of organizational form that is right for them. Sometimes, one form works better than another. The business's founders may fail to take into account disadvantages, such as double taxation with corporations.

Disclosure of Information.
Corporations must make information available to their owners, usually through an annual report to shareholders. The annual report contains financial information about the firm's profits, sales, facilities and equipment, and debts, as well as descriptions of the company's operations, products, and plans for the future. Public corporations must also file reports with the Securities and Exchange Commission (SEC), the government regulatory agency that regulates securities such as stocks and bonds. The larger the firm, the more data the SEC requires. Because all reports filed with the SEC are available to the public, competitors can access them. Additionally, complying with securities laws takes time.

Employee-Owner Separation.
Many employees are not stockholders of the company for which they work. This separation of owners and

DID YOU KNOW?

The first corporation with a net income of more than $1 billion in one year was General Motors, with a net income in 1955 of $1,189,477,082.[b]

Stacy Flynn first realized how much the apparel industry pollutes the environment during a trip to China. She stepped out of the car and could barely see through the smog generated by China's local textile industry. Flynn started working on producing recycled fibers and collaborating with apparel makers to turn textile waste into sustainable pieces. She and her co-founder eventually developed the private company Evrnu, a research and development firm whose technology is able to convert post-consumer apparel waste into new fibers called regenerative fiber. Evrnu is the only company that has been able to develop this process.

As a privately held company, Evrnu is able to retain tight control over the direction of the company while choosing the investors it partners with. One of these investors is Closed Loop Partners, an investment firm focused on sustainable manufacturing. Evrnu is licensing its NuCycl technology which converts pre- and post-consumer textile materials into recyclable new fibers to companies such as Adidas and Target. With these new partnerships, Evrnu has raised more than $9.1 million in investments. According to the World Wildlife Fund, it takes about 2,700 liters (or 700 gallons) of water to produce the cotton needed to make one T-shirt. Evrnu is ready to change these numbers. Its process uses 98 percent less water than would be consumed making new cotton apparel.

While the past few years have been spent refining the technology, Flynn is now ready to lead the company toward commercialization. Evrnu has already garnered the interest of large apparel companies with goals to increase their sustainable processes. It partnered with Levi Strauss to develop a line of jeans made from regenerated fiber. Evrnu has also developed an "early-adopter program" for its technology. Stella-McCartney and Target have already joined with the intent to launch their own lines.[c]

Critical Thinking Questions

1. How do private companies have more control than public corporations?
2. What are some of the advantages of a privately-held company over a sole proprietorship?
3. Why might private ownership be more beneficial to a small tech company like Evrnu?

employees may cause employees to feel that their work benefits only the owners. Employees without an ownership stake do not always see how they fit into the corporate picture and may not understand the importance of profits to the health of the organization. If managers are part owners but other employees are not, management–labor relations take on a different, sometimes difficult, aspect from those in partnerships and sole proprietorships. However, this situation is changing as more corporations establish employee stock ownership plans (ESOPs), which give shares of the company's stock to its employees. Such plans build a partnership between employee and employer and can boost productivity because they motivate employees to work harder so that they can earn dividends from their hard work as well as from their regular wages.

OTHER TYPES OF OWNERSHIP

In this section, we take a brief look at joint ventures, S corporations, limited liability companies, and cooperatives–businesses formed for special purposes.

Joint Ventures

A **joint venture** is a partnership established for a specific project or for a limited time. The partners in a joint venture may be individuals or organizations, as in the case of the international joint ventures discussed in the chapter "Business in a Borderless World." Control of a joint venture may be shared equally, or one partner may control decision making. Joint ventures are especially popular in situations that call for large investments, such as extraction of natural resources and the development of new products. Joint ventures can even take place between businesses and governments. For example, Sony set up joint ventures to make and sell PlayStation consoles and games in China.[25]

S Corporations

An **S corporation** is a form of business ownership that is taxed as though it were a partnership. Net profits or losses of the corporation pass to the owners, thus eliminating double taxation. The benefit of limited liability is retained. Formally known as Subchapter S Corporations, they have become a popular form of business ownership for entrepreneurs and represent almost half of all corporate filings.[26] The owners of an S corporation get the benefits of tax advantages and limited liability. Advantages of S corporations include the simple method of taxation, the limited liability of shareholders, perpetual life, and the ability to shift income and appreciation to others. Avoiding double taxation is reason enough for approximately 4.6 million U.S. companies to operate as S corporations.[27] Disadvantages include restrictions on the number (100) and types (individuals, estates, and certain trusts) of shareholders and the difficulty of formation and operation. S corporations are mainly small businesses

Limited Liability Companies

A **limited liability company (LLC)** is a form of business ownership that provides limited liability, as in a corporation, but is taxed like a partnership. Although relatively new in the United

joint venture a partnership established for a specific project or for a limited time.

S corporation corporation taxed as though it were a partnership with restrictions on shareholders.

limited liability company (LLC) form of ownership that provides limited liability and taxation like a partnership but places fewer restrictions on members.

Fiat Chrysler Automobiles (FCA) US LLC is the automaker that designs, manufactures, sells, and distributes brands like Jeep, Dodge, and Ram. FCA US is an example of a limited liability company.

Steve Lagreca/Shutterstock

the LLC form of ownership is to protect the members' personal assets in case of lawsuits. LLCs are flexible, simple to run, and do not require the members to hold meetings, keep minutes, or make resolutions, all of which are necessary in corporations. Mrs. Fields Famous Brands LLC—known for its cookies and brownies—is an example of a limited liability company.[29]

Cooperatives

Another form of organization in business is the **cooperative** or **co-op**, an organization composed of individuals or small businesses that have banded together to reap the benefits of belonging to a larger organization. Berkshire Co-op Market, for example, is a grocery store cooperative based in Massachusetts; Ocean Spray is a cooperative of cranberry farmers.[30] REI operates a bit differently because it is owned by consumers rather than farmers or small businesses. A co-op is set up not to make money as an entity. It exists so that its members can become more profitable or save money. Co-ops are generally expected to operate without profit or to create only enough profit to maintain the co-op organization.

Many cooperatives exist in small farming communities. The co-op stores and markets grain; orders large quantities of fertilizer, seed, and other supplies at discounted prices; and reduces costs and increases efficiency with good management. A co-op can purchase supplies in large quantities and pass the savings on to its members. It also can help distribute the products of its members more efficiently than each could on an individual basis. A cooperative can advertise its members' products and thus generate demand. Ace Hardware, a cooperative of independent hardware store owners, allows its members to share in the savings that result from buying supplies in large quantities; it also provides advertising, which individual members might not be able to afford on their own.

cooperative (co-op)
an organization composed of individuals or small businesses that have banded together to reap the benefits of belonging to a larger organization.

States, LLCs have existed for many years abroad. For example, Kano Computing Ltd., a build-it-yourself computer startup aiming to help teach the next generation of kids how to program and code, is based in London. The company got its start as a Kickstarter project that raised $1.5 million.[28] Professionals such as lawyers, doctors, and engineers often use the LLC form of ownership. Many consider the LLC a blend of the best characteristics of corporations, partnerships, and sole proprietorships. One of the major reasons for

"MEAT" THE VEGETARIAN BUTCHER

De Vegetarische Slager (DVS) is a Dutch vegetarian food producer. DVS started with founder Jaap Korteweg's initiative toward an organic and animal-friendly diet. At the end of the 20th century, swine fever and mad cow disease had killed many people in the Netherlands. During this period, Jaap tried to find vegetarian alternatives but missed the taste and texture of meat. Jaap spent 10 years searching and developing meat-like vegetarian products. He self-funded the experiments with capital from his existing business and partnered with scientists from Wageningen

University & Research. In 2010, he founded DVS to market his products to the world.

Korteweg incorporated DVS in the Netherlands as a BV. This is the most frequently used legal entity in the Netherlands for business purposes and is the equivalent of a limited liability company (LLC) in the United States. DVS has since become a sizable business with 4,000 stores in 17 countries and was purchased by Unilever. To earn such an achievement, DVS has focused extensively on product quality. From day one, the development team at DVS committed to producing plant-based

products resembling meats without compromising taste or texture.[d]

Critical Thinking Questions

1. What are the benefits of a limited liability company?

2. Describe the type of liability founder Jaap Korteweg had under his chosen business model.

3. What benefits does self-funding a business have over other types of funding?

TRENDS IN BUSINESS OWNERSHIP: MERGERS AND ACQUISITIONS

Companies large and small achieve growth and improve profitability by expanding their operations, often by developing and selling new products or selling current products to new groups of customers in different geographic areas. Such growth, when carefully planned and controlled, is usually beneficial to the firm and ultimately helps it reach its goal of enhanced profitability. But companies also grow by merging with or purchasing other companies.

A **merger** occurs when two companies (usually corporations) combine to form a new company. An **acquisition** occurs when one company purchases another, generally by buying most of its stock. The acquired company may become a subsidiary of the buyer, or its operations and assets may be merged with those of the buyer. In an effort to diversify beyond the car industry, Ford acquired Spin, an electric scooter startup; Chariot, a commuter shuttle service; Autonomic, a vehicle connectivity platform; and more.[31] The government sometimes scrutinizes mergers and acquisitions in an attempt to protect customers from monopolistic practices. For example, the decision to authorize the merger of AT&T and Time Warner was carefully analyzed. After a federal judge approved the merger, the Justice Department appealed the verdict due to antitrust concerns.[32] In some cases, acquisitions could end up harming the acquiring company. Google paid $3.2 billion for smart-home company Nest Labs.[33] The company was just one of many that Google acquired during the year. While these acquisitions diversified Google's service offerings, some believed that Google was investing in companies of which it had little knowledge. Since Google restructured to become a holding firm called Alphabet Inc., divisions such as Google Nest are now operated as semi-independent businesses.[34] Acquisitions sometimes involve the purchase of a division or some other part of a company rather than the entire company. Table 4.7 highlights the largest mergers of all time.

When firms that make and sell similar products to the same customers merge, it is known as a *horizontal merger*, as when Martin Marietta and Lockheed, both defense contractors, merged to form Lockheed Martin. Horizontal mergers, however, reduce the number of corporations competing within an industry, and for this reason they are usually reviewed carefully by federal regulators before the merger is allowed to proceed.

When companies operating at different but related levels of an industry merge, it is known as a *vertical merger*. In many instances, a vertical merger results when one corporation merges with one of its customers or suppliers. For example, if Burger King were to purchase a large Idaho potato farm—to ensure a ready supply of potatoes for its french fries—a vertical merger would result.

A *conglomerate merger* results when two firms in unrelated industries merge. For example, the purchase of Sterling Drug, a pharmaceutical firm, by Eastman Kodak, best known for its films and cameras, represented a conglomerate merger because the two companies were of different industries. (Kodak later sold Sterling Drug to a pharmaceutical company.)

When a company (or an individual), sometimes called a *corporate raider,* wants to acquire or take over another company, it first offers to buy some or all of the other company's stock at a premium over its current price in a *tender offer*. For example, photo service provider Snapfish completed its tender offer for shares of CafePress, a custom merchandise retailer.[35] Most such offers are "friendly," with both groups agreeing to the proposed deal, but some are "hostile," when the second company does not want to be taken over.

To head off a hostile takeover attempt, a threatened company's managers may use one or more of several techniques. They may ask stockholders not to sell to the raider, file a lawsuit in an effort to abort the takeover, institute a *poison pill* as Energizer did (in which the firm allows stockholders to buy more shares of stock at prices lower than the current market value) or *shark repellant* (in which management requires a large majority of stockholders to approve the takeover), or seek a *white knight* (a more acceptable firm that is willing to acquire the threatened company). In some cases, management may take the company private or even take on more debt so that the heavy debt obligation will "scare off" the raider.

merger the combination of two companies (usually corporations) to form a new company.

acquisition the purchase of one company by another, usually by buying its stock.

▼ **TABLE 4.7** The Largest Mergers of All Time

Rank	Acquirer	Target	Transaction Value (in billions)
1.	Vodafone	Mannesmann AG	$180
2.	America Online (AOL)	Time Warner	$165
3.	Verizon Communications	Vodafone	$130
4.	Dow Chemical	DuPont	$130
5.	AB InBev	SABMiller	$104

CVS Health, a drugstore and pharmacy company, joined forces with Aetna, a health care company, in a vertical merger.

Richard Drew/AP/Shutterstock

leveraged buyout (LBO) a purchase in which a group of investors borrows money from banks and other institutions to acquire a company (or a division of one), using the assets of the purchased company to guarantee repayment of the loan.

In a **leveraged buyout (LBO)**, a group of investors borrows money from banks and other institutions to acquire a company (or a division of one), using the assets of the purchased company to guarantee repayment of the loan. In some LBOs, as much as 95 percent of the buyout price is paid with borrowed money, which eventually must be repaid.

Because of the explosion of mergers, acquisitions, and leveraged buyouts in the 1980s and 1990s, financial journalists coined the term *merger mania*. Many companies joined the merger mania simply to enhance their own operations by consolidating them with the operations of other firms. Mergers and acquisitions enabled these companies to gain a larger market share in their industries, acquire valuable assets such as new products or plants and equipment, and lower their costs. Mergers also represent a means of making profits quickly, as was the case during the 1980s when many companies' stock was undervalued. Quite simply, such companies represent a bargain to other companies that can afford to buy them. Additionally, deregulation of some industries has permitted consolidation of firms within those industries for the first time, as is the case in the banking and airline industries.

Some people view mergers and acquisitions favorably, pointing out that they boost corporations' stock prices and market value, to the benefit of their stockholders. In many instances, mergers enhance a company's ability to meet foreign competition in an increasingly global marketplace. Additionally, companies that are victims of hostile takeovers generally streamline their operations, reduce unnecessary staff, cut costs, and otherwise become more efficient with their operations, which benefits their stockholders whether or not the takeover succeeds.

Critics, however, argue that mergers hurt companies because they force managers to focus their efforts on avoiding takeovers rather than managing effectively and profitably. Some companies have taken on a heavy debt burden to stave off a takeover, later to be forced into bankruptcy when economic downturns left them unable to handle the debt. Mergers and acquisitions also can damage employee morale and productivity, as well as the quality of the companies' products.

Many mergers have been beneficial for all involved; others have had damaging effects for the companies, their employees, and customers. No one can say whether mergers will continue to slow, but many experts say the utilities, telecommunications, financial services, natural resources, computer hardware and software, gaming, managed health care, and technology industries are likely targets. ■

BUILDING YOUR SOFT SKILLS

BY HANDLING CONFLICT

Being able to effectively handle conflict is an important soft skill and one that is especially important in certain partnerships. Conduct some research on how to resolve conflicts. What are the five guidelines you think are most important to follow, and why?

Team Exercise

Form groups and find examples of mergers and acquisitions. Mergers can be broken down into traditional mergers, horizontal mergers, and conglomerate mergers. When companies are found, note how long the merger or acquisition took, if there were any requirements by the government before approval of the merger or acquisition, and if any failed mergers or acquisitions were found that did not achieve government approval. Report your findings to the class, and explain what the companies hoped to gain from the merger or acquisition.

WANT TO BE AN ENTREPRENEUR? // Know Which Form of Business Is Best for You /

If you have a good idea and want to turn it into a business, you are not alone. Small businesses are popping up all over the United States, and the concept of entrepreneurship is hot. Entrepreneurs seek opportunities and creative ways to make profits. Business emerges in a number of different organizational forms, each with its own advantages and disadvantages. Sole proprietorships are the most common form of business organization in the United States. They tend to be small businesses and can take pretty much any form—anything from a hair salon to a scuba shop, from an organic produce provider to a financial advisor. Proprietorships are everywhere serving consumers' wants and needs. Proprietorships have a big advantage in that they tend to be simple to manage—decisions get made quickly when the owner and the manager are the same person and they are fairly simple and inexpensive to set up. Rules vary by state, but at most all you will need is a license from the state.

Many people have been part of a partnership at some point in their life. Group work in school is an example of a partnership. If you ever worked as a DJ on the weekend with your friend and split the profits, then you have experienced a partnership. Partnerships can be either general or limited. General partners have unlimited liability and share completely in the management, debts, and profits of the business. Limited partners, on the other hand, consist of at least one general partner and one or more limited partners who do not participate in the management of the company but share in the profits. This form of partnership is used more often in risky investments where the limited partner stands only to lose his or her initial investment. Real estate limited partnerships are an example of how investors can minimize their financial exposure, given the poor performance of the real estate market in recent years. Although it has its advantages, partnership is the least utilized form of business. Part of the reason is that all partners are responsible for the actions and decisions of all other partners, whether or not all of the partners were involved. Usually, partners will have to write up articles of partnership that outline respective responsibilities in the business. Even in states where it is not required, it is a good idea to draw up this document as a way to cement each partner's role and hopefully minimize conflict. Unlike a corporation, proprietorships and partnerships both expire upon the death of one or more of those involved.

Corporations tend to be larger businesses, but do not need to be. A corporation can consist of nothing more than a small group of family members. In order to become a corporation, you will have to file in the state under which you wish to incorporate. Each state has its own procedure for incorporation, meaning there are no general guidelines to follow. You can make your corporation private or public, meaning the company issues stocks, and shareholders are the owners. While incorporating is a popular form of organization because it gives the company an unlimited lifespan and limited liability (meaning that if your business fails, you cannot lose personal funds to make up for losses), there is a downside. You will be taxed as a corporation and as an individual, resulting in double taxation. No matter what form of organization suits your business idea best, there is a world of options out there for you if you want to be or experiment with being an entrepreneur.

small business, entrepreneurship, and franchising

Jonathan Weiss/Alamy Stock Photo

LEARNING OBJECTIVES

After reading this chapter, you will be able to:

LO 5-1 Define *entrepreneurship* and *small business*.

LO 5-2 Explain the importance of small business in the U.S. economy and why certain fields attract small business.

LO 5-3 Specify the advantages of small-business ownership.

LO 5-4 Analyze the disadvantages of small-business ownership and the reasons why many small businesses fail.

LO 5-5 Describe how to start a small business and what resources are needed.

LO 5-6 Evaluate the demographic, technological, and economic trends that are affecting the future of small business.

LO 5-7 Explain why many large businesses are trying to "think small."

Although many business students go to work for large corporations upon graduation, others may choose to start their own business or find employment opportunities in small organizations. Small businesses employ about half of all private-sector employees.[1] Each small business represents the vision of its owners to succeed through providing new or better products. Small businesses are the heart of the U.S. economic and social system because they offer opportunities and demonstrate the freedom of people to make their own destinies. Today, the entrepreneurial spirit is growing around the world, from Russia and China to India, Germany, Brazil, and Mexico. Countries with the healthiest "entrepreneurship ecosystems" include the United States, Canada, Australia, Denmark, and Sweden.[2] This chapter surveys the world of entrepreneurship and small business. First, we define entrepreneurship and small business and examine the role of small business in the American economy. Then, we explore the advantages and disadvantages of small-business ownership and analyze why small businesses succeed or fail. Next, we discuss how an entrepreneur goes about starting a business and the challenges facing small businesses today. Finally, we look at entrepreneurship in larger organizations. ■

LO 5-1 Define *entrepreneurship* and *small business*.

THE NATURE OF ENTREPRENEURSHIP AND SMALL BUSINESS

In the chapter "The Dynamics of Business and Economics," we defined an *entrepreneur* as a person who risks his or her wealth, time, and effort to develop for profit an innovative product or way of doing something. **Entrepreneurship** is the process of creating and managing a business to achieve desired objectives. Many large businesses you may recognize (Levi Strauss and Co., Procter & Gamble, McDonald's, Dell, Microsoft, and Google) all began as small businesses based on the visions of their founders. Some entrepreneurs who start small businesses have the ability to see emerging trends; in response, they create a company to provide a product that serves customer needs. For example, rather than inventing a major new technology, an innovative company may take advantage of technology to create new markets, such as Amazon. Or it may offer a familiar product that has been improved or placed in a unique retail environment, such as Starbucks and its coffee shops. A company may innovate by focusing on a particular market segment and delivering a combination of features that consumers in that segment could not find anywhere else. The sharing economy, or gig economy, can use technology to connect service providers or homeowners. Porch was founded as a way to connect homeowners with contractors. Founder Matt Ehrlichman conceived of the idea after becoming frustrated with problems in building his own house. Porch's software provides a more transparent way to link homeowners with licensed professionals. More than 2 million home improvement projects have been facilitated through the site and app, earning the company more than $1 billion in revenue.[3]

Success requires creativity, innovation, and entrepreneurship, and it requires more than a formal education. It requires the

entrepreneurship
the process of creating and managing a business to achieve desired objectives.

> " ALTHOUGH THESE ENTREPRENEURS OFTEN START THEIR OWN NONPROFIT ORGANIZATIONS, THEY CAN ALSO OPERATE FOR-PROFIT ORGANIZATIONS COMMITTED TO SOLVING SOCIAL ISSUES. "

microentrepreneur entrepreneurs who develop businesses with five or fewer employees.

social entrepreneurs individuals who use entrepreneurship to address social problems.

small business any independently owned and operated business that is not dominant in its competitive area and does not employ more than 500 people.

Small Business Administration (SBA) an independent agency of the federal government that offers managerial and financial assistance to small businesses.

ability to learn and develop skills and knowledge and be an independent thinker. Consider that Steve Jobs (Apple), Richard Branson (Virgin Group), Larry Ellison (co-founder and former CEO of Oracle), and Michael Dell (Dell) did not graduate from college. Mark Zuckerberg dropped out of Harvard after his sophomore year to focus on Facebook. Bill Gates, co-founder of Microsoft, also dropped out of Harvard after his sophomore year. Of course, smaller businesses do not have to evolve into such highly visible companies to be successful, but those entrepreneurial efforts that result in rapidly growing businesses gain visibility along with success. Table 5.1 lists successful entrepreneurs of innovative companies.

The entrepreneurship movement is accelerating, and many new, smaller businesses are emerging. Many entrepreneurs with five or fewer employees are considered **microentrepreneurs**. Technology once available only to the largest firms can now be obtained by a small business. Websites, podcasts, online videos, social media, cellular phones, and even expedited delivery services enable small businesses to be more competitive with today's giant corporations. Small businesses can also form alliances with other companies to produce and sell products in domestic and global markets.

Another growing trend among small businesses is social entrepreneurship. **Social entrepreneurs** are individuals who use entrepreneurship to address social problems. They operate by the same principles as other entrepreneurs but view their organizations as vehicles to create social change. Although these

entrepreneurs often start their own nonprofit organizations, they can also operate for-profit organizations committed to solving social issues. Karissa Bodnar, the founder of Thrive Causemetics, is an example of a social entrepreneur. Bodnar founded Thrive Causemetics with the purpose of distributing products and financial support to giving partners, like Ronald McDonald House Charities and Make-A-Wish Foundation, for every product purchased.[4] Shamayim Harris is restoring rundown homes in Michigan's Highland Park, an impoverished city of 10,000 in the Detroit metro area. Through seed grants and crowdfunding, she is helping to develop a self-sustaining community.[5]

What Is a Small Business?

This question is difficult to answer because smallness is relative. In this book, we will define a **small business** as any independently owned and operated business that is not dominant in its competitive area and does not employ more than 500 people. Microentrepreneurs, sometimes called micropreneurs, that employ five or fewer employees are growing rapidly. A local Mexican restaurant may be the most patronized Mexican restaurant in your community, but because it does not dominate the restaurant industry as a whole, the restaurant can be considered a small business. This definition is similar to the one used by the **Small Business Administration (SBA)**, an independent agency of the federal government that offers managerial and financial assistance to small businesses. On its website, the SBA outlines the first steps in starting a small business and offers a wealth of information to current and potential small-business owners.

The Role of Small Business in the American Economy

No matter how you define a small business, one fact is clear: They are vital to the American economy. As you can see in Table 5.2, more than 99 percent of all U.S. firms are classified as small businesses, and they employ about half of private workers. Small firms are also important as exporters, representing 98 percent of U.S. exporters of goods and contributing 33 percent of the value of exported goods.[6] In addition, small businesses are largely responsible for fueling job creation and innovation. Small businesses also provide opportunities for minorities and women to succeed in business. Women own more than 10 million businesses nationwide, with great success in the professional services, retail, communication, and administrative services areas.[7] The number of minority-owned businesses is also

▼ **TABLE 5.1** Great Entrepreneurs of Innovative Companies

Company	Entrepreneur
Hewlett-Packard	Bill Hewlett, David Packard
Walt Disney Productions	Walt Disney
Starbucks	Howard Schultz
Amazon	Jeff Bezos
Dell	Michael Dell
Microsoft	Bill Gates
23andMe	Anne Wojcicki
Goodr	Jasmine Crowe
Google	Larry Page, Sergey Brin
Ben & Jerry's	Ben Cohen, Jerry Greenfield
Ford	Henry Ford
General Electric	Thomas Edison

▼ TABLE 5.2 Importance of Small Businesses to Our Economy

Small firms represent 99.9 percent of all employer firms.

Small firms create 1.8 million net new jobs each year.

Small firms hire approximately 58.9 percent of high-tech workers (such as scientists, engineers, computer programmers, and others).

Small firms with fewer than 100 employees have the largest share of small business employment.

Small firms employ nearly half of all private-sector employees.

Small firms employ more than 80 percent of construction workers.

Source: U.S. Small Business Administration Office of Advocacy, "2019 Small Business Profile," https://cdn.advocacy.sba.gov/wp-content/uploads/2019/04/23142719/2019-Small-Business-Profiles-US.pdf (accessed May 29, 2020).

growing. According to the U.S. Small Business Administration, 30 percent of all businesses are minority-owned.[8] For example, Mexican-born José de Jesus Legaspi went into the real estate business and focused his market niche on inner-city areas with a high percentage of Hispanic consumers. When Legaspi decided to begin investing in struggling malls, he refashioned the malls he acquired as cultural centers appealing to Hispanic consumers of all generations. One of his malls, renamed La Gran Plaza, went from being 20 percent occupied to 80 percent.[9]

Job Creation. The energy, creativity, and innovative abilities of small-business owners have resulted in jobs for many people. About 1.8 million net new jobs annually are created by small businesses.[10] Figure 5.1 shows the top industries, such as agriculture, forestry, and fishing and hunting, for small business employment.

Many small businesses today are being started because of encouragement from larger ones. Many new jobs are also created by big-company/small-company alliances. Whether through formal joint ventures, supplier relationships, or product or marketing cooperative projects, the rewards of collaborative relationships are creating numerous jobs for small-business owners and their employees. In India, for example, many small information technology (IT) firms provide IT services to global markets. Because of lower costs, international companies can often find Indian businesses to provide their information-processing solutions.[11]

Innovation. Perhaps one of the most significant strengths of small businesses is their ability to innovate,

bringing significant benefits to customers. Consider Away, a line of premium direct-to-consumer luggage sold at an affordable price. The stylish suitcases feature 360-degree spinning wheels, durable zippers, and a battery pack for charging electronics. Away turned profitable and began taking away market share from established competitors just two years after launching because of its cult following.[12] Andrew Blackmon co-founded the online tuxedo rental service The Black Tux. There was such extreme interest in the service after a single mention in *GQ Magazine* that it quickly ran into supply chain issues. The company was able to decrease turnaround times with manufacturers and improve its supply chain. Both of these businesses provide an important service that many people want.

Small firms produce more than half of all innovations. Among the important 20th-century innovations by U.S. small firms are the airplane, the audio tape recorder, fiber-optic examining equipment, the heart valve, the optical scanner, the pacemaker, the personal computer, soft contact lenses, the Internet, and the zipper. Artificial intelligence will create new opportunities for innovation. The ability of computers to perform tasks that normally require human intelligence will provide the ability to create new businesses. The simulation of human behavior will permit facial recognition, speech recognition, decision making, and the control of robots to do tasks associated with people. Small businesses will have improved ability to compete with large businesses because the technology is becoming available and affordable. Customer service, marketing, human resources, supply chains, and manufacturing will all be more efficient to develop and manage. Artificial intelligence will provide the opportunity for new business models for startups. Companies

▼ FIGURE 5.1 Top Industries for Small Business Employment

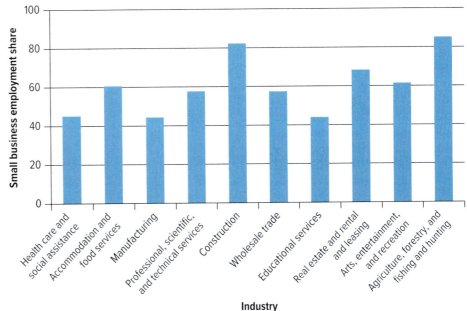

Source: U.S. Small Business Administration Office of Advocacy, "2019 Small Business Profile," https://cdn.advocacy.sba.gov/wp-content/uploads/2019/04/23142719/2019-Small-Business-Profiles-US.pdf (accessed May 29, 2020).

in the early stage of development will have the ability to be highly independent and maximize all the elements that create value. The barrier to enter and advance a new business will be easier.

The innovation of successful firms takes many forms. For instance, franchises make up approximately 3 percent of all small businesses.[13] Many of today's largest businesses started off as small firms that used innovation to achieve success. Small businessman Ray Kroc found a new way to sell hamburgers and turned his ideas into one of the most successful fast-food franchises in the world—McDonald's. David Galboa co-founded the successful company Warby Parker, an online retailer that sells stylish glasses at lower prices. Warby Parker is a social enterprise that gives a pair of glasses to seeing-impaired individuals in developing countries for every pair of glasses sold. The company has sold more than 1 million pairs of glasses.[14] Entrepreneurs provide fresh ideas and usually have greater flexibility to change than do large companies.

The retailing industry is particularly attractive to entrepreneurs.
Lynne Neuman/Shutterstock

LO 5-2 Explain the importance of small business in the U.S. economy and why certain fields attract small business.

Industries That Attract Small Business

Small businesses are found in nearly every industry, but retailing and wholesaling, services, manufacturing, and high technology are especially attractive to entrepreneurs. These fields are relatively easy to enter and require low initial financing. Small-business owners in these industries also find it easier to focus on specific groups of consumers; new firms in these industries initially suffer less from heavy competition than do established firms.

Retailing. Retailers acquire goods from producers or wholesalers and sell them to consumers. Main streets, shopping centers, and malls are generally lined with independent music stores, sporting-goods stores, dry cleaners, boutiques, drugstores, restaurants, caterers, service stations, and hardware stores that sell directly to consumers. Retailing attracts entrepreneurs because gaining experience and exposure in retailing is relatively easy. Additionally, an entrepreneur opening a new retail store or establishing a new website does not have to spend the large sums of money for the equipment and distribution systems that a manufacturing business requires. All that a new retailer needs is the ability to understand the market and provide a product that satisfies a need. However, it is important for entrepreneurs to anticipate the costs of opening a retail

or wholesale business beforehand. Some entrepreneurs turn to crowdfunding platforms such as Kickstarter to launch their business.[15]

Many opportunities exist for nonstore retailing as well. Nonstore retailing involves selling products outside of a retail facility. There are two types of nonstore retailing: direct marketing—which uses the telephone, catalogs, and other media to give consumers an opportunity to place orders by mail, telephone, or the Internet—and direct selling. Nonstore retailing is an area that provides great opportunity for entrepreneurs because of a lower cost of entry. Smaller businesses can engage in a form of direct marketing by featuring their products on eBay, Amazon, or Etsy. Etsy, an online marketplace, connects 1.9 million sellers with 33.4 million buyers.[16]

Direct selling involves the marketing of products to ultimate consumers through face-to-face sales presentations at home, in the workplace, and in party environments. Well-known direct selling companies include Amway, Avon, Herbalife, and Mary Kay. The cost of getting involved in direct selling is low and often involves buying enough inventory to get started. Many people view direct selling as a part-time business opportunity. Often, those who become independent contractors for direct selling companies are enthusiastic about the product and have the opportunity to recruit other distributors and receive commissions on their sales.

Wholesaling. Wholesalers provide both goods and services to producers and retailers. They can assist their customers with almost every business function. Wholesalers supply products to industrial, retail, and institutional users for resale or for use in making other products. Wholesaling activities range from planning and negotiating for supplies, promoting, and distributing (warehousing and transporting) to providing management and merchandising assistance to clients. Wholesalers are extremely important for many products,

In Lancaster County, Pennsylvania, some of the freshest fruits and vegetables are up for auction. Since 1985, the Leola Produce Auction has supported other small businesses—specifically, Amish farmers selling produce. The auction runs efficiently with almost no technology. Instead, employees use clipboards to record the results of each auction.

The auction operates twice a week and makes around $7 million annually through auction fees and sales of food and drinks. It offers a centralized, high-traffic location for selling produce. Amish farmers who use Leola's services are essentially small-business owners; many used to sell their goods through roadside stands. Some also used to sell goods through cooperative agreements where they pooled resources to guarantee that each farmer would make some money each crop cycle. However, the Amish people were not happy with the fees associated with cooperatives, so the auction was created.

The auction has a variety of regular business buyers. Grocery stores are the biggest buyer. Grocers from as far as Washington, D.C., come to the auction. The grocery stores can place a large markup on the produce they win at the auction because the quantities they buy are so large. Some restaurants like to bid at the auction to provide their customers with popular farm-to-table meals.

The Leola Produce Auction is an efficient middleman for produce buyers and sellers.

It gives farmers a place to sell their goods, while buyers can purchase high-quality produce in large quantities. The auction itself benefits from auction fees and through concession sales. Thanks to the auction, everybody wins.[a]

Critical Thinking Questions

1. What type of business does Leola Produce Auction operate in?

2. Describe how Leola Produce Auction acts as a middleman for buyers and sellers.

3. What type of consumer does Leola Produce Auction appear to predominately target?

---

especially consumer goods, because of the marketing activities they perform. Although it is true that wholesalers themselves can be eliminated, their functions must be passed on to some other organization such as the producer or another intermediary, often a small business. Frequently, small businesses are closer to the final customers and know what it takes to keep them satisfied. Some smaller businesses find their real niche as a service provider or distributor of other firms' products. John Hinnen created a snow slugger that could make snowballs and be used to defend against snowball attacks. The toy company Wham-O picked the product up to manufacture for Hinnen.[17]

Services. The service sector includes businesses that do not actually produce tangible goods. Services include intangible products that involve a performance, inauguration, or any effort to provide something of value that cannot be physically possessed. Services can also be part of the wholesale market and involve any product that is intangible and therefore cannot be touched. The service sector accounts for 80 percent of U.S. jobs, excluding farmworkers.[18] Real estate, insurance and personnel agencies, barbershops, banks, television and computer repair shops, copy centers, dry cleaners, and accounting firms are all service businesses. Services also attract individuals–such as beauticians, morticians, jewelers, doctors, and veterinarians—whose skills are not usually required by large firms. Many of these service providers are retailers who provide their services to ultimate consumers.

José Neves founded his company, Farfetch, to assist retail luxury boutiques in putting their inventory online. The services provide an opportunity for stores to track their fashion brands from payment and shipping, to customer service and in-store returns.[19]

Manufacturing. Manufacturing goods can provide unique opportunities for small businesses. For example, Irene Rhodes founded Consumer Fire Products by using her background in engineering to create a system that sprays a biodegradable protective foam on a house when a wildfire is nearby.[20] Small businesses sometimes have an advantage over large firms because they can customize products to meet specific customer needs and wants. Such products include custom artwork, jewelry, clothing, and furniture.

Technology. *High technology* is a broad term used to describe businesses that depend heavily on advanced scientific and engineering knowledge. People who were able to innovate or identify new markets in the fields of computers, biotechnology, genetic engineering, robotics, and other markets have become today's high-tech giants. One innovative technology was developed by a teenager interested in virtual reality. Only a few years ago, virtual reality was considered a dead technology past its prime. However, when 19-year-old Palmer Luckey developed a virtual gaming headset, it caught the attention of programmer John Carmack. Together, they brought virtual reality to a new level for gamers. The company, Oculus Rift, was sold to

sharing economy an economic model involving the sharing of underutilized resources.

Facebook for $2 billion.[21] In general, high-technology businesses require greater capital and have higher initial startup costs than do other small businesses. Many of the biggest, nonetheless, started out in garages, basements, kitchens, and dorm rooms.

Sharing Economy.

The past decade has seen a rise in the **sharing economy**, an economic model involving the sharing of underutilized resources. Under this model, entrepreneurs earn income by renting out an underutilized resource such as lodging or vehicles.[22] The ride-sharing service Uber is the company most associated with the sharing economy. Rather than employing people outright, Uber acts more as a "labor broker," providing a mobile app that connects buyers (passengers) with sellers (drivers).[23] Although Uber does maintain control over variables such as rates, drivers act as independent contractors taking on jobs whenever or wherever they desire. Airbnb is another well-known company operating in the sharing economy. Its website connects those in need of lodging with sellers of those services.

Bird, Lime, Lyft, and Spin are all examples of electric scooters. The companies pay people to collect, recharge, and distribute the scooters daily.

Arne Beruldsen/Shutterstock

and not employees, some states, such as California, are raising the bar classifying workers, making it harder for companies to hire workers as contractors. In addition, Uber and Airbnb often are in conflict with local regulatory rules about lodging or ride

> ## "The sharing economy offers opportunities for those who want to be their own entrepreneurs or want additional income even though they have another job.

The sharing economy is often referred to as the "gig economy" because independent contractors earn income going from job to job.[24] The sharing economy offers opportunities for those who want to be their own entrepreneurs or want additional income even though they have another job. Ilise Benun, fired from her second job out of college, started Marketing Mentor to help creative professionals find clients with large budgets. Currently 34 percent of the U.S. workforce consists of independent gig workers that are self-employed.[25] Services offered through this model often cost less than more traditional services. It is even taking market share away from established firms. For instance, Airbnb is now twice as valuable as Hilton. The company is buying related companies to move into a wider tourism market.[26] ShareRing, a blockchain-driven marketplace for the sharing economy, aims to combine all sharing platforms into one app so users do not have to download and register for individual apps and services.[27]

Despite the opportunities in the sharing economy, Uber and similar firms have been experiencing pressure over whether workers are independent contractors or employees. While the U.S. Department of Labor agrees Uber drivers are contractors

sharing. As independent contractors, workers act as their own bosses and pay their own taxes and benefits, unlike employees of a firm. In spite of the controversy, however, overall perception of the sharing economy appears to be high. According to one study, approximately 86 percent of respondents believe the sharing economy makes life more affordable, while 78 percent believe the sharing of underutilized resources reduces waste.[28]

> **LO 5-3** Specify the advantages of small-business ownership.

ADVANTAGES OF SMALL-BUSINESS OWNERSHIP

There are many advantages to establishing and running a small business. These can be categorized into personal advantages and business advantages. Table 5.3 lists some of the traits that can help entrepreneurs succeed.

Trait	Definition	Trait	Definition
Intuitive	Using one's intuition to derive what's true without conscious reasoning	Innovative	Being able to come up with new and creative ideas
Productive	Being able to produce large amounts of something during a specific time period	Risk-taker	Having the ability to pursue risky endeavors despite the possibility of failure
Resourceful	Understanding how to use and spend resources wisely	Persistent	Continuing in a certain action in spite of obstacles
Charismatic	Having the ability to inspire others behind a central vision	Friendly	Being able to have mutually beneficial interactions with people

Independence

Independence is probably one of the leading reasons that entrepreneurs choose to go into business for themselves. Being a small-business owner means being your own boss. Many people start their own businesses because they believe they will do better for themselves than they could do by remaining with their current employer or by changing jobs. They may feel stuck on the corporate ladder and that no business would take them seriously enough to fund their ideas. Sometimes people who venture forth to start their own small business are those who simply cannot work for someone else. Such people may say that they just do not fit the "corporate mold." In a survey of top entrepreneurs, ambition, ability, and a timeless work ethic were important to success.[29]

More often, small-business owners just want the freedom to choose whom they work with, the flexibility to pick where and when to work, and the option of working in a family setting. The availability of a company website, social media, and other Internet resources make it easy to start a business and work from home.

Costs

As already mentioned, small businesses often require less money to start and maintain than do large ones. Of top entrepreneurs, 64 percent used personal savings to start their business, with 9 percent using their credit card.[30] Obviously, a firm with just 14 people spends less money on wages and salaries, rent, utilities, and other expenses than does a firm employing tens of thousands of people in several large facilities. Rather than maintain the expense of keeping separate departments for accounting, advertising, and legal counseling, small businesses often hire other firms (sometimes small businesses themselves) to supply these services as they are needed. Additionally, small-business owners can sometimes rely on friends and family members to help them save money by volunteering to work on a difficult project.

Flexibility

With small size comes the flexibility to adapt to changing market demands. Small businesses usually have only one layer of management–the owners. Decisions therefore can be made and

AMS CLOTHING GEARS UP FOR SPORTSWEAR BATTLE

Although Nike, Adidas, and Puma dominate the sportswear industry, Australian entrepreneur Luke Westcott is challenging these apparel empires. Westcott created AMS Clothing Company to outfit smaller, seemingly overlooked African countries with soccer jerseys for players and fans. He cites these markets as huge business opportunities with little competition.

The path for Wescott was not easy. He had to find the right business partners who would listen to his ideas. In 2016, he met with a rebel leader from South Sudan during the height of its civil war who wished to purchase jerseys from him. Westcott traveled to Sierra Leone during the Ebola epidemic and agreed to supply jerseys to the national team. No other apparel maker was willing to risk sending representatives to the country.

Westcott maintains a supply chain that begins in Australia, runs through factories in China, and ends with the jerseys being shipped and delivered throughout Africa. He charges $10 per jersey, compared to the $100 Nike and Adidas jerseys made in Kenya. The AMS jerseys also serve as a superior alternative to $8 counterfeit jerseys made of inferior-quality inputs.[b]

Critical Thinking Questions

1. What are the advantages of serving an underserved market?

2. In what type of competition is AMS Clothing competing: pure competition, monopolistic competition, oligopoly, or monopoly? Explain your reasoning.

3. How may the laws of supply and demand enable a small company like AMS Clothing to become profitable by serving a market niche?

Some entrepreneurs choose to start their businesses from scratch so they can run their businesses as they see fit. While they might start off small and struggle to attract customers, they are not limited by the restrictions of a franchise agreement.

Arina P Habich/Shutterstock

executed quickly. In larger firms, decisions about even routine matters can take weeks because they must pass through multiple levels of management before action is authorized. When Taco Bell introduces a new product, for example, it must first research what consumers want, then develop the product and test it before introducing it nationwide—a process that sometimes takes years. An independent snack shop, however, can develop and introduce a new product (perhaps to meet a customer's request) in a much shorter time. In fact, 56 percent of successful small-business CEOs say they use social media to collect feedback on products.[31]

Focus

Small firms can focus their efforts on a precisely defined market niche—that is, a specific group of customers. Many large corporations must compete in the mass market or for large market segments. Smaller firms can develop products for particular groups of customers or to satisfy a need that other companies have not addressed. For example, Megan Tamte launched a chain of boutiques called Evereve targeted toward young mothers. As a young mother herself, she recognized the many problems mothers faced when they take their young children out shopping. Evereve stores were built with double-wide aisles to accommodate strollers, large dressing rooms, and play areas for children. It has since opened 85 stores and experienced 20 percent annual sales growth.[32] By targeting small niches or product needs, businesses can sometimes avoid competition from larger firms, helping them to grow into stronger companies.

Reputation

Reputation, or how a firm is perceived by its various stakeholders, is highly significant to an organization's success. Small firms, because of their capacity to focus on narrow niches, can develop enviable reputations for quality and service.

DID YOU KNOW?

About 20 percent of small businesses fail to make it past the first year of operation.[c]

A good example of a small business with a formidable reputation is W. Atlee Burpee and Co., which has the country's premier bulb and seed catalog. Burpee has an unqualified returns policy (complete satisfaction or your money back) that demonstrates a strong commitment to customer satisfaction.

LO 5-4 Analyze the disadvantages of small-business ownership and the reasons why many small businesses fail.

DISADVANTAGES OF SMALL-BUSINESS OWNERSHIP

The rewards associated with running a small business are so enticing that it's no wonder many people dream of it. However, as with any undertaking, small-business ownership has its disadvantages.

High Stress Level

A small business is likely to provide a living for its owner, but not much more (although there are exceptions as some examples in this chapter have shown). There are ongoing worries about competition, employee problems, new equipment, expanding inventory, rent increases, or changing market demand. In addition to other stresses, small-business owners tend to be victims of physical and psychological stress. The small-business person is often the owner, manager, sales force, shipping and receiving clerk, bookkeeper, and custodian. Having to multitask can result in long hours for most small-business owners. Many creative persons fail, not because of their business concepts, but rather because of difficulties in managing their business. Fear of failure is the most common concern when starting a business.[33]

High Failure Rate

Despite the importance of small businesses to our economy, there is no guarantee of success. Half of all businesses fail within the first five years.[34] Restaurants are a case in point. Look around your own neighborhood, and you can probably spot the locations of several restaurants that are no longer in business. While there were more independent, small restaurants than chains before the COVID-19 (coronavirus) pandemic, it was estimated that over half would go out of business after the pandemic. Chains such as Chipotle, Arby's, McDonald's, and Burger King had an advantage with quick service adjustments and their fast food business model.

Small businesses fail for many reasons (see Table 5.4). A poor business concept—such as

▼ **TABLE 5.4** Challenges in Starting a New Business

1. Underfunded (not providing adequate startup capital)
2. Not understanding your competitive niche
3. Lack of effective utilization of websites and social media
4. Lack of a marketing and business plan
5. If operating a retail store, poor site selection
6. Pricing mistakes–too high or too low
7. Underestimating the time commitment for success
8. Not finding complementary partners to bring in additional experience
9. Not hiring the right employees and/or not training them properly
10. Not understanding legal and ethical responsibilities

insecticides for garbage cans (research found that consumers are not concerned with insects in their garbage)—will produce disaster nearly every time. Expanding a hobby into a business may work if a genuine market niche exists, but all too often people start such a business without identifying a real need for the good or service. Other notable causes of small-business failure include the burdens imposed by government regulation, insufficient funds to withstand slow sales, and vulnerability to competition from larger companies. Three major causes of small-business failure deserve a close look: undercapitalization, managerial inexperience or incompetence, and inability to cope with growth.

Undercapitalization.
The shortest path to failure in business is **undercapitalization**, the lack of funds to operate a business normally. Too many entrepreneurs think that all they need is enough money to get started, that the business can survive on cash generated from sales soon thereafter. But almost all businesses suffer from seasonal variations in sales, which make cash tight, and few businesses make money from the start. Many small rural operations cannot obtain financing within their own communities because small rural banks often lack the necessary financing expertise or assets sizable enough to counter the risks involved with small-business loans. That is why personal savings and loans from family members are top sources for financing a small business. For startups, personal bank loans represent less than 10 percent of the sources of starting capital.[35] Without sufficient funds, the best small-business idea in the world will fail. Consider Necco Wafers, the heart-shaped pressed sugar Valentine's Day candy bearing messages including "Kiss Me" and "Be Mine." The firm was started by an English Immigrant in 1847 and is the oldest confectionary company in America. Today, the still small company makes 630 million wafers a year. In 2018, the Necco Wafer brand was purchased by Spangler Candy Company, and the product returned to the market in 2020.[36]

Managerial Inexperience or Incompetence.
Poor management is the cause of many business failures. Just because an entrepreneur has a brilliant vision for a small business does not mean he or she has the knowledge or experience to manage a growing business effectively. A person who is good at creating great product ideas and marketing them may lack the skills and experience to make good management decisions in hiring, negotiating, finance, and control. Moreover, entrepreneurs may neglect those areas of management they know little about or find tedious, at the expense of the business's success.

Inability to Cope with Growth.
Sometimes, the very factors that are advantages for a small business turn into serious disadvantages when the time comes to grow. Growth often requires the owner to give up a certain amount of direct authority, and it is frequently hard for someone who has called all the shots to give up control. It has often been said that the greatest impediment to the success of a business is the entrepreneur. Similarly, growth requires specialized management skills in areas such as credit analysis and promotion—skills that the founder may lack or not have time to apply. The founders of many small businesses, including Dell Computers, found that they needed to bring in more experienced managers to help manage their companies through growing pains.

Poorly managed growth probably affects a company's reputation more than anything else, at least initially. And products that do not arrive on time or goods that are poorly made can quickly reverse

Zynga Inc., a social game developer and creator of mobile games like FarmVille and Words with Friends, expanded too quickly and had to let go hundreds of employees.

JHVEPhoto/Shutterstock

business plan a precise statement of the rationale for a business and a step-by-step explanation of how it will achieve its goals.

a success. The principal immediate threats to small and mid-sized businesses include rising inflation, energy and other supply shortages or cost escalations, and excessive household and/or corporate debt. For this reason, some small-business owners choose to stay small and are not interested in wide-scale growth. These micropreneurs operate small-scale businesses with no more than five employees. It is estimated that 95 percent of small businesses are microbusinesses.[37]

LO 5-5 Describe how to start a small business and what resources are needed.

STARTING A SMALL BUSINESS

We've told you how important small businesses are and why they succeed and fail, but *how do you go about* starting your own business in the first place? To start any business, large or small, you must have some kind of general idea. Sam Walton, founder of Walmart stores, had a vision of a discount retailing enterprise that spawned the world's largest retailing empire and changed the way companies look at business. Next, you need to devise a strategy to guide planning and development in the business. Finally, you must make decisions about form of ownership; the financial resources needed; and whether to acquire an existing business, start a new one, or buy a franchise.

The Business Plan

A key element of business success is a **business plan**—a precise statement of the rationale for the business and a step-by-step

explanation of how it will achieve its goals. The business plan should include an explanation of the business, an analysis of the competition, estimates of income and expenses, and other information. It should also establish a strategy for acquiring sufficient funds to keep the business going. The U.S. SBA website provides an overview of a plan for small businesses to use to gain financing. Many financial institutions decide whether to loan a small business money based on its business plan. A good business plan should act as a guide and reference document—not a shackle that limits the business's flexibility and decision-making ability. The business plan must be revised periodically to ensure that the firm's goals and strategies adapt to changes in the environment. Business plans allow companies to assess market potential, determine price and manufacturing requirements, identify optimal distribution channels, and refine product selection. It is also important to evaluate and update the business plan to account for changes in the company. Salem, Oregon-based Rich Duncan Construction learned this the hard way. The company rewrote part of its business plan after 14 years to account for high growth rates and identify weaknesses that needed to be addressed.[38]

Forms of Business Ownership

After developing a business plan, the entrepreneur has to decide on an appropriate legal form of business ownership—whether it is best to operate as a sole proprietorship, partnership, or corporation—and to examine the many factors that affect that decision, which we explored in the chapter, "Options for Organizing Business."

Financial Resources

The expression "it takes money to make money" holds especially true in developing a business enterprise. To make money from a small business, the owner must first provide or obtain money (capital) to get started and to keep it running smoothly. Even a small retail store will probably need at least $50,000

THE ROOT OF BRIOGEO'S SUCCESS

Nancy Twine founded Briogeo, a natural haircare line, in 2013. Today, Briogeo products can be found at Sephora, Nordstrom, and Net-a-Porter. Briogeo is the fastest growing hair care brand at Sephora.

After graduating from the University of Virginia, Twine took a job at Goldman Sachs trading commodities. Twine began studying and learning about the beauty care markets. She realized there was a huge increase in skin care products focused on more natural ingredients but not much in this area for hair care. She began working with chemists to find a hair care

formula that was all natural but could still perform at the level of the competition.

Once Twine started running tests, the costs got too high and she needed an investor. Twine picked mostly angel investors, more known for investing in tech companies. Yet the investors who invested with Twine believed her business idea would succeed. With this funding Twine was able to land her first two orders from Urban Outfitters and a Los Angeles boutique. In 2014, Sephora agreed to launch Briogeo on its website. Briogeo, with $35 million in revenue, has turned a profit

every year it has been on the market. Briogeo's success stems from Twine's ability to recognize an unfilled market need and leverage this to create a high-growth company with a lucrative future.[d]

Critical Thinking Questions

1. How did Nancy Twine use entrepreneurial skills to develop a successful hair care company?
2. What type of industry does Briogeo operate in?
3. What type of financing did Nancy Twine end up using to start her business?

Small-business owners often use debt financing from banks or the Small Business Administration to start their own organizations.

Vico Collective/Erik Palmer/Blend Images LLC

in initial financing to rent space, purchase or lease necessary equipment and furnishings, buy the initial inventory, and provide working capital. For example, children's hair bow startup Wunderkin operates in a 5,000-square-foot space where rent is $10,500 per month.[39] Of all startups, 90 percent start with less than $100,000, with almost 50 percent of these business ventures starting with less than $5,000.[40] Often, the small-business owner has to put up a significant percentage of the necessary capital. Ben Chestnut and Dan Kurizius are the sole owners of Mailchimp, a marketing and e-mail automation platform with a valuation of $4.2 billion. Because Mailchimp doesn't have any investors, each owner has a $2.1 billion stake in the company.[41] Few new business owners have a large amount of their own capital and must look to other sources for additional financing. Opendoor buys and resells houses. It borrows about 90 percent of the purchase price of a home, and they operate in 21 cities. Therefore, they have to find investors to loan funds or borrow from banks.[42]

Equity Financing.

The most important source of funds for any new business is the owner. Many owners include among their personal resources ownership of a home, the accumulated value in a life insurance policy, or a savings account. A new business owner may sell or borrow against the value of such assets to obtain funds to operate a business. Additionally, the owner may bring useful personal assets—such as a computer, desks and other furniture, a car or truck—as part of his or her ownership interest in the firm. Such financing is referred to as *equity financing* because the owner uses real personal assets rather than borrowing funds from outside sources to get started in a new business. The owner can also provide working capital by reinvesting profits into the business or simply by not drawing a full salary.

Small businesses can also obtain equity financing by finding investors for their operations. They may sell stock in the business to family members, friends, employees, or other investors. **Venture capitalists** are persons or organizations that agree to provide some funds for a new business in exchange for an ownership interest or stock. For example, FreightWaves, a startup in Chattanooga, Tennessee, is a database platform that aggregates millions of sources and data points in order to deliver and publish insights about how factors like weather, technology, regulations, and the economy affect freight markets. The company has raised more than $40 million from venture capital investors.[43] Venture capitalists hope to purchase the stock of a small business at a low price and then sell the stock for a profit after the business has grown successful. In 2010, identical twins Brandon and Bradley Deyo launched Mars Reel, a company that showcases highlight films of high school athletes over platforms like Snapchat, YouTube, and Twitter. The twins came up with the idea after submitting highlight clips of themselves playing basketball in an attempt to earn college scholarships. Mars Reel has received more than $4.7 million in funding from investors like LeBron James, Drake, and *USA Today*.[44] Although these forms of equity financing have helped many small businesses, they require that the small-business owner share the profits of the business—and sometimes control, as well—with the investors.

Debt Financing.

New businesses can borrow more as they become established. Banks are the main suppliers of external financing to small businesses. On the federal level, the SBA offers financial assistance to qualifying businesses. Medhi Zarhloul of Crazy Pita Rotisserie & Grill in Henderson, Nevada, was named among the Persons of the Year by SBA. SBA loans allow companies such as Five Star Guitars to acquire retail space, employ salespeople, and serve specific target markets.[45] They can also look to family and friends as sources for long-term loans or other assets, such as computers or an automobile, that are exchanged for an ownership interest in a business. In such cases, the business owner can usually structure a favorable repayment schedule and sometimes negotiate an interest rate below current bank rates. If the business goes bad, however, the emotional losses for all concerned may greatly exceed the money involved. Anyone lending a friend or family member money for a venture should state the agreement clearly in writing before any money changes hands.

The amount a bank or other institution is willing to loan depends on its assessment of the venture's likelihood of success and of the entrepreneur's ability to repay the loan. The bank will often require the entrepreneur to put up *collateral*, a financial interest in the property or fixtures of the business, to guarantee payment of the debt. Additionally, the small-business owner may have to provide personal property as collateral, such as his or her home, in which case the loan is called a *mortgage*. If the small business fails to repay the loan, the lending institution may eventually claim and sell the collateral or mortgage to recover its loss.

Banks and other financial institutions can also grant a small business a *line of credit*—an agreement by which a financial institution promises to lend a business a predetermined sum on

venture capitalists persons or organizations that agree to provide some funds for a new business in exchange for an ownership interest or stock.

franchise a license to sell another's products or to use another's name in business, or both.

franchiser the company that sells a franchise.

franchisee the purchaser of a franchise.

demand. A line of credit permits an entrepreneur to take quick advantage of opportunities that require external funding. Small businesses may obtain funding from their suppliers in the form of a *trade credit*—that is, suppliers allow the business to take possession of the needed goods and services and pay for them at a later date or in installments. Occasionally, small businesses engage in *bartering*—trading their own products for the goods and services offered by other businesses. For example, an accountant may offer accounting services to an office supply firm in exchange for office supplies and equipment. Three students from Michigan Tech were having trouble landing jobs out of school. As a result, they got together and launched the career site, Handshake. In order to grow the company, the founders acquired seed funding and issued Series A and Series B bonds to fund the business. Now, Handshake is the leading early talent network, serving 900 schools, 5 million students, and 500,000 employers.[46]

Additionally, some community groups sponsor loan funds to encourage the development of particular types of businesses. State and local agencies may guarantee loans, especially to minority business people or for development in certain areas.

Approaches to Starting a Small Business

Starting from Scratch versus Buying an Existing Business.
Although entrepreneurs often start new small businesses from scratch much the way we have discussed in this section, they may elect instead to buy an existing business. This has the advantage of providing a built-in network of customers, suppliers, and distributors and reducing some of the guesswork inherent in starting a new business from the ground up. Actor Sarah Michelle Gellar co-founded Foodstirs, a baking brand, after being dismissed by countless investors. Gellar leveraged her brand based on her ability to get on talk shows and promote the baking mix and prepared foods with high-quality ingredients. Their one-minute mug cake was picked up by 8,000 Starbucks stores.[47] However, an entrepreneur who buys an existing business also takes on any problems the business already has.

Franchising.
Many small-business owners find entry into the business world through franchising. A license to sell another's products or to use another's name in business, or both, is a **franchise**. The company that sells a franchise is the **franchiser**. Dunkin', Subway, and Jiffy Lube are well-known franchisers with national visibility. The purchaser of a franchise is called a **franchisee**.

The franchisee acquires the rights to a name, logo, methods of operation, national advertising, products, and other elements associated with the franchiser's business in return for a financial commitment and the agreement to conduct business in accordance with the franchiser's standard of operations. The initial fee to join a franchise varies greatly. In addition, franchisees buy equipment, pay for training, and obtain a mortgage or lease. The franchisee also pays the franchiser a monthly or annual fee based on a percentage of sales or profits. In return, the franchisee often receives building specifications and designs, site recommendations, management and accounting support, and perhaps most importantly, immediate name recognition. Visit the website of the International Franchise Association to learn more on this topic.

The practice of franchising first began in the United States in the 19th century when Singer used it to sell sewing machines. This method of goods distribution soon became commonplace in the automobile, gasoline, soft drink, and hotel industries. The concept of franchising grew especially rapidly during the 1960s, when it expanded to diverse industries. Table 5.5 shows the 10 fastest growing franchises.

The entrepreneur will find that franchising has both advantages and disadvantages. Franchising allows a franchisee the opportunity to set up a small business relatively quickly, and because of its association with an established brand, a franchise outlet often reaches the break-even point faster than an independent business would. Franchisees commonly report the following advantages:

- Management training and support.
- Brand-name appeal.
- Standardized quality of goods and services.
- National and local advertising programs.
- Financial assistance.
- Proven products and business formats.
- Centralized buying power.

▼ **TABLE 5.5** Fastest Growing Franchises

Top 10 Fastest Growing Franchises
1. Supercuts
2. Jan-Pro Franchising International Inc.
3. Reis & Irvy's
4. Cruise Planners
5. Taco Bell
6. Planet Fitness
7. Stratus Building Solutions
8. Dunkin'
9. Orangetheory Fitness
10. Goosehead Insurance Agency LLC

Source: "2020 Fastest Growing Granchises Ranking," *Entrepreneur,* https://www.entrepreneur.com/franchises/fastestgrowing (accessed May 29, 2020).

- Site selection and territorial protection.
- Greater chance for success.[48]

However, the franchisee must sacrifice some freedom to the franchiser. Some shortcomings experienced by franchisees include:

- Franchise fees and profit sharing with the franchiser.
- Strict adherence to standardized operations.
- Restrictions on purchasing.
- Limited product line.
- Possible market saturation.
- Less freedom in business decisions.[49]

Strict uniformity is the rule rather than the exception. Entrepreneurs who want to be their own bosses are often frustrated with the restrictions of a franchise.

Help for Small-Business Managers

Because of the crucial role that small business and entrepreneurs play in the U.S. economy, a number of organizations offer programs to improve the small-business owner's ability to compete. These include entrepreneurial training programs and programs sponsored by the SBA. Such programs provide small-business owners with invaluable assistance in managing their businesses, often at little or no cost to the owner.

Entrepreneurs can learn critical marketing, management, and finance skills in seminars and college courses. In addition, knowledge, experience, and judgment are necessary for success in a new business. While knowledge can be communicated and some experiences can be simulated in the classroom, good judgment must be developed by the entrepreneur. Local chambers of commerce and the U.S. Department of Commerce offer information and assistance helpful in operating a small business. National publications such as *Inc.* and *Entrepreneur* share statistics, advice, tips, and success/ failure stories. Additionally, most urban areas have weekly business journals/newspapers that provide stories on local businesses as well as on business techniques that a manager or small business can use.

The SBA offers many types of management assistance to small businesses, including counseling for firms in difficulty, consulting on improving operations, and training for owner/managers and their employees. Among its many programs, the SBA funds Small Business Development Centers (SBDCs). These are business clinics, usually located on college campuses, that provide counseling at no charge and training at only a nominal charge. SBDCs are often the SBA's principal means of providing direct management assistance.

The Service Corps of Retired Executives (SCORE) and the Active Corps of Executives (ACE) are volunteer agencies funded by the SBA to provide advice for owners of small firms. Both are staffed by experienced managers whose talents and knowledge the small firms could not ordinarily afford. SCORE

has more than 10,000 volunteers at over 250 local chapters across the country.[50] The SBA also has organized Small Business Institutes (SBIs) on almost 500 university and college campuses in the United States. Seniors, graduate students, and faculty at each SBI provide onsite management counseling.

Finally, the small-business owner can obtain advice from other small-business owners, suppliers, and even customers. A customer may approach a small business it frequents with a request for a new product, for example, or a supplier may offer suggestions for improving a manufacturing process. Networking— building relationships and sharing information with colleagues—is vital for any businessperson, whether you work for a huge corporation or run your own small business. Incubators, or organizations created to accelerate the development and success of startup organizations, often provide network opportunities and potential capital to jumpstart a business.[51] Communicating with other business owners is a great way to find ideas for dealing with employees and government regulation, improving processes, or solving problems. New technology is making it easier to network. For example, some states are establishing social networking sites for the use of their businesses to network and share ideas.

LO 5-6 Evaluate the demographic, technological, and economic trends that are affecting the future of small business.

THE FUTURE FOR SMALL BUSINESS

Although small businesses are crucial to the economy, their size and limited resources can make them more vulnerable to turbulence and change in the marketplace than large businesses.[52] Next, we take a brief look at the demographic, technological, and economic trends that will have the most impact on small business in the future.

Demographic Trends

America's baby boom started in 1946 and ended in 1964. The baby boomer generation consists of 75 million Americans.[53] This segment of the population is wealthy, but many small businesses do not actively pursue it. Some exceptions, however, include Gold Violin, which sells designer canes and other products online and through a catalog, and LifeSpring Nutrition, which delivers nutritional meals and snacks directly to the customer. Industries such as travel, financial planning, and health care will continue to grow as boomers age. Many experts believe that the boomer demographic is the market of the future.

Other consumers, comprising a market with a huge potential for small business, that have surpassed baby boomers as

The Latino population is the biggest and fastest growing minority segment in the U.S.—and a lucrative market for businesses looking for ways to meet the segment's many needs.

Vico Collective/Erik Palmer/Blend Images LLC

▼ **TABLE 5.6** Most Business-Friendly States

1. North Carolina
2. Texas
3. Utah
4. Virginia
5. Florida
6. Georgia
7. Tennessee
8. Washington
9. Colorado
10. Idaho

Source: "Best States for Business," *Forbes,* www.forbes.com/best-states-for-business/list/ (accessed May 29, 2020).

environment.[56] Working remotely is more acceptable to these groups than previous generations, and virtual communication may become as important as face-to-face meetings.[57]

Also to be considered are the growing number of immigrants living in the United States, who now represent more than 17 percent, or 27.6 million, of the total U.S. workforce. The largest employer of legal immigrants is retail, followed by educational services and non-hospital health care services.[58] This vast group provides still another greatly untapped market for small businesses. Retailers who specialize in ethnic products, and service providers who offer bi- or multilingual employees, will find a large amount of business potential in this market. Table 5.6 ranks top states in the United States for small businesses and startups.

Technological and Economic Trends

Advances in technology have opened up many new markets to small businesses. Undoubtedly, the Internet will continue to provide new opportunities for small businesses. Slack is a cloud-based app that allows teams to engage in efficient collaboration through cloud-based computing. The company is now valued at $20 billion.[59] In the advertisement, Slack shows how a human resources manager can use the platform to quickly and efficiently field questions from employees. Technology has also enabled the substantial growth of entrepreneurs working out of their houses, known as home-based businesses. Many of today's largest businesses started out in homes, including Mary Kay, Ford, and Apple. Approximately 50 percent of small businesses are based out of the home.[60] Technological advancements have increased the ability of

the United States' largest living generation are called millennials or Generation Y.[54] Millennials number around 83 million and possess a number of unique characteristics.[55] Born between 1981 and 1997, this cohort is not solely concerned about money. Those that fall into this group tend to be concerned with advancement, recognition, and improved capabilities. They tend to need direct, timely feedback and frequent encouragement and recognition. Millennials do well when training sessions combine entertainment with learning. The generation after Millennials is Gen Z, which accounts for 61 million people in the United States. This group, which is starting to enter the workforce, tends to seek a fun, flexible work

> **"Approximately 50 percent of small businesses are based out of the home."**

Anna can field questions about the new vacation policy, without calling an all-company meeting.

That's collaboration in Slack.

Learn more at **slack.com**

Slack is a collaboration hub that supports small businesses with cloud-based communication systems and tools.

Source: Slack

home-based businesses to interact with customers and operate effectively.[61]

Technological advances and an increase in service exports have created new opportunities for small companies to expand their operations abroad. Changes in communications and technology can allow small companies to customize their services quickly for international customers. Also, free trade agreements and trade alliances are helping to create an environment in which small businesses have fewer regulatory and legal barriers.

In recent years, economic turbulence has provided both opportunities and threats for small businesses. As large information technology companies such as Cisco, Oracle, and Sun Microsystems had to recover from an economic slowdown and an oversupply of Internet infrastructure products, some smaller firms found new niche markets. Smaller companies can react quickly to change and can stay close to their customers. While well-funded dot-coms were failing, many small businesses were learning how to use the Internet to promote themselves and sell products online. For example, arts and crafts dealers and makers of specialty products found they could sell their wares on existing websites, such as eBay and Etsy. Service providers related to tourism, real estate, and construction also found they could reach customers through their own or existing websites.

Deregulation of the energy market and interest in alternative fuels and in fuel conservation have spawned many small businesses. Southwest Windpower Inc. manufactures and markets small wind turbines for producing electric power for homes, sailboats, and telecommunications. As entrepreneurs begin to realize that worldwide energy markets are valued in the hundreds of billions of dollars, the number of innovative companies entering this market will increase. In addition, many small businesses have the desire and employee commitment to purchase such environmentally friendly products. New Belgium Brewing Company received the U.S. Environmental Protection Agency and Department of Energy Award for leadership in conservation for making a 10-year commitment to purchase wind energy.

The future for small business remains promising. The opportunities to apply creativity and entrepreneurship to serve customers are unlimited. Large companies such as Walmart, with 2.2 million employees around the world, often adapt slowly to changes in the environment, whereas small businesses can adapt immediately.[62] This flexibility provides small businesses with a definite advantage over large companies.

LO 5-7 Explain why many large businesses are trying to "think small."

MAKING BIG BUSINESSES ACT "SMALL"

The continuing success and competitiveness of small businesses through rapidly changing conditions in the business world have led many large corporations to take a closer look at what makes their smaller rivals tick. More and more firms are emulating small businesses in an effort to improve their own bottom line. Beginning in the 1980s and continuing through the present, the buzzword in business has been to *downsize* or

BUILDING YOUR SOFT SKILLS

BY STARTING YOUR OWN BUSINESS

Starting your own business requires solid soft skills such as communication, leadership, self-management, time management, and people skills. Imagine you are going to launch your own dream business. What three soft skills would you most need in order to succeed, and why? How might you go about building these soft skills if you do not currently have them?

right-size to reduce management layers, corporate staff, and work tasks in order to make the firm more flexible, resourceful, and innovative. Many well-known U.S. companies—including IBM, Ford, Apple, General Electric, Xerox, and 3M—have downsized to improve their competitiveness, as have German, British, and Japanese firms. Other firms have sought to make their businesses "smaller" by making their operating units function more like independent small businesses, each responsible for its profits, losses, and resources. Of course, some large corporations, such as Southwest Airlines, have acted like small businesses from their inception, with great success.

Trying to capitalize on small-business success in introducing innovative new products, more and more companies are attempting to instill a spirit of entrepreneurship into even the largest firms. In major corporations, **intrapreneurs**, like entrepreneurs, take responsibility for, or "champion," the development of innovations of any kind *within* the larger organization.[63] Often, they use company resources and time to develop a new product for the company. ◼

Team Exercise

Explore successful global franchises. Go to the companies' websites and find the requirements for applying for three franchises. The chapter provides examples of successful franchises. What do the companies provide, and what is expected to be provided by the franchiser? Compare and contrast each group's findings for the franchises researched. For example, at Subway, the franchisee is responsible for the initial franchise fee, finding locations, leasehold improvements and equipment, hiring employees and operating restaurants, and paying an 8 percent royalty to the company and a fee into the advertising fund. The company provides access to formulas and operational systems, store design and equipment ordering guidance, a training program, an operations manual, a representative on site during opening, periodic evaluations and ongoing support, and informative publications.

DO YOU KNOW // How to Make a Small Business Survive? /

In times when jobs are scarce, many people turn to entrepreneurship as a way to find employment. As long as there are unfulfilled needs from consumers, there will be a demand for entrepreneurs and small businesses. Entrepreneurs and small-business owners have been, and will continue to be, a vital part of the U.S. economy, whether in retailing, wholesaling, manufacturing, technology, or services. Creating a business around your idea has a lot of advantages. For many people, independence is the biggest advantage of forming their own small business, especially for those who do not work well in a corporate setting and like to call their own shots. Smaller businesses are also cheaper to start up than large ones in terms of salaries, infrastructure, and equipment. Smallness also provides a lot of flexibility to change with the times. If consumers suddenly start demanding new and different products, a small business is more likely to deliver quickly.

Starting your own business is not easy, especially in slow economic times. Even in a good economy, taking an idea and turning it into a business has a very high failure rate. The possibility of failure can increase even more when

money is tight. Reduced revenues and expensive materials can hurt a small business more than a large one because small businesses have fewer resources. When people are feeling the pinch from rising food and fuel prices, they tend to cut back on other expenditures—which could potentially harm your small business. The increased cost of materials will also affect your bottom line. However, several techniques can help your company survive:

- Set clear payment schedules for all clients. Small businesses tend to be worse about collecting payments than large ones, especially if the clients are acquaintances. However, you need to keep cash flowing into the company in order to keep business going.
- Take the time to learn about tax breaks. A lot of people do not realize all of the deductions they can claim on items such as equipment and health insurance.
- Focus on your current customers, and don't spend a lot of time looking for new ones. It is far less expensive for a company to keep its existing customers happy.
- Although entrepreneurs and small-business owners are more likely to be friends with their

customers, do not let this be a temptation to give things away for free. Make it clear to your customers what the basic price is for what you are selling and charge for extra features, extra services, etc.

- Make sure the office has the conveniences employees need—like a good coffee maker and other drinks and snacks. This will not only make your employees happy, but it will also help maintain productivity by keeping employees closer to their desks.
- Use your actions to set an example. If money is tight, show your commitment to cutting costs and making the business work by doing simple things like taking the bus to work or bringing a sack lunch every day.
- Don't forget to increase productivity in addition to cutting costs. Try not to focus so much attention on cost cutting that you don't try to increase sales.

In unsure economic times, these measures should help new entrepreneurs and small-business owners sustain their businesses. Learning how to run a business on a shoestring is a great opportunity to cut the fat and to establish lean, efficient operations.[64]

the nature
of management

Monkey Business Images/Shutterstock

LEARNING OBJECTIVES

After reading this chapter, you will be able to:

LO 6-1 Explain management's role in the achievement of organizational objectives.

LO 6-2 Describe the major functions of management.

LO 6-3 Distinguish among three levels of management and the concerns of managers at each level.

LO 6-4 Specify the skills managers need in order to be successful.

LO 6-5 Summarize the systematic approach to decision making used by many business managers.

For any organization—small or large, for profit or nonprofit—to achieve its objectives, it must have resources to support operations; employees to make and sell the products; and financial resources to purchase additional goods and services, pay employees, and generally operate the business. To accomplish this, it must also have one or more managers to plan, organize, staff, direct, and control the work that goes on.

This chapter introduces the field of management. It examines and surveys the various functions, levels, and areas of management in business. The skills that managers need for success and the steps that lead to effective decision making are also discussed. ■

LO 6-1 Explain management's role in the achievement of organizational objectives.

THE IMPORTANCE OF MANAGEMENT

Management is a process designed to achieve an organization's objectives by using its resources effectively and efficiently in a changing environment. *Effectively* means having the intended result; *efficiently* means accomplishing the objectives with a minimum of resources. **Managers** make decisions about the use of the organization's resources and are concerned with planning, organizing, directing, and controlling the organization's activities so as to reach its objectives. Consider Waze, Google's crowdsourcing map app that taps data from 130 million users to deliver information on traffic patterns and infrastructure problems. Management of Waze sells location-based advertising and traffic data. For example, the firm helped plan the launch of carpool or ride-sharing programs to help commuters, provided organizational structure for the launch, and was involved in directing and controlling implementation of the service.[1] Management is universal. It takes place not only in business but also in government, the military, labor unions, hospitals, schools, and religious groups—any organization requiring the coordination of resources.

Every organization must acquire resources (people, services, raw materials, equipment, finances, and information) to effectively pursue its objectives and coordinate their use to turn out a final good or service. Employees are one of the most important resources in helping a business attain its objectives. Hiring people to carry out the work of the organization is known as **staffing**. Beyond recruiting people for positions within the firm, managers must determine what skills are needed for specific jobs, how to motivate and train employees, how much to pay, what benefits to provide, and how to prepare employees for higher-level jobs in the firm at a later date. U.S. companies are focusing more on increasing benefits and bonuses rather than salary. This gives more instant gratification to employees for exceptional work and provides a safety net for employers in case of a downturn in the economy.[2] Sometimes, they must also make the difficult decision to reduce the workforce. This is known as **downsizing**, the elimination of significant numbers of employees from an organization. During the COVID-19 (coronavirus) pandemic, many companies downsized in 2020. While some downsizing was temporary due to closures and a decrease in demand for certain products, some layoffs became permanent.[3] After a

management a process designed to achieve an organization's objectives by using its resources effectively and efficiently in a changing environment.

managers those individuals in organizations who make decisions about the use of resources and who are concerned with planning, organizing, staffing, directing, and controlling the organization's activities to reach its objectives.

staffing the hiring of people to carry out the work of the organization.

downsizing the elimination of a significant number of employees from an organization.

As a result of over-hiring, Snap Inc., the parent company of Snapchat, cut more than 220 workers, including 120 engineers.[a]

BigTunaOnline/Shutterstock

downsizing situation, an effective manager will promote optimism and positive thinking and minimize criticism and fault-finding. These elements of staffing will be explored in detail in the "Motivating the Workforce" and "Managing Human Resources" chapters.

Acquiring suppliers is another important part of managing resources and ensuring that products are made available to customers. As firms reach global markets, companies such as PepsiCo, Corning, and Charles Schwab enlist hundreds of diverse suppliers that provide goods and services to support operations. A good supplier maximizes efficiencies and provides creative solutions to help the company reduce expenses and reach its objectives. Finally, the manager needs adequate financial resources to pay for essential activities. Primary funding comes from owners and shareholders, as well as banks and other financial institutions. All these resources and activities must be coordinated and controlled if the company is to earn a profit. Organizations must also have adequate supplies of resources of all types, and managers must carefully coordinate their use if they are to achieve the organization's objectives.

LO 6-2 Describe the major functions of management.

MANAGEMENT FUNCTIONS

To harmonize the use of resources so that the business can develop, produce, and sell products, managers engage in a series of activities: planning, organizing, directing, and controlling (Figure 6.1). Although this book discusses each of the four functions separately, they are interrelated; managers may perform two or more of them at the same time.

Planning

Planning, the process of determining the organization's objectives and deciding how to accomplish them, is the first function of management. Planning is a crucial activity because it designs the

WeWork, a leader in the shared co-working space industry, has declared its mission to be to create a world where people work to make a life, not just a living.

Yonhap/Epa/REX/Shutterstock

map that lays the groundwork for the other functions. It involves forecasting events and determining the best course of action from a set of options or choices. The plan itself specifies what should be done, by whom, where, when, and how. For some managers, one major decision that requires extensive planning is selecting the right type of automation for warehouses and distribution facilities. Data gathering is a major phase of the planning process to determine what the facilities need and which automation can maximize order efficiency. Potential pitfalls in this process that managers should plan for include being swayed by advanced technology that is not needed, under-automating the facility, or over-automating the facility.[4] All businesses—from the smallest restaurant to the largest multinational corporation—need to develop plans for achieving success. But before an organization can plan a course of action, it must first determine what it wants to achieve.

Mission. A **mission**, or mission statement, is a declaration of an organization's fundamental

▼**FIGURE 6.1** *The Functions of Management*

Managers

Planning	Organizing	Directing	Controlling
activities to achieve the organization's objectives	resources and activities to achieve the organization's objectives	employees' activities toward achievement of objectives	the organization's activities to keep it on course

purpose and basic philosophy. It seeks to answer the question: "What business are we in?" Good mission statements are clear and concise statements that explain the organization's reason for existence. A well-developed mission statement, no matter what the industry or size of business, will answer five basic questions:

1. Who are we?
2. Who are our customers?
3. What is our operating philosophy (basic beliefs, values, ethics, etc.)?
4. What are our core competencies and competitive advantages?
5. What are our responsibilities with respect to being a good steward of environmental, financial, and human resources?

A mission statement that delivers a clear answer to these questions provides the foundation for the development of a strong organizational culture, a good marketing plan, and a coherent business strategy. The Walt Disney Company's mission is to "entertain, inform and inspire people around the globe through the power of unparalleled storytelling, reflecting the iconic brands, creative minds and innovative technologies that make ours the world's premier entertainment company."[5]

Goals.

A goal is the result that a firm wishes to achieve. A company almost always has multiple goals, which illustrates the complex nature of business. A goal has three key components: an attribute sought, such as profits, customer satisfaction, or product quality; a target to be achieved, such as the

want to have money and assets left over after paying off business expenses. Objectives regarding competitive advantage are generally stated in terms of percentage of sales increase and market share, with the goal of increasing those figures. Efficiency objectives involve making the best use of the organization's resources. Growth objectives relate to an organization's ability to adapt and to get new products to the marketplace in a timely fashion. One of the most important objectives for businesses is sales. In the United States, the consumption of bottled water surpassed soda for the first time. To take advantage of this, Pepsi launched LIFEWTR, and Fiji advertised its water to an audience of more than 111 million during the Super Bowl.[6] Objectives provide direction for all managerial decisions; additionally, they establish criteria by which performance can be evaluated.

Plans.

There are three general types of plans for meeting objectives—strategic, tactical, and operational. A firm's highest managers develop its **strategic plans**, which establish the long-range objectives and overall strategy or course of action

> ## "Strategic plans must take into account the organization's capabilities and resources, the changing business environment, and organizational objectives."

volume of sales or extent of management training to be completed; and a time frame, which is the time period in which the goal is to be attained. Sometimes goals have unintended consequences. When Wells Fargo set goals for salespeople to generate new accounts, they did not intend for their employees to fraudulently set up new accounts without the customer's knowledge. Incidents such as this do tremendous damage to reputation, brand, and customer attraction and retention. To be successful at achieving goals, it is necessary to know what is to be achieved, how much, when, and how succeeding at a goal is to be determined.

Objectives.

Objectives, the ends or results desired by an organization, derive from the organization's mission. A business's objectives may be elaborate or simple. Common objectives relate to profit, competitive advantage, efficiency, and growth. The principal difference between goals and objectives is that objectives are generally stated in such a way that they are measurable. Organizations with profit as an objective

by which the firm fulfills its mission. Strategic plans generally cover periods of one year or longer. They include plans to add products, purchase companies, sell unprofitable segments of the business, issue stock, and move into international markets. For example, Combekk, a Dutch firm that makes knives and tools, set an objective to increase sales by introducing a heavyweight pot called a Dutch Oven that cost $450. The 100 percent recycled iron collected from bridges and former train rails has an added value to help create an incredible sales success.[7] Strategic plans must take into account the organization's capabilities and resources, the changing business environment, and organizational objectives. Plans should be market-driven, matching customers' desire for value with operational capabilities, processes, and human resources.[8]

Tactical plans are short range and designed to implement the activities and objectives specified in the strategic plan. These plans, which usually cover a period of one year or less, help keep the organization on the course established in the strategic plan. General Motors, for instance, developed tactical plans to release redesigned versions of its vehicles that target millennials as part of its strategic plan to grow market share and reduce rental deliveries.[9] Because tactical plans allow the organization to react to changes in the environment while continuing to focus on the company's overall strategy, management must periodically review and update them. Declining performance or failure to meet objectives set out in tactical plans are possible reasons for revising them. The differences between the two types of planning result in different activities in the short term versus the long term. For instance, a strategic plan might include the use of social media to reach consumers. A tactical plan could involve finding ways to increase traffic to the site or promoting premium content to those who visit the site. A fast-paced and ever-changing market requires companies to develop short-run or tactical plans to deal with the changing environment.

Many traditional retailers have been under enormous pressure because of online providers such as Amazon. A retailing organization may have a five-year strategic plan that calls for store closures and revamping their sales structure. The tactical part of the plan would address which stores to close and the timeline, how to boost their online presence, and how to handle employee separation and layoffs. Tactical plans are designed to execute the overall strategic plan. Because of their short-term nature, they are easier to adjust or abandon if changes in the environment or the company's performance so warrant.

Operational plans are very short term and specify what actions specific individuals, work groups, or departments need to accomplish in order to achieve the tactical plan and, ultimately, the strategic plan. They apply to details in executing activities in one month, week, or even day. For example, a work group may be assigned a weekly production quota to ensure there are sufficient products available to elevate market share (tactical goal) and ultimately help the firm be number one in its product category (strategic goal). Returning to our retail store example, operational plans may specify the schedule for opening one new store, hiring and training new employees, obtaining merchandise, and opening for actual business.

Another element of planning is **crisis management** or **contingency planning**, which deals with potential disasters such as product tampering, oil spills, fire, earthquake, computer viruses, global pandemics, or even a reputation crisis due to unethical or illegal conduct by one or more employees. Unfortunately, many businesses do not have updated contingency plans to handle the types of crises that their companies might encounter.

After KFC's chicken shortage in the UK went viral on Twitter, the fast-food company acknowledged the issue in a timely manner, addressed guest concerns on social media, and published a series of ads apologizing for the supply chain error.
Ray Tang/REX/Shutterstock

According to the Federal Emergency Management Agency (FEMA), approximately 40 percent of small businesses do not reopen after a disaster.[10] Businesses that have well-thought-out contingency plans tend to respond more effectively when problems occur than do businesses that lack such planning.

Many companies—including Ashland Oil, H. J. Heinz, and Johnson & Johnson—have crisis management teams to deal specifically with problems, permitting other managers to continue to focus on their regular duties. Some companies even hold periodic disaster drills to ensure that their employees know how to respond when a crisis does occur. After the COVID-19 pandemic, many companies reevaluated their crisis management plans. The supply chain, for example, was instantly crippled as demand for certain items (e.g., toilet paper) skyrocketed while demand for other products (e.g., gas) plummeted. This highlighted the need for thorough supply chain mapping. Crisis management plans generally cover maintaining business operations throughout a crisis and communicating with the public, employees, and officials about

REBECCA RAY DESIGNS HAS IT IN THE BAG

Founded in 1998 in Chagrin Falls, Ohio, Rebecca Yuhasz Smith's retail and wholesale company, Rebecca Ray Designs, grew out of her love of animals and the sporting lifestyle. Rebecca partnered with Amish communities in Ohio and Pennsylvania to create and sell equestrian-themed luxury handbags.

As both manager and founder, Rebecca had to plan the organization's goals, organize different job functions, lead others to develop and sell the products, and control activities needed for achieving objectives. Luxury bags are hand-sewn by Amish women with peddle powered sewing machines, while Amish harness-makers hand-make the company's leather products. No electricity is used to make the products.

In 2007, Rebecca Ray Designs won the category of *Country Living* magazine's Pitch Your Product competition. Rebecca wanted to expand, but she underestimated the human resources skills needed. After hiring sales representatives, the number of boutiques selling Rebecca Ray Designs grew.

Today, Rebecca's luxury products include handbags, accessories, belts, and home decor. In her managerial role, Rebecca turned Rebecca Ray Designs into a successful high-fashion business. Due to her reputation for quality, the Kentucky Derby used Rebecca Ray-designed gift bags for its VIP guests.[b]

🔴 Critical Thinking Questions

1. What management skills did Rebecca Yuhasz Smith need to found her successful business?

2. How does Rebecca Yuhasz Smith use the four functions of management to operate her business?

3. What types of decisions did Rebecca Yuhasz Smith need to make as her business grew?

---

the nature of and the company's response to the problem. Communication is especially important to minimize panic and damaging rumors; it also demonstrates that the company is aware of the problem and plans to respond.

Sometimes, disasters occur that no one can anticipate, but companies can still plan for how to react to the disaster. There can be a major crisis when supply that is time sensitive is disrupted. That's what happened to KFC in the UK when it pared back its logistics network to cut expenses. The move resulted in two-thirds of its outlets without chicken for several days.[11] The award-winning print ad campaign KFC released to apologize for the shortage helped the company maintain its reputation. Incidents such as this highlight the importance of planning for crises and the need to respond publicly and quickly when a disaster occurs.

Organizing

Rarely are individuals in an organization able to achieve common goals without some form of structure. **Organizing** is the structuring of resources and activities to accomplish objectives in an efficient and effective manner. Managers organize by reviewing plans and determining what activities are necessary to implement them; then, they divide the work into small units and assign it to specific individuals, groups, or departments. As companies reorganize for greater efficiency, more often than not, they are organizing work into teams to handle core processes such as new product development instead of organizing around traditional departments such as marketing and production. Organizing occurs continuously because change is inevitable.

Organizing is important for several reasons. It helps create synergy, whereby the effect of a whole system equals more than that of its parts. It also establishes lines of authority, improves communication, helps avoid duplication of resources, and can improve competitiveness by speeding up decision making. Procter & Gamble underwent a major, multiyear reorganization cutting more than 36,000 jobs. Major changes in staffing and structure present challenges and opportunities for companies such as P&G.[12]

A business model relates to how a firm is organized to operate and provide value to stakeholders. It is the map or blueprint for running a business—a conceptual tool for organizing how a business operates.[13] Examples of business models include a Subway franchise, Avon direct selling, Amazon and online retailing, and Netflix's subscription business model that provides access to

> **organizing** the structuring of resources and activities to accomplish objectives in an efficient and effective manner.

MANAGERS MAY MOTIVATE EMPLOYEES BY PROVIDING INCENTIVES—SUCH AS THE PROMISE OF A RAISE OR PROMOTION—FOR THEM TO DO A GOOD JOB.

directing motivating and leading employees to achieve organizational objectives.

controlling the process of evaluating and correcting activities to keep the organization on course.

top managers the president and other top executives of a business, such as the chief executive officer (CEO), chief financial officer (CFO), and chief operations officer (COO), who have overall responsibility for the organization.

entertainment. General business models relate to manufacturing to create a product or a distribution that resells to retailors. Today many businesses are trying to create new business models that focus on business sectors such as the sharing economy. Uber and Airbnb provide access but not ownership of products. In the future, many business models will emerge related to the digital economy, driverless vehicles, robotics, drones, and artificial intelligence. Artificial intelligence will allow managers to gain extraordinary control over their workers as well as forecasting demand, developing customer relationships, and managing the supply chain. New business models will develop around artificial intelligence systems.[14] Because organizing is so important, we'll take a closer look at it in the chapter titled "Organization, Teamwork, and Communication."

Directing

During planning and organizing, staffing occurs and management must direct the employees. **Directing** is motivating and leading employees to achieve organizational objectives. Good directing involves telling employees what to do and when to do it through the implementation of deadlines and then encouraging them to do their work. For example, as a sales manager, you would need to learn how to motivate salespersons, provide leadership, teach sales teams to be responsive to customer needs, and manage organizational issues as well as evaluate sales results. Finally, directing also involves determining and administering appropriate rewards and recognition. All managers are involved in directing, but it is especially important for lower-level managers who interact daily with the employees operating the organization. For example, an assembly-line supervisor for Frito-Lay must ensure that her workers know how to use their equipment properly and have the resources needed to carry out their jobs safely and efficiently, and she must motivate her workers to achieve their expected output of packaged snacks.

Managers may motivate employees by providing incentives—such as the promise of a raise or promotion—for them to do a good job. But most workers want more than money from their jobs: They need to know that their employer values their ideas and input. Managers should give younger employees some decision-making authority as soon as possible. Smart managers, therefore, ask workers to contribute ideas for reducing costs, making equipment more efficient, improving customer service, or even developing new products. This participation also serves to increase employee morale. Recognition and appreciation are often the best motivators. Employees who understand more

about their effect on the financial success of the company may be induced to work harder for that success, and managers who understand the needs and desires of workers can encourage their employees to work harder and more productively. The motivation of employees is discussed in detail in the chapter titled "Motivating the Workforce."

Controlling

Planning, organizing, staffing, and directing are all important to the success of an organization, whether its objective is earning a profit or something else. But what happens when a firm fails to reach its goals despite a strong planning effort? **Controlling** is the process of evaluating and correcting activities to keep the organization on course. Control involves five activities: (1) measuring performance, (2) comparing present performance with standards or objectives, (3) identifying deviations from the standards, (4) investigating the causes of deviations, and (5) taking corrective action when necessary.

Controlling and planning are closely linked. Planning establishes goals and standards. By monitoring performance and comparing it with standards, managers can determine whether performance is on target. When performance is substandard, management must determine why and take appropriate actions to get the firm back on course. In short, the control function helps managers assess the success of their plans. You might relate this to your performance in this class. If you did not perform as well on early projects or exams, you must take corrective action such as increasing studying or using website resources to achieve your overall objective of getting an A or B in the course. When the outcomes of plans do not meet expectations, the control process facilitates revision of the plans. Control can take many forms such as visual inspections, testing, and statistical modeling processes. The basic idea is to ensure that operations meet requirements and are satisfactory to reach objectives.

The control process also helps managers deal with problems arising outside the firm. For example, if a firm is the subject of negative publicity, management should use the control process to determine why, and to guide the firm's response.

LO 6-3 Distinguish among three levels of management and the concerns of managers at each level.

TYPES OF MANAGEMENT

All managers—whether the sole proprietor of a jewelry store or the hundreds of managers of a large company such as Home Depot—perform the four functions just discussed. In the case of the jewelry store, the owner handles all the functions, but in a large company with more than one manager, responsibilities must be divided and delegated. This division of responsibility is generally achieved by establishing levels of management and areas of specialization—finance, marketing, and so on.

FIGURE 6.2 Levels of Management Planning

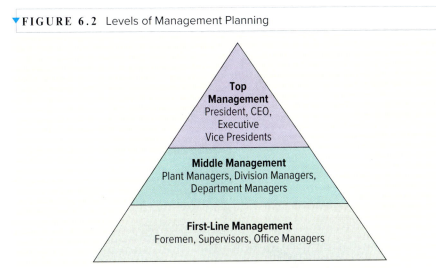

Levels of Management

As we have hinted, many organizations have multiple levels of management—top management, middle management, and first-line (or supervisory) management. These levels form a pyramid, as shown in Figure 6.2. As the pyramid shape implies, there are generally more middle managers than top managers and still more first-line managers. Very small organizations may have only one manager (typically, the owner), who assumes the responsibilities of all three levels. Large businesses have

DID YOU KNOW?

Only 6.6 percent of *Fortune* 500 CEOs are women.ᶜ

▼**FIGURE 6.3**
Importance of Management Functions to Managers in Each Level

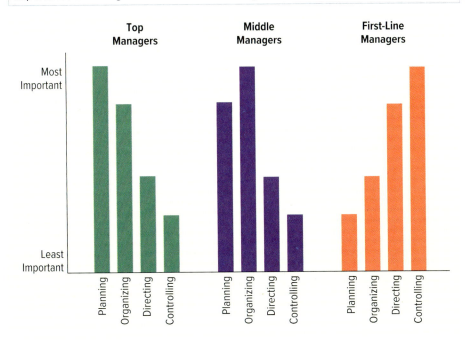

many managers at each level to coordinate the use of the organization's resources. Managers at all three levels perform all four management functions, but the amount of time they spend on each function varies, as we shall see (Figure 6.3).

Top Management. In businesses, **top managers** include the president and other top executives, such as the chief executive officer (CEO), chief financial officer (CFO), and chief operations officer (COO), who have overall responsibility for the organization. For example, the CEO of a company manages the overall strategic direction of the company and plays a key role in representing the company to stakeholders. The COO is responsible for daily operations of the company. The COO reports to the CEO and is often considered the number two in command. In public corporations, even the CEO has a boss, which is the board of directors. With technological advances accelerating and privacy concerns increasing, many companies are adding a new executive in the form of a chief privacy officer (CPO). The position of privacy officer has grown and the International Association of Privacy Professionals now have more than 50,000 members in 100 countries.¹⁵ In government, top management refers to the president, a governor, or a mayor or city manager; in education, a chancellor of a university or a superintendent of education.

Top-level managers spend most of their time planning. They make the organization's strategic decisions, decisions that focus on an overall scheme or key idea for using resources to take advantage of opportunities. They decide whether to add products, acquire companies, sell unprofitable business segments, and move into foreign markets. Top managers also represent their company to the public and to government regulators.

Given the importance and range of top management's decisions, top managers generally have many years of varied experience and command top salaries. In addition to salaries, top managers' compensation packages typically include bonuses, long-term incentive awards, stock, and stock options. Table 6.1 lists the compensation packages of different CEOs. Top management may also get perks and special treatment that is criticized by stakeholders.

Compensation committees are increasingly working with boards of directors and CEOs to attempt to keep pay in line with performance in order to benefit stockholders and key stakeholders. The majority of major companies cite their concern about attracting capable leadership for the CEO and other top executive positions in their organizations. However, many firms are trying to curb criticism of excessive executive compensation by trying to align CEO compensation with performance. In other words, if the company performs poorly, the CEO will not be paid as well. This type of compensation method is making a difference.[16] Chipotle struggled for several years following *E. coli* outbreaks in its restaurants. The co-CEOs had their pay

▼ **TABLE 6.1** Compensation Packages of CEOs

CEO	Company	Total Compensation
Sundar Pichai	Alphabet Inc.	$280.6 million
Robert H. Swan	Intel Corp	$66.9 million
Lisa T. Su	Advanced Micro Devices Inc.	$58.5 million
Miguel Patricio	Kraft Heinz Co.	$43.3 million
Satya Nadella	Microsoft Corp	$42.9 million

Source: Grant Suneson, "50 Highest Paid CEOs in 2019," *USA Today,* May 19, 2020, https://www.usatoday.com/story/money/2020/05/19/50-highest-paid-ceos-in-2019/111783524/ (accessed June 1, 2020).

Lowe's CEO Marvin Ellison has a base salary of approximately $1.45 million.

MediaPunch/REX/Shutterstock

LOWE'S UNDERGOES A MAJOR REMODEL

In an effort to improve performance, home improvement retailer Lowe's hired former JCPenney CEO Marvin Ellison as its leader. Ellison promised a massive overhaul to make Lowe's more competitive against Home Depot and online retailers.

As a top manager, Ellison provided the strategic direction for Lowe's. He wasted little time, eliminating the positions of chief operating officer and three other leadership roles. Ellison created new leadership positions that were not top senior executive roles, such as executive vice president of stores. Although restructuring management positions is risky, Ellison made decisions he believed would help the company concentrate more on its operations.

Ellison shut down Orchard Supply Hardware chain stores, which were previously purchased by Lowe's, in an effort to streamline the company. Recognizing that job loss at the stores might harm employee morale, Ellison offered these employees priority consideration for Lowe's store positions as well as job placement assistance and severance packages.

Under Ellison's leadership, Lowe's also made changes to its product offering, cutting back on low-selling inventory. Using his analytical skills, Ellison determined that retail tactics were insufficient to promote higher-performing products. In response, Lowe's changed store layout by placing high-selling items in promotional areas near the end of aisles and prioritizing placement of high-tech items for smart homes. He hired

leaders experienced on the sales floor to help executives understand daily store operations. Ellison's "remodel" paid off during the COVID-19 (coronavirus) pandemic when sales surged due to home do-it-yourself projects. Overall, with these measures, Lowe's performance has steadily improved.[d]

Critical Thinking Questions

1. What type of managerial skills is Marvin Ellison exhibiting in his decisions to overhaul Lowe's?

2. Describe ways in which Marvin Ellison is demonstrating the four management functions.

3. Outline the six steps of decision making that Marvin Ellison likely used in his decision to shut down Orchard Supply Hardware stores.

▼ **TABLE 6.2** Five Rules of Successful Diversity Recruiting

Rule	Action
1. Involve employees	Educate all employees on the tangible benefits of diversity recruiting to garner support and enthusiasm for those initiatives.
2. Communicate diversity	Prospective employees are not likely to become excited about joining your company just because you say that your company is diversity-friendly; they need to see it.
3. Support diversity initiatives and activities	By supporting community-based diversity organizations, your company will generate the priceless word-of-mouth publicity that will lead qualified diversity candidates to your company.
4. Delegate resources	If you are serious about diversity recruiting, you will need to spend some money getting your message out to the right places.
5. Promote your diversity initiatives	Employers need to sell their company to prospective diversity employees and present them with a convincing case as to why their company is a good fit for the diversity candidate.

Source: Adapted from Juan Rodriguez, "The Five Rules of Successful Diversity Recruiting," *Diversityjobs.com*, www.diversityjobs.com/Rules-of-Successful Diversity-Recruiting (accessed February 25, 2010).

cut in half, and the stock underperformed, losing 30 percent of its value in one year. Unsuccessful management has negative consequences for leaders, whereas successful management translates into happy stockholders who are willing to compensate their top executives fairly and in line with performance.[17]

Workforce diversity is an important issue in today's corporations. Effective managers at enlightened corporations have found that diversity is good for workers and for the bottom line. Putting together different kinds of people to solve problems often results in better solutions. Kaiser Permanente has been recognized by DiversityInc for its culture of diversity and inclusiveness. The company has minorities in top management positions at a level 66.6 percent higher than the other top 10 companies on the list. Executive compensation is tied to diversity, diversity metrics, and progress in growing supplier diversity.[18] A diverse workforce is better at making decisions regarding issues related to consumer diversity. Reaching fast-growing demographic groups such as Hispanics, African Americans, Asian Americans, and others will be beneficial to large companies as they begin to target these markets.[19] Managers from companies devoted to workforce diversity devised five rules that make diversity recruiting work (see Table 6.2).

Diversity concerns also relate to gender equality. Gender equality relates to pay, promotions, respect, and how one is treated in the workplace. The higher ranks in management often have significantly fewer women than men, and the women often receive lower pay, although Starbucks has achieved equal pay and career advancement for women. In addition, women occupy only 15 percent of board of director seats globally.[20] Diversity is explored in greater detail in the chapter titled "Managing Human Resources."

Middle Management.

Rather than making strategic decisions about the whole organization, **middle managers** are responsible for tactical and operational planning that will implement the general guidelines established by top management. Thus, their responsibility is more narrowly focused than that

of top managers. Middle managers are involved in the specific operations of the organization and spend more time organizing than other managers. In business, plant managers, division managers, and

middle managers
those members of an organization responsible for the tactical planning that implements the general guidelines established by top management.

IT managers are responsible for implementing, maintaining, and controlling technology applications including cyber defense systems like Darktrace.

Source: Darktrace

financial managers
those who focus on obtaining needed funds for the successful operation of an organization and using those funds to further organizational goals.

production and operations managers those who develop and administer the activities involved in transforming resources into goods, services, and ideas ready for the marketplace.

human resources managers those who handle the staffing function and deal with employees in a formalized manner.

marketing managers
those who are responsible for planning, pricing, and promoting products and making them available to customers.

information technology (IT) managers those who are responsible for implementing, maintaining, and controlling technology applications in business, such as computer networks.

administrative managers those who manage an entire business or a major segment of a business; they are not specialists but coordinate the activities of specialized managers.

first-line managers
those who supervise both workers and the daily operations of an organization.

▼ **TABLE 6.3** Areas of Management

Manager	Function
Financial manager	Focus on obtaining the money needed for the successful operation of the organization and using that money in accordance with organizational goals.
Production and operations manager	Develop and administer the activities involved in transforming resources into goods, services, and ideas ready for the marketplace.
Human resources manager	Handle the staffing function and deal with employees in a formalized manner.
Marketing manager	Responsible for planning, pricing, and promoting products and making them available to customers through distribution.
Information technology (IT) manager	Responsible for implementing, maintaining, and controlling technology applications in business, such as computer networks.
Administrative manager	Manage an entire business or a major segment of a business; do not specialize in a particular function.

department managers make up middle management. The product manager for laundry detergent at a consumer products manufacturer, the department chairperson in a university, and the head of a state public health department are all middle managers. The ranks of middle managers have been shrinking as more and more companies downsize to be more productive.

First-Line Management.
Most people get their first managerial experience as **first-line managers**, those who supervise workers and the daily operations of the organization. They are responsible for implementing the plans established by middle management and directing workers' daily performance on the job. They spend most of their time directing and controlling. Common titles for first-line managers are foreman, supervisor, and office manager.

Areas of Management
At each level, there are managers who specialize in the basic functional areas of business: finance, production and operations, human resources (personnel), marketing, IT, and administration.

Each of these management areas is important to a business's success. For instance, a firm cannot survive without someone obtaining needed financial resources (financial managers) or

staff (human resources managers). The Darktrace advertisement, for example, appeals to information technology (IT) managers who are responsible for technology applications in business such as Google Cloud Platforms. Darktrace is an artificial intelligence (AI) cyber defense company. While larger firms will most likely have all of these managers, and even more depending upon that particular firm's needs, in smaller firms, these important tasks may fall onto the owner or a few employees. Yet whether or not companies have managers for specific areas, every company must have someone responsible for obtaining financial resources, transforming resources into finished products for the marketplace, hiring and/or dealing with staff, marketing goods and services, handling the firm's information technology resources, and managing a business segment or the overall business. These different types of managers are discussed in more detail in Table 6.3.

LO 6-4 Specify the skills managers need in order to be successful.

SKILLS NEEDED BY MANAGERS
Managers are typically evaluated using the metrics of how effective and efficient they are. Managing effectively and efficiently requires certain skills—technical expertise, conceptual skills, analytical skills, human relations skills, and leadership. Table 6.4 describes some of the roles managers may fulfill.

Technical Expertise
Managers need **technical expertise**, the specialized knowledge and training required to perform jobs related to their area of management. Accounting managers need to be able to

technical expertise the specialized knowledge and training needed to perform jobs that are related to particular areas of management.

conceptual skills the ability to think in abstract terms and to see how parts fit together to form the whole.

analytical skills the ability to identify relevant issues, recognize their importance, understand the relationships between them, and perceive the underlying causes of a situation.

human relations skills the ability to deal with people, both inside and outside the organization.

leadership the ability to influence employees to work toward organizational goals.

▼ **TABLE 6.4** Managerial Roles

General Role Category	Specific Role	Example Activity
Interpersonal	Figure	Attending award banquet
	Liaison	Coordinating production schedule with supply manager
	Leadership	Conducting performance appraisal for subordinates
Informational	Monitor	Contacting government regulatory agencies
	Disseminator	Conducting meetings with subordinates to pass along safety policy
	Spokesperson	Meeting with consumer group to discuss product safety
Decisional	Entrepreneur	Changing work process
	Disturbance handler	Deciding which unit moves into new facilities
	Resource allocator	Deciding who receives new computer equipment
	Negotiator	Settling union grievance

Source: Roles developed by management professor Henry Mintzberg.

perform accounting jobs, and production managers need to be able to perform production jobs. Although a production manager may not actually perform a job, he or she needs technical expertise to train employees, answer questions, provide guidance, and solve problems. Technical skills are most needed by first-line managers and are least critical to top-level managers.

Conceptual Skills

Conceptual skills, the ability to think in abstract terms, and to see how parts fit together to form the whole, are needed by all managers, but particularly top-level managers. Top management must be able to evaluate continually where the company will be in the future. Conceptual skills also involve the ability to think creatively. Recent scientific research has revealed that creative thinking, which is behind the development of many innovative products and ideas, can be learned. As a result, IBM, AT&T, GE, Hewlett-Packard, Intel, and other top U.S. firms hire creative consultants to teach their managers how to think creatively.

Analytical Skills

Analytical skills refer to the ability to identify relevant issues and recognize their importance, understand the relationships between them, and perceive the underlying causes of a situation. When managers have identified critical factors and causes, they can take appropriate action. All managers need

> **People skills are especially important in hospitals, airline companies, banks, and other organizations that provide services.**

to think logically, but this skill is probably most important to the success of top-level managers. To be analytical, it is necessary to think about a broad range of issues and to weigh different options before taking action. Because analytical skills are so important, questions that require analytical skills are often a part of job interviews. Questions such as "Tell me how you would resolve a problem at work if you had access to a large amount of data?" may be part of the interview process. The answer would require the interviewee to try to explain how to sort data to find relevant facts that could resolve the issue. Analytical thinking is required in complex or difficult situations where the solution is often not clear. Resolving ethical issues often requires analytical skills.

Human Relations Skills

People skills, or **human relations skills**, are the ability to deal with people, both inside and outside the organization. Those who can relate to others, communicate well with others, understand the needs of others, and show a true appreciation for others are generally more successful than managers who lack such skills. People skills are especially important in hospitals, airline companies, banks, and other organizations that provide services. For example, Southwest Airlines places great value on its employees. New hires go through extensive training to teach employees about the airline and its reputation for impeccable customer service. All employees in management positions at Southwest take mandatory leadership classes that address skills related to listening, staying in touch with employees, and handling change without compromising values.

LO 6-5 Summarize the systematic approach to decision making used by many business managers.

LEADERSHIP

Leadership is the ability to influence employees to work toward organizational goals. Strong leaders manage and pay attention to the culture of their organizations and the needs of their employees. Table 6.5 offers some requirements for successful leadership.

leadership the ability to influence employees to work toward organizational goals.

Managers often can be classified into three types based on their leadership style. *Autocratic leaders* make all the decisions and then tell employees what must be done and how to do it. They generally use their authority and economic rewards to get employees to comply with their directions. Martha Stewart is an example of an autocratic leader. She built up her media empire by paying close attention to every detail.[21] *Democratic leaders* involve their employees in decisions. The manager presents a situation and encourages his or her subordinates to express opinions and contribute ideas. The manager then considers the employees' points of view and makes the decision. Herb Kelleher, co-founder of Southwest Airlines, had a democratic leadership style. Under his leadership, employees were encouraged to discuss concerns and provide input.[22] *Free-rein leaders* let their employees work without much interference. The manager sets performance standards and allows employees to find their own ways to meet them. For this style to be effective, employees must know what the standards are, and they must be motivated to attain them. The free-rein style of leadership can be a powerful motivator because it demonstrates a great deal of trust and confidence in the employee. Warren Buffett, CEO of Berkshire Hathaway, exhibits free-rein leadership among the managers who run the company's various businesses.

Twitter CEO Jack Dorsey believes in a democratic leadership style.
Roger Askew/Shutterstock

The effectiveness of the autocratic, democratic, and free-rein styles depends on several factors. One consideration is the type of employees. An autocratic style of leadership is generally best for stimulating unskilled, unmotivated employees; highly skilled, trained, and motivated employees may respond better to democratic or free-rein leadership styles. Employees who have been involved in decision making generally require less supervision than those not similarly involved. Other considerations are the manager's abilities and the situation itself. When a situation requires quick decisions, an autocratic style of leadership may be best because the manager does not have to consider input from a lot of people. If a special task force must be set up to solve a quality-control problem, a normally democratic manager may give free rein to the task force.

Many managers, however, are unable to use more than one style of leadership. Some are incapable of allowing their subordinates to participate in decision making, let alone make any decisions. What leadership style is "best" depends on specific circumstances, and effective managers will strive to adapt their leadership style as circumstances warrant. Many organizations offer programs to develop good leadership skills. Warren Buffett, chair of Berkshire Hathaway, has developed dozens of exemplary leaders with proven track records. Leadership continuity is important to all firms.[23] When plans fail, very often leaders are held responsible for what goes wrong. For example, Wells

▼ **TABLE 6.5** Requirements for Successful Leadership

- Communicate objectives and expectations.
- Gain the respect and trust of stakeholders.
- Develop shared values.
- Acquire and share knowledge.
- Empower employees to make decisions.
- Be a role model for appropriate behavior.
- Provide rewards and take corrective action to achieve goals.

Rubrik CEO Bipul Sinha invites all of his employees to board meetings to empower employees with information and embrace transparency.

David Paul Morris/Bloomberg via Getty Images

Fargo CEO John Stumpf resigned before probably being fired for oversight of a bank that opened more than 3.5 million fake accounts for customers.[24]

Another type of leadership style that has been gaining in popularity is *authentic leadership.* Authentic leadership is a bit different from the other three leadership styles because it is not exclusive. Both democratic and free-rein leaders could qualify as authentic leaders depending upon how they conduct themselves among stakeholders. Authentic leaders are passionate about the goals and mission of the company, display corporate values in the workplace, and form long-term relationships with stakeholders.[25] Chobani founder and CEO Hamdi Ulukaya feels a deep responsibility to consumers and employees. He believes in equitable polices for employees and embraces diversity, especially related to immigrants and refugees. He wants to stand for something more than profit.[26]

While leaders might incorporate different leadership styles depending on the business and the situation, all leaders must be able to align employees behind a common vision to be effective.[27] Strong leaders also realize the value that employees can provide by participating in the firm's corporate culture. It is important that companies develop leadership training programs for employees. Because managers cannot oversee everything that goes on in the company, empowering employees to take more responsibility for their decisions can aid in organizational growth and productivity. Leaders often change directions when they see opportunities. Founder and CEO Michael Preysman of online clothing retailer Everlane said he would open no brick-and-mortar stores. But, based on demand, he opened minimalist glass storefronts in Manhattan, Brooklyn, Boston, Los Angeles, Palo Alto, and San Francisco.[28]

Employee Empowerment

Businesses are increasingly realizing the benefits of participative corporate cultures characterized by employee empowerment. **Employee empowerment** occurs when employees are provided with the ability to take on responsibilities and make decisions about their jobs. Employee empowerment does not mean that managers are not needed. Managers are important for guiding employees, setting goals, making major decisions, and other responsibilities emphasized throughout this chapter. However, a participative corporate culture has been found to be beneficial because employees in these companies feel like they are taking an active role in the firm's success.

Leaders who wish to empower employees adopt systems that support an employee's ability to provide input and feedback on company decisions. *Participative decision making,* a type of decision making that involves both manager and employee input, supports employee empowerment within the organization. One of the best ways to encourage participative decision making is through employee and managerial training. As mentioned earlier, employees should be trained in leadership skills, including teamwork, conflict resolution, and decision making. Managers should also be trained in ways to empower employees to make decisions while also guiding employees through challenging situations in which the right decision might not be so clear.[29]

A section on leadership would not be complete without a discussion of leadership in teams. In today's business world, decisions made by teams are becoming the norm. Employees at Zappos, for instance, often work in teams and are encouraged to make decisions that they believe will reinforce the company's mission and values. Teamwork has often been an effective way for encouraging employee empowerment. Although decision making in teams is collective, the most effective teams are those in which all employees are encouraged to contribute their ideas and recommendations. Because each employee can bring in his or her own unique insights, teams often result in innovative ideas or decisions that would not have been reached by only one or two people. Michelle Peluso, IBM's senior vice president of digital sales and chief marketing officer, tries to pull designers and data scientists, as well as marketers, together in teams. For example, she has teams attend sessions where they review and refine their work using only mobile devices to better understand how consumers use their products.[30] However, truly empowering employees in team decision making can be difficult. It is quite common for more outspoken employees to dominate the team and others to engage in groupthink, in which team members go with the majority rather than what they think is the right decision. Training employees to listen to one another and then provide relevant feedback can help to prevent these common challenges. Another way is to rotate the team leader so that no one person can assume dominancy.[31]

DECISION MAKING

Managers make many different kinds of decisions, such as the hours in a workday, which employees to hire, what products to introduce, and what price to charge for a product. Decision making is important in all management functions and at all levels, whether the decisions are on a strategic, tactical, or operational level. A systematic approach using the following six steps usually leads to more effective decision making: (1) recognizing and defining the decision situation, (2) developing options to resolve the situation, (3) analyzing the options, (4) selecting the best option, (5) implementing the decision, and (6) monitoring the consequences of the decision (Figure 6.4).

Recognizing and Defining the Decision Situation

The first step in decision making is recognizing and defining the situation. The situation may be negative—for example, huge losses on a particular product—or positive—for example, an opportunity to increase sales.

brainstorming a technique in which group members spontaneously suggest ideas to solve a problem.

Situations calling for small-scale decisions often occur without warning. Situations requiring large-scale decisions, however, generally occur after some warning signs. Effective managers pay attention to such signals. Declining profits, small-scale losses in previous years, inventory buildup, and retailers' unwillingness to stock a product are signals that may foreshadow huge losses to come. If managers pay attention to such signals, problems can be contained.

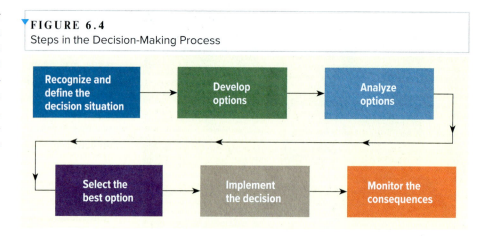

FIGURE 6.4
Steps in the Decision-Making Process

Once a situation has been recognized, management must define it. Losses reveal a problem—for example, a failing product. One manager may define the situation as a product quality problem; another may define it as a change in consumer preference. These two viewpoints may lead to vastly different solutions. The first manager, for example, may seek new sources of raw materials of better quality. The second manager may believe that the product has reached the end of its lifespan and decide to discontinue it. This example emphasizes the importance of carefully defining the problem rather than jumping to conclusions.

Developing Options

Once the decision situation has been recognized and defined, the next step is to develop a list of possible courses of action. The best lists include both standard and creative plans. **Brainstorming**, a technique in which group members

POTBELLY SANDWICHED IN A CROWDED MARKET

In 1977, Peter Hastings and his wife owned a Chicago antique shop. They began using the shop's potbelly stove to toast and sell sandwiches to customers, and the store soon became popular for its gourmet fare. Today, Potbelly Sandwich Shop has more than 400 locations in the United States, Canada, the United Kingdom, and the Middle East. However, the successful chain is struggling with overexpansion and differentiating itself among a crowded sandwich market. Alan Johnson took over as CEO to reinvigorate the company.

Johnson renamed sandwiches to make them stand out and reduced the number of menu items to exert greater control over quality. During

the overhaul of Potbelly's management team, Johnson hired former executive sous chef Ryan LaRoche to help direct the creation and improvement of menu items. The company also directed employees to offer customers additional items to purchase along with their sandwiches.

Johnson hoped these measures, as well as initiatives like a more extensive customer loyalty program, would draw more customers and differentiate Potbelly sandwiches from competitors. Though sales increased for a time, the COVID-19 (coronavirus) pandemic severely impacted U.S. restaurants in 2020. Potbelly chose to permanently close multiple under-performing shops to improve profitability.[e]

Critical Thinking Questions

1. Describe how Potbelly, under Johnson's leadership, is engaging in the four management functions.

2. Do you think Johnson's plans are more operational, tactical, strategic, or a combination? Explain your reasoning.

3. As Johnson works to increase sales and revamp the company, do you think an autocratic, democratic, or free-rein leadership style would be most effective? Explain your reasoning.

spontaneously suggest ideas to solve a problem, is an effective way to encourage creativity and explore a variety of options. As a general rule, more time and expertise are devoted to the development stage of decision making when the decision is of major importance. For example, after years of losses, Sears Holding Corp. has raised doubts about its ability to keep operating. Former CEO Edward Lampert reportedly ignored those around him as he cut money on advertising and inventory while raising prices. After filing for bankruptcy protection, Sears secured a loan of $350 million to keep the retailer operating while reorganizing.[32] When the decision is of less importance, less time and expertise will be spent on this stage. Options may be developed individually, by teams, or through analysis of similar situations in comparable organizations. Creativity is a very important part of selecting the most viable option. Creativity depends on new and useful ideas, regardless of where they originate or the method used to create them. The best option can range from a required solution to an identified problem or a volunteered solution to an observed problem by an outside work group member.[33]

Analyzing Options

After developing a list of possible courses of action, management should analyze the practicality and appropriateness of each option. An option may be deemed impractical because of a lack of financial resources, legal restrictions, ethical and social responsibility considerations, authority constraints, technological constraints, economic limitations, or simply a lack of information and expertise. For example, after experiencing the greatest loss since the U.S. government bailed out American International Group Inc., the company's directors looked at options related to then-CEO Peter Hancock, who did not achieve desired performance.[34]

When assessing appropriateness, the decision maker should consider whether the proposed option adequately addresses the situation. When analyzing the consequences of an option, managers should consider its impact on the situation and on the organization as a whole. For example, when considering a price cut to boost sales, management must think about the consequences of the action on the organization's cash flow and consumers' reaction to the price change.

Selecting the Best Option

When all courses of action have been analyzed, management must select the best one. Selection is often a subjective procedure because many situations do not lend themselves to quantitative analysis. The best option always relates to analyzing risks and trade-offs. For example, how Amazon uses its Alexa virtual assistant involves many alternatives. A decision had to be made whether the voice-activated device could store bank accounts data and make payments with all the risk associated with this service. Nearly all options create dilemmas that create an assistant of risks and rewards.[35] Of course, it is not always necessary to select only one option and reject all others; it may be possible to select and use a combination of several options.

Implementing the Decision

To deal with the situation at hand, the selected option or options must be put into action. Implementation can be fairly simple or very complex, depending on the nature of the decision. For example, China is a country where almost everything is purchased online. Walmart meets this challenge by crowdsourcing delivery drivers, such as Uber drivers with cell phones and scooters to provide one-hour delivery within about a two-mile radius from 161 Walmart supermarkets. This is an example of making changes to adjust to current consumer behavior in purchasing groceries.[36] Effective implementation of a decision to abandon a product, close a plant, purchase a new business, or something similar requires planning. For example, when a product is dropped, managers must decide how to handle distributors and customers and what to do with the idle production facility. Additionally, they should anticipate resistance from people within the organization. (People tend to resist change because they fear the unknown.) Finally, management should be ready to deal with the unexpected consequences. No matter how well planned implementation is, unforeseen problems will arise. Management must be ready to address these situations when they occur.

Monitoring the Consequences

After managers have implemented the decision, they must determine whether it has accomplished the desired result. Without proper monitoring, the consequences of decisions may not be known quickly enough to make efficient changes. If the desired result is achieved, management can reasonably conclude that it made a good choice. If the desired result is not achieved, further analysis is warranted. Was the decision simply wrong, or did the situation change? Should some other option have been implemented?

If the desired result is not achieved, management may discover that the situation was incorrectly defined from the beginning. That may require starting the decision-making process all over again. Finally, management may determine that the decision was good even though the desired results have not yet shown up, or it may determine a flaw in the decision's implementation. In the latter case, management would not change the decision but would change the way in which it is implemented.

MANAGEMENT IN PRACTICE

Management is not exact and calculated. There is no mathematical formula for managing an organization and achieving organizational goals, although many managers passionately wish for one. Managers plan, organize, direct, and control, but management expert John P. Kotter says even these functions can be boiled down to two basic activities:

1. Figuring out what to do despite uncertainty, great diversity, and an enormous amount of potentially relevant information.

2. Getting things done through a large and diverse set of people despite having little direct control over most of them.[37]

agenda a calendar, containing both specific and vague items, that covers short-term goals and long-term objectives.

networking the building of relationships and sharing of information with colleagues who can help managers achieve the items on their agendas.

Managers spend as much as 75 percent of their time working with others—not only with subordinates but with bosses, people outside their hierarchy at work, and people outside the organization itself. In these interactions, they discuss anything and everything remotely connected with their business.

Managers spend a lot of time establishing and updating an agenda of goals and plans for carrying out their responsibilities. An **agenda** contains both specific and vague items, covering short-term goals and long-term objectives. Like a calendar, an agenda helps the manager figure out what must be done and how to get it done to meet the objectives set by the organization. Technology tools such as smartphones can help managers manage their agendas, contacts, communications, and time.

Managers also spend a lot of time **networking**—building relationships and sharing information with colleagues who can help them achieve the items on their agendas. Managers spend much of their time communicating with a variety of people and participating in activities that, on the surface, do not seem to have much to do with the goals of their organization. Nevertheless, these activities are crucial to getting the job done. Networks are not limited to immediate subordinates and bosses; they include other people in the company as well as customers, suppliers, and friends. These contacts provide managers with information and advice on diverse topics. Managers ask, persuade, and push members of their network in order to get information and to get things done. Networking helps managers carry out their responsibilities. Social media sites have increased the ability of both managers and subordinates to network. Internal social networks such as Yammer allow employees to connect with one another, while social networks such as Facebook or Twitter enable managers to connect with customers. Sales managers are even using social networks to communicate with their distributors. LinkedIn has been used for job networking and is gaining in popularity among the younger generation as an alternative to traditional job hunting. Some speculate that social networks might eventually replace traditional résumés and job boards.[38]

Finally, managers spend a great deal of time confronting the complex and difficult challenges of the business world today. Some

Websites like LinkedIn help managers and employees network to achieve their professional goals.

dennizn/Shutterstock

Team Exercise

Form groups and assign the responsibility of locating examples of crisis management implementation for companies dealing with natural disasters (explosions, fires, earthquakes, etc.), technology disasters (viruses, plane crashes, compromised customer data, etc.), health crises (pandemics, etc.), or ethical or legal disasters. How did these companies communicate with key stakeholders? What measures did the company take to provide support to those involved in the crisis? Report your findings to the class.

of these challenges relate to rapidly changing technology (especially in production and information processing), increased scrutiny of individual and corporate ethics and social responsibility, the impact of social media, the changing nature of the workforce, new laws and regulations, increased global competition and more challenging foreign markets, declining educational standards (which may limit the skills and knowledge of the future labor and customer pool), and time itself—that is, making the best use of it. But such diverse issues cannot simply be plugged into a computer program that supplies correct, easy-to-apply solutions. It is only through creativity and imagination that managers can make effective decisions that benefit their organizations. ∎

BUILDING YOUR SOFT SKILLS

BY BECOMING A BETTER LEADER

Leadership is an important soft skill for many managers. But can you learn how to become a better leader? Many people think so. Research how to become a better leader on the Internet. What are five suggestions that reputable sources offer? Choose one and list one concrete way that you can implement it in order to improve your leadership skills.

WHAT KIND OF MANAGER // Do You Want to Be? /

Managers are needed in a wide variety of organizations. Experts suggest that employment will increase by millions of jobs in upcoming years. But the requirements for the jobs become more demanding with every passing year—with the speed of technology and communication increasing by the day, and the stress of global commerce increasing pressures to perform. However, if you like a challenge and if you have the right kind of personality, management remains a viable field. Even as companies are forced to restructure, management remains a vital role in business. For example, the Bureau of Labor Statistics projects that demand for financial managers will grow by 16 percent, much faster than average, between 2018 and 2020.[39]

Salaries for managerial positions remain strong overall. While pay can vary significantly depending on your level of experience, the firm where you work, and the region of the country where you live, below is a list of the nationwide median incomes for a variety of different managers:

Computer and Information Systems
 Managers: $146,360
Advertising, Promotions, and Marketing
 Managers: $135,900
Financial Managers: $129,890
Sales Managers: $126,640
Human Resource Managers: $116,720[40]

In short, if you want to be a manager, there are opportunities in almost every field. There may be fewer middle management positions available in firms, but managers remain a vital part of most industries and will continue to be long into the future—especially as navigating global business becomes ever more complex.

chapter seven

organization, teamwork, and communication

GaudiLab/Shutterstock

LEARNING OBJECTIVES

After reading this chapter, you will be able to:

LO 7-1 Explain the importance of organizational culture.

LO 7-2 Describe how organizational structures develop.

LO 7-3 Describe how specialization and departmentalization help an organization achieve its goals.

LO 7-4 Determine how organizations assign responsibility for tasks and delegate authority.

LO 7-5 Compare and contrast some common forms of organizational structure.

LO 7-6 Distinguish between groups and teams.

LO 7-7 Identify the types of groups that exist in organizations.

LO 7-8 Describe how communication occurs in organizations.

An organization's structure determines how well it makes decisions and responds to problems, and it influences employees' attitudes toward their work. A suitable structure can minimize a business's costs and maximize its efficiency. Even companies that operate within the same industry may utilize different organizational structures. For example, in the consumer electronics industry, Samsung is organized as a conglomerate with separate business units or divisions. Samsung is largely decentralized. Apple, under CEO Tim Cook, has moved from a hierarchical structure to a more collaborative approach among divisions.[1] On the other hand, Ford Motor Co.'s board views the CEO, Jim Hackett, as being in charge of the firm's strategy in a more hierarchical structure.[2] A manufacturing firm, like Ford, may require more leadership and control from the top.

Because a business's structure can so profoundly affect its success, this chapter will examine organizational structure in detail. First, we discuss how an organization's culture affects its operations. Then we consider the development of structure, including how tasks and responsibilities are organized through specialization and departmentalization. Next, we explore some of the forms organizational structure may take. Finally, we consider communications within business. ■

LO 7-1 Explain the importance of organizational culture.

ORGANIZATIONAL CULTURE

One of the most important aspects of organizing a business is determining its **organizational culture**, a firm's shared values, beliefs, traditions, philosophies, rules, and role models for behavior. Also called corporate culture, an organizational culture exists in every organization, regardless of size, organizational type, product, or profit objective. Sometimes behaviors, programs, and policies enhance and support the organizational culture. For instance, the sixth-largest accounting firm, Grant Thornton, established an unlimited vacation policy to give its employees more freedom. Less than 1 percent of American firms have this policy, but it seems to be growing in companies like Netflix, where employees have greater autonomy. Some speculate, however, that these policies will only work at firms with employees who are already highly motivated to work hard and are less likely to take vacations in the first place.[3] A firm's culture may be expressed formally through its mission statement, codes of ethics, memos, manuals, and ceremonies, but it is more commonly expressed informally. Examples of informal expressions of culture include dress codes (or the lack thereof), work habits, extracurricular activities, and stories. Employees often learn the accepted standards through discussions with co-workers.

McDonald's has organizational cultures focused on quality, service, cleanliness, and value. Nordstrom stresses a culture of excellent customer service. As a result, employees are empowered to use their best judgment in delivering the best services.[4] When such values are shared by all members of an organization, they will be expressed in its relationships with customers. However, organizational cultures that fail to understand the values of their customers may experience rejection. The values and integrity of customers must always be considered. Google's culture is focused more on metrics and sales of advertising than customer values. Companies such as Cisco have pulled advertisements from

organizational culture a firm's shared values, beliefs, traditions, philosophies, rules, and role models for behavior.

Google embraces a corporate culture that focuses on employee happiness. The tech company offers perks and benefits like in-office gyms and fitness areas, free meals, and more.
Uladzik Kryhin/Shutterstock

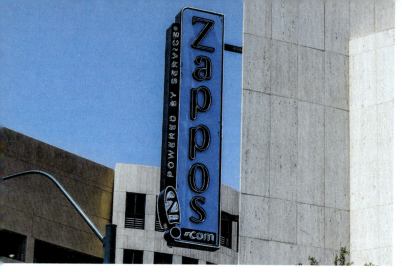

The Zappos tagline "Powered by Service" emphasizes the company's focus on its customers.

Jonathan Weiss/Alamy Stock Photo

structure the arrangement or relationship of positions within an organization.

organizational chart a visual display of the organizational structure, lines of authority (chain of command), staff relationships, permanent committee arrangements, and lines of communication.

YouTube because of concerns over the possibility of appearing next to sensitive material.[5]

Organizational culture helps ensure that all members of a company share values and suggests rules for how to behave and deal with problems within the organization. When Kevin Johnson became the CEO of Starbucks, he had to embrace the corporate culture that founder and former CEO Howard Schultz built. Employees like to work at Starbucks because of the firm's culture. It was troubling to executives when a Starbucks manager in Philadelphia had two minority customers removed from the restaurant. The company's move to support their ethical organizational culture was swift and decisive. They offered a half day of racial sensitivity training in the vast majority of their company-owned restaurants.[6] The key to success in any organization is satisfying stakeholders, especially customers. Establishing a positive organizational culture sets the tone for all other decisions, including building an efficient organizational structure.

LO 7-2 Describe how organizational structures develop.

DEVELOPING ORGANIZATIONAL STRUCTURE

Structure is the arrangement or relationship of positions within an organization. Rarely is an organization, or any group of individuals working together, able to achieve common objectives without some form of structure, whether that structure is explicitly defined or only implied. A professional baseball team such as the Colorado Rockies is a business organization with

an explicit formal structure that guides the team's activities so that it can increase game attendance, win games, and sell souvenirs such as T-shirts. But even an informal group playing softball for fun has an organization that specifies who will pitch, catch, bat, coach, and so on. Governments and nonprofit organizations also have formal organizational structures to facilitate the achievement of their objectives. Getting people to work together efficiently and coordinating the skills of diverse individuals require careful planning. Developing appropriate organizational structures is, therefore, a major challenge for managers in both large and small organizations.

An organization's structure develops when managers assign work tasks and activities to specific individuals or work groups and coordinate the diverse activities required to reach the firm's objectives. When Best Buy, for example, has a sale, the store manager must work with the advertising department to make the public aware of the sale, with department managers to ensure that extra salespeople are scheduled to handle the increased customer traffic, and with merchandise buyers to ensure that enough sale merchandise is available to meet expected consumer demand. All the people occupying these positions must work together to achieve the store's objectives.

The best way to begin to understand how organizational structure develops is to consider the evolution of a new business such as a clothing store. At first, the business is a sole proprietorship in which the owner does everything—buys, prices, and displays the merchandise; does the accounting and tax records; and assists customers. As the business grows, the owner hires a salesperson and perhaps a merchandise buyer to help run the store. As the business continues to grow, the owner hires more salespeople. The growth and success of the business now require the owner to be away from the store frequently, meeting with suppliers, engaging in public relations, and attending trade shows. Thus, the owner must designate someone to manage the salespeople and maintain the accounting, payroll, and tax functions. If the owner decides to expand by opening more stores, still more managers will be needed. Figure 7.1 shows these stages of growth with three **organizational charts** (visual displays of organizational structure, chain of command, and other relationships).

Growth requires organizing—the structuring of human, physical, and financial resources to achieve objectives in an effective and efficient manner. Growth necessitates hiring people who have specialized skills. With more people and greater specialization, the organization needs to develop a formal structure to function efficiently. Often organizations undergo structural changes when the current structure is no longer deemed effective. For instance, Zappos, an online shoe and clothing retailer, adopted an organizational structure called a *holacracy*, a structure in which job titles are abandoned, traditional managers are eliminated, and authority is distributed to teams. After several years, Zappos adjusted its strategy by bringing back managers while retaining a circular hierarchy.[7] Zappos has a major focus on service, but its structure might not work for a manufacturing

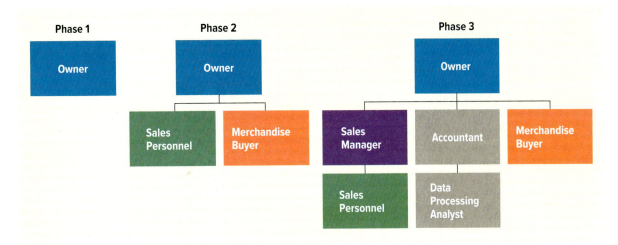

firm like Ford that is more hierarchical in its structure. As we shall see, structuring an organization requires that management assign work tasks to specific individuals and departments and assign responsibility for the achievement of specific organizational objectives.

LO 7-3 Describe how specialization and departmentalization help an organization achieve its goals.

ASSIGNING TASKS

For a business to earn profits from the sale of its products, its managers must first determine what activities are required to achieve its objectives. At Celestial Seasonings, for example, employees must purchase herbs from suppliers, dry the herbs and place them in tea bags, package and label the tea, and then ship the packages to grocery stores around the country. Other necessary activities include negotiating with supermarkets and other retailers for display space, developing new products, planning advertising, managing finances, and managing employees. All these activities must be coordinated, assigned to work groups, and controlled. Two important aspects of assigning these work activities are specialization and departmentalization.

Specialization

After identifying all activities that must be accomplished, managers then break these activities down into specific tasks that can be handled by individual employees. This division of labor into small, specific tasks and the assignment of employees to do a single task is called **specialization**.

The rationale for specialization is efficiency. People can perform more efficiently if they master just one task rather than

all tasks. In *The Wealth of Nations,* 18th-century economist Adam Smith discussed specialization, using the manufacture of straight pins as an example. Individually, workers could produce 20 pins a day when each employee produced complete pins. Thus, 10 employees working independently of each other could produce 200 pins a day. However, when one worker drew the wire, another straightened it, a third cut it, and a fourth ground the point, 10 workers could produce 48,000 pins per day.[8] To save money and achieve the benefits of specialization, some companies outsource and hire temporary workers to provide key skills. Many highly skilled, diverse, experienced workers are available through temp agencies.

specialization the division of labor into small, specific tasks and the assignment of employees to do a single task.

Specialization means workers do not waste time shifting from one job to another, and training is easier. However, efficiency is not the only motivation for specialization. Specialization also occurs when the activities that must be performed within an organization are too numerous for one person to handle. Recall the example of the clothing store. When the business was young and small, the owner could do everything; but when the business grew, the owner needed help waiting on customers, keeping the books, and managing other business activities.

Overspecialization can have negative consequences. Employees may become bored and dissatisfied with their jobs, and the result of their unhappiness is likely to be poor quality work, more injuries, and high employee turnover. In extreme cases, employees in crowded specialized electronic plants are unable to form working relationships with one another. In some factories in Asia, workers are cramped together and overworked. Fourteen global vehicle manufacturers pledged to increase their oversight of the factories in their supply chain to ensure human rights

departmentalization
the grouping of jobs into working units usually called departments, units, groups, or divisions.

and healthy working conditions. However, the task is monumental for these global companies because their supply chains encompass many different countries with different labor practices, and it can be difficult to oversee the operations of dozens of supplier and subcontractors.[9] This is why some manufacturing firms allow job rotation so that employees do not become dissatisfied and leave. Although some degree of specialization is necessary for efficiency, because of differences in skills, abilities, and interests, all people are not equally suited for all jobs. We examine some strategies to overcome these issues in the chapter titled "Motivating the Workforce."

Departmentalization

After assigning specialized tasks to individuals, managers next organize workers doing similar jobs into groups to make them easier to manage. **Departmentalization** is the grouping of jobs into working units usually called departments, units, groups, or divisions. As we shall see, departments are commonly organized by function, product, geographic region, or customer (Figure 7.2). Most companies use more than one departmentalization plan to enhance productivity. For instance, many consumer goods manufacturers have departments for specific product lines (beverages, frozen dinners, canned goods, and so on) as well as departments dealing with legal, purchasing,

▼**FIGURE 7.2** Departmentalization

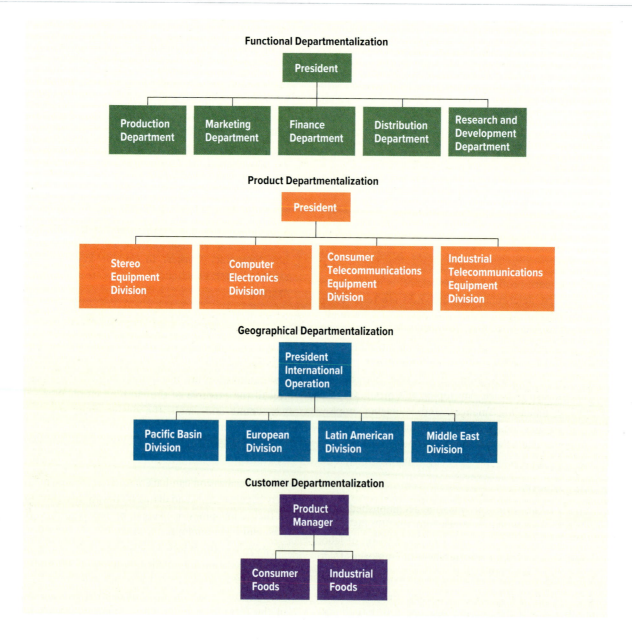

functional departmentalization
the grouping of jobs that perform similar functional activities, such as finance, manufacturing, marketing, and human resources.

product departmentalization
the organization of jobs in relation to the products of the firm.

geographical departmentalization
the grouping of jobs according to geographic location, such as state, region, country, or continent.

finance, human resources, and other business functions. For smaller companies, accounting can be set up online, almost as an automated department. Accounting software can handle electronic transfers so you never have to worry about a late bill. Many city governments also have departments for specific services (e.g., police, fire, waste disposal) as well as departments for legal, human resources, and other business functions.

Functional Departmentalization.

Functional departmentalization groups jobs that perform similar functional activities, such as finance, manufacturing, marketing, and human resources. Each of these functions is managed by an expert in the work done by the department—an engineer supervises the production department; a financial executive supervises the finance department. This approach is common in small organizations. PopSockets uses functional departmentalization with Brand Protection, Design & Development, Finance, Human Resources, IT, Marketing, and Operations.[10] A weakness of functional departmentalization is that because it tends to emphasize departmental units rather than the organization as a whole, decision making that involves more than one department may be slow, and it requires greater coordination. Thus, as businesses grow, they tend to adopt other approaches to organizing jobs.

Product Departmentalization.

Product departmentalization, as you might guess, organizes jobs around the products of the firm. Unilever has global units, including personal care, foods, refreshment, and home care.[11] Each division develops and implements its own product plans, monitors the results, and takes corrective action as necessary. Functional activities—production, finance, marketing, and others—are located within each product division. Consequently, organizing by products duplicates functions and resources and emphasizes the product rather than achievement of the organization's overall objectives. However, it simplifies decision making and helps coordinate all activities related to a product or product group. PepsiCo is organized into seven business units: (1) PepsiCo Beverages North America; (2) Frito-Lay North America; (3) Quaker Foods North America; (4) Latin America; (5) Europe; (6) Africa, Middle East, South Asia; and (7) Asia Pacific, Australia/New Zealand,

The Coca-Cola Company has five operating regions: Asia Pacific; Europe, Middle East & Africa; Latin America; North America; and Bottling Investments.

Testing/Shutterstock

China. PepsiCo has actually adopted a combination of two types of departmentalization. While it clearly uses product departmentalization in North America, the company also chooses to divide its segments into geographic regions—a type of geographic departmentalization.[12]

Geographical Departmentalization.

Geographical departmentalization groups jobs according to geographic location, such as a state, region, country, or continent. Diageo, the premium beverage company known for brands such as Johnnie Walker and Tanqueray, is organized into five geographic regions, allowing the company to get closer to its customers and respond more quickly and efficiently to regional competitors.[13] Multinational corporations often use a geographical approach because of vast differences between different regions. Coca-Cola, General Motors, and Caterpillar are organized by region. However, organizing by region requires a large administrative staff and control system to coordinate operations, and tasks are duplicated among the different regions.

> **"Organizing by region requires a large administrative staff and control system to coordinate operations, and tasks are duplicated among the different regions."**

customer departmentalization the arrangement of jobs around the needs of various types of customers.

delegation of authority giving employees not only tasks but also the power to make commitments, use resources, and take whatever actions are necessary to carry out those tasks.

responsibility the obligation, placed on employees through delegation, to perform assigned tasks satisfactorily and be held accountable for the proper execution of work.

accountability the principle that employees who accept an assignment and the authority to carry it out are answerable to a superior for the outcome.

centralized organization a structure in which authority is concentrated at the top and very little decision-making authority is delegated to lower levels.

Customer Departmentalization. Customer departmentalization arranges jobs around the needs of various types of customers. This allows companies to address the unique requirements of each group. Airlines, such as British Airways and Southwest Airlines, provide prices and services customized for either business/frequent travelers or infrequent/vacationing customers. Customer departmentalization, like geographical departmentalization, does not focus on the organization as a whole and therefore requires a large administrative staff to coordinate the operations of the various groups.

LO 7-4 Determine how organizations assign responsibility for tasks and delegate authority.

ASSIGNING RESPONSIBILITY

After all workers and work groups have been assigned their tasks, they must be given the responsibility to carry them out. Management must determine to what extent it will delegate responsibility throughout the organization and how many employees will report to each manager.

Delegation of Authority

Delegation of authority means not only giving tasks to employees but also empowering them to make commitments, use resources, and take whatever actions are necessary to carry out those tasks. Let's say a marketing manager at Nestlé has assigned an employee to design a new package that is less wasteful (more environmentally responsible) than the current package for one of the company's frozen dinner lines. To carry out the assignment, the employee needs access to information and the authority to make certain decisions on packaging materials, costs, and so on. Without the authority to carry out the assigned task, the employee would have to get the approval of others for every decision and every request for materials.

As a business grows, so do the number and complexity of decisions that must be made; no one manager can handle them all. 3M delegates authority to its employees by encouraging them to share ideas and make decisions. 3M believes employee ideas can have such an impact on the firm that it encourages them to spend 15 percent of their time working on and sharing their own projects. This "15 percent culture" has created the collaboration that drives innovation in the company.[14] Delegation of authority frees a manager to concentrate on larger issues, such as planning or dealing with problems and opportunities.

Delegation also gives a **responsibility**, or obligation, to employees to carry out assigned tasks satisfactorily and holds them accountable for the proper execution of their assigned work. The principle of **accountability** means that employees who accept an assignment and the authority to carry it out are answerable to a superior for the outcome. While there can be delegation of authority with employee responsibility, the manager delegating still is accountable for oversight of the final result. Returning to the Nestlé example, if the packaging design prepared by the employee is unacceptable or late, the employee must accept the blame. If the new design is innovative, attractive, and cost-efficient, as well as environmentally responsible, or is completed ahead of schedule, the employee will accept the credit.

The process of delegating authority establishes a pattern of relationships and accountability between a superior and his or her subordinates. The president of a firm delegates responsibility for all marketing activities to the vice president of marketing. The vice president accepts this responsibility and has the authority to obtain all relevant information, make certain decisions, and delegate any or all activities to his or her subordinates. The vice president, in turn, delegates all advertising activities to the advertising manager, all sales activities to the sales manager, and so on. These managers then delegate specific tasks to their subordinates. However, the act of delegating authority to a subordinate does not relieve the superior of accountability for the delegated job. Even though the vice president of marketing delegates work to subordinates, he or she is still ultimately accountable to the president for all marketing activities.

Degree of Centralization

The extent to which authority is delegated throughout an organization determines its degree of centralization.

Centralized Organizations. In a **centralized organization**, authority is concentrated at the top, and very little decision-making authority is delegated to lower levels. Although decision-making authority in centralized organizations rests with top levels of management, a vast amount of responsibility for carrying out daily and routine procedures is delegated to even the lowest levels of the organization. Many government

SUGAR BOWL BAKERY IS A SWEET SUCCESS

In the 1980s, a family of refugees from Vietnam came to the United States to start a new life. Brothers Tom, Binh, Andrew, Sam, and Paul Ly had a deeply ingrained spirit of teamwork. Despite limited baking experience, the brothers saved $40,000 and decided to purchase a struggling coffee shop in San Francisco to make Chinese doughnuts. To purchase the shop, they worked any jobs they could find and pooled together their money.

After the bakery opened, the brother shared operational responsibility. Andrew Ly took English language night courses so he could build business connections and promote the company. To improve their pastry selection, they sent their nephew to culinary school and hired a baker from a local competitor. Sugar Bowl Bakery grew to seven retail locations which became difficult to manage. When the economy slowed in 2008, the brothers sold their retail operations and the food service distribution to concentrate on selling to high-volume retailers like Walmart.

While Sugar Bowl Bakery began as a coffee and donut shop, today its dessert products are manufactured with modern technology and can be found in nationwide retailers including Starbucks, Costco, and Walgreens. The bakery is most well-known for its Madeleines, bite-sized brownies and 600-layer Petite Palmiers. It is still very much a team endeavor, with Andrew Ly as CEO and several second-generation children working at the bakery. This culture of shared responsibility has led to continual success for over 30 years. Today it is one of the largest minority-owned bakeries in the United States.[a]

💬 Critical Thinking Questions

1. How do the founders of Sugar Bowl Bakery use teamwork to make their bakery a success?

2. How do you think communication contributed to Sugar Bowl Bakery's current status?

3. Do you think Sugar Bowl has a centralized or decentralized structure? Why?

The United States Postal Service is a centralized organization which limits routine business decisions post offices can make.

Jonathan Weiss/Shutterstock

organizations, including the U.S. Army, the Postal Service, and the IRS, are centralized.

Businesses tend to be more centralized when the decisions to be made are risky and when low-level managers are not highly skilled in decision making. In the banking industry, for example, authority to make routine car loans is given to all loan managers, while the authority to make high-risk loans, such as for a large residential development, may be restricted to upper-level loan officers.

Overcentralization can cause serious problems for a company, in part because it may take longer for the organization as a whole to implement decisions and to respond to changes and problems on a regional or national scale. To avoid this, brands often test new product offerings at their retailers regionally to get feedback and make improvements before rolling out nationally. For example, McDonald's tested fresh beef in its Quarter Pounder regionally in the United States. The success of the tests allowed McDonald's to engage in a national rollout. The move was in response to competitors promoting their fresh beef and casting McDonald's frozen beef in a negative light.[15] Centralized decision making can also prevent front-line service employees from providing insights and recommendations to improve the customer experience as well as reporting and resolving problems.

> **decentralized organization** an organization in which decision-making authority is delegated as far down the chain of command as possible.

Decentralized Organizations.
A **decentralized organization** is one in which decision-making authority is delegated as far down the chain of command as possible. Decentralization is characteristic of organizations that operate in complex, unpredictable environments. Businesses that face intense competition often decentralize to improve responsiveness and enhance creativity. Lower-level managers who interact with the external environment often develop a good understanding of it and thus are able to react quickly to changes. Johnson & Johnson has a very decentralized, flat organizational structure.

Delegating authority to lower levels of managers may increase the organization's productivity. Decentralization requires that lower-level managers have strong decision-making skills. Ritz Carlton decentralized the ability to resolve guest issues by empowering employees with a discretionary spending budget. Hotel managers all the way down to entry-level employees can use up to $2,000 per guest to make them happy. This prevents upper management from having to approve individual resolutions.[16] In recent years, the trend has been toward more decentralized organizations, and some of the largest and most successful companies, including GE, IBM, Google, and Nike, have decentralized decision-making authority. Decentralization can be a key to being better, not just bigger. Nonprofit organizations can benefit from decentralization as well.

Span of Management

How many subordinates should a manager manage? There is no simple answer. Experts generally agree, however, that top managers should not directly supervise more than four to eight people, while lower-level managers who supervise routine tasks are capable of managing a much larger number of subordinates. For example, the manager of the finance department may supervise 25 employees, whereas the vice president of finance may supervise only five managers. **Span of management** (also called *span of control*) refers to the number of subordinates who report to a particular manager. A *wide span of management or control* exists when a manager directly supervises a very large number of employees. A *narrow span of management or control* exists when a manager directly supervises only a few subordinates (Figure 7.3). The United States Postal Service has varying spans of management. Its distribution operations supervisors have a 1:12 span of control (i.e., one supervisor for every 12 employees), while supervisors at international service centers have a 1:25 span of control.[17]

Should the span of management be wide or narrow? To answer this question, several factors need to be considered. A narrow span of management is appropriate when superiors and subordinates are not in close proximity, the manager has many responsibilities in addition to the supervision, the interaction between superiors and subordinates is frequent, and problems are common. However, when superiors and subordinates are located close to one another, the manager has few responsibilities other than supervision, the level of interaction between superiors and subordinates is low, few problems arise, subordinates are highly competent, and a set of specific operating procedures governs the activities of managers and their subordinates, a wide span of management will be more appropriate. Narrow spans of management are typical in centralized organizations, while wide spans of management are more common in decentralized firms.

Organizational Layers

Complementing the concept of span of management is **organizational layers**, the levels of management in an organization. Organizational layers relate to a description of the layers and number of layers in the organizational structure. Span of management or control covered in the last section is the number of subordinates, functions, or people that have need to be managed. A company with many layers of managers is considered tall; in a tall organization, the span of management is narrow (see Figure 7.3). Because each manager supervises only a few subordinates, many layers of management are necessary to carry out the operations of the business. For example, CVS has a tall organization structure with layers including branch managers, district leaders, district managers, operations managers, retail store managers, and more.[18] Because there are more managers in tall organizations than in flat organizations, administrative costs are usually higher. Communication is slower because information must pass through many layers.

Organizations with few layers are flat and have wide spans of management. When managers supervise a large number of employees, fewer management layers are needed to conduct the organization's activities. Managers in flat organizations typically perform more administrative duties than managers in tall organizations because there are fewer of them. They also spend more time supervising and working with subordinates.

▼ **FIGURE 7.3** Span of Management: Wide Span and Narrow Span

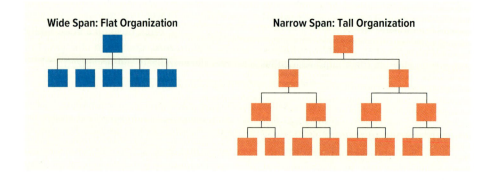

Wide Span: Flat Organization

Narrow Span: Tall Organization

Elon Musk founded SpaceX with the dream of resetting the standard for what is possible with rockets and space travel. Its rocket, Falcon 9, launched two astronauts into space in 2020, the first astronauts to orbit from U.S. soil in nine years. Falcon 9's success had its share of setbacks, with two failed launches that cast doubt on the company's abilities. However, SpaceX was able to recover—thanks in large part to president and COO Gwynne Shotwell.

Shotwell recognizes the value of strong communication and teamwork. As president, she knows she must align SpaceX's 6,000 employees behind a common vision. Shotwell seems well-suited to SpaceX's self-driven organizational culture. After spending a decade working for large aerospace companies like Aerospace Corp. and Microcosm, Shotwell took a risk and started working for the small startup SpaceX. Shotwell became the seventh employee to join the team as head of business development. The organizational culture inspired by Musk means that employees are always collaborating on how to make his seemingly impossible ideas into a reality.

Shotwell balances Musk as a less emotional and steadier leader for the day-to-day activities of the company. This involves pulling the company through crises. In 2016, one of the rockets exploded, an event she credits as a turning point in her career. Shotwell quickly realized that as the leader of the company, she needed to display confidence to the other employees. SpaceX investigators teamed up with each other to investigate the cause of the explosion. They were able to determine that the issue was due to the fuel tank. With this knowledge and Shotwell's support, SpaceX corrected for its mistakes and returned to flight three months later.[b]

🔵 Critical Thinking Questions

1. What characteristics does Gwynne Shotwell have that makes her a good fit for SpaceX's organizational culture?

2. How does SpaceX display teamwork to overcome challenges?

3. How do you think strong communication skills helped Gwynne Shotwell lead SpaceX through its explosion crisis?

Many of the companies that have decentralized also flattened their structures and widened their spans of management, often by eliminating layers of middle management. As mentioned earlier in this chapter, Johnson & Johnson has both a decentralized and flat organizational structure.

> **LO 7-5** Compare and contrast some common forms of organizational structure.

FORMS OF ORGANIZATIONAL STRUCTURE

Along with assigning tasks and the responsibility for carrying them out, managers must consider how to structure their authority relationships—that is, what structure the organization itself will have and how it will appear on the organizational chart. Common forms of organization include line structure, line-and-staff structure, multidivisional structure, and matrix structure.

Line Structure

The simplest organizational structure, **line structure**, has direct lines of authority that extend from the top manager to employees at the lowest level of the organization. For example, a convenience store employee at 7-Eleven may report to an assistant manager, who reports to the store manager, who reports to a regional manager, or, in an independent store, directly to the owner (Figure 7.4). This structure has a clear chain of command, which enables managers to make decisions quickly.

A mid-level manager facing a decision must consult only one person, his or her immediate supervisor. However, this structure requires that managers possess a wide range of knowledge and

> **line structure** the simplest organizational structure, in which direct lines of authority extend from the top manager to the lowest level of the organization.

▼**FIGURE 7.4** Line Structure

Convenience Store

Owner — Manager — Assistant Manager — Hourly Employee

line-and-staff structure a structure having a traditional line relationship between superiors and subordinates and also specialized managers—called staff managers—who are available to assist line managers.

restructure to change the basic structure of an organization.

multidivisional structure a structure that organizes departments into larger groups called divisions.

skills. They are responsible for a variety of activities and must be knowledgeable about them all. Line structures are most common in small businesses.

Line-and-Staff Structure

The **line-and-staff structure** has a traditional line relationship between superiors and subordinates, and specialized managers—called staff managers—are available to assist line managers (Figure 7.5). Line managers can focus on their area of expertise in the operation of the business, while staff managers provide advice and support to line departments on specialized matters such as finance, engineering, human resources, and the law. Staff managers do not have direct authority over line managers or over the line manager's subordinates, but they do have direct authority over subordinates in their own departments. However, line-and-staff organizations may experience problems with overstaffing and ambiguous lines of communication. Additionally, employees may become frustrated because they lack the authority to carry out certain decisions.

Multidivisional Structure

As companies grow and diversify, traditional line structures become difficult to coordinate, making communication difficult and decision making slow. When the weaknesses of the structure—the "turf wars," miscommunication, and working at cross-purposes—exceed the benefits, growing firms tend to **restructure**, or change the basic structure of an organization. Growing firms tend to restructure into the divisionalized form. A **multidivisional structure** organizes departments into larger groups called divisions. Just as departments might be formed on the basis of geography, customer, product, or a combination of these, so too divisions can be formed based on any of these methods of organizing. Within each of these divisions, departments may be organized by product, geographic region, function, or some combination of all three. Indra Nooyi, former CEO of PepsiCo, rearranged the company's organizational structure after taking the helm. Prior to her tenure, PepsiCo was

▼**FIGURE 7.5** Line-and-Staff Structure

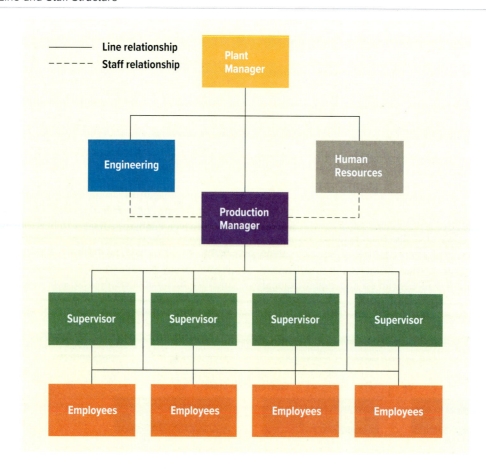

organized geographically. She created new units that span international boundaries and make it easier for employees in different geographic regions to share business practices.[19]

Multidivisional structures permit delegation of decision-making authority, allowing divisional and department managers to specialize. They allow those closest to the action to make the decisions that will affect them. Delegation of authority and divisionalized work also mean that better decisions are made faster, and they tend to be more innovative. Most importantly, by focusing each division on a common region, product, or customer, each is more likely to provide products that meet the needs of its particular customers. However, the divisional structure inevitably creates work duplication, which makes it more difficult to realize the economies of scale that result from grouping functions together.

Matrix Structure

Another structure that attempts to address issues that arise with growth, diversification, productivity, and competitiveness, is the matrix. A **matrix structure**, also called a project management structure, sets up teams from different departments, thereby creating two or more intersecting lines of authority (Figure 7.6). One of the first organizations to design and implement a matrix structure was the National Aeronautics and Space Administration (NASA) for the space program because it needed to coordinate different projects at the same time. The matrix structure superimposes project-based departments on the more traditional,

> **matrix structure** a structure that sets up teams from different departments, thereby creating two or more intersecting lines of authority; also called a project management structure.

▼**FIGURE 7.6** Matrix Structure

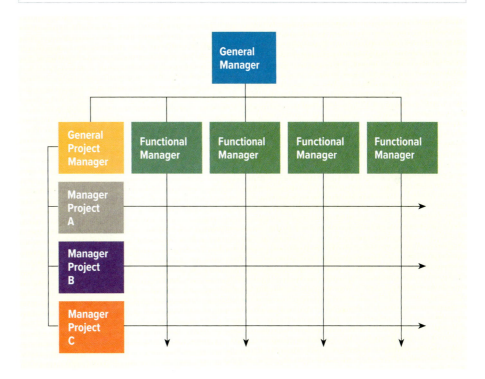

group two or more individuals who communicate with one another, share a common identity, and have a common goal.

team a small group whose members have complementary skills; have a common purpose, goals, and approach; and hold themselves mutually accountable.

function-based departments. Project teams bring together specialists from a variety of areas to work together on a single project, such as developing a new fighter jet. In this arrangement, employees are responsible to two managers—functional managers and project managers. Matrix structures are usually temporary: Team members typically go back to their functional or line department after a project is finished. However, more firms are becoming permanent matrix structures, creating and dissolving project teams as needed to meet customer needs. The aerospace industry was one of the first to apply the matrix structure, but today it is used by universities and schools, accounting firms, banks, and organizations in other industries.

Matrix structures provide flexibility, enhanced cooperation, and creativity, and they enable the company to respond quickly to changes in the environment by giving special attention to specific projects or problems. However, they are generally expensive and quite complex, and employees may be confused as to whose authority has priority—the project manager's or the immediate supervisor's.

and organizational success. Some experts now believe that highest productivity results only when groups become teams.[20]

Traditionally, a **group** has been defined as two or more individuals who communicate with one another, share a common identity, and have a common goal. A **team** is a small group whose members have complementary skills; have a common purpose, goals, and approach; and hold themselves mutually accountable.[21] Think of a team like a sports team. Members of a basketball team have different skill sets and work together to score and win the game. All teams are groups, but not all groups are teams. Table 7.1 points out some important differences between them. Work groups emphasize individual work products, individual accountability, and even individual leadership. Your class is a group that can further be separated into teams of two or three classmates. Work teams share leadership roles, have both individual and mutual accountability, and create collective work products. In other words, a work group's performance depends on what its members do as individuals, while a team's performance is based on creating a knowledge center and a competency to work together to accomplish a goal. On the other hand, it is also important for team members to retain their individuality and avoid becoming just "another face in the crowd." The purpose of teams should be toward collaboration versus collectivism. Although the team is working toward a common goal, it is important that all team members actively contribute their ideas and work together to achieve this common goal.[22]

LO 7-6 Distinguish between groups and teams.

THE ROLE OF GROUPS AND TEAMS IN ORGANIZATIONS

Regardless of how they are organized, most of the essential work of business occurs in individual work groups and teams, so we'll take a closer look at them now. There has been a gradual shift toward an emphasis on teams and managing them to enhance individual

LO 7-7 Identify the types of groups that exist in organizations.

The type of groups an organization establishes depends on the tasks it needs to accomplish and the situation it faces. Some specific kinds of groups and teams include committees, task forces, project teams, product-development teams, quality-assurance teams, and self-directed work teams. All of these can be *virtual teams*—employees in different locations who rely on e-mail, audio conferencing, Internet, videoconferencing (e.g., Zoom),

▼ **TABLE 7.1** Differences between Groups and Teams

Working Group	Team
Has strong, clearly focused leader	Has shared leadership roles
Has individual accountability	Has individual and group accountability
Has the same purpose as the broader organizational mission	Has a specific purpose that the team itself delivers
Creates individual work products	Creates collective work products
Runs efficient meetings	Encourages open-ended discussion and active problem-solving meetings
Measures its effectiveness indirectly by its effects on others (e.g., financial performance of the business)	Measures performance directly by assessing collective work products
Discusses, decides, and delegates	Discusses, decides, and does real work together

Source: Robert Gatewood, Robert Taylor, and O. C. Ferrell, *Management: Comprehension Analysis and Application,* (New York: McGraw-Hill Education, 1995), p. 427.

committee a permanent, formal group that performs a specific task.

task force a temporary group of employees responsible for bringing about a particular change.

project teams groups similar to task forces that normally run their operation and have total control of a specific work project.

product-development teams a specific type of project team formed to devise, design, and implement a new product.

or other collaboration tools to accomplish their goals. For example, Trello, a visual project management platform, has a marketing team that is completely virtual, meeting three times per week via video conference and connecting through collaboration tools like Slack and Google Drive.[23] Virtual teams are becoming a part of everyday business, accelerated by the COVID-19 (coronavirus) pandemic.[24] Virtual teams have also opened up opportunities for different companies. For instance, inside salespeople use virtual technology such as e-mail and social media to connect with prospects and clients.[25]

Committees

A **committee** is usually a permanent, formal group that does some specific task. For example, many firms have a compensation or finance committee to examine the effectiveness of these areas of operation as well as the need for possible changes. Ethics committees are formed to develop and revise codes of ethics, suggest methods for implementing ethical standards, and review specific issues and concerns.

Task Forces

A **task force** is a temporary group of employees responsible for bringing about a particular change. They typically come from across all departments and levels of an organization. Task force membership is usually based on expertise rather than organizational position. Occasionally, a task force may be formed from individuals outside a company. Coca-Cola has often used task forces to address problems and provide recommendations for improving company practices or products. While some task forces might last a few months, others last for years. When Coca-Cola faced lawsuits alleging discrimination practices in hiring and promotion, it developed a five-year task force to examine pay and promotion practices among minority employees. Its experiences helped Coca-Cola realize the advantages of having a cross-functional task force made up of employees from different departments, and it continued to use task forces to tackle major company issues. Other companies that have also recognized the benefits of task forces include IBM, Prudential, and General Electric.[26]

Teams

Teams are becoming far more common in the U.S. workplace as businesses strive to enhance productivity and global competitiveness. In general, teams have the benefit of being able to pool members' knowledge and skills and make greater use of them than can individuals working alone. Team building is becoming increasingly popular in organizations, with around half of executives indicating their companies had team-building training. Teams require

Florida State University formed a temporary Brand Development Task Force comprised of campus leaders to refine and develop the university's brand.

Mario Houben/CSM/REX/Shutterstock

harmony, cooperation, synchronized effort, and flexibility to maximize their contribution.[27] Teams can also create more solutions to problems than can individuals. Furthermore, team participation enhances employee acceptance of, understanding of, and commitment to team goals. Teams motivate workers by providing internal rewards in the form of an enhanced sense of accomplishment for employees as they achieve more, and external rewards in the form of praise and certain perks. Consequently, they can help get workers more involved. They can help companies be more innovative, and they can boost productivity and cut costs.

According to psychologist Ivan Steiner, team productivity peaks at about five team members. People become less motivated and group coordination becomes more difficult after this size. Jeff Bezos, Amazon CEO, says that he has a "two-pizza rule": If a team cannot be fed by two pizzas, it is too large. Keep teams small enough where everyone gets a piece of the action.[28]

Project Teams. **Project teams** are similar to task forces, but normally they run their operation and have total control of a specific work project. Like task forces, their membership is likely to cut across the firm's hierarchy and be composed of people from different functional areas. They are almost always temporary, although a large project, such as designing and building a new airplane at Boeing Corporation, may last for years.

Product-development teams are a special type of project team formed to devise, design, and implement a new product. Sometimes product-development teams exist within a functional area—research

quality-assurance teams (or quality circles) small groups of workers brought together from throughout the organization to solve specific quality, productivity, or service problems.

self-directed work team (SDWT) a group of employees responsible for an entire work process or segment that delivers a product to an internal or external customer.

and development—but now they more frequently include people from numerous functional areas and may even include customers to help ensure that the end product meets the customers' needs. Intel informs its product development process through indirect input from customers. It has a social scientist on staff who leads a research team on how customers actually use products. This is done mainly by observation and asking questions. Once enough information is gathered, it is relayed to the product-development team and incorporated into Intel's designs.[29]

Quality-Assurance Teams.

Quality-assurance teams, sometimes called **quality circles**, are fairly small groups of workers brought together from throughout the organization to solve specific quality, productivity, or service problems. Although the *quality circle* term is not as popular as it once was, the concern about quality is stronger than ever. Companies such as IBM and Xerox as well as companies in the automobile industry have used quality circles to shift the organization to a more participative culture. The use of teams to address quality issues will no doubt continue to increase throughout the business world.

Self-Directed Work Teams.

A **self-directed work team (SDWT)** is a group of employees responsible for an entire work process or segment that delivers a product to an internal or external customer.[30] SDWTs permit the flexibility to change rapidly to meet the competition or respond to customer needs. The defining characteristic of an SDWT is the extent to which it is empowered or given authority to make and implement work decisions. Thus, SDWTs are designed to give employees a feeling of "ownership" of a whole job. Employees at 3M as well as an increasing number of companies encourage employees to be active to perform a function or operational task. With shared team responsibility for work outcomes, team members often have broader job assignments and cross-train to master other jobs, thus permitting greater team flexibility.

LO 7-8 Describe how communication occurs in organizations.

COMMUNICATING IN ORGANIZATIONS

Communication within an organization can flow in a variety of directions and from a number of sources, each using both oral and written forms of communication. The success of communication systems within the organization has a tremendous effect on the overall success of the firm. Communication mistakes can lower productivity and morale.

Alternatives to face-to-face communications—such as meetings—are growing, thanks to technology such as voicemail, e-mail, social media, video conferencing, and online newsletters. Many companies use internal networks called intranets to share information with employees. Intranets increase communication across different departments and levels of management and help with the flow of everyday business activities. Another innovative approach is cloud computing. Rather than using physical products, companies using cloud computing technology can access computing resources and information over a network. Cloud computing allows companies to have more control over computing resources and can be less expensive than hardware or software. Salesforce.com uses cloud computing in its customer relationship management solutions.[31] Companies can even integrate aspects of social media into their intranets, allowing employees to post comments and pictures, participate in polls, and create group calendars. However, increased access to the Internet at work has also created many problems, including employee abuse of company e-mail and Internet access.[32] The increasing use of e-mail as a communication tool

Cloud-based tools like Dropbox, iCloud, Google Drive, Salesforce, and more are transforming internal communication at companies. They allow employees to share documents, collaborate with their teams, and even work from home.

Krisztian Bocsi/Bloomberg/Getty Images

Type	Definition	Examples
Upward	Flows from lower to higher levels of the organization	Progress reports, suggestions for improvement, inquiries, grievances
Downward	Traditional flow of communication from upper organizational levels to lower organizational levels	Directions, assignments of tasks and responsibilities, performance feedback, details about strategies and goals, speeches, employee handbooks, job descriptions
Horizontal	Exchange of information among colleagues and peers on the same organizational level, such as across or within departments, who inform, support, and early coordinate activities both within the department and between other departments	Task forces, project teams, communication from the finance department to the marketing department concerning budget requirements
Diagonal	When individuals from different levels and different departments communicate	A manager from the finance department communicates with a lower-level manager from the marketing department

also inundates employees and managers with e-mails, making it easier to overlook individual communications. For this reason, it is advised that employees place a specific subject in the subject line, keep e-mails brief, and avoid using e-mail if a problem would be better solved through telephone contact or face-to-face interaction.[33]

Formal and Informal Communication

Formal channels of communication are intentionally defined and designed by the organization. They represent the flow of communication within the formal organizational structure, as shown on organizational charts. Table 7.2 describes the different forms of formal communication. Traditionally, formal communication patterns were classified as vertical and horizontal, but with the increased use of teams and matrix structures, formal communication may occur in a number of patterns (Figure 7.7).

Along with the formal channels of communication shown on an organizational chart, all firms communicate informally as well. Communication between friends, for instance, cuts across department, division, and even management-subordinate boundaries. Such friendships and other nonwork social relationships comprise the *informal organization* of a firm, and their impact can be great.

The most significant informal communication occurs through the **grapevine**, an informal channel of communication, separate from management's formal, official communication channels. Grapevines exist in all organizations. Information passed along the grapevine may relate to the job or organization, or it may be gossip and rumors unrelated to either. The accuracy of grapevine information has been of great concern to managers.

Managers can turn the grapevine to their advantage. Using it as a "sounding device" for possible new policies is one example. Managers can obtain valuable information from the grapevine that could improve decision making. Some organizations use the grapevine to their advantage by floating ideas, soliciting feedback, and reacting accordingly. People love to gossip, and managers need to be aware that grapevines exist in every organization. Managers who understand how the grapevine works also can use it to their advantage by feeding it facts to squelch rumors and incorrect information. For instance, rather than confronting employees about gossip and placing them on the defense, some employers ask employees—especially those who are the spreaders of gossip—for assistance in squelching the untrue rumors. This tactic turns employees into advocates for sharing truthful information.[34]

grapevine an informal channel of communication, separate from management's formal, official communication channels.

Monitoring Communications

Technological advances and the increased use of electronic communication in the workplace have made monitoring its use

▼**FIGURE 7.7** The Flow of Communication in an Organizational Hierarchy

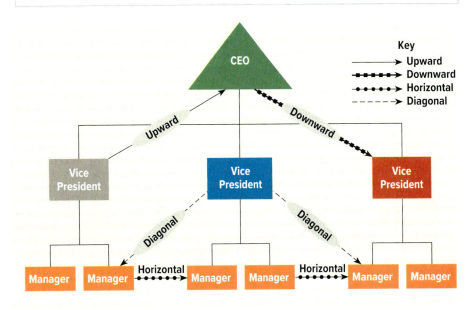

Hitachi Social Innovation allows employers globally to implement AI tools to increase happiness, improve productivity, and reduce costs.

Source: Hitachi Corporation

necessary for most companies. Failing to monitor employees' use of e-mail, social media, and the Internet can be costly. Many companies require that employees sign and follow a policy on appropriate Internet use. These agreements often require that employees will use corporate computers only for work-related activities. Additionally, some companies use software programs and surveillance apps to monitor employee computer usage.[35] Instituting practices that show respect for employee privacy but do not abdicate employer responsibility are increasingly necessary in today's workplace. Merck, for instance, has a section on employee privacy in its code of conduct that reassures both current and former employees that their information will be protected and used only for legitimate business purposes.[36]

Artificial intelligence (AI) is having a significant impact on workplace monitoring, benchmarking, and understanding how employees "feel" about their jobs. More than 40 percent of employers globally have implemented AI processes within their organization. In the advertisement, Hitachi promotes its AI tools to achieve various business goals including increasing happiness, improving productivity, and reducing costs. Hitachi has developed technology to monitor worker behavior data using artificial intelligence and gives businesses advice for improving happiness. With such an understanding of employee attitudes, you can correct or improve the negative experiences in the workplace and enhance the positive ones. Software companies have developed artificial intelligence tools that can make routine human resource decisions such as hiring, firing, and raises. There are concerns that AI technology might incorporate biases that can lead to discriminatory decision making.[37]

Improving Communication Effectiveness

Without effective communication, the activities and overall productivity of projects, groups, teams, and individuals will be diminished. Communication is an important area for a firm to address at all levels of management. Apple supplier Foxconn is one example of how essential communication is to a firm. Despite criticisms of unfair labor conditions, the Fair Labor Association determined that Foxconn had formal procedures in place at its factories to prevent many major accidents. However, it concluded that the firm had a communication problem. These procedures were not being communicated to the factory workers, contributing to unsafe practices and two tragic explosions.[38]

One of the major issues of effective communication is in obtaining feedback. If feedback is not provided, then communication will be ineffective and can drag down overall performance. Managers should always encourage feedback, including concerns and challenges about issues. Listening is a skill that involves hearing, and most employees listen much more than they actively communicate to others. Therefore, managers should encourage employees to provide feedback—even if it is negative. It is interesting to note that employees list a failure to listen to their concerns as a top complaint in the workplace.[39] Employees often notice issues that managers overlook, and employee feedback can alert managers to these issues. This will allow the organization to identify strengths and weaknesses and make adjustments when needed. At the same time, strong feedback mechanisms help to empower employees as they feel that their voices are being heard.

Interruptions can be a serious threat to effective communication. Various activities can interrupt the message. For example, interjecting a remark can create discontinuance in the

STRONG AND EFFECTIVE COMMUNICATION CHANNELS ARE A REQUIREMENT FOR COMPANIES TO DISTRIBUTE INFORMATION TO DIFFERENT LEVELS OF THE COMPANY.

communication process or disrupt the uniformity of the message. Even small interruptions can be a problem if the messenger cannot adequately understand or interpret the communicator's message. One suggestion is to give the communicator space or time to make another statement rather than quickly responding or making your own comment.

Strong and effective communication channels are a requirement for companies to distribute information to different levels of the company. Businesses have several channels for communication, including face-to-face, e-mail, phone, and written communication (e.g., memos). Each channel has advantages and disadvantages, and some are more appropriate to use than others. For instance, a small task requiring little instruction might be communicated through a short memo or e-mail. An in-depth task would most likely require a phone conversation or face-to-face contact. E-mail has become especially helpful for businesses, and both employees and managers are increasingly using e-mail rather than phone conversations. However, it is important that employees use e-mail correctly. Inappropriate use of e-mail can include forwarding sexually explicit or otherwise offensive material. Additionally, many employees have used work e-mail accounts to send personal information. This may be against company policy. E-mail sent from corporate accounts is the property of the firm, so employees should exert caution in making sure their e-mail messages contain appropriate content. It is, therefore, important for companies to communicate their e-mail policies throughout the organization. Communicators using e-mail, whether managers or employees, must exert caution before pushing that "Send" button.

The use of Zoom and Webex for video conferencing, team collaboration, and even daily communication between employees is changing the work environment. During the COVID-19 pandemic employees were forced to work from home. Many continued to work from home on a permanent basis due to increases in productivity. Employees developed new communication skills that were more effective than traditional e-mail.

E-mail is a dominant form of workplace communication in many offices. Employees need to be coached on best practices in using their e-mail so that it's not a distraction or disruptive to productivity. On average, users check their e-mail every 11 minutes, and 84 percent have their e-mail up at all times. On average, we receive 87 e-mails each day, with 70 percent being opened within six seconds of their receipt. It takes us just over a minute to transition to our original tasks interrupted by e-mail. Some guidance on best practices in managing workplace productivity suggests that it's best to check your e-mail every 45 minutes. Also, responding too quickly and during evenings and weekends can increase stress and diminish productivity.[40]

Team Exercise

Assign the responsibility of providing the organizational structure for a company one of your team members has worked for. Was your organization centralized or decentralized in terms of decision making? Would you consider the span of control to be wide or narrow? Were any types of teams, committees, or task forces utilized in the organization? Report your work to the class.

Communication is necessary in helping every organizational member understand what is expected of him or her. Many business problems can be avoided if clear communication exists within the company. Even the best business strategies are of little use if those who will oversee them cannot understand what is intended. Communication might not seem to be as big of a concern to management as finances, human resources, and marketing, but in reality, it can make the difference between successful implementation of business activities or failure. ■

ORGANIZATION, TEAMWOK, AND COMMUNICATION // Are You Ready to Apply These Skills on the Job? /

Jobs dealing with organizational culture and structure are usually at the top of the organization. If you want to be a CEO or high-level manager, you will help shape these areas of business. On the other hand, if you are an entrepreneur or small-business person, you will need to make decisions about assigning tasks, departmentalization, and assigning responsibility. Even managers in small organizations have to make decisions about decentralization, span of management, and forms of organizational structure. Micro-entrepreneurs with five or fewer employees still have to make decisions about assigning tasks and whether to work as a group or a team. While these decisions may be part of your job, there are usually no job titles dealing with these specific areas. Specific jobs that attempt to improve organizational culture could include ethics and compliance positions as well as those who are in charge of communicating memos, manuals, and policies that help establish the culture. These positions will be in communications, human resources, and positions that assist top organizational managers.

Teams are becoming more common in the workplace, and it is possible to become a member of a product development group or quality assurance team. There are also human resource positions that encourage teamwork through training activities. The area of corporate communications provides lots of opportunities for specific jobs that facilitate communication systems. Thanks to technology, there are job positions to help disseminate information through online newsletters, intranets, or internal computer networks to share information to increase collaboration. In addition to the many advances using electronic communications, there are technology concerns that create new job opportunities. Monitoring workplace communications such as the use of e-mail and the Internet has created new industries. There have to be internal controls in the organization to make sure that the organization does not engage in any copyright infringement. If this is an area of interest, there are specific jobs that provide an opportunity to use your technological skills to assist in maintaining appropriate standards in communicating and using technology.

If you go to work for a large company with many divisions, you can expect a number of positions dealing with the tasks discussed here. If you go to work for a small company, you will probably engage in most of these tasks as a part of your position. Organizational flexibility requires individual flexibility, and those employees willing to take on new domains and challenges will be the employees who survive and prosper in the future.

chapter eight

chapter 8

managing operations
and supply chains

Zapp2Photo/Shutterstock

LEARNING OBJECTIVES

After reading this chapter, you will be able to:

LO 8-1 Define *operations management.*

LO 8-2 Differentiate between operations and manufacturing.

LO 8-3 Explain how operations management differs in manufacturing and service firms.

LO 8-4 Describe the elements involved in planning and designing an operations system.

LO 8-5 Specify some techniques managers may use to manage the logistics of transforming inputs into finished products.

LO 8-6 Assess the importance of quality in operations management.

All organizations create products—goods, services, or ideas—for customers. Thus, organizations as diverse as Tesla, Subway, UPS, and a public hospital share a number of similarities relating to how they transform resources into the products we enjoy. Most hospitals use similar admission procedures, while online social media companies, like Facebook and TikTok, use their technology and operating systems to create social networking opportunities and sell advertising. Such similarities are to be expected. But even organizations in unrelated industries take similar steps in creating goods or services. The check-in procedures of hotels and commercial airlines are comparable, for example. The way Subway assembles a sandwich and the way Tesla assembles a car are similar (both use multiple employees in an assembly line). These similarities are the result of operations management, the focus of this chapter.

Here, we discuss the role of production or operations management in acquiring and managing the resources necessary to create goods and services. Production and operations management involve planning and designing the processes that will transform those resources into finished products, managing the movement of those resources through the transformation process, and ensuring that the products are of the quality expected by customers. ■

THE NATURE OF OPERATIONS MANAGEMENT

Operations management (OM), the development and administration of the activities involved in transforming resources into goods and services, is of critical importance. Operations managers oversee the transformation process and the planning and designing of operations systems, managing logistics, quality, and productivity. Quality and productivity have become fundamental aspects of operations management because a company that cannot make products of the quality desired by consumers, using resources efficiently and effectively, will not be able to remain in business. OM is the "core" of most organizations because it is responsible for the creation of the organization's goods and services. Some organizations like General Motors produce tangible products, but service is an important part of the total product for the customer.

Historically, operations management has been called "production" or "manufacturing" primarily because of the view that it was limited to the manufacture of physical goods. Its focus was on methods and techniques required to operate a factory efficiently. The change from "production" to "operations" recognizes the increasing importance of organizations that provide services and ideas. Additionally, the term *operations* represents an interest in viewing the operations function as a whole rather than simply as an analysis of inputs and outputs.

Today, OM includes a wide range of organizational activities and situations outside of manufacturing, such as health care, food service, banking, entertainment, education, transportation, and charity. Thus, we use the terms **manufacturing** and **production** interchangeably to represent the activities and processes used in making *tangible* products, whereas we use the broader term **operations** to describe those processes used in the making of *both tangible and intangible products*. Manufacturing provides tangible products such as the Apple Watch, and operations also provides intangibles such as a stay at Wyndham Hotels and Resorts.

operations management (OM) the development and administration of the activities involved in transforming resources into goods and services.

manufacturing the activities and processes used in making tangible products; also called production.

production the activities and processes used in making tangible products; also called manufacturing.

operations the activities and processes used in making both tangible and intangible products.

inputs the resources—such as labor, money, materials, and energy—that are converted into outputs.

outputs the goods, services, and ideas that result from the conversion of inputs.

The Transformation Process

At the heart of operations management is the transformation process through which **inputs** (resources such as labor, money, materials, and energy) are converted into **outputs** (goods, services, and ideas). The transformation process combines inputs in predetermined ways using different equipment, administrative procedures, and technology to create a product (Figure 8.1). To ensure that this process generates quality products efficiently, operations managers control the process by taking measurements (feedback) at various points in the transformation process and comparing them to previously established standards. If there is any deviation between the actual and desired outputs, the manager may take some sort of corrective action. For example, if an airline has a standard of 90 percent of its flights departing on time but only 80 percent depart on time, a 10 percentage point negative deviation exists. All adjustments made to create a satisfying product are a part of the transformation process.

Transformation may take place through one or more processes. In a business that manufactures oak furniture, for example, inputs pass through several processes before being turned into the final outputs—furniture that has been designed to meet the desires of customers (Figure 8.2). The furniture maker must first strip the oak trees of their bark and saw them into appropriate sizes—one step in the transformation process. Next, the firm dries the strips of oak lumber, a second form of transformation. Third, the dried wood is routed into its appropriate shape and made smooth. Fourth, workers assemble and treat the wood pieces, then stain or varnish the piece of assembled furniture. Finally, the completed piece of furniture is stored until it can be shipped to customers at the appropriate time. Of course, many businesses choose to eliminate some of these stages by purchasing already processed materials—lumber, for example—or outsourcing some tasks to third-party firms with greater expertise.

LO 8-3 Explain how operations management differs in manufacturing and service firms.

Operations Management in Service Businesses

Different types of transformation processes take place in organizations that provide services, such as airlines, colleges, and most nonprofit organizations. An airline transforms inputs such as employees, time, money, and equipment through processes such as booking flights, flying airplanes, maintaining equipment, and training crews. The output of these processes is flying passengers and/or packages to their destinations. In a nonprofit organization like Denver Rescue Mission, inputs such as money, food, and volunteer time and labor are used to transform raw materials into meals for needy families. In this setting, transformation processes include fundraising and promoting the cause in order to gain new volunteers and donations of supplies, as well as preparing ingredients, prepping food, and serving hot meals. Transformation processes occur in all organizations, regardless of what they produce or their objectives. For most organizations, the ultimate objective is for the produced outputs to be worth more than the combined costs of the inputs.

FIGURE 8.1 The Transformation Process of Operations Management

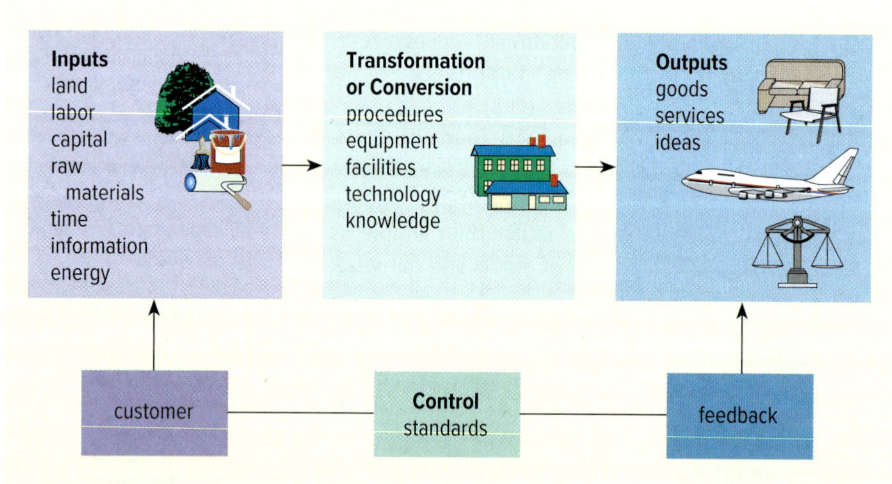

FIGURE 8.2
Inputs, Outputs, and Transformation Processes in the Manufacture of Oak Furniture

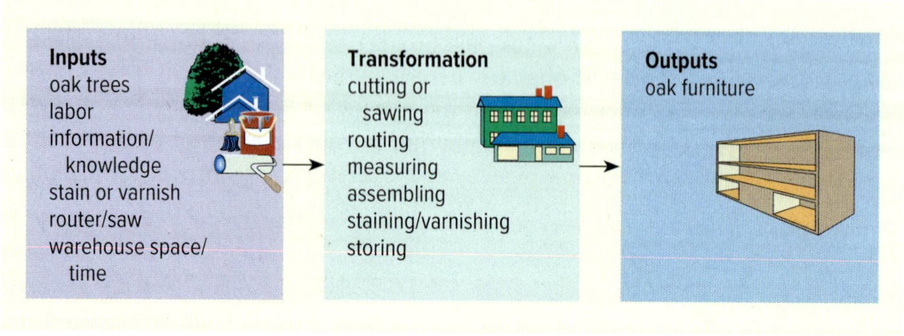

Service Characteristics	Examples
Intangibility	Going to a concert or sports event such as baseball, basketball, or football
Inseparability of production and consumption	Going to a chiropractor; air travel; veterinary services
Perishability	Seats at a speaker's presentation
Customization	Haircut; legal services; tax consultation
Customer contact	Restaurants; retailing such as Macy's

Sources: Adapted from Valerie A. Zeithaml, A. Parasuraman, and Leonard L. Berry, *Delivering Quality Service: Balancing Customer Perceptions and Expectations* (New York: Free Press, 1990); K. Douglas Hoffman and John E.G. Bateson, *Essentials of Services Marketing* (Mason, OH; Cengage Learning, 2001); Ian P. McCarthy, Leyland Pitt, and Pierre R. Berthon, "Service Customization Through Dramaturgy," *Mass Customization*, 2011, pp. 45–65.

Unlike tangible goods, services effectively are actions or performances that must be directed toward the consumers who use them. Thus, there is a significant customer-contact component to most services. Examples of high-contact services include health care, real estate, tax preparation, and food service. The amount of training for service or customer-contact personnel can vary significantly depending on the business, industry, or culture of the company. For example, first-year, full-time employees at the Container Store receive 200 hours of training compared to an eight-hour average for the industry. The Container Store culture embraces the importance of employees, stating that one great person equals three good people.[1] Low-contact services, such as the online auction-and-purchase services provided by eBay, often have a strong high-tech component. Table 8.1 shows common characteristics of services.

Regardless of the level of customer contact, service businesses strive to provide a standardized process, and technology offers an interface that creates an automatic and structured response. The ideal service provider will be high tech and high touch.

Amazon, Wegmans, and Patagonia are consistently recognized for their positive corporate reputation in the annual Axios Harris corporate reputation survey.

piotrkt/123RF

Amazon, for instance, has one of the highest customer service ratings. It provides a site that is easily navigable, and it has fast shipping times to deliver high-quality customer service. Amazon, through the commitment of CEO Jeff Bezos, encourages customers to e-mail him with any concerns. He routes the messages to the appropriate Amazon employee, asking for an explanation of why the problem occurred and how it can be prevented in the future.[2] Thus, service organizations must build their operations around good execution, which comes from hiring and training excellent employees, developing flexible systems, customizing services, and maintaining adjustable capacity to deal with fluctuating demand.[3]

Another challenge related to service operations is that the output is generally intangible and even perishable. Few services can be saved, stored, resold, or returned.[4] A seat on an airline or a table in a restaurant, for example, cannot be sold or used at a later date. Because of the perishability of services, it can be extremely difficult for service providers to accurately estimate the demand in order to match the right supply of a service. If an airline overestimates demand, for example, it will still have to fly each plane even with empty seats. For example, as a result of overestimating demand during the winter, Scandinavian airlines SAS cut 1,500 flights from its schedule.[5] The flight costs the same regardless of whether it is 50 percent full or 100 percent full, but the former will result in much higher costs per passenger. If the airline underestimates demand, the result can be long lines of annoyed customers or even the necessity of bumping some customers off of an overbooked flight.

Businesses that manufacture tangible goods and those that provide services or ideas are similar yet different. For example, both types of organizations must make design and operating decisions. Most goods are manufactured prior to purchase, but most services are performed after purchase. Flight attendants at Southwest Airlines, hotel service personnel at The Ritz Carlton, and even the Denver Broncos football team engage in performances that are a part of the total product. Though manufacturers and service providers often perform similar activities, they also differ in several respects. We can classify these differences in five basic ways.

Nature and Consumption of Output. First, manufacturers and service providers differ in the nature and consumption of their output. For example, the term *manufacturer* implies a firm that makes tangible products. A service provider, on the other hand, produces more intangible outputs such as U.S. Postal Service delivery of priority mail or a business stay in a Westin hotel. As mentioned earlier, the very nature of the service provider's product requires a higher degree of customer contact. Moreover, the actual performance of the service typically occurs at the point of consumption. At the Westin, business travelers may be very pleased with the Heavenly Bed and Shower System, both proprietary and luxury amenities. Or, customers may like getting points through their reward membership or upgrades based on their status with Starwood Preferred

Blaze Pizza's inputs are components such as pepperoni, mozzarella, mushrooms, onions, and sausage, while its outputs are customized pizzas.

Sorbis/Shutterstock

Guests. Automakers, on the other hand, can separate the production of a car from its actual use, but the service dimension requires closer contact with the consumer. Manufacturing, then, can occur in an isolated environment, away from the customer. However, service providers, because of their need for customer contact, are often more limited than manufacturers in selecting work methods, assigning jobs, scheduling work, and exercising control over operations. For this reason, Starbucks uses artificial intelligence (AI) to help store managers predict staffing needs and create schedules.[6] The quality of the service experience is often controlled by a service-contact employee. However, some hospitals are studying the manufacturing processes and quality control mechanisms applied in the automotive industry in an effort to improve their service quality. By analyzing work processes to find unnecessary steps to eliminate and using teams to identify and address problems as soon as they occur, these hospitals are slashing patient waiting times, decreasing inventories of wheelchairs, readying operating rooms sooner, and generally moving patients through their hospital visit more quickly, with fewer errors, and at a lower cost.[7]

Uniformity of Inputs.
A second way to classify differences between manufacturers and service providers has to do with the uniformity of inputs. Manufacturers typically have more control over the amount of variability of the resources they use than do service providers. For example, each customer calling Fidelity Investments is likely to require different services due to differing needs, whereas many of the tasks required to manufacture a Ford Focus are the same across each unit of output. Consequently, the products of service organizations tend to be more "customized" than those of their manufacturing counterparts. Consider, for example, a haircut versus a bottle of shampoo. The haircut is much more likely to incorporate your specific desires (customization) than is the bottle of shampoo.

Uniformity of Output.
Manufacturers and service providers also differ in the uniformity of their output, the final product. Because of the human element inherent in providing services, each service tends to be performed differently. Not all grocery checkers, for example, wait on customers in the same way. If a barber or stylist performs 15 haircuts in a day, it is unlikely that any two of them will be exactly the same. Consequently, human and technological elements associated with a service can result in a different day-to-day or even hour-to-hour performance of that service. The service experience can even vary at McDonald's or Burger King despite the fact that the two chains employ very similar procedures and processes. Moreover, no two customers are exactly alike in their perception of the service experience. Health care offers another excellent example of this challenge. Every diagnosis, treatment, and surgery varies because every individual is different. In manufacturing, the high degree of automation available allows manufacturers to generate uniform outputs and, thus, the operations are more effective and efficient. For example, we expect luxury bicycles—such as the Giant TCR Advanced SL Disc, which sells for up to $10,500—to have extremely high standards for quality and performance.

Labor Required.
A fourth point of difference is the amount of labor required to produce an output. Service providers are generally more labor-intensive (require more labor) because of the high level of customer contact, perishability of the output (must be consumed immediately), and high degree of variation of inputs and outputs (customization). For example, Adecco provides temporary support personnel. Each temporary worker's performance determines Adecco's product quality. A manufacturer, on the other hand, is likely to be more capital-intensive because of the machinery and technology used in the mass production of highly similar goods. For instance, it would take a considerable investment for Ford to make an electric car that has batteries with a longer life.

Measurement of Productivity.
The final distinction between service providers and manufacturers involves the measurement of productivity for each output produced. For manufacturers, measuring productivity is fairly straightforward because of the tangibility of the output and its high degree of uniformity. For the service provider, variations in demand (e.g., higher demand for air travel in some seasons than in others), variations in service requirements from job to job, and the intangibility of the product make productivity measurement more difficult. Consider, for example, how much easier it is to measure the productivity of employees involved in the production of Intel computer processors as opposed to those serving the needs of Prudential Securities' clients.

It is convenient and simple to think of organizations as being either manufacturers or service providers as in the preceding discussion. In reality, however, most organizations are a combination of the two, with both tangible and intangible qualities embodied in what they produce. For example, Samsung provides customer services such as toll-free hotlines and warranty protection, while banks may sell checks and other tangible products that complement their primarily intangible product offering. Thus, we consider "products" to include both tangible physical goods and intangible service offerings. It is the level of tangibility of its principal product that tends to classify a company as either a manufacturer or a service provider. From an OM standpoint, this level of tangibility greatly influences the nature of the company's operational processes and procedures.

> **Before a company can produce any product, it must first decide what it will produce and for what group of customers.**

LO 8-4   Describe the elements involved in planning and designing an operations system.

PLANNING AND DESIGNING OPERATIONS SYSTEMS

Before a company can produce any product, it must first decide what it will produce and for what group of customers. It must then determine what processes it will use to make these products as well as the facilities it needs to produce them. These decisions comprise operations planning. Although planning was once the sole realm of the production and operations department, today's successful companies involve all departments within an organization, particularly marketing and research and development, in these decisions.

Planning the Product

Before making any product, a company first must determine what consumers want and then design a product to satisfy that want. Most companies use marketing research (discussed in the chapter titled "Customer-Driven Marketing") to determine the kinds of goods and services to provide and the features they must possess. Twitter and Facebook provide new opportunities for businesses to discover what consumers want, then design the product accordingly. Less than 50 percent of companies use social media in the new-product-development process.[8] Marketing research can also help gauge the demand for a product and how much consumers are willing to pay for it. But, when a market's environment changes, firms have to be flexible. Marketing research is advancing from wearables that measure skin response to geo-located survey delivery. Artificial intelligence (AI) can be used to measure people's expressions as they watch events.[9]

SUNNY SKIES AHEAD FOR WEATHER INSIGHTS

Every type of weather has impacts on businesses. IBM partnered with Oxford Economics to survey 1,000 global corporate-level executives to see how weather affects their organizations. Half stated that weather insights can create competitive advantages where they can start to reduce costs when weather strikes and increase revenues. All respondents said improving their use of weather data could reduce annual legal, insurance, and risk mitigation costs, while 99 percent said that they could also reduce operational costs.

However, 69 percent are uncertain how weather data creates value. Difficulty integrating weather data into operational processes, understanding how weather affects decision making, and gathering data are areas where organizations can turn negative impacts into positives. Organizations should start with a clear strategy and understanding of how weather affects their business functions.

Subway, Campbell's, and Panera Bread are known for their research and weather predictions as a way to optimize product offerings with the fluctuations in customer demands. Accurate weather predictions help businesses make more informed decisions, from determining whether to stock up on certain inventory to modifying supply chain orders to predicting if the weather will affect shipping and delivery. Every industry can find positives when it comes to accurate weather predictions.

NASCAR and The Weather Company, a subsidiary of IBM, made a multiyear agreement to optimize weather-related decision making for NASCAR. NASCAR gained access to The Weather Company's weather data and used a weather station at each race to improve race operations and fan engagement. This information helped NASCAR "minimize delays" and improved customer experiences. NASCAR is one organization that is taking advantage of weather data to optimize its business functions.[a]

Critical Thinking Questions

1. What are some ways that accurate weather predictions can be used to improve business operations?

2. How do you think weather affects a company's supply chain?

3. How can NASCAR use the data from The Weather Company to improve operations and create better customer satisfaction?

JUST Inc., the company behind JUST Mayo, spent six years developing its latest product JUST Egg, an egg-free, scrambled egg product.

Tada Images/Shutterstock

standardization the making of identical, interchangeable components or products.

modular design the creation of an item in self-contained units, or modules, that can be combined or interchanged to create different products.

customization making products to meet a particular customer's needs or wants.

Developing a product can be a lengthy, expensive process. For example, Uber and Volvo partnered to create a driverless car. The $300 million alliance paired Volvo's manufacturing and design expertise together with Uber's ridesharing market and a staff that increasingly consists of former employees of Carnegie Mellon University's robotics department.[10] Uber and Volvo unveiled their first production car, the XC90 SUV.[11] Most companies work to reduce development time and costs. By joining together, companies can pool their resources and reduce the time it takes to develop new products. Once a firm has developed an idea for a product that customers will buy, it must then plan how to produce the product.

Within a company, the engineering or research and development department is charged with turning a product idea into a workable design that can be produced economically. In smaller companies, a single individual (perhaps the owner) may be solely responsible for this crucial activity. Regardless of who is responsible for product design, planning does not stop with a blueprint for a product or a description of a service; it must also work out efficient production of the product to ensure that enough is available to satisfy consumer demand. How does a company like Snapper transform steel, aluminum, and other materials into a mower design that satisfies consumer and environmental requirements? Operations managers must plan for the types and quantities of materials needed to produce the product, the skills and quantity of people needed to make the product, and the actual processes through which the inputs must pass in their transformation to outputs.

Designing the Operations Processes

Before a firm can begin production, it must first determine the appropriate method of transforming resources into the desired product. Often, consumers' specific needs and desires dictate a process. A state's needs for toll booths for its highway systems may be very structured and consistent, and engineering and manufacturing would be standardized. On the other hand, a bridge often must be customized so that it is appropriate for the site and expected load; furthermore, the bridge must be constructed on site rather than in a factory. Typically, products are designed to be manufactured by one of three processes: standardization, modular design, or customization.

Standardization.
Most firms that manufacture products in large quantities for many customers have found that they can make them cheaper and faster by standardizing designs. **Standardization** is making identical, interchangeable components or even complete products. With standardization, a customer may not get exactly what he or she wants, but the product generally costs less than a custom-designed product. Television sets, ballpoint pens, and tortilla chips are standardized products; most are manufactured on an assembly line. Standardization speeds up production and quality control and reduces production costs. And, as in the example of the toll booths, standardization provides consistency so that customers who need certain products to function uniformly all the time will get a product that meets their expectations. Standardization becomes more complex on a global scale because different countries have different standards for quality. To help solve this problem, the International Organization for Standardization (ISO) has developed a list of global standards that companies can adopt to assure stakeholders that they are complying with the highest quality, environmental, and managerial guidelines. ISO standards are discussed later in the chapter.

Modular Design.
Modular design involves building an item in self-contained units, or modules, that can be combined or interchanged to create different products. The Container Store, for example, uses the modular design in many of its storage solutions. This allows for customers to mix and match components for customized design. Because many modular components are produced as integrated units, the failure of any portion of a modular component usually means replacing the entire component. Modular design allows products to be repaired quickly, thus reducing the cost of labor, but the component itself is expensive, raising the cost of repair materials. Many automobile manufacturers use modular design in the production process. Manufactured homes are built on a modular design and often cost about one-fourth the cost of a conventionally built house.

Customization.
Customization is making products to meet a particular customer's needs or wants. Products produced in this way are generally unique. Such products include repair services, photocopy services, custom artwork, jewelry, and furniture, as well as large-scale products such as bridges, ships, and

computer software. Lancôme sells Le Teint Particulier, a custom foundation with 72,000 possibilities. After customers have their skin tone scanned and select their skin type and desired coverage, the foundation is made on the spot. Because of the complexities of offering a customized product, the foundation is only available at select Nordstrom locations.[12] Mass customization relates to making products that meet the needs or wants of a large number of individual customers. The customer can select the model, size, color, style, or design of the product. Dell can customize a computer with the exact configuration that fits a customer's needs. Services such as fitness programs and travel packages can also be custom designed for a large number of individual customers. For both goods and services, customers get to make choices and have options to determine the final product.

Blockchain. Blockchain information technology could alter processes throughout virtually every industry including supply chain, health care, and even online advertising. The blockchain is a secure, public database (or ledger) that records all transactions and is spread across multiple computers. The global blockchain is difficult to tamper with and growing rapidly. By 2030, the business value added by blockchain is expected to reach $3.1 trillion.[13] In the age of tech-savvy consumers and continuous innovation, the adoption of blockchain technology is occurring quicker than ever. Microsoft, for example, is using blockchain technology for Xbox's digital contracts to track digital media content, rights, and royalties for content creators. The technology reduces fraud and improves efficiency.[14] Blockchain technology continues to be tested by companies across all industries and could change the way we do almost anything.

DID YOU KNOW?

Hershey's has the production capacity to make 390,000 Kit Kats per day.[b]

Dell is well known for mass customization. Customers select a base model computer then customize the graphics card, hard drive, keyboard, battery, display, and more.

Jonathan Weiss/Shutterstock

Planning Capacity

Planning the operational processes for the organization involves two important areas: capacity planning and facilities planning. The term **capacity** basically refers to the maximum load that an organizational unit can carry or operate. The unit of measurement may be a worker or machine, a department, a branch, or even an entire plant. Maximum capacity can be stated in terms of the inputs or outputs provided. For example, an electric plant might state plant capacity in terms of the maximum number of kilowatt-hours that can be produced without causing a power outage, while a restaurant might state capacity in terms of the maximum number of customers who can be effectively—comfortably and courteously—served at any one particular time.

Efficiently planning the organization's capacity needs is an important process for the operations manager. Capacity levels that fall short can result in unmet demand, and consequently, lost customers. On the other hand, when there is more capacity available than needed, operating costs are driven up needlessly due to unused and often expensive resources. To avoid such situations, organizations must accurately forecast demand and then plan capacity based on these forecasts. Another reason for the importance of efficient capacity planning has to do with long-term commitment of resources. Often, once a capacity decision—such as factory size—has been implemented, it is very difficult to change the decision without incurring substantial costs. Large companies have come to realize that although change can be expensive, not adjusting to future demand and stakeholder desires will be more expensive in the long run. Responding to consumers' concern for the environment, Toyota and its subsidiaries have acquired ISO 14001 certification for environmental management at many of its locations worldwide.[15] These systems help firms monitor their impact on the environment.

Planning Facilities

Once a company knows what process it will use to create its products, it then can design and build an appropriate facility in which to make them. Many products are manufactured in factories, but others are produced in stores, at home, or where the product ultimately will be used. Companies must decide where to locate their operations facilities, what layout is best for producing their particular product, and even what technology to apply to the transformation process.

Many firms are developing both a traditional organization for customer contact and a virtual organization. Charles Schwab Corporation, a securities brokerage and investment company, maintains traditional offices and has developed complete telephone and Internet services for customers. Through its website,

fixed-position layout
a layout that brings all resources required to create the product to a central location.

project organization
a company using a fixed-position layout because it is typically involved in large, complex projects such as construction or exploration.

process layout a layout that organizes the transformation process into departments that group related processes.

intermittent organizations
organizations that deal with products of a lesser magnitude than do project organizations; their products are not necessarily unique but possess a significant number of differences.

product layout a layout requiring that production be broken down into relatively simple tasks assigned to workers, who are usually positioned along an assembly line.

continuous manufacturing organizations
companies that use continuously running assembly lines, creating products with many similar characteristics.

computer-assisted design (CAD) the design of components, products, and processes on computers instead of on paper.

investors can obtain personal investment information and trade securities over the Internet without leaving their home or office.

Facility Location.
Where to locate a firm's facilities is a significant question because, once the decision has been made and implemented, the firm must live with it due to the high costs involved. When a company decides to relocate or open a facility at a new location, it must pay careful attention to factors such as proximity to market, availability of raw materials, availability of transportation, availability of power, climatic influences, availability of labor, community characteristics (quality of life), and taxes and inducements. Inducements and tax reductions have become an increasingly important criterion in recent years. To increase production and to provide incentives for small startups, many states are offering tax inducements for solar companies. State governments are willing to forgo some tax revenue in exchange for job growth, getting in on a burgeoning industry, as well as the good publicity generated by the company. However, it is still less expensive for many firms to use overseas factories. Apple has followed the lead of other major companies by locating its manufacturing facilities in Asia to take advantage of lower labor and production costs. The facility-location decision is complex because it involves the evaluation of many factors, some of which cannot be measured with precision. Because of the long-term impact of the decision, however, it is one that cannot be taken lightly.

Facility Layout.
Arranging the physical layout of a facility is a complex, highly technical task. Some industrial architects specialize in the design and layout of certain types of businesses. There are three basic layouts: fixed-position, process, and product.

A company using a **fixed-position layout** brings all resources required to create the product to a central location. The

product—perhaps an office building, house, hydroelectric plant, or bridge—does not move. A company using a fixed-position layout may be called a **project organization** because it is typically involved in large, complex projects such as construction or exploration. Project organizations generally make a unique product, rely on highly skilled labor, produce very few units, and have high production costs per unit.

Firms that use a **process layout** organize the transformation process into departments that group related processes. A metal fabrication plant, for example, may have a cutting department, a drilling department, and a polishing department. A hospital may have cardiology, urgent care, neurology, obstetrics and gynecology units, and so on. These types of organizations are sometimes called **intermittent organizations**, which deal with products of a lesser magnitude than do project organizations, and their products are not necessarily unique but possess a significant number of differences. Doctors, makers of custom-made cabinets, commercial printers, and advertising agencies are intermittent organizations because they tend to create products to customers' specifications and produce relatively few units of each product. Because of the low level of output, the cost per unit of product is generally high.

The **product layout** requires that production be broken down into relatively simple tasks assigned to workers, who are usually positioned along an assembly line. Workers remain in one location, and the product moves from one worker to another. Each person in turn performs his or her required tasks or activities. Companies that use assembly lines are usually known as **continuous manufacturing organizations**, so named because once they are set up, they run continuously, creating products with many similar characteristics. Examples of products produced on assembly lines are automobiles, television sets, vacuum cleaners, toothpaste, and meals from a cafeteria. Continuous manufacturing organizations using a product layout are characterized by the standardized product they produce, the large number of units produced, and the relatively low unit cost of production.

Many companies actually use a combination of layout designs. For example, an automobile manufacturer may rely on an assembly line (product layout) but may also use a process layout to manufacture parts.

Technology.
Every industry has a basic, underlying technology that dictates the nature of its transformation process. Today business models are changing how the transformation process occurs. As mentioned earlier, blockchain information systems, AI, and computer integrated systems are driving changes throughout all industries.

Computers were introduced in the late 1950s by IBM. The operations function makes great use of computers in all phases of the transformation process. **Computer-assisted design (CAD)**, for example, helps engineers design components, products, and processes on the computer instead of on paper. CAD software is used to develop a 3D image. Then, the CAD file is sent to the printer. The printer is able to use layers of liquid, powder, paper, or metal to construct a 3D model.[16]

Computer-assisted manufacturing (CAM) goes a step further, employing specialized computer systems to actually guide and control the transformation processes. Such systems can monitor the transformation process, gathering information about the equipment used to produce the products and about the product itself as it goes from one stage of the transformation process to the next. The computer provides information to an operator who may, if necessary, take corrective action. In some highly automated systems, the computer itself can take corrective action.

Using **flexible manufacturing**, computers can direct machinery to adapt to different versions of similar operations. For example, with instructions from a computer, one machine can be programmed to carry out its function for several different versions of an engine without shutting down the production line for refitting.

The use of drones in business operations will vastly change the technology landscape. Drones refer to unmanned aerial vehicles and have long been used in military operations. Amazon is pursuing methods to use drones for package delivery. Amazon has secured a patent to allow it to drop packages delivered by its fleet of drones by parachute. The Federal Aviation Administration is in the process of establishing a new air traffic control system. Currently, only select companies have been approved to fly drones beyond visual line of sight.[17] It is surprising that drones have not played a larger role thus far; the adoption of drones in organizations could increase and greatly impact everything from shipping to logistics and delivery in the near future. For example, one of the current common uses of this technology involves drones sending automatic signals for reorder when an order has been placed or when inventory for a product is low and thus greatly improves inventory management. Whether it is adapting drones to a specific company to increase efficiency and capability or expanding the available applications as a whole, it is evident that drones could potentially handle many activities associated with operations.[18]

AI relates to machine (computer) learning that is able to perform activities and tasks that usually require human intelligence such as decisions, visual perception, and speech recognition. In short, it makes computers act like humans. According to the Brookings Institution, AI could disrupt 25 percent of U.S. jobs, but the timeline is uncertain. However, many predict AI will create more jobs than it takes, including new roles that do not exist today. This should be especially true in manufacturing supply chain operations and distribution. Robotic processes will include software bots with AI capabilities to perform tasks including object recognition. Robots are also becoming increasingly useful in the transformation process. These "steel-collar" workers have become particularly important in industries such as nuclear power, hazardous-waste disposal, ocean research, and space construction and maintenance, in which human lives would otherwise be at risk. Robots are used in

numerous applications by companies around the world. Many assembly operations—cars, electronics, metal products, plastics, chemicals, and numerous other products—depend on industrial robots. The economic impact of robots was quantified by two economists who found that for every robot per 1,000 employees, up to six employees lost their jobs and wages fell by three-fourths of a percent.[19]

Researchers continue to make more sophisticated robots, extending their use beyond manufacturing and space programs to various industries, including laboratory research, education, medicine, and household activities. There are many advantages in using robotics, such as more successful surgeries, re-shoring manufacturing activities back to America, energy conservation, and safer work practices. The United States is the fourth largest market for industrial robots. The strongest market is China, with a 40 percent share of the market for industrial robots projected by the end of the decade.[20]

When all these technologies—CAD/CAM, flexible manufacturing, robotics, computer systems, and more—are integrated, the result is **computer-integrated manufacturing (CIM)**, a complete system that designs products, manages machines and materials, and controls the operations function. Companies adopt CIM to boost productivity and quality and reduce costs. Such technology, and computers in particular, will continue to make strong inroads into operations on two fronts—one dealing with the technology involved in manufacturing and one dealing with the administrative functions and processes used by operations managers. The operations manager must be willing to work with computers and other forms of technology and to develop a high degree of computer literacy.

Sustainability and Manufacturing

Manufacturing and operations systems are moving quickly to establish environmental sustainability and minimize negative impact on the natural environment. Sustainability deals with conducting activities in such a way as to provide for the long-term well-being of the natural environment, including all biological entities. Sustainability issues are becoming increasingly important to stakeholders and consumers, as they pertain to the future health of the planet. The Hershey Company is committed to working toward a long-term, sustainable cocoa supply, protecting the natural environment as a part of its "Cocoa for Good" sustainability initiative.[21] Some sustainability issues include pollution of the land, air, and water, climate change, waste management, deforestation, urban sprawl, protection of biodiversity, and

computer-assisted manufacturing (CAM) manufacturing that employs specialized computer systems to actually guide and control the transformation processes.

flexible manufacturing the direction of machinery by computers to adapt to different versions of similar operations.

computer-integrated manufacturing (CIM) a complete system that designs products, manages machines and materials, and controls the operations function.

More than 76 percent of Adobe workspaces are LEED-certified buildings, emphasizing the company's focus on sustainability.[c]

Katherine Welles/Shutterstock

MANAGING THE SUPPLY CHAIN

A major function of operations is **supply chain management**, which refers to connecting and integrating all parties or members of the distribution system in order to satisfy customers.[24] Supply chain is a part of distribution that will be discussed in more detail in the chapter titled "Dimensions of Marketing Strategy," where we cover marketing channels, which are the groups of organizations that make decisions about moving products from producers to consumers. We discuss supply chains here because it is a major component of operations within a business. It may help to think of the firms involved in a total distribution system as existing along a conceptual line, the combined impact of which results in an effective supply chain. Firms that are "upstream" in the supply chain (e.g., suppliers) and "downstream" (e.g., wholesalers and retailers) work together to serve customers and generate competitive advantage. Supply chain management requires marketing managers to work with other managers in operations, logistics, and procurement.

Procurement involves the processes to obtain resources to create value through sourcing, purchasing, and recycling materials and information. Procurement for many is synonymous with "buying" or "purchasing," but this is only a small part of what goes into the procurement activities within a supply chain. Decisions about where the supplies (including services) come from are very important. They are not just about price but also relate to where they are sourced and the integrity of the supplier. Also, recycling impact on the environment after consumption is an important consideration. An important process is the creation of a digital platform to link everything from production to consumer and involves sensors, mobile devices, cameras, and other systems that capture information for procurement. We discuss purchasing more in the next section.

Logistical concerns involve physical distribution and the selection of transportation modes. In transportation, digital networks that integrate the movement of products provide insights to import service and reduce cost. Inbound logistics, outbound logistics, and third-party logistics are all important pieces of these transportation nodes. *Inbound logistics* involves the movement of the raw materials, packaging, information, and other goods and services from the suppliers to the producers. Similarly, *outbound logistics* follows the finished products and information from the business customers and then to the final consumer. In order to pull this transportation process together, some companies use *third-party logistics*, which involves employing outside firms to move goods

supply chain management

connecting and integrating all parties or members of the distribution system in order to satisfy customers.

genetically modified foods. New Belgium Brewing is another company that illustrates green initiatives in operations and manufacturing. New Belgium was the first brewery to adopt 100 percent wind-powered electricity, reducing carbon emissions by 1,800 metric tons a year.

New Belgium Brewing demonstrates that reducing waste, recycling, conserving, and using renewable energy not only protect the environment but can also gain the support of stakeholders. Green operations and manufacturing can improve a firm's reputation along with customer and employee loyalty, leading to improved profits.

Much of the movement to green manufacturing and operations is the belief that global warming and climate change must decline. In the United States, roughly 40 percent of carbon dioxide emissions are accounted for by buildings; however, Leadership in Energy and Environmental Design (LEED)-certified buildings maintain a 34 percent lower emissions rate and consume 25 percent less energy, 11 percent less water, and reduce more than 80 million tons of waste.[22] Companies such as General Motors, Ford, and Tesla have responded by doubling down on electric vehicles. Tesla also makes sure that its manufacturing facilities operate sustainably by installing solar panels and other renewable sources of energy. Green products produced through green operations and manufacturing are our future. Cities around the United States are taking leadership roles, with Portland, Oregon, standing out as a leader in environmental initiatives. Portland boasts expansive parks, mass transit, sustainable eating, bicycle parking spots, and electricity-producing exercycles.[23] Government initiatives provide space for businesses to innovate their green operations and manufacturing.

Old Dominion Freight Line is a shipping company with regional as well as national services from shipping to supply chain consulting.

Source: Old Dominion Freight Line

Drones from U.S. company Zipline International deliver blood and medical supplies to Ghana hospitals to improve the country's supply chain.

Stephanie Aglietti/AFP/Getty Images

because they can transport them more efficiently than the company can themselves. One example is Old Dominion Freight Line. In the ad, Old Dominion highlights its ocean and air freight services for international shipments. With predictive analytics and AI orders, transportation decisions can be made based on customers' defined requirements, costs, and service options.[25]

Manufacturers, distributors, and retailers need to communicate with their supply-chain partners to provide real-time information. This provides the opportunity to advance capabilities and efficiencies in the supply chain. For these same reasons, and with so many variables, logistical disruptions can be massively harmful to the ability to adequately satisfy customer expectations and can even be fatal to the firm. Logistics management is just as important in managing services, enabling and communicating with partners. For example, health care providers must rely on manufacturers and distributors to perform many supply-chain activities from various unrelated items; food, medicine, and supplies that meet required standard logistics involve deliveries from vendors with inventories that accommodate the ability to provide health care services.

AI is moving rapidly across supply chain functions. AI has the potential to make the world more efficient in predictable, physical work such as assembly lines, packaging, shipping, and other repetitive tasks. Transportation, operations, and even purchasing can be implemented by machine learning. Self-driving trucks and other vehicles can be efficient, dependable, and less expensive in the long run. Additionally, drone technology has its challenges

but, as noted earlier, is nevertheless growing rapidly, with some estimating that drone services overall are worth more than $127 billion globally, $23 billion coming from transport. For example, Amazon is paving the way for new innovation with its ideas regarding consumer goods delivery. With skepticism and public safety concerns from consumers, Amazon is working more with lower-value, less fragile items to begin with before straying from traditional delivery methods for other goods. Amazon and drone technology as a whole could completely change the way logistics and the supply chain operate in the future.[26]

Blockchain, mentioned previously, is an emerging information technology that will change supply chain relationships. It is a distributed ledger that can manage blocks of information without the control of intermediaries or third parties. Information can be added but not deleted. Information asymmetry will be eliminated so all supply chain members will have almost total information regarding the product. This can empower buyers all the way to retail consumers. This information technology will make supply chain management the coordination center of operations, procurement, and logistics. As a result, AI and blockchain have tremendous supply chain implications. For example, Walmart is requiring all produce to be tracked from the field to the store. Carrefour S.A. customers can scan a chicken to determine when the egg was hatched, what food was consumed, what hormones were used, and other information that could relate to the product's quality. These advances in technology continue to push supply chain to one of the most important functions in business. Consumers are increasingly concerned with an important question: "How are our products being made?" Fair trade, organic food products, working conditions, child labor, concerns with sending jobs overseas, and regulatory mandates create major factors in decision making about operations. Technology in operations is driving a more digital enterprise system. Robotics, predictive analytics, the Internet of Things (IoT), driverless cars, drones, automation in identification of inventory, blockchain technology, AI, and network

purchasing the buying of all the materials needed by the organization; also called procurement.

inventory all raw materials, components, completed or partially completed products, and pieces of equipment a firm uses.

inventory optimization tools are changing the landscape of operations. By making profitable and responsible use of the materials and products sourced to them, and utilizing the information and capabilities afforded them through logistics, operational personnel can create extensive financial and brand value.

In this section, we look at elements of supply chain, including purchasing, managing inventory, outsourcing, and scheduling, which are vital tasks in the transformation of raw materials into finished goods. To illustrate logistics, consider a hypothetical small business—we'll call it Rushing Water Canoes Inc.—that manufactures aluminum canoes, which it sells primarily to sporting goods stores and river-rafting expeditions. Our company also makes paddles and helmets, but the focus of the following discussion is the manufacture of the company's quality canoes as they proceed through the logistics process.

Procurement

Purchasing is a part in procurement involved in the buying of all the materials needed by the organization. The purchasing department aims to obtain items of the desired quality in the right quantities at the lowest possible cost. Rushing Water Canoes, for example, must procure not only aluminum and other raw materials, and various canoe parts and components but also machines and equipment, manufacturing supplies (oil, electricity, and so on), and office supplies in order to make its canoes. People in the purchasing department locate and evaluate suppliers of these items. They must constantly be on the lookout for new materials or parts that will do a better job or cost less than those currently being used. The purchasing function can be quite complex and is one area made much easier and more efficient by technological advances. Advanced AI can uncover the highest value opportunities and empower organizations to unlock savings and increase profit.[27]

Not all companies purchase all of the materials needed to create their products. Oftentimes, they can make some components more economically and efficiently than can an outside supplier. On the other hand, firms sometimes find that it is uneconomical to make or purchase an item, and instead arrange to lease it from another organization. Many organizations lease equipment such as copiers that are costly to own and maintain and where significant product improvements occur over time. Whether to purchase, make, or lease a needed item generally depends on cost, as well as on product availability and supplier reliability.

Managing Inventory

Once the items needed to create a product have been procured, some provision has to be made for storing them until they are needed. Every raw material, component, completed or partially completed product, and piece of equipment a firm uses—its **inventory**—must be accounted for, or controlled. There are three basic types of inventory. *Finished-goods inventory* includes those products that are ready for sale, such as a fully assembled automobile ready to ship to a dealer. *Work-in-process inventory* consists of those products that are partly completed or are in some stage of the transformation process. At McDonald's, a cooking hamburger represents work-in-process inventory because it must go through several more stages before it can be sold to a customer. *Raw materials inventory* includes all the materials that have been purchased to be used as inputs for making other products. Nuts and bolts are raw materials for an automobile manufacturer, while hamburger patties, vegetables, and buns are raw materials for the fast-food restaurant. Our fictional Rushing Water Canoes has an inventory of materials for making canoes, paddles, and helmets, as well as its inventory of finished products for sale to consumers. **Inventory control** is the process of determining how many supplies and goods are needed and keeping track of quantities on hand, where each item is, and who is responsible for it.

Operations management must be closely coordinated with inventory control. The production of televisions, for example, cannot be planned without some knowledge of the availability of all the necessary materials—the chassis, picture tubes, color guns, and so forth. Also, each item held in inventory—any type of inventory—carries with it a cost. For example, storing fully assembled televisions in a warehouse to sell to a dealer at a future date requires not only the use of space but also the purchase of insurance to cover any losses that might occur due to fire or other unforeseen events.

Inventory managers spend a great deal of time trying to determine the proper inventory level for each item. The answer to the question of how many units to hold in inventory depends on variables such as the usage rate of the item, the cost of maintaining the item in inventory, future costs of inventory and other procedures associated with ordering or making the item, and the cost of the item itself. For example, radio-frequency identification (RFID) is a wireless system composed of tags and readers that use radio waves to communicate information (tags communicate to readers) through every phase of handling inventory. RFID has a broad range of applications, particularly throughout the supply chain, and has immensely improved shipment tracking and reduced cycle times. This technology can be used in everything from inventory control to helping to prevent the distribution of counterfeit drugs and medical devices.[28] Several approaches may be used to determine how many units of a given item should be procured at one time and when that procurement should take place.

The Economic Order Quantity Model.

To control the number of items maintained in inventory, managers need to determine how much of any given item they should order. One popular approach is the **economic order quantity (EOQ) model**, which identifies the optimum number of items to order to minimize the costs of managing (ordering, storing, and using) them.

Just-in-Time Inventory Management.

An increasingly popular technique is **just-in-time (JIT) inventory management**, which eliminates waste by using smaller quantities of materials that arrive "just in time" for use in the transformation process and, therefore, require less storage space and other inventory management expense. JIT minimizes inventory by providing an almost continuous flow of items from suppliers to the production facility. Many U.S. companies—including, IBM, Hewlett-Packard and Harley Davidson—have adopted JIT to reduce costs and boost efficiency.

Let's say that Rushing Water Canoes uses 20 units of aluminum from a supplier per day. Traditionally, its inventory manager might order enough for one month at a time: 440 units per order (20 units per day times 22 workdays per month). The expense of such a large inventory could be considerable because of the cost of insurance coverage, recordkeeping, rented storage space, and so on. The just-in-time approach would reduce these costs because aluminum would be purchased in smaller quantities, perhaps in lot sizes of 20, which the supplier would deliver once a day. Of course, for such an approach to be effective, the supplier must be extremely reliable and relatively close to the production facility.

On the other hand, there are some downsides to just-in-time inventory management that marketers must take into account. During the COVID-19 (coronavirus) pandemic, many companies temporarily halted operations. In the case of a global pandemic, having only enough inventory to meet current needs could create delays in production and hurt the company's bottom line. For this reason, some suggest today's supply chains have become too lean.[29]

Material-Requirements Planning.

Another inventory management technique is **material-requirements planning (MRP)**, a planning system that schedules the precise quantity of materials needed to make the product. The basic components of MRP are a master production schedule, a bill of materials, and an inventory status file. At Rushing Water Canoes (RWC), for example, the inventory-control manager will look at the production schedule to determine how many canoes the company plans to make. He or she will then prepare a bill of materials—a list of all the materials needed to make that quantity of canoes. Next, the manager will determine the quantity of these items that RWC already holds in inventory (to avoid ordering excess materials) and then develop a schedule for ordering and accepting delivery of the right quantity of materials to satisfy the firm's

inventory control the process of determining how many supplies and goods are needed and keeping track of quantities on hand, where each item is, and who is responsible for it.

economic order quantity (EOQ) model a model that identifies the optimum number of items to order to minimize the costs of managing (ordering, storing, and using) them.

just-in-time (JIT) inventory management a technique using smaller quantities of materials that arrive "just in time" for use in the transformation process and therefore require less storage space and other inventory management expense.

material-requirements planning (MRP) a planning system that schedules the precise quantity of materials needed to make the product.

TARGET AIMS FOR BULLSEYE WITH SUPPLY CHAIN IMPROVEMENTS

Target, alongside other retailers, is constantly competing for the same share of the market place. Target invested $5 billion toward improving its supply chain and technology infrastructure in a two-year period, including raising its delivery time standards for suppliers and investing in same-day delivery. Then, Target tested a new distribution strategy in order to make its stores quicker at restocking and distributing to stores and customers.

Target's "replenish cycle" took days, but its new distribution strategy reduces that cycle down to hours. In Target's smaller stores, located in more urban areas, the company reduced the amount of inventory it has. Instead of large shipments of inventory, Target makes smaller deliveries to fulfill exactly what the stores need. This is more of a just-in-time approach to inventory management, which reduces waste and allows stores to get exactly what they need when they need it.

Target also acquired Shipt, a same-day grocery delivery service that delivers directly to consumers' doors. Shipt allows Target to compete directly against same-day delivery services offered by Amazon Fresh. Additionally, Target added fresh groceries and adult beverages to its drive up and pickup services. Using tools like these new distribution strategies and Shipt, Target is staying relevant against its competitors. Along with the new distribution strategy, Target is integrating its distribution and fulfillment operations into a new warehouse management system.[e]

🔵 Critical Thinking Questions

1. Describe the many ways Target is trying to improve its supply chain in order to compete.

2. Why might changes to its inventory management improve Target's distribution?

3. What are some of the risks of adopting a just-in-time approach?

> ## "Many companies elect to outsource some aspects of their operations to companies that can provide these products more efficiently, at a lower cost, and with greater customer satisfaction."

needs. Because of the large number of parts and materials that go into a typical production process, MRP must be done on a computer. It can be, and often is, used in conjunction with just-in-time inventory management.

Outsourcing

Increasingly, outsourcing has become a component of supply chain management in operations. As we mentioned in the chapter titled "Business in a Borderless World," outsourcing refers to the contracting of manufacturing or other tasks to independent companies. The use of these outside firms, called third parties, is related to outsourcing logistical services. Many companies elect to outsource some aspects of their operations to companies that can provide these products more efficiently, at a lower cost, and with greater customer satisfaction. Globalization has put pressure on supply chain managers to improve speed and balance resources against competitive pressures. Companies outsourcing to China, in particular, face heavy regulation, high transportation costs, inadequate facilities, and unpredictable supply chain execution. Therefore, suppliers need to provide useful, timely, and accurate information about every aspect of the quality requirements, schedules, and solutions to dealing with problems. Companies that hire suppliers must also make certain that their suppliers are following company standards; failure to do so could lead to criticism of the parent company.

Many high-tech firms have outsourced the production of chips, computers, and telecom equipment to Asian companies. The hourly labor costs in countries such as China, India, and Vietnam are far less than in the United States, Europe, or even Mexico. These developing countries have improved their manufacturing capabilities, infrastructure, and technical and business skills, making them more attractive regions for global sourcing. For instance, Nike outsources almost all of its production to Asian countries such as China and Vietnam. On the other hand, the cost of outsourcing halfway around the world must be considered in decisions. While information technology is often outsourced today, transportation, human resources, services, and even marketing functions can be outsourced. Our hypothetical Rushing Water Canoes might contract with a local janitorial service to clean its offices and with a local accountant to handle routine bookkeeping and tax-preparation functions.

▼ **TABLE 8.2** Top Outsourcing Providers

Company	Services
KPMG	Auditing, tax services, and advisory services
Accenture	Management consulting, technology, and outsourcing
Canon Business Process Services	Business process services, document management, and managed workforce services
CBRE	Commercial real estate services
Kelly Outsourcing and Consulting Group	Talent management solutions

Source: International Association of Outsourcing, *The Global Outsourcing 100*, 2020, https://www.iaop.org/Content/25/195/5148 (accessed June 2, 2020).

Outsourcing, once used primarily as a cost-cutting tactic, has increasingly been linked with the development of competitive advantage through improved product quality, speeding up the time it takes products to get to the customer, and increasing overall supply chain efficiencies. Table 8.2 describes five of the top 100 global outsourcing providers that assist mainly in information technology. Outsourcing allows companies to free up time and resources to focus on what they do best and to create better opportunities to focus on customer satisfaction. Many executives view outsourcing as an innovative way to boost productivity and remain competitive against low-wage offshore factories. However, outsourcing may create conflict with labor and negative public opinion when it results in U.S. workers being replaced by lower-cost workers in other countries.

Routing and Scheduling

After all materials have been procured and their use determined, managers must then consider the **routing**, or sequence of operations through which the product must pass. Therefore, routing and scheduling is an important part of operations in the supply chain. For example, before employees at Rushing Water Canoes can form aluminum sheets into a canoe, the aluminum must be cut to size. Likewise, the canoe's flotation material must be installed before workers can secure the wood seats. The sequence depends on the product specifications developed by the engineering department of the company.

Once management knows the routing, the actual work can be scheduled. **Scheduling** assigns the tasks to be done to departments or even specific machines, workers, or teams. At Rushing Water, cutting aluminum for the company's canoes might be scheduled to be done by the "cutting and finishing" department on machines designed especially for that purpose.

Many approaches to scheduling have been developed, ranging from simple trial and error to highly sophisticated computer programs. One popular method is the *Program Evaluation and Review Technique (PERT)*, which identifies all the major activities or events required to complete a project, arranges them in a sequence or path, determines the critical path, and estimates the time required for each event. Producing a McDonald's Big Mac, for example, involves removing meat, cheese, sauce, and vegetables from the refrigerator; grilling the hamburger patties; assembling the ingredients; placing the completed Big Mac in its package; and serving it to the customer (Figure 8.3). The cheese, pickles, onions, and sauce cannot be put on before the

routing the sequence of operations through which the product must pass.

scheduling the assignment of required tasks to departments or even specific machines, workers, or teams.

▼**FIGURE 8.3** A Hypothetical PERT Diagram for a McDonald's Big Mac

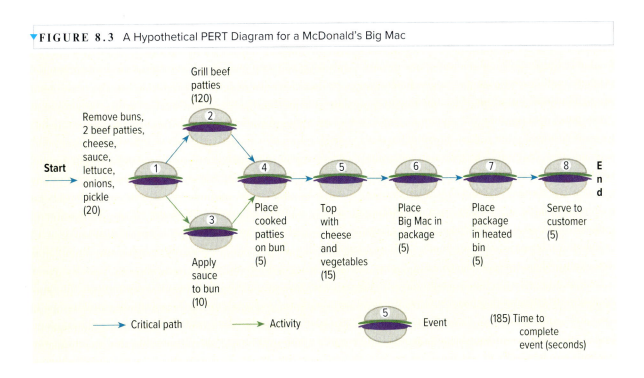

quality control the processes an organization uses to maintain its established quality standards.

total quality management (TQM) a philosophy that uniform commitment to quality in all areas of an organization will promote a culture that meets customers' perceptions of quality.

hamburger patty is completely grilled and placed on the bun. The path that requires the longest time from start to finish is called the *critical path* because it determines the minimum amount of time in which the process can be completed. If any of the activities on the critical path for production of the Big Mac fall behind schedule, the sandwich will not be completed on time, causing customers to wait longer than they usually would.

LO 8-6 Assess the importance of quality in operations management.

MANAGING QUALITY

Quality, like cost and efficiency, is a critical element of operations management because defective products can quickly ruin a firm. Quality reflects the degree to which a good or service meets the demands and requirements of customers. Customers are increasingly dissatisfied with the quality of service provided by many airlines. Table 8.3 gives the rankings of U.S. airlines in certain operational areas. Determining quality can be difficult because it depends on customers' perceptions of how well the product meets or exceeds their expectations. For example, customer satisfaction on airlines can vary wildly depending on individual customers' perspectives. The airline industry is notorious for its dissatisfied customers. Flight delays are a common complaint from airline passengers; 20 percent of all flights arrive late.[30] However, most consumers select airlines based on price, route, schedule, or membership or status with the airline's frequent-flyer program.

The fuel economy of an automobile or its reliability (defined in terms of frequency of repairs) can be measured with some degree of precision. Although automakers rely on their own measures of vehicle quality, they also look to independent sources such as the J.D. Power & Associates annual initial quality survey for confirmation of their quality assessment and for consumer perceptions of quality for the industry, as indicated in Table 8.4.

It is especially difficult to measure quality characteristics when the product is a service. A company has to decide exactly which quality characteristics it considers important and then define those characteristics in terms that can be measured. The inseparability of production and consumption and the level of customer contact influence the selection of characteristics of the service that are most important. Employees in high-contact services such as hairstyling, education, and legal services—and even the barista at Starbucks—are an important part of the product.

The Malcolm Baldrige National Quality Award is given each year to companies that meet rigorous standards of quality. The Baldrige criteria are (1) leadership, (2) information and analysis, (3) strategic planning, (4) human resource development and management, (5) process management, (6) business results, and (7) customer focus and satisfaction. The criteria have become a worldwide framework for driving business improvement. Recent honorees include Adventist Health White Memorial (health care), Center for Organ Recovery & Education (nonprofit), City of Germantown (nonprofit), Howard Community College (education), Illinois Municipal Retirement Fund (nonprofit), and Mary Greeley Medical Center (health care).[31]

Quality is so important that we need to examine it in the context of operations management. **Quality control** refers to the processes an organization uses to maintain its established quality standards. Quality has become a major concern in many organizations, particularly in light of intense foreign competition and increasingly demanding customers. To regain a competitive edge, a number of firms have adopted a total quality management approach. **Total quality management (TQM)** is

▼ **TABLE 8.3** Airline Scorecard (Best to Worst)

Airline	Overall Rank	On-Time Arrival	Canceled Flights	Extreme Delays	2-Hour Tarmac Delays	Mishandled Baggage	Involuntary Bumping	Complaints
Delta	1	1	1	3	6	4	1	3
Alaska	2	2	4	1	5	6	5	2
Southwest	2	4	8	2	1	3	6	1
Allegiant	4	5	2	4	2	1	8	6
Spirit	5	3	6	5	4	5	4	9
JetBlue	6	8	3	9	7	7	3	4
Frontier	7	9	5	8	3	2	7	8
United	8	7	7	7	8	8	2	5
American	9	6	9	6	9	9	9	7

Source: Scott McCartney, "The Best and Worst U.S. Airlines of 2019," *The Wall Street Journal*, January 15, 2020, https://www.wsj.com/articles/the-best-and-worst-u-s-airlines-of-2019-11579097301 (accessed June 2, 2020).

statistical process control a system in which management collects and analyzes information about the production process to pinpoint quality problems in the production system.

ISO 9000 a series of quality assurance standards designed by the International Organization for Standardization (ISO) to ensure consistent product quality under many conditions.

▼ **TABLE 8.4** Top 10 J.D. Power & Associates Initial Automobile Quality Study

1.	Genesis
2.	Kia
3.	Hyundai
4.	Ford
5.	Lincoln
6.	Chevrolet
7.	Nissan
8.	Dodge
9.	Lexus
10.	Toyota

Source: J.D. Power, "New-Vehicle Quality Stalls After Four Years of Improvement, J.D. Power Finds," June 19, 2019, https://www.jdpower.com/business/press-releases/2019-initial-quality-study-iqs (accessed June 2, 2020).

a philosophy that uniform commitment to quality in all areas of the organization will promote a culture that meets customers' perceptions of quality. It involves coordinating efforts to improve customer satisfaction, increasing employee participation, forming and strengthening supplier partnerships, and facilitating an organizational culture of continuous quality improvement. TQM requires constant improvements in all areas of the company as well as employee empowerment.

Continuous improvement of an organization's goods and services is built around the notion that quality is free; by contrast, *not* having high-quality goods and services can be very expensive, especially in terms of dissatisfied customers.[32] A primary tool of the continuous improvement process is *benchmarking,* the measuring and evaluating of the quality of the organization's goods, services, or processes as compared with the quality produced by the best-performing companies in the industry.[33] Benchmarking lets the organization know where it stands competitively in its industry, thus giving it a goal to aim for over time. Now that online digital media are becoming more important in businesses, benchmarking tools are also becoming more popular. These tools allow companies to monitor and compare the success of their websites as they track traffic to their site versus competitors' sites.

Companies employing TQM programs know that quality control should be incorporated throughout the transformation process, from the initial plans to the development of a specific product through the product and production-facility design processes to the actual manufacture of the product. In other words, they view quality control as an element of the product itself, rather than as simply a function of the operations process. When a company makes the product correctly from the outset, it eliminates the need to rework defective products, expedites the transformation process itself, and allows employees to make better use of their time and materials. One method through which many companies have tried to improve quality is **statistical process control**, a system in which management collects and analyzes information about the production process to pinpoint quality problems in the production system.

International Organization for Standardization (ISO)

Regardless of whether a company has a TQM program for quality control, it must first determine what standard of quality it desires and then assess whether its products meet that standard. Product specifications and quality standards must be set so the company can create a product that will compete in the marketplace. Rushing Water Canoes, for example, may specify that each of its canoes has aluminum walls of a specified uniform thickness, that the front and back be reinforced with a specified level of steel, and that each contain a specified amount of flotation material for safety. Production facilities must be designed that can produce products with the desired specifications.

Quality standards can be incorporated into service businesses as well. A hamburger chain, for example, may establish standards relating to how long it takes to cook an order and serve it to customers, how many fries are in each order, how thick the burgers are, or how many customer complaints might be acceptable. Once the desired quality characteristics, specifications, and standards have been stated in measurable terms, the next step is inspection.

The International Organization for Standardization (ISO) has created a series of quality management standards—**ISO 9000**—designed to ensure the customer's quality standards are met. The standards provide a framework for documenting how a certified business keeps records, trains employees, tests products, and fixes defects. To obtain ISO 9001 certification, an independent

Lockheed Martin Aeronautics Company in Fort Worth, Texas, has achieved ISO 14001 certification.

Ronald Martinez/Getty Images

ISO 14000 a comprehensive set of environmental standards that encourages a cleaner and safer world by promoting a more uniform approach to environmental management and helping companies attain and measure improvements in their environmental performance.

ISO 19600 a comprehensive set of guidelines for compliance management that address risks, legal requirements, and stakeholder needs.

auditor must verify that a business's factory, laboratory, or office meets the quality standards spelled out by the International Organization for Standardization. The certification process can require significant investment, but for many companies, the process is essential to being able to compete. Thousands of companies have been certified, including General Electric Analytical Instruments, which has applied ISO standards to everything from the design to the manufacturing practices of its global facilities.[34] Certification has become a virtual necessity for doing business in Europe in some high-technology businesses. ISO 9002 certification was established for service providers.

ISO 14000 is a comprehensive set of environmental standards that encourages a cleaner and safer world. ISO 14000 is a valuable standard because currently considerable variation exists between the regulations in different nations, and even regions within a nation. These variations make it difficult for organizations committed to sustainability to find acceptable global solutions to problems. The goal of the ISO 14000 standards is to promote a more uniform approach to environmental management and to help companies attain and measure improvements in their environmental performance. **ISO 19600** provides guidance for establishing, developing, implementing, evaluating, maintaining, and improving an effective and responsive compliance management system within an organization. The guidelines are applicable to all types of organizations. The extent of the application of these guidelines depends on the size, structure, nature, and complexity of the organization. This guidance is based on the principles of good governance, transparency, and sustainability.[35]

Inspection

Inspection reveals whether a product meets quality standards. Some product characteristics may be discerned by fairly simple inspection techniques—weighing the contents of cereal boxes or measuring the time it takes for a customer to receive his or her hamburger. As part of the ongoing quality assurance program at Hershey Foods, all wrapped Hershey Kisses are checked, and all imperfectly wrapped kisses are rejected. Other inspection techniques are more elaborate. Automobile manufacturers use automated machines to open and close car doors to test the durability of latches and hinges. The food-processing and pharmaceutical industries use various chemical tests to determine the quality of their output. Rushing Water Canoes might use a special device that can precisely measure the thickness of each canoe wall to ensure that it meets the company's specifications.

Organizations normally inspect purchased items, work-in-process, and finished items. The inspection of purchased items and finished items takes place after the fact; the inspection of work-in-process is preventive. In other words, the purpose of inspection of purchased items and finished items is to determine what the quality level is. For items that are being worked on—an automobile moving down the assembly line or a canoe being assembled—the purpose of the inspection is to find defects before the product is completed so that necessary corrections can be made.

Sampling

An important question relating to inspection is how many items should be inspected. Should all canoes produced by Rushing Water be inspected or just some of them? Whether to inspect 100 percent of the output or only part of it is related to the cost of the inspection process, the destructiveness of the inspection process (some tests last until the product fails), and the potential cost of product flaws in terms of human lives and safety.

Some inspection procedures are quite expensive, use elaborate testing equipment, destroy products, and/or require a significant number of hours to complete. In such cases, it is usually desirable to test only a sample of the output. If the sample passes inspection, the inspector may assume that all the items in the lot from which the sample was drawn would also pass inspection. By using principles of statistical inference, management can employ sampling techniques that ensure a relatively high probability of reaching the right conclusion—that is, rejecting a lot that does not meet standards and accepting a lot that does. Nevertheless, there will always be a risk of making an incorrect conclusion—accepting a population that *does not* meet standards (because the sample was satisfactory) or rejecting a population that *does* meet standards (because the sample contained too many defective items).

Sampling is likely to be used when inspection tests are destructive. Determining the life expectancy of light bulbs by turning them on and recording how long they last would be foolish: There is no market for burned-out light bulbs. Instead, a generalization based on the quality of a sample would be applied to the entire population of light bulbs from which the sample was drawn. However, human lives and safety often depend on the proper functioning of specific items, such as the navigational systems installed in commercial airliners. For such items, even though the inspection process is costly, the potential cost of flawed systems is too great not to inspect 100 percent of the output.

INTEGRATING OPERATIONS AND SUPPLY CHAIN MANAGEMENT

Managing operations and supply chains can be complex and challenging due to the number of independent organizations that must perform their responsibilities in creating product quality. Managing supply chains requires constant vigilance and the ability to make quick tactical changes. When allegations arose that seafood sold in the United States may have come from forced labor on ships around Thailand, companies had to immediately investigate these allegations. Therefore, managing the various partners involved in supply chains and operations is important because many stakeholders hold the firm responsible for appropriate conduct related to product quality. This requires that the company exercise oversight over all suppliers involved in producing a product. Encouraging suppliers to report problems, issues, or concerns requires excellent communication systems to obtain feedback. Ideally, suppliers will report potential problems before they reach the next level of the supply chain, which reduces damage. As new technology advances, supply chain management is becoming one of the most important areas of marketing. Integrating all members of the distribution system through advances in transportation and technology is the driving force to promote change. Because the supply chain cuts across accounting, production, inventory management, warehousing, information technology, transportation, and other functions with a network of alliances and partnerships with marketing channel members, it is of strategic importance to the organization.

Despite the challenges of monitoring global operations and supply chains, there are steps businesses can take to manage these risks. All companies who work with global suppliers should adopt a Global Supplier Code of Conduct and ensure that it is effectively communicated. Additionally, companies should encourage compliance and procurement employees to work together to find ethical suppliers at reasonable costs. Those in procurement are concerned with the costs of obtaining materials for the company. As a result, supply chain and procurement managers must work together to make operational decisions to ensure the selection of the best suppliers from an ethical and cost-effective standpoint. Businesses must also work to make certain that their supply chains are diverse. Having only a few suppliers in one area can disrupt operations should a disaster strike. During the COVID-19 pandemic, consumers quickly changed consumption patterns disrupting supply chains. Food going to restaurants was not needed yet grocery stores had shortages. It was difficult to quickly shift operations, supplies, packaging, and transportation to serve these two different markets. This illustrated the importance of supply chains in the economy and the need for contingency planning.

Finally, companies must perform regular audits on its suppliers and take action against those found to be in violation of company standards.[36] Kellogg's offers a Global Supplier Code of Conduct on its website in 13 different languages, showing the importance of having access to the code throughout its supply chain.[37] ▪

Team Exercise

Form groups and assign the responsibility of finding companies that outsource their production to other countries. What are the key advantages of this outsourcing decision? Do you see any drawbacks or weaknesses in this approach? Why would a company not outsource when such a tactic can be undertaken to cut manufacturing costs? Report your findings to the class.

CAREERS ABOUND // in Operations Management /

While you might not have been familiar with terms such as *supply chain* or *logistics* or *total quality management* before taking this course, careers abound in the operations management field. You will find these careers in a wide variety of organizations—manufacturers, retailers, transportation companies, third-party logistics firms, government agencies, and service firms. Approximately $1.3 trillion is spent on transportation, inventory, and related logistics activities, and logistics alone accounts for more than 8 percent of U.S. gross domestic product.[38] Closely managing how a company's inputs and outputs flow from raw materials to the end consumer is vital to a firm's success. Successful companies also need to ensure that quality is measured and actively managed at each step.

Supply chain managers have a tremendous impact on the success of an organization. These managers are engaged in every facet of the business process, including planning, purchasing, production, transportation, storage and distribution, customer service, and more. Their performance helps organizations control expenses, boost sales, and maximize profits.

Warehouse managers are a vital part of manufacturing operations. A typical warehouse manager's duties include overseeing and recording deliveries and pickups, maintaining inventory records and the product tracking system, and adjusting inventory levels to reflect receipts and disbursements. Warehouse managers also have to keep in mind customer service and employee issues. Warehouse managers can earn up to $60,000 in some cases.

Operations management is also required in service businesses. With more than 80 percent of the U.S. economy in services, jobs exist for services operations. Many service contact operations require standardized processes that often use technology to provide an interface that provides an automatic quality performance. Consider jobs in health care, the travel industry, fast food, and entertainment. Think of any job or task that is a part of the final product in these industries. Even an online retailer such as Amazon has a transformation process that includes information technology and human activities that facilitate a transaction. These services have a standardized process and can be evaluated based on their level of achieved service quality.

Total quality management is becoming a key attribute for companies to ensure that quality pervades all aspects of the organization. Quality assurance managers make a median salary of $79,685. These managers monitor and advise on how a company's quality management system is performing and publish data and reports regarding company performance in both manufacturing and service industries.[39]

chapter nine

motivating the
workforce

Tony Tallec/Alamy Stock Photo

After reading this chapter, you will be able to:

LO 9-1 Explain why the study of *human relations* is important.

LO 9-2 Summarize early studies that laid the groundwork for understanding employee motivation.

LO 9-3 Compare and contrast the human relations theories of Abraham Maslow and Frederick Herzberg.

LO 9-4 Investigate various theories of motivation, including Theories X, Y, and Z; equity theory; expectancy theory; and goal-setting theory.

LO 9-5 Describe some of the strategies that managers use to motivate employees.

Because employees do the actual work of the business and influence whether the firm achieves its objectives, most top managers agree that employees are an organization's most valuable resource. To achieve organizational objectives, employees must have the motivation, ability (appropriate knowledge and skills), and tools (proper training and equipment) to perform their jobs. The chapter titled "Managing Human Resources" covers topics such as those listed earlier. This chapter focuses on how to motivate employees.

We examine employees' needs and motivation, managers' views of workers, and several strategies for motivating employees. Managers who understand the needs of their employees can help them reach higher levels of productivity and thus better contribute to the achievement of organizational goals. ◼

LO 9-1   Explain why the study of *human relations* is important.

NATURE OF HUMAN RELATIONS

What motivates employees to perform on the job is the focus of **human relations**, the study of the behavior of individuals and groups in organizational settings. In business, human relations involves motivating employees to achieve organizational objectives efficiently and effectively. The field of human relations has become increasingly important over the years as businesses strive to understand how to boost workplace morale, maximize employees' productivity and creativity, and motivate their ever-more-diverse employees to be more effective.

Motivation is an inner drive that directs a person's behavior toward goals. A goal is the satisfaction of some need, and a need is the difference between an actual state and a desired state. Both needs and goals can be motivating. Motivation explains why people behave as they do; similarly, a lack of motivation explains, at times, why people avoid doing what they should do. Motivating employees to do the wrong things or for the wrong reasons can be problematic, however. At Wells Fargo, for instance, employees created at least 3.5 million fake customer accounts to meet unrealistic sales goals. The company paid millions in fines.[1] On the other hand, motivating employees to achieve realistic company objectives can greatly enhance an organization's productivity.

A person who recognizes or feels a need is motivated to take action to satisfy the need and achieve a goal (Figure 9.1). Consider a person who takes a job as a salesperson. If that person's

human relations the study of the behavior of individuals and groups in organizational settings.

motivation an inner drive that directs a person's behavior toward goals.

Motivation is important both in business and outside of it. For instance, coaches motivate athletes before major games to increase their chances they will play their best.

Chris Brown/CSM/Shutterstock

▼**FIGURE 9.1**   The Motivation Process

Need

↓

Goal-Directed Behavior

↓

Need Satisfaction

performance is far below other salespeople's, that person will likely recognize a need to increase sales. To satisfy that need and achieve success, the person may try to acquire new insights from successful salespeople or obtain additional training to improve sales skills. In addition, a sales manager might try different means to motivate the salesperson to work harder and to improve his or her skills. Human relations is concerned with the needs of employees, their goals and how they try to achieve them, and the impact of those needs and goals on job performance.

Effectively motivating employees helps keep them engaged in their work. Engagement involves emotional involvement and commitment. Being engaged results in carrying out the expectations and obligations of employment. Many employees are actively engaged in their jobs, while others are not. Some employees do the minimum amount of work required to get by, and some employees are completely disengaged. Mastercard motivates employees with career planning, promoting from within, and job rotation opportunities to help employees advance.[2]

Motivating employees to stay engaged is a key responsibility of management. For example, to test if his onsite production managers were fully engaged in their jobs, former Van Halen frontman David Lee Roth placed a line in the band's rider asking for a bowl of M&M'S with the brown ones removed. It was a means for the band to test local stage production crews' attention to detail. Because their shows were highly technical, David Lee Roth would demand a complete recheck of everything if he found brown M&M'S in the bowl.[3]

One prominent aspect of human relations is **morale** on employees' attitudes toward their jobs, employers, and colleagues. High morale contributes to high levels of productivity, high returns to stakeholders, and employee loyalty. Conversely, low morale may cause high rates of absenteeism and turnover (when employees quit or are fired and must be replaced by new employees). Some companies go to great lengths to retain employees and value their contributions. Apple is a great example of how to motivate employees with its benefits and corporate culture—demonstrated in an average employee retention of five years. Besides traditional benefits, Apple employees receive 25 percent off Apple products; four weeks paid leave to expectant mothers with 14 weeks after delivery; and its AppleCare College Program, which helps student employees pay tuition. Employees on Glassdoor gave Apple's benefits 4.5 out of 5 stars.[4]

Employees are motivated by their perceptions of extrinsic and intrinsic rewards. An **intrinsic reward** is the personal satisfaction and enjoyment that you feel from attaining a goal. For example, in this class you may feel personal enjoyment in learning how business works and aspire to have a career in business or to operate your own business one day. **Extrinsic rewards** are benefits and/or recognition that you receive from someone else. In this class, your grade is extrinsic recognition of your efforts and success in the class. In business, praise and recognition, pay increases, and bonuses are extrinsic rewards. If you believe that your job provides an opportunity to contribute to society or the environment, then that aspect would represent an intrinsic reward. Both intrinsic and extrinsic rewards

BURGERVILLE'S EMPLOYEE MOTIVATION STRATEGY IS HOT OFF THE GRILL

Founded by George Propstra in 1961, Burgerville has 42 restaurants spread throughout the northwest United States. With the mission to "serve with love," Burgerville strives to achieve this mission not only for its customers, but among employees as well.

Burgerville is committed to creating a culture where employees advance. It empowers employees by paying competitively within the industry, and it places high precedence on employee input and feedback. It pays 20 percent higher than the industry average and offers health insurance premiums for employees working at least 25 hours weekly—a rarity in fast food.

Along with health care benefits, Burgerville offers employees career opportunities with professional development programs, scholarships, and educational reimbursements. When the company promotes employees for higher-level roles, it tends to promote employees from within the company instead of looking externally. These motivational techniques have significantly improved employee retention. Burgerville has an employee retention rate twice the industry average.

Despite this higher retention rate, Burgerville is not without criticism from employees. In 2018 employees at a Portland Burgerville voted to unionize. The employees walked out on strike in 2019 and successfully renegotiated wage proposals. This highlights the complexities that can exist in employer–employee relationships.[a]

Critical Thinking Questions:

1. Is health care a hygiene factor or a motivational factor?

2. Burgerville offers development programs to help employees advance. Which need does this meet on Maslow's hierarchy of needs?

3. Do Burgerville managers seem to adopt a Theory X approach or a Theory Y approach to managing employees? Explain your reasoning.

▼ **TABLE 9.1** How to Retain Good Employees

1. Offer training and mentoring
2. Create a positive organizational culture
3. Build credibility through communication
4. Blend compensation, benefits, and recognition
5. Encourage referrals and don't overlook internal recruiting
6. Give coaching and feedback
7. Provide growth opportunities
8. Create work/life balance and minimize stress
9. Foster trust, respect and confidence in senior leadership

Source: Sarah K. Yazinski, "Strategies for Retaining Employees and Minimizing Turnover," *HR.BLR.com,* August 3, 2009, https://hr.blr.com/whitepapers/Staffing-Training/Employee-Turnover/Strategies-for-Retaining-Employees-and-Minimizing- (accessed June 8, 2020).

that have been applied to workers with varying degrees of success. A brief discussion of two of these theories—the classical theory of motivation and the Hawthorne studies—provides a background for understanding the present state of human relations.

Classical Theory of Motivation

The birth of the study of human relations can be traced to time and motion studies conducted at the turn of the century by Frederick W. Taylor and Frank and Lillian Gilbreth. Their studies analyzed how workers perform specific work tasks in an effort to improve the employees' productivity. These efforts led to the application of scientific principles to management.

contribute to motivation that stimulates employees to do their best in contributing to business goals.

Respect, involvement, appreciation, adequate compensation, promotions, a pleasant work environment, and a positive organizational culture are all morale boosters. Patagonia, for instance, has a positive organizational culture that encourages employees to act ethically and contribute their ideas. Ensuring that employee values are aligned with the company's values is extremely important for Patagonia. The company prides itself on charitable giving and doing what's right, and it hires individuals accordingly. For example, employees were the ones to suggest that the company give away all Black Friday sales to environmental organizations. The idea was accepted by CEO Rose Marcario within 30 minutes via text message.[5]

DID YOU KNOW?

Absenteeism costs U.S. employers about $225.8 billion annually.[b]

According to the **classical theory of motivation**, money is the sole motivator for workers. Taylor suggested that workers who were paid more would produce more, an idea that would benefit both companies and workers. To improve productivity, Taylor thought that managers should break down each job into its component tasks (specialization), determine the best way to perform each task, and specify the output to be achieved by a worker performing the task. Taylor also believed that incentives would motivate employees to be more productive. Thus, he suggested that managers link workers' pay directly to their output. He developed the piece-rate system, under which employees were paid a certain amount for each unit they produced; those who exceeded their quota were paid a higher rate per unit for all the units they produced.

Table 9.1 lists some ways to retain and motivate good employees. Many companies offer a diverse array of benefits designed to improve the quality of employees' lives and increase their morale and satisfaction. Some of the "best companies to work for" offer onsite day care, concierge services (e.g., dry cleaning, shoe repair, prescription renewal), domestic partner benefits to same-sex couples, and fully paid sabbaticals.

LO 9-2 Summarize early studies that laid the groundwork for understanding employee motivation.

HISTORICAL PERSPECTIVES ON EMPLOYEE MOTIVATION

Throughout the 20th century, researchers have conducted numerous studies to try to identify ways to motivate workers and increase productivity. From these studies have come theories

We can still see Taylor's ideas in practice today in the use of financial incentives for productivity. Moreover, companies are increasingly striving to relate pay to performance at both the hourly and managerial level. Incentive planners choose an individual incentive to motivate and reward their employees. In contrast, team incentives are used to generate partnership and collaboration to accomplish organizational goals. Boeing develops sales teams for most of its products, including commercial airplanes. The team dedicated to each product shares in the sales incentive program.

More and more corporations are tying pay to performance in order to motivate—even up to the CEO level. The topic of executive pay has become controversial in recent years, and many corporate boards of directors have taken steps to link executive compensation more closely to corporate performance. Despite changes in linking pay to performance, there are many CEOs who receive extremely large compensation packages. Sundar Pichai, CEO of Alphabet Inc., received a compensation package of more than $280 million and is one of the highest paid CEOs in the United States.[6]

> COMPANIES ARE INCREASINGLY STRIVING TO RELATE PAY TO PERFORMANCE AT BOTH THE HOURLY AND MANAGERIAL LEVEL. "

Like most managers of the early 20th century, Taylor believed that satisfactory pay and job security would motivate employees to work hard. However, later studies showed that other factors are also important in motivating workers.

The Hawthorne Studies

Elton Mayo and a team of researchers from Harvard University wanted to determine what physical conditions in the workplace—such as light and noise levels—would stimulate employees to be most productive. From 1924 to 1932, they studied a group of workers at the Hawthorne Works Plant of the Western Electric

Some companies let people bring their pets to work as an added incentive to make the workplace feel more friendly.

Image Source Plus/Alamy Stock Photo

Company and measured their productivity under various physical conditions.

What the researchers discovered was quite unexpected and very puzzling: Productivity increased regardless of the physical conditions. This phenomenon has been labeled the Hawthorne effect. When questioned about their behavior, the employees expressed satisfaction because their co-workers in the experiments were friendly and, more importantly, because their supervisors had asked for their help and cooperation in the study. In other words, they were responding to the attention they received, not the changing physical work conditions. The researchers concluded that social and psychological factors could significantly affect productivity and morale. The United Services Automobile Association (USAA) has a built-in psychological factor that influences employee morale. The work of the financial services company serves military and veteran families, which enlivens employees. This shows how important it is for employees to feel like their work matters.

The Hawthorne experiments marked the beginning of a concern for human relations in the workplace. They revealed that human factors do influence workers' behavior and that managers who understand the needs, beliefs, and expectations of people have the greatest success in motivating their workers.

LO 9-3 Compare and contrast the human relations theories of Abraham Maslow and Frederick Herzberg.

THEORIES OF EMPLOYEE MOTIVATION

The research of Taylor, Mayo, and many others has led to the development of a number of theories that attempt to describe what motivates employees to perform. In this section, we discuss some of the most important of these theories. The successful implementation of ideas based on these theories will vary, of course, depending on the company, its management, and its employees. It should be noted, too, that what worked in the past may no longer work today. Good managers must have the ability to adapt their ideas to an ever-changing, diverse group of employees.

Maslow's Hierarchy of Needs

Psychologist Abraham Maslow theorized that people have five basic needs: physiological, security, social, esteem, and

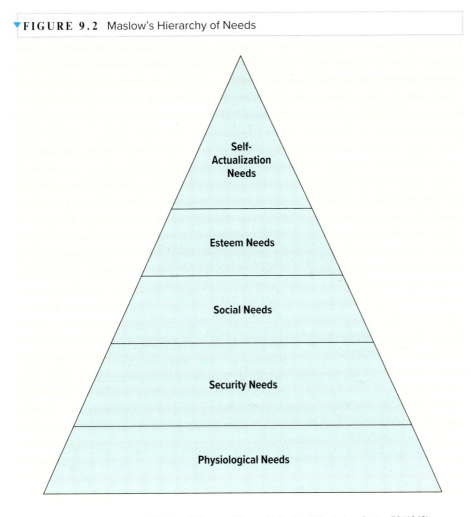

▼ **FIGURE 9.2** Maslow's Hierarchy of Needs

Self-Actualization Needs

Esteem Needs

Social Needs

Security Needs

Physiological Needs

Source: Adapted from Abraham H. Maslow, "A Theory of Human Motivation," *Psychology Review* 50 (1943), pp. 370–396. American Psychology Association.

Maslow's hierarchy a theory that arranges the five basic needs of people— physiological, security, social, esteem, and self-actualization—into the order in which people strive to satisfy them.

physiological needs the most basic human needs to be satisfied—water, food, shelter, and clothing.

security needs the need to protect oneself from physical and economic harm.

social needs the need for love, companionship, and friendship—the desire for acceptance by others.

esteem needs the need for respect—both self-respect and respect from others.

self-actualization needs the need to be the best one can be; at the top of Maslow's hierarchy.

self-actualization. **Maslow's hierarchy** arranges these needs into the order in which people strive to satisfy them (Figure 9.2).

Physiological needs, the most basic and first needs to be satisfied, are the essentials for living—water, food, shelter, and clothing. According to Maslow, humans devote all their efforts to satisfying physiological needs until they are met. Only when these needs are met can people focus their attention on satisfying the next level of needs—security.

Security needs relate to protecting yourself from physical and economic harm. Actions that may be taken to achieve security include reporting a dangerous workplace condition to management, maintaining safety equipment, and purchasing insurance with income protection in the event you become unable to work. Once security needs have been satisfied, people may strive for social goals.

Social needs are the need for love, companionship, and friendship—the desire for acceptance by others. To fulfill social needs, a person may try many things: making friends with a co-worker, joining a group, volunteering at a hospital, throwing a party, and so on. Once their social needs have been satisfied, people attempt to satisfy their need for esteem.

Esteem needs relate to respect—both self-respect and respect from others. One aspect of esteem needs is competition—the need to feel that you can do something better than anyone else. Competition often motivates people to increase their productivity. Esteem needs are not as easily satisfied as the needs at lower levels in Maslow's hierarchy because they do not always provide tangible evidence of success. However, these needs can be realized through rewards and increased involvement in organizational activities. Until esteem needs are met, people focus their attention on achieving respect. When they feel they have achieved some measure of respect, self-actualization becomes the major goal of life.

Self-actualization needs, at the top of Maslow's hierarchy, mean being the best you can be. Self-actualization involves maximizing your potential. Self-actualized people tend to feel that they are living life to its fullest in every way. For J.K. Rowling, self-actualization might mean being praised as one of the best fiction writers in the world; for actress Viola Davis, it might mean winning an Oscar.

hygiene factors
aspects of Herzberg's theory of motivation that focus on the work setting and not the content of the work; these aspects include adequate wages, comfortable and safe working conditions, fair company policies, and job security.

motivational factors
aspects of Herzberg's theory of motivation that focus on the content of the work itself; these aspects include achievement, recognition, involvement, responsibility, and advancement.

Maslow's theory maintains that the more basic needs at the bottom of the hierarchy must be satisfied before higher-level goals can be pursued. Thus, people who are hungry and homeless are not concerned with obtaining respect from their colleagues. Only when physiological, security, and social needs have been more or less satisfied do people seek esteem. Maslow's theory also suggests that if a low-level need is suddenly reactivated, the individual will try to satisfy that need rather than higher-level needs. Many laid-off workers probably shift their focus from high-level esteem needs to the need for security. Managers should learn from Maslow's hierarchy that employees will be motivated to contribute to organizational goals only if they are able to first satisfy their physiological, security, and social needs through their work.

Herzberg's Two-Factor Theory

In the 1950s, psychologist Frederick Herzberg proposed a theory of motivation that focuses on the job and on the environment where work is done. Herzberg studied various factors relating to the job and their relation to employee motivation and concluded that they can be divided into hygiene factors and motivational factors (Table 9.2).[7]

Hygiene factors, which relate to the work setting and not to the content of the work, include adequate wages, comfortable and safe working conditions, fair company policies, and job security. These factors do not necessarily motivate employees to excel, but their absence may be a potential source of dissatisfaction and high turnover. Employee safety and comfort are clearly hygiene factors.

Many people feel that a good salary is one of the most important job factors, even more important than job security and the chance to use one's mind and abilities. Salary and security, two of the hygiene factors identified by Herzberg, make it possible for employees to satisfy the physiological and security needs identified by Maslow. However, the presence of hygiene factors is unlikely to motivate employees to work harder. For example, many people do not feel motivated to pursue a career as a gastroenterologist (doctors who specialize in the digestive system). The average annual salary of the job is more than $379,000; however, patients do not look forward to the visits and the process is fairly routine.[8]

Motivational factors, which relate to the content of the work itself, include achievement, recognition, involvement, responsibility, and advancement. The absence of motivational factors may not result in dissatisfaction, but their presence is likely to motivate employees to excel. Many companies are beginning to employ methods to give employees more responsibility and control and to involve them more in their work, which serves to motivate them to higher levels of productivity and quality. Hotels are adopting more employee-centric processes in order to better their offerings. Service businesses, such as hotels and airlines, recognize the benefit of happy employees—they are not only 12 percent more productive, but they work to generate happy customers. Many companies who value employee happiness consider the following benefits, where possible: implementing flexible hours and the ability to work from home (the average commute is over 25 minutes), making the office "pet friendly," maintaining a break room with recreational items (ping pong, video games, etc.), and celebrating successes and special occasions.[9]

Herzberg's motivational factors and Maslow's esteem and self-actualization needs are similar. Workers' low-level needs (physiological and security) have largely been satisfied by minimum-wage laws and occupational-safety standards set by various government agencies and are therefore not motivators. Consequently, to improve productivity, management should focus on satisfying workers' higher-level needs (motivational factors) by providing opportunities for achievement, involvement, and advancement and by recognizing good performance.

▼ **TABLE 9.2** Herzberg's Hygiene and Motivational Factors

Hygiene Factors	Motivational Factors
Company policies	Achievement
Supervision	Recognition
Working conditions	Work itself
Relationships with peers, supervisors, and subordinates	Responsibility
Salary	Advancement
Security	Personal growth

Google's employee-friendly offices feature elements like basketball courts, pinball machines, and photo booths to foster creativity and make work more enjoyable.

Daniel Brenner/Bloomberg/Getty Images

McGregor's Theory X and Theory Y

In *The Human Side of Enterprise,* Douglas McGregor related Maslow's ideas about personal needs to management. McGregor contrasted two views of management—the traditional view, which he called Theory X, and a humanistic view, which he called Theory Y.

According to McGregor, managers adopting **Theory X** assume that workers generally dislike work and must be forced to do their jobs. They believe that the following statements are true of workers:

1. The average person naturally dislikes work and will avoid it when possible.

2. Most workers must be coerced, controlled, directed, or threatened with punishment to get them to work toward the achievement of organizational objectives.

3. The average worker prefers to be directed and to avoid responsibility, has relatively little ambition, and wants security.[10]

Managers who subscribe to the Theory X view maintain tight control over workers, provide almost constant supervision, try to motivate through fear, and make decisions in an autocratic fashion, eliciting little or no input from their subordinates.

The Theory X style of management focuses on physiological and security needs and virtually ignores the higher needs discussed by Maslow. Computer Science Corporation seemed to adopt the Theory X perspective when it initiated an employee ranking system that ranked 40 percent of employees as below expectations. Employees felt that the system was unfair and the company did not have a good work/life balance. The outcry was so intense that Computer Science Corporation eventually relaxed some of its ratings criteria.[11]

The Theory X view of management does not take into account people's needs for companionship, esteem, and personal growth, whereas Theory Y, the contrasting view of management, does. Managers subscribing to the **Theory Y** view assume that workers like to work and that under proper conditions employees will seek out responsibility in an attempt to satisfy their social, esteem, and self-actualization needs. McGregor describes the assumptions behind Theory Y in the following way:

1. The expenditure of physical and mental effort in work is as natural as play or rest.

2. People will exercise self-direction and self-control to achieve objectives to which they are committed.

Theory X McGregor's traditional view of management whereby it is assumed that workers generally dislike work and must be forced to do their jobs.

Theory Y McGregor's humanistic view of management whereby it is assumed that workers like to work and that under proper conditions employees will seek out responsibility in an attempt to satisfy their social, esteem, and self-actualization needs.

A PERFECT FIT: PATAGONIA'S PASSIONATE EMPLOYEES

What type of organization lets employees take off during the day to go surfing? The answer is Patagonia, an outdoor clothing and gear company. When founder Yvon Chouinard first developed the company, he was not interested in pursuing profits as the firm's main goal. Instead, he wanted to improve the planet. New employees are hired based in large part on their passion for the firm's goals.

Chouinard decided that the company would produce only products of the highest quality and manufactured in the most responsible way. He selected the following mission statement: "Build the best product, cause no unnecessary harm, use business to inspire and implement solutions to the environmental crisis." Patagonia ensures

employees understand and support these values, using a mix of in-person training, video training, and online instruction to help employees learn about company expectations.

Patagonia creates excitement for the company's mission with a fun, informal work environment for employees. It instituted a flextime policy that allows employees to go surfing during the day and provides on-site child care. Solar panels, Tibetan prayer flags, and sheds full of rescued or recuperating owls and hawks are all a part of corporate headquarters.

Patagonia also developed an internship program that enables employees to leave the company for two months to volunteer at the environmental organization of their choice. At

Patagonia, employees are viewed as important partners toward advancing environmental preservation.[c]

Critical Thinking Questions

1. How does Patagonia use training and a fun, informal work environment to encourage employees to support Patagonia's mission?

2. Why do you think Yvon Chouinard decided to make his company so focused on employee satisfaction?

3. Do you think that an informal work environment that provides employees freedom to take off during the day will be harmful or helpful in the long run? Why?

Theory Z a management philosophy that stresses employee participation in all aspects of company decision making.

equity theory an assumption that how much people are willing to contribute to an organization depends on their assessment of the fairness, or equity, of the rewards they will receive in exchange.

3. People will commit to objectives when they realize that the achievement of those goals will bring them personal reward.

4. The average person will accept and seek responsibility.

5. Imagination, ingenuity, and creativity can help solve organizational problems, but most organizations do not make adequate use of these characteristics in their employees.

6. Organizations today do not make full use of workers' intellectual potential.[12]

Obviously, managers subscribing to the Theory Y philosophy have a management style very different from managers subscribing to the Theory X philosophy. Theory Y managers maintain less control and supervision; do not use fear as the primary motivator; and are more democratic in decision making, allowing subordinates to participate in the process. Theory Y managers address the high-level needs in Maslow's hierarchy as well as physiological and security needs. For example, H&R Block is empowering its employees to have "extra help" in interpreting the 74,000 pages of tax code. Employees can use IBM's Watson, a computer system that answers questions using artificial intelligence, to assist them in analyzing returns and maximizing customer refunds. This empowerment gives employees the ability to offer more personalized service and improve customer satisfaction in return.[13] Today, Theory Y enjoys widespread support and may have displaced Theory X.

Theory Z

Theory Z is a management philosophy that stresses employee participation in all aspects of company decision making. It was first described by William Ouchi in his book, *Theory Z—How American Business Can Meet the Japanese Challenge.*[14] Theory Z incorporates many elements associated with the Japanese approach to management, such as trust and intimacy, but Japanese ideas have been adapted for use in the United States. In a Theory Z organization, managers and workers share responsibilities; the management style is participative; and employment is long term and, often, lifelong. Japan has faced a significant period of slowing economic progress and competition from China and other Asian nations. This has led to experts questioning Theory Z, particularly at firms such as Sony and Toyota. On the other hand, Theory Z results in employees feeling organizational ownership. Research has found that such feelings of ownership may produce positive attitudinal and behavioral effects for employees.[15] In a Theory Y organization, managers focus on assumptions about the nature of the worker. The two theories can be seen as complementary. Table 9.3 compares Theory X, Theory Y, and Theory Z.

Equity Theory

According to **equity theory**, how much people are willing to contribute to an organization depends on their assessment of the fairness, or equity, of the rewards they will receive in exchange. In a fair situation, workers receive rewards proportional to the contribution they make to the organization. However, in practice, equity is a subjective notion. Workers regularly develop personal input-output ratios by taking stock of their contributions (inputs) to the organization in time, effort, skills, and experience and assessing the rewards (outputs) offered by the organization in pay, benefits, recognition, and promotions. Workers compare their ratios to the input-output ratio of some other person's "comparison other," who may be a co-worker, a friend working in another organization, or an "average" of several people working in the organization. If the two ratios are close, workers will feel that they are being treated equitably.

Let's say you have a high-school education and earn $25,000 a year. When you compare your input-output ratio with that of a co-worker who has a college degree and makes $35,000 a year, you will probably feel that you are being paid fairly. However, if you perceive that your personal input-output ratio is lower than that of your college-educated co-worker, you may feel that you are being treated unfairly and be motivated to seek change. Or if you learn that your co-worker who makes $35,000 has only a high-school diploma, you may feel cheated by your employer. To achieve equity, you could try to increase your outputs by asking for a raise or promotion. You could also try to have your co-worker's inputs increased or have your co-worker's outputs decreased. Failing to achieve equity, you may be motivated to look for a job at a different company.

▼ **TABLE 9.3** Comparisons of Theories X, Y, and Z

	Theory X	Theory Y	Theory Z
Countries that use this style	China	United States	Japan
Philosophy	Tight control over workers	Assume workers will seek out responsibility and satisfy social needs	Employee participation in all aspects of company decision making
Job description	Considerable specialization	Less control and supervision; address higher levels of Maslow's hierarchy	Trust and intimacy with workers sharing responsibilities
Control	Tight control	Commitment to objectives with self-direction	Relaxed but required expectations
Worker welfare	Limited concern	Democratic	Commitment to worker's total lives
Responsibility	Managerial	Collaborative	Participative

Equity theory might explain why many consumers are upset about CEO compensation. Although the job of the CEO can be incredibly stressful, the fact that they take home millions in compensation, bonuses, and stock options has been questioned. The high unemployment rate coupled with the misconduct that occurred at some large corporations prior to the recession contributed largely to consumer frustration with executive compensation packages. To counter this perception of pay inequality, several corporations have now begun to tie CEO compensation with company performance. If the company performs poorly for the year, then firms such as Goldman Sachs will cut bonuses and other compensation.[16] While lower compensation rates might appease the general public, some companies are worried that lower pay might deter talented individuals from wanting to assume the position of CEO at their firms.

Because almost all the issues involved in equity theory are subjective, they can be problematic. Author David Callahan has argued that feelings of inequity may underlie some unethical or illegal behavior in business.[17] Employee theft costs U.S. companies about $50 billion per year.[18] Some employees may take company resources to restore what they perceive to be an inequity (inadequate pay, working hours, or other deficient benefits).[19] The FBI notes that employee theft is one of the fastest-growing crimes in the United States.[20] Callahan believes that employees who do not feel they are being treated equitably may be motivated to equalize the situation by lying, cheating, or otherwise "improving" their pay, perhaps by stealing.[21] Managers should try to avoid equity problems by ensuring that rewards are distributed on the basis of performance and that all employees clearly understand the basis for their pay and benefits.

Expectancy Theory

Psychologist Victor Vroom described **expectancy theory**, which states that motivation depends not only on how much a person wants something but also on the person's perception of how likely he or she is to get it. A person who wants something and has reason to be optimistic will be strongly motivated. For example, say you really want a promotion. And let's say because you have taken some night classes to improve your skills, and moreover, have just made a large, significant sale, you feel confident that you are qualified and able to handle the new position. Therefore, you are motivated to try to get the promotion. In contrast, if you do not believe you are likely to get what you want, you may not be motivated to try to get it, even though you really want it.

Goal-Setting Theory

Goal-setting theory refers to the impact that setting goals has on performance. According to this philosophy, goals act as motivators to focus employee efforts on achieving certain performance outcomes. Setting goals can positively affect performance because goals help employees direct their efforts and attention toward the outcome, mobilize their efforts, develop consistent behavior patterns, and create strategies to obtain desired outcomes.[22] When Cinnabon introduced two new hot chocolates, Ghirardelli and Cinnamon Roll, it had specific goals for sales. To support these sales goals and generate awareness of the new drinks, the company might have employees at the counter suggest these new options or offer other forms of promotional support.

In 1954, Peter Drucker introduced the term *management by objectives (MBO)* that has since become important to goal-setting theory. MBO refers to the need to develop goals that both managers and employees can understand and agree upon.[23] This requires managers to work with employees to set personal objectives that will be used to further organizational objectives. By linking managerial objectives with personal objectives, employees often feel a greater sense of commitment toward achieving organizational goals. Hewlett-Packard was an early adopter of MBO as a management style.[24]

expectancy theory
the assumption that motivation depends not only on how much a person wants something but also on how likely he or she is to get it.

goal-setting theory
refers to the impact that setting goals has on performance.

LO 9-5 Describe some of the strategies that managers use to motivate employees.

STRATEGIES FOR MOTIVATING EMPLOYEES

Based on the various theories that attempt to explain what motivates employees, businesses have developed several strategies for motivating their employees and boosting morale and productivity. Some of these techniques include behavior modification and job design, as well as the already described employee involvement programs and work teams.

> "Managers should try to avoid equity problems by ensuring that rewards are distributed on the basis of performance and that all employees clearly understand the basis for their pay and benefits."

behavior modification changing behavior and encouraging appropriate actions by relating the consequences of behavior to the behavior itself.

reinforcement theory the theory that behavior can be strengthened or weakened through the use of rewards and punishments.

job rotation movement of employees from one job to another in an effort to relieve the boredom often associated with job specialization.

job enlargement the addition of more tasks to a job instead of treating each task as separate.

Behavior Modification

Behavior modification involves changing behavior and encouraging appropriate actions by relating the consequences of behavior to the behavior itself. Behavior modification is the most widely discussed application of **reinforcement theory**, the theory that behavior can be strengthened or weakened through the use of rewards and punishments. The concept of behavior modification was developed by psychologist B. F. Skinner. Skinner found that behavior that is rewarded will tend to be repeated, while behavior that is punished will tend to be eliminated. For example, employees who know that they will receive a bonus such as an expensive restaurant meal for making a sale over $2,000 may be more motivated to make sales. Workers who know they will be punished for being tardy are likely to make a greater effort to get to work on time.

However, the two strategies may not be equally effective. Punishing unacceptable behavior may provide quick results but may lead to undesirable long-term side effects, such as employee dissatisfaction and increased turnover. In general, rewarding appropriate behavior is a more effective way to modify behavior.

Job Design

Herzberg identified the job itself as a motivational factor. Managers have several strategies that they can use to design jobs to help improve employee motivation. These include job rotation, job enlargement, job enrichment, and flexible scheduling strategies.

Job Rotation. **Job rotation** allows employees to move from one job to another in an effort to relieve the boredom that is often associated with job specialization. Businesses often turn to specialization in hopes of increasing productivity, but there is a negative side effect to this type of job design: Employees become bored and dissatisfied, and productivity declines. Job rotation reduces this boredom by allowing workers to undertake a greater variety of tasks and by giving them the opportunity to learn new skills. With job rotation, an employee spends a specified amount of time performing one job and then moves on to another, different job. The worker eventually returns to the initial job and begins the cycle again. Table 9.4 offers additional benefits of job rotation.

PricewaterhouseCoopers promotes job rotation to allow employees to learn new skills.
ricochet64/Shutterstock

Job rotation is a good idea, but it has one major drawback. Because employees may eventually become bored with all the jobs in the cycle, job rotation does not totally eliminate the problem of boredom. Job rotation is extremely useful, however, in situations where a person is being trained for a position that requires an understanding of various units in an organization. Many businesses and departments understand the benefits of job rotation. Roughly 44 percent of CFOs said their companies promote job rotation. Finance employees can end up in accounting operations, finance, internal audit, compliance, and tax—and can benefit from the diverse exposure and experience.[25] Many executive training programs require trainees to spend time learning a variety of specialized jobs. Job rotation is also used to cross-train today's self-directed work teams.

Job Enlargement. **Job enlargement** adds more tasks to a job instead of treating each task as separate. Like job rotation, job enlargement was developed to overcome the boredom associated with specialization. The rationale behind this strategy is

▼ **TABLE 9.4** Benefits of Job Rotation

1. Exposure to a diversity of viewpoints
2. Motivating ongoing lifelong learning
3. Preparing for promotion and leadership roles
4. Building specific skills and abilities
5. Supporting recruitment efforts
6. Boosting overall productivity
7. Retaining employees

Source: Tim Hird, "The Lasting Benefits of Job Rotation," *Treasury & Risk*, January 24, 2017, https://www.treasuryandrisk.com/sites/treasuryandrisk/2017/01/24/the-lasting-benefits-of-job-rotation/ (accessed June 8, 2020).

that jobs are more satisfying as the number of tasks performed by an individual increases. Employees sometimes enlarge, or craft, their jobs by noticing what needs to be done and then changing tasks and relationship boundaries to adjust. Individual orientation and motivation shape opportunities to craft new jobs and job relationships. Job enlargement strategies have been more successful in increasing job satisfaction than have job rotation strategies. IBM, AT&T, and Maytag are among the many companies that have used job enlargement to motivate employees.

Job Enrichment.
Job enrichment incorporates motivational factors such as opportunity for achievement, recognition, responsibility, and advancement into a job. It gives workers not only more tasks within the job, but more control and authority over the job. Job enrichment programs enhance a worker's feeling of responsibility and provide opportunities for growth and advancement when the worker is able to take on the more challenging tasks. Hyatt Hotels Corporation and Clif Bar use job enrichment to improve the quality of work life for their employees. The potential benefits of job enrichment are great, but it requires careful planning and execution.

Flexible Scheduling Strategies.
Many U.S. workers work a traditional 40-hour workweek consisting of five 8-hour days with fixed starting and ending times. Facing problems of poor morale and high absenteeism as well as a diverse workforce with changing needs, many managers have turned to flexible scheduling strategies such as flextime, compressed workweeks, job sharing, part-time work, and telecommuting.

Flextime is a program that allows employees to choose their starting and ending times, as long as they are at work during a specified core period (Figure 9.3). FlexJobs defines flexible jobs as those that are professional, have a flexible schedule, include a telecommuting component, and are part-time or freelance.[26] It does not reduce the total number of hours that employees work; instead, it gives employees more flexibility in choosing which hours they work. A firm may specify that employees must be present from 10:00 a.m. to 3:00 p.m. One employee may choose to come in at 7:00 a.m. and leave at the end of the core time, perhaps to attend classes at a nearby college after work. Another employee, a mother who lives in the suburbs, may come in at 9:00 a.m. in order to have time to drop off her children at a day care center and commute by public transportation to her job. Flextime provides many benefits, including improved ability to recruit and retain workers who wish to balance work and home life. Customers can be better served by allowing customer service over longer hours, workstations and

Flextime provides many benefits, including improved ability to recruit and retain workers who wish to balance work and home life.

job enrichment the incorporation of motivational factors, such as opportunity for achievement, recognition, responsibility, and advancement, into a job.

flextime a program that allows employees to choose their starting and ending times, provided that they are at work during a specified core period.

compressed workweek a four-day (or shorter) period during which an employee works 40 hours.

▼**FIGURE 9.3** Flextime, Showing Core and Flexible Hours

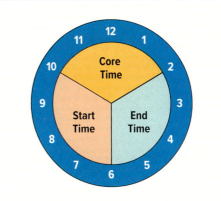

facilities can be better utilized by staggering employee use, and rush hour traffic may be reduced. In addition, flexible schedules have been associated with an increase in job satisfaction on the part of employees. More flexible schedules are associated with higher job satisfaction, less burnout, and better work-to-family balance.[27]

Related to flextime are the scheduling strategies of the compressed workweek and job sharing. The **compressed workweek** is a four-day (or shorter) period in which an employee works 40 hours. Under such a plan, employees typically work 10 hours per day for four days and have a three-day weekend. Lockheed Martin offers a compressed workweek called 9/80, which allows employees to work 80 hours across 9 business days instead of the traditional 10, resulting in an extra day off every two weeks.[28] The compressed workweek reduces the company's operating expenses because its actual hours of operation are reduced. It is also sometimes used by parents who want to have more days off to spend with their families. Millennials and Generation Z are groups of employees who value flexibility in their work schedules. Industries and companies that are the largest flextime employers include medical and health (Kaiser Permanente), education and training (Kaplan), computer and IT (VMWare), administrative (Kelly Services),

Tony Hsieh, CEO of online shoe and clothing retailer Zappos, believes satisfied employees who buy into the firm's culture are the key to delivering the "WOW customer service" for which the company has become known. When Amazon acquired Zappos for $1.2 billion, it was under the condition that Zappos could function independently and maintain its employee-centered environment.

Zappos strives to make work enjoyable. Days at Zappos may include Nerf wars, office parades, ugly sweater days, or donut eating contests. Hsieh believes that by attracting talented people and employees who enjoy their work, great service and brand power naturally develop. Employees must embrace the company's culture and dedication to customer service to succeed. Zappos has fired employees who did not fit in with its culture, even if they performed good work.

Employees at Zappos have strong decision-making authority, essential in allowing them to offer customized services. There is no limit to how long call-center employees can talk to customers about customer-service issues—one employee talked with a customer for more than 10 hours. Employees engage in Zappos's participative culture by actively working together toward problem-solving and identifying solutions.

Hsieh has placed such value on employee decision-making he made the controversial decision to reorganize Zappos as a holacracy, which removes the standard business hierarchy for a self-management system where employees are empowered to input their own decision making. Hsieh decided that this was the best way Zappos could maintain its culture and continue to grow.[d]

Critical Thinking Questions

1. Describe some of the ways Zappos motivates its employees.

2. Where does employee empowerment fall on Maslow's hierarchy of needs?

3. Why do you think Zappos places such emphasis on employees who will embrace its company culture?

---

job sharing
performance of one full-time job by two people on part-time hours.

sales (SAP, AT&T), customer services (Williams & Sonoma), and accounting and finance (PricewaterhouseCoopers).[29]

Job sharing occurs when two people do one job. One person may work from 8:00 a.m. to 12:30 p.m.; the second person comes in at 12:30 p.m. and works until 5:00 p.m. Job sharing gives both people the opportunity to work as well as time to fulfill other obligations, such as parenting or school. With job sharing, the company has the benefit of the skills of two people for one job, often at a lower total cost for salaries and benefits than one person working eight hours a day would be paid.

Two other flexible scheduling strategies attaining wider use include allowing full-time workers to work part-time for a certain period and allowing workers to work at home either full- or part-time. Employees at some firms may be permitted to work part-time for several months in order to care for a new baby or an elderly parent or just to slow down for a little while to "recharge their batteries." When the employees return to full-time work, they are usually given a position comparable to their original full-time position. Other firms are allowing employees to telecommute or telework (work at home a few days of the week), staying connected via computers and telephones. Most telecommuters tend to combine going into the office with working from home. At Dell, for instance, 60 percent of employees leverage flexible work arrangements.[30]

Although many employees ask for the option of working at home to ease the responsibilities of caring for family members, some have discovered that they are more productive at home without the distractions of the workplace. Workers like telecommuting because they can improve their overall productivity through a variety of means, besides just saving on driving time. They do not have office distractions such as people coming into their workspace to talk and office politics to detract from their

Working remotely is becoming increasingly common. Telecommuting, job sharing, and flextime can be beneficial for employees who cannot work normal work hours.

nd3000/Shutterstock

productivity.[31] Other employees, however, have discovered that they are not suited for working at home. For telecommuting to work, it must be a feasible alternative and must not create significant costs for the company.[32] Work-at-home programs can also help reduce overhead costs for businesses. For example, some companies used to maintain a surplus of office space but have reduced the surplus through employee telecommuting, "hoteling" (being assigned to a desk through a reservation system), and "hot-desking" (several people using the same desk but at different times). During the COVID-19 (coronavirus) pandemic, many businesses began to experience the benefits of telecommuting. Many decided to embrace remote working arrangements permanently.

Companies are turning to flexible work schedules to provide more options to employees who are trying to juggle their work duties with other responsibilities and needs. Preliminary results indicate that flexible scheduling plans increase job satisfaction, which, in turn, leads to increases in productivity. Some recent research, however, has indicated there are potential problems with telecommuting. Some managers are reluctant to adopt the practice because the pace of change in today's workplace is faster than ever, and telecommuters may be left behind or actually cause managers more work in helping them stay abreast of changes. Some employers also worry that telecommuting workers create a security risk by creating more opportunities for computer hackers or equipment thieves. Some employees have found that working outside the office may hurt career advancement opportunities, and some report that instead of helping them balance work and family responsibilities, telecommuting increases the strain by blurring the barriers between the office and home. Co-workers call at all hours, and telecommuters are apt to continue to work when they are not supposed to (after regular business hours or during vacation time).

Businesses have come up with different ways to motivate employees, including rewards such as trophies and plaques to show the company's appreciation.

Caiaimage/Paul Bradbury/Getty Images

BUILDING YOUR SOFT SKILLS

BY STAYING MOTIVATED

Motivated employees are often happy employees. This chapter discussed a number of ways that companies try to keep employees motivated. Consider yourself and how you stay motivated to complete your education. Do you find that you are more intrinsically motivated or extrinsically motivated? Why do you think that is? Consider stumbling blocks you have in keeping motivated (such as cell phone distractions). List your top three stumbling blocks and how you can avoid them.

Importance of Motivational Strategies

Motivation is more than a tool that managers can use to foster employee loyalty and boost productivity. It is a process that affects all the relationships within an organization and influences many areas such as pay, promotion, job design, training opportunities, and reporting relationships. Employees are motivated by the nature of the relationships they have with their supervisors, by the nature of their jobs, and by characteristics of the organization. Table 9.5 shows companies with excellent motivational strategies, along with the types of strategies they use to motivate employees. Even the economic environment can change an employee's

Team Exercise

Form groups and outline a compensation package that you would consider ideal in motivating an employee, recognizing performance, and assisting the company in attaining its cost-to-performance objectives. Think about the impact of intrinsic and extrinsic motivation and recognition. How can flexible scheduling strategies be used effectively to motivate employees? Report your compensation package to the class.

motivation. In a slow growth or recession economy, sales can flatten or decrease and morale can drop because of the need to cut jobs. The firm may have to work harder to keep good employees and to motivate all employees to work to overcome obstacles. In good economic times, employees may be more demanding and be on the lookout for better opportunities. New rewards or incentives may help motivate workers in such economies. Motivation tools, then, must be varied as well. Managers can further nurture motivation by being honest, supportive, empathic, accessible, fair, and open. Motivating employees to increase satisfaction and productivity is an important concern for organizations seeking to remain competitive in the global marketplace. ■

Company	Motivational Strategies
3M	Gives employees 15 percent of their time to pursue own projects
Google	Perks include a massage every other week, free gourmet lunches, tuition reimbursement, a volleyball court, and time to work on own projects
Whole Foods	Employees receive 20–30 percent discounts on company products, the opportunity to gain stock options, and the ability to make major decisions in small teams
Patagonia	Provides areas for yoga and aerobics, in-house child care services, organic food in its café, and opportunities to go surfing during the day
The Container Store	Provides more than 260 hours of employee training and hosts "We Love Our Employees" Day
Southwest Airlines	Gives employees permission to interact with passengers as they see fit, provides free or discounted flights, and hosts the "Adopt-a-Pilot" program to connect pilots with students across the nation
Nike	Offers tuition assistance, product discounts, onsite fitness centers, and the ability for employees to give insights on how to improve the firm
Apple	Creates a fast-paced, innovative work environment where employees are encouraged to debate ideas
Marriott International	Offers discounts at hotels across the world as well as free hotel stays and travel opportunities for employees with exceptional service
Zappos	Creates a fun, zany work environment for employees and empowers them to take as much time as needed to answer customer concerns

WOULD YOU BE GOOD // at Motivating a Workforce? /

If you are good at mediation, smoothing conflict, and have a good understanding of motivation and human relations theories, then you might be a good leader, human resource manager, or training expert. Most organizations, especially as they grow, will need to implement human relations programs. These are necessary to teach employees about sensitivity to other cultures, religions, and beliefs, as well as for teaching the workforce about the organization so that they understand how they fit in the larger picture. Employees need to appreciate the benefits of working together to make the firm run smoothly, and they also need to understand how their contributions help the firm. To stay motivated, most employees need to feel like what they do each day contributes something of value to the firm. Disclosing information and including employees in decision-making processes will also help employees feel valuable and wanted within the firm.

There are many different ways employers can reward and encourage employees. However, employers must be careful when considering what kinds of incentives to use. Different cultures value different kinds of incentives more highly than others. For example, a Japanese worker would probably not like it if she were singled out from the group and given a large cash bonus as a reward for her work. Japanese workers tend to be more group oriented, and therefore, anything that singles out individuals would not be an effective way of rewarding and motivating. American workers, on the other hand, are very individualistic, and a raise and public praise might be more effective. However, what might motivate a younger employee (bonuses, raises, and perks) may not be the same as what motivates a more seasoned, experienced, and financially successful employee (recognition, opportunity for greater influence, and increased training). Motivation is not an easy thing to understand, especially as firms become more global and more diverse.

Another important part of motivation is enjoying where you work and your career opportunities. Here is a list of the best places to do business and start careers in the United States, according to *Forbes* magazine. Chances are, workers who live in these places have encountered fewer frustrations than those placed at the bottom of the list and, therefore, would probably be more content with where they work.[33]

▼ Best Places for Businesses and Careers

Rank	Metro Area	Job Growth Rank	Population
1.	Seattle, WA	39	3,048,100
2.	Dallas, TX	16	5,007,200
3.	Raleigh, NC	22	1,362,500
4.	Denver, CO	32	2,932,400
5.	Portland, OR	45	2,478,800
6.	Provo, UT	1	633,800
7.	Charlotte, NC	20	2,569,200
8.	Austin, TX	9	2,168,300
9.	Olympia, WA	19	286,400
10.	Des Moines, IA	77	655,400

Source: "The Best Places for Business and Careers," *Forbes*, https://www.forbes.com/best-places-for-business/list/ (accessed June 8, 2020).

Jacob Ammentorp Lund/Ammentorp/123RF

chapter 10 ten

managing
human resources

LEARNING OBJECTIVES

After reading this chapter, you will be able to:

LO 10-1 Explain the significance of human resource management.

LO 10-2 Summarize the processes of recruiting and selecting human resources for a company.

LO 10-3 Describe how workers are trained and their performance appraised.

LO 10-4 Identify the types of turnover companies may experience.

LO 10-5 Explain why turnover is an important issue.

LO 10-6 Specify the various ways a worker may be compensated.

LO 10-7 Evaluate some of the issues associated with unionized employees, including collective bargaining and dispute resolution.

LO 10-8 Describe the importance of diversity in the workforce.

If a business is to achieve success, it must have sufficient numbers of employees who are qualified and motivated to perform the required duties. Thus, managing the quantity (from hiring to firing) and quality (through training, compensating, and so on) of employees is an important business function. Meeting the challenge of managing increasingly diverse human resources effectively can give a company a competitive edge in a global marketplace.

This chapter focuses on the quantity and quality of human resources. First, we look at how human resource managers plan for, recruit, and select qualified employees. Next, we look at training, appraising, and compensating employees—aspects of human resource management designed to retain valued employees. Along the way, we'll also consider the challenges of managing unionized employees and workplace diversity.

THE NATURE OF HUMAN RESOURCE MANAGEMENT

In the "Dynamics of Business and Economics" chapter, *human resources* was defined as labor, the physical and mental abilities that people use to produce goods and services. **Human resource management (HRM)** refers to all the activities involved in determining an organization's human resource needs, as well as acquiring, training, and compensating people to fill those needs. Human resource managers are concerned with maximizing the satisfaction of employees and motivating them to meet organizational objectives productively. In some companies, this function is called personnel management.

HRM has increased in importance over the past few decades, in part because managers have developed a better understanding of human relations through the work of Maslow, Herzberg, and others. How employees are treated is also important to consumers. The conduct of an organization has an impact on the attitudes and behaviors of consumers. In a LinkedIn survey, almost 90 percent of millennials would consider accepting a lower salary from a company with similar values to their own.[1] Moreover, the human resources themselves are changing. Employees today are concerned not only about how much a job pays; they are concerned also with job satisfaction, personal performance, recreation, benefits, the work environment, and their opportunities for advancement. Today's workforce includes significantly more women, Blacks, Hispanics, and other minorities, as well as disabled and older workers, than in the past. Human resource managers must be aware of these changes and leverage them to increase the productivity of their employees. Every manager practices some of the functions of human resource management at all times.

human resource management (HRM) all the activities involved in determining an organization's human resources needs, as well as acquiring, training, and compensating people to fill those needs.

Today's organizations are more diverse, with a greater range of women, minorities, and older workers.
Rawpixel.com/Shutterstock

PLANNING FOR HUMAN RESOURCE NEEDS

When planning and developing strategies for reaching the organization's overall objectives, a company must consider whether it will have the human resources necessary to carry out its plans. After determining how many employees and what skills are needed to satisfy the overall plans, the human resource department (which may range from the owner in a small business to hundreds of people in a large corporation) ascertains how many employees the company currently has and how many will be retiring or otherwise leaving the organization during the planning period. With this information, the human resource manager can then forecast how many more employees the company will need to hire and what qualifications they must have or determine if lay-offs are required to meet demand more efficiently. HRM planning also requires forecasting the availability of people in the workforce who will have the necessary qualifications to meet the organization's future needs. The human resource manager then develops a strategy for satisfying the organization's human resource needs. As organizations strive to increase efficiency through outsourcing, automation, or learning to effectively use temporary workers, hiring needs can change dramatically.

Next, managers analyze the jobs within the organization so that they can match the human resources to the available

list the skills, knowledge, and education needed to fulfill a particular occupation (e.g., human resources).[2] A **job specification** describes the qualifications necessary for a specific job, in terms of education (some jobs require a college degree), experience, personal characteristics (ads frequently request outgoing, hard-working persons), and physical characteristics. Both the job description and job specification are used to develop recruiting materials such as newspapers, trade publications, and online advertisements.

LO 10-2 Summarize the processes of recruiting and selecting human resources for a company.

RECRUITING AND SELECTING NEW EMPLOYEES

After forecasting the firm's human resource needs and comparing them to existing human resources, the human resource manager should have a general idea of how many new employees the firm needs to hire. With the aid of job analyses, management can then recruit and select employees who are qualified to fill specific job openings.

Recruiting

Recruiting means forming a pool of qualified applicants from which management can select employees. There are two sources from which to develop this pool of applicants—internal and external.

> ## "Managers use the information obtained through a job analysis to develop job descriptions and job specifications."

assignments. **Job analysis** determines, through observation and study, pertinent information about a job—the specific tasks that comprise it; the knowledge, skills, and abilities necessary to perform it; and the environment in which it will be performed. Managers use the information obtained through a job analysis to develop job descriptions and job specifications.

A **job description** is a formal, written explanation of a specific job that usually includes job title, tasks to be performed (for instance, waiting on customers), relationship with other jobs, physical and mental skills required (such as lifting heavy boxes or calculating data), duties, responsibilities, and working conditions. Job seekers might turn to online websites or databases to help find job descriptions for specific occupations. For instance, the Occupational Information Network has an online database with hundreds of occupational descriptors. These descriptors

Internal sources of applicants include the organization's current employees. Many firms have a policy of giving first consideration to their own employees—or promoting from within. The cost of hiring current employees to fill job openings is inexpensive when compared with the cost of hiring from external sources, and it is good for employee morale. However, hiring from within creates another job vacancy to be filled.

External sources of applicants consist of advertisements in newspapers and professional journals, employment agencies, colleges, vocational schools, recommendations from current employees, competing firms, unsolicited applications, online websites, and social networking sites such as LinkedIn.

Internships are also a good way to solicit for potential employees. Many companies hire college students or recent graduates to low-paying internships that give them the opportunity to get hands-on experience on the job. If the intern proves to be a good fit, an organization may then hire the intern as a full-time worker.

There are also hundreds of websites where employers can post job openings and job seekers can post their résumés, including Monster, USAJobs, SimplyHired, and CareerBuilder. TheLadders.com is a website that focuses on career-driven professionals who make salaries of $100,000 or more. Employers looking for employees for specialized jobs can use more focused sites such as ComputerWork which lists jobs for people in technical careers. Increasingly, companies can turn to their own websites for potential candidates: Nearly all of the *Fortune 500* firms provide career websites where they recruit, provide employment information, and take applications.

Using these sources of applicants is generally more expensive than hiring from within, but it may be necessary if there are no current employees who meet the job specifications or there are better-qualified people outside of the organization. Recruiting for entry-level managerial and professional positions is often carried out on college and university campuses. For managerial or professional positions above the entry level, companies sometimes depend on employment agencies or executive search firms, sometimes called *headhunters*, that specialize in luring qualified people away from other companies. Employers are also increasingly using professional social networking sites such as LinkedIn (the most popular), Facebook, Instagram, Twitter, and blogs as recruitment tools.[3]

> **selection** the process of collecting information about applicants and using that information to make hiring decisions.

Selection

Selection is the process of collecting information about applicants and using that information to decide which ones to hire. It includes the application itself, as well as interviewing, testing, and reference checking. This process can be quite lengthy and expensive and is increasingly being completed online. Online job applications take from 1 minute to 52 minutes to complete, with a median completion time of 13 minutes. The longer the application process, the more applicants drop out and don't complete the application. *Business News Daily* found that 30 percent of candidates and 57 percent of those earning more than $100,000 will not spend more than 15 minutes on an application. With this in mind, AT&T revamped its online applications, cutting the number of screenshots by 50 percent. Its dropout rate fell 55 percent and generated 100,000 more

LinkedIn, a social network for professionals, has more than 660 million users.

aradaphotography/Shutterstock

desirable, quality applicants.[4] Companies are working to improve the online application process to attract the best pool of candidates for the job. Such rigorous scrutiny is necessary to find those applicants who can do the work expected and fit into the firm's structure and culture. If an organization finds the "right" employees through its recruiting and selection process, it will not have to spend as much money later in recruiting, selecting, and training replacement employees. Many companies have turned to artificial intelligence (AI) to support the recruitment and hiring process. AI has the ability to perform repetitive tasks such as scanning résumés for minimum qualifications. Some experts are concerned AI tools could lead to unintended bias so it's important to monitor equity algorithms.

The Application. In the first stage of the selection process, the individual fills out an application form and perhaps has a brief interview. The application form asks for the applicant's name, address, telephone number, education, and previous work experience. The goal of this stage of the selection process is to get acquainted with the applicants and to weed out those who are obviously not qualified for the job. For employees with work experience, most companies ask for the following information before contacting a potential candidate: current salary, reason for seeking a new job, years of experience, availability, and level of interest in the position. In addition to identifying obvious qualifications, the application can provide subtle clues about whether a person is appropriate for a particular job. For example, an applicant who gives unusually creative answers may be perfect for a position at an advertising agency; a person who turns in an application with incomplete sentences or errors probably would not be appropriate for a technical job requiring precise adjustments. Most companies exclusively accept online applications. To get a better view of the fit between the applicant and the company, the online application contains a questionnaire that asks applicants more specific questions, from how they might react in a certain situation to personality attributes like self-esteem or ability to interact with people.

The Interview. The next phase of the selection process involves interviewing applicants. Table 10.1 lists some of the most common questions asked by interviewers. The interviewer can answer the applicant's questions about the requirements for the job, compensation, working conditions, company policies, organizational culture, and so on. A potential employee's questions may be just as revealing as his or her answers. Today's students might be surprised to have an interviewer ask them about their social media activity. Currently, these are legal questions for an interviewer to ask, although some states have passed laws banning employers from asking applicants to divulge their user names and passwords to their private accounts.[5] Approximately 70 percent of recruiters use social media sites to screen job candidates.[6] It is also legal and common for companies to monitor employee work habits and e-mails. While this can be important for monitoring outside threats such as hacking or information leaks, employees might view this as the company's way of saying it does not trust them.

▼ **TABLE 10.1** Most Common Questions Asked during the Interview

1. What are your strengths?
2. What are your weaknesses?
3. Why are you interested in working for this company?
4. Where do you see yourself in five years? Ten years?
5. Why do you want to leave your current company?
6. Why was there a gap in your employment between [insert date] and [insert date]?
7. What can you offer us that someone else can not?
8. What are three things your former manager would like you to improve on?
9. Are you willing to relocate?
10. Are you willing to travel?

Source: "50 Most Common Interview Questions," *Glassdoor,* October 21, 2019, https://www.glassdoor.com/blog/common-interview-questions/ (accessed June 9, 2020).

Testing. Another step in the selection process is testing. Ability and performance tests are used to determine whether an applicant has the skills necessary for the job. Aptitude, IQ, or personality tests may be used to assess an applicant's potential for a certain kind of work as well as the applicant's ability to fit into the organization's culture. One of the most commonly used tests is the Myers-Briggs Type Indicator. The Myers-Briggs Type Indicator Test is used worldwide by millions of people each year. Although polygraph ("lie detector") tests were once a common technique for evaluating the honesty of applicants, in 1988 their use was restricted to specific government jobs and those involving security or access to drugs. Applicants may also undergo physical examinations to determine their suitability for some jobs, and many companies require applicants to be screened for illegal drug use.

Drug and alcohol abuse can be particularly damaging to business. There is a growing opioid addiction in this country, with more than 70 percent of employers impacted by prescription drug misuse. Of those, 65 percent feel justified in terminating employees for this abuse.[7] The cost to companies for dealing with drug and alcohol abuse is staggering; abuse of prescription painkillers alone is estimated to cost companies $42 billion due to lost productivity or absenteeism.[8] Small businesses may have a higher percentage of these employees because they do not engage in systematic drug testing. E-cigarettes are another growing concern. Many organizations have restrictions on cigarette use, but these policies do not necessarily apply to e-cigarettes. As e-cigarette use grows among employees, companies are having to establish policies and requirements for their proper use.[9]

Reference Checking. Before making a job offer, the company should always check an applicant's references. Reference checking usually involves verifying educational background and previous work experience. An Internet search is often done to determine social media activities or other public activities. Some of the employment trends related to background checks include the fact that criminal background checks are increasingly being

Personality tests such as Myers-Briggs are used to assess an applicant's potential for a certain kind of job. For instance, extroversion and a love of people would be good qualities for a retail job.

stockphoto mania/Shutterstock

delayed until after the interview or offer has been extended. With the growth in the gig and sharing economy, there will be more background checks for contingent workers. More companies will engage in continuous or ongoing background checks to keep the workplace safe. Social media screening will continue as nearly half of those using the technique find information that casts a negative light on the candidate.[10] Public companies are likely to do more extensive background searches to make sure applicants are not misrepresenting themselves.

Background checking is important because applicants may misrepresent themselves on their applications or résumés. Research has shown that those who are willing to exaggerate or lie on their résumés are more likely to engage in unethical behaviors.[11] As Table 10.2 illustrates, most of the common résumé lies relate to the applicant's college experience.

Reference checking is a vital, albeit often overlooked, stage in the selection process. Managers charged with hiring should be aware, however, that many organizations will confirm only that

▼ **TABLE 10.2** Top Ten Most Common Résumé Lies

1. Education
2. Employment dates
3. Technical skills
4. Previous employment history
5. Foreign language fluency
6. GPA
7. Previous job descriptions
8. Graduation year
9. Promotions
10. Salary

Source: "20 Most Common Lies on Resumes and Why Applicants Get Caught," *Skillsroads.com,* https://skillroads.com/blog/most-common-lies-on-resumes (accessed June 9, 2020).

an applicant is a former employee, perhaps with beginning and ending work dates, and will not release details about the quality of the employee's work.

Title VII of the Civil Rights Act prohibits discrimination in employment and created the Equal Employment Opportunity Commission.

Legal Issues in Recruiting and Selecting

Legal constraints and regulations are present in almost every phase of the recruitment and selection process, and a violation of these regulations can result in lawsuits and fines. Therefore, managers should be aware of these restrictions to avoid legal problems. Some of the laws affecting human resource management are discussed here.

Because one law pervades all areas of human resource management, we'll take a quick look at it now. **Title VII of the Civil Rights Act** of 1964 prohibits discrimination in employment. It also created the Equal Employment Opportunity Commission (EEOC), a federal agency dedicated to increasing job opportunities for women and minorities and eliminating job discrimination based on race, religion, color, gender identity, sexual orientation national origin, or handicap. As a result of Title VII, employers must not impose sex distinctions in job specifications, job descriptions, or newspaper advertisements. In 2019, workplace discrimination charges filed with the EEOC were 72,675. The top five types of discrimination include retaliation, race, disability, sex, and age.[12] The Civil Rights Act of 1964 also outlaws the use of discriminatory tests for applicants. Aptitude tests and other indirect tests must be validated; in other words, employers must be able to demonstrate that scores on such tests are related to job performance so that no one race has an advantage in taking the tests or is alternatively discriminated against. Diversity still has room for improvement, particularly in management. Only 7.4 percent of Fortune 500 companies have a woman CEO and less than 1 percent have a Black CEO.[13]

Other laws affecting HRM include the Americans with Disabilities Act (ADA), which prevents discrimination against disabled persons. It also classifies people with AIDS as handicapped and, consequently, prohibits using a positive AIDS test as reason to deny an applicant employment. The Age Discrimination in Employment Act specifically outlaws discrimination based on age. Its focus is banning hiring practices that discriminate against people 40 years and older. Generally, when companies need employees, recruiters head to college campuses, and when downsizing is necessary, many older workers are offered early retirement. Forced retirement based on age, however, is generally considered to be illegal in the United States, although claims of forced retirement still abound. Indeed, there are many benefits that companies are realizing in hiring older workers. Some of these benefits include the fact that they are more dedicated, punctual, honest, and detail-oriented; are good listeners; take pride in their work; exhibit good organizational skills; are efficient and confident; are mature; can be seen as role models; have good communication skills; and offer

The Department of Labor has oversight over workplace safety, wages and work hours, unemployment benefits, and more. It often files lawsuits against firms that it believes are treating workers unfairly and violating labor laws.

B Christopher/Alamy Stock Photo

orientation

familiarizing newly hired employees with fellow workers, company procedures, and the physical properties of the company.

training teaching employees to do specific job tasks through either classroom development or on-the-job experience.

an opportunity for a reduced labor cost because of already having insurance plans.[14]

The Equal Pay Act mandates that men and women who do equal work must receive the same wage. Wage differences are acceptable only if they are attributed to seniority, performance, or qualifications. It is estimated that women make 80 cents on the dollar what their male counterparts make. The wage gap increases for African American and Hispanic women, at 62.5 percent and 54.4 percent what their male counterparts make, respectively.[15] While gender wage gaps vary by industry, a financial analytics company found that the wage gap tends to decrease among jobs that pay lower wages, at just under 5 percent. Professions with the lowest wage gaps include transportation, storage, and distribution managers; stock clerks and order fillers; and counselors (female counselors actually earn more on average than male counselors). The widest gap is among personal financial advisors, estimated to be at

55.6 percent.[16] However, despite the wage inequalities that still exist, women are becoming increasingly accepted in the workplace. The working mother is no longer a novelty; in fact, many working mothers seek the same amount of achievement as any other worker—with or without children.

DEVELOPING THE WORKFORCE

Once the most qualified applicants have been selected, have been offered positions, and have accepted their offers, they must be formally introduced to the organization and trained so they can begin to be productive members of the workforce. **Orientation** familiarizes the newly hired employees with fellow workers, company procedures, and the physical properties of the company. It generally includes a tour of the building; introductions to supervisors, co-workers, and subordinates; and the distribution of organizational manuals describing the organization's policy on vacations, absenteeism, lunch breaks, company benefits, and so on. Orientation also involves socializing the new employee into the ethics and culture of the new company. Many larger companies now show videos of procedures, facilities, and key personnel in the organization to help speed the adjustment process.

LO 10-3 Describe how workers are trained and their performance appraised.

Training and Development

Although recruiting and selection are designed to find employees who have the knowledge, skills, and abilities the company needs, new employees still must undergo **training** to learn how to do their specific job tasks. *On-the-job training* allows workers to learn by actually performing the tasks of the job, while *classroom training* teaches employees with lectures, conferences, videos, case studies, and web-based training. McDonald's has always had a strong training presence at Hamburger University. With major management transitions and plans for 4,000

"ALTHOUGH RECRUITING AND SELECTION ARE DESIGNED TO FIND EMPLOYEES WHO HAVE THE KNOWLEDGE, SKILLS, AND ABILITIES THE COMPANY NEEDS, NEW EMPLOYEES STILL MUST UNDERGO TRAINING TO LEARN HOW TO DO THEIR SPECIFIC JOB TASKS."

McDonald's Hamburger University, with locations in Chicago, Tokyo, London, Sydney, Munich, Shanghai, and São Paulo, provides learning and training for its employees and partners to build long-lasting careers.

Qilai Shen/Bloomberg/Getty Images

about the quality of the firm's selection, training, and development activities.

Performance appraisals may be objective or subjective. An objective assessment is quantifiable. For example, a Westinghouse employee might be judged by how many circuit boards the employee typically produces in one day or by how many of the employee's boards have defects. A RE/MAX real estate agent might be judged by the number of listings the agent has shown or the number of sales the agent has closed. A company can also use tests as an objective method of assessment. Whatever method they use, managers must take into account the work environment when they appraise performance objectively.

When jobs do not lend themselves to objective appraisal, the manager must relate the employee's performance to some other standard. One popular tool used in subjective assessment is the ranking system, which lists various performance factors on which the manager ranks employees against each other. Although used by many large companies, ranking systems are unpopular with many employees. Qualitative criteria, such as teamwork and communication skills, used to evaluate employees are generally hard to gauge. Such grading systems have triggered employee lawsuits that allege discrimination in grade/ranking assignments. For example, one manager may grade a company's employees one way, while another manager grades a group more harshly depending on the managers' grading style. If layoffs occur, then employees graded by the second manager may be more likely to lose their jobs. Other criticisms of grading systems include unclear wording or inappropriate words that a manager may unintentionally write in a performance evaluation, like *youthful* or *attractive* to describe an employee's appearance. These liabilities can all be fodder for lawsuits should employees allege that they were treated

company-owned restaurants to become franchises, the company is now investing in a virtual training platform through cloud-based technology to reach many of these new global operators.[17]

Some companies will go even further and ask a more experienced individual in the organization to mentor a new employee. **Mentoring** involves supporting, training, and guiding an employee in his or her professional development. Mentoring provides employees with more of a one-on-one interaction with somebody in the organization who not only teaches them but also acts as their supporter as they progress in their jobs. Another benefit of mentoring is that companies can use this process to attract talent from underrepresented areas. For instance, mentoring has been suggested as a way to attract more women into male-dominated industries.

Development is training that augments the skills and knowledge of managers and professionals. Training and development are also used to improve the skills of employees in their present positions and to prepare them for increased responsibility and job promotions. Training is, therefore, a vital function of human resource management. At The Container Store, for example, first-year sales personnel receive more than 200 hours of formal training about the company's products versus an industry average of eight hours.[18] Companies are engaging in more experiential and involvement-oriented training exercises for employees. Use of role-plays, simulations, and online training methods are becoming increasingly popular in employee training.

Assessing Performance

Assessing employees' performance—their strengths and weaknesses on the job—is one of the most difficult tasks for managers. However, performance appraisal is crucial because it gives employees feedback on how they are doing and what they need to do to improve. It also provides a basis for determining how to compensate and reward employees, and it generates information

Performance appraisals are important because they provide employees with feedback on how well they are doing as well as areas for improvement.

bluedog studio/Shutterstock

turnover occurs when employees quit or are fired and must be replaced by new employees.

promotion a persuasive form of communication that attempts to expedite a marketing exchange by influencing individuals, groups, and organizations to accept goods, services, and ideas.

transfer a move to another job within the company at essentially the same level and wage.

separations employment changes involving resignation, retirement, termination, or layoff.

unfairly. Therefore, it is crucial that managers use clear language in performance evaluations and be consistent with all employees.

Another performance appraisal method used by many companies is the 360-degree feedback system, which provides feedback from a panel that typically includes superiors, peers, and subordinates. Because of the tensions it may cause, peer appraisal appears to be difficult for many. However, companies that have success with 360-degree feedback tend to be open to learning, willing to experiment, and are led by executives who are direct about the expected benefits as well as the challenges.[19] Managers and leaders with a high emotional intelligence (sensitivity to their own as well as others' emotions) assess and reflect upon their interactions with colleagues on a daily basis. In addition, they conduct follow-up analysis on their projects, asking the right questions and listening carefully to responses without getting defensive of their actions.[20]

Another trend occurring at some companies is the decrease of negative employee feedback. Executives have begun to recognize that hard tactics can harm employee confidence. Negative feedback tends to overshadow positive feedback, so employees may get discouraged if performance reviews are phrased too negatively. At the same time, it is important for managers to provide constructive criticism on employee weaknesses in addition to their strengths so workers know what to expect and how they are viewed.[21]

Whether the assessment is objective or subjective, it is vital that managers discuss the results with their employees, so that they know how well they are doing their jobs. The results of a performance appraisal become useful only when they are communicated, tactfully, to employees and presented as a tool to allow the employees to grow and improve in their positions and beyond. Performance appraisals are also used to determine whether an employee should be promoted, transferred, or terminated from the organization.

LO 10-4 Identify the types of turnover companies may experience.

Turnover

Turnover, which occurs when employees quit or are fired and must be replaced by new employees, results in lost productivity from the vacancy, costs to recruit replacement employees,

Many companies in recent years are choosing to downsize by eliminating jobs. Reasons for downsizing might be due to financial constraints or the need to become more productive and competitive.
belterz/iStockphoto

management time devoted to interviewing, training, and socialization expenses for new employees. Gallup research shows that approximately 75 percent of the reasons for voluntary turnover involve areas that management can influence.[22] Companies can therefore significantly impact turnover rates. Of course, turnover is not always an unhappy occasion when it takes the form of a promotion or transfer.

A **promotion** is an advancement to a higher-level job with increased authority, responsibility, and pay. In some companies and most labor unions, seniority—the length of time a person has been with the company or at a particular job classification—is the key issue in determining who should be promoted. Most managers base promotions on seniority only when they have candidates with equal qualifications. Managers prefer to base promotions on merit.

A **transfer** is a move to another job within the company at essentially the same level and wage. Transfers allow workers to obtain new skills or to find a new position within an organization when their old position has been eliminated because of automation or downsizing.

Separations occur when employees resign, retire, are terminated, or are laid off. Employees may be terminated, or fired, for poor performance, violation of work rules, absenteeism, and so on. Businesses have traditionally been able to fire employees *at will*—that is, for any reason other than for race, religion, sex, or age, or because an employee is a union organizer. However, recent legislation and court decisions now require that companies fire employees fairly, for just cause only. Managers must take care, then, to warn employees when their performance is unacceptable and may lead to dismissal, elevating the importance of performance evaluations. They should also document all problems and warnings in employees' work records. To avoid the possibility of lawsuits from individuals who may feel they have been fired unfairly, employers should provide clear, business-related reasons for any firing, supported by written documentation if possible. Employee disciplinary procedures

wage/salary survey a study that tells a company how much compensation comparable firms are paying for specific jobs that the firms have in common.

wages financial rewards based on the number of hours the employee works or the level of output achieved.

▼ **TABLE 10.3** Actions You Should and Shouldn't Take When You Are Terminated

1. Do not criticize your boss who terminated you.
2. Do not take files or property that is not yours.
3. Do try to get a reference letter.
4. Do not criticize your former employer during job interviews.
5. Do look to the future and be positive about new job opportunities.

should be carefully explained to all employees and should be set forth in employee handbooks. Table 10.3 illustrates what to do and what *not* to do when you are terminated.

LO 10-5 Explain why turnover is an important issue.

Many companies have downsized in recent years, laying off tens of thousands of employees in their effort to become more productive and competitive. Layoffs are sometimes temporary; employees may be brought back when business conditions improve. When layoffs are to be permanent, employers often help employees find other jobs and may extend benefits while the employees search for new employment. Such actions help lessen the trauma of the layoffs. Fortunately, there are several business areas that are choosing not to downsize.

A well-organized human resource department strives to minimize losses due to separations and transfers because recruiting and training new employees is very expensive. Note that a high turnover rate in a company may signal problems with the selection and training process, the compensation program, or even the type of company. To help reduce turnover, companies have tried a number of strategies, including giving employees more interesting job responsibilities (job enrichment), allowing for increased job flexibility, and providing more employee benefits. When employees do choose to leave the organization, the company will often ask them to participate in an *exit interview*. An exit interview is a survey used to determine why the employee is leaving the organization. The company hopes that this feedback will alert them to processes they can improve upon to dissuade valuable employees from leaving in the future.

LO 10-6 Specify the various ways a worker may be compensated.

COMPENSATING THE WORKFORCE

People generally don't work for free, and how much they are paid for their work is a complicated issue. Also, designing a fair compensation plan is an important task because pay and benefits represent a substantial portion of an organization's expenses. Wages that are too high may result in the company's products being priced too high, making them uncompetitive in the market. Wages that are too low may damage employee morale and result in costly turnover. Remember that compensation is one of the hygiene factors identified by Herzberg.

Designing a fair compensation plan is a difficult task because it involves evaluating the relative worth of all jobs within the business while allowing for individual efforts. Compensation for a specific job is typically determined through a **wage/salary survey**, which tells the company how much compensation comparable firms are paying for specific jobs that the firms have in common. Compensation for individuals within a specific job category depends on both the compensation for that job and the individual's productivity. Therefore, two employees with identical jobs may not receive exactly the same pay because of individual differences in performance.

Financial Compensation

Financial compensation falls into two general categories—wages and salaries. **Wages** are financial rewards based on the number of hours the employee works or the level of output achieved. Wages based on the number of hours worked are called time wages. The federal minimum wage is $7.25 per hour for covered nonexempt workers.[23] Tipped wages may be $2.13 per hour as long as tips plus the wage of $2.13 per hour equal the minimum wage of $7.25 per hour, although some states require minimum wage and then tips added on top.[24] Many states also mandate minimum wages; in the case where this conflicts with the federal minimum wage, the higher of the two wages prevails. There may even be differences between city and state minimum wages. In Maryland, the minimum wage is $11, whereas its next door neighbor Washington D.C. has a minimum wage of $15.[25] Time wages are appropriate when employees are continually interrupted and when quality is more important than quantity. Assembly-line workers, clerks, and maintenance personnel are commonly paid on a time-wage basis. The advantage of time wages is the ease of computation. The disadvantage is that time wages provide no incentive to increase productivity. In fact, time wages may encourage employees to be less productive.

To overcome these disadvantages, many companies pay on an incentive system, using piece wages or commissions. Piece wages are based on the level of output achieved. A major advantage of piece wages is that they motivate employees to supervise their own activities and to increase output. Skilled craftworkers are often paid on a piece-wage basis.

commission an incentive system that pays a fixed amount or a percentage of the employee's sales.

salary a financial reward calculated on a weekly, monthly, or annual basis.

bonuses monetary rewards offered by companies for exceptional performance as incentives to further increase productivity.

profit sharing a form of compensation whereby a percentage of company profits is distributed to the employees whose work helped to generate them.

benefits nonfinancial forms of compensation provided to employees, such as pension plans, health insurance, paid vacation and holidays, and the like.

The other incentive system, **commission**, pays a fixed amount or a percentage of the employee's sales. Skincare direct seller Rodan + Fields uses independent contractors to sell its products. Consultants earn commissions on whatever products they sell. This method motivates employees to sell as much as they can. Some companies also combine payment based on commission with time wages or salaries.

A **salary** is a financial reward calculated on a weekly, monthly, or annual basis. Salaries are associated with white-collar workers such as office personnel, executives, and professional employees. Although a salary provides a stable stream of income, salaried workers may be required to work beyond usual hours without additional financial compensation.

In addition to the basic wages or salaries paid to employees, a company may offer **bonuses** for exceptional performance as an incentive to increase productivity further. Many workers receive a bonus as a "thank you" for good work and an incentive to continue working hard. Many owners and managers are recognizing that simple bonuses and perks foster happier employees and reduce turnover. Bonuses are especially popular among Wall Street firms. Wall Street executives' bonuses rise when the United States has an improving economy and strong performance in the financial sector.[26]

Another form of compensation is **profit sharing**, which distributes a percentage of company profits to the employees whose work helped to generate those profits. Some profit-sharing plans involve distributing shares of company stock to employees. Usually referred to as *ESOPs*—employee stock ownership plans— they have been gaining popularity in recent years. One reason for the popularity of ESOPs is the sense of partnership that they create between the organization and employees. Profit sharing can also motivate employees to work hard because increased productivity and sales mean that the profits or the stock dividends will increase. Many organizations offer employees a stake in the company through stock purchase plans, ESOPs, or stock investments through 401(k) plans. Companies are adopting broad-based stock option plans to build a stronger link between employees' interests and the organization's interests. Businesses have found employee stock options a great way to boost productivity and increase morale.

Onsite child care is just one of the benefits large companies have begun to offer employees.

Ariel Skelley/Blend Images/Getty Images

Benefits

Benefits are nonfinancial forms of compensation provided to employees, such as pension plans for retirement; health, disability, and life insurance; holidays and paid days off for vacation or illness; credit union membership; health programs; child care; elder care; assistance with adoption; and more. According to the Bureau of Labor Statistics, employer costs for employee compensation in the United States averaged $34.72 per hour worked. Wages and salaries accounted for more than 68 percent of these costs, while benefits account for more than 31 percent of the cost.[27] Such benefits increase employee security and, to a certain extent, their morale and motivation.

Although health insurance is a common benefit for full-time employees, rising health care costs have forced a growing number of employers to trim this benefit. Even government workers, whose wages and benefits used to be virtually guaranteed safe, have seen reductions in health care and other benefits. On the other hand, employee loyalty tends to increase when employees feel that the firm cares about them. Starbucks recognizes the importance of how benefits can significantly affect an employee's health and well-being. As a result, it offers its part-time employees health insurance. Additionally, Starbucks began offering employees a benefit called College Achievement Plan in which it will pay full tuition for employees to finish a bachelor's degree at Arizona State University.[28]

A benefit increasingly offered is the employee assistance program (EAP). Each company's EAP is different, but most offer counseling for and assistance with those employees' personal problems that might hurt their job performance if not addressed. The most common counseling services offered include drug- and alcohol-abuse treatment programs, fitness

PAY DAY: EMPLOYERS CHOOSE BONUSES OVER RAISES

Since the Great Recession, companies have begun awarding more bonuses and benefits like vacation time and 401(k) contributions. Bonuses allow companies greater flexibility with wages while giving employees incentives to meet goals. The trend of bonuses continues to increase. Bonuses are growing at a faster rate than salary and wage increases. In recent years, bonus compensation accounted for 12.7 percent of compensation budgets, while salary increases were 2.9 percent.

Bonuses give companies the flexibility to lower costs during economic downturns and reward employees when financial performance is good. While bonuses can be a great compensation system, they may not always be the right solution. For instance, during the COVID-19 (coronavirus) pandemic, retailers offered frontline essential workers temporary wage increases. The biggest downside to bonuses is that they are not guaranteed. Companies have found that cutting bonuses is more favorable than cutting salaries during economic downturns. On the other hand, bonuses can lead to increased compensation for top performers. Companies can use bonuses to reward top performers they deem as strategically important without having to raise wages for all employees. Bonuses are a great tool to attract top-tier talent.

The Tax Cuts and Jobs Act of 2017 led to increased media coverage about corporate bonuses. Companies like Comcast and AT&T gave out one-time lump sums to their employees because of the act. Other companies are taking a different approach. Amazon increased the minimum wage of all hourly employees to $15 an hour. This came at the cost of cutting bonuses, incentives, and employee stock option plans. Amazon's situation highlights the trade-offs many companies must make between increasing salaries or providing bonuses for exceptional performance.[b]

Critical Thinking Questions

1. What are some of the benefits of bonuses for companies and employees?

2. What might be some disadvantages of bonuses for employees?

3. Do you think that lowering bonuses to increase salaries for the entire workforce will disincentivize top performers at companies?

---

programs, smoking-cessation clinics, stress-management clinics, financial counseling, family counseling, and career counseling. Home Depot offers an employee assistance program that is called CARE/Solutions for Life. The program focuses on three areas: free financial consultation by phone; free legal consultation; and three free face-to-face counseling sessions to assist with personal, family, or work life.[29] EAPs help reduce costs associated with poor productivity, absenteeism, and other workplace issues by helping employees deal with personal problems that contribute to these issues. For example, exercise and fitness programs reduce health insurance costs by helping employees stay healthy. Family counseling may help workers trying to cope with a divorce or other personal problems to better focus on their jobs.

Companies try to provide the benefits they believe their employees want, but diverse people may want different things. In recent years, some single workers have felt that co-workers with spouses and children seem to get "special breaks" and extra time off to deal with family issues. Some companies use flexible benefit programs to allow employees to choose the benefits they would like, up to a specified amount.

Fringe benefits include sick leave, vacation pay, pension plans, health plans, and any other extra compensation. Many states and cities are adopting new policies on sick leave that mandate a certain number of paid sick days a worker can take. It is often lower-wage employees who do not receive paid sick leave, yet they are the ones who usually cannot afford to take a day off if it is unpaid.[30] *Soft benefits* include perks that help balance life and work. They include onsite child care, spas, food service, and even laundry services and hair salons. These soft benefits motivate employees and give them more time to focus on their job. They also inspire loyalty to the company. Facebook is known for its positive work/life balance and for the numerous benefits it provides employees. The importance of management fueling a positive work/life balance of employees can be seen through Facebook's constant employee support after the Cambridge Analytica breach. Employees' attitudes toward the firm remained unwavering, with many saying the anger at Facebook by the public is misplaced. In fact, Facebook's rating on Glassdoor remained between 4.5 and 4.6 out of 5, even after the breach was announced.[31]

Cafeteria benefit plans provide a financial amount to employees so that they can select the specific benefits that fit their needs. The key is making benefits flexible, rather than giving employees identical benefits. As firms go global, the need for cafeteria or flexible benefit plans becomes even more important. For some employees, benefits are a greater motivator and differentiator in jobs than wages. For many Starbucks employees who receive health insurance when working part-time, this benefit could be the most important compensation. Over the past two decades, the list of fringe benefits offered by employers has grown dramatically, and new benefits are being added every year.

labor unions employee organizations formed to deal with employers for achieving better pay, hours, and working conditions.

collective bargaining the negotiation process through which management and unions reach an agreement about compensation, working hours, and working conditions for the bargaining unit.

labor contract the formal, written document that spells out the relationship between the union and management for a specified period of time—usually two or three years.

picketing a public protest against management practices that involves union members marching and carrying antimanagement signs at the employer's plant.

LO 10-7 Evaluate some of the issues associated with unionized employees, including collective bargaining and dispute resolution.

MANAGING UNIONIZED EMPLOYEES

Employees who are dissatisfied with their working conditions or compensation have to negotiate with management to bring about change. Dealing with management on an individual basis is not always effective, however, so employees may organize themselves into **labor unions** to deal with employers and to achieve better pay, hours, and working conditions. Organized employees are backed by the power of a large group that can hire specialists to represent the entire union in its dealings with management. Union workers make significantly more than nonunion employees. The United States has roughly 10.5 percent of wage and salary workers who are members of unions. On average, the median usual weekly earnings of unionized full-time and salary workers are about $200 more than their nonunion counterparts.[32]

However, union growth has slowed in recent years, and prospects for growth do not look good. One reason is that most blue-collar workers, the traditional members of unions, have already been organized. Factories have become more automated and need fewer blue-collar workers. The United States has shifted from a manufacturing to a service economy, further reducing the demand for blue-collar workers. Moreover, in response to foreign competition, U.S. companies are scrambling to find ways to become more productive and cost-efficient. Job enrichment programs and participative management have blurred the line between management and workers. Because workers' say in the way plants are run is increasing, their need for union protection is decreasing. Many workers do not see the benefits of union membership if they do not have complaints or grievances against their employers.[33]

Nonetheless, labor unions have been successful in organizing blue-collar manufacturing, government, and health care

> The United States has shifted from a manufacturing to a service economy, further reducing the demand for blue-collar workers.

workers, as well as smaller percentages of employees in other industries. Consequently, significant aspects of HRM, particularly compensation, are dictated to a large degree by union contracts at many companies. Therefore, we'll take a brief look at collective bargaining and dispute resolution in this section.

Collective Bargaining

Collective bargaining is the negotiation process through which management and unions reach an agreement about compensation, working hours, and working conditions for the bargaining unit (Figure 10.1). The objective of negotiations is to reach agreement about a **labor contract**, the formal, written document that spells out the relationship between the union and management for a specified period of time, usually two or three years.

In collective bargaining, each side tries to negotiate an agreement that meets its demands; compromise is frequently necessary. Management tries to negotiate a labor contract that permits the company to retain control over things like work schedules; the hiring and firing of workers; production standards; promotions, transfers, and separations; the span of management in each department; and discipline. Unions tend to focus on contract issues such as magnitude of wages; better pay rates for overtime, holidays, and undesirable shifts; scheduling of pay increases; and benefits. These issues will be spelled out in the labor contract, which union members will vote to either accept (and abide by) or reject.

Many labor contracts contain a *cost-of-living escalator* (or *adjustment*) *(COLA) clause*, which calls for automatic wage increases during periods of inflation to protect the "real" income of the employees. During tough economic times, unions may be forced to accept *givebacks*—wage and benefit concessions made to employers to allow them to remain competitive or, in some cases, to survive and continue to provide jobs for union workers.

Resolving Disputes

Sometimes, management and labor simply cannot agree on a contract. Most labor disputes are handled through collective bargaining or through grievance procedures. When these processes break down, however, either side may resort to more drastic measures to achieve its objectives.

Labor Tactics. **Picketing** is a public protest against management practices and involves union members marching (often waving antimanagement signs and placards) at the employer's plant or work site. Picketing workers hope that their signs will arouse sympathy for their demands from the public and from other unions. Picketing may occur as a protest or in conjunction with a strike.

Strikes (employee walkouts) are one of the most effective weapons labor has. By striking, a union makes carrying out the normal operations of a business difficult at best and impossible at worst. Strikes receive widespread publicity, but they remain a weapon of last resort. However, in extreme cases, workers may organize a strike with the help of unions and coalitions. McDonald's employees in St. Louis went on strike in 2020 amid

---

strikes employee walkouts; one of the most effective weapons labor has.

boycott an attempt to keep people from purchasing the products of a company.

lockout management's version of a strike, wherein a work site is closed so that employees cannot go to work.

strikebreakers people hired by management to replace striking employees; called "scabs" by striking union members.

---

the COVID-19 (coronavirus) pandemic over unsafe working conditions, lost hours, and pay cuts.[34] While it is mostly the case that the mere threat of a strike is enough to make management back down, there are times when the issues are heatedly debated and regulatory agencies become involved.[35]

A **boycott** is an attempt to keep people from purchasing the products of a company. In a boycott, union members are asked not to do business with the boycotted organization. Some unions may even impose fines on members who ignore the boycott. To gain further support for their objectives, a union involved in a boycott may also ask the public—through picketing and advertising—not to purchase the products of the picketed firm.

Management Tactics. Management's version of a strike is the **lockout**; management actually closes a work site so that employees cannot go to work. Lockouts are used, as a general rule, only when a union strike has partially shut down a plant and it seems less expensive for the plant to close completely. Honeywell workers, after a 10-month lockout, returned to their jobs after agreeing to a new contract with management. More than 350 employees in Indiana and New York returned to work where replacement workers had been filling their jobs.[36]

Strikebreakers, called "scabs" by striking union members, are people hired by management to replace striking employees. Managers hire strikebreakers to continue operations and reduce the losses associated with strikes—and to show the unions that they will not bow to their demands. Strikebreaking is generally a last-resort measure for management because it does great damage to the relationship between management and labor.

Outside Resolution. Management and union members normally reach

---

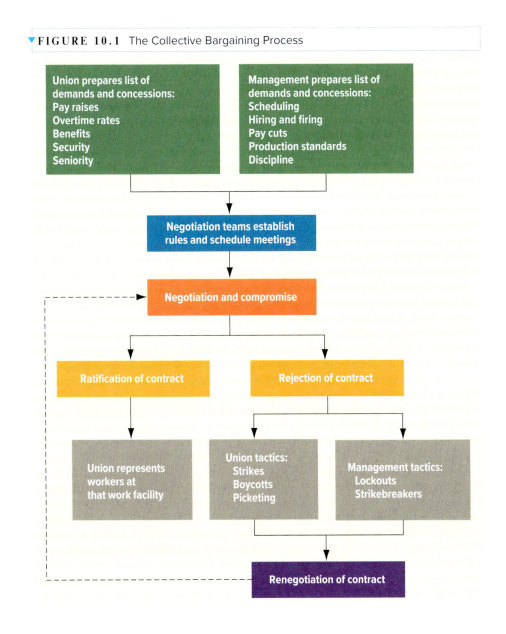

▼ **FIGURE 10.1** The Collective Bargaining Process

Union prepares list of demands and concessions:
Pay raises
Overtime rates
Benefits
Security
Seniority

Management prepares list of demands and concessions:
Scheduling
Hiring and firing
Pay cuts
Production standards
Discipline

Negotiation teams establish rules and schedule meetings

Negotiation and compromise

Ratification of contract

Rejection of contract

Union represents workers at that work facility

Union tactics:
Strikes
Boycotts
Picketing

Management tactics:
Lockouts
Strikebreakers

Renegotiation of contract

---

conciliation a method of outside resolution of labor and management differences in which a third party is brought in to keep the two sides talking.

mediation a method of outside resolution of labor and management differences in which the third party's role is to suggest or propose a solution to the problem.

arbitration settlement of a labor/ management dispute by a third party whose solution is legally binding and enforceable.

diversity the participation of different ages, genders, races, ethnicities, nationalities, and abilities in the workplace.

mutually agreeable decisions without outside assistance. Sometimes though, even after lengthy negotiations, strikes, lockouts, and other tactics, management and labor still cannot resolve a contract dispute. In such cases, they have three choices: conciliation, mediation, and arbitration. **Conciliation** brings in a neutral third party to keep labor and management talking. The conciliator has no formal power over union representatives or over management. The conciliator's goal is to get both parties to focus on the issues and to prevent negotiations from breaking down. Like conciliation, **mediation** involves bringing in a neutral third party, but the mediator's role is to suggest or propose a solution to the problem. With **arbitration**, a neutral third party is brought in to settle the dispute, but the arbitrator's solution is legally binding and enforceable. Generally, arbitration takes place on a voluntary basis—management and labor must agree to it, and they usually split the cost (the arbitrator's fee and expenses) between them. Occasionally, management and labor submit to *compulsory arbitration*, in which an outside party (usually the federal government) requests arbitration as a means of eliminating a prolonged strike that threatens to disrupt the economy.

THE IMPORTANCE OF WORKFORCE DIVERSITY

Customers, employees, suppliers—all the participants in the world of business—come in different ages, genders, races, ethnicities, nationalities, and abilities, a truth that business has come to label **diversity**. Understanding this diversity means recognizing and accepting differences as well as valuing the unique perspectives such differences can bring to the workplace.

LO 10-8 Describe the importance of diversity in the workforce.

The Characteristics of Diversity

When managers speak of diverse workforces, they typically mean differences in gender and race. While gender and race are important characteristics of diversity, others are also important. We can divide these differences into primary and secondary characteristics of diversity. In the lower segment of Figure 10.2, sexual orientation, age, gender, race, ethnicity, and abilities represent *primary characteristics* of diversity. In the upper section of Figure 10.2 are eight *secondary characteristics* of diversity—education, work background, income, marital status, parental status, military experience, religious beliefs, geographic location. We acquire, change, and discard these characteristics as we progress through our lives.

Defining characteristics of diversity as either primary or secondary enhances our understanding, but we must remember that each person is defined by the interrelation of all characteristics. In dealing with diversity in the workforce, managers must consider the complete person—not one or a few of a person's differences.

▼ **FIGURE 10.2** Characteristics of Diversity

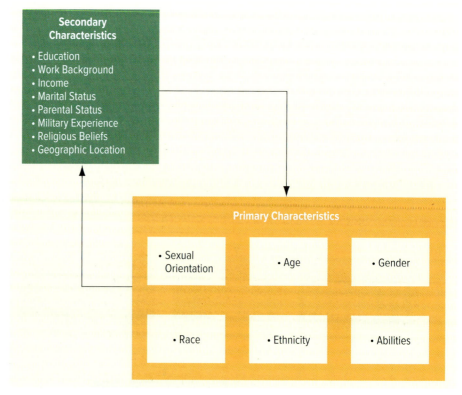

Secondary Characteristics
- Education
- Work Background
- Income
- Marital Status
- Parental Status
- Military Experience
- Religious Beliefs
- Geographic Location

Primary Characteristics
- Sexual Orientation
- Age
- Gender
- Race
- Ethnicity
- Abilities

Source: Marilyn Loden and Judy B. Rosener, *Workforce America! Managing Employee Diversity as a Vital Resource* (New York: McGraw-Hill, 1991), p. 20.

Why Is Diversity Important?

The U.S. workforce is becoming increasingly diverse. Once dominated by white men, today's workforce includes significantly more women, Blacks, Hispanics, and other minorities, as well as disabled and older workers. The Census Bureau predicts that by 2044, minorities will be the majority in the United States[37] These groups have traditionally faced discrimination and higher unemployment rates and have been denied opportunities to assume leadership roles in corporate America. Consequently, more and more companies are trying to improve HRM programs to recruit, develop, and retain more diverse employees to better serve their diverse customers. Some firms are providing special programs such as sponsored affinity groups, mentoring programs, and special career development opportunities. Silicon Valley startup Social Capital and its CEO Chamath Palihapitiya have focused on investing in and nurturing more startups in some of the controversial industries like education and health care because they are imperative and typically handicapped by bias or perceived risk. Their program, Capital-as-a-Service (CAAS), automates early investment decisions and thus eliminates bias against unconventional startups. CAAS received 30,000 applications from startups and invested in 30, with half the funded CEOs being nonwhite and 40 percent female.[38] Table 10.4 shows the top companies for minorities according to a study by *DiversityInc.* Effectively managing diversity in the workforce involves cultivating and valuing its benefits and minimizing its problems.

▼ **TABLE 10.4** Top 10 Companies for Diversity

1. Marriott International, Inc.
2. Hilton
3. Eli Lilly and Company
4. ADP
5. Accenture
6. Mastercard
7. Comcast NBCUniversal
8. Abbott
9. TIAA
10. Toyota Motor North America, Inc.

Source: DiversityInc, "The 2020 DiversityInc Top 50 Companies for Diversity," https://www.diversityinc.com/the-2020-top-50-diversityinc/ (accessed June 8, 2020).

The Benefits of Workforce Diversity

There are a number of benefits to fostering and valuing workforce diversity, including the following:

1. More productive use of a company's human resources.

2. Reduced conflict among employees of different ethnicities, races, religions, and sexual orientations as they learn to respect each other's differences.

3. More productive working relationships among diverse employees as they learn more about and accept each other.

WOMEN "LEAN IN" TO LEADERSHIP

More companies are recognizing the advantages of a diverse workforce. However, despite positive changes, men still vastly outnumber women in the executive suite, also known as the C-suite. Sheryl Sandberg, chief operating officer of Facebook, wrote a popular book called *Lean In: Women, Work, and the Will to Lead* about women in the workforce that empowers women to take on leadership roles.

Sandberg's book addresses the fact that while women are obtaining degrees at a higher rate than men and are aspiring to have high-paying careers after college, they often fall behind their male colleagues. Women are more likely than men to quit their jobs or scale back their hours after having children.

Research has indicated that the pay gap between genders widens as women progress in their careers because women are more likely to take off from work to take care of children. It is notable that the gap shrinks once female workers are beyond their child-bearing years.

Getting to the C-suite is difficult, but Sandberg wants to encourage both women and businesses to see that female executives can not only maintain a strong work-life balance but also make strong leaders. Susan Wojcicki, CEO of YouTube; Hanneke Smits, CEO of Newton Investment Management Company in the UK; and Karen Finerman, CEO of Metropolitan Capital Advisors and a panelist on CNBC's *Fast Money,* demonstrate that women can be business leaders without having to sacrifice family. Thanks to Sandberg's *Lean In,* 44,000 Lean In circles have been established globally. These circles consist of small groups of women who meet to provide education, expert advice, and discussion about leadership. The idea is to gain new skills and expand the ability to influence others.[c]

Critical Thinking Questions

1. Do you think *Lean In* and Lean In circles will have a long-term beneficial impact?

2. Describe some ways that companies can support women in leadership.

3. In what ways can both men and women maintain a strong work/life balance?

Some of the major benefits of diversity include a wider range of employee perspectives, greater innovation and creativity, and the ability to target a diverse customer base more effectively.

Inti St Clair/Blend Images

affirmative action programs legally mandated plans that try to increase job opportunities for minority groups by analyzing the current pool of workers, identifying areas where women and minorities are underrepresented, and establishing specific hiring and promotion goals, with target dates, for addressing the discrepancy.

4. Increased commitment to and sharing of organizational goals among diverse employees at all organizational levels.

5. Increased innovation and creativity as diverse employees bring new, unique perspectives to decision-making and problem-solving tasks.

6. Increased ability to serve the needs of an increasingly diverse customer base.[39]

Companies that do not value their diverse employees are likely to experience greater conflict, as well as prejudice and discrimination. Among individual employees, for example, racial slurs and gestures, sexist comments, and other behaviors by co-workers harm the individuals at whom such behavior is directed. The victims of such behavior may feel hurt, depressed, or even threatened and may suffer from lowered self-esteem, all of which harm their productivity and morale. In such cases, women and minority employees may simply leave the firm, wasting the time, money, and other resources spent on hiring and training them. When discrimination comes from a supervisor, employees may also fear for their jobs. A discriminatory atmosphere not only can harm productivity and increase turnover but it may also subject a firm to costly lawsuits and negative publicity.

Astute businesses recognize that they need to modify their human resource management programs to target the needs of *all* their diverse employees as well as the needs of the firm itself. They realize that the benefits of diversity are long term in nature and come only to those organizations willing to make the commitment. Most importantly, as workforce diversity becomes a valued organizational asset, companies spend less time managing conflict and more time accomplishing tasks and satisfying customers, which is, after all, the purpose of business.

Affirmative Action

Many companies strive to improve their working environment through **affirmative action programs**, legally mandated plans that try to increase job opportunities for minority groups by analyzing the current pool of workers; identifying areas where women and minorities are underrepresented; and establishing specific hiring and promotion goals, along with target dates, for meeting those goals to resolve the discrepancy. Affirmative action began in 1965 as Lyndon B. Johnson issued the first of a series of presidential directives. It was designed to make up for past hiring and promotion prejudices, to overcome workplace discrimination, and to provide equal employment opportunities for Blacks and whites. Since then, minorities have made solid gains. California passed a bill that requires public companies in the state to have at least one woman on the board of directors.[40]

Legislation passed in 1991 reinforces affirmative action but prohibits organizations from setting hiring quotas that might result in reverse discrimination. Reverse discrimination occurs when a company' policies force it to consider only minorities or women instead of concentrating on hiring the person who is best qualified. More companies are arguing that affirmative action stifles their ability to hire the best employees, regardless of their minority status. Because of these problems, affirmative action became politically questionable. Recent social unrest has placed more emphasis on creating plans and commitments to hire and support minorities. Managers need to ensure that there is no discrimination in any of the firms operations. This includes promotions and top management positions.

EMPLOYEE RELATIONSHIPS AND SEXUAL HARASSMENT

Sexual harassment in the workplace has become one of the biggest ethical and legal challenges facing corporations. The U.S. Equal Employment Opportunity Commission (EEOC) defines sexual harassment as:

> Unwelcome sexual advances, requests for sexual favors, and other verbal or physical conduct of a sexual nature . . . when this conduct explicitly or implicitly affects an individual's employment, unreasonably interferes with an individual's work performance or creates an intimidating, hostile, or offensive work environment.[41]

Sexual harassment is a term used to describe unwanted behavior anywhere from suggestive remarks to sexual assault. In recent years, many high-profile executives have been cast out of their companies due to sexual harassment claims by employees. Corporations are developing training and programs to address employee relationships.

Sexual harassment has become rampant in Hollywood as well as in many corporate cultures. Leslie Moonves, a notable television executive at CBS, was forced to resign in 2018 after sexual harassment claims were made by more than two dozen women.

Moonves was accused of canceling a television show after one of his victims refused his advances.[42] This type of sexual harassment is referred to as "quid pro quo" harassment, which translates to "something for something." With quid pro quo harassments, victims are forced into situations in which they are not comfortable as a result of the fear of being fired or being passed up for promotions. CBS has since hired its first female president, Susan Zirinsky.[43]

Another type of sexual harassment in the workplace is known as a hostile work environment. In this situation, victims are put in uncomfortable positions where inappropriate behavior is pervasive and unwanted jokes or touching can occur. Uber's former CEO Travis Kalanick was forced to resign after former employees came forward with harassment claims against the company. More than 215 cases of sexual harassment were reported to Uber, and more than 20 employees were fired because of the claims.[44] Uber was said to have a hostile work environment where employees often made inappropriate remarks and shared sexually explicit material at work, which created an unsafe working environment.

One way that victims can get help is through the EEOC. The EEOC is the agency that administers and enforces civil rights laws for workplace discrimination. The EEOC has reported a 50 percent increase in sexual harassment suits since 2017. The EEOC was able to recover nearly $70 million through litigation on sexual harassment issues.[45] A study found that 81 percent of women and 43 percent of men have experienced sexual harassment.[46]

Women are typically seen as the most common victim of sexual harassment, but men are not immune to sexual harassment. About 17 percent of sexual harassment claims filed with the EEOC are made by men.[47] Male-on-male harassment and sexual-based hazing are common types of harassment that men face. Men are typically less likely to report sexual harassment in the workplace. Some common reasons are that men are afraid of being mocked, or they believe that men can't be sexually harassed by women.

Over the past few years, sexual harassment has become a national issue signaled by the #MeToo era. Pressure has been put on companies to create policies that protect and help their employees. The #MeToo era was fueled by the accusations of sexual abuse and harassment against Harvey Weinstein, a noted Hollywood movie producer. Many high-profile actresses have come forward with accusations of abuse and harassment. Recently, Google and Facebook were pressured into changing policies on sexual harassment. Previously, employees at Google and Facebook required their employees to settle sexual-harassment claims through private arbitration. Both companies changed their policies to allow employees to pursue harassment claims in court.[48]

As sexual harassment concerns rise, corporations are responding by implementing training programs to prevent the behavior. Employees are trained on what actions can constitute sexual harassment and what words and phrases may be considered harassment. California implemented a law that requires employers to provide sexual harassment training to their employees at least every two years.[49] Training is designed to help educate employees on what behavior is deemed unacceptable while also providing information on policies and how victims can receive help.

The #MeToo movement is generally a touchy topic for most companies. However, some companies have tried to address sexual harassment concerns publicly. Gillette released a controversial advertisement criticizing men and challenging them to exhibit better behavior.[50] The ad showcased several men who were shown sexually harassing women and young boys that were bullying other young boys. Some companies have created controversial ads to show that their values are aligned with their customers. The ad became controversial related to the role of a firm changing attitudes and cultural values. Companies like Gillette are trying to demonstrate that sexual harassment is a societal issue that should not be tolerated.

TRENDS IN MANAGEMENT OF THE WORKFORCE

Advances in technology, the Great Recession, and the plunge in the global economy due to the COVID-19 (coronavirus) pandemic have had a major impact on employment. Employee benefits, especially health care, remain a significant and controversial issue. The nature of the workplace is changing as well. Microentrepreneurs, small-scale businesses with no more than five employees, are growing rapidly. The gig economy where individuals move from one project to another is growing quickly as well. The sharing economy (online gig economy) is providing opportunities for independent contractors to own their businesses and contract their time and resources as they see fit. The rise of Uber, Airbnb, and Lyft illustrates this new form of employment. Space is also increasingly shared among employees and small businesses, a new trend called *coworking.* Companies such as WeWork and Industrious Office are capitalizing on these coworking opportunities by offering flexible, agile workspaces to businesses ranging from freelancers to *Fortune* 500 companies.[51]

This new job market has been supported by smartphones, tablet computers, and other technologies. However, a major challenge with the

DID YOU KNOW?

The largest employer in the world is the U.S. Department of Defense, with 2.87 million employees. The largest private employer is Walmart, with 2.3 million employees.[d]

increasing use of smartphones and tablet computers is the blurring between leisure and work time, with some employers calling employees after hours.[52] Employees themselves are mixing work and personal time by using social media in the office. This is requiring companies to come up with new policies that limit how employees can use social media in the workplace. On the other hand, it is estimated that 40 percent of full-time workers log more than 50 hours per week, while 20 percent log more than 60 hours. Many in this country are concerned about burnout and the negative impact that these work schedules can have on productivity.[53] Clearly, technology is changing the dynamics of the workplace in both positive and negative ways.

It is important for human resource managers to be aware of legal issues regarding worker rights. Strict criteria—such as having management responsibilities, having advanced degrees, or making more than $455 a week—determine whether an employee is exempt from overtime pay.[54] Interestingly, employees who "rant" about their employers on Facebook can receive some form of legal protection. Under the National Labor Relations Act of 1935, certain private-sector employees are allowed to complain about working conditions and pay—which seems to apply to social media sites as well. Threats, on the other hand, are not protected. Even then, however, courts sometimes differ from employers as to what constitutes a threat.[55]

Despite the grim outlook of the past few years, hiring trends are on the rise. While many companies eliminated jobs during the COVID-19 pandemic—either temporarily or permanently—new jobs were created during this time as well in the areas of healthcare and tech.[56] This uptick in hiring will require firms not only to know about relevant employee laws but also to understand how benefits and employee morale can contribute to overall productivity. Many of the most successful firms have discovered ways to balance costs with the well-being of their employees. ▪

Team Exercise

Form groups and go to Monster.com and look up job descriptions for positions in business (account executive in advertising, marketing manager, human resource director, production supervisor, financial analyst, bank teller, etc.). What are the key requirements for the position that you have been assigned (education, work experience, language/ computer skills, etc.)? Does the position announcement provide a thorough understanding of the job? Was any key information that you would have expected omitted? Report your findings to the class.

ARE YOU READY // for a Job in Human Resources? /

Managing human resources is a challenging and creative facet of a business. It is the department that handles the recruiting, hiring, training, and firing of employees. Because of the diligence and detail required in hiring and the sensitivity required in firing, human resource managers have a broad skill set. Human resources, therefore, is vital to the overall functioning of the business because, without the right staff, a firm will not be able to effectively carry out its plans. Like in basketball, a team is only as strong as its individual players, and those players must be able to work together to enhance strengths and downplay weaknesses. In addition, a good human resource manager can anticipate upcoming needs and changes in the business, hiring in line with the dynamics of the market and organization.

Once a good workforce is in place, human resource managers must ensure that employees are properly trained and oriented and that they clearly understand some elements of what the organization expects. Hiring new people is expensive, time consuming, and turbulent; thus, it is imperative that all employees are carefully selected, trained, and motivated so that they will remain committed and loyal to the company. This is not an easy task, but it is one of the responsibilities of the HR manager. Even with references, a résumé, background checks, and an interview, it can be hard to tell how a person will fit in the organization; therefore, the HR manager needs to have skills to be able to anticipate how every individual will "fit in." HR jobs include compensation, labor relations, benefits, training, ethics, and compliance managers. All of the tasks associated with the interface with hiring, developing, and maintaining employee motivation come into play in human resource management. Jobs are diverse and salaries will depend on responsibilities, education, and experience.

One of the major considerations for an HR manager is workforce diversity. A multicultural, multiethnic workforce consisting of all genders will help to bring in a variety of viewpoints and improve the quality and creativity of organizational decision making. Diversity is an asset and can help a company from having blind spots or harmony in thought, background, and perspective, which stifles good team decisions. However, a diverse workforce can present some management challenges. Human resource management is often responsible for managing diversity training and compliance to make sure employees do not violate the ethical culture of the organization or break the law. Different people have different goals, motivations, and ways of thinking about issues that are informed by their culture, religion, and the people closest to them. No one way of thinking is more right or more wrong than others, and they are all valuable. A human resource manager's job can become very complicated, however, because of diversity. To be good at human resources, you should be aware of the value of differences, strive to be culturally sensitive, and ideally should have a strong understanding and appreciation of different cultures and religions. Human resources managers' ability to manage diversity and those differences will affect their overall career success.

customer-driven marketing

13_Phunkod/Shutterstock

LEARNING OBJECTIVES

After reading this chapter, you will be able to:

LO 11-1 Define *marketing.*

LO 11-2 Describe the exchange process.

LO 11-3 Specify the functions of marketing.

LO 11-4 Explain the marketing concept and its implications for developing marketing strategies.

LO 11-5 Examine the development of a marketing strategy, including market segmentation and marketing mix.

LO 11-6 Describe how marketers conduct marketing research and study buying behavior.

LO 11-7 Summarize the environmental forces that influence marketing decisions.

Marketing involves planning and executing the development, pricing, promotion, and distribution of ideas, goods, and services to create exchanges that satisfy individual and organizational goals. These activities ensure that the products consumers want to buy are available at a price they are willing to pay and that consumers are provided with information about product features and availability. Organizations of all sizes and objectives engage in these activities.

In this chapter, we focus on the basic principles of marketing. First we define and examine the nature of marketing. Then we look at how marketers develop marketing strategies to satisfy the needs and wants of their customers. Next we discuss buying behavior and how marketers use research to determine what consumers want to buy and why. Finally, we explore the impact of the environment on marketing activities. ■

LO 11-1   Define *marketing*.

NATURE OF MARKETING

A vital part of any business undertaking, **marketing** is a group of activities designed to expedite transactions by creating, distributing, pricing, and promoting goods, services, and ideas.

Companies find that communicating with customers through social media sites can enhance customer relationships and create value for their brands.

Chinnapong/Shutterstock

These activities create value by allowing individuals and organizations to obtain what they need and want. A business cannot achieve its objectives unless it provides something that customers value. But just creating an innovative product that meets many users' needs isn't sufficient in today's volatile global marketplace. Products must be conveniently available, competitively priced, and uniquely promoted.

marketing a group of activities designed to expedite transactions by creating, distributing, pricing, and promoting goods, services, and ideas.

Marketing is an important part of a firm's overall strategy. Other functional areas of the business—such as operations, finance, and all areas of management—must be coordinated with marketing decisions. Marketing has the important function of providing revenue to sustain a firm. Only by creating trust and effective relationships with customers can a firm succeed in the long run. Businesses try to respond to consumer wants and needs and to anticipate changes in the environment. Unfortunately, it is difficult to understand and predict what consumers want: Motives are often unclear; few principles can be applied consistently; and markets tend to fragment, each desiring customized products, new value, or better service.

It is important to note what marketing is not: It is not manipulating consumers to get them to buy products they do not want. It is not just advertising and selling; it is a systematic approach to satisfying consumers. Marketing focuses on the many activities—planning, pricing, promoting, and distributing products—that foster exchanges. Unfortunately, the mass media and movies sometimes portray marketing as unethical or as not

exchange the act of giving up one thing (money, credit, labor, goods) in return for something else (goods, services, or ideas).

adding value to business. In this chapter, we point out that marketing is essential and provides important benefits in making products available to consumers.

LO 11-2 Describe the exchange process.

The Exchange Relationship

At the heart of all business is the **exchange**, the act of giving up one thing (money, credit, labor, goods) in return for something else (goods, services, or ideas). Businesses exchange their goods, services, or ideas for money or credit supplied by customers in a voluntary *exchange relationship,* illustrated in Figure 11.1. The buyer must feel good about the purchase, or the exchange will not continue. If your cell phone service works everywhere, you will probably feel good about using its services. But if you have a lot of dropped calls, you will probably use another phone service next time.

For an exchange to occur, certain conditions are required. As indicated by the arrows in Figure 11.1, buyers and sellers must be able to communicate about the "something of value" available to each. An exchange does not necessarily take place just because buyers and sellers have something of value to exchange. Each participant must be willing to give up his or her respective "something of value" to receive the "something" held by the other. You are willing to exchange your "something of value"—your money or credit—for soft drinks, football tickets, or new shoes because you consider those products more valuable or more important than holding on to your cash or credit potential.

When you think of marketing products, you may think of tangible things—cars, smartphones, or books, for example. What most consumers want, however, is a way to get a job done, solve a problem, or gain some enjoyment. You may purchase a Dyson vacuum cleaner not because you want a vacuum cleaner, but because you want clean carpets. Starbucks serves coffee drinks at a premium price, providing convenience, quality, and an inviting environment. It claims that it is not in the "coffee business serving people" but is in the "people business serving coffee." Therefore, the tangible product itself may not be as important as the image or the benefits associated with the product. This intangible "something of value" may be capability gained from using a product or the image evoked by it, or even the brand name. Good examples of items with brand names that are easy to remember include ColourPop Lippie Stix, Tide detergent, and the Ford Mustang. The label or brand name, such as Ravenswood or Smoking Loon wine, may also offer the added bonus of being a conversation piece in a social environment.

LO 11-3 Specify the functions of marketing.

Functions of Marketing

Marketing focuses on a complex set of activities that must be performed to accomplish objectives and generate exchanges. These activities include buying, selling, transporting, storing, grading, financing, marketing research, and risk taking.

Buying. Everyone who shops for products (consumers, stores, businesses, governments) decides whether and what to buy. A marketer must understand buyers' needs and desires to determine what products to make available.

Selling. The exchange process is expedited through selling. Marketers usually view selling as a persuasive activity that is accomplished through promotion (advertising, personal selling, sales promotion, publicity, and packaging).

Transporting. Transporting is the process of moving products from the seller to the buyer. Marketers focus on transportation costs and services.

Storing. Like transporting, storing is part of the physical distribution of products and includes warehousing goods. Warehouses hold some products for lengthy periods in order to create time utility. Time utility has to do with being able to satisfy demand in a timely manner. This especially pertains to a seasonal good such

▼ **FIGURE 11.1** The Exchange Process: Giving Up One Thing in Return for Another

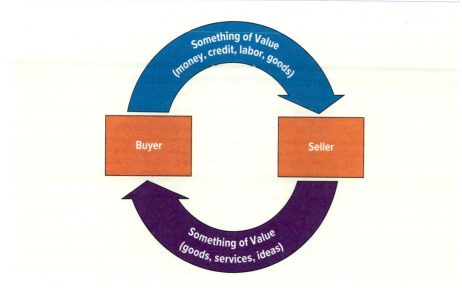

as orange juice. Fresh oranges are only available for a few months annually, but consumers demand juice throughout the entire year. Sellers must arrange for cold storage of orange juice concentrate so that they can maintain a steady supply all of the time.

Grading. Grading refers to standardizing products by dividing them into subgroups and displaying and labeling them so that consumers clearly understand their nature and quality. Many products, such as meat, steel, and fruit, are graded according to a set of standards that often are established by the state or federal government.

Financing. For many products, especially large items such as automobiles, refrigerators, and new homes, the marketer arranges credit to expedite the purchase.

Marketing Research. Through research, marketers ascertain the need for new goods and services. By gathering information regularly, marketers can detect new trends and changes in consumer tastes.

Risk Taking. Risk is the chance of loss associated with marketing decisions. Developing a new product creates a chance of loss if consumers do not like it enough to buy it. Spending money to hire a sales force or to conduct marketing research also involves risk. The implication of risk is that most marketing decisions result in either success or failure.

Creating Value with Marketing

Value is an important element of managing long-term customer relationships and implementing the marking concept. We view **value** as a customer's subjective assessment of benefits relative to costs in determining the worth of a product (customer value = customer benefits − customer costs).

Customer benefits include anything a buyer receives in an exchange. Hotels and motels, for example, basically provide a room with a bed and bathroom, but each firm provides a different level of service, amenities, and atmosphere to satisfy its guests. Motel 6 offers the minimum services necessary to maintain a quality, efficient, low-price overnight accommodation. In contrast, the Ritz-Carlton provides every imaginable service a guest might desire and strives to ensure that all service is of the highest quality. Customers judge which type of accommodation offers them the best value according to the benefits they desire and their willingness and ability to pay for the costs associated with the benefits.

Customer costs include anything a buyer must give up to obtain the benefits the product provides. The most obvious cost is the monetary price of the product, but nonmonetary costs can be equally important in a customer's determination of value. Two nonmonetary costs are the time and effort customers expend to find and purchase desired products. To reduce time and effort, a company can increase product availability, thereby making it more convenient for buyers to purchase the firm's products. Another nonmonetary cost is risk, which can be reduced by offering good basic warranties for an additional charge. Another

risk-reduction strategy is increasingly popular in today's catalog/telephone/Internet shopping environment. Vistaprint for example, uses a guarantee to reduce the risk involved in ordering merchandise from its catalogs, and many online retailers like Nordstrom and Sephora offer free return shipping.

In developing marketing activities, it is important to recognize that customers receive benefits based on their experiences. For example, many computer buyers consider services such as fast delivery, ease of installation, technical advice, and training assistance to be important elements of the product. Customers also derive benefits from the act of shopping and selecting products. These benefits can be affected by the atmosphere or environment of a store, such as Red Lobster's nautical/seafood theme.

value a customer's subjective assessment of benefits relative to costs in determining the worth of a product.

marketing concept the idea that an organization should try to satisfy customers' needs through coordinated activities that also allow it to achieve its own goals.

> **LO 11-4** Explain the marketing concept and its implications for developing marketing strategies.

The Marketing Concept

A basic philosophy that guides all marketing activities is the **marketing concept**, the idea that an organization should try to satisfy customers' needs through coordinated activities that

Drones provide an example of a product that is based on advanced technology but is finding many uses from being a toy or recreational product to commercial uses. The marketing concept is based on the philosophy that consumers purchase the satisfaction and value they derive from a product not the product itself.

Doxieone Photography/Moment Open/Getty Images

also allow it to achieve its own goals. According to the marketing concept, a business must find out what consumers desire and then develop the good, service, or idea that fulfills their needs or wants. The business must then get the product to the customer. In addition, the business must continually alter, adapt, and develop products to keep pace with changing consumer needs and wants. For instance, after removing artificial dyes

store in Paris rejected her perfume in the 1960s, she "accidentally" dropped a bottle on the floor where nearby customers could get a whiff of it. So many asked about the scent that Galeries Lafayette was obliged to place an order. Lauder ultimately built an empire using then-unheard-of tactics like free samples and gifts with purchase to market her "jars of hope."[2]

> ## "Businesses must continually alter, adapt, and develop products to keep pace with changing consumer needs and wants."

from its cereals, General Mills decided to bring back its brightly colored Trix cereal after receiving more than 20,000 customer complaints over 18 months.[1] To remain competitive, companies must be prepared to add to or adapt their product lines to satisfy customers' desires for new fads or changes in habits. For example, to appeal to the growing health and wellness market, Oscar Mayer introduced a line of natural meat and cheese plates that are advertised as containing no artificial ingredients, artificial preservatives, or added nitrates or nitrites. Each business must determine how best to implement the marketing concept, given its own goals and resources.

Trying to determine customers' true needs is increasingly difficult because no one fully understands what motivates people to buy things. However, Estée Lauder, founder of her namesake cosmetics company, had a pretty good idea. When a prestigious

Although customer satisfaction is the goal of the marketing concept, a business must also achieve its own objectives, such as boosting productivity, reducing costs, or achieving a percentage of a specific market. If it does not, it will not survive. For example, Lenovo could sell computers for $50 and give customers a lifetime guarantee, which would be great for customers but not so great for Lenovo. Obviously, the company must strike a balance between achieving organizational objectives and satisfying customers.

To implement the marketing concept, a firm must have good information about what consumers want, adopt a consumer orientation, and coordinate its efforts throughout the entire organization; otherwise, it may be awash with goods, services, and ideas that consumers do not want or need. Successfully implementing the marketing concept requires that a business

VIRTUAL REALITY CONCEALS THE WORLD, AUGMENTED REALITY IMPROVES IT

Imagine observing a historical building. All of a sudden, facts about the building pop into view. Augmented reality gives a view of the real environment that is enhanced by digitally generated information. Snapchat filters, Minecraft Earth, and sports broadcast drawings to analyze plays are just a few ways we use AR today.

Companies want to take this further with headsets and other devices that will enhance the AR experience. However, while organizations feel there is a demand for AR, they recognize that to satisfy customer needs, they will need to develop headsets and devices that customers will want to wear. AR leaders like Microsoft are having a difficult time creating

wearable headsets that aren't bulky and awkward. Apple purchased Akonia Holographics, a startup that makes AR lenses. Many think they will be the first creators of a sleek design.

Marketers have additional obstacles to face. The GPS system is not accurate for distances greater than 30 feet and often doesn't work well indoors. Incorporating cutting-edge technology can be expensive, resulting in a higher-priced product. While technophiles (technology-lovers) are often willing to pay high prices for the newest technology, other market segments may be less willing. Privacy concerns with AR might dissuade consumer segments who are worried that image-recognition software could make it

possible for outside parties to observe their private lives. AR companies need to decide which marketing segmentation approach works best based upon the consumers they want to target.[a]

Critical Thinking Questions

1. How are AR makers trying to overcome obstacles to embrace the marketing concept?

2. What type of variables do you think AR marketers are most likely to use to segment the market?

3. If you were a marketer of new AR headsets, what type of market segmentation approach would you adopt to reach consumer segments? Explain your reasoning.

view the customer's perception of value as the ultimate measure of work performance and improving value, and the rate at which this is done, as the measure of success.[3] Everyone in the organization who interacts with customers—*all* customer-contact employees—must know what customers want. They are selling ideas, benefits, philosophies, and experiences—not just goods and services.

Someone once said that if you build a better mousetrap, the world will beat a path to your door. Suppose you do build a better mousetrap. What will happen? Actually, consumers are not likely to beat a path to your door because the market is so competitive. A coordinated effort by everyone involved with the mousetrap is needed to sell the product. Your company must reach out to customers and tell them about your mousetrap, especially how your mousetrap works better than those offered by competitors. If you do not make the benefits of your product widely known, in most cases, it will not be successful. One reason that Apple is so successful is because of its stores. Apple's more than 500 national and international retail stores market computers and electronics in a way unlike any other computer manufacturer or retail establishment. The upscale stores, located in high-rent shopping districts, show off Apple's products in modern, spacious settings to encourage consumers to try new things—like making a movie on a computer.[4] So for some companies, like Apple, you need to create stores to sell your product to consumers. You could also find stores that are willing to sell your product to consumers for you. In either situation, you must implement the marketing concept by making a product with satisfying benefits and making it available and visible.

Orville Wright said that an airplane is "a group of separate parts flying in close formation." This is what most companies are trying to accomplish: They are striving for a team effort to deliver the right good or service to customers. A breakdown at any point in the organization—whether it be in production, purchasing, sales, distribution, or advertising—can result in lost sales, lost revenue, and dissatisfied customers.

Evolution of the Marketing Concept

The marketing concept may seem like the obvious approach to running a business and building relationships with customers. However, businesspeople are not always focused on customers when they create and operate businesses. Many companies fail to grasp the importance of customer relationships and fail to implement customer strategies. A firm's marketing department needs to share information about customers and their desires with the entire organization. Our society and economic system have changed over time, and marketing has become more important as markets have become more competitive. Although this is an oversimplification, these time periods help us to understand how marketing has evolved. There have always been some firms that have practiced the marketing concept.

With consumer preferences rapidly evolving, Oscar Mayer is changing to satisfy a growing target market by advertising its natural snacks.

Source: Oscar Mayer

The Production Orientation. During the second half of the 19th century, the Industrial Revolution was well under way in the United States. New technologies, such as electricity, railroads, internal combustion engines, and mass-production techniques, made it possible to manufacture goods with ever increasing efficiency. Together with new management ideas and ways of using labor, products poured into the marketplace, where demand for manufactured goods was strong.

The Sales Orientation. By the early part of the 20th century, supply caught up with and then exceeded demand, and businesspeople began to realize they would have to "sell" products to buyers. During the first half of the 20th century, businesspeople viewed sales as the primary means of increasing profits in what has become known as a sales orientation. Those who adopted the sales orientation perspective believed the most important marketing activities were personal selling and advertising. Today, some people still inaccurately equate marketing with a sales orientation.

The Market Orientation.

By the 1950s, some businesspeople began to recognize that even efficient production and extensive promotion did not guarantee sales. These businesses, and many others since, found that they must first determine what customers want and then produce it, rather than making the products first and then trying to persuade customers that they need them. Managers at General Electric first suggested that the marketing concept was a companywide philosophy of doing business. As more organizations realized the importance of satisfying customers' needs, U.S. businesses entered the marketing era, one of market orientation. A **market orientation** requires organizations to gather information about customer needs, share that information throughout the entire firm, and use it to help build long-term relationships with customers. Market orientation is linked to new product innovation by developing a strategic focus to explore and develop new products to serve target markets.[5] For example, the popular outdoor store REI allows consumers to return most products within one year for a full refund. Electronics have a shorter window for returns. A "user-friendly" return policy helps REI better serve its customers' desires to return merchandise without time pressures.[6] Top executives, marketing managers, nonmarketing managers (those in production, finance, human resources, and so on), and customers all become mutually dependent and cooperate in developing and carrying out a market orientation.

Nonmarketing managers must communicate with marketing managers to share information important to understanding the customer. Consider the nearly 130-year history of Wrigley's gum. In 1891, the gum was given away to promote sales of baking powder (the company's original product). The gum was launched as its own product in 1893, and after four generations of Wrigley family CEOs, the company continues to reinvent itself and focus on consumers. Eventually, the family made the decision to sell the company to Mars. Wrigley now functions as a stand-alone subsidiary of Mars. The deal combined such popular brands as Wrigley's gums and Life Savers with Mars' M&M'S, Snickers, and Skittles to form the world's largest confectionary company.

Trying to assess what customers want, which is difficult to begin with, is further complicated by the rate at which trends, fashions, and tastes can change. Businesses today want to satisfy customers and build meaningful long-term relationships with them. It is more efficient and less expensive for the company to retain existing customers and even increase the amount of business each customer provides the organization than to find new customers. Most companies' success depends on increasing the amount of repeat business; therefore, relationship building between company and customer is key. Many companies are turning to technologies associated with customer relationship management to help build relationships and boost business with existing customers. For example, Birchbox, a beauty subscription service, looks to its social media networks to collect and respond to customer feedback. The company uses Facebook to create educational posts to help its subscribers learn how to

KRAFT HEINZ PLAYS KETCHUP

The world of condiments has become increasingly competitive over the past decade. This holds especially true for mayonnaise. Companies like Hellmann's and Kraft Heinz are struggling to hold their market share on mayonnaise as health food trends grow and smaller companies try to fill that niche. However, Kraft Heinz has a plan to adapt to trends and grow its market share.

With growing health trends, consumers are more conscious of what they are eating. This has led to a decline in mayonnaise because of its high fat content. As consumers move away from traditional mayo, new brands have popped up offering healthier versions of mayo that substitute traditional oil with healthier ingredients

like avocado oil. In response, Kraft Heinz has expanded its product selection to include healthier options and new flavors like roasted garlic and spicy chipotle flavors.

Kraft Heinz has also invested in advertisement campaigns designed to market its new flavors like Mayochup, which is a combination of mayonnaise and ketchup. The campaign asked consumers to vote for whether they wanted Mayochup in stores. Once Heinz made the decision to launch, it advertised in a variety of media targeting different consumer demographics, including foodie, "top-tier lifestyle," social, and major media outlets.

Heinz has been hard at work to compete by refining its product, offering substitutes, and

creating ad campaigns. In the very competitive condiment space where tastes can change overnight, Heinz has a tough task to stay a nationally recognized brand.[b]

Critical Thinking Questions

1. How are evolving consumer perceptions changing Heinz mayonnaise products?

2. Describe how Heinz used consumer interaction as a form of marketing research. What type of data did it collect, primary or secondary?

3. What type of segmentation variables is Heinz using for its Mayochup advertising?

use the products received in each monthly Birchbox.[7] A market orientation involves being responsive to ever-changing customer needs and wants.

Although it might be easy to dismiss customer relationship management as time-consuming and expensive, this mistake could destroy a company. Customer relationship management (CRM) is important in a market orientation because it can result in loyal and profitable customers. Without loyal customers, businesses would not survive; therefore, achieving the full profit potential of each customer relationship should be the goal of every marketing strategy. At the most basic level, profits can be obtained through relationships by acquiring new customers, enhancing the profitability of existing customers, and extending the duration of customer relationships. The profitability of loyal customers throughout their relationship with the company (their lifetime customer value) should not be underestimated. Starbucks, for example, is estimated to have a customer lifetime value of more than $14,000.[8]

Communication remains a major element of any strategy to develop and manage long-term customer relationships. By providing multiple points of interactions with customers—that is, websites, telephone, social media, e-mail, and personal contact—companies can personalize customer relationships.[9] Like many online retailers, Amazon stores and analyzes purchase data in an attempt to understand each customer's interests. This information helps the online retailer improve its ability to satisfy individual customers and thereby increase sales of books, music, movies, and other products to each customer. The ability to identify individual customers allows marketers to shift their focus from targeting groups of similar customers to increasing their share of an individual customer's purchases. Regardless of the medium through which communication occurs, customers should ultimately be the drivers of marketing strategy because they understand what they want. Customer relationship management systems should ensure that marketers listen to customers in order to respond to their needs and concerns and build long-term relationships.

LO 11-5 Examine the development of a marketing strategy, including market segmentation and marketing mix.

DEVELOPING A MARKETING STRATEGY

To implement the marketing concept and customer relationship management, a business needs to develop and maintain a **marketing strategy**, a plan of action for developing, pricing, distributing, and promoting products that meet the needs of specific customers. This definition has two major components: selecting a target market and developing an appropriate marketing mix to satisfy that target market.

Selecting a Target Market

A **market** is a group of people who have a need, purchasing power, and the desire and authority to spend money on goods, services, and ideas. A **target market** is a more specific group of consumers on whose needs and wants a company focuses its marketing efforts. Target markets can be further segmented into business markets and consumer markets.

Business-to-business marketing (B2B) involves marketing products to customers who will use the product for resale, direct use in daily operations, or direct use in making other products. John Deere, for instance, sells earth-moving equipment to construction firms and tractors to farmers. Most people, however, tend to think of *business-to-consumer marketing (B2C)*, or marketing directly to the end consumer. Sometimes products are used by both types of markets. For example, Glo Skin Beauty sells its cosmetics and skin care products wholesale to salons and spas as well as to consumers directly via its website.

Marketing managers may define a target market as a relatively small number of people within a larger market, or they may define it as the total market (Figure 11.2). Rolls-Royce, for example, targets its products at a very exclusive, high-income market—people who want the ultimate in prestige in an automobile. On the other hand, Ford Motor Company manufactures a variety of vehicles including Lincolns, Mercurys, and Ford Trucks in order to appeal to varied tastes, needs, and desires.

Some firms use a **total-market approach**, in which they try to appeal to everyone and assume that all buyers have similar needs and wants. Sellers of salt, sugar, and many agricultural products use a total-market approach because everyone is a potential consumer of these products. This approach is also referred to as *mass marketing*. Most firms, though, use **market segmentation** and divide the total market into groups of people. A **market segment** is a collection of individuals, groups, or organizations who share one or more characteristics and thus have relatively similar product needs and desires. For example, women are a large market segment. At the household level, segmentation can identify each woman's social

marketing strategy a plan of action for developing, pricing, distributing, and promoting products that meet the needs of specific customers.

market a group of people who have a need, purchasing power, and the desire and authority to spend money on goods, services, and ideas.

target market a specific group of consumers on whose needs and wants a company focuses its marketing efforts.

total-market approach an approach whereby a firm tries to appeal to everyone and assumes that all buyers have similar needs.

market segmentation a strategy whereby a firm divides the total market into groups of people who have relatively similar product needs.

market segment a collection of individuals, groups, or organizations who share one or more characteristics and thus have relatively similar product needs and desires.

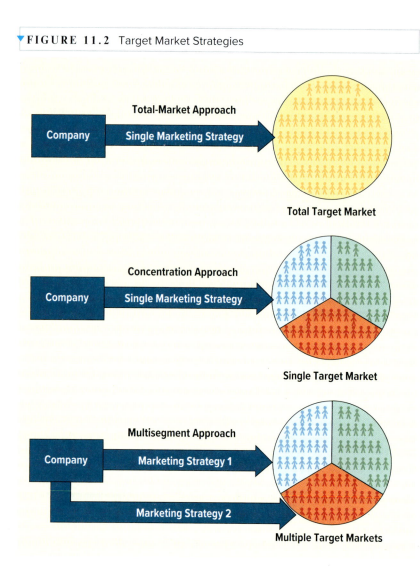

and bounds. Table 11.1 shows the buying power in the United States by race/ethnicity. Companies will have to learn how to most effectively reach these growing segments. Companies use market segmentation to focus their efforts and resources on specific target markets so that they can develop a productive marketing strategy. Two common approaches to segmenting markets are the concentration approach and the multisegment approach.

Market Segmentation Approaches. In the **concentration approach**, a company develops one marketing strategy for a single market segment. The concentration approach allows a firm to specialize, focusing all its efforts on the one market segment. Porsche, for example, directs all its marketing efforts toward high-income individuals who want to own high-performance vehicles. A firm can generate a large sales volume by penetrating a single market segment deeply. The concentration approach may be especially effective when a firm can identify and develop products for a segment ignored by other companies in the industry.

In the **multisegment approach**, the marketer aims its marketing efforts at two or more segments, developing a marketing strategy for each. Many firms use a multisegment approach that includes different advertising messages for different segments. Companies also develop product variations to appeal to different market segments. The U.S. Post Office, for example, offers personalized stamps, while Mars Inc. sells personalized M&M'S. Many other firms also attempt to use a multisegment approach to market segmentation, such as the manufacturer of Raleigh bicycles, which has designed separate marketing strategies for racers, tourers, commuters, and children.

concentration approach a market segmentation approach whereby a company develops one marketing strategy for a single market segment.

multisegment approach a market segmentation approach whereby the marketer aims its efforts at two or more segments, developing a marketing strategy for each.

attributes, culture, and stages in life to determine preferences and needs.

Another market segment on which many marketers are focusing is the growing Asian population in the United States with a population of more than 20 million and buying power of more than $1.2 trillion. The Hispanic population is also growing with buying power of more than $1.7 trillion.[10] For instance, online retail giant Amazon includes Spanish-language options to its site.[11] The companies hope to create relationships with Hispanic consumers in order to gain their loyalty. One of the challenges for marketers in the future will be to effectively address an increasingly racially diverse United States. In future decades, the purchasing power of minority market segments is set to grow by leaps

▼ **TABLE 11.1** Buying Power in the United States by Race/Ethnicity

	Share of US Population	Share of Buying Power	Buying Power	Percent Increase in Buying Power*
White	76.20%	81.7%	$13.2 trillion	39.50%
Black	13.40%	8.9%	$1.4 trillion	48.10%
Asian	6.30%	7.1%	$1.2 trillion	89.50%
Latinx	18.60%	10.7%	$1.7 trillion	69.10%
American Indian	1.30%	0.8%	$126.8 billion	51.80%
Multiracial	2.80%	1.6%	$253.9 billion	73.60%

***Percent increase in buying power between 2010–2019.**

Source: Catalyst, "Buying Power: Quick Take," April 27, 2020, https://www.catalyst.org/research/buying-power/ (accessed June 9, 2020).

Niche marketing is a narrow market segment focus when efforts are on one small, well-defined group that has a unique, specific set of needs. For example, Chrome Industries was founded in Boulder, Colorado, to make unique, durable bags for bike messengers. This target market showed such affinity for the product that the company has since expanded with a variety of bags as well as clothing and shoes.[12] Niche segments are usually very small compared to the total market for the products. Freshpet makes all-natural gourmet pet food that mimics the type of food humans like. This company is targeting a growing niche of pet owners who want the best food for their pets.[13]

For a firm to successfully use a concentration or multisegment approach to market segmentation, several requirements must be met:

1. Consumers' needs for the product must be heterogeneous.
2. The segments must be identifiable and divisible.
3. The total market must be divided in a way that allows estimated sales potential, cost, and profits of the segments to be compared.
4. At least one segment must have enough profit potential to justify developing and maintaining a special marketing strategy.
5. The firm must be able to reach the chosen market segment with a particular market strategy.

Bases for Segmenting Markets.
Companies segment markets on the basis of several variables:

1. *Demographic*—age, sex, race, ethnicity, income, education, occupation, family size, religion, social class. These characteristics are often closely related to customers' product needs and purchasing behavior, and they can be readily measured. For example, yogurt companies often segment by age: nonfat, high protein yogurt for adults and easy-to-eat tubes for children.

2. *Geographic*—climate, terrain, natural resources, population density, subcultural values. These influence consumer needs and product usage. Climate, for example, influences consumer purchases of clothing, automobiles, heating and air conditioning equipment, and leisure activity equipment.

3. *Psychographic*—personality characteristics, motives, lifestyles. Soft-drink marketers provide their products in several types of packaging, including two-liter bottles and cases of cans, to satisfy different lifestyles and motives.

4. *Behavioristic*—some characteristic of the consumer's behavior toward the product. These characteristics commonly involve some aspect of product use. Benefit segmentation is also a type of behavioristic segmentation. For instance, low-fat, low-carb food products would target those who desire the benefits of a healthier diet.

> **marketing mix** the four marketing activities—product, price, promotion, and distribution—that the firm can control to achieve specific goals within a dynamic marketing environment.

Developing a Marketing Mix

The second step in developing a marketing strategy is to create and maintain a satisfying marketing mix. The **marketing mix** refers to four marketing activities—product, price, distribution, and promotion—that the firm can control to achieve specific

---

FORD'S F-150 RACES AHEAD

For more than 40 years, Ford's F-150 has been the best-selling vehicle in the United States. It beat out the Toyota Corolla as the most sold vehicle worldwide, doubly impressive as the world market has a smaller taste for trucks than does the United States. Ford's successful marketing of the F-150 makes it a role model for other companies.

One reason Ford has stayed on top is that it knows the market. Over the years, Ford has kept a conservative body style for the F-150 and made performance a priority. This allows Ford to attract customers who fit more of the standard truck owner mold. Also, as owning a truck has become more popular among suburbanites, the F-150 has led the market in comfort and technology. For example, as the market shifts to cleaner vehicles, Ford announced plans to create an electric version of the F-150.

Because Ford has multiple customer segments, the company has adopted a multisegment approach. Within the Ford F-150, there are engine types that range from a 2.7-liter V6 all the way to a 5.0-liter V8. Ford has seven different models of its F-150, ranging in price from $28,745 to $67,735.

As Ford invests in electric and hybrid models, Ford must find a way to market greener cars to its core market by focusing on other attributes. Ford plans to focus on other unique benefits of an electric engine like how it can function as a mobile generator for keeping beer cold or preparing coffee for a camping trip. Because Ford continually seeks to understand its customers, it can market new versions of the F-150 to target more environmentally-friendly consumers while not alienating its core markets.[c]

Critical Thinking Questions

1. Why does a multisegment approach seem to work for Ford?
2. How do you think knowing its market has allowed Ford to branch off into different markets for its F-150 trucks?
3. What types of segmentation variables does Ford likely use to target different types of consumers?

▼ FIGURE 11.3 The Marketing Mix: Product, Price, Promotion, and Distribution

Marketing Environment

price a value placed on an object exchanged between a buyer and a seller.

goals within a dynamic marketing environment (Figure 11.3). The buyer or the target market is the central focus of all marketing activities. Amazon is well known for its implementation of the marketing mix. It routinely engages in research and development to create new products like its digital assistant Echo. It promotes its products through advertising, social media, and media events. Best Buy and other retailers provide these products at a premium price to convey their quality and effectiveness.

Product. A product—whether a good, a service, an idea, or some combination—is a complex mix of tangible and intangible attributes that provide satisfaction and benefits. A *good* is a physical entity you can touch. A Nissan Rogue, a Nerf Blaster, and pets available for adoption at an animal shelter are examples of goods. A *service* is the application of human and mechanical efforts to people or objects to provide intangible benefits to customers. Air travel, dry cleaning, haircuts, facials, banking, insurance, medical care, and day care are examples of services. *Ideas* include concepts, philosophies, images, and issues. For instance, an attorney, for a fee, may advise you about what rights you have in the event that the IRS decides to audit your tax return. Other marketers of ideas include political parties, churches, and schools.

A product has emotional and psychological as well as physical characteristics that include everything that the buyer receives from an exchange. This definition includes supporting services such as installation, guarantees,

DID YOU KNOW?

During its first year of operation, sales of Coca-Cola averaged just nine drinks per day for total first-year sales of $50. Today, Coca-Cola products are consumed at the rate of 1.9 billion drinks per day.[d]

product information, and promises of repair. For example, in an advertisement, Subaru highlights both physical and psychological characteristics of its Subaru Ascent. It is an eight-passenger vehicle with standard symmetrical all-wheel drive. Subaru highlights it has been Kelley Blue Book's Most Trusted Brand for four years running to appeal to consumers who desire a safe vehicle. Products usually have both favorable and unfavorable attributes; therefore, almost every purchase or exchange involves trade-offs as consumers try to maximize their benefits and satisfaction and minimize unfavorable attributes.

Products are among a firm's most visible contacts with consumers. If they do not meet consumer needs and expectations, sales will be difficult, and product life spans will be brief. On the other hand, Silicon Valley car maker Tesla has overtaken market values of Ford and General Motors. Although its sales of cars are modest, Tesla's growth reflects the belief that electric motors are the future and Tesla is best positioned to bring advanced self-driving technology to the highways.[14] The product is an important variable—often the central focus—of the marketing mix; the other variables (price, promotion, and distribution) must be coordinated with product decisions.

Price. Almost anything can be assessed by a **price**, a value placed on an object exchanged between a buyer and a seller. Although the seller usually establishes the price, it may be negotiated between the buyer and the seller. The buyer usually exchanges purchasing power—income, credit, wealth—for the satisfaction or utility associated with a product. Because financial price is the measure of value commonly used in an exchange, it quantifies value and is the basis of most market exchanges.

Marketers view price as much more than a way of assessing value, however. It is a key element of the marketing mix because it relates directly to the generation of revenue and profits. Digital services such as Disney+ and Spotify follow a subscription-based pricing model. Subscription pricing is gaining popularity. Prices can also be changed quickly to stimulate demand or respond to competitors' actions. The sudden increase in the cost of commodities such as oil can create price increases or a drop in consumer demand for a product. When gas prices rise,

Subaru highlights vehicle safety in its Subaru Ascent advertisement.

Source: Subaru

consumers purchase more fuel-efficient cars; when prices fall, consumers return to larger vehicles.[15]

Distribution. Distribution (sometimes referred to as "place" because it helps to remember the marketing mix as the "4Ps") is making products available to customers in the quantities desired. For example, consumers can stream a movie or go to the movie theater. Intermediaries, usually wholesalers and retailers, perform many of the activities required to move products efficiently from producers to consumers or industrial buyers. These activities involve transporting, warehousing, materials handling, and inventory control, as well as packaging and communication.

Critics who suggest that eliminating wholesalers and other intermediaries would result in lower prices for consumers do not recognize that eliminating intermediaries would not do away with the need for their services. Other institutions would have to perform those services, and consumers would still have to pay for them. In addition, in the absence of wholesalers, all producers would have to deal directly with retailers or customers, keeping voluminous records and hiring extra people to deal with customers. Supply chain management (SCM) involves maintaining a flow of products through physical distribution activities. This includes acquiring resources, inventory, and the interlinked networks that make products available to customers through purchasing, logistics, and operations. SCM has become very important to the success of online marketers. Consider Amazon, the largest and most successful online retailer, which takes on typical wholesale and retail functions by storing inventory in warehouses and is developing its own shipping and delivery capacity. As an online retailer, it provides easy online access and customer service.[16] Companies now can make their products available throughout the world without maintaining facilities in each country. For instance, Pandora, Spotify, and Apple Music have benefited from the ability to stream music over the Internet. Customers can listen to music for free with commercial interruptions, or they can pay to upgrade to listen without commercials. Pandora has 63.5 million active users, while Spotify has 271 million and Apple Music has 60 million.[17]

Promotion. Promotion is a persuasive form of communication that attempts to expedite a marketing exchange by influencing individuals, groups, and organizations to accept goods, services, and ideas. Promotion includes advertising, personal selling, publicity, and sales promotion, all of which we will look at more closely in the "Dimensions of Marketing Strategy" chapter.

The aim of promotion is to communicate directly or indirectly with individuals, groups, and organizations to facilitate exchanges. When marketers use advertising and other forms of promotion, they must effectively manage their promotional resources and understand product and target-market characteristics to ensure that these promotional activities contribute to the firm's objectives.

Most major companies have set up websites on the Internet to promote themselves and their products. For example, L'Oréal operates Makeup.com, a beauty website that discusses beauty trends and shares makeup tutorials using products from L'Oréal brands like Urban Decay, Maybelline, and NYX.[18] While traditional advertising media such as television, radio, newspapers, and magazines remain important, digital advertising on websites and social media sites is growing. Not only can digital advertising be less expensive, but advertising offerings such as Google Ads allow companies to only pay when users click on the link or advertisement.[19] Additionally, social media sites offer advertising opportunities for both large and small companies. Firms can create a Facebook page and post corporate updates for free. Not to be outdone, Twitter also allows advertisers to purchase Promoted Tweets on the site. Promoted Tweets are just like regular tweets (except for the name), allowing users to respond or re-tweet them to their friends.[20]

distribution making products available to customers in the quantities desired.

promotion a persuasive form of communication that attempts to expedite a marketing exchange by influencing individuals, groups, and organizations to accept goods, services, and ideas.

MARKETING RESEARCH AND INFORMATION SYSTEMS

Before marketers can develop a marketing mix, they must collect in-depth, up-to-date information about customer needs. **Marketing research** is a systematic, objective process of getting information about potential customers to guide marketing decisions. Such information might include data about the age,

from respondents. If you've ever participated in a telephone survey about a product, recorded your TV viewing habits for ACNielsen or Arbitron, or even responded to a political opinion poll, you provided the researcher with primary data. Primary data must be gathered by researchers who develop a method to observe phenomena or research respondents. Many companies use "mystery shoppers" to visit their retail establishments and report on whether the stores were adhering to the companies' standards of service. These undercover customers document their observations of store appearance, employee effectiveness, and customer treatment. Mystery shoppers provide valuable information that helps companies improve their organizations and refine their marketing strategies.[22] Companies also use surveys and focus groups to gauge customer opinion. Table 11.2

> ## BEFORE MARKETERS CAN DEVELOP A MARKETING MIX, THEY MUST COLLECT IN-DEPTH, UP-TO-DATE INFORMATION ABOUT CUSTOMER NEEDS.

marketing research a systematic, objective process of getting information about potential customers to guide marketing decisions.

primary data marketing information that is observed, recorded, or collected directly from respondents.

income, ethnicity, gender, and educational level of people in the target market, their preferences for product features, their attitudes toward competitors' products, and the frequency with which they use the product. For instance, marketing research has revealed that consumers often make in-store purchase decisions in three seconds or less.[21] Marketing research is vital because the marketing concept cannot be implemented without information about customers.

A marketing information system is a framework for accessing information about customers from sources both inside and outside the organization. Inside the organization, there is a continuous flow of information about prices, sales, and expenses. Outside the organization, data are readily available through private or public reports and census statistics, as well as from many other sources. Computer networking technology provides a framework for companies to connect to useful databases and customers with instantaneous information about product acceptance, sales performance, and buying behavior. This information is important to planning and marketing strategy development.

Two types of data are usually available to decision makers. **Primary data** are observed, recorded, or collected directly

shows the companies regarded as having the best customer service. A weakness of surveys is that respondents are sometimes untruthful in order to avoid seeming foolish or ignorant. Although focus groups can be more expensive than surveys, they allow marketers to understand how consumers express themselves as well as observe their behavior patterns.[23]

Some methods for marketing research use passive observation of consumer behavior and open-ended questioning techniques. Called ethnographic or observational research, the approach

▼ **TABLE 11.2** Companies with the Best Customer Service

Rank	Brand
1	Disney Cruise Line
2	Neiman Marcus
3	The Ritz-Carlton
4	Edward Jones
5	Chick-fil-A
6	L.L.Bean
7	National Storage Affiliates
8	Embassy Suites
9	Publix
10	Beau Coup

Source: "America's Best Customer Service 2020," *Newsweek,* https://www.newsweek.com/americas-best-customer-service-2020 (accessed June 9, 2020).

can help marketers determine what consumers really think about their products and how different ethnic or demographic groups react to them.

Secondary data are compiled inside or outside the organization for some purpose other than changing the current situation. Marketers typically use information compiled by the U.S. census bureau and other government agencies, databases created by marketing research firms, as well as sales and other internal reports, to gain information about customers. For example, the average television viewership for NASCAR declined from 7.6 million to 3.759 million in only 4 years. In addition, the audience is becoming older. This finding could indicate the need for additional research to determine approaches to increase viewership.[24]

Online Marketing Research

The marketing of products and collecting of data about buying behavior—information on what people actually buy and how they buy it—represents marketing research of the future. New information technologies are changing the way businesses learn about their customers and market their products. Interactive multimedia research, or *virtual testing,* combines sight, sound, and animation to facilitate the testing of concepts as well as packaging and design features for consumer products. The evolving development of telecommunications and computer technologies is allowing marketing researchers quick and easy access to a growing number of online services and a vast database of potential respondents.

Marketing research can use digital media and social networking sites to gather useful information for marketing decisions. Sites such as Twitter, Facebook, and LinkedIn can be good substitutes for focus groups. Online surveys can serve as an alternative to mail, telephone, or personal interviews. There are fewer

Coffee shops and restaurants attempt to influence consumers' buying behavior by offering free Wi-Fi and a comfortable retail environment. Businesses can also gather data about their customers with Wi-Fi services like Purple, Aislelabs, and Yelp WiFi.

Image Source

landlines, in fact, more than half of households have a cell phone but no landline telephones.[25]

Social networks are a great way to obtain information from consumers who are willing to share their experiences about products and companies. In a way, this process identifies those consumers who develop an identity or passion for certain products, as well as those consumers who have concerns about quality or performance. It is possible for firms to tap into existing online social networks and simply "listen" to what consumers have on their mind. Firms can also encourage consumers to join a community or group so that they can share their opinions with the business.

A good outcome from using social networks is the opportunity to reach new voices and gain varied perspectives on the creative process of developing new products and promotions. For instance, Kickstarter gives aspiring entrepreneurs the ability to market their ideas online. Funders can then choose whether to fund those ideas in return for a finished product or a steep discount.[26] To some extent, social networking is democratizing design by welcoming consumers to join in the development process for new products.[27]

Online surveys are becoming an important part of marketing research. Traditionally, the process of conducting surveys online involved sending questionnaires to respondents either through e-mail or through a website. However, digital communication has increased the ability of marketers to conduct polls on blogs and social networking sites. The benefits of online market research include lower costs and quicker feedback. For instance, LEGO encourages fans to submit their own ideas for LEGO sets on their LEGO Ideas crowdsourcing platform. Other fans can vote on the ideas, and enough votes make the idea eligible for review and possible commercialization. This allows LEGO to solicit creative ideas from passionate fans at low cost.[28] By monitoring consumers' feedback, companies can understand customer needs and adapt their goods or services.

Finally, *marketing analytics* uses data that has been collected to measure, interpret, and evaluate marketing decisions. This emerging area uses advanced software that can track, store, and analyze data. Marketing research has been advanced with big data and data analytics. Big data involves large data sets that can provide the opportunity for advanced analysis to provide information for marketing decisions. Marketing analytics is becoming an increasingly important part of a company's marketing activities that are integrated into daily decision making. Dashboards are a data management tool that provide visual information related to sales, inventory, and product information as well as key performance indicators related to financial results. The ability of marketing analytics to harness trillions of gigabytes of data provides marketing research findings on demand. Marketing analytics can use artificial intelligence (AI) to turn

buying behavior the decision processes and actions of people who purchase and use products.

perception the process by which a person selects, organizes, and interprets information received from his or her senses.

motivation an inner drive that directs a person's behavior toward goals.

learning changes in a person's behavior based on information and experience.

attitude knowledge and positive or negative feelings about something.

personality the organization of an individual's distinguishing character traits, attitudes, or habits.

social roles a set of expectations for individuals based on some position they occupy.

data into new ways of making marketing decisions. For example, retailer H&M has been using big data alongside AI to determine fashion trends and consumer preferences. By using the big data analytics, it has been able to predict what the market will want in the future months ahead of time. Also, H&M has been able to create personalized recommendations for individual customers with products selected by algorithms. Through big data, the extent of services and personalization provided has increased dramatically.[29] Additionally, frequent-flyer programs enable airlines to track individual information about customers, using databases that can help airlines understand what different customers want, and treat customers differently depending on their flying habits and overall value to the company. Airlines, hotels, and other service providers are also increasingly gathering a greater 'share of customer,' as discussed below, by tying a company branded credit card to enhance overall value for the user and the customer. Many airlines require you fly certain levels of mileage and charge a minimum dollar value to their credit card to retain premium benefits. Relationship-building efforts like frequent-flyer and credit card programs have been shown to increase customer value.[30]

BUYING BEHAVIOR

Carrying out the marketing concept is impossible unless marketers know what, where, when, and how consumers buy; conducting marketing research into the factors that influence buying behavior helps marketers develop effective marketing strategies. **Buying behavior** refers to the decision processes and actions of people who purchase and use products. It includes the behavior of both consumers purchasing products for personal or household use and organizations buying products for business use. Marketers analyze buying behavior because a firm's marketing strategy should be guided by an understanding of buyers. For instance, men's shopping habits are changing. Men's shopping habits used to be more targeted and fast. Today, they tend to buy more clothes on impulse, search websites or mobile phones for style ideas, and try out new brands. As a result, retailers have begun expanding the men's areas in their stores.[31] Both

psychological and social variables are important to an understanding of buying behavior.

Psychological Variables of Buying Behavior

Psychological factors include the following:

- **Perception** is the process by which a person selects, organizes, and interprets information received from that person's senses, as when experiencing an advertisement or touching a product to better understand it.

- **Motivation**, as we said in the "Motivating the Workforce" chapter, is an inner drive that directs a person's behavior toward goals. A customer's behavior is influenced by a set of motives rather than by a single motive. A buyer of a tablet computer, for example, may be motivated by ease of use, ability to communicate with the office, and price.

- **Learning** brings about changes in a person's behavior based on information and experience. For instance, a smartphone app that provides digital news or magazine content could eliminate the need for print copies. If a person's actions result in a reward, that person is likely to behave the same way in similar situations. If a person's actions bring about a negative result, however—such as feeling ill after eating at a certain restaurant—that person will probably not repeat that action.

- **Attitude** is knowledge and positive or negative feelings about something. For example, a person who feels strongly about protecting the environment may refuse to buy products that harm the earth and its inhabitants.

- **Personality** refers to the organization of an individual's distinguishing character traits, attitudes, or habits. Although market research on the relationship between personality and buying behavior has been inconclusive, some marketers believe that the type of car or clothing a person buys reflects that person's personality.

Social Variables of Buying Behavior

Social factors include **social roles**, which are a set of expectations for individuals based on some position they occupy. A person may have many roles: parent, spouse, student, executive. Each of these roles can influence buying behavior. Consider a parent choosing an automobile. As a parent, that person might prefer to purchase a safe, gasoline-efficient car such as a Volvo. The person's environmentally supportive work colleagues might encourage the use of public transportation and Uber instead of buying a car. Because millennials tend to prefer vehicles that represent how they see themselves, even that person's children might want different vehicles: one might want a Ford Explorer to take on camping trips, while the other might prefer a cool, classy car such as a Ford Mustang.[32] Thus, in choosing which car to buy, the parent's buying behavior may be affected by the opinions and experiences of family and friends and by that person's role as a parent and employee.

Other social factors include reference groups, social classes, and culture.

- **Reference groups** include families, professional groups, civic organizations, and other groups with whom buyers identify and whose values or attitudes they adopt. A person may use a reference group as a point of comparison or a source of information. A person new to a community may ask other group members to recommend a family doctor, for example.

- **Social classes** are determined by ranking people into higher or lower positions of respect. Criteria vary from one society to another. People within a particular social class may develop common patterns of behavior. People in the upper-middle class, for example, might buy a Lexus or a BMW as a symbol of their social class.

- **Culture** is the integrated, accepted pattern of human behavior, including thought, speech, beliefs, actions, and artifacts. Culture determines what people wear and eat and where they live and travel. Many Hispanic Texans and New Mexicans, for example, buy *masa harina,* the corn flour used to prepare fresh tortillas, which are basic to Southwestern and Mexican cuisine.

Understanding Buying Behavior

Although marketers try to understand buying behavior, it is extremely difficult to explain exactly why a buyer purchases a particular product. The tools and techniques for analyzing consumers are not exact. Marketers may not be able to determine accurately what is highly satisfying to buyers, but they know that trying to understand consumer wants and needs is the best way to satisfy them. Marriott International's Innovation Lab, for instance, tests out new hotel designs for its brands to target millennials and other desirable demographics. Wi-Fi, lighting, and more soundproof rooms are among the top desirable traits travelers desire. Another trend is that travelers are not unpacking their suitcases as much. As a result, Marriott has begun reducing the size of closets and the number of hangers to save room.[33]

LO 11-7 Summarize the environmental forces that influence marketing decisions.

THE MARKETING ENVIRONMENT

A number of external forces directly or indirectly influence the development of marketing strategies; the following political, legal, regulatory, social, competitive, economic, and technological forces comprise the marketing environment.

- *Political, legal, and regulatory forces*—laws and regulators' interpretation of laws, law enforcement and regulatory activities, regulatory bodies, legislators and legislation, and political actions of interest groups. Specific laws, for example, require that advertisements be truthful and that all health claims be documented.

- *Social forces*—the public's opinions and attitudes toward issues such as living standards, ethics, the environment, lifestyles, and quality of life. For example, social concerns have led marketers to design and market safer toys for children.

- *Competitive and economic forces*—competitive relationships such as those in the technology industry, unemployment, purchasing power, and general economic conditions (prosperity, recession, depression, recovery, product shortages, and inflation).

- *Technological forces*—computers and other technological advances that improve distribution, promotion, and new product development.

reference groups groups with whom buyers identify and whose values or attitudes they adopt.

social classes a ranking of people into higher or lower positions of respect.

culture the integrated, accepted pattern of human behavior, including thought, speech, beliefs, actions, and artifacts.

Marketing requires creativity and consumer focus because environmental forces can change quickly and dramatically. Changes can arise from social concerns and economic forces such as price increases, product shortages, and altering levels of demand for commodities. The COVID-19 (coronavirus) pandemic swiftly changed buying behavior as many Americans were urged to stay home and many lost their jobs. Consumer spending on essentials increased while spending on discretionary categories decreased.[34] Recently, climate change, global warming, and the impact of carbon emissions on our environment have become social concerns and are causing businesses to rethink marketing strategies. These environmental issues have persuaded governments to institute stricter limits on greenhouse gas emissions. *Newsweek* magazine ranks the top "Green Companies" each year. Recent highly ranked companies include Cisco Systems, Ecolab Inc., Hasbro, Sealed Air Corp., and Best Buy.[35]

Because such environmental forces are interconnected, changes in one may cause changes in others. Consider that because of evidence linking children's consumption of soft drinks and fast foods to health issues such as obesity, diabetes, and osteoporosis, marketers of such products have experienced negative publicity and calls for legislation regulating the sale of soft drinks in public schools.

Although the forces in the marketing environment are sometimes called uncontrollables, they are not totally so. A marketing manager can influence some environmental variables. For example, businesses can lobby legislators to dissuade them from passing unfavorable legislation. From a social responsibility perspective, firms like BMW try to make a positive contribution. The BMW Ultimate Drive program involves specially marked BMWs that drive across the United States to increase breast cancer awareness and raise funds for breast cancer research. BMW donates

Marketing Environment

$1 to the Susan G. Komen Breast Cancer Foundation for every mile these cars are test driven by participants.[36] Figure 11.4 shows the variables in the marketing environment that affect the marketing mix and the buyer.

IMPORTANCE OF MARKETING TO BUSINESS AND SOCIETY

As this chapter has shown, marketing is a necessary function to reaching consumers, establishing relationships, and creating revenue. While some critics might view marketing as a way to change what consumers want, marketing is essential in communicating the value of goods and services. For consumers, marketing is necessary to ensure that they get the products they desire at the right places in the right quantities at a reasonable price. From the perspective of businesses, marketing is necessary in order to form valuable relationships with customers to increase profitability and customer support.

It is not just for-profit businesses that engage in marketing activities. Nonprofit organizations, government institutions, and even people must market themselves to spread awareness and achieve desired outcomes. All organizations must reach their target markets,

BUILDING YOUR SOFT SKILLS

BY CONSIDERING YOUR PERSONAL BRAND

This chapter discussed some basic principles of marketing that focus on ensuring that products consumers want to buy are provided at a price they want to pay. Consider the way you market yourself to potential employers. What is your "personal brand"? Try to develop a brief statement that outlines your unique value and articulates why hiring you would be a positive decision for employers. Be as specific as you can, and be sure you emphasize the soft skills you have. If you're struggling, search online for some samples you can use as models.

Team Exercise

Form groups and assign the responsibility of finding examples of companies that excel in one dimension of the marketing mix (price, product, promotion, and distribution). Provide several company and product examples, and defend why this would be an exemplary case. Present your research to the class.

communicate their offerings, and establish high-quality services. For instance, nonprofit organization The Leukemia and Lymphoma Society uses print, radio, web, and other forms of media to market its Team in Training racing events to recruit participants and solicit support. Without marketing, it would be nearly impossible for organizations to connect with their target audiences. Marketing is, therefore, an important contributor to business and societal well-being. ■

DO YOU HAVE WHAT IT TAKES // to Get a Job in Marketing? /

You probably did not think as a child how great it would be to grow up and become a marketer. That's because, often, marketing is associated with sales jobs, but opportunities in marketing, public relations, product management, advertising, e-marketing, and customer relationship management and beyond represent almost one-third of all jobs in today's business world. To enter any job in the marketing field, you must balance an awareness of customer needs with business knowledge while mixing in creativity and the ability to obtain useful information to make smart business decisions.

Marketing starts with understanding the customer. Marketing research is a vital aspect in marketing decision making and presents many job opportunities. Market researchers survey customers to determine their habits, preferences, and aspirations. Activities include concept testing, product testing, package testing, test-market research, and new-product research. Salaries vary, depending on the nature and level of the position as well as the type, size, and location of the firm. A market analyst may make between $40,000 and $78,000, while a market research director earns a median salary of more than $111,000.

One of the most dynamic areas in marketing is direct marketing, where a seller solicits a response from a consumer using direct communications methods such as telephone, online communication, direct mail, or catalogs. Jobs in direct marketing include buyers, catalog managers, research/mail-list managers, or order fulfillment managers. Most positions in direct marketing involve planning and market analysis. Some require the use of databases to sort and analyze customer information and sales history.

Use of the Internet for retail sales is growing, and the Internet continues to be very useful for business-to-business sales. E-marketing offers many career opportunities, including customer relationship management (CRM). CRM helps companies market to customers through relationships, maintaining customer loyalty. Information technology plays a huge role in such marketing jobs because you need to combine technical skills and marketing knowledge to effectively communicate with customers. Job titles include e-marketing manager, customer relationship manager, and e-services manager. A CRM manager earns a median salary of approximately $68,000, and experienced individuals may earn as much as $113,000.

A job in any of these marketing fields will require a strong sense of the current trends in business and marketing. Customer service is vital to many aspects of marketing, so the ability to work with customers and to communicate their needs and wants is important. Marketing is everywhere, from the corner grocery or local nonprofit organization to the largest multinational corporations, making it a shrewd choice for an ambitious and creative person. We will provide additional job opportunities in marketing in the "Dimensions of Marketing Strategy" chapter.[37]

dimensions of
marketing strategy

Tinnaporn Sathapornnanont/Shutterstock

LEARNING OBJECTIVES

After reading this chapter, you will be able to:

LO 12-1 Describe the role of product in the marketing mix, including how products are developed, classified, and identified.

LO 12-2 Explain the importance of price in the marketing mix, including various pricing strategies a firm might employ.

LO 12-3 Identify factors affecting distribution decisions, such as marketing channels and intensity of market coverage.

LO 12-4 Specify the activities involved in promotion, as well as promotional strategies and promotional positioning.

The key to developing a marketing strategy is selecting a target market and maintaining a marketing mix that creates long-term relationships with customers. Getting just the right mix of product, price, promotion, and distribution is critical if a business is to satisfy its target customers and achieve its own objectives (implement the marketing concept).

In the "Customer-Driven Marketing" chapter, we introduced the marketing concept and the various activities important in developing a marketing strategy. In this chapter, we'll take a closer look at the four dimensions of the marketing mix—product, price, distribution, and promotion—used to develop the marketing strategy. As we mentioned in the "Customer-Driven Marketing" chapter, sometimes the marketing mix is called the 4Ps with distribution referred to as place. The focus of these marketing mix elements is a marketing strategy that builds customer relationships and satisfaction. ■

THE MARKETING MIX

The marketing mix is the part of marketing strategy that involves decisions regarding controllable variables. After selecting a target market, marketers have to develop and manage the dimensions of the marketing mix to give their firm an advantage over competitors. Successful companies offer at least one dimension of value usually associated with a marketing mix element that surpasses all competitors in the marketplace in meeting customer expectations. However, this does not mean that a company can ignore the other dimensions of the marketing mix; it must maintain acceptable, and if possible distinguishable, differences in the other dimensions as well.

Walmart, for example, emphasizes price ("Save money, live better"). Procter & Gamble is well known for its products with top consumer brands such as Tide, Cheer, Crest, Ivory, and Head & Shoulders. Many successful marketers have worked with advertising agencies to create catchy jingles to help consumers recall ads. Campbell Soup's "Mmm Mmm Good," McDonald's "I'm lovin' it," and Coca-Cola's "I'd like to Teach the World to Sing" are all iconic jingles.[1] Finally, Amazon has become so successful by having a highly efficient distribution system.

LO 12-1 Describe the role of product in the marketing mix, including how products are developed, classified, and identified.

PRODUCT STRATEGY

As mentioned previously, the term *product* refers to goods, services, and ideas. Because the product is often the most visible of the marketing mix dimensions, managing product decisions is crucial. In this section, we'll consider product development, classification, mix, life cycle, and identification.

Developing New Products

Each year, thousands of products are introduced, but few of them succeed. Even established firms launch unsuccessful products. For example, GM discontinued its subcompact car, the Chevy Sonic, after years of poor sales.[2] Figure 12.1 shows the different steps in the product development process. Before introducing a new product, a business must follow a multistep process: idea development, the screening of new ideas, business analysis, product development, test marketing, and commercialization. A firm can take considerable time to get a product ready for the market: It took more than 20 years for the first photocopier, for example. Additionally, sometimes an idea or product prototype might be shelved only to be returned to later. Former Apple CEO Steve Jobs admitted that the iPad actually came before the iPhone in the product development process. Once it was realized that the scrolling mechanism he was thinking of using could be used to develop a phone, the iPad

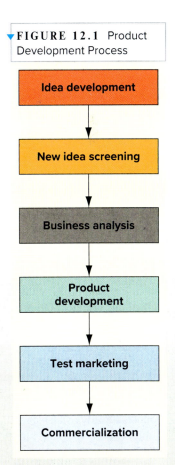

▼ **FIGURE 12.1** Product Development Process

- Idea development
- New idea screening
- Business analysis
- Product development
- Test marketing
- Commercialization

test marketing a trial minilaunch of a product in limited areas that represent the potential market.

commercialization the full introduction of a complete marketing strategy and the launch of the product for commercial success.

idea was placed on a shelf for the time being. Apple later returned to develop the product and released the iPad in 2010.[3]

Idea Development.
New ideas can come from marketing research, engineers, and outside sources such as advertising agencies and management consultants. Nike has a separate division—Nike Sport Research Lab—where scientists, athletes, engineers, and designers work together to develop technology of the future. The teams research ideas in biomechanics, perception, athletic performance, and physiology to create unique, relevant, and innovative products. These final products are tested in environmental chambers with real athletes to ensure functionality and quality before being introduced into the market.[4] As we said in the "Customer-Driven Marketing" chapter, ideas sometimes come from customers, too. Other sources are brainstorming and intracompany incentives or

marketers to screen ideas. Most new-product ideas are rejected during screening because they seem inappropriate or impractical for the organization.

Business Analysis.
Business analysis is a basic assessment of a product's compatibility in the marketplace and its potential profitability. Both the size of the market and competing products are often studied at this point. The most important question relates to market demand: How will the product affect the firm's sales, costs, and profits?

Product Development.
If a product survives the first three steps, it is developed into a prototype that should reveal the intangible attributes it possesses as perceived by the consumer. Product development is often expensive, and few product ideas make it to this stage. New product research and development costs vary. Adding a new color to an existing item may cost $100,000 to $200,000, but launching a completely new product can cost millions of dollars. During product development, various elements of the marketing mix must be developed for testing. Copyrights, tentative advertising

> ## "USING THE INTERNET TO ENCOURAGE COLLABORATION REPRESENTS A RICH OPPORTUNITY FOR MARKETERS TO SCREEN IDEAS."

rewards for good ideas. New ideas can even create a company. When Jeff Bezos came up with the idea to sell books over the Internet in 1992, he had no idea it would evolve into the world's largest online retailer. After failing to convince his boss of the value of his idea, Bezos left to start Amazon.[5]

New Idea Screening.
The next step in developing a new product is idea screening. In this phase, a marketing manager should look at the organization's resources and objectives and assess the firm's ability to produce and market the product. Important aspects to be considered at this stage are consumer desires; the competition; technological changes; social trends; and political, economic, and environmental considerations. Basically, there are two reasons new products succeed: They are able to meet a need or solve a problem better than products already available, or they add variety to the product selection currently on the market. Bringing together a team of knowledgeable people—including designers, engineers, marketers, and customers—is a great way to screen ideas. Using the Internet to encourage collaboration represents a rich opportunity for

copy, packaging, labeling, and descriptions of a target market are integrated to develop an overall marketing strategy.

Test Marketing.
Test marketing is a trial minilaunch of a product in limited areas that represent the potential market. It allows a complete test of the marketing strategy in a natural environment, giving the organization an opportunity to discover weaknesses and eliminate them before the product is fully launched. For example, Waymo LLC, a leader in the driverless-car industry, tested its commercial robo-taxi service in Phoenix to a pool of just 400 families.[6] Because test marketing requires significant resources and expertise, market research companies like Nielsen can assist firms in test marketing their products. Figure 12.2 shows a sample of test markets that marketing research firms often use to test products to predict how successful they might be on a nationwide scale.

Commercialization.
Commercialization is the full introduction of a complete marketing strategy and the launch of the product for commercial success. During commercialization, the

DID YOU KNOW?

Less than 20 percent of new products succeed in the marketplace. The success rate for consumer goods is about 51 percent.[a]

The Museum of Failure in Los Angeles is the largest collection of failed products and services such as Colgate Beef Lasagna, which was originally launched in the 1980s.

ROBYN BECK/AFP/Getty Images

family use; they are not intended for any purpose other than daily living. They can be further classified as convenience products, shopping products, and specialty products on the basis of consumers' buying behavior and intentions.

- *Convenience products,* such as beverages, granola bars, gasoline, and batteries, are bought frequently, without a lengthy search, and often for immediate consumption. Consumers spend virtually no time planning where to purchase these products and usually accept whatever brand is available.

- *Shopping products,* such as computers, smartphones, clothing, and sporting goods, are purchased after the consumer has compared competitive products and "shopped around." Price, product features, quality, style, service, and image all influence the decision to buy.

- *Specialty products,* such as motorcycles, designer clothing, art, and rock concerts, require even greater research and shopping effort. Consumers know what they want and go out of their way to find it; they are not willing to accept a substitute.

Business products are used directly or indirectly in the operation or manufacturing processes of businesses. They are usually purchased for the operation of an organization or the production of other products; thus, their purchase is tied to specific goals and objectives. They too can be further classified:

- *Raw materials* are natural products taken from the earth, oceans, and recycled solid waste. Iron ore, bauxite, lumber, cotton, and fruits and vegetables are examples.

firm gears up for full-scale production, distribution, and promotion. Firms such as AquAdvantage Salmon are getting ready to release genetically modified salmon into the market. The Food and Drug Administration has approved the salmon as fit for consumption. However, even with federal regulatory approval, AquAdvantage may face hurdles because of consumer and environmental groups.[7]

Classifying Products

Products are usually classified as either consumer products or industrial products. **Consumer products** are for household or

- *Major equipment* covers large, expensive items used in production. Examples include earth-moving equipment, stamping machines, and robotic equipment used on auto assembly lines.

- *Accessory equipment* includes items used for production, office, or management purposes, which usually do not become part of the final product. Computers, calculators, and hand tools are examples.

- *Component parts* are finished items, ready to be assembled into the company's final products. Tires, window glass, batteries, and spark plugs are component parts of automobiles.

- *Processed materials* are things used directly in production or management operations but are not readily identifiable as component parts. Varnish, for example, is a processed material for a furniture manufacturer.

▼**FIGURE 12.2** Common Test Market Cities

**Market Decisions
Test Market Locations**

Portland
Albany
Columbus
Boise
Peoria
Evansville
Provo
Colorado Springs
St. Louis
Lexington
Little Rock
Charlotte
Charleston
Tucson
Jacksonville
Baton Rouge

■ Permanent Test Markets ("Data Markets")

★ Additional "Custom" Test Markets

Source: The Nielsen Company

product line a group of closely related products that are treated as a unit because of similar marketing strategy, production, or end-use considerations.

product mix all the products offered by an organization.

- *Supplies* include materials that make production, management, and other operations possible, such as paper, pencils, paint, cleaning supplies, and so on.
- *Industrial services* include financial, legal, marketing research, security, janitorial, and exterminating services. Purchasers decide whether to provide these services internally or to acquire them from an outside supplier.

Product Line and Product Mix

Product relationships within an organization are of key importance. A **product line** is a group of closely related products that are treated as a unit because of a similar marketing strategy. At Colgate-Palmolive, for example, the personal-care product line includes deodorant, body wash, bar soap, liquid soap, and toiletries for men. A **product mix** is all the products offered by an organization. Figure 12.3 displays a sampling of the product mix and product lines of the Colgate-Palmolive Company.

Product Life Cycle

Like people, products are born, grow, mature, and eventually die. Some products have very long lives. Ivory Soap was introduced in 1879 and still exists (although competition leading to decreased sales may soon put the future of Ivory Soap in question). In contrast, a new computer chip is usually outdated within a year because of technological breakthroughs and rapid changes in the computer industry. There are four stages in the life cycle of a product: introduction, growth, maturity, and decline (Figure 12.4). The stage a product is in helps determine marketing strategy. In the personal computer industry, desktop computers are in the decline stage, laptop computers have reached the maturity stage, and tablet computers are currently in the growth stage of the product life cycle (although growth has slowed in recent years). Manufacturers of these products are adopting different advertising and pricing strategies to maintain or increase demand for these types of computers.

In the *introductory stage*, consumer awareness and acceptance of the product are limited, sales are zero, and profits are negative. Profits are negative because the firm has spent money on research, development, and marketing to launch the product. Chipotle introduced a series of healthy menu options named "Lifestyle Bowls." They are targeted at customers who are interested in trendy diets like Whole30 and Keto. Only time will tell

FIGURE 12.3 A Sampling of Colgate-Palmolive's Product Mix and Product Lines in North America

← Product Mix →

↕ Product Lines

Oral Care	Personal Care	Home Care	Pet Nutrition
Toothpaste	*Deodorant*	*Dishwashing*	Hill's Prescription Diet
Colgate Total	Speed Stick 24/7	*Glo Regular*	Hill's Science Diet
Colgate Optic White	Lady Speed Stick Roll-on	*Glo Professional*	Hill's Healthy Advantage
Colgate Sensitive	Lady Speed Stick Invisible	*Axion Paste*	
Colgate MaxFresh	Tom's of Maine	*Axion Gel*	
Colgate Kids		Palmolive	
Tom's of Maine Toothpaste	*Body Wash*	AJAX	
Tom's of Maine Children's Toothpaste	Softsoap	Dermassage	
	Irish Spring		
Mouthwashes		*Fabric Conditioner*	
Colgate Total	*Bar Soap*	Suavitel Liquid Fabric Conditioners	
Colgate Optic White	Irish Spring	Suavitel Ultra Liquid Fabric Conditioners	
Colgate Kids	Softsoap	Suavitel Fragrance Pearls	
Tom's of Maine Mouthwash		Suavitel Fast Dry Fabric Conditioners	
Tom's of Maine Children's	*Liquid Soap*	Suavitel Complete	
Mouthwash	Softsoap		
		Household cleaner	
Toothbrushes	*Toiletries for Men*	Murphy Oil Soap	
Colgate 360°	Afta	Fabuloso	
Colgate MaxFresh	Skin Bracer	AJAX	
Colgate Kids			
Colgate Total			
Colgate Optic White			

Source: Colgate-Palmolive, "Colgate-Palmolive Brands," https://www.colgatepalmolive.com/en-us/brands (accessed June 10, 2020).

branding the process of naming and identifying products.

▼ FIGURE 12.4 The Life Cycle of a Product

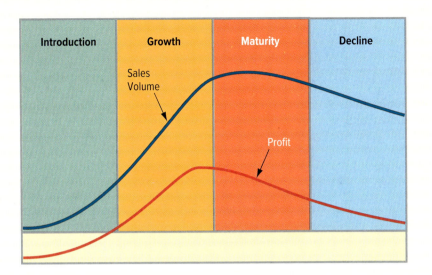

if these new menu items will take off.[8] During the introductory stage, marketers focus on making consumers aware of the product and its benefits. It is not unusual for technology products to go quickly through the life cycle as the rate of new technology innovations continues to increase. The smartwatch product category, for example, rapidly moved from the introductory stage to the growth stage. The smartwatch market is expected to become a $96 billion market by 2027.[9] Innovation of this type is welcomed by consumers and the public at large. Table 12.1 shows some familiar products at different stages of the product life cycle. Sales accelerate as the product enters the growth stage of the life cycle.

In the *growth stage*, sales increase rapidly and profits peak, then start to decline. One reason profits start to decline during the growth stage is that new companies enter the market, driving prices down and increasing marketing expenses. Drones for both recreational and business uses are growing rapidly and are a good example of a product in the growth stage. During the growth stage, the firm tries to strengthen its position in the market by emphasizing the product's benefits and identifying market segments that want these benefits.

Sales continue to increase at the beginning of the *maturity stage*, but then the sales curve peaks and starts to decline while profits

continue to decline. This stage is characterized by severe competition and heavy expenditures. In the United States, soft drinks have hit the maturity stage. For example, the best-selling sodas are Coca-Cola, Diet Coke, Pepsi, Mountain Dew, Dr Pepper, Sprite, and Diet Pepsi. This represents a move to less sugary drinks as consumers have also turned to flavored water, bottled water, and tea. The soft-drink market is highly competitive, with many alternative products for consumers.[10]

During the *decline stage*, sales continue to fall rapidly. Profits also decline and may even become losses as prices are cut and necessary marketing expenditures are made. As profits drop, firms may eliminate certain models or items. To reduce expenses and squeeze out any remaining profits, marketing expenditures may be cut back, even though such cutbacks accelerate the sales decline. Finally, plans must be made for phasing out the product and introducing new ones to take its place. Consoles for video games are often phased out and a new one takes its place. Nintendo's launch of the Switch that has a 6.2-inch touchscreen allows taking games on the go but required developing a strong lineup of game titles.[11]

At the same time, it should be noted that product stages do not always go one way. Some products that have moved to the maturity stage or to the decline stage can still rebound through redesign or new uses for the product. For example, United Record Pressing LLC is enjoying the new interest in vinyl records. The company produces 30 to 40 percent of all vinyl records available in stores. This new interest in vinyl signals a resurgence in the sales of vinyl records to consumers and has created a growth mode for this privately held company—as well as a commitment to the company's rich musical history, which dates back to 1949.[12]

Identifying Products

Branding, packaging, and labeling can be used to identify or distinguish one product from others. As a result, they are key marketing activities that help position a product appropriately for its target market.

▼ TABLE 12.1 Products at Different Stages of the Product Life Cycle

Introduction	Growth	Maturity	Decline
Ultra HD 4K television	3D printers	Laptop computer	Desktop computers
Home assistants	Airbnb lodging sharing	Disney theme parks	Landline phones
Hydrogen fuel automobiles	Keto products	Soft drinks	Print newspaper

Branding. Branding is the process of naming and identifying products. A *brand* is a name, term, symbol, design, or combination that identifies a product and distinguishes it from other products. Consider that Google and Band-Aid are brand names that

trademark a brand that is registered with the U.S. Patent and Trademark Office and is thus legally protected from use by any other firm.

manufacturer brands brands initiated and owned by the manufacturer to identify products from the point of production to the point of purchase.

private distributor brands brands, which may cost less than manufacturer brands, that are owned and controlled by a wholesaler or retailer.

generic products products with no brand name that often come in simple packages and carry only their generic name.

packaging the external container that holds and describes the product.

---

are used to identify entire product categories, much like Xerox has become synonymous with photocopying and Kleenex with tissues. Protecting a brand name is important in maintaining a brand identity. The world's 10 most valuable brands are shown in Table 12.2. The brand name is the part of the brand that can be spoken and consists of letters, words, and numbers—such as WD-40 lubricant. A *brand mark* is the part of the brand that is a distinctive design, such as the silver star on the hood of a Mercedes or McDonald's golden arches logo. A **trademark** is a brand that is registered with the U.S. Patent and Trademark Office and is thus legally protected from use by any other firm.

Two major categories of brands are manufacturer brands and private distributor brands. **Manufacturer brands** are brands initiated and owned by the manufacturer to identify products from the point of production to the point of purchase. Kellogg's, Sony, and Chevron are examples. **Private distributor brands**, which may be less expensive than manufacturer brands, are owned and controlled by a wholesaler or retailer, such as Nice! (Walgreens), Pantry Essentials (Safeway), 365 Everyday Value (Whole Foods), Great Value (Walmart), and Trader Joe's. The names of private brands do not usually identify their manufacturer. While private-label brands were once considered cheaper and of poor quality, such as Walmart's Ol'Roy dog food, many private-label brands are increasing in quality and image and are competing with national brands. Even Amazon has noticed the lucrative opportunities of private-label brands. The firm developed its own private-label clothing brand.[13] Today, there are

private-label brands in nearly every food and beverage category, and the private-label food and beverage market is expected to grow by nearly 5 percent annually.[14] Manufacturer brands are fighting hard against private distributor brands to retain their market share.

Another type of brand that has developed is **generic products**—products with no brand name at all. They often come in plain simple packages that carry only the generic name of the product—peanut butter, tomato juice, aspirin, dog food, and so on. They appeal to consumers who may be willing to sacrifice quality or product consistency to get a lower price. Sales of generic brands have significantly decreased in recent years, although generic pharmaceuticals are commonly purchased due to their lower prices.

Companies use two basic approaches to branding multiple products. In one, a company gives each product within its complete product mix its own brand name. Unilever sells many well-known consumer products—Dove, Axe, Knorr, Hellman's, Dermalogica—each individually branded. This branding policy ensures that the name of one product does not affect the names of others, and different brands can be targeted at different segments of the same market, increasing the company's market share (its percentage of the sales for the total market for a product). Another approach to branding is to develop a family of brands with each of the firm's products carrying the same name or at least part of the name. Gillette, Sara Lee, and IBM use this approach. Finally, consumers may react differently to domestic versus foreign brands. The quality of Chinese brands may be questioned compared to German or U.S. brands.

Packaging. The **packaging**, or external container that holds and describes the product, influences consumers' attitudes and their buying decisions. Surveys have shown that consumers are willing to pay more for certain packaging attributes. For example, after facing criticism for its cardboard packaging, Kylie Cosmetics released higher-quality plastic eyeshadow palettes.[15] One of the attributes includes clearly stated nutrition and ingredient labeling, especially those characteristics indicating whether a product is organic, gluten-free, or environmentally friendly. Recyclable and biodegradable packaging is also popular.[16] For example, the advertisement for Hormel Natural Choice Bacon shows product packaging that lists "no preservatives" and "100% natural" to help its product stand out. It is estimated that consumers' eyes linger only 2.5 seconds on each product on an average shopping trip; therefore, product packaging should be designed to attract and hold consumers' attention.

▼ **TABLE 12.2** The 10 Most Valuable Brands in the World

Rank	Brand	Brand Value ($ billion)	Brand Value (% change from prior year)
1	Apple	205.5	12
2	Google	167.7	27
3	Microsoft	125.3	20
4	Amazon	97.0	37
5	Facebook	88.9	–6
6	Coca-Cola	59.2	3
7	Samsung	53.1	11
8	Disney	52.2	10
9	Toyota	44.6	0
10	McDonalds	43.8	6

Source: "The World's Most Valuable Brands," *Forbes,* https://www.forbes.com/powerful-brands/list/#tab:rank (accessed June 10, 2020).

A package can perform several functions, including protection, economy, convenience, and promotion. IKEA is constantly trying to investigate new ways for more efficient packaging to save on shipping costs.[17] Packaging can also be used to appeal to emotions. For example, pet food packaging appeals to the emotions of pet owners with illustrations of animals happily running, eating, or looking serene.[18] On the other hand, organizations must also exert caution before changing the designs of highly popular products. For example, Coca-Cola released a new global design for its products that features the traditional red as the main color. The "one brand" strategy is to create a unified global presence for its flagship soda.

Labeling.
Labeling, the presentation of important information on the package, is closely associated with packaging. The content of a label, often required by law, may include ingredients or content, nutrition facts (calories, fat, etc.), care instructions, suggestions for use (such as recipes), the manufacturer's address and toll-free number, website, and other useful information. This information can have a strong impact on sales. The labels of many products, particularly food and drugs, must carry warnings, instructions, certifications, or manufacturers' identifications.

Product Quality.
Quality reflects the degree to which a good, service, or idea meets the demands and requirements of customers. Quality products are often referred to as reliable,

Hormel includes the attributes "no preservatives" and "100% natural" on its product packaging to help differentiate its bacon to consumers.

Source: Hormel

labeling the presentation of important information on a package.

quality the degree to which a good, service, or idea meets the demands and requirements of customers.

durable, easily maintained, easily used, a good value, or a trusted brand name. The level of quality is the amount of quality that a product possesses, and the consistency of quality depends on the product maintaining the same level of quality over time.

Quality of service is difficult to gauge because it depends on customers' perceptions of how well the service meets or exceeds their expectations. In other words, service quality is judged by consumers, not the service providers. For this reason, it is quite common for perceptions of quality to fluctuate from year to year. For instance, Volkswagen suffered significant reputational and financial impact from its emissions scandal with attempting to cover up the actual emissions impact of its diesel vehicles. VW faced buybacks, repairs, and financial settlements with defrauded customers.

Consumers expect quality projects and truthful and transparent information.[19] A bank may define service quality as employing friendly and knowledgeable employees, but the bank's customers may be more concerned with waiting time, ATM access, security, and statement accuracy. Similarly, an airline traveler considers on-time arrival, on-board Internet or TV connections, and satisfaction with the ticketing and boarding process. The American Customer Satisfaction Index produces customer satisfaction scores for 10 economic sectors, 44 industries, and more than 300 companies. The latest results show that overall customer satisfaction was 75.4 (out of a possible 100), with increases in some industries balancing out drops in others.[20] Reynolds Kitchens used an in-home study to inform its advertisement, which promotes that three out of four prefer Reynolds Kitchens Quick Cut Plastic Wrap over Glad Cling Wrap. Table 12.3 shows the customer satisfaction rankings of some of the most popular personal care and cleaning product companies.

The quality of services provided by businesses on the Internet can be gauged by consumers on such sites as ConsumerReports.org and the Better Business Bureau. The subscription service offered by ConsumerReports.org provides consumers with a

▼ **TABLE 12.3** Personal Care and Cleaning Products Customer Satisfaction Ratings

Company	Score
Procter & Gamble	85
Clorox	84
Colgate-Palmolive	82
Unilever	80
Henkel	77
Johnson & Johnson	77

Source: American Customer Satisfaction Index, "ACSI Nondurable Products Report," 2019, https://www.theacsi.org/news-and-resources/customer-satisfaction-reports/reports-2019/acsi-nondurable-products-report-2018-2019/acsi-nondurable-products-report-2018-2019-download (accessed June 10, 2020).

First founded in 1967 in California, Trader Joe's is composed of more than 500 stores in 42 states. One of Trader Joe's biggest assets is uniqueness. Despite its large reach, Trader Joe's exudes the same neighborhood-store atmosphere that it did back in 1967. It maintains smaller facilities and product lines than comparable stores, stocking only about 4,000 items compared to the 50,000 stocked by the typical grocery store. Inventory control has been a key advantage in reducing costs and focusing on a limited number of quality products.

Trader Joe's also sets itself apart with its private-label products. More than 80 percent of Trader Joe's stock consists of private-label products, giving Trader Joe's management more control over the supply chain. The private-label products prevent the company from relying too heavily on any one supplier, and as a result, Trader Joe's can offer lower prices than rival Whole Foods. Trader Joe's also recognizes consumers' changing demands for more sustainable and ethical products. In 2012, Trader Joe's made the decision to sell only sustainable seafood and not carry products containing genetically modified ingredients. This approach to its product selection has increased Trader Joe's reputation for selling quality products that meet customer needs. In 2018, the company announced plans to improve the sustainability of its product packaging.

Additionally, Trader Joe's excels at quality and supplier relations. The company employs product developers who travel the world looking for the best product/price combinations. Trader Joe's charges less in fees and is known for on-time payments with suppliers. Further, Trader Joe's only expands into areas that can support this streamlined distribution system. With its popularity continuing to rise, customers seem impressed by the way Trader Joe's is redefining the grocery shopping experience.[b]

Critical Thinking Questions

1. Which elements of the marketing strategy does Trader Joe's seem to particularly excel at?

2. What advantages do private distributor brands offer over manufacturer and generic brands?

3. Describe how Trader Joe's distribution strategy helps to save on costs.

To promote the quality of its Quick Cut Plastic Wrap, Reynolds Kitchens shared the results of an in-home study on plastic wrap preference.

Source: Reynolds Kitchens

view of digital marketing sites' business, security, and privacy policies, while the Better Business Bureau is dedicated to promoting responsibility both online and in-store. As consumers join in by posting business and product reviews on the Internet on sites such as Yelp, the public can often get a much better idea of the quality of certain goods and services. Quality can also be associated with where the product is made. For example, "Made in USA" labeling can be perceived as having a different value and quality. This includes strict laws on how much of a product can be made outside of the United States to still qualify for the "Made in USA" label. There are differences in the perception of quality and value between U.S. consumers and Europeans when comparing products made in the United States, Japan, Korea, and China.[21] Chinese brands are usually perceived as lower quality, while Japanese and Korean products are perceived as being of higher quality. However, China is trying to change consumer perceptions of its low brand quality. The increase in middle and upper classes in China has stimulated a rise in Chinese-branded luxury goods.[22]

LO 12-2 Explain the importance of price in the marketing mix, including various pricing strategies a firm might employ.

PRICING STRATEGY

Previously, we defined price as the value placed on an object exchanged between a buyer and a seller. Buyers' interest in price stems from their expectations about the usefulness of a product or the satisfaction they may derive from it. Because buyers have limited resources, they must allocate those resources to obtain the products they most desire. They must decide whether the benefits gained in an exchange are worth the buying power sacrificed. Almost anything of value can be assessed by a price. Many factors may influence the evaluation of value, including time constraints, price levels, perceived quality, and motivations to use available information about prices.[23] Figure 12.5 illustrates a method for calculating the value of a product. Indeed, consumers vary in their response to price: Some focus solely on the lowest price, while others consider quality or the prestige associated with a product and its price. Some types of consumers are increasingly "trading up" to more status-conscious products, such as automobiles, home appliances, restaurants, and even pet food, yet remain price-conscious for other products such as cleaning and grocery goods. In setting prices, marketers must consider not just a company's cost to produce a good or service, but the perceived value of that item in the marketplace. Products' perceived value has benefited marketers at Starbucks, Sub-Zero, BMW, and Petco—which can charge premium prices for high-quality, prestige products—as well as Sam's Clubs and Costco—which offer basic household products at everyday low prices.

Price is a key element in the marketing mix because it relates directly to the generation of revenue and profits. In large part, the ability to set a price depends on the supply of and demand for a product. For most products, the quantity demanded goes up as the price goes down, and as the price goes up, the quantity demanded goes down. Changes in buyers' needs, variations in the effectiveness of other marketing mix variables, the presence of substitutes, and competition can influence demand. Faced with competition from online razor startups such as Harry's and Dollar Shave Club, Gillette saw its market share drop significantly, causing the company to reduce prices.[24]

Price is probably the most flexible variable in the marketing mix. Although it may take years to develop a product, establish channels of distribution, and design and implement promotion, a product's price may be set and changed in a few minutes. Under certain circumstances, of course, the price may not be so flexible, especially if government regulations prevent dealers from controlling prices. Of course, price also depends on the cost to manufacture a good or provide a service or idea. A firm may temporarily sell products below cost to match competition, to generate cash flow, or even to increase market share, but in the long run, it cannot survive by selling its products below cost.

price skimming charging the highest possible price that buyers who want the product will pay.

penetration price a low price designed to help a product enter the market and gain market share rapidly.

Pricing Objectives

Pricing objectives specify the role of price in an organization's marketing mix and strategy. They usually are influenced not only by marketing mix decisions but also by finance, accounting, and production factors. Maximizing profits and sales, boosting market share, maintaining the status quo, and survival are four common pricing objectives.

Specific Pricing Strategies

Pricing strategies provide guidelines for achieving the company's pricing objectives and overall marketing strategy. They specify how price will be used as a variable in the marketing mix. Significant pricing strategies relate to the pricing of new products, psychological pricing, reference pricing, and price discounting.

Pricing New Products.
Setting the price for a new product is critical: The right price leads to profitability; the wrong price may kill the product. In general, there are two basic strategies to setting the base price for a new product. **Price skimming** is charging the highest possible price that buyers who want the product will pay. Price skimming is used with luxury items. Price skimming is often used to allow the company to generate much-needed revenue to help offset the costs of research and development. Conversely, a **penetration price** is a low price designed to help a product enter the market and gain market share rapidly. When Netflix entered the market, it offered its rentals at prices much lower than the average rental stores and did not charge late fees. Netflix quickly gained market share and eventually drove many rental stores out of business. Penetration pricing is less flexible than price skimming; it is more difficult

▼ **FIGURE 12.5** Calculating the Value of a Product

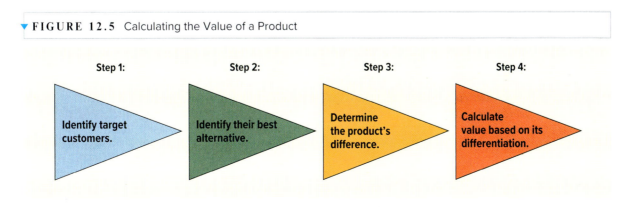

Step 1: Identify target customers.

Step 2: Identify their best alternative.

Step 3: Determine the product's difference.

Step 4: Calculate value based on its differentiation.

to raise a penetration price than to lower a skimming price. Penetration pricing is used most often when marketers suspect that competitors will enter the market shortly after the product has been introduced.

Psychological Pricing.
Psychological pricing encourages purchases based on emotional rather than rational responses to the price. For example, the assumption behind *even/odd pricing* is that people will buy more of a product for $9.99 than $10 because it seems to be a bargain at the odd price. The assumption behind *symbolic/prestige pricing* is that high prices connote high quality. Thus the prices of certain fragrances and cosmetics are set artificially high to give the impression of superior quality. Some over-the-counter drugs are priced high because consumers associate a drug's price with potency.

Reference Pricing.
Reference pricing is a type of psychological pricing in which a lower-priced item is compared to a more expensive brand in hopes that the consumer will use the higher price as a comparison price. The main idea is to make the item appear less expensive compared with other alternatives. For example, Walmart might place its Great Value brand next to a manufacturer's brand such as Hefty or Heinz so that the Great Value brand will look like a better deal.

Price Discounting.
Temporary price reductions, or **discounts**, are often employed to boost sales. Although there are many types, quantity, seasonal, and promotional discounts are among the most widely used. Quantity discounts reflect the economies of purchasing in large volumes. Seasonal discounts to buyers who purchase goods or services out of season help even out production capacity. Promotional discounts attempt to improve sales by advertising price reductions on selected products to increase customer interest. Often, promotional pricing is geared toward increased profits. For instance, bare-bones German grocery chain Aldi is attempting to compete against Trader Joe's as it expands in the United States through the offering of higher-end food and price discounts.[25] Aldi has about 1,900 stores in the U.S. and plans to open more.[26]

DISTRIBUTION STRATEGY

In the "Managing Operations and Supply Chains" chapter, we discussed supply chain management that involves connecting and integrating all members of the supply chain. While supply chain management involves operations, procurement, and logistics, we take a closer look at the role of marketing channels and logistics management.

The best products in the world will not be successful unless companies make them available where and when customers want to buy them. In this section, we will explore dimensions of distribution strategy, including the channels through which products are distributed, the intensity of market coverage, and the physical handling of products during distribution.

Marketing Channels

A **marketing channel**, or channel of distribution, is a group of organizations that moves products from their producer to customers. Marketing channels make products available to buyers when and where they desire to purchase them. Organizations that bridge the gap between a product's manufacturer and the ultimate consumer are called *middlemen*, or intermediaries. They create time, place, and ownership utility. Two intermediary organizations are retailers and wholesalers.

Retailers buy products from manufacturers (or other intermediaries) and sell them to consumers for home and household use rather than for resale or for use in producing other products. Dick's Sporting Goods, for example, buys products from Nike and other manufacturers and resells them to consumers. By bringing together an assortment of products from competing producers, retailers create utility. Retailers arrange for products to be moved from producers to a convenient retail establishment (place utility). They maintain hours of operation for their retail stores to make merchandise available when consumers want it (time utility). They also assume the risk of ownership of inventories (ownership utility). Table 12.4 describes various types of general merchandise retailers.

Amazon represents an Internet retailer business model that is disrupting the competitive structure of retail markets. Traditional retailers are developing their own online operations to compete with Amazon. The company accounts for 5 percent of retail spending and 49 percent of e-commerce sales in America and is growing rapidly.[27] While currently only half the size of the largest retailer, Walmart, it is the largest online retailer. Amazon is changing the nature of competition in the retail environment. The company sells almost every retail item and is challenging department and other retail stores. Also,

Amazon allows other retailers to use its e-commerce platform, warehouses, and other services.[28] In many ways, Amazon has remade retailing. The company even expanded into brick-and-mortar stores with Amazon Books, Amazon Go, and more.[29]

General merchandise retailers, especially department stores, are feeling the competitive threat, with Macy's, Sears, and others closing stores.[30] Online retailers, such as Amazon, pose a competitive threat to traditional retailers, undercutting store-based sellers on prices and options of many products. Many sporting goods store chains have gone out of business, but Dick's Sporting Goods is one that remains very successful today.[31]

Another type of retail is **direct marketing**, which is the use of nonpersonal media to communicate products, information, and the opportunity to purchase via

direct marketing the use of nonpersonal media to communicate products, information, and the opportunity to purchase via media such as mail, telephone, or the Internet.

▼ **TABLE 12.4** General Merchandise Retailers

Type of Retailer	Description	Examples
Department store	Large, full-service stores organized by departments	Nordstrom, Macy's, Neiman Marcus
Internet retailer	A direct marketer providing most products over the Internet	Amazon, Alibaba
Discount store	Offers less services than department stores; store atmosphere reflects value pricing	Walmart, Stein Mart, Target
Convenience store	Small, self-service stores carrying many items for immediate consumption	Circle K, 7-Eleven, Allsup's
Supermarket	Large stores carrying most food items as well as nonfood items for daily family use	Trader Joe's, Albertsons, Wegmans
Superstore	Very large stores that carry most food and nonfood products that are routinely purchased	Super Walmart, Meijer
Hypermarket	The largest retail stores that take the foundation of the discount store and provide even more food and nonfood products	Carrefour, Tesco Extra
Warehouse club	Large membership establishments with food and nonfood products and deep discounts	Costco, BJ's Wholesale Club, Sam's Club
Warehouse showroom	Large facilities with products displayed that are often retrieved from a less expensive adjacent warehouse	IKEA, Cost Plus

direct selling the marketing of products to ultimate consumers through face-to-face sales presentations at home or in the workplace.

wholesalers intermediaries who buy from producers or from other wholesalers and sell to retailers.

media such as mail, telephone, or the Internet. For example, Duluth Trading has stores but specializes in catalog marketing, especially with products such as jeans, work boots, and hats. Amazon—which is more or less an online catalog—is another example of a direct marketer. Another form of non-store retailing is **direct selling**, which involves the marketing of products to ultimate consumers through face-to-face sales presentations at home or in the workplace. The top three global direct selling companies are Amway, Avon, and Herbalife. Most individuals who engage in direct selling work on a part-time basis because they like the product and often sell to their own social networks. This channel grew during the COVID-19 (coronavirus) pandemic as social media was used for person-to-person connections and products shipped directly from the producer.

Wholesalers are intermediaries who buy from producers or from other wholesalers and sell to retailers. They usually do not sell in significant quantities to ultimate consumers. Wholesalers perform the functions listed in Table 12.5.

Wholesalers are extremely important because of the marketing activities they perform, particularly for consumer products. Although it is true that wholesalers can be eliminated, their functions must be passed on to some other entity, such as the producer, another intermediary, or even the customer. Wholesalers help consumers and retailers by buying in large quantities, then selling to retailers in smaller quantities. By stocking an assortment of products, wholesalers match products to demand. Sysco is a food wholesaler for the food services industry. The company provides food, preparation, and serving products to restaurants, hospitals, and other institutions that provide meals outside of the home.[32] *Merchant wholesalers* like Sysco take title to the goods, assume risks, and sell to other wholesalers, business customers, or retailers. *Agents* negotiate sales, do not own products, and perform a limited number of functions in exchange for a commission.

Channels for Consumer Products.
Typical marketing channels for consumer products are shown in Figure 12.6. In channel A, the product moves from the producer directly to the consumer. Farmers who sell their fruit and vegetables to consumers at roadside stands or farmers' markets use a direct-from-producer-to-consumer marketing channel.

> **Wholesalers are extremely important because of the marketing activities they perform, particularly for consumer products.**

In channel B, the product goes from producer to retailer to consumer. This type of channel is used for products such as college textbooks, automobiles, and appliances. In channel C, the product is handled by a wholesaler and a retailer before it reaches the consumer. Producer-to-wholesaler-to-retailer-to-consumer marketing channels distribute a wide range of products including refrigerators, televisions, soft drinks, cigarettes, clocks, watches, and office products. In channel D, the product goes to an agent, a wholesaler, and a retailer before going to the consumer. This long channel of distribution is especially useful for convenience products. Candy and some produce are often sold by agents who bring buyers and sellers together.

Services are usually distributed through direct marketing channels because they are generally produced *and* consumed simultaneously. For example, you cannot take a haircut home for later use. Many services require the customer's presence and participation: The sick patient must visit the physician to receive treatment; the child must be at the day care center to receive care; the tourist must be present to sightsee and consume tourism services.

▼ **TABLE 12.5** Major Wholesaling Functions

Logistics management	• Inventory management • Transportation • Warehousing • Materials handling
Promotion	• Personal selling • Publicity • Sales promotion • Advertising
Inventory control and data processing	• Management information systems • Inventory control • Transaction monitoring • Financial and accounting data analysis
Risk-taking	• Inventory decisions • Product deterioration • Theft control
Financing and budgeting	• Investment capital • Credit management • Managing cash flow and receivables
Marketing research and information systems	• Conducting primary market research • Analyzing big data • Utilizing marketing analytics

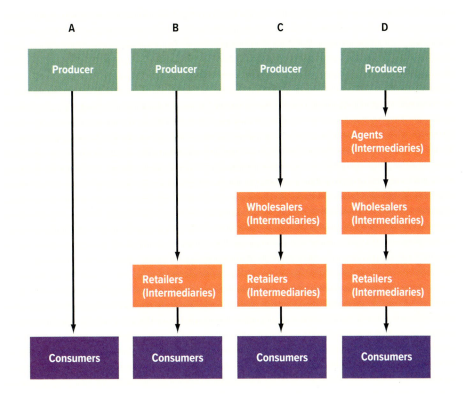

Channels for Business Products. In contrast to consumer goods, more than half of all business products, especially expensive equipment or technically complex products, are sold through direct marketing channels. Business customers like to communicate directly with producers of such products to gain the technical assistance and personal assurances that only the producer can offer. For this reason, business buyers prefer to purchase expensive and highly complex mainframe computers directly from IBM, Unisys, and other mainframe producers. Other business products may be distributed through channels employing wholesaling intermediaries such as industrial distributors and/or manufacturer's agents.

Supply Chain Management. In an effort to improve distribution channel relationships among manufacturers and other channel intermediaries, supply chain management creates alliances between channel members. In the "Managing Operations and Supply Chains" chapter, we defined supply chain management as connecting and integrating all parties or members of the distribution system in order to satisfy customers. It involves long-term partnerships among marketing channel members working together to reduce costs, waste, and unnecessary movement in the entire marketing channel in order to satisfy customers. It goes beyond traditional channel members (producers, wholesalers, retailers, customers) to include *all* organizations involved in moving products from the producer to the ultimate customer. In a survey of business managers, a disruption in the supply chain was viewed as the number-one crisis that could decrease revenue.[33] This type of crisis was seen in action during the COVID-19 pandemic when the global supply chain was disrupted as a result of shutdown factories and

DRINKFINITY GOES BUST

Over the past two decades, non-diet soda sales have dropped 25 percent. This led PepsiCo to develop more health-conscious beverages. PepsiCo introduced Drinkfinity, a "water-enhancer" that featured a 20-ounce reusable water bottle and recyclable flavor pods. When punctured, the pods infused the water with one of 10 non-artificial flavors made from ingredients like fruit juice concentrates and superfoods.

Instead of using its worldwide store presence, PepsiCo adopted a direct distribution channel. Drinkfinity was only sold through its e-commerce website. Whereas a name brand soda is about $0.40 per can, a four-pack of Drinkfinity capsules cost $6. Before the capsules were used, the Drinkfinity water bottle had to be purchased with a retail price of about $20.

Though Drinkfinity was a more environmentally-friendly product, the barriers to adoption, including price, were too much for consumers to overcome. Less than two years after the product was first introduced, Pepsi attempted a relaunch with a new bottle design and three new flavors. The relaunch was not enough to garner excitement, and the brand folded a few short months later.[d]

🔵 Critical Thinking Questions

1. Why do you think PepsiCo used a direct distribution channel to sell its Drinkfinity beverages in the United States?

2. What value did Drinkfinity beverages offer consumers to offset the higher price?

3. Why do you think Drinkfinity failed?

logistics management involves planning, implementing, and controlling the flow and storage of products and information from the point of origin to consumption.

transportation the shipment of products to buyers.

warehousing the design and operation of facilities to receive, store, and ship products.

stay-at-home orders. It highlighted the need for supply chain mapping and contingency planning.

Firms can be either upstream or downstream in a supply chain relationship. When a firm is upstream, it is usually suppliers that send their goods down the stream to wholesalers and retailers. When a firm is downstream, it receives goods from suppliers further up the stream. Good managers are able to manage inventory effectively and procure their goods from sustainable sources.

The focus shifts from one of selling to the next level in the channel to one of selling products *through* the channel to a satisfied ultimate customer. Information, once provided on a guarded, "as-needed" basis, is now open, honest, and ongoing. Perhaps most importantly, the points of contact in the relationship expand from one-on-one at the salesperson-buyer level to multiple interfaces at all levels and in all functional areas of the various organizations. Predictive analytics are being used for forecasting and coordinating the integration of supply chain members. For example, Amazon ships products before it receives a customer order based upon predictive models that relate to customer purchasing history.[34]

Logistics Management

Logistics management involves planning, implementing, and controlling the flow and storage of products and information

Amazon has fulfillment centers across the country from Lakeland, Florida, to San Bernardino, California.

SWNS/Alamy Stock Photo

from the point of origin to consumption. Logistics refers to more than simply the physical transport of goods and materials. There is also a need to quickly and accurately share information.

Transportation. **Transportation**, the shipment of products to buyers, creates time and place utility for products, and thus is a key element in the flow of goods and services from producer to consumer. The five major modes of transportation used to move products between cities in the United States are railways, motor vehicles, inland waterways, pipelines, and airways.

Railroads are a cost-effective method of transportation for many products. Heavy commodities, foodstuffs, raw materials, and coal are examples of products carried by railroads. Trucks have greater flexibility than railroads because they can reach more locations. Trucks handle freight quickly and economically, offer door-to-door service, and are more flexible in their packaging requirements than are ships or airplanes. Air transport offers speed and a high degree of dependability but is the most expensive means of transportation; transport by ship is less expensive and is the slowest form. Pipelines are used to transport petroleum, natural gas, semi-liquid coal, wood chips, and certain chemicals. Pipelines have the lowest costs for products that can be transported via this method. Many products can be moved most efficiently by using more than one mode of transportation.

Factors affecting the selection of a mode of transportation include cost, capability to handle the product, reliability, and availability; and, as suggested, selecting transportation modes requires trade-offs. Unique characteristics of the product and consumer desires often determine the mode selected.

Warehousing. **Warehousing** is the design and operation of facilities to receive, store, and ship products. A warehouse facility receives, identifies, sorts, and dispatches goods to storage; stores them; recalls, selects, or picks goods; assembles the shipment; and finally, dispatches the shipment.

Companies often own and operate their own private warehouses that store, handle, and move their own products. Firms might want to own or lease a private warehouse when their goods require special handling and storage or when it has large warehousing needs in a specific geographic area. Private warehouses are beneficial because they provide customers with more control over their goods. However, fixed costs for maintaining these warehouses can be quite high.[35] They can also rent storage and related distribution services from public warehouses. While public warehouses store goods for more than one company, providing firms with less control over distribution, they are often less expensive than private warehouses and are useful for seasonal production or low-volume storage.[36] For example, Next Level Resource Partners offers warehousing services and fulfillment including picking, packing, and shipping products for clients like Pure Barre, Mineral Fusion, and Flywheel.[37] Regardless of whether a private or a public warehouse is used, warehousing is important because it makes products available for shipment to match demand at different geographic locations.

Materials Handling. **Materials handling** is the physical handling and movement of products in warehousing and transportation. Handling processes may vary significantly due to product characteristics. Efficient materials-handling procedures increase a warehouse's useful capacity and improve customer service. Well-coordinated loading and movement systems increase efficiency and reduce costs.

Intensity of Market Coverage

A major distribution decision is how widely to distribute a product—that is, how many and what type of outlets should carry it. The intensity of market coverage depends on buyer behavior, as well as the nature of the target market and the competition. Wholesalers and retailers provide various intensities of market coverage and must be selected carefully to ensure success. Market coverage may be intensive, selective, or exclusive.

Intensive distribution makes a product available in as many outlets as possible. Because availability is important to purchasers of convenience products such as toothpaste, yogurt, candy, beverages, and chewing gum, a nearby location with a minimum of time spent searching and waiting in line is most important to the consumer. To saturate markets intensively, wholesalers and many varied retailers try to make the product available at every location where a consumer might desire to purchase it. ZoomSystems provides robotic vending machines for products beyond candy and drinks. Zoom has 1,500 machines in airports and hotels across the United States. Through partnering with different companies, today's ZoomShops sell a variety of brands, including products from The Honest Company, Best Buy, Macy's, and Nespresso.[38]

Selective distribution uses only a small number of all available outlets to expose products. It is used most often for products that consumers buy only after shopping and comparing price, quality, and style. Many products sold on a selective basis require salesperson assistance, technical advice, warranties, or repair service to maintain consumer satisfaction. Typical products include automobiles, major appliances, clothes, and furniture. Ralph Lauren is a brand that uses selective distribution.

Exclusive distribution exists when a manufacturer gives an intermediary the sole right to sell a product in a defined geographic territory. Such exclusivity provides an incentive for a dealer to handle a product that has a limited market. Exclusive distribution is the opposite of intensive distribution in that products are purchased and consumed over a long period of time, and service or information is required to develop a satisfactory sales relationship. Products distributed on an exclusive basis include high-quality musical instruments, yachts, airplanes, and high-fashion leather goods. For example, Singapore's Triple Pte is the exclusive distributor for Under Armour in Southeast Asia.[39]

Importance of Distribution in a Marketing Strategy

Distribution decisions are among the least flexible marketing mix decisions. Products can be changed over time, prices can be changed quickly, and promotion is usually changed regularly. But distribution decisions often commit resources and establish contractual relationships that are slow to change. As a company attempts to expand into new markets, it may require a complete change in distribution. Moreover, if a firm does not manage its marketing channel in the most efficient manner and provide the best service, then a new competitor will evolve to create a more effective distribution system. The growth of online retailing is increasing consumers' expectations for more choices, faster delivery, order status updates, and easy returns at no extra cost. Amazon is transforming the supply chain, and retailers such as Target are revamping their distribution systems to use digital technology to develop a smart network.[40] Target began introducing remodeled stores as part of its goal of creating a smart network where its stores, digital channels, and supply chain work together to support the guest.[41]

materials handling the physical handling and movement of products in warehousing and transportation.

intensive distribution a form of market coverage whereby a product is made available in as many outlets as possible.

selective distribution a form of market coverage whereby only a small number of all available outlets are used to expose products.

exclusive distribution the awarding by a manufacturer to an intermediary of the sole right to sell a product in a defined geographic territory.

Lee, an American denim company, uses an intensive distribution strategy by making their jeans available in as many outlets as possible.

Francis Dean/Corbis/Getty Images

PROMOTION STRATEGY

integrated marketing communications
coordinating the promotion mix elements and synchronizing promotion as a unified effort.

advertising a paid form of nonpersonal communication transmitted through a mass medium, such as television commercials or magazine advertisements.

The role of promotion is to communicate with individuals, groups, and organizations to facilitate an exchange directly or indirectly. It encourages marketing exchanges by attempting to persuade individuals, groups, and organizations to accept goods, services, and ideas. Promotion is used not only to sell products but also to influence opinions and attitudes toward an organization, person, or cause. For example, for the Super Bowl, Audi emphasized the use of electric vehicles, Anheuser promoted wind power, and Olay aimed a commercial specifically at women in an effort to create emotional appeal and make viewers think about current issues. However, not all the corporate social responsibility commercials find success. Companies risk alienating audience members with overly political advertisements. Regardless of purpose, the main goal of the companies airing these Super Bowl advertisements is to stand apart from one another and make the viewer feel something.[42] Most people probably equate promotion with advertising, but it also includes personal selling, publicity, and sales promotion. The role that these elements play in a marketing strategy is extremely important.

The Promotion Mix

Advertising, personal selling, publicity, and sales promotion are collectively known as the promotion mix because a strong promotion program results from the careful selection and blending of these elements. The process of coordinating the promotion mix elements and synchronizing promotion as a unified effort is called **integrated marketing communications**. When planning promotional activities, an integrated marketing communications approach results in the desired message for customers. Different elements of the promotion mix are coordinated to play their appropriate roles in delivery of the message on a consistent basis. Integrated communication creates a reason for purchase.

Advertising. Perhaps the best-known form of promotion, **advertising** is a paid form of nonpersonal communication transmitted through a mass medium, such as television commercials, magazine advertisements, or online ads. Pharmaceutical firms have long used advertisements to promote medications for lifestyle conditions. However, more recently it has begun releasing advertisements promoting life-saving, often expensive, medications that

specialist doctors prescribe.[43] Commercials featuring celebrities, customers, or unique creations serve to grab viewers' attention and pique their interest in a product. Venus Williams, an American professional tennis champion, worked with Alcon on its campaign for Systane Lubricant Eye Drops. The advertisement creates awareness for dry eye and appeals to athletes as well as those who suffer from this condition. On the other hand, there are downsides to using celebrity endorsers when they act inappropriately. Nike has terminated or suspended contracts with celebrity endorsers for domestic violence allegations and doping allegations.

An **advertising campaign** involves designing a series of advertisements and placing them in various media to reach a particular target audience. The basic content and form of an advertising campaign are a function of several factors. A product's features, uses, and benefits affect the content of the campaign message and individual ads. Characteristics of the people in the target audience–gender, age, education, race, income, occupation, lifestyle, and other attributes–influence both content and form. When Procter & Gamble promotes Crest toothpaste to children, the company emphasizes daily brushing and cavity control, whereas it promotes tartar control and whiter teeth when marketing to adults. To communicate effectively, advertisers use

Brands often partner with celebrity endorsers to promote their products. Alcon worked with Venus Williams, tennis star, to launch its eye drops, Systane Complete.

Source: Alcon

words, symbols, and illustrations that are meaningful, familiar, and attractive to people in the target audience.

An advertising campaign's objectives and platform also affect the content and form of its messages. If a firm's advertising objectives involve large sales increases, the message may include hard-hitting, high-impact language and symbols. When campaign objectives aim at increasing brand awareness, the message may use much repetition of the brand name and words and illustrations associated with it. Thus, the advertising platform is the foundation on which campaign messages are built.

Advertising media are the vehicles or forms of communication used to reach a desired audience. Print media include newspapers, magazines, direct mail, and billboards, while electronic media include television, radio, Internet, and mobile advertising. Choice of media obviously influences the content and form of the message. Effective outdoor displays and short broadcast spot announcements require concise, simple messages. Magazine and newspaper advertisements can include considerable detail and long explanations. Because several kinds of media offer geographic selectivity, a precise message can be tailored to a particular geographic section of the target audience. For example, a company advertising in *Time* might decide to use one message in the New England region and another in the rest of the nation. A company may also choose to advertise in only one region. Such geographic selectivity lets a firm use the same message in different regions at different times. On the other hand, some companies are willing to pay extensive amounts of money to reach national audiences. Marketers spent approximately $5 million for one 30-second advertising slot during the Super Bowl due to its national reach and popularity.[44]

The use of online advertising is increasing. However, advertisers are demanding more for their ad dollars and proof that they are working, which is why Google Ads only charges companies when users click on the ad. Certain types of ads are more popular than pop-up ads and banner ads that consumers find annoying. One technique is to blur the lines between television and online advertising. TV commercials may point viewers to a website for more information, where short "advertainment" films continue the marketing message. Marketers might also use the Internet to show advertisements or videos that were not accepted by mainstream television. People for the Ethical Treatment of Animals (PETA) often develop racy commercials that are denied Super Bowl spots. However, these ads can be viewed online through YouTube and other sites.[45]

Infomercials—typically 30-minute blocks of radio or television air time featuring a celebrity or upbeat host talking about and demonstrating a product—have evolved as an advertising method. Under Armour teamed with famed Olympic athlete Michael Phelps to create a day in his life called "The Water Diviner." The writing, visuals, and lighting make this a compelling piece and won its recognition by *Advertising Age* as one of the top 10 best branded content partnerships. As the most decorated Olympian in history, there remains significant fascination with Michael Phelps, and Under Armour has found an innovative way to create a partnership that enhances its branding.[46] Toll-free numbers and website addresses are usually provided so consumers can conveniently purchase the product or obtain additional information. Although many consumers and companies have negative feelings about infomercials, apparently they get results.

Personal Selling. Personal selling is direct, two-way communication with buyers and potential buyers. For many products—especially large, expensive ones with specialized uses, such as cars, appliances, and houses–interaction between a salesperson and the customer is probably the most important promotional tool.

Personal selling is the most flexible of the promotional methods because it gives marketers the greatest opportunity to communicate specific information that might trigger a purchase. Only personal selling can zero in on a prospect and attempt to persuade that person to make a purchase. Although personal selling has a lot of advantages, it is one of the costliest forms of promotion. A sales call on an industrial customer can cost more than $400.

There are three distinct categories of salespersons: order takers (e.g., retail sales clerks and route salespeople), creative

Personal selling is important with high-risk items such as medical tools and devices. Sales representatives can assist customers in discussing the benefits of a product, financing arrangements, and any warranties or guarantees.

Blend Images/ERproductions Ltd/Getty Images

publicity nonpersonal communication transmitted through the mass media but not paid for directly by the firm.

sales promotion direct inducements offering added value or some other incentive for buyers to enter into an exchange.

salespersons (e.g., automobile, furniture, and insurance salespeople), and support salespersons (e.g., customer educators and goodwill builders who usually do not take orders). For most of these salespeople, personal selling is a six-step process:

1. *Prospecting:* Identifying potential buyers of the product.

2. *Approaching:* Using a referral or calling on a customer without prior notice to determine interest in the product.

3. *Presenting:* Getting the prospect's attention with a product demonstration.

4. *Handling objections:* Countering reasons for not buying the product.

5. *Closing:* Asking the prospect to buy the product.

6. *Following up:* Checking customer satisfaction with the purchased product.

Publicity. **Publicity** is nonpersonal communication transmitted through the mass media but not paid for directly by the firm. A firm does not pay the media cost for publicity and is not identified as the originator of the message; instead, the message is presented in news story form. Obviously, a company can benefit from publicity by releasing to news sources newsworthy messages about the firm and its involvement with the public. Many companies have *public relations* departments to try to gain favorable publicity and minimize negative publicity for the firm.

Although advertising and publicity are both carried by the mass media, they differ in several major ways. Advertising messages tend to be informative, persuasive, or both; publicity is mainly informative. Advertising is often designed to have an immediate impact or to provide specific information to persuade a person to act; publicity describes what a firm is doing, what products it is launching, or other newsworthy information, but seldom calls for action. When advertising is used, the organization must pay for media time and select the media that will best reach target audiences. The mass media willingly carry publicity because they believe it has general public interest. Advertising can be repeated a number of times; most publicity appears in the mass media once and is not repeated.

Advertising, personal selling, and sales promotion are especially useful for influencing an exchange directly. Publicity is extremely important when communication focuses on a company's activities and products and is directed at interest groups, current and potential investors, regulatory agencies, and society in general.

A variation of traditional advertising is buzz marketing, in which marketers attempt to create a trend or acceptance of a product. Companies seek out trendsetters in communities and get them to "talk up" a brand to their friends, family, co-workers, and others. One unusual method that Nagoya, Japan, used to attract more job applicants to the city was adopting a spokes-ape. The city used an ape at the local zoo that not only became a recruitment tool, with his face on posters and T-shirts, but also a national celebrity.[47] Other marketers using the buzz technique include Hebrew National ("mom squads" grilled the company's hot dogs) and Red Bull (its sponsorship of the stratosphere space diving project). The idea behind buzz marketing is that an accepted member of a particular social group will be more credible than any form of paid communication.[48] The concept works best as part of an integrated marketing communication program that also includes traditional advertising, personal selling, sales promotion, and publicity.

A related concept is viral marketing, which describes the concept of getting Internet users to pass on ads and promotions to others. For example, Canadian Tire, an automotive company based in Toronto, uploaded two 60-second ads during the summer Olympics that attracted viral attention. In one, a group of kids invite a boy in a wheelchair to play basketball. The video attracted more than 200 million views and almost 4 million shares. Positive opinion of Canadian Tire increased by 13 percent.[49]

Sales Promotion. **Sales promotion** involves direct inducements offering added value or some other incentive for buyers to enter into an exchange. Sales promotions are generally easier to measure and less expensive than advertising. The major tools of sales promotion are store displays, premiums, samples and demonstrations, coupons, contests and sweepstakes, refunds, and trade shows. Coupon-clipping in particular became common due to the recent recession. While coupons in the past decade traditionally had a fairly low redemption rate, with about 2 percent being redeemed, the recent recession caused an upsurge in coupon usage. There has also been a major upsurge in the use of mobile coupons, or coupons sent to consumers over mobile devices. The redemption rate for mobile coupons is eight times higher than that of traditional coupons.[50] While coupons can be a valuable tool in sales promotion, they cannot be relied upon to stand by themselves, but should be part of an overall promotion mix. Sales promotion stimulates customer purchasing and increases dealer effectiveness in selling products. It is used to enhance and supplement other forms of promotion. Sampling a product may also encourage consumers to buy. This is why many grocery stores provide free samples in the hopes of influencing consumers' purchasing decisions. In a given year, almost three-fourths of consumer product companies may use sampling.

Promotion Strategies: To Push or to Pull

In developing a promotion mix, organizations must decide whether to fashion a mix that pushes or pulls the product

Ibotta is a digital coupon app that allows users to select deals and receive cash back from retailers like Kroger and Target after scanning their receipts.

Joe Amon/The Denver Post/Getty Images

(Figure 12.7). A **push strategy** attempts to motivate intermediaries to push the product down to their customers. When a push strategy is used, the company attempts to motivate wholesalers and retailers to make the product available to their customers. Sales personnel may be used to persuade intermediaries to offer the product, distribute promotional materials, and offer special promotional incentives for those who agree to carry the product. For example, salespeople from pharmaceutical companies will often market new products to doctors in the hope that the doctors will recommend their products to their clients.

A **pull strategy** uses promotion to create consumer demand for a product so that consumers exert pressure on marketing channel members to make it available. For example, Mountain Dew regularly does a limited release of its Baja Blast flavor every few years to stoke demand. The soda company brought back the fan-favorite flavor for a limited time only after its followers on Twitter championed the hashtag #bringbajablastback.[51] Many brands like Parmer Water Company, Cinnabon, and Campbell's have used Twitter to encourage followers to demand the brand's products at their local grocery store. Additionally, offering free samples prior to a product rollout encourages consumers to request the product from their favorite retailer.

A company can use either strategy, or it can use a variation or combination of the two. The exclusive use of advertising indicates a pull strategy. Personal selling to marketing channel members indicates a push strategy. The allocation of promotional resources to various marketing mix elements probably determines which strategy a marketer uses.

Objectives of Promotion

The marketing mix a company uses depends on its objectives. It is important to recognize that promotion is only one element of the marketing strategy and must be tied carefully to the goals of the firm, its overall marketing objectives, and the other elements

push strategy an attempt to motivate intermediaries to push the product down to their customers.

pull strategy the use of promotion to create consumer demand for a product so that consumers exert pressure on marketing channel members to make it available.

▼ **FIGURE 12.7** Push and Pull Strategies

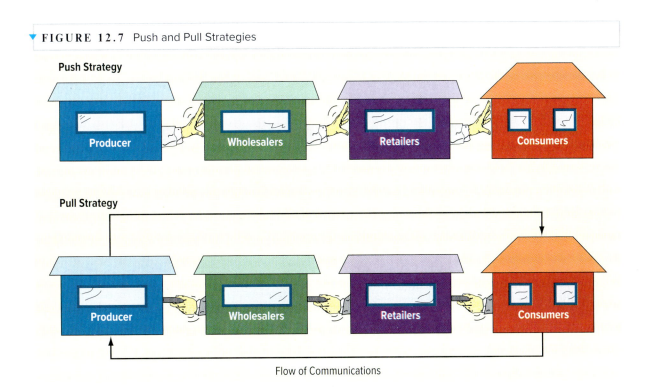

Flow of Communications

of the marketing strategy. Firms use promotion for many reasons, but typical objectives are to stimulate demand, to stabilize sales, and to inform, remind, and reinforce customers.

Increasing demand for a product is probably the most typical promotional objective. Stimulating demand, often through advertising, publicity, and sales promotion, is particularly important when a firm is using a pull strategy.

Another goal of promotion is to stabilize sales by maintaining the status quo—that is, the current sales level of the product. During periods of slack or decreasing sales, contests, prizes, vacations, and other sales promotions are sometimes offered to customers to maintain sales goals. Advertising is often used to stabilize sales by making customers aware of slack use periods. For example, auto manufacturers often provide rebates, free options, or lower-than-market interest rates to stabilize sales and thereby keep production lines moving during temporary slowdowns. A stable sales pattern allows the firm to run efficiently by maintaining a consistent level of production and storage and utilizing all its functions so that it is ready when sales increase.

An important role of any promotional program is to inform potential buyers about the organization and its products. A major portion of advertising in the United States, particularly in daily newspapers, is informational. Providing information about the availability, price, technology, and features of a product is very important in encouraging a buyer to move toward a purchase decision. Nearly all forms of promotion involve an attempt to help consumers learn more about a product and a company. Blendtec, the powerful kitchen blender, developed videos showing its blender pulverizing everything from rakes to marbles and even Apple iPads. The "Will It Blend" videos have attracted more than 289 million views and have attracted 870,000 subscribers. Humor and the unexpected are key contributors to viral marketing success.[52]

Promotion is also used to remind consumers that an established organization is still around and sells certain products that have uses and benefits. Often advertising reminds customers that they may need to use a product more frequently or in certain situations. Pennzoil, for example, has run television commercials reminding car owners that they need to change their oil every 3,000 miles to ensure proper performance of their cars.

Reinforcement promotion attempts to assure current users of the product that they have made the right choice and tells them how to get the most satisfaction from the product. Also, a company could release publicity statements through the news media about a new use for a product. Additionally, firms can have salespeople communicate with current and potential customers about the proper use and maintenance of a product—all in the hope of developing a repeat customer.

Promotional Positioning

Promotional positioning uses promotion to create and maintain an image of a product in buyers' minds. It is a natural result of market segmentation. In both promotional positioning and market segmentation, the firm targets a given product or brand at a portion of the total market. A promotional strategy helps differentiate the product and makes it appeal to a particular market segment. For example, to appeal to safety-conscious consumers, Volvo heavily promotes the safety and crashworthiness of Volvo automobiles in its advertising. Promotion can be used to change or reinforce an image. Effective promotion influences customers and persuades them to buy.

IMPORTANCE OF MARKETING STRATEGY

Marketing creates value through the marketing mix. For customers, value means receiving a product in which the benefit of the product outweighs the cost, or price paid for it. For marketers, value means that the benefits (usually monetary) received from selling the product outweigh the costs it takes to develop and sell it. This requires carefully integrating the marketing mix into an effective marketing strategy. One misstep could mean a loss in profits, whether it be from a failed product idea, shortages or oversupply of a product, a failure to effectively promote the product, or prices that are too high or too low. And while some of these marketing mix elements can be easily fixed, other marketing mix elements such as distribution can be harder to adapt.

On the other hand, firms that develop an effective marketing mix to meet customer needs will gain competitive advantages over those that do not. Often, these advantages occur when the firm excels at one or more elements of the marketing mix.

BUILDING YOUR SOFT SKILLS

BY DEVELOPING YOUR PERSONAL BRAND

In the previous chapter's Building Your Soft Skills exercise, you worked on developing a brief statement that outlines your unique value and your personal brand. Consider the personal brand statement you've developed. What are three concrete things you can do to enhance your personal brand? For example, if part of your unique value is that you are passionate about your field, how can you demonstrate that passion?

Aldi has a reputation for low prices, while Christian Louboutin is known for its high-quality, luxury shoes. However, exceling at one element of the marketing mix does not mean that a company can neglect the others. The best product cannot succeed if consumers do not know about it or if they cannot find it in stores. Additionally, firms must constantly monitor the market environment to understand

how demand is changing and whether adaptations in the marketing mix are needed. It is therefore essential that every element of the marketing mix be carefully evaluated and synchronized with the marketing strategy. Only then will firms be able to achieve the marketing concept of providing products that satisfy customers' needs while allowing the organization to achieve its goals.

ARE YOU INTERESTED // in Becoming a Marketing Manager? /

Many jobs in marketing are closely tied to the marketing mix functions: distribution, product, promotion, and price. Often the job titles could be sales manager, distribution or supply chain manager, advertising account executive, or store manager.

A distribution manager arranges for transportation of goods within firms and through marketing channels. Transportation can be costly, and time is always an important factor, so minimizing their effects is vital to the success of a firm. Distribution managers must choose one or a combination of transportation modes from a vast array of options, taking into account local, federal, and international regulations for different freight classifications; the weight, size, and fragility of products to be shipped; time schedules; and loss and damage ratios. Manufacturing firms are the largest employers of distribution managers.

A product manager is responsible for the success or failure of a product line. This requires a general knowledge of advertising, transportation modes, inventory control, selling and sales management, promotion, marketing research, packaging, and pricing. Frequently, several years of selling and sales management experience are prerequisites for such a position as well as college training in business administration. Being a product manager can be rewarding both financially and psychologically.

Some of the most creative roles in the business world are in the area of advertising. Advertising pervades our daily lives, as businesses and other organizations try to grab our attention and tell us about what they have to offer. Copywriters, artists, and account executives in advertising must have creativity, imagination, artistic talent, and expertise in expression and persuasion. Advertising is an area of business in which a wide variety of educational backgrounds may be useful, from degrees in advertising itself, to journalism or liberal arts degrees. Common entry-level positions in an advertising agency are found in the traffic department, account service (account coordinator), or the media department (media assistant). Advertising jobs are also available in many manufacturing or retail firms, nonprofit organizations, banks, professional associations, utility companies, and other arenas outside of an advertising agency.

Although a career in retailing may begin in sales, there is much more to retailing than simply selling. Many retail personnel occupy management positions, focusing on selecting and ordering merchandise, promotional activities, inventory control, customer credit operations, accounting, personnel, and store security. Many specific examples of retailing jobs can be found in large department stores. A section manager coordinates inventory and promotions and interacts with buyers, salespeople, and consumers. The buyer's job is fast-paced, often involving much travel and pressure. Buyers must be open-minded and foresighted in their hunt for new, potentially successful items. Regional managers coordinate the activities of several retail stores within a specific geographic area, usually monitoring and supporting sales, promotions, and general procedures. Retail management can be exciting and challenging. Growth in retailing is expected to accompany the growth in population and is likely to create substantial opportunities in the coming years.

While a career in marketing can be very rewarding, marketers today agree that the job is getting tougher. Many advertising and marketing executives say the job has gotten much more demanding in the past 10 years, viewing their number one challenge as balancing work and personal obligations. Other challenges include staying current on industry trends or technologies, keeping motivated/inspired on the job, and measuring success. If you are up to the challenge, you may find that a career in marketing is just right for you to utilize your business knowledge while exercising your creative side as well.

chapter 13

digital marketing and social media

Rawpixel.com/Shutterstock

LEARNING OBJECTIVES

After reading this chapter, you will be able to:

LO 13-1 Recognize the increasing value of digital media and digital marketing in strategic planning.

LO 13-2 Demonstrate the role of digital marketing in today's business environment.

LO 13-3 Show how digital media affect the marketing mix.

LO 13-4 Illustrate how businesses can use different types of social networking media.

LO 13-5 Explain online monitoring and analytics for social media.

LO 13-6 Identify legal and ethical considerations in digital media.

The Internet and information technology have dramatically changed the environment for business. Marketers' new ability to convert all types of communications into digital media has created efficient, inexpensive ways of connecting businesses and consumers and has improved the flow and the usefulness of information. Businesses have the information they need to make more informed decisions, and consumers have access to a greater variety of products and more information about choices and quality. This has resulted in a shift in the balance of power between consumer and marketer.[1]

The defining characteristic of information technology in the 21st century is accelerating change. New systems and applications advance so rapidly that it is almost impossible to keep up with the latest developments. Startup companies emerge with systems that quickly overtake existing approaches to digital media. When Google first arrived on the scene, a number of search engines were fighting for dominance. With its fast, easy-to-use search engine, Google became number one and is now challenging many industries, including advertising, mobile phones, and book publishing. Social media continues to advance as the channel most observers believe will dominate digital communication in the near future. Today, people spend more time on social networking sites, such as TikTok, than they spend on e-mail.

In this chapter, we first provide some key definitions related to digital marketing and social media. Next, we discuss using digital media in business and marketing. We look at marketing mix considerations when using digital media and pay special attention to social networking. Then we focus on digital marketing strategies—particularly new communication channels like social networks. We take a close look at media sharing, mobile marketing, applications, and widgets. Next the importance of online monitoring and analytics is discussed. Then we examine using digital media to learn about consumers. Finally, we examine the legal and social issues associated with information technology, digital media, and e-business. ■

LO 13-1 Recognize the increasing value of digital media and digital marketing in strategic planning.

GROWTH AND BENEFITS OF DIGITAL COMMUNICATION

Let's start with a clear understanding of our focus in this chapter. First, we can distinguish e-business from traditional business by noting that conducting **e-business** means carrying out the goals of business through the use of the Internet. **Digital media** are electronic media that function using digital codes—when we refer to digital media, we mean media available via computers and other digital devices, including mobile and wireless ones like smartphones.

Digital marketing uses all digital media, including the Internet and mobile and interactive channels, to develop communication and exchanges with customers. Digital marketing is a term we will use often because we are interested in all types of digital communications, regardless of the electronic channel that transmits the data. Digital marketing goes beyond the Internet and includes mobile phones, banner ads, digital outdoor marketing, and social networks.

The Internet has created tremendous opportunities for businesses to forge relationships with consumers and business customers, target markets more precisely, and even reach previously inaccessible markets at home and around the world. The Internet also facilitates business transactions, allowing companies to network with manufacturers, wholesalers, retailers, suppliers, and outsource firms to serve customers more quickly and more efficiently. The telecommunication opportunities created by the Internet have set the stage for digital marketing's development and growth.

e-business carrying out the goals of business through utilization of the Internet.

digital media electronic media that function using digital codes via computers, cellular phones, smartphones, and other digital devices that have been released in recent years.

digital marketing uses all digital media, including the Internet and mobile and interactive channels, to develop communication and exchanges with customers.

Consumers are increasingly turning to mobile apps to access company information, earn loyalty rewards, and purchase products.

Monika Wisniewska/Shutterstock

Digital communication offers a completely new dimension in connecting with others. Some of the characteristics that distinguish digital from traditional communication are addressability, interactivity, accessibility, connectivity, and control. These terms are discussed in Table 13.1.

LO 13-2 Demonstrate the role of digital marketing in today's business environment.

USING DIGITAL MEDIA IN BUSINESS

The phenomenal growth of digital media has provided new ways of conducting business. Given almost instant communication with precisely defined consumer groups, firms can use real-time exchanges to create and stimulate interactive communication, forge closer relationships, and learn more accurately about consumer and supplier needs. Consider how Amazon is taking on department stores and big box stores such as Walmart and Home Depot.[2] In fact, store closings doubled in recent years with the rise of online shopping.[3] Many of you may not remember a world before Amazon because it has completely transformed how many people shop.

Because it is fast and inexpensive, digital communication is making it easier for businesses to conduct marketing research, provide and obtain price and product information, and advertise, as well as to fulfill their business goals by selling goods and services online. Even the U.S. government engages in digital marketing activities—marketing everything from Treasury bonds and other financial instruments to oil-drilling leases and wild horses. Procter & Gamble uses the Internet as a fast, cost-effective means for marketing research, judging consumer demand for potential new products by inviting online consumers to sample new-product prototypes and provide feedback. If a product gets rave reviews from the samplers, the company might decide to introduce it. Many companies turn to software companies like Salesforce for digital marketing automation and marketing analytics. In the advertisement, Salesforce highlights a recent marketing research survey in an effort to demonstrate its abilities in data-driven insights.

New businesses and even industries are evolving that would not exist without digital media. Vimeo is a video website founded by filmmakers to share creative videos. The site lets users post or view videos from around the world. Vimeo now has more than 1.2 million paid subscribers.[4]

The reality, however, is that Internet markets are more similar to traditional markets than they are different. Thus, successful digital marketing strategies, like traditional business strategies, focus on creating products that customers need or want, not merely developing a brand name or reducing the costs associated with online transactions. Instead of changing all industries, digital technology has had much more impact in certain industries where the cost of business and customer transactions has

▼ **TABLE 13.1** Characteristics of Digital Marketing

Characteristic	Definition	Example
Addressability	The ability of the marketer to identify customers before they make a purchase	Amazon installs cookies on a user's computer that allows it to identify the owner when he or she returns to the website.
Interactivity	The ability of customers to express their needs and wants directly to the firm in response to its marketing communications	Texas Instruments interacts with its customers on its Facebook page by answering concerns and posting updates.
Accessibility	The ability for marketers to obtain digital information	Google can use web searches done through its search engine to learn about customer interests.
Connectivity	The ability for consumers to be connected with marketers along with other consumers	Volition Beauty's website encourages customers to submit their makeup and skin care product ideas, which can then be voted on by other users for the chance to be created.
Control	The customer's ability to regulate the information they view as well as the rate and exposure to that information	Consumers use Kayak to discover the best travel deals.

been very high. For example, investment trading is less expensive online because customers can buy and sell investments, such as stocks and mutual funds, on their own. Firms such as Charles Schwab Corp., the biggest online brokerage firm, have been innovators in promoting online trading. Traditional brokers such as Merrill Lynch have had to follow with online trading for their customers.

Digital media can also improve communication within and between businesses. In the future, most significant gains will come from productivity improvements within businesses. Communication is a key business function, and improving the speed and clarity of communication can help businesses save time and improve employee problem-solving abilities. Digital media can be a communications backbone that helps to store knowledge, information, and records in management information systems so co-workers can access it when faced with a problem to solve. A well-designed management information system that utilizes digital technology can, therefore, help reduce confusion, improve organization and efficiency, and facilitate clear communications. Given the crucial role of communication and information in business, the long-term impact of digital media on economic growth is substantial, and it will inevitably grow over time.

The dynamic nature of digital marketing can quickly change opportunities and create challenges. For example, digital assistants now function as a personal information manager and are being used to assist professionals in medicine, engineering, and other business areas. Smartphones, social networking, drones, and driverless cars are shaping a new marketing environment. While digital marketing has many benefits, challenges exist, especially in giving up privacy to use digital media.[5]

Salesforce promotes its digital marketing automation and marketing analytics solutions by advertising its data-driven insights on consumers and buyers. The advertisement states 86 percent of customers report that trust and loyalty go hand-in-hand.

Source: Salesforce

LO 13-3 Show how digital media affect the marketing mix.

DIGITAL MEDIA AND THE MARKETING MIX

While digital marketing shares some similarities with conventional marketing techniques, a few valuable differences stand out. First, digital media make customer communications faster and interactive. Second, digital media help companies reach new target markets more easily, affordably, and quickly than ever before. Finally, digital media help marketers utilize new resources in seeking out and communicating with customers. One of the most important benefits of digital marketing is the ability of marketers and customers to easily share information. Through websites, social networks, and other digital media, consumers can learn about everything they consume and use in their lives, ask questions, voice complaints, indicate preferences, and otherwise communicate about their needs and desires. For example, IBM's digital assistant allows IBM customers to identify and digitally interact with key experts through a variety of platforms. IBM's Watson is an assistant in cognitive computing impacting fields as diverse as finance, medicine, and education. Many marketers use e-mail, mobile phones, social media, wikis, media sharing, blogs, videoconferencing, and other technologies to coordinate activities and communicate with employees, customers, and suppliers. Twitter, considered both a social network and a micro-blog, illustrates how these digital technologies can combine to create new communication opportunities.

Nielsen Marketing Research revealed that consumers now spend more time on social networking sites than they do on e-mail, and social network use is still growing. Figure 13.1 shows the popularity of each social media platform over the years. With digital media, even small businesses can reach new markets through these inexpensive communication channels. Brick-and-mortar companies like Walmart utilize online catalogs and company websites and blogs to supplement their retail stores. Internet companies like Zappos that lack physical stores let customers post reviews of their purchases on their websites, creating company-sponsored communities. Amazon is taking

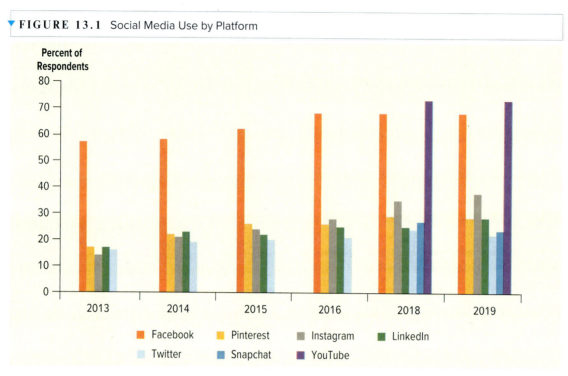

▼ FIGURE 13.1 Social Media Use by Platform

Note: U.S. adults. Pre-2018 telephone poll data are not available for YouTube, Snapchat, or WhatsApp.

Source: Pew Research Center survey conducted January 8–February 7, 2019. Trend data from previous Pew Research Center surveys.

on department stores and big box stores such as Walmart and Home Depot. Department stores such as Macy's and Sears have had to close hundreds of stores and some shopping centers have gone out of business.[6]

One aspect of marketing that has not changed with digital media is the importance of achieving the right marketing mix. Product, distribution, promotion, and pricing are as important as ever for successful online marketing strategies. More than 54 percent of the world's population now uses the Internet.[7] That means it is essential for businesses large and small to use digital media effectively, not only to grab or maintain market share, but also

tailor their goods and services to meet these needs, and continually upgrade them to remain competitive. The connectivity created by digital media provides the opportunity for adding services and can enhance product benefits. Some products, such as online games, applications, and virtual worlds, are only available via digital media. The 1.8 million iOS applications available in the App Store, for instance, provide examples of products that are only available in the digital world.[8] Businesses can often offer more items online than they could in a retail store.

The ability to access information for any product can have a major impact on buyer decision making. However, with larger

THE ABILITY TO ACCESS INFORMATION FOR ANY PRODUCT CAN HAVE A MAJOR IMPACT ON BUYER DECISION MAKING. 🙰

to streamline their organizations and offer customers entirely new benefits and convenience. Let's look at how businesses are using digital media to create effective marketing strategies on the web.

Product Considerations. Like traditional marketers, digital marketers must anticipate consumer needs and preferences,

companies now launching their own extensive marketing campaigns, and with the constant sophistication of digital technology, many businesses are finding it necessary to upgrade their product offerings to meet consumer needs. For example, Volition, a skin care and cosmetics company, crowdsources its new product ideas from its customers. If an idea makes it past the Volition team, tens of thousands of people in the Volition community will vote online whether the product should be produced and then receive a discount if the product is voted in. Using their fan base for new ideas has led to unique and innovative products, and as consumers share their product ideas to their social networks for support from friends and family, awareness increases for this beauty community.[9] The Internet provides a major resource for learning more about consumer wants and needs.

Distribution Considerations.

The Internet is a new distribution channel for making products available at the right time, at the right place, and in the right quantities. Marketers' ability to process orders electronically and increase the speed of communications via the Internet reduces inefficiencies, costs, and redundancies while increasing speed throughout the marketing channel. Shipping times and costs have become an important consideration in attracting customers, prompting many companies to offer consumers low shipping costs or next-day delivery. Although consumers still flock to brick-and-mortar stores to purchase items, they tend to spend less time shopping because they have already determined what they want online. Approximately 88 percent of U.S. consumers research shoes, toys, clothing, and other items on the Internet before going to the store. Online shopping is also significantly increasing, with 209 million U.S. consumers finding and purchasing items online. Convenience and constant availability are two major reasons consumers prefer to shop online.[10]

Many online retailers, such as Birchbox, Blue Nile and Warby Parker, have established a presence in the traditional brick-and-mortar realm to create a physical presence and increase awareness. Unlike most, Blue Nile's shops, called a "Webroom," are showrooms only, meaning customers can touch and feel the products, but all orders are placed online, saving the company money in distribution costs and real estate costs associated with large storefronts. This trend is a result of increased online competition, as well as a trend toward **omni-channel retailing**, where retailers offer a seamless experience on mobile, desktop, or traditional retail spaces. For example, many retailers aim to offer consistent product assortments and pricing on all channels as well as streamline the return process. A customer may research a purchase online, shop in-store, browse an in-store digital catalog, and then use a coupon from the retailer's app at checkout. A survey revealed 73 percent of shoppers use multiple channels while shopping, making a seamless shopping experience a way to differentiate a retailer from its competitors. The survey revealed customers that research online before in-store

shopping led to 13 percent more in sales among omni-channel shoppers.[11]

Promotion Considerations.

Perhaps one of the best ways businesses can utilize digital media is for promotion purposes—whether they are increasing brand awareness, connecting with consumers, or taking advantage of social networks or virtual worlds (discussed later) to form relationships and generate positive publicity or "buzz" about their products. Thanks to online promotion, consumers can be more informed than ever, including reading customer-generated content before making purchasing decisions. Consumer consumption patterns are radically changing, and marketers must adapt their promotional efforts to meet them.

With the rise of bloggers and social media stars like Zach King and Eva Gutowski, brands are turning to influencers to promote their products. Brands identify influencers who align with their brand image and often pay them for an endorsement or send complimentary product in exchange for a review. Roughly

> ## "Thanks to online promotion, consumers can be more informed than ever, including reading customer-generated content before making purchasing decisions."

22 percent of businesses are seeing higher customer purchases through influencer marketing than traditional channels like e-mail and web search marketing.[12] Brands can contact influencers directly or use paid platforms like BrandBacker to identify ideal partners and manage campaigns. Influenster is a product sampling program that puts products in the hands of influencers and micro-influencers in exchange for authentic, user-generated content on social media. With a community of more than 6.5 million, brands are able to identify users who fall into their target demographic through data collected on the platform along with pre-qualification surveys. Once a user receives a set of products, Influenster drives social posts, in-store actions, and product reviews by incentivizing the influencers with a "Brand Badge." To receive the digital badge and retain membership privileges, users must participate in activities dictated by the brand, such as writing a review on a blog, posting a photo on Instagram, or uploading video using the products on YouTube.[13]

Pricing Considerations.

Price is the most flexible element of the marketing mix. Digital marketing can enhance the value of products by providing extra benefits such as service, information, and convenience. Through digital media, discounts and other promotions can be quickly communicated. As consumers have become better informed about their options, the demand for low-priced products has grown, leading to the creation of deal sites where consumers can directly compare prices. Expedia, for instance, provides consumers with a wealth of travel information about everything from flights to hotels that lets them compare benefits and prices. Many marketers offer buying incentives like online coupons or free samples to generate consumer demand for their products. For the business that wants to compete on price, digital marketing provides unlimited opportunities.

Facebook is the number one social media platform with more than 2.6 billion monthly active users.

easy camera/Shutterstock

Social Media Marketing

Social media marketing involves obtaining communications with consumers through social media sites. Social media marketing enables firms to promote a message and create online conversations through multiple platforms. Large markets can be targeted and reached through paid media, owned media, and earned media.[14] Paid media includes traditional print and broadcast but is now joined by paid advertising on social networks such as Facebook and Twitter. Marketers can place ads on Google just like they place an ad on television. On Facebook, which has more than 7 million advertisers, brands can pay to boost posts, create compelling photo carousel ads, promote their page, and more.[15] In addition to placing ads, marketers can own their own media outlets and create messages on social networks. Most firms have owned websites but can also develop profiles on websites such as Facebook and LinkedIn. Finally, markets can have earned media when consumers are communicating on social media sites. These digital word-of-mouth posts or interactions can promote a product or firm. Although it is not controllable like advertising, if the communication is positive, it increases sales.[16]

User-generated content relates to consumers who create, converse, rate, collect, join, or simply read online materials. Marketers can't always access the creative efforts of consumers who post or publish on publicly accessible websites, such as blogs, like A Beautiful Mess, or on social networking sites such as LinkedIn. These user-generated sites often involve self-disclosure, where consumers share their knowledge, interests, and desire to join or associate with others. Participating in discussions to connect and network with others is a major motivating factor to influence others or to promote an interest or cause. There are many critics involved in user-generated content. These consumers post evaluations on blogs or post ratings and reviews. If you have ever posted a product review or rated a movie, you have engaged in this activity. Evaluating what critics post should be an important part in a company's digital marketing strategy. Of course, consumers read ratings to aid their shopping purchases. Yelp is one of the most comprehensive review sites on products and businesses. With more than 170 million reviews, Yelp continues to expand its platform, adding Questions and Answers for users to ask venue-specific questions for other users to answer.[17] Therefore, these rating sites can be helpful to collect information used in marketing research and to monitor firm reputation.

Marketers need to analyze their target markets and determine the best social media approach to support marketing objectives. Social media should be included in both the corporate and marketing strategy. It should be a part of the firm's marketing plan and implementation efforts. Social media can be used to monitor target market competitors and understand the social and economic environment as a whole. Social media has the potential of building campaigns that produce advocates and enthusiasts of a firm's products. For example, Penguin Teen, a publisher of teen and young adult books, uses TikTok to share book teasers and news to its engaged fans. The brand has amassed millions of likes on its videos, rewarding its most engaged fans with free books.[18] Marketing should be focused on relationship building and social media can influence consumer behavior and deliver value to the firm.

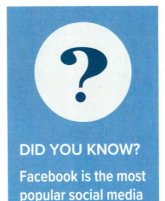

> **LO 13-4** Illustrate how businesses can use different types of social networking media.

CONSUMER-GENERATED MARKETING AND DIGITAL MEDIA

While digital marketing has generated exciting opportunities for companies to interact with their customers, digital media are also more consumer-driven than traditional media. Internet users are creating and reading consumer-generated content as never before and are having a profound effect on marketing in the process.

Two factors have sparked the rise of consumer-generated information:

1. The increased tendency of consumers to post their own thoughts, opinions, reviews, and product discussions through blogs or digital media.

2. Consumers' tendencies to trust other consumers over corporations. Consumers often rely on the recommendations of friends, family, and fellow consumers when making purchasing decisions.

Marketers who know where online users are likely to express their thoughts and opinions can use these forums to interact with them, address problems, and promote their companies. Types of digital media in which Internet users are likely to participate include social networks, blogs, wikis, video-sharing sites, podcasts, virtual reality sites, and mobile applications. Let's look a little more closely at each.

Social Networks

The increase in social networking across the world is exponential. It is estimated that today's adults spend nearly 2.5 hours on social media per day.[19] As social networks evolve, both marketers and the owners of social networking sites are realizing the opportunities such networks offer—an influx of advertising dollars for site owners and a large reach for the advertiser. As a result, marketers have begun investigating and experimenting with promotion on social networks.

Facebook. Facebook is the most popular social networking site in the world. Facebook users create profiles, which they can make public or private, and then search the network for people with whom to connect. The social networking giant has surpassed 2.3 billion users. It has also acquired a number of companies as it expands into other services, including Instagram, WhatsApp, and Oculus.[20] Facebook also has a video feature that enables the sharing and tagging of videos.[21]

For this reason, many marketers are turning to Facebook to market products, interact with consumers, and gain free publicity. Consumers can follow brands or pages they are interested in. Boosted posts, one of the features Facebook has to offer businesses, allows companies to develop an advertisement quickly from a post on their timelines, select the people they would like the advertisement to target, and select the budget they want to spend. Boosted posts appear higher up in the News Feeds of the advertisement's target market.[22] Facebook Messenger, which has the ability to facilitate large group video chats, is one of Facebook's competitive advantages. Facebook Messenger is a distinct improvement over its WhatsApp and competitor's products including Snap Inc.'s Snapchat, Apple's FaceTime, and Google Duo, which allow one-to-one communication.[23]

Additionally, social networking sites are useful for relationship marketing, or the creation of relationships that mutually benefit the business and customer. According to Hubspot, 71 percent of consumers are likely to make purchases based on social media referrals.[24] As a result, firms are spending more time on the quality of their Facebook interactions. Ritz-Carlton, for instance, spends a significant amount of time analyzing its social media conversations and reaching out to noncustomers. Businesses are shifting their emphasis from selling a product or promoting a brand to developing beneficial relationships in which brands are used to generate a positive outcome for the consumer.[25]

Twitter. Twitter is a hybrid of a social networking site and a micro-blogging site that asks users one simple question: "What's happening?" Members can post answers of up to 280 characters, which are then available for their "followers" to read. It sounds simple enough, but Twitter's effect on digital media has been immense. The site quickly progressed from a novelty to a social networking staple, attracting millions of viewers each month.[26] About 82 percent access the site from their mobile devices.[27]

Although 280 characters may not seem like enough for companies to send an effective message, shorter social media messages appear to be more effective. Tweets shorter than 100 characters are found to have a 17 percent higher engagement rate with users, and Facebook has shown similar data.[28] These efforts are having an impact; more than half of Twitter's active and monthly users follow companies or brands.[29]

Like other social networking tools, Twitter is also being used to build, or in some cases rebuild, customer relationships. For example, MoonPie uses Twitter to interact with consumers. MoonPie has been recognized for its humorous tweets and one-liners that have attracted viral attention.[30] On the other hand, approximately 70 percent of companies ignore complaints on Twitter. This failure acts as a missed opportunity to address customer concerns and maintain strong relationships.[31]

Snapchat. While Snap Inc. admits it may never achieve profitability, posting a net loss of approximately $1 billion in recent years, investors see value in Snapchat, which has more than 31 million daily active users.[32] The mobile app, launched in 2011, allows users to send messages and disappearing photos and videos to friends. The parent company prefers to think of itself as a camera company rather than a social media company and plans to release more lifestyle products like Spectacles, camera glasses sold at Snapchat pop-up shops, outside of its social media platform.[33] Marketers are looking at Snapchat as an opportunity to reach their young, highly engaged audience. Brands like Taco Bell and Sour Patch Kids have taken to Snapchat to engage with their audiences.

Snapchat, which features skippable, vertical video ads and custom photo filters, is used mostly by users under the age of 34. In fact, 79 percent of daily users are between 18 and 34.[34] Sponsored Lenses are also shoppable, taking augmented reality (AR) to the next level. For example, L'Oréal was one of the first brands to invest in shoppable AR on the platform, allowing users to virtually try on lipsticks before they buy. In the advertisement for L'Oréal Voluminous Lash Paradise Mascara, there is a small Snapchat logo in the lower corner to encourage customers to follow the brand. One of Snapchat's biggest

L'Oréal includes the social media icons for Snapchat and Instagram in its mascara advertisement.

Source: L'Oreal

challenges will be scaling its advertising dollars to achieve its revenue goals.

YouTube. Purchased by Google for $1.65 billion, YouTube allows users to upload and share videos worldwide. Users watch a billion hours of YouTube videos every day, making this popular video platform an important part of marketing strategy.[35] Though brands use the platform to release original video content, consumers far outnumber them on the platform. For example, beauty brands on YouTube are outnumbered by beauty vloggers in beauty searches by 14 to 1.[36] This makes it challenging for brands to control messaging about their products on the platform.

YouTube continues to diversify its video offering with YouTube Premium and YouTube TV. YouTube Premium expands upon the original platform, allowing users to pay for ad-free and offline video and original programming from top creators. As more homes cancel their cable packages, YouTube TV is an affordable alternative. For $49.99 per month, users can watch ABC, CBS, and NBC among other top networks, positioning the service as a competitor to Sling TV and DirecTV Now.[37]

TikTok. TikTok is a video-sharing platform that specializes in short-form mobile video. Unlike other video platforms, TikTok encourages users to build off of other user's content. For instance, a user can create a video using another person's audio or share a duet video, a feature that displays two videos simultaneously side-by-side. Audio is an important component of the TikTok app, acting as a launchpad for musical artists. TikTok's popularity has skyrocketed in recent years, with the platform surpassing 800 million active users. The platform is particularly popular among Gen Z and Millennials.[38]

TikTok is known for its meme culture, dancing videos, challenges, and comedic sketches. By embracing this style, companies can make their brand visible on the platform. For example, Urban Decay Cosmetics challenged its fans to create a video promoting the company's All Nighter Setting Spray with the hashtag #allnighterlegend in the caption. The company's original video only accrued 65,000 views, but videos uploaded by users to the branded hashtag earned a cumulative 33.3 million views.[39]

LinkedIn. LinkedIn is the top networking site for businesses and business professionals. This networking tool allows users

the blog post and spread it across the Internet after the original's removal. In other cases, a positive review of a good or service posted on a popular blog can result in large increases in sales. Thus, blogs can represent a potent threat or opportunity to marketers.

Rather than trying to eliminate blogs that cast their companies in a negative light, some firms are using their own blogs, or employee blogs, to answer consumer concerns or defend their corporate reputations. Bill Marriott, son of the founder of Marriott International, maintains a blog called "Marriott on the Move" where he not only discusses the hotel business but also posts on a number of insightful business and inspirational topics to engage his readers.[43] As blogging changes the face of media, smart companies are using it to build enthusiasm for their products and create relationships with consumers.

Wikis are websites where users can add to or edit the content of posted articles. One of the best known is Wikipedia, an online encyclopedia with more than 52 million entries in more than 309

blogs web-based journals in which writers can editorialize and interact with other Internet users.

wikis websites where users can add to or edit the content of posted articles.

> ❝ **There is too much at stake financially for marketers to ignore wikis and blogs.** ❞

to post a public profile, similar to a résumé, connect with colleagues, find job listings, and join private groups. Eighty percent of B2B marketers say LinkedIn is an effective business lead generator.[40] This platform can also be used to spread brand awareness and for corporate recruiting. HubSpot, an inbound marketing and sales platform with more than 440,000 followers, uses LinkedIn to spread its content, promote free webinars, and increase awareness around inbound marketing.[41]

Blogs and Wikis

Today's marketers must recognize that the impact of consumer-generated material like blogs and wikis and their significance to online consumers have increased a great deal. **Blogs** (short for web logs) are web-based journals in which writers can editorialize and interact with other Internet users. More than three-fourths of Internet users read blogs.[42]

Blogs give consumers power, sometimes more than companies would like. Bloggers can post whatever they like about a company or its products, whether their opinions are positive or negative, true or false. For instance, although companies sometimes force bloggers to remove blogs, readers often create copies of

languages on nearly every subject imaginable.[44] Wikipedia is one of the 10 most popular sites on the web, and because much of its content can be edited by anyone, it is easy for online consumers to add detail and supporting evidence and to correct inaccuracies in content. Wikipedia used to be completely open to editing, but in order to stop vandalism, the site had to make some topics off-limits that are now editable only by a small group of experts.

Like all digital media, wikis have advantages and disadvantages for companies. Wikis about controversial companies like Walmart and Nike often contain negative publicity about things such as workers' rights violations. However, monitoring relevant wikis can provide companies with a better idea of how consumers feel about the company or brand. Some companies also use wikis as internal tools for teams working on projects that require a great deal of documentation.[45]

There is too much at stake financially for marketers to ignore wikis and blogs. Despite this fact, statistics show that only about 36 percent of *Fortune* 500 companies have a corporate blog.[46] Marketers who want to form better customer relationships and promote their company's products must not underestimate the power of these two media outlets.

Media Sharing

Businesses can also share their corporate messages in more visual ways through media sharing sites. Media sharing sites allow marketers to share photos, videos, and podcasts. Media sharing sites are more limited in scope in how companies interact with consumers. They tend to be more promotional than reactive. This means that while firms can promote their products through videos or photos, they usually do not interact with consumers through personal messages or responses. At the same time, the popularity of these sites provides the potential to reach a global audience of consumers.

Video-sharing sites allow virtually anybody to upload videos, from professional marketers at *Fortune* 500 corporations to the average Internet user. Some of the most popular video-sharing sites include YouTube, Vimeo, and Dailymotion. Video-sharing sites give companies the opportunity to upload ads and informational videos about their products. A few videos become viral at any given time, and although many of these gain popularity because they embarrass the subject in some way, others reach viral status because people find them entertaining. **Viral marketing** occurs when a message gets sent from person to person. It can be an extremely effective tool for marketers—particularly on the Internet, where one click can send a message to dozens or hundreds of people simultaneously. Marketers are taking advantage of the viral nature of video-sharing sites like YouTube, either by creating their own unique videos or advertising on videos that have already reached viral status. Purple released a "Raw Egg Test" video on YouTube to demonstrate the support its mattress provides. To date the video has more than 187 million views.[47]

Posting videos on digital media sites also allows amateur entrepreneurs to showcase their talents for the chance to become successful. Michelle Phan started off posting makeup tutorials to YouTube in 2007. Her videos took off, catching the interest of women across the country who valued Phan's beauty advice.[48] She founded IPSY, a beauty subscription service that delivers its subscribers deluxe samples of popular cosmetics brands like Tarte and Ofra. IPSY, which reached profitability within its first six months of operation, is the largest beauty subscription in the world and the third-largest subscription service overall.[49]

Photo-sharing sites allow users to upload and share their photos and short videos with the world. Well-known photo-sharing sites include Flickr, Google Photos, Amazon Prime Photos, Photobucket, and Instagram. Instagram is the most popular mobile photo-sharing application. Instagram, owned by Facebook, allows users to be creative with their photos by using filters and tints and then sharing them with their friends. Chobani uses Instagram to build communities and suggest new uses for its yogurt products.[50] To compete against Snapchat, Instagram introduced Instagram Stories, a way for its users to send their friends messages that disappear in 24 hours.[51] Instagram is one of the fastest growing social networks.[52] With more and more people using mobile apps or accessing the Internet through their smartphones, the use of photo sharing through mobile devices is likely to increase.

Other sites are emerging that take photo sharing to a new level. Pinterest is a photo-sharing bulletin board site that combines photo sharing with elements of bookmarking and social networking. Users can share photos and images among other Internet users, communicating mostly through images that they "pin" to their boards. Other users can "repin" these images to their boards, follow each other, "like" images, and make comments. Pinterest added a feature called Lens that allows users to take a picture of an object and find a list of pins with similar-looking objects, further establishing the platform as a discovery tool for shopping.[53] They also released functionality that allows users to filter hair and beauty search results by skin tone ranges.[54] Marketers have found that an effective way of marketing through Pinterest is to post images conveying a certain emotion that represents their brand.[55] Because Pinterest users create boards that deal with their interests, marketers also have a chance to develop marketing messages encouraging users to purchase the product or brand that interests them. Pinterest hopes to learn how to influence a customer to proceed from

Verizon sold Yahoo's photo sharing site Flickr to independent image hosting company SmugMug. Though SmugMug planned to continue to operate Flickr separately without making changes to its plans or rates, the company admitted Flickr was operating at a loss.

showing interest in a product to having an intent to purchase. This knowledge will be helpful to advertisers marketing through Pinterest's website.[56]

Photo sharing represents an opportunity for companies to market themselves visually by displaying snapshots of company events, company staff, and/or company products. Nike, Audi, and MTV have all used Instagram in digital marketing campaigns. Zales Jewelers has topic boards on Pinterest featuring rings as well as other themes of love, including songs, wedding cakes, and wedding dresses.[57] Digital marketing companies are also scanning photos and images on photo-sharing sites to gather insights about how brands are being displayed or used. They hope to offer these insights to big-name companies such as Kraft. The opportunities for marketers to use photo-sharing sites to gather information and promote brands appear limitless.[58]

Podcasts are audio or video files that can be downloaded from the Internet via a subscription that automatically delivers new content to listening devices or personal computers. Popular podcast apps include Pocket Casts, Apple Podcasts, Google Podcasts, and Overcast. Podcasting offers the benefit of convenience, giving users the ability to listen to or view content when and where they choose. The markets podcasts reach are ideal for marketers, especially the 18–34 demographic, which includes the young and affluent.[59] They also affect consumer buying habits. For instance, listening to nutrition podcasts while in the grocery store increases the likelihood that shoppers will purchase healthier items.[60]

As podcasting continues to spread, radio stations and television networks like CBC Radio, NPR, MSNBC, and PBS are creating podcasts of their shows to profit from this growing trend. Many companies like GE, eBay, and Basecamp hope to use podcasts to create brand awareness, promote their products, and encourage customer loyalty.

podcast audio or video file that can be downloaded from the Internet with a subscription that automatically delivers new content to listening devices or personal computers.

Mobile Marketing

As digital marketing becomes increasingly sophisticated, consumers are beginning to utilize mobile devices like smartphones as a highly functional communication method. The smartphone and tablet have changed the way consumers communicate, and a growing number of travelers are using their smartphones to find online maps, travel guides, and taxis. In industries such as hotels, airlines, and car rental agencies, mobile phones have become a primary method for booking reservations and communicating about services. Other marketing uses of mobile phones include sending shoppers timely messages related to discounts and shopping opportunities.[61] For these reasons, mobile marketing has exploded in recent years—mobile phones have become an important part of our everyday lives and can even affect how we shop. For instance, it is estimated that shoppers who are distracted by their phones in-store increased their unplanned purchases by 12 percent over those who are not.[62] To avoid being left behind, brands must recognize the importance of mobile marketing.

E-commerce sales on smartphones are also rapidly growing and account for about half of total online sales.[63] This makes it essential for companies to understand how to use mobile tools to create effective campaigns. Figure 13.2 breaks down smartphone use in the United States. Some of the more common mobile marketing tools include the following:

THE MUSIC INDUSTRY GETS A TUNE UP

After a 20-year downturn, the music industry is rebounding. Today, streaming music is as simple as going onto Spotify, Pandora, Apple Music, or a number of other music-streaming sites. More consumers are paying for music-streaming services to get greater access to music and avoid listening to advertisements. This is increasing royalties for the featured artists because they can make money from each service. More than half of the music industry's revenue comes from streaming services.

Streaming has an advantage because it offers consumers instant access and consumption. This form of digital marketing is profitable because it provides a vast number of products (music selections) instantly (without the need for a physical location or intermediary) at a low price. For about $10 month, users can purchase a paid subscription to a streaming service and gain access to thousands of songs. Promoting these services are simple with Internet advertising.

The ease of delivery to the consumer is beneficial to both consumers and streaming services—so much so that competition among the music-streaming industry is heating up. While Spotify, Pandora, and Apple dominate the market, other companies are quickly jumping on board. Amazon introduced Amazon Music that integrates with its Alexa products so Alexa owners can hear their music simply by speaking. YouTube introduced YouTube Music Premium, an ad-free service for $9.99. Thanks to music streaming, the music industry is on the rise again. Music is easier to consume than ever, and artists are banding up to create a better product.[c]

🔵 Critical Thinking Questions

1. How does music streaming display the digital characteristics of marketing, such as greater accessibility and connectivity?

2. Describe how music streaming utilizes the marketing mix.

3. What ethical issues do you think might occur as music streaming continues to increase?

FIGURE 13.2 App Categories Mobile Users Spent the Most Time On

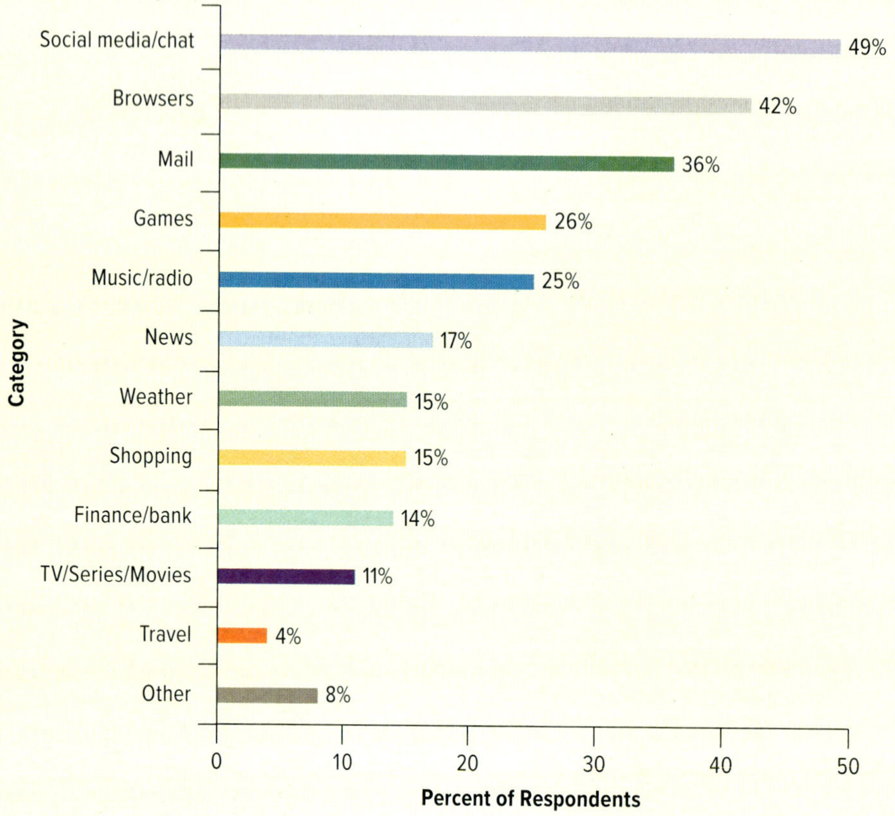

Category	Percent of Respondents
Social media/chat	49%
Browsers	42%
Mail	36%
Games	26%
Music/radio	25%
News	17%
Weather	15%
Shopping	15%
Finance/bank	14%
TV/Series/Movies	11%
Travel	4%
Other	8%

Note: ages 18–64; in the past 30 days
Source: Ipsos MORI, "Something for Everyone: Why the Growth of Mobile Apps is Good News for Brands," sponsored by Google, August 1, 2017.

- *SMS messages:* SMS messages are text messages of 160 characters or less. SMS messages have been an effective way to send coupons to prospective customers.[64]

- *Multimedia messages:* Multimedia messaging takes SMS messaging a step further by allowing companies to send video, audio, photos, and other types of media over mobile devices.

- *Mobile advertisements:* Mobile advertisements are visual advertisements that appear on mobile devices. Companies might choose to advertise through search engines, websites, or even games accessed on mobile devices. Mobile accounts for more than half of digital ad spending.[65]

- *Mobile websites:* Mobile websites are websites designed for mobile devices. More than 50 percent of e-commerce website traffic now comes through mobile devices.[66]

- *Location-based networks:* Location-based networks are built for mobile devices. A popular location-based network is Google's Waze, a GPS navigation app that crowdsources route details and traffic alerts with 130 million active monthly users.[67] Location-based services are also critical for ride-sharing apps (e.g., Uber and Lyft) or apps that offer store locators, proximity-based marketing, travel information, roadside assistance, and more.[68]

- *Mobile applications:* Mobile applications (known as *apps*) are software programs that run on mobile devices and give users access to certain content.[69] Businesses release apps to help consumers access more information about their company or to provide incentives. Apps are discussed in further detail in the next section.

Applications and Widgets

Applications (apps) are adding an entirely new layer to the marketing environment as Americans are estimated to spend 5.4 hours per day on smartphones using apps.[70] The most important feature of apps is the convenience and cost savings they offer to the consumer. Certain apps allow consumers to scan a product's barcode and then compare it with the prices of identical products in other stores. Mobile apps also enable customers to download in-store discounts. An estimated 81 percent of American adults have smartphones, so businesses cannot afford to miss out on the chance to profit from these new trends.[71] The advertisement for *The Economist,* a world news and economics publication, features its app, which provides subscribers with additional features like morning briefings for a personalized experience, audio articles for on-the-go listening, bookmarking for easy article access, and more.

To remain competitive, companies are beginning to use mobile marketing to offer additional incentives to consumers. As Unilever expands into Southeast Asia, it developed a mobile campaign that gives consumers rewards in exchange for providing Unilever with certain information about themselves, such as shopping habits.[72] Another mobile tool that marketers have found useful is QR codes. While QR codes used to require scanning apps, smartphone cameras now have built-in QR code readers. The camera app recognizes the code and opens a link, video, or image on the phone's screen. Marketers are using QR codes to promote their companies and offer consumer discounts.[73]

Mobile payments are also gaining traction, and companies like Google are working to capitalize on this opportunity.[74] Google Wallet and Apple Pay are mobile apps that store credit card information on the smartphone. When the shopper is ready to check out, he or she can tap the phone at the point of sale for the transaction to be registered.[75] Square is a company launched by Twitter co-founder Jack Dorsey. The company provides organizations with smartphone swiping devices for credit cards as well as tablets that can be used to tally purchases. Bitcoin is a virtual peer-to-peer currency that can be used to make a payment via smartphone. Smaller organizations have begun to accept Bitcoin at some of their stores. The success of mobile payments in revolutionizing the shopping experience will largely depend upon retailers adopting this payment system, but companies such as Starbucks are already jumping at the opportunity.

Widgets are small bits of software on a website, desktop, or mobile device that perform a simple purpose, such as providing stock quotes or blog updates. Marketers might use widgets to display news headlines, clocks, or games on their web pages.[76] For example, CNBC uses widgets to send alerts and financial news to subscribers. Widgets have been used by companies as a form of viral marketing—users can download the widget and send it to their friends with a click of a button.[77] Widgets downloaded to a user's desktop can update the user on the latest company or product information, enhancing relationship marketing between companies and their fans. Hotels, restaurants, and other tourist locations can download TripAdvisor widgets to their websites. These widgets display the latest company reviews, rewards, and other TripAdvisor content directly to the company's website.[78] Widgets are an innovative digital marketing tool to personalize web pages, alert users to the latest company information, and spread awareness of the company's products.

The Economist app adds value to its subscriptions with access to additional features and curated content.

Source: The Economist

LO 13-5 Explain online monitoring and analytics for social media.

ONLINE MONITORING AND ANALYTICS

Without digital media monitoring and evaluation, it will not be possible to maximize resources and minimize costs in social media marketing. The strength of measurement relates to the ability to have online analytics and metrics. Social media monitoring involves activities to track, measure, and evaluate a firm's digital marketing initiatives.[79] An advantage of digital marketing evaluations is that there are methods to capture the metrics that indicate the outcomes of strategies. Therefore, establishing an expected level of performance against actual performance can be compared. Metrics develop from listening and tracking. For example, a firm could set up a hashtag and promote it.

TABLE 13.2 Google Analytics

Real time	Data updates are live so you can see pageviews, top social traffic, top referrals, top keywords, top active pages, and top locations in real time.
Audience	Audience reports provide insight into demographics, interests, geography, behavior, mobile use, and more.
Acquisition	In-bound traffic is monitored through acquisition reports, allowing you to compare traffic from search, referrals, e-mail, and social media.
Behavior	Use RSS feeds. Add tags to web pages or photos. "Vote" for websites online.
Conversions	Google Analytics allows users to set goals and objectives to monitor web conversions, like signing up for an e-mail newsletter or completing a purchase.

M&M'S has used crowdsourcing to let consumers vote on new limited edition flavors.

Roman Samokhin/123RF

Metrics can be quantitative or qualitative. For example, click-through rate (CTR) determines the percentage of consumers who clicked on a link on a site as a quantitative measure. In addition, a qualitative metric could relate how consumers feel about a product.

Key performance indicators (KPIs) should be embedded at the onset of a social media strategy that can allow almost real-time measurement and evaluation. This provides a foundation for making iterative changes to implementation and tactical execution. Marketing analytics uses tools and methods to measure and interpret the effectiveness of marketing activities. Applying analytics to social media performance can help develop better targeted social media campaigns. Selecting valid metrics requires specific objectives that the social media strategy is to obtain. Objectives that are quantitative could include the number of likes on an Instagram post or the CTR of a Facebook post.

A comprehensive performance evaluation requires gathering all valid metrics and understanding the way the strategy meets performance standards or underperforms based on expectations. One way to approach this is to use Google Analytics, the largest analytics platform monitoring more than 30 million websites.[80] The Google Analytics dashboard is broken down into five sections: real time, audience, acquisition, behavior, and conversions. Table 13.2 explains the function of each section. Using this tool allows you to identify your website's strengths and weaknesses and uncover opportunities for growth. For example, you may find that organic search traffic is very high, but that your social media traffic is quite low, or you may see a spike in weekday traffic while weekends are slow. KPIs for your social media strategy can include likes, shares, reach, engagement rate, CTR, and conversions. In the conversions dashboard, marketers can set up custom conversion goals to see the impact social media has on their business.

By analyzing rich site traffic data, marketers can better understand their customers and measure the effectiveness of their marketing efforts. For example, PBS uses Google Analytics to monitor the web performance for multiple properties and track key events like user registrations and video views. After analyzing search engine trends, PBS experienced 30 percent more site traffic in the first year after implementation.[81] Google Analytics is arguably the most robust web analytics tool available, and it is free to anyone with a Google account. A premium version, Google Analytics 360 Suite, designed to help companies target potential customers, is available for even more in-depth analytics. The tool identifies someone's habits from web and television to mobile, competing with companies like Salesforce and Oracle.[82]

USING DIGITAL MEDIA TO LEARN ABOUT CONSUMERS

Marketing research and information systems can use digital media and social networking sites to gather useful information about consumers and their preferences. Sites such as Twitter and Facebook can be good substitutes for focus groups. Online surveys can serve as an alternative to mail, telephone, or personal interviews.

Crowdsourcing describes how marketers use digital media to find out the opinions or needs of the crowd (or potential markets). Communities of interested consumers join sites like Threadless, which designs T-shirts, or Crowdspring, which creates logos and print and web designs. These companies give interested consumers opportunities to contribute and give feedback on product ideas. Crowdsourcing lets companies gather and utilize consumers' ideas in an interactive way when creating new products.

Consumer feedback is an important part of the digital media equation. Ratings and reviews have become exceptionally popular. Online reviews are estimated to influence the buying decisions of approximately 97 percent of U.S. consumers.[83] Retailers such as Amazon, Netflix, and Priceline allow consumers to post comments on their sites about the goods and services they sell. Today, most online shoppers search the Internet for ratings and reviews before making major purchase decisions.

While consumer-generated content about a firm can be either positive or negative, digital media forums do allow businesses to closely monitor what their customers are saying. In the case of negative feedback, businesses can communicate with consumers to address problems or complaints much more easily than through traditional communication channels. Yet despite the ease and obvious importance of online feedback, many companies do not yet take full advantage of the digital tools at their disposal.

LO 13-6 Propose recommendations to a marketer's dilemma.

LEGAL AND SOCIAL ISSUES IN INTERNET MARKETING

The extraordinary growth of information technology, the Internet, and social networks has generated many legal and social issues for consumers and businesses. These issues include privacy concerns, the risk of identity theft and online fraud, and the need to protect intellectual property. The FTC rules for online marketing are the same as for any other form of communication or advertising. These rules help maintain the credibility of the Internet as an advertising medium. To avoid deception, all online communication must tell the truth and cannot mislead consumers. In addition, all claims must be substantiated. If online communication is unfair and causes injury that is substantial and not reasonably avoidable and is not outweighed by other benefits, it is considered deceptive. The FTC identifies risk areas for online communication and issues warnings to consumers as misconduct is reported. Some of the areas include testimonials and endorsements, warranties and guarantees, free products, and mail and telephone orders. The FTC periodically joins with other law enforcement agencies to monitor the Internet for potentially false or deceptive online claims, including fraud, privacy, and intellectual property issues. We discuss these in this section, as well as steps that individuals, companies, and the government have taken to address them.

Privacy

Businesses have long tracked consumers' shopping habits with little controversy. However, observing the contents of a consumer's shopping cart or the process a consumer goes through when choosing a box of cereal generally does not result in the collection of specific, personally identifying data. Although using credit cards, shopping cards, and coupons forces consumers to

give up a certain degree of anonymity in the traditional shopping process, they can still choose to remain anonymous by paying cash. Shopping on the Internet, however, allows businesses to track them on a far more personal level, from the contents of their online purchases to the websites they favor. Current technology has made it possible for marketers to amass vast quantities of personal information, often without consumers' knowledge, and to share and sell this information to interested third parties.

How is personal information collected on the web? Many sites follow users online by storing a "cookie," or an identifying string of text, on users' computers. Cookies permit website operators to track how often a user visits the site, what he or she looks at while there, and in what sequence. They also allow website visitors to customize services, such as virtual shopping carts, as well as the particular content they see when they log onto a web page. Users have the option of turning off cookies on their machines, but nevertheless, the potential for misuse has left many consumers uncomfortable with this technology.

While the United States does not have a comprehensive consumer data protection law, the European Union passed the General Data Protection Regulation (GDPR) which requires businesses to acquire permission from consumers in order to collect their data. The legislation applies to any company doing business with EU citizens.[84] While consumers may welcome such added protections, web advertisers, who use consumer information to better target advertisements to online consumers, see it as a threat. In response to impending legislation, many web advertisers are attempting self-regulation in order to stay ahead of the game. For instance, the Digital Advertising Alliance (DAA) adopted privacy guidelines for online advertisers and created a "trusted mark" icon that websites adhering to their guidelines can display. However, because it is self-regulatory, not all digital advertisers will choose to participate in its programs.[85]

Identity theft costs consumers more than $16 billion each year.

Africa Studio/Shutterstock

identity theft when criminals obtain personal information that allows them to impersonate someone else in order to use their credit to access financial accounts and make purchases.

online fraud any attempt to conduct fraudulent activities online.

Transparency

Influencer marketing, as we discussed earlier as a form of promotion, is relatively new compared with other forms of advertising, so it should be no surprise there have been road bumps for early adopters. Due to concerns about dishonest advertising, the Federal Trade Commission (FTC) requires influencers to clearly disclose any connection they have with brands they promote. Neglecting to make a disclosure is viewed as deceptive advertising. Cases have been filed against Warner Bros. Home Entertainment and Lord & Taylor, which paid various influencers to promote their products without disclosures. According to the FTC, any level of compensation must be disclosed, whether a partnership is paid or an influencer strictly receives free product.[86]

Identity Theft and Online Fraud

Identity theft occurs when criminals obtain personal information that allows them to impersonate someone else in order to use the person's credit to access financial accounts and make purchases. This requires organizations to implement increased security measures to prevent database theft. As you can see in Figure 13.3, the most common complaints relate to employment or tax-related fraud, credit card fraud, phone/utilities fraud, bank fraud, loan/lease fraud, and government documents/benefits fraud. Sadly, cyberthieves have started targeting children's identities as they offer criminals "a clean slate" for them to commit fraud, such as applying for loans or credit cards.[87]

The Internet's relative anonymity and speed make possible both legal and illegal access to databases storing Social Security numbers, drivers' license numbers, dates of birth, mothers' maiden names, and other information that can be used to establish a credit card or bank account in another person's name in order to make fraudulent transactions. One growing scam used to initiate identity theft fraud is the practice of *phishing*, whereby con artists counterfeit a well-known website and send out e-mails directing victims to it. There, visitors find instructions to reveal sensitive information such as their credit card numbers. Phishing scams have faked websites for PayPal and the Federal Deposit Insurance Corporation.

Some identity theft problems are resolved quickly, while other cases take weeks and hundreds of dollars before a victim's bank balances and credit standings are restored. To deter identity theft, the National Fraud Center wants financial institutions to implement new technologies such as digital certificates, digital signatures, and biometrics—the use of fingerprinting or retina scanning.

Online fraud includes any attempt to purposely deceive online. Many cybercriminals use hacking to commit online fraud. Hackers break into websites and steal users' personal information. Home Depot, Target, and JPMorgan are some notable cases where cybercriminals hacked into these companies' systems and stole information. Sony experienced a devastating attack that shut down its entire computer network and resulted in the theft of 27 gigabytes of files.[88]

Using a different password for each website users visit is another important way to avoid becoming the victim of online fraud. Passwords should be complex enough that a cybercriminal cannot easily guess it. However, many consumers do not do this because of the hassle it takes in remembering complex passwords for multiple sites.[89]

Credit card fraud is a major type of fraud that occurs online. Some companies, such as Apple, are releasing credit cards with advanced security features such as one-time unique dynamic security codes that replace the static three-digit CVV. In the case of Apple, the company does not store the user's transaction history or spending habits, so the data cannot be shared or sold to third parties as

▼ **FIGURE 13.3** Main Sources of Identity Theft

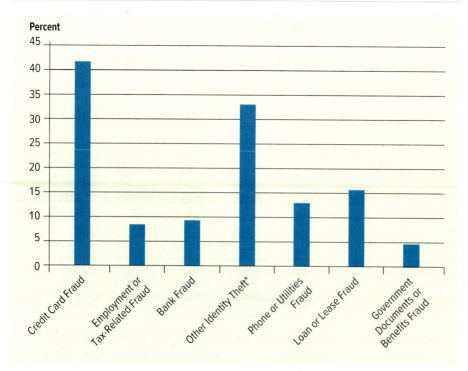

* Other includes email or social media, evading the law, insurance, medical services, online shopping or payment account, and securities accounts.

Source: *Consumer Sentinel Network Data Book 2019,* Federal Trade Commission.

traditional credit card companies do.[90] Privacy advocates advise that the best way to stay out of trouble is to avoid giving out personal information, such as Social Security numbers or credit card information, unless the site is definitely legitimate.

Intellectual Property Theft and Other Illegal Activities

In addition to protecting personal privacy, Internet users and others want to protect their rights to property they may create, including songs, movies, books, and software. Such intellectual property consists of the ideas and creative materials developed to solve problems, carry out applications, and educate and entertain others.

Although intellectual property is generally protected by patents and copyrights, losses from the illegal copying of computer programs, music, movies, and books reach billions of dollars each year in the United States alone. This has become a particular problem with digital media sites. YouTube has often faced lawsuits on intellectual property infringement. With millions of users uploading content to YouTube, it can be hard for Google to monitor and remove all the videos that may contain copyrighted materials.

Illegal sharing of content is another major intellectual property problem. Consumers rationalize the pirating of software, videogames, movies, and music for a number of reasons. First, many feel they just don't have the money to pay for what they want. Second, because their friends engage in piracy and swap digital content, some users feel influenced to engage in this activity. Others enjoy the thrill of getting away with something with a low risk of consequences. And finally, some people feel being tech-savvy allows them to take advantage of the opportunity to pirate content.[91]

Illicit online marketing is also becoming a serious issue for law enforcement across the globe. The ease of the Internet and the difficulty in pinpointing perpetrators are leading drug buyers to deal in illegal drugs over the Internet. Websites that deal in illegal drugs are looking increasingly legitimate, even employing marketing strategies and customer service.[92] Sales of counterfeit goods are another problem. Knockoffs of popular products seized by federal officials annually are valued at more than $1 billion. Counterfeit products, particularly from overseas, are thriving

Team Exercise

Develop a digital marketing promotion for a local sports team. Use Twitter, Facebook, and other social networking media to promote ticket sales for next season's schedule. In your plan, provide specific details and ideas for the content you would use on the sites. Also, describe how you would encourage fans and potential fans to go to your site. How would you use digital media to motivate sports fans to purchase tickets and merchandise and attend games?

FAKE OUT: AMAZON KICKS COUNTERFEITS TO THE CURB

The rise of the electronic retailers (e-tailers) has created an avenue for small brands to market their products. However, these same avenues are allowing counterfeiters to cut into their businesses. For instance, Amazon's simple process for listing products has created an onslaught of counterfeit listings that make it difficult for consumers to distinguish what is real. Counterfeiters register with Amazon, list their products alongside the authentic product, and undercut the price. Amazon's price algorithms often locate the lower price and recommend the counterfeit product. Amazon claims that less than 0.1 percent of listings were flagged for potential infringements, and it acts on of 95 percent of complaints on brand-registered products within eight hours.

Large companies face the same issues that small businesses do. Apple filed a lawsuit against Mobile Star LLC for producing counterfeit chargers and marketing them as authentic via the Fulfilled by Amazon program. Birkenstock and Nike ceased partnerships with Amazon due to the number of counterfeits and the inability to police them.

E-tailers are taking measures to fight the fakes. Amazon requires third-party sellers to provide proof they are licensed to sell items from Adidas, Asics, Hasbro, Nike, and Samsung. Additionally, the company committed $400 million to invest in personnel and machine learning tools to fight fraud and abuse. eBay established a Verified Rights Owner program that allows intellectual property owners and licensed sellers to report phony listings. Alibaba created the Big Data Anti-Counterfeiting Alliance with 20 international brands to remove fake goods from its site and worked with Chinese authorities to seize $207 million worth of fake items. Alibaba is also applying data analytics and technology like blockchain to fight fraudulent listings before the rights holders flag them, with a reported 97 percent of all takedowns occurring before a purchase.[d]

Critical Thinking Questions

1. What types of legal and social issues in Internet marketing do counterfeit products create on e-retailing sites?

2. What responsibility do e-retailers like Amazon have to consumers in ensuring the items sold on their sites are authentic?

3. As e-retailers like Alibaba grow in global popularity, what additional challenges do you think e-retailers will face regarding the sale of counterfeit products on their sites?

on the Internet because they can be shipped directly to customers without having to be examined by customs officials when shipped through ports. Some firms, including UGG Boots, use online services allowing users to type in the address to verify whether the electronic retailer is a legitimate seller.[93]

DIGITAL MEDIA'S IMPACT ON MARKETING

To be successful in business, you need to know much more than how to use a social media site to communicate with friends. Developing a strategic understanding of how digital marketing can make business more efficient and productive is increasingly necessary. If you are thinking of becoming an entrepreneur, then the digital world can open doors to new resources and customers. Smartphones, mobile broadband, and webcams are among the tools that can make the most of an online business world, creating greater efficiency at less cost. For example, rather than using traditional phone lines, Skype helps people make and receive calls via the Internet and provides free video calling and text messaging for about 10 percent of the cost of a landline.[94] It is up to businesses and entrepreneurs to develop strategies that achieve business success using existing and future technology, software, and networking opportunities.

Traditional businesses accustomed to using print media can find the transition to digital challenging. New media may require employees with new skills or additional training for current employees. There is often a gap between technical knowledge of how to develop sites and how to develop effective digital marketing strategies to enhance business success. Determining the correct blend of traditional and new media requires careful consideration; the mix will vary depending on the business, its size, and its target market. Future career opportunities will require skills in both traditional and digital media areas so that marketers properly understand and implement marketing strategies that help businesses achieve a competitive advantage. ■

WHAT DOES IT MEAN // to Be a Digital Marketer? /

The business world has grown increasingly dependent on digital marketing to maintain communication with stakeholders. Reaching customers is often a major concern, but digital marketing can also be used to communicate with suppliers, concerned community members, and special interest groups about issues related to sustainability, safety practices, and philanthropic activities. Many types of jobs exist: account executive directors of social media and director of marketing for digital products, as well as digital advertisers, online marketers, global digital marketers, and brand managers are prominently listed on career opportunity websites.

Entrepreneurs are taking advantage of the low cost of digital marketing, building social networking sites to help market their products. In fact, some small businesses such as specialty publishing, personal health and beauty, and other specialty products can use digital marketing as the primary channel for reaching consumers. Many small businesses are posting signs outside their stores with statements such as "Follow us on Twitter" or "Check out our Facebook page."

To utilize digital marketing, especially social networking, requires more than information technology skills related to constructing websites, graphics, videos, podcasts, etc. Most importantly, one must be able to determine how digital media can be used in implementing a marketing strategy. All marketing starts with identifying a target market and developing a marketing mix to satisfy customers. Digital marketing is just another way to reach customers, provide information, and develop relationships. Therefore, your opportunity for a career in this field is greatly based on understanding the messages, desired level of interactivity, and connectivity that helps achieve marketing objectives.

As social media use skyrockets, digital marketing professionals will be in demand. The experience of many businesses and research indicate digital marketing is a powerful way to increase brand exposure and generate traffic. In fact, a study conducted on Social Media Examiner found that 85 percent of marketers surveyed believe generating exposure for their business is their number-one advantage in Internet marketing. As consumers use social networking for their personal communication, they will be more open to obtaining information about products through this channel. Digital marketing could be the fastest growing opportunity in business.

To prepare yourself for a digital marketing career, learn not only the technical aspects but also how social media can be used to maximize marketing performance. According to Glassdoor, a social media manager's average base pay is $50,000 while a digital marketing manager's average base pay is $70,000.

accounting and
financial statements

Chrispictures/Shutterstock

LEARNING OBJECTIVES

After reading this chapter, you will be able to:

LO 14-1 Describe the different uses of accounting information.

LO 14-2 Demonstrate the accounting process.

LO 14-3 Examine the various components of an income statement in order to evaluate a firm's "bottom line."

LO 14-4 Interpret a company's balance sheet to determine its current financial position.

LO 14-5 Analyze financial statements, using ratio analysis, to evaluate a company's performance.

Although you may cover some of this material in your accounting course, reading this chapter will only strengthen your understanding of accounting. What professors find is that a little duplication and repetition goes a long way in helping the brain retain material. Accounting is the financial "language" that organizations use to record, measure, and interpret all of their financial transactions and records and is very important in business. All businesses—from a small family farm to a giant corporation—use the language of accounting to make sure they track their use of funds, measure profitability, and budget for future expenditures. Nonbusiness organizations such as charities and governments also use accounting to demonstrate to donors and taxpayers how well they use their funds to meet their stated objectives.

This chapter explores the role of accounting in business and its importance in making business decisions. First, we discuss the uses of accounting information and the accounting process. Then, we briefly look at some simple financial statements and accounting tools that are useful in analyzing organizations worldwide. ■

LO 14-1 Describe the different uses of accounting information.

THE NATURE OF ACCOUNTING

Simply stated, **accounting** is the recording, measurement, and interpretation of financial information. Large numbers of people and institutions, both within and outside businesses, use accounting tools to evaluate organizational operations. The Financial Accounting Standards Board has been setting the principles and standards of financial accounting and reporting in the private sector since 1973. Its mission is to establish and improve standards of financial accounting and reporting for the guidance and education of the public, including issuers, investors, auditors, and users of financial information. However, accounting scandals at the turn of the last century resulted when many accounting firms and businesses failed to abide by generally accepted accounting principles, or GAAP. Consequently, the federal government has taken a greater role in making rules, requirements, and policies for accounting firms and businesses through the Securities and Exchange Commission's (SEC) Public Company Accounting Oversight Board (PCAOB). For example, the PCAOB has the ability to file a disciplinary order against a firm or individual that either temporarily or permanently prohibits that firm or individual from practicing accounting. To better understand the importance of accounting, we must first understand who prepares accounting information and how it is used.

Accountants

Many of the functions of accounting are carried out by public or private accountants.

Public Accountants.

Individuals and businesses can hire a **certified public accountant (CPA)**, an individual who has been certified by the state in which he or she practices to provide accounting services ranging from the preparation of financial records and the filing of tax returns to complex audits of corporate financial records. Certification gives a public accountant the right to express, officially, an unbiased opinion regarding the accuracy of the client's financial statements. Most public accountants are either self-employed or members of large public accounting firms such as Ernst & Young, KPMG, Deloitte, and PricewaterhouseCoopers, together referred to as "the Big Four." In addition, many CPAs work for one of the second-tier accounting firms that are much smaller than the Big Four. Table 14.1 shows the number of employees at the most prestigious accounting firms. Vault.com uses a weighted ranking system based on survey results to create a score that represents work-life quality issues to reflect the prestige of the firm. Note that not all of the prestigious firms are ranked high in work-life quality.

accounting the recording, measurement, and interpretation of financial information.

certified public accountant (CPA) an individual who has been state certified to provide accounting services ranging from the preparation of financial records and the filing of tax returns to complex audits of corporate financial records.

Rank	Firm	Employees	Location
1	PwC (PricewaterhouseCoopers) LLP	58,133	New York, NY
2	Deloitte LLP	80,000	New York, NY
3	Ernst & Young LLP (EY)	45,000	New York, NY
4	KPMG LLP	31,000	New York, NY
5	Grant Thornton LLP	7,530	Chicago, IL
6	BDO USA LLP	5,395	Chicago, IL
7	RSM US LLP	9,560	Chicago, IL
8	Baker Tilly Virchow Kraus LLP	2,800	Chicago, IL
9	Crowe LLP	4,100	Chicago, IL
10	Moss Adams LLP	2,500	Seattle, WA

Note: U.S. only, does not include international operations.

Source: *"Most Prestigious Accounting Firms,"* Vault.com, https://www.vault.com/best-companies-to-work-for/accounting/most-prestigious-accounting-firms (accessed August 28, 2020).

private accountants
accountants employed by large corporations, government agencies, and other organizations to prepare and analyze their financial statements.

certified management accountants (CMAs)
private accountants who, after rigorous examination, are certified by the Institute of Management Accountants and who have some managerial responsibility.

Although there will always be companies and individual money managers who can successfully hide illegal or misleading accounting practices for a while, eventually they are exposed. After the accounting scandals of Enron and Worldcom in the early 2000s, Congress passed the Sarbanes-Oxley Act, which required firms to be more rigorous in their accounting and reporting practices. Sarbanes-Oxley made accounting firms separate their consulting and auditing businesses and punished corporate executives with potential jail sentences for inaccurate, misleading, or illegal accounting statements. This seemed to reduce the accounting errors among nonfinancial companies, but declining housing prices exposed some of the questionable practices by banks and mortgage companies. Only five years after the passage of the Sarbanes-Oxley Act, the world experienced a financial crisis starting in 2008—part of which was due to excessive risk taking and inappropriate accounting practices. Many banks failed to understand the true state of their financial health. Banks also developed questionable lending practices and investments based on subprime mortgages made to individuals who had poor credit. When housing prices declined and people suddenly found that they owed more on their mortgages than their homes were worth, they began to default. To prevent a depression, the government intervened and bailed out some of the United States' largest banks. Congress passed the Dodd-Frank Act in 2010 to strengthen the oversight of financial institutions. This act gave the Federal Reserve Board the task of implementing the legislation. This legislation limits the types of assets commercial banks can buy; the amount of capital they must maintain; and the use of derivative instruments such as options, futures, and structured investment products. However, at the Economics Club of New York on February 16, 2017, Alan Greenspan, the former chair of the Federal Reserve Board, was quoted as saying the Dodd-Frank Act is one of the worst pieces of legislation he has ever seen.

A growing area for public accountants is *forensic accounting*, which is accounting that is fit for legal review. It involves analyzing financial documents in search of fraudulent entries or financial misconduct. Functioning as much like detectives as accountants, forensic accountants have been used since the 1930s. Many auditing firms are expanding their forensic or fraud-detection services. Additionally, many forensic accountants root out evidence of "cooked books" for federal agencies like the Federal Bureau of Investigation or the Internal Revenue Service. The Association of Certified Fraud Examiners, which certifies accounting professionals as *certified fraud examiners (CFEs)*, has grown to more than 85,000 members.[1]

Private Accountants.
Large corporations, government agencies, and other organizations may employ their own **private accountants** to prepare and analyze their financial statements. With titles such as controller, tax accountant, or internal auditor, private accountants are deeply involved in many of the most important financial decisions of the organizations for which they work. Private accountants can be CPAs and may become **certified management accountants (CMAs)** by passing a rigorous examination by the Institute of Management Accountants.

Accounting or Bookkeeping?
The terms *accounting* and *bookkeeping* are often mistakenly used interchangeably. Much narrower and far more mechanical than accounting, bookkeeping is typically limited to the routine, day-to-day recording of business transactions. Bookkeepers are responsible for obtaining and recording the information that accountants require to analyze a firm's financial position. They generally require less training than accountants. Accountants, on the other hand, usually complete course work beyond their basic four- or five-year college accounting degrees. This additional training allows accountants not only to record financial information

DID YOU KNOW?

Corporate fraud costs are estimated at $5 trillion annually.[a]

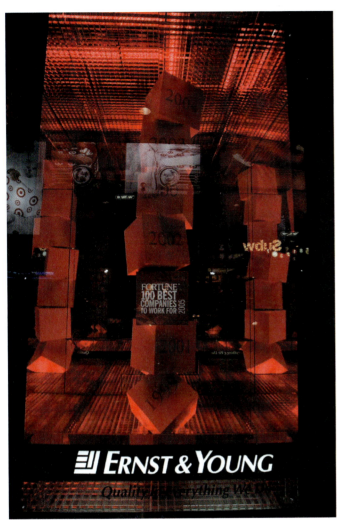

Ernst & Young is part of the Big Four, or the four largest international accounting firms. The other three are KPMG, PricewaterhouseCoopers, and Deloitte.

Lars Niki

Basically, managers and owners use financial statements (1) to aid in internal planning and control and (2) for external purposes such as reporting to the Internal Revenue Service, stockholders, creditors, customers, employees, and other interested parties. Figure 14.1 shows some of the users of the accounting information generated by organizations and other stakeholders.

Internal Uses. Managerial accounting refers to the internal use of accounting statements by managers in planning and directing the organization's activities. Perhaps management's greatest single concern is **cash flow**, the movement of money through an organization over a daily, weekly, monthly, or yearly basis. Obviously, for any business to succeed, it needs to generate enough cash to pay its bills as they fall due. However, it is not at all unusual for highly successful and rapidly growing companies to struggle to make payments to employees, suppliers, and lenders because of an inadequate cash flow. One common reason for a so-called cash crunch, or shortfall, is poor managerial planning.

Managerial accountants also help prepare an organization's **budget**, an internal financial plan that forecasts expenses and income over a set period of time. It is not unusual for an organization to prepare separate daily, weekly, monthly, and yearly budgets. Think of a budget as a financial map, showing how the company expects to move from Point A to Point B over a specific period of time. While most companies prepare *master budgets* for the entire firm, many also prepare budgets for smaller segments of the organization such as divisions, departments, product lines, or projects. "Top-down" master budgets begin at the upper management level and filter down to the individual department level, while "bottom-up" budgets start at the department or project level

managerial accounting the internal use of accounting statements by managers in planning and directing the organization's activities.

cash flow the movement of money through an organization over a daily, weekly, monthly, or yearly basis.

budget an internal financial plan that forecasts expenses and income over a set period of time.

but to understand, interpret, and even develop the sophisticated accounting systems necessary to classify and analyze complex financial information.

The Uses of Accounting Information

Accountants summarize the information from a firm's business transactions in various financial statements (which we'll look at in a later section of this chapter) for a variety of stakeholders, including managers, investors, creditors, and government agencies. Many business failures may be directly linked to ignorance of the information "hidden" inside these financial statements. Likewise, most business successes can be traced to informed managers who understand the consequences of their decisions. While maintaining and even increasing short-run profits is desirable, the failure to plan sufficiently for the future can easily lead an otherwise successful company to insolvency and bankruptcy court.

▼**FIGURE 14.1** The Users of Accounting Information

INTERNAL USERS	EXTERNAL USERS
Boards of directors	Government
Owners	Creditors
Managers	Stockholders
Accountants	Employees
Business analysts	Customers

annual report
summary of a firm's financial information, products, and growth plans for owners and potential investors.

and are combined at the chief executive's office. Generally, the larger and more rapidly growing an organization, the greater will be the likelihood that it will build its master budget from the ground up.

Regardless of focus, the principal value of a budget lies in its breakdown of cash inflows and outflows. Expected operating expenses (cash outflows such as wages, materials costs, and taxes) and operating revenues (cash inflows in the form of payments from customers) over a set period of time are carefully forecast and subsequently compared with actual results. Deviations between the two serve as a "trip wire" or "feedback loop" to launch more detailed financial analyses in an effort to pinpoint trouble spots and opportunities.

External Uses. Managers also use accounting statements to report the business's financial performance to outsiders. Such statements are used for filing income taxes, obtaining credit from lenders, and reporting results to the firm's stockholders. They become the basis for the information provided in the official corporate **annual report**,

UNITED STATES
SECURITIES AND EXCHANGE COMMISSION
Washington, D.C. 20549

FORM 10-K

☒ ANNUAL REPORT PURSUANT TO SECTION 13 OR 15(d) OF THE SECURITIES EXCHANGE ACT OF 1934

For the fiscal year ended January 26, 2020

OR

☐ TRANSITION REPORT PURSUANT TO SECTION 13 OR 15(d) OF THE SECURITIES EXCHANGE ACT OF 1934

Commission file number: 0-23985

NVIDIA CORPORATION
(Exact name of registrant as specified in its charter)

Delaware	94-3177549
(State or other jurisdiction of Incorporation or Organization)	(I.R.S. Employer Identification No.)

2788 San Tomas Expressway Santa Clara, California 95051 (408) 486-2000

(Address, including zip code, and telephone number, including area code, of principal executive offices) Securities registered pursuant to Section 12(b) of the Act:

Title of each class Trading Symbol(s) Name of each exchange on which registered

Common Stock, $0.001 par value per share	NVDA	The Nasdaq Global Select Market

Securities registered pursuant to Section 12(g) of the Act:
None

The annual report is a summary of the firm's financial information, products, and growth plans for owners and potential investors. Many investors look at a firm's annual report to determine how well the company is doing financially.

Source: U.S. Securities and Exchange Commission.

a summary of the firm's financial information, products, and growth plans for owners and potential investors. While frequently presented between slick, glossy covers, the single most important component of an annual report is the signature of a certified public accountant attesting that the required financial statements are an accurate reflection of the underlying financial condition of the firm. Financial statements meeting these conditions are termed *audited*. The primary external users of audited accounting information are government agencies, stockholders and potential investors, lenders, suppliers, and employees.

During the global financial crisis, it was discovered that Greece had been engaging in deceptive accounting practices using financial techniques to hide massive amounts of debt from its public balance sheets. Eventually, the markets figured out the country might not be able to pay off its creditors. The European Union and the International Monetary Fund bailed out Greece with loans and credit relief, but tied to this was the message to "get your financial house in order."

Many states have huge pension fund deficits and some have been borrowing from pension funds to help balance their budgets which only compounds the problem. To make matters worse, the COVID-19 (coronavirus) pandemic in 2020 caused major financial difficulties for states as they had to cover unemployment benefits and fight the virus with unexpected medical costs. States like New York, Illinois, Connecticut, New Jersey, and Louisiana were hardest hit because of their high population density cities like Chicago and New Orleans.

Financial statements evaluate the return on stockholders' investments and the overall quality of the firm's management team. As a result, poor performance, as documented in the financial statements, often results in changes in top management.

Potential investors study the financial statements in a firm's annual report to determine whether the company meets its investment requirements and whether the returns from a given firm are likely to compare favorably with other similar companies. NVIDIA's annual financial statement submitted to the Securities and Exchange Commission, called Form 10-K, can be seen on the previous page.

Banks and other lenders look at financial statements to determine a company's ability to meet current and future debt obligations if a loan or credit is granted. To determine this ability, a short-term lender examines a firm's cash flow to assess its ability to repay a loan quickly with cash generated from sales. A long-term lender is more interested in the company's profitability and indebtedness to other lenders. In the advertisement, HSBC highlights its insights into global business and modern trade through its Navigator survey. HSBC, based in London, is the seventh largest bank in the world and the largest bank in Europe.[3] HSBC offers loans for everything from personal use to global business. Evaluating financial statements is an important step in the lending process for banks like HSBC.

Labor unions and employees use financial statements to establish reasonable expectations for salary and other benefit

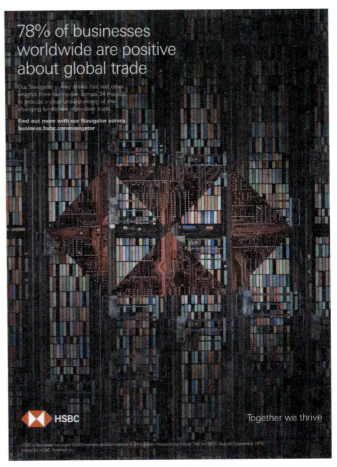

As one of the biggest banks in the world, HSBC specializes in loans, mortgages, savings, investments, and credit cards. The data provided can be used in financial statements.

Source: HSBC

requests. Just as firms experiencing record profits are likely to face added pressure to increase employee wages, so too are employees unlikely to grant employers wage and benefit concessions without considerable evidence of financial distress.

LO 14-2 Demonstrate the accounting process.

THE ACCOUNTING PROCESS

Many view accounting as a primary business language. It is of little use, however, unless you know how to "speak" it. Fortunately, the fundamentals—the accounting equation and the double-entry bookkeeping system—are not difficult to learn. These two concepts serve as the starting point for all currently accepted accounting principles.

Artificial intelligence (AI) is a type of technology that allows machines to perform decision-based tasks previously left to humans. To some accountants, the words "artificial intelligence" mean goodbye jobs. Kai Fu Lee, an AI expert and former Google executive, believes 40 percent of all jobs will be replaced by automation in the next two decades.

On the other hand, AI is currently being used to supplement accountants, not replace them. The director of accounting firm Raedan believes AI is the next step in automation and efficiency provided by cloud software. He believes AI will increase time savings, reduce errors, and aid compliance. In turn, this will allow accountants to spend time on more meaningful tasks, while AI can cover tasks like data entry.

AI may also increase employee satisfaction, empowering accountants to focus more on tasks they find enjoyable. Especially at the Big Four accounting firms, retention is difficult. Employees become exhausted from the amount of work and number of hours they have to put in. If AI can be used to automate some of this work, accountants would suffer less from burnout.

AI has so many advantages for businesses that many are adopting their own systems. For instance, PricewaterhouseCoopers has developed its own AI system called GL.ai. This system identifies anomalies in its clients' general ledger systems. According to a recent survey of 3,000+ business executives, more than 80 percent of executives believe AI leads to a competitive advantage, and 79 percent believe it will increase their company's productivity. AI will disrupt jobs and businesses of all kinds. However, professionals should not be scared to jump on the AI train because it is likely that AI will disrupt businesses for the better.[c]

Critical Thinking Questions

1. Describe some of the advantages of AI to the accounting industry.

2. GL.ai, the AI system adopted by PricewaterhouseCoopers, helps identify anomalies in its clients' general ledger systems. Why do you think this is important?

3. If AI can take over basic accounting tasks such as data entry, do you think this will improve the services accountants offer to their customers? Why or why not?

---

assets a firm's economic resources, or items of value that it owns, such as cash, inventory, land, equipment, buildings, and other tangible and intangible things.

liabilities debts that a firm owes to others.

owners' equity equals assets minus liabilities and reflects historical values.

accounting equation assets equal liabilities plus owners' equity.

The Accounting Equation

Accountants are concerned with reporting an organization's assets, liabilities, and owners' equity. To help illustrate these concepts, consider a hypothetical floral shop called Anna's Flowers, owned by Anna Rodriguez. A firm's economic resources, or items of value that it owns, represent its **assets**—cash, inventory, land, equipment, buildings, and other tangible and intangible things. The assets of Anna's Flowers include counters, refrigerated display cases, flowers, decorations, vases, cards, and other gifts, as well as something known as "goodwill," which in this case is Anna's reputation for preparing and delivering beautiful floral arrangements on a timely basis. **Liabilities**, on the other hand, are debts the firm owes to others. Among the liabilities of Anna's Flowers are a loan from the Small Business Administration and money owed to flower suppliers and other creditors for items purchased. The **owners' equity** category contains all of the money that has ever been contributed to the company that never has to be paid back. The funds can come from investors who have given money or assets to the company, or it can come from past profitable operations. In the case of Anna's Flowers, if Anna were to sell off, or liquidate, her business, any money left over after selling all the shop's assets and paying off its liabilities would comprise her owners' equity. The relationship among assets, liabilities, and owners' equity is a fundamental concept in accounting and is known as the **accounting equation**:

$$\text{Assets} = \text{Liabilities} + \text{Owners' equity}$$

The owners' equity portion of this florist's balance sheet includes the money she has put into the firm.

Jose Luis Pelaez Inc/Blend Images LLC

Double-Entry Bookkeeping

Double-entry bookkeeping is a system of recording and classifying business transactions in separate accounts in order to maintain the balance of the accounting equation. Returning to Anna's Flowers, suppose Anna buys $325 worth of roses on credit from the Antique Rose Emporium to fill a wedding order. When she records this transaction, she will list the $325 as a liability or a debt to a supplier. At the same time, however, she will also record $325 worth of roses as an asset in an account known as "inventory." Because the assets and liabilities are on different sides of the accounting equation, Anna's accounts increase in total size (by $325) but remain in balance:

$$\text{Assets} = \text{Liabilities} + \text{Owners'' equity}$$
$$\$325 = \$325$$

Thus, to keep the accounting equation in balance, each business transaction must be recorded in two separate accounts.

In the final analysis, all business transactions are classified as assets, liabilities, or owners' equity. However, most organizations further break down these three accounts to provide more specific information about a transaction. For example, assets may be broken down into specific categories such as cash, inventory, and equipment, while liabilities may include bank loans, supplier credit, and other debts.

Figure 14.2 shows how Anna used the double-entry bookkeeping system to account for all of the transactions that took place in her first month of business. These transactions include her initial investment of $2,500, the loan from the Small Business Administration, purchases of equipment and inventory, and the purchase of roses on credit. In her first month of business, Anna generated revenues of $2,000 by selling $1,500 worth of inventory. Thus, she deducts, or (in accounting notation that is appropriate for assets) *credits*, $1,500 from inventory and adds, or *debits*, $2,000 to the cash account. The difference between Anna's $2,000 cash inflow and her $1,500 outflow is represented by a credit to owners' equity because it is money that belongs to her as the owner of the flower shop.

The Accounting Cycle

In any accounting system, financial data typically pass through a four-step procedure sometimes called the **accounting cycle**. The steps include examining source documents, recording transactions in an accounting journal, posting recorded transactions, and preparing financial statements. Figure 14.3 shows how Anna works through them. Traditionally, all of these steps were performed using paper, pencils, and erasers (lots of erasers!), but today, the process is often fully computerized.

double-entry bookkeeping a system of recording and classifying business transactions that maintains the balance of the accounting equation.

accounting cycle the four-step procedure of an accounting system: examining source documents, recording transactions in an accounting journal, posting recorded transactions, and preparing financial statements.

▼**FIGURE 14.2** The Accounting Equation and Double-Entry Bookkeeping for Anna's Flowers

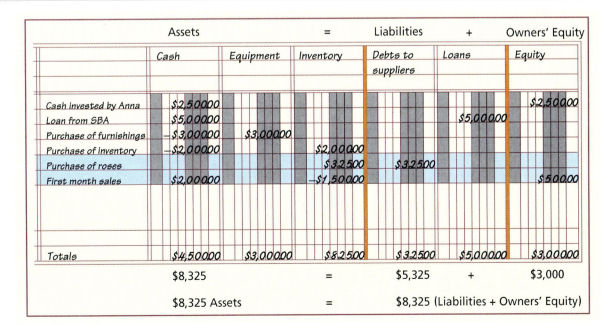

	Assets			=	Liabilities	+	Owners' Equity
	Cash	Equipment	Inventory	Debts to suppliers	Loans		Equity
Cash invested by Anna	$2,500.00						$2,500.00
Loan from SBA	$5,000.00				$5,000.00		
Purchase of furnishings	–$3,000.00	$3,000.00					
Purchase of inventory	–$2,000.00		$2,000.00				
Purchase of roses			$325.00	$325.00			
First month sales	$2,000.00		–$1,500.00				$500.00
Totals	$4,500.00	$3,000.00	$825.00	$325.00	$5,000.00		$3,000.00
	$8,325			=	$5,325	+	$3,000
	$8,325 Assets			=	$8,325 (Liabilities + Owners' Equity)		

Step 1: Source documents show that a transaction took place.

Step 2: The transaction is recorded in the journal.

Step 3: The transaction is posted to the general ledger under the appropriate account (asset, liability, or some further breakdown of these main accounts).

Step 4: At the end of the accounting period, the ledger is used to prepare the firm's financial statements.

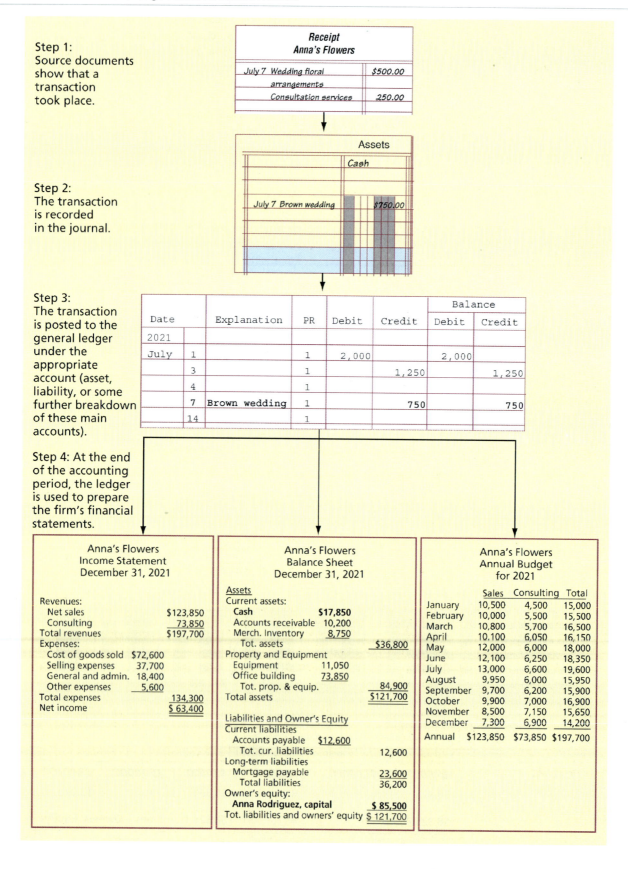

Receipt
Anna's Flowers

July 7 Wedding floral arrangements	$500.00
Consultation services	250.00

Assets

Cash

July 7 Brown wedding $750.00

Date		Explanation	PR	Debit	Credit	Balance Debit	Balance Credit
2021							
July	1		1	2,000		2,000	
	3		1		1,250		1,250
	4		1				
	7	Brown wedding	1		750		750
	14		1				

Anna's Flowers
Income Statement
December 31, 2021

Revenues:		
Net sales		$123,850
Consulting		73,850
Total revenues		$197,700
Expenses:		
Cost of goods sold	$72,600	
Selling expenses	37,700	
General and admin.	18,400	
Other expenses	5,600	
Total expenses		134,300
Net income		$ 63,400

Anna's Flowers
Balance Sheet
December 31, 2021

Assets
Current assets:

Cash	**$17,850**	
Accounts receivable	10,200	
Merch. Inventory	8,750	
Tot. assets		$36,800

Property and Equipment

Equipment	11,050	
Office building	73,850	
Tot. prop. & equip.		84,900
Total assets		$121,700

Liabilities and Owner's Equity
Current liabilities

Accounts payable	$12,600	
Tot. cur. liabilities		12,600

Long-term liabilities

Mortgage payable		23,600
Total liabilities		36,200

Owner's equity:

Anna Rodriguez, capital	**$ 85,500**
Tot. liabilities and owners' equity	$ 121,700

Anna's Flowers
Annual Budget
for 2021

	Sales	Consulting	Total
January	10,500	4,500	15,000
February	10,000	5,500	15,500
March	10,800	5,700	16,500
April	10,100	6,050	16,150
May	12,000	6,000	18,000
June	12,100	6,250	18,350
July	13,000	6,600	19,600
August	9,950	6,000	15,950
September	9,700	6,200	15,900
October	9,900	7,000	16,900
November	8,500	7,150	15,650
December	7,300	6,900	14,200
Annual	$123,850	$73,850	$197,700

Step One: Examine Source Documents. Like all good managers, Anna Rodriguez begins the accounting cycle by gathering and examining source documents—checks, credit card receipts, sales slips, and other related evidence concerning specific transactions.

Step Two: Record Transactions. Next, Anna records each financial transaction in a **journal**, which is basically just a time-ordered list of account transactions. While most businesses keep a general journal in which all transactions are recorded, some classify transactions into specialized journals for specific types of transaction accounts.

Step Three: Post Transactions. Anna next transfers the information from her journal into a **ledger**, a book or computer program with separate files for each account. This process is known as *posting.* At the end of the accounting period (usually yearly, but occasionally quarterly or monthly), Anna prepares a *trial balance*, a summary of the balances of all the accounts in the general ledger. If, upon totaling, the trial balance doesn't balance (that is, the accounting equation is not in balance), Anna or her accountant must look for mistakes (typically an error in one or more of the ledger entries) and correct them. If the trial balance is correct, the accountant can then begin to prepare the financial statements.

Step Four: Prepare Financial Statements. The information from the trial balance is also used to prepare the company's financial statements. In the case of public corporations and certain other organizations, a CPA must *attest*, or certify, that the organization followed generally accepted accounting principles in preparing the financial statements. When these statements have been completed, the organization's books are "closed," and the accounting cycle begins anew for the next accounting period.

FINANCIAL STATEMENTS

The end result of the accounting process is a series of financial statements. The income statement, the balance sheet, and the statement of cash flows are the best-known examples of financial statements. They are provided to stockholders and potential investors in a firm's annual report as well as to other relevant outsiders such as creditors, government agencies, and the Internal Revenue Service.

It is important to recognize that not all financial statements follow precisely the same format. The fact that different organizations generate income in different ways suggests that when it comes to financial statements, one size definitely does not fit all. Manufacturing firms, service providers, and nonprofit organizations each use a different set of accounting principles

or rules upon which the public accounting profession has agreed. As we have already mentioned, these are sometimes referred to as *generally accepted accounting principles (GAAP).* Each country has a different set of rules that the businesses within that country are required to use for their accounting process and financial statements. However, a number of countries have adopted a standard set of accounting principles known as International Financial Reporting Standards. The United States has discussed adopting these standards to create a more standardized system of reporting for global investors. Moreover, as is the case in many other disciplines, certain concepts have more than one name. For example, *sales* and *revenues* are often interchanged, as are *profits*, *income*, and *earnings.* Table 14.2 lists a few common equivalent terms that should help you decipher their meaning in accounting statements.

journal a time-ordered list of account transactions.

ledger a book or computer file with separate sections for each account.

income statement a financial report that shows an organization's profitability over a period of time—month, quarter, or year.

LO 14-3 Examine the various components of an income statement in order to evaluate a firm's "bottom line."

The Income Statement

The question, "What's the bottom line?" derives from the income statement, where the bottom line shows the overall profit or loss of the company after taxes. Thus, the **income statement** is a financial report that shows an organization's profitability over

▼ **TABLE 14.2** Equivalent Terms in Accounting

Term	Equivalent Term
Revenues	Sales
	Goods or services sold
Gross profit	Gross income
	Gross earnings
Operating income	Operating profit
	Earnings before interest and taxes (EBIT)
	Income before interest and taxes (IBIT)
Income before taxes (IBT)	Earnings before taxes (EBT) Profit before taxes (PBT)
Net income (NI)	Earnings after taxes (EAT)
	Profit after taxes (PAT)
Income available to common stockholders	Earnings available to common stockholders

revenue the total amount of money received from the sale of goods or services, as well as from related business activities.

cost of goods sold the amount of money a firm spent to buy or produce the products it sold during the period to which the income statement applies.

a period of time, be that a month, quarter, or year. By its very design, the income statement offers one of the clearest possible pictures of the company's overall revenues and the costs incurred in generating those revenues. Other names for the income statement include profit and loss (P&L) statement or operating statement. A sample income statement in word form with line-by-line explanations is presented in Table 14.3, while Table 14.4 presents recent income statements of Nvidia. The income statement indicates the firm's profitability or income (the bottom line), which is derived by subtracting the firm's expenses from its revenues.

Revenue. **Revenue** is the total amount of money received (or promised) from the sale of goods or services, as well as from other business activities such as the rental of property and investments. Nonbusiness entities typically obtain revenues through donations from individuals and/or grants from governments and private foundations. One of the controversies in accounting has been when a business should recognize revenue. For instance, should an organization book revenue during a project or after the project is completed? Differences in revenue recognition have caused similar organizations to book different accounting results. Generally accepted practice is that firms should book revenue when "it satisfies a performance obligation by transferring a promised good or service to a customer."[4]

For most manufacturing and retail concerns, the next major item included in the income statement is the **cost of goods sold**, the amount of money the firm spent (or promised to

▼ **TABLE 14.3** Sample Income Statement

Company Name for the Year Ended December 31	
Revenues (sales)	Total dollar amount of products sold (includes income from other business services such as rental-lease income and interest income).
Less: Cost of goods sold	The cost of producing the goods and services, including the cost of labor and raw materials as well as other expenses associated with production.
Gross profit	The income available after paying all expenses of production.
Less: Selling and administrative expense	The cost of promoting, advertising, and selling products as well as the overhead costs of managing the company. This includes the cost of management and corporate staff. One noncash expense included in this category is depreciation, which approximates the decline in the value of plant and equipment assets due to use over time. In most accounting statements, depreciation is not separated from selling and administrative expenses. However, financial analysts usually create statements that include this expense.
Income before interest and taxes (operating income or EBIT)	This line represents all income left over after operating expenses have been deducted. This is sometimes referred to as operating income because it represents all income after the expenses of operations have been accounted for. Occasionally, this is referred to as EBIT, or earnings before interest and taxes.
Less: Interest expense	Interest expense arises as a cost of borrowing money. This is a financial expense rather than an operating expense and is listed separately. As the amount of debt and the cost of debt increase, so will the interest expense. This covers the cost of both short-term and long-term borrowing.
Income before taxes (earnings before taxes—EBT)	The firm will pay a tax on this amount. This is what is left of revenues after subtracting all operating costs, depreciation costs, and interest costs.
Less: Taxes	The tax rate is specified in the federal tax code.
Net income	This is the amount of income left after taxes. The firm may decide to retain all or a portion of the income for reinvestment in new assets. Whatever it decides not to keep will usually be paid out in dividends to its stockholders.
Less: Preferred dividends	If the company has preferred stockholders, they are first in line for dividends. That is one reason their stock is called "preferred."
Income to common stockholders	This is the income left for the common stockholders. If the company has a good year, there may be a lot of income available for dividends. If the company has a bad year, income could be negative. The common stockholders are the ultimate owners and risk takers. They have the potential for very high or very poor returns because they get whatever is left after all other expenses.
Earnings per share	Earnings per share is found by taking the income available to the common stockholders and dividing by the number of shares of common stock outstanding. This is income generated by the company for each share of common stock.

gross income revenues minus the cost of goods sold required to generate the revenues.

profit the difference between what it costs to make and sell a product and what a customer pays for it.

expenses the costs incurred in the day-to-day operations of an organization.

depreciation the process of spreading the costs of long-lived assets such as buildings and equipment over the total number of accounting periods in which they are expected to be used.

spend) to buy and/or produce the products it sold during the accounting period. This figure may be calculated as follows:

Cost of goods sold = Beginning inventory + Interim purchases − Ending inventory

Let's say that Anna's Flowers began an accounting period with an inventory of goods for which it paid $5,000. During the period, Anna bought another $4,000 worth of goods, giving the shop a total inventory available for sale of $9,000. If, at the end of the accounting period, Anna's inventory was worth $5,500, the cost of goods sold during the period would have been $3,500

($5,000 + $4,000 − $5,500 = $3,500). If Anna had total revenues of $10,000 over the same period of time, subtracting the cost of goods sold ($3,500) from the total revenues of $10,000 yields the store's **gross income** or **profit** (revenues minus the cost of goods sold required to generate the revenues): $6,500. In the case of Nvidia shown in Table 14.4, the company bundles "the cost of goods sold" with sales, general and administrative costs, so it is not an item they wish to highlight.

Expenses. **Expenses** are the costs incurred in the day-to-day operations of an organization. Three common expense accounts shown on income statements are (1) selling, general, and administrative expenses; (2) research, development, and engineering expenses; and (3) interest expenses (remember that the costs directly attributable to selling goods or services are included in the cost of goods sold). Selling expenses include advertising and sales salaries. General and administrative expenses include salaries of executives and their staff and the costs of owning and maintaining the general office. Research and development costs include scientific, engineering, and marketing personnel and the equipment and information used to design and build prototypes and samples. Interest expenses include the direct costs of borrowing money.

The number and type of expense accounts vary from organization to organization. Included in the general and administrative category is a special type of expense known as **depreciation**, the process of spreading the costs of long-lived assets such as buildings and equipment over the total number of accounting periods in which they are expected to be used. Consider a manufacturer that purchases a $100,000 machine expected to last about 10 years. Rather than showing an expense of $100,000 in the first year and no expense for that equipment over the next nine years, the manufacturer is allowed to report depreciation expenses of $10,000 per year in each of the next 10 years because that better matches the cost of the machine to the years the machine is used. Each time this depreciation is "written off" as an expense, the book value of the machine is also reduced by $10,000.

▼ **TABLE 14.4** Nvidia Corporation and Subsidiaries Consolidated Statements of Income (in millions, except per share data)

	Year Ended		
	January 26, 2020	January 27, 2019	January 28, 2018
Revenue	$10,918	$11,716	$9,714
Cost of revenue	4,150	4,545	3,892
Gross profit	6,768	7,171	5,822
Operating expenses			
Research and developement	2,829	2,376	1,797
Sales, general and administrative	1,093	991	815
Total operating expenses	3,922	3,367	2,612
Income from operations	2,846	3,804	3,210
Interest income	178	136	69
Interest expense	(52)	(58)	(61)
Other, net	(2)	14	(22)
Total other income (expense)	124	92	(14)
Income before income tax	2,970	3,896	3,196
Income tax expense (benefit)	174	(245)	149
Net income	$ 2,796	$ 4,141	$3,047
Net income per share			
Basic	$ 4.59	$ 6.81	$ 5.09
Diluted	$ 4.52	$ 6.63	$ 4.82
Weighted average shares used in per share computation:			
Basic	609	608	599
Diluted	618	625	632

net income the total profit (or loss) after all expenses, including taxes, have been deducted from revenue; also called net earnings.

balance sheet a "snapshot" of an organization's financial position at a given moment.

The fact that the equipment has a zero value on the firm's balance sheet when it is fully depreciated (in this case, after 10 years) does not necessarily mean that it can no longer be used or is economically worthless. Indeed, in some industries, machines used every day have been reported as having no book value whatsoever for more than 30 years.

Net Income. **Net income** (or net earnings) is the total profit (or loss) after all expenses, including taxes, have been deducted from revenue. Generally, accountants divide profits into individual sections such as operating income and earnings before interest and taxes. Like most companies, Nvidia presents not only the current year's results, but also the previous two years' income statements to permit comparison of performance from one period to another.

Net income is very sensitive to the corporate tax rate, and in 2017, Congress implemented the Tax Cut and Jobs Act which became effective in 2018. The United States switched to a territorial tax system consistent with most developed countries so that income is taxed in the country where it was earned. For example, income generated in France is taxed at the French tax rate and not the U.S. rate. The law also reduced the statutory rate on corporate income from 35 percent to 21 percent which made it more comparable to rates in most developed countries.

Temporary Nature of the Income Statement Accounts. Companies record their operational activities in the revenue and expense accounts during an accounting period. Gross profit, earnings before interest and taxes, and net income are the results of calculations made from the revenues and expenses accounts; they are not actual accounts. At the end of each accounting period, the dollar amounts in all the revenue and expense accounts are moved into an account called "Retained Earnings," one of the owners' equity accounts. Revenues increase owners' equity, while expenses decrease it. The resulting change in the owners' equity account is exactly equal to the net income. This shifting of dollar values from the revenue and expense accounts allows the firm to begin the next accounting period with zero balances in those accounts. Zeroing out the balances enables a company to count how much it has sold and how many expenses have been incurred during a period of time. The basic accounting equation (Assets = Liabilities + Owners' equity) will not balance until the revenue and expense account balances have been moved or "closed out" to the owners' equity account.

One final note about income statements: You may remember that corporations may choose to make cash payments called

Walmart is the largest company in the United States, with more than $524 billion in revenue.

Quality HD/Shutterstock

dividends to shareholders out of their net earnings. When a corporation elects to pay dividends, it decreases the cash account (in the assets category of the balance sheet) as well as a capital account (in the owners' equity category of the balance sheet). During any period of time, the owners' equity account may change because of the sale of stock (or contributions/withdrawals by owners), the net income or loss, or the dividends paid.

LO 14-4 Interpret a company's balance sheet to determine its current financial position.

The Balance Sheet

The second basic financial statement is the **balance sheet**, which presents a "snapshot" of an organization's financial position at a given moment. As such, the balance sheet indicates what the organization owns or controls and the various sources of the funds used to pay for these assets, such as bank debt or owners' equity.

The balance sheet takes its name from its reliance on the accounting equation: Assets *must* equal liabilities plus owners' equity. Table 14.5 provides a sample balance sheet in word form with line-by-line explanations. Unlike the income statement, the balance sheet does not represent the result of transactions completed over a specified accounting period. Instead, the balance sheet is, by definition, an accumulation of all financial transactions conducted by an organization since its founding. Following long-established traditions, items on the balance sheet are listed on the basis of their original cost less accumulated depreciation, rather than their present values.

Typical Company	December 31
Assets	This is the major category for all physical, monetary, or intangible goods that have some dollar value.
Current assets	Assets that are either cash or are expected to be turned into cash within the next 12 months.
Cash	Cash or checking accounts.
Marketable securities	Short-term investments in securities that can be converted to cash quickly (liquid assets).
Accounts receivable	Cash due from customers in payment for goods received. These arise from sales made on credit.
Inventory	Finished goods ready for sale, goods in the process of being finished, or raw materials used in the production of goods.
Prepaid expense	A future expense item that has already been paid, such as insurance premiums or rent.
Total current assets	The sum of the above accounts.
Fixed assets	Assets that are long term in nature and have a minimum life expectancy that exceeds one year.
Investments	Assets held as investments rather than assets owned for the production process. Most often, the assets include small ownership interests in other companies.
Gross property, plant, and equipment	Land, buildings, and other fixed assets listed at original cost.
Less: Accumulated depreciation	The accumulated expense deductions applied to all plant and equipment over their life. Land may not be depreciated. The total amount represents, in general, the decline in value as equipment gets older and wears out. The maximum amount that can be deducted is set by the U.S. Federal Tax Code and varies by type of asset.
Net property, plant, and equipment	Gross property, plant, and equipment minus the accumulated depreciation. This amount reflects the book value of the fixed assets and not their value if sold.
Other assets	Any other asset that is long term and does not fit into the preceding categories. It could be patents or trademarks.
Total fixed assets	The sum of the above accounts.
Total assets	The sum of all the asset values.
Liabilities and stockholders' equity	This is the major category. Liabilities refer to all indebtedness and loans of both a long-term and short-term nature. Stockholders' equity refers to all money that has been contributed to the company over the life of the firm by the owners.
Current liabilities	Short-term debt expected to be paid off within the next 12 months.
Accounts payable	Money owed to suppliers for goods ordered. Firms usually have between 30 and 90 days to pay this account, depending on industry norms.
Wages payable	Money owed to employees for hours worked or salary. If workers receive checks every two weeks, the amount owed should be no more than two weeks' pay.
Taxes payable	Firms are required to pay corporate taxes quarterly. This refers to taxes owed based on earnings estimates for the quarter.
Notes payable	Short-term loans from banks or other lenders.
Other current liabilities	The other short-term debts that do not fit into the preceding categories.
Total current liabilities	The sum of the preceding accounts.
Long-term liabilities	All long-term debt that will not be paid off in the next 12 months.
Long-term debt	Loans of more than one year from banks, pension funds, insurance companies, or other lenders. These loans often take the form of bonds, which are securities that may be bought and sold in bond markets.
Deferred income taxes	This is a liability owed to the government but not due within one year.
Other long-term liabilities	Any other long-term debt that does not fit the preceding two categories.
Total long-term liabilities	The sum of the preceding accounts.
Total liabilities	The sum of all liability values.

(Continued)

Typical Company	December 31
Stockholders' equity	The following three categories are the owners' investment in the company.
Common stock	The tangible evidence of ownership is a security called common stock. The par value is stated value and does not indicate the company's worth.
Capital in excess of par (a.k.a. contributed capital)	When shares of stock were sold to the owners, they were recorded at the price at the time of the original sale. If the price paid was $10 per share, the extra $9 per share would show up in this account at 100,000 shares times $9 per share, or $900,000.
Retained earnings	The total amount of earnings the company has made during its life and not paid out to its stockholders as dividends. This account represents the owners' reinvestment of earnings into company assets rather than payments of cash dividends. This account does not represent cash.
Total stockholders' equity	This is the sum of the preceding equity accounts representing the owners' total investment in the company.
Total liabilities and stockholders' equity	The total short-term and long-term debt of the company plus the owners' total investment. This combined amount *must* equal total assets.

current assets assets that are used or converted into cash within the course of a calendar year; also called short-term assets.

accounts receivable money owed a company by its clients or customers who have promised to pay for the products at a later date.

current liabilities a firm's financial obligations to short-term creditors, which must be repaid within one year.

accounts payable the amount a company owes to suppliers for goods and services purchased with credit.

accrued expenses all unpaid financial obligations incurred by an organization.

Balance sheets are often presented in two different formats. The traditional balance sheet format placed the organization's assets on the left side and its liabilities and owners' equity on the right. More recently, a vertical format, with assets on top followed by liabilities and owners' equity, has gained wide acceptance. Nvidia's balance sheet is presented in Table 14.6. In the sections that follow, we'll briefly describe the basic items found on the balance sheet; we'll take a closer look at a number of these in the "Financial Management and Securities Markets" chapter.

Assets. All asset accounts are listed in descending order of *liquidity*—that is, how quickly each could be turned into cash. **Current assets**, also called short-term assets, are those that are used or converted into cash within the course of a calendar year. Cash is followed by temporary investments, accounts receivable, and inventory, in that order. **Accounts receivable** refers to money owed the company by its clients or customers who have promised to pay for the products at a later date. Accounts receivable usually includes an allowance for bad debts that management does not expect to collect. The bad-debts adjustment is normally based on historical collections experience and is deducted from the accounts receivable balance to present a more realistic view of the payments likely to be received in the future, called net receivables. Inventory may be

held in the form of raw materials, work-in-progress, or finished goods ready for delivery.

Long-term or fixed assets represent a commitment of organizational funds of at least one year. Items classified as fixed include long-term investments, such as plants and equipment, and intangible assets, such as corporate "goodwill," or reputation, as well as patents and trademarks.

Liabilities. As seen in the accounting equation, total assets must be financed either through borrowing (liabilities) or through owner investments (owners' equity). **Current liabilities** include a firm's financial obligations to short-term creditors, which must be repaid within one year, while long-term liabilities have longer repayment terms. **Accounts payable** represents amounts owed to suppliers for goods and services purchased with credit. For example, if you buy gas with a Shell credit card, the purchase represents an account payable for you (and an account receivable for Shell). Other liabilities include wages earned by employees but not yet paid and taxes owed to the government. Occasionally, these accounts are consolidated into an **accrued expenses** account, representing all unpaid financial obligations incurred by the organization.

Owners' Equity. Owners' equity includes the owners' contributions to the organization along with income earned by the organization and retained to finance continued growth and development. If the organization were to sell off all of its assets and pay off all of its liabilities, any remaining funds would belong to the owners. Not surprisingly, the accounts listed as owners' equity on a balance sheet may differ dramatically from company to company. Corporations sell stock to investors, who then become the owners of the firm. Many corporations issue two, three, or even more different classes of common and preferred stock, each with different dividend payments and/or voting rights. Google has three classes of stock, with the class B stock having more voting rights than class A shares. These are

▼ TABLE 14.6 NVIDIA Corporation and Subsidiaries Consolidated Balance Sheets (in millions, except par value)

	January 26, 2020	January 27, 2019
Assets		
Current assets:		
Cash and cash equivalents	$10, 896	$ 782
Marketable securities	1	6,640
Accounts receivable, net	1,657	1,424
Inventories	979	1,575
Prepaid expenses and other current assets	157	136
Total current assets	13,690	10,557
Property and equipment, net	1,674	1,404
Operating lease assets	618	—
Goodwill	618	618
Intangible assets, net	49	45
Deferred income tax assets	548	560
Other assets	118	108
Total assets	$ 17,315	$13,292
Liabilities and shareholders' equity		
Current liabilities:		
Accounts payable	$ 687	$ 511
Accrued and other current liabilities	1,097	818
Total current liabilities	1,784	1,329
Long-term debt	1,991	1,988
Long-term operating lease liabilities	561	—
Other long-term liabilities	775	633
Total liabilities	5,111	3,950
Commitments and contingencies		
Shareholders' equity:		
Preferred stock, $.001 par value; 2 shares authorized; none issued	—	—
Common stock, $.001 par value; 2,000 shares authorized; 955 shares issued and 612 outstanding as of January 26, 2020; 945 shares issued and 606 outstanding as of January 27, 2019	1	1
Additional paid-in capital	7,045	6,051
Treasury stock, at cost (342 shares in 2020 and 339 shares in 2019)	(9,814)	(9,263)
Accumulated other comprehensive income (loss)	1	(12)
Retained earnings	14,971	12,565
Total shareholders' equity	12,204	9,342
Total liabilities and shareholders' equity	$ 17,315	$13,292

sometimes called founder's shares and allow the founders to maintain control over the company even though they do not own the majority of the shares. Ford Motor has the same type of voting structure. Because each type of stock issued represents a different claim on the organization, each must be represented by a separate owners' equity account, called contributed capital.

The Statement of Cash Flows

The third primary financial statement is called the **statement of cash flows**, which explains how the company's cash changed from the beginning of the accounting period to the end. Cash, of course, is an asset shown on the balance sheet, which provides a snapshot of the firm's financial position at one point in time. However, many investors and other users of financial statements want more information about the cash flowing into and out of the firm than is provided on the balance sheet in order to better understand the company's financial health. The statement of cash flows takes the cash balance from one year's balance sheet and compares it with the next while providing detail about how the firm used the cash. Table 14.7 presents Nvidia statement of cash flows.

The change in cash is explained through details in three categories: cash from (used for) operating activities, cash from (used

for) financing activities, and cash from (used for) investing activities.

Cash from operating activities is calculated by combining the changes in the revenue accounts, expense accounts, current asset accounts, and current liability accounts. This category of cash flows includes all the accounts on the balance sheet that relate to computing revenues and expenses for the accounting period. If this amount is a positive number, as it is for Nvidia, then the business is making extra cash that it can use to invest in increased long-term capacity or to pay off debts such as loans or bonds.

Cash from investing activities is calculated from changes in the long-term or fixed asset accounts. If this amount is negative, as is the case with Nvidia, we can see that the company bought $489 million of property and equipment. It also purchased $1.461 billion of marketable securities and sold $3.365 billion of investments and had $4.744 billion of investments mature for a total positive cash flow of $6.145 billion.

Cash from financing activities is calculated from changes in the long-term liability accounts and the contributed capital accounts in owners' equity. If this amount is negative, the company is likely paying off long-term debt or returning contributed capital to investors. In the case of Nvidia, it paid dividends of $390 million, received $149 million from employees purchasing stock through employee plans, and it paid taxes of $551 million on restricted stock distributed to employees.

▼ **TABLE 14.7** NVIDIA Corporation and Subsidiaries Consolidated Statements of Cash Flows (in millions)

	Year Ended		
	January 26, 2020	January 27, 2019	January 28, 2018
Cash flows from operating activities:			
Net income	$2,796	$4,141	$3,047
Adjustments to reconcile net income to net cash provided by operating activities:			
Stock-based compensation expense	844	557	391
Depreciation and amortization	381	262	199
Deferred income taxes	18	(315)	(359)
Loss on early debt conversions	—	—	19
Other	5	(45)	20
Changes in operating assets and liabilities:			
Accounts receivable	(233)	(149)	(440)
Inventories	597	(776)	—
Prepaid expenses and other assets	77	(55)	21
Accounts payable	194	(135)	90
Accrued and other current liabilities	54	256	33
Other long-term liabilities	28	2	481
Net cash provided by operating activities	4,761	3,743	3,502

(Continued)

	Year Ended		
	January 26, 2020	**January 27, 2019**	**January 28, 2018**
Cash flows from investing activities:			
Proceeds from maturities of marketable securities	4,744	7,232	1,078
Proceeds from sales of marketable securities	3,365	428	863
Purchases of marketable securities	(1,461)	(11,148)	(36)
Purchases of property and equipment and intangible assets	(489)	(600)	(593)
Investments and other, net	(14)	(9)	(36)
Proceeds from sale of long-lived assets and investments	–	–	2
Net cash provided by (used in) investing activities	6,145	(4,097)	1,278
Cash flows from financing activities:			
Payments related to repurchases of common stock	–	(1,579)	(909)
Repayment of Convertible Notes	–	(16)	(812)
Dividends paid	(390)	(371)	(341)
Proceeds related to employee stock plans	149	137	139
Payments related to tax on restricted stock units	(551)	(1,032)	(612)
Other	–	(5)	(9)
Net cash used in financing activities	(792)	(2,866)	(2,544)
Change in cash and cash equivalents	10,114	(3,220)	2,236
Cash and cash equivalents at beginning of period	782	4,002	1,766
Cash and cash equivalents at end of period	$10,896	$ 782	$4,002

LO 14-5 Analyze financial statements, using ratio analysis, to evaluate a company's performance.

RATIO ANALYSIS: ANALYZING FINANCIAL STATEMENTS

The income statement shows a company's profit or loss, while the balance sheet itemizes the value of its assets, liabilities, and owners' equity. Together, the two statements provide the means to answer two critical questions: (1) How much did the firm make or lose? and (2) How much is the firm presently worth based on historical values found on the balance sheet? **Ratio analysis**, calculations that measure an organization's financial health, brings the complex information from the income statement and balance sheet into sharper focus so that managers, lenders, owners, and other interested parties can measure and compare the organization's productivity, profitability, and financing mix with other similar entities.

As you know, a ratio is simply one number divided by another, with the result showing the relationship between the two numbers. For example, we measure fuel efficiency with miles per gallon. This is how we know that 55 mpg in a Toyota Prius is much better than the average car. We use ratios in all sports, such as earned run and batting averages in baseball, field goal percentage in basketball, and percentage of passes completed in football. But, to make sense out of ratios, you have to know what you want to measure. Financial ratios are used to weigh and evaluate a firm's performance. An absolute value such as earnings of $70,000 or accounts receivable of $200,000 almost never provides as much useful information as a well-constructed ratio. Whether those numbers are good or bad depends on their relation to other numbers. If a company earned $70,000 on $700,000 in sales (a 10 percent return), such an earnings level might be quite satisfactory. The president of a company earning this same $70,000 on sales of $7 million (a 1 percent return), however, should probably start looking for another job!

ratio analysis calculations that measure an organization's financial health.

profitability ratios ratios that measure the amount of operating income or net income an organization is able to generate relative to its assets, owners' equity, and sales.

profit margin net income divided by sales.

return on assets net income divided by assets.

return on equity net income divided by owners' equity; also called return on investment (ROI).

asset utilization ratios ratios that measure how well a firm uses its assets to generate each $1 of sales.

receivables turnover sales divided by accounts receivable.

inventory turnover sales divided by total inventory.

Ratios by themselves are not very useful. What matters is the relationship of the calculated ratios to the previous years performance, comparison to its competitors and the company's stated goals. Remember, while the profitability, asset utilization, liquidity, debt ratios, and per share data we'll look at here can be very useful, you will never see the forest by looking only at the trees.

Profitability Ratios

Profitability ratios measure how much operating income or net income an organization is able to generate relative to its assets, owners' equity, and sales. The numerator (top number) used in these examples is always the net income after taxes. Common profitability ratios include profit margin, return on assets, and return on equity. The following examples are based on the 2020 income statement and balance sheet for Nvidia, as shown in Tables 14.4 and 14.6. Except where specified, all data are expressed in millions of dollars.

The **profit margin**, computed by dividing net income by sales, shows the overall percentage of profits earned by the company. It is based solely upon data obtained from the income statement. The higher the profit margin, the better the cost controls within the company and the higher the return on every dollar of revenue. Nvidia's profit margin is calculated as follows:

$$\text{Profit margin} = \frac{\text{Net income}}{\text{Sales}}$$
$$= \frac{\$2,796}{\$10,918}$$
$$= 25.61\%$$

Thus, for every $1 in sales, Nvidia generated profits after taxes of slightly more than 25 cents.

Return on assets, net income divided by assets, shows how much income the firm produces for every dollar invested in assets. A company with a low return on assets is probably not using its assets very productively—a key managerial failing. For

> **Stockholders are always concerned with how much money they will make on their investment, and they frequently use the return on equity ratio as one of their key performance yardsticks.**

its computation, the return on assets calculation requires data from both the income statement and the balance sheet.

$$\text{Return on assets} = \frac{\text{Net income}}{\text{Total assets}}$$
$$= \frac{\$2,796}{\$17,315}$$
$$= 16.15\%$$

In the case of Nvidia, every $1 of assets generated a return of 16.15 percent, or profits of 16.15 cents per dollar.

Stockholders are always concerned with how much money they will make on their investment, and they frequently use the return on equity ratio as one of their key performance yardsticks. **Return on equity** (also called return on investment [ROI]), calculated by dividing net income by owners' equity, shows how much income is generated by each $1 the owners have invested in the firm. Obviously, a low return on equity means low stockholder returns and may indicate a need for immediate managerial attention. Because some assets may have been financed with debt not contributed by the owners, the value of the owners' equity is usually considerably lower than the total value of the firm's assets. Nvidia's return on equity is calculated as follows:

$$\text{Return on equity} = \frac{\text{Net income}}{\text{Stockholders' equity}}$$
$$= \frac{\$2,796}{\$12,204}$$
$$= 22.91\%$$

For every dollar invested by Nvidia stockholders, the company earned a 22.91 percent return, or 22.91 cents per dollar invested.

Asset Utilization Ratios

Asset utilization ratios measure how well a firm uses its assets to generate each $1 of sales. Obviously, companies using their assets more productively will have higher returns on assets than their less efficient competitors. Similarly, managers can use asset utilization ratios to pinpoint areas of inefficiency in their operations. These ratios (receivables turnover, inventory turnover, and total asset turnover) relate balance sheet assets to sales, which are found on the income statement.

The **receivables turnover**, sales divided by accounts receivable, indicates how many times a firm collects its accounts receivable in one year. It also demonstrates how quickly a firm is able to collect payments on its credit sales. Obviously, no payments means no profits. Nvidia collected its receivables 6.59 times per year, which translates to about 55 days that receivables are outstanding. These ratios are based on a 360 day year. This is most likely due to the trade terms it gives its corporate customers.

$$\text{Receivables turnover} = \frac{\text{Sales}}{\text{Receivables}}$$

$$= \frac{\$10{,}918}{\$1{,}657}$$

$$= 6.59 \text{ times per year}$$

Inventory turnover, sales divided by total inventory, indicates how many times a firm sells and replaces its inventory over the course of a year. A high inventory turnover ratio may indicate great efficiency but may also suggest the possibility of lost sales due to insufficient stock levels. Nvidia's inventory turnover indicates that it replaced its inventory 11.15 times last year, or about every 32 days.

$$\text{Inventory turnover} = \frac{\text{Sales}}{\text{Inventory}}$$

$$= \frac{\$10{,}918}{\$979}$$

$$= 11.15 \text{ times per year}$$

Accountants often like to calculate inventory turnover using cost of goods sold in the numerator because inventory is carried on the books at cost and so is cost of goods sold. Financial analysts prefer sales in the numerator to measure the efficiency of inventory in producing revenues. Nvidia makes very expensive high-end computer chips that power video games and powerful servers used in cloud operations. Their inventory turnover is quite good.

Total asset turnover, sales divided by total assets, measures how well an organization uses all of its assets in creating sales. It indicates whether a company is using its assets productively. Nvidia generated $0.63 in sales for every $1 in total corporate assets. The cause of this low total asset turnover is the large cash balance that Nvidia has on its balance sheet. Cash does not produce sales income. At the end of the fiscal year more than 62 percent of its assets were held in cash or cash equivalents.

$$\text{Total asset turnover} = \frac{\text{Sales}}{\text{Total assets}}$$

$$= \frac{\$10{,}918}{\$17{,}315}$$

$$= 0.63 \text{ times per year}$$

Liquidity Ratios

Liquidity ratios compare current (short-term) assets to current liabilities to indicate the speed with which a company can turn its assets into cash to meet debts as they fall due. High liquidity ratios may satisfy a creditor's need for safety, but ratios that are too high may indicate that the organization is not using its current assets efficiently. Liquidity ratios are generally best examined in conjunction with asset utilization ratios because high turnover ratios imply that cash is flowing through an organization very quickly—a situation that dramatically reduces the need for the type of reserves measured by liquidity ratios.

The **current ratio** is calculated by dividing current assets by current liabilities. Nvidia's current ratio indicates that for every $1 of current liabilities, the firm had $7.67 of current assets on hand. This very high current ratio is also due to the $10.896 billion of cash, and cash equivalents, on hand, which is part of the current asset total.

$$\text{Current ratio} = \frac{\text{Current assets}}{\text{Current liabilities}}$$

$$= \frac{\$13{,}690}{\$1{,}784}$$

$$= 7.67 \text{ times}$$

The **quick ratio** (also known as the **acid test**) is a far more stringent measure of liquidity because it eliminates inventory, the least liquid current asset. It measures how well an organization can meet its current obligations without resorting to the sale of its inventory. Because Nvidia carries a small amount of inventory, the quick ratio at 7.13 times is almost the same as the current ratio.

$$\text{Quick ratio} = \frac{\text{Current assets} - \text{Inventory}}{\text{Current liabilities}}$$

$$= \frac{\$13{,}690 - \$979}{\$1{,}784}$$

$$= 7.13 \text{ times}$$

Debt Utilization Ratios

Debt utilization ratios provide information about how much debt an organization is using relative to other sources of capital, such as owners' equity. Because the use of debt carries an interest charge that must be paid regularly regardless of profitability, debt financing is much riskier than equity. Unforeseen negative events such as recessions affect heavily indebted firms to a far greater extent than those financed exclusively with

debt to total assets ratio a ratio indicating how much of the firm is financed by debt and how much by owners' equity.

times interest earned ratio operating income divided by interest expense.

per share data data used by investors to compare the performance of one company with another on an equal, per share, basis.

earnings per share net income or profit divided by the number of stock shares outstanding.

dividends per share the actual cash received for each share owned.

owners' equity. Because of this and other factors, the managers of most firms tend to keep debt-to-asset levels below 50 percent. However, firms in very stable and/or regulated industries, such as electric utilities, often are able to carry debt ratios well in excess of 50 percent with no ill effects.

The **debt to total assets ratio** indicates how much of the firm is financed by debt and how much by owners' equity. To find the value of Nvidia's total debt, you must add current liabilities to long-term debt and other liabilities or simply subtract stockholders' equity from total assets.

$$\text{Debt to total assets} = \frac{\text{Debt (Assets} - \text{Equity)}}{\text{Total assets}}$$

$$= \frac{\$17,315 - \$12,204}{\$17,315}$$

$$= 30\%$$

Thus, for every $1 of Nvidia's total assets, 30 percent is financed with debt. The remaining 70 percent is provided by owners' equity.

The **times interest earned ratio**, operating income divided by interest expense, is a measure of the safety margin a company has with respect to the interest payments it must make to its creditors. A low times interest earned ratio indicates that even a small decrease in earnings may lead the company into financial straits. We find that interest expense on the income statement was 52 million and that it has gone down by a small amount over the last several years. Putting this into the calculation, we find that interest expense is covered 54.73 times by operating income. This is a very high number which shows that Nvidia would have no problem paying its interest on its debt. In fact lenders would be happy to loan Nvidia money.

$$\text{Times interest earned} = \frac{\text{Income before interest and taxes}}{\text{Interest}}$$

$$= \frac{\$2,846}{\$52}$$

$$= 54.73 \text{ times}$$

Per Share Data

Investors may use **per share data** to compare the performance of one company with another on an equal, or per share, basis. Generally, the more shares of stock a company issues, the less income is available for each share.

Earnings per share is calculated by dividing net income or profit by the number of shares of stock outstanding. This ratio is important because yearly changes in earnings per share, in combination with other economy-wide factors, determine

a company's overall stock price. When earnings go up, so does a company's stock price—and so does the wealth of its stockholders.

$$\text{Diluted earnings per share} = \frac{\text{Net income}}{\text{Number of shares outstanding (diluted)}}$$

$$= \frac{\$2,796}{618}$$

$$= \$4.52$$

We can see from the income statement that Nvidia's earnings per share are up and down between 2018 and 2020, and this is because the computer chip industry is somewhat cyclical as newer and faster chips come into the market every several years. So, rather than a steady increase year after year, investors can expect big ups and downs in earnings. You can see from the income statement that diluted earnings per share include more shares than the basic calculation; this is because diluted shares include potential shares that could be issued due to the exercise of stock options or the conversion of certain types of debt into common stock. Investors generally pay more attention to diluted earnings per share than basic earnings per share.

Dividends per share are paid by the corporation to the stockholders for each share owned. The payment is made from earnings after taxes by the corporation but is taxable income to the stockholder. Thus, dividends result in double taxation: The corporation pays tax once on its earnings, and the stockholder pays tax a second time on his or her dividend income. Nvidia—with almost $11 billion in revenue—is a young, growing company compared to Intel with approximately $75 billion in revenue. It only pays a small dividend, and as you can see on the income statement it spends a lot on research and development. Note that the shares listed on the income statement versus shares listed as outstanding on the balance sheet are not the same. Share count for earnings per share are weighted average shares over the year. The shares on the balance sheet are those outstanding at the year's end and do not necessarily represent the shares on which dividends were actually paid. Nvidia does not show dividends on the income statement and so you have to look on the statement of cash flows for total dividends paid.

$$\text{Dividends per share} = \frac{\text{Dividends paid}}{\text{Number of shares outstanding (year end)}}$$

$$= \frac{\$390}{609}$$

$$= \$0.64$$

Though three of the four Big Four accounting firms have women in high-level positions, a large gap exists between the number of men and women who make it to partner or principal. Approximately 61 percent of accountants and auditors in the United States are women, and 51 percent of all full-time staff at CPA firms are women. Women make up 47 percent of senior managers but only 24 percent of partners and principals.

Statistics also show that women are extremely underrepresented among accounting-firm partners who head audit engagement of some U.S companies. Out of the S&P 100 companies, only 11 percent of the engagement partners are women. Engagement partners are the lead representatives for client engagements. These numbers show that women are not being assigned to as many large clients as men.

One former Big Four accountant claims the discrepancy might not be due to the firms themselves. Instead, many women quit before making it to partner. Big Four firms are known to have very competitive cultures, requiring long hours. Accounting firm leaders have started to address these challenges by looking into creating a more family-friendly environment so accountants can take advantage of opportunities and achieve work/life balance. If successful, these changes may lead to more women taking on a partner or principal role in the accounting field—not only increasing diversity in leadership but also possibly decreasing the high turnover rates at these firms.[d]

Critical Thinking Questions

1. What are some reasons women might not be as represented among the partners or principals of the Big Four accounting firms?

2. Describe the corporate culture at the Big Four accounting firms. What might be done to make it more family friendly?

3. Do you think accounting firms should work to create a better work/life balance for employees with families, or should accountants expect to work long hours and make sacrifices if they choose to work for the Big Four?

IMPORTANCE OF INTEGRITY IN ACCOUNTING

The financial crisis and the recession that followed provided another example of a failure in accounting reporting. Many firms attempted to exploit loopholes and manipulate accounting processes and statements. Banks and other financial institutions often held assets off their books by manipulating their accounts. If the accountants, the SEC, and the bank regulators had been more careful, these types of transactions would have been discovered and corrected.

On the other hand, strong compliance to accounting principles creates trust among stakeholders. Accounting and financial planning is important for all organizational entities, even cities. The City of Maricopa in Arizona received the Government Finance Officers Association of the United States and Canada (GFOA) Distinguished Budget Presentation Award for its governmental budgeting. The city scored proficient in its policy, financial plan, operations guide, and communications device. Integrity in accounting is crucial to creating trust, understanding the financial position of an organization or entity, and making financial decisions that will benefit the organization.[5]

BUILDING YOUR SOFT SKILLS

BY THINKING ABOUT ETHICS

As an employee and even as a student, you may have to turn in expense reports for reimbursement. Approximately 14 percent of all fraud relates to expense report fraud. Some employees charge items that are for personal use, and others get blank receipts and fill in an amount greater than the expense. Think about your own personal ethics and explain how you will handle expense reimbursements. What if your colleagues tell you to add an extra amount because you probably forgot to include some other expenses?

Team Exercise

You can look at websites such as Yahoo! Finance (http://finance.yahoo.com/), under the company's "key statistics" link, to find many of its financial ratios, such as return on assets and return on equity. Have each member of your team look up a different company, and explain why you think there are differences in the ratio analysis for these two ratios among the selected companies.

It is most important to remember that integrity in accounting processes requires ethical principles and compliance with both the spirit of the law and professional standards in the accounting profession. Most states require accountants preparing to take the CPA exam to take accounting ethics courses. Transparency and accuracy in reporting revenue, income, and assets develops trust from investors and other stakeholders.

WOULD YOU MAKE // a Good Accountant? /

Do you like numbers and finances? Are you detail oriented, a perfectionist, and highly accountable for your decisions? If so, accounting may be a good field for you. If you are interested in accounting, there are always job opportunities available no matter the state of the economy. Accounting is one of the most secure job options in business. Of course, becoming an accountant is not easy. You will need at least a bachelor's degree in accounting to get a job, and many positions require additional training. Many states demand coursework beyond the 120 to 150 credit hours collegiate programs require for an accounting degree. If you are really serious about getting into the accounting field, you will probably want to consider getting your master's in accounting and taking the CPA exam. The field of accounting can be complicated, and the extra training provided through a master's in accounting program

will prove invaluable when you go out looking for a good job. Accounting is a volatile discipline affected by changes in legislative initiatives.

With corporate accounting policies changing constantly and becoming more complex, accountants are needed to help keep a business running smoothly and within the bounds of the law. In fact, the number of jobs in the accounting and auditing field are expected to increase 10 percent between 2016 and 2026. Jobs in accounting tend to pay quite well, with the median salary standing at $69,350. If you go on to get your master's degree in accounting, expect to see an even higher starting wage. Of course, your earnings could be higher or lower than these averages, depending on where you work, your level of experience, the firm, and your particular position.

Accountants are needed in the public and the private sectors, in large and small firms,

in for-profit and not-for-profit organizations. Accountants in firms are generally in charge of preparing and filing tax forms and financial reports. Public-sector accountants are responsible for checking the veracity of corporate and personal records in order to prepare tax filings. Basically, any organization that has to deal with money and/ or taxes in some way or another will be in need of an accountant, either for in-house service or occasional contract work. Requirements for audits under the Sarbanes-Oxley Act and rules from the Public Company Accounting Oversight Board are creating more jobs and increased responsibility to maintain internal controls and accounting ethics. The fact that accounting rules and tax filings tend to be complex virtually ensures that the demand for accountants will never decrease.[6] ■

fifteen

money and the
financial system

Panuwat Phimpha/Shutterstock

LEARNING OBJECTIVES

After reading this chapter, you will be able to:

LO 15-1 Define *money*, its functions, and its characteristics.

LO 15-2 Describe various types of money.

LO 15-3 Specify how the Federal Reserve Board manages the money supply and regulates the American banking system.

LO 15-4 Compare and contrast commercial banks, savings and loan associations, credit unions, and mutual savings banks.

LO 15-5 Distinguish among nonbanking institutions such as insurance companies, pension funds, mutual funds, and finance companies.

LO 15-6 Analyze the challenges ahead for the banking industry.

From Wall Street to Main Street, both overseas and at home, money is the one tool used to measure personal and business income and wealth. **Finance** is the study of how money is managed by individuals, companies, and governments. This chapter introduces you to the role of money and the financial system in the economy. Of course, if you have a checking account, automobile insurance, a college loan, or a credit card, you already have personal experience with some key players in the financial world.

We begin our discussion with a definition of money and then explore some of the many forms money may take. Next, we examine the roles of the Federal Reserve Board and other major institutions in the financial system. Finally, we explore the future of the finance industry and some of the changes likely to occur over the course of the next several years. ■

LO 15-1 Define *money*, its functions, and its characteristics.

MONEY IN THE FINANCIAL SYSTEM

Strictly defined, **money**, or *currency*, is anything generally accepted in exchange for goods and services. Materials as diverse as salt, cattle, fish, rocks, shells, and cloth, as well as precious metals such as gold, silver, and copper, have long been used by various cultures as money. Most of these materials were limited-supply commodities that had their own value to society (e.g., salt can be used as a preservative and shells and metals as jewelry). The supply of these commodities therefore determined the supply of "money" in that society. The next step

fiduciary, or fiat, monetary system. In the United States, paper money is really a government "note" or promise, worth the value specified on the note.

Functions of Money

No matter what a particular society uses for money, its primary purpose is to enable a person or organization to trade money for a good or a service. These desires may be for entertainment actions like funding party expenses; operating actions, such as paying for rent, utilities, or employees; investing actions, such as buying property or equipment; or financing actions, such as starting or growing a business. Money serves three important functions: as a medium of exchange, a measure of value, and a store of value.

finance the study of how money is managed by individuals, companies, and governments.

money anything generally accepted in exchange for goods and services; also called currency.

> "No matter what a particular society uses for money, its primary purpose is to enable a person or organization to trade money for a good or a service."

was the development of "IOUs," or slips of paper that could be exchanged for a specified supply of the underlying commodity. "Gold" notes, for instance, could be exchanged for gold, and the money supply was tied to the amount of gold available. While paper money was first used in North America in 1685 (and even earlier in Europe), the concept of *fiat money*—a paper money not readily convertible to a precious metal such as gold—did not gain full acceptance until the Great Depression in the 1930s. The United States abandoned its gold-backed currency standard largely in response to the Great Depression and converted to a

Medium of Exchange. Before fiat money, the trade of goods and services was accomplished through *bartering*—trading one good or service for another of similar value. There had to be a simpler way, and that was to decide on a single item—money—that can be freely converted to any other good upon agreement between parties.

Measure of Value. As a measure of value, money serves as a common standard or yardstick of the value of goods and services. For example, $2 will buy a dozen large eggs and

$25,000 will buy a nice car in the United States. In Japan, where the currency is known as the yen, these same transactions would cost about 210 yen and 2.75 million yen, respectively. Money, then, is a common denominator that allows people to compare the different goods and services that can be consumed on a particular income level. While a star athlete and a minimum-wage earner are paid vastly different wages, each uses money as a measure of the value of their yearly earnings and purchases.

Store of Value.

As a store of value, money serves as a way to accumulate wealth (buying power) until it is needed. For example, a person making $1,000 per week who wants to buy a $500 computer could save $50 per week for each of the next 10 weeks. Unfortunately, the value of stored money is directly dependent on the health of the economy. If, due to rapid inflation, all prices double in one year, then the purchasing power value of the money would fall by half. On the other hand, deflation occurs when prices of goods fall. Deflation might seem like a good thing for consumers, but in many ways it can be just as problematic as inflation. Periods of major deflation often lead to decreases in wages and increases in debt burdens.[1] Deflation also tends to be an indicator of problems in the economy. Deflation usually indicates slow economic growth and falling prices. Over the past 25 years, we have seen deflation in Japan, and Europe has continued to struggle with deflation off and on since the financial crisis. Given a choice, central banks like the Federal Reserve would rather have a small amount of inflation of 2 to 3 percent than deflation.

Characteristics of Money

To be used as a medium of exchange, money must be acceptable, divisible, portable, stable in value, durable, and difficult to counterfeit.

Acceptability.

To be effective, money must be readily acceptable for the purchase of goods and services and for the settlement of debts. Acceptability is probably the most important characteristic of money: If people do not trust the value of money, businesses will not accept it as a payment for goods and services, and consumers will have to find some other means of paying for their purchases.

Divisibility.

Given the widespread use of quarters, dimes, nickels, and pennies in the United States, it is no surprise that the principle of divisibility is an important one. With barter, the lack of divisibility often makes otherwise preferable trades impossible, as would be an attempt to trade a steer for a loaf of bread. For money to serve effectively as a measure of value, all items must be valued in terms of comparable units—dimes for a piece of bubble gum, quarters for laundry machines, and dollars (or dollars and coins) for everything else.

Portability.

Clearly, for money to function as a medium of exchange, it must be easily moved from one location to the next.

The euro, yen, and U.S. dollar are all examples of currency.
Wara1982/Shutterstock

Large colored rocks could be used as money, but you couldn't carry them around in your wallet. Paper currency and metal coins, on the other hand, are capable of transferring vast purchasing power into small, easily carried (and hidden!) bundles. Few Americans realize it, but more U.S. currency is in circulation outside the United States than within. The U.S. Federal Reserve reports that as of June 2020 there was $1.91 trillion of U.S. currency in circulation.[2] Some countries, such as Panama, even use the U.S. dollar as their currency.

Stability.

Money must be stable and maintain its declared face value. A $10 bill should purchase the same amount of goods or services from one day to the next. The principle of stability allows people who wish to postpone purchases and save their money to do so without fear that it will decline in value. As mentioned earlier, when economic conditions cause prices to rise, the same amount of money buys fewer and fewer goods and services. In some countries with very high inflation, people spend their money as fast as they can in order to keep it from losing any more of its value. Instability destroys confidence in a nation's money and its ability to store value and serve as an effective medium of exchange. It also has an impact on other countries. Ultimately, people faced with spiraling price increases avoid the increasingly worthless paper money at all costs, storing all of their savings in the form of real assets such as gold and land.

Durability.

Money must be durable. The crisp new dollar bills you trade for products at the mall will make their way all around town for about six years before being replaced (see

Table 15.1). Were the value of an old, faded bill to fall in line with the deterioration of its appearance, the principles of stability and universal acceptability would fail (but, no doubt, fewer bills would pass through the washer!). Although metal coins, due to their much longer useful life, would appear to be an ideal form of money, paper currency is far more portable than metal because of its light weight. Today, coins are used primarily to provide divisibility.

Difficulty to Counterfeit.

Finally, to remain stable and enjoy universal acceptance, it almost goes without saying that money must be very difficult to counterfeit—that is, to duplicate illegally. Every country takes steps to make counterfeiting difficult. Most use multicolored money, and many use specially watermarked papers that are virtually impossible to duplicate. However, it is becoming increasingly easy for counterfeiters to print money.[3] This illegal printing of money is fueled by hundreds of people who often circulate only small amounts of counterfeit bills. Even rogue governments such as North Korea are known to make counterfeit U.S. currency. To thwart the problem of counterfeiting, the U.S. Treasury Department redesigned the U.S. currency, starting with the $20 bill in 2003, the $50 bill in 2004, the $10 bill in 2006, the $5 bill in 2008, and the $100 bill in 2013.[4]

DID YOU KNOW?

Less than 0.01% of money in circulation in the U.S. is counterfeit.[a]

U.S. money includes subtle colors in addition to the traditional green, as well as enhanced security features, such as a watermark, security thread, and color-shifting ink.[5] Many countries are discontinuing large-denominated bills that are used in illegal trade such as drugs or terrorism. The idea is that it is more difficult to transport or hide €100 notes than €500 notes. Although counterfeiting is not as much of an issue with coins, U.S. metal coins are usually worth more for the metal than their face value. It has begun to cost more to manufacture coins than what they are worth monetarily.

As Table 15.2 indicates, it costs more to produce pennies and nickels than their face value. For example, we can see that in 2019 it cost $0.0199 to produce a one-cent piece, or 99 percent more than it was worth. However, what the U.S. Mint loses on pennies and nickels it makes up for with

The U.S. government redesigns currency to stay ahead of counterfeiters and protect the public.

zefart/Shutterstock

▼ TABLE 15.1 Life Expectancy of Money

How long is the life span of U.S. paper money?

When currency is deposited with a Federal Reserve Bank, the quality of each note is evaluated by sophisticated processing equipment. Notes that meet the strict quality criteria—that is, they are still in good condition—continue to circulate, while those that do not are taken out of circulation and destroyed. This process determines the life span of a Federal Reserve note.

Life span varies by denomination. One factor that influences the life span of each denomination is how the denomination is used by the public. For example, $100 notes are often used as a store of value. This means that they pass between users less frequently than lower denominations that are more often used for transactions, such as $5 notes. Thus, $100 notes typically last longer than $5 notes.

Denomination	Estimated Life Span*
$ 1	6.6 years
$ 5	4.7 years
$ 10	5.3 years
$ 20	7.8 years
$ 50	12.2 years
$100	22.9 years

*Estimated life spans as of December 2018. Because the $2 note does not widely circulate, we do not publish its estimated life span.

Source: Board of Governors of the Federal Reserve System, "How Long Is the Life Span of U.S. Paper Money?" www.federalreserve.gov/faqs/how-long-is-the-life-span-of-us-paper-money.htm (accessed May 26, 2020).

▼ TABLE 15.2 Costs to Produce U.S. Coins

Fiscal Year	Penny	Nickel	Dime	Quarter	Total Profit from Coins (Millions)
2019	$0.0199	$0.0762	$0.0373	$0.0901	$318.3
2018	$0.0206	$0.0753	$0.0372	$0.0888	$321.1
2017	$0.0182	$0.0666	$0.0333	$0.0824	$391.5
2016	$0.0150	$0.0632	$0.0308	$0.0763	$578.7
2015	$0.0143	$0.0744	$0.0354	$0.0844	$540.9
2014	$0.0166	$0.0809	$0.0391	$0.0895	$289.1
2013	$0.0183	$0.0941	$0.0456	$0.0105	$137.4
2012	$0.0200	$0.1009	$0.0499	$0.1130	$105.9
2011	$0.0241	$0.1118	$0.0565	$0.1114	$348.8

Source: Various annual reports of the U.S. Mint.

checking account money stored in an account at a bank or other financial institution that can be withdrawn without advance notice; also called a demand deposit.

savings accounts accounts with funds that usually cannot be withdrawn without advance notice; also known as time deposits.

money market accounts accounts that offer higher interest rates than standard bank rates but with greater restrictions.

certificates of deposit (CDs) savings accounts that guarantee a depositor a set interest rate over a specified interval as long as the funds are not withdrawn before the end of the period—six months or one year, for example.

credit cards means of access to preapproved lines of credit granted by a bank or finance company.

profits on dimes, quarters, and dollars. The U.S. $1 coin proved to be so unpopular that the U.S. Mint discontinued producing it after 2013. Profits fluctuate over time because of the rising and falling costs of copper, zinc, and nickel, but dimes and quarters have always been profitable for the U.S. Mint.

LO 15-2 Describe various types of money.

Types of Money

While paper money and coins are the most visible types of money, the combined value of all of the printed bills and all of the minted coins is actually rather insignificant when compared with the value of money kept in checking accounts, savings accounts, and other monetary forms.

You probably have a **checking account** (also called a *demand deposit*), money stored in an account at a bank or other financial institution that can be withdrawn without advance notice. One way to withdraw funds from your account is by writing a *check*, a written order to a bank to pay the indicated individual or business the amount specified on the check from money already on deposit. Figure 15.1 explains the significance of the numbers found on a typical U.S. check. As legal instruments, checks serve as a substitute for currency and coins and are preferred for many transactions due to their lower risk of loss. If you lose a $100 bill, anyone who finds or steals it can spend it. If you lose a blank check, however, the risk of catastrophic loss is quite low. Not only does your bank have a sample of your signature on file to compare with a suspected forged signature, but you can render the check immediately worthless by means of a stop-payment order at your bank.

There are several types of checking accounts, with different features available for different monthly fee levels or specific minimum account balances. Some checking accounts earn interest (a small percentage of the amount deposited in the account that the bank pays to the depositor). One such interest-bearing checking account is the *NOW (Negotiable Order of Withdrawal) account* offered by most financial institutions. The interest rate paid on such accounts varies with the interest rates available in the economy but is typically quite low (more recently less than 1 percent but in the past between 2 and 5 percent).

Savings accounts (also known as *time deposits*) are accounts with funds that usually cannot be withdrawn without advance notice and/or have limits on the number of withdrawals per period. While seldom enforced, the "fine print" governing most savings accounts prohibits withdrawals without two or three days' notice. Savings accounts are not generally used for transactions or as a medium of exchange, but their funds can be moved to a checking account or turned into cash.

Money market accounts are similar to interest-bearing checking accounts, but with more restrictions. Generally, in exchange for slightly higher interest rates, the owner of a money market account can write only a limited number of checks each month, and there may be a restriction on the minimum amount of each check.

Certificates of deposit (CDs) are savings accounts that guarantee a depositor a set interest rate over a specified interval of time as long as the funds are not withdrawn before the end of the interval—six months, one year, or seven years, for example. Money may be withdrawn from these accounts prematurely only after paying a substantial penalty. In general, the longer the term of the CD, the higher is the interest rate it earns. As with all interest rates, the rate offered and fixed at the time the account is opened fluctuates according to economic conditions.

Credit cards allow you to promise to pay at a later date by using preapproved lines of credit granted by a bank or finance company. They are a popular substitute for cash payments because of their convenience, easy access to credit, and acceptance by merchants around the world. The institution that issues the credit card guarantees payment of a credit charge to merchants and assumes responsibility for collecting the money from the cardholders. Card issuers charge a transaction fee to the merchants for performing the credit check, guaranteeing the payment, and collecting the payment. The fee is typically between 2 and 5 percent, depending on the type of card. American Express fees are usually higher than those for Visa and Mastercard.

The original American Express cards required full payment at the end of each month, but American Express now offers credit cards similar to Visa, Mastercard, and Discover that allow cardholders to make installment payments and carry a maximum balance. There is a minimum monthly payment with interest charged on the remaining balance. Some people pay off their credit cards monthly, while other make monthly payments. Charges for unpaid balances can run 18 percent or higher at an

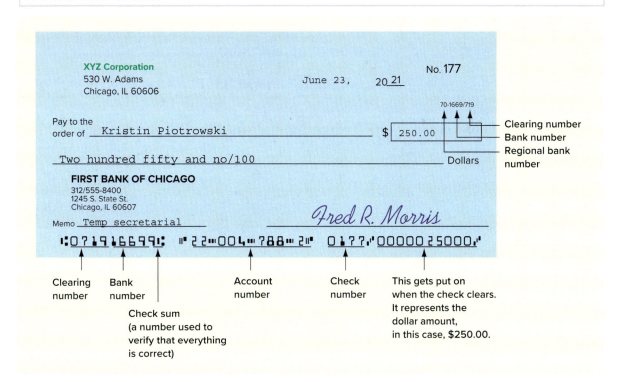

annual rate, making credit card debt one of the most expensive ways to borrow money.

Besides the major credit card companies, many stores—Target, Saks Fifth Avenue, Macy's, Bloomingdales, and others—have their own branded credit cards. They use credit rating agencies to check the credit of the cardholders and they generally make money on the finance charges. **Reward cards** are credit cards that carry a benefit to the user. For example, gas stations such as Mobil and Shell have branded credit cards so that when you use the card you save five or six cents per gallon. Others—such as airline cards for American, Delta, and United—reward you with miles that you can use for flights. And there are cash-back credit cards that give you 1 percent or more cash back on everything you spend.

The Credit CARD (Card Accountability Responsibility and Disclosure) Act of 2009 was passed to regulate the practices of credit card companies. The law limited the ability of card issuers to raise interest rates, limited credit to young adults, gave people more time to pay bills, and made clearer due dates on billing cycles, along with several other provisions. For college students, the most important part of the law is that young adults under the age of 21 have to have an adult co-signer or show proof that they have enough income to handle the debt limit on the card.

This act is important to all companies and cardholders. Research indicates that approximately 40 percent of lower- and middle-income households use credit cards to pay for basic necessities. Yet there is also good news. The average credit card debt for lower- and middle-income households has decreased in recent years. On the other hand, studies also show that college students tend to

lack the financial literacy needed to understand credit cards and their requirements. Therefore, vulnerable segments of the population, such as college students, should be careful about which credit cards to choose and how often they use them.[6]

A **debit card** looks like a credit card but works like a check. The use of a debit card results in a direct, immediate, electronic payment from the cardholder's checking account to a merchant or other party. While they are convenient to carry and profitable for banks, they lack credit features, offer no purchase "grace period," and provide no hard "paper trail." Debit cards are gaining more acceptance with merchants, and consumers like debit cards because of the ease of getting cash from an increasing number of ATM machines. Financial institutions also want consumers to use debit cards because they reduce the number of teller transactions and check processing costs. Some cash management accounts at retail brokers like Merrill Lynch offer deferred debit cards. These act like a credit card but debit to the cash management account once a month. During that time, the cash earns a money market return.

Traveler's checks, money orders, and cashier's checks are other forms of "near money." Although each is slightly different from the others, they all share a common characteristic: A financial

reward cards credit cards made available by stores that carry a benefit to the user.

debit card a card that looks like a credit card but works like a check; using it results in a direct, immediate, electronic payment from the cardholder's checking account to a merchant or third party.

Federal Reserve Board an independent agency of the federal government established in 1913 to regulate the nation's banking and financial industry; also called "the Fed."

institution, bank, credit company, or neighborhood currency exchange issues them in exchange for cash and guarantees that the purchased note will be honored and exchanged for cash when it is presented to the institution making the guarantee.

Credit Card Fraud. More and more computer hackers have managed to steal credit card and debit card information and either use the information for Internet purchases or actually make a card exactly the same as the stolen card. Losses on credit card theft run into the billions, but consumers are usually not liable for the losses. However, consumers should be careful with debit cards because once the money is out of the account, the bank and credit card companies cannot get it back. Debit cards do not have the same level of protection as credit cards.

Cryptocurrency. A new type of money called cryptocurrency has become popular over the last several years with technology-oriented people. Bitcoin is the most popular, but it has a fluctuating price, which makes it less desirable than fiat money like dollars, yens, and euros that are backed by governments. It also does not have a stable value or portability. But it does work in a digital economy with instantaneous payments where the transaction size is large and the value of the cryptocurrency is known by both the buyer and the seller. Cryptocurrencies are not favored by governments because the transactions are impossible to track. This makes them very useful for illegal transactions and international currency transactions that can't be traced. For example, cybercriminals who hack computer systems with ransomware often require payment in a cryptocurrency because the transfer can't be traced.

Credit cards have many advantages, including being able to buy expensive items and pay them off a little at a time. However, this can easily lead an individual to incur spiraling credit card debt that is hard to pay off.

Piotr Adamowicz/123RF

THE AMERICAN FINANCIAL SYSTEM

The U.S. financial system fuels our economy by storing money, fostering investment opportunities, and making loans for new businesses and business expansion as well as for homes, cars, and college educations. This amazingly complex system includes banking institutions, nonbanking financial institutions such as finance companies, and systems that provide for the electronic transfer of funds throughout the world. Over the past 20 years, the rate at which money turns over, or changes hands, has increased exponentially. Different cultures place unique values on saving, spending, borrowing, and investing. The combination of this increased turnover rate and increasing interactions with people and organizations from other countries has created a complex money system. First, we need to meet the guardian of this complex system.

The Federal Reserve System

The guardian of the American financial system is the **Federal Reserve Board**, or "the Fed," as it is commonly called, an independent agency of the federal government established in 1913 to regulate the nation's banking and financial industry. The Chair of the Board of Governors of the Federal Reserve system is the executive officer and serves a four-year term beginning in the middle of the president's term and ending in the middle of the next president's term. This is thought to help the Fed maintain its independence from political pressure from the president. The Federal Reserve System is organized into 12 regions, each with a Federal Reserve Bank that serves its defined area (Figure 15.2). All the Federal Reserve banks except those in Boston and Philadelphia have regional branches. The Cleveland Federal Reserve Bank, for example, is responsible for branch offices in Pittsburgh and Cincinnati.

The Federal Reserve Board is the chief economic policy arm of the United States. Working with Congress and the president, the Fed tries to create a positive economic environment capable of sustaining low inflation, high levels of employment, a balance in international payments, and long-term economic growth. To this end, the Federal Reserve Board has five major responsibilities:

1. to conduct monetary policy;
2. to promote financial system stability;
3. to supervise and regulate financial institutions and activities;
4. to foster payment and settlement system safety and efficiency; and
5. to promote consumer protection and community development.

─── Boundaries of Federal Reserve Districts	○ Federal Reserve Bank Cities
─── Boundaries of Federal Reserve Branch Territories	● Federal Reserve Branch Cities
⊙ Board of Governors of the Federal Reserve System	■ Federal Reserve Bank Facility

Monetary Policy. The Fed controls the amount of money available in the economy through **monetary policy**. Without this intervention, the supply of and demand for money might not balance. This could result in either rapid price increases (inflation) because of too little money or economic recession and a slowdown of price increases (disinflation) because of too little growth in the money supply. In very rare cases (the depression of the 1930s), the United States has suffered from deflation, when the actual purchasing power of the dollar has increased as prices declined. To effectively control the supply of money in the economy, the Fed must have a good idea of how much money is in circulation at any given time. This has become increasingly challenging because the global nature of our economy means that more and more U.S. dollars are circulating overseas. Using several different measures of the money supply, the Fed establishes specific growth targets that, presumably, ensure a close balance between money supply and money demand. The Fed fine-tunes money growth by using four basic tools: open market operations, reserve requirements, the discount rate, and credit controls (see Table 15.3). There is generally a lag of 6 to 18 months before the effect of these charges shows up in economic activity.

Open market operations refer to decisions to buy or sell U.S. Treasury bills (short-term debt issued by the U.S. government; also called T-bills) and other investments in the open market. The actual purchase or sale of the investments is performed by the New York Federal Reserve Bank. This monetary tool, the most commonly employed of all Fed operations, is performed almost daily in an effort to control the money supply.

When the Fed buys securities, it writes a check on its own account to the seller of the investments. When the seller of the investments (usually a large bank) deposits the check, the Fed transfers the balance from the Federal Reserve account into the seller's account, thus increasing the supply of money in the economy and, hopefully, fueling economic growth. The opposite occurs when the Fed sells investments. The buyer writes a check to the Federal Reserve, and when the funds are transferred out of the purchaser's

monetary policy means by which the Fed controls the amount of money available in the economy.

open market operations decisions to buy or sell U.S. Treasury bills (short-term debt issued by the U.S. government) and other investments in the open market.

▼ **TABLE 15.3** Fed Tools for Regulating the Money Supply

Activity	The Intended Effect on the Money Supply and the Economy
Buy government securities	The money supply increases; economic activity increases.
Sell government securities	The money supply decreases; economic activity slows down.
Raise discount rate	Interest rates increase; the money supply decreases; economic activity slows down.
Lower discount rate	Interest rates decrease; the money supply increases; economic activity increases.
Increase reserve requirements	Banks make fewer loans; the money supply declines; economic activity slows down.
Decrease reserve requirements	Banks make more loans; the money supply increases; economic activity increases.
Relax credit controls	More people are encouraged to make major purchases, increasing economic activity.
Restrict credit controls	People are discouraged from making major purchases, decreasing economic activity.

reserve requirement
the percentage of deposits that banking institutions must hold in reserve.

discount rate the rate of interest the Fed charges to loan money to any banking institution to meet reserve requirements.

account, the amount of money in circulation falls, slowing economic growth to a desired level.

The second major monetary policy tool is the **reserve requirement**, the percentage of deposits that banking institutions must hold in reserve ("in the vault," as it were). Funds so held are not available for lending to businesses and consumers. For example, a bank holding $10 million in deposits, with a 10 percent reserve requirement, must have reserves of $1 million. If the Fed were to reduce the reserve requirement to, say, 5 percent, the bank would need to keep only $500,000 in reserves. The bank could then lend to customers the $500,000 difference between the old reserve level and the new lower reserve level, thus increasing the supply of money. Because the reserve requirement has such a powerful effect on the money supply, the Fed does not change it very often, relying instead on open market operations most of the time.

The third monetary policy tool, the **discount rate**, is the rate of interest the Fed charges to loan money to any banking institution

Conversely, when the Fed wants to decrease the money supply, it raises the discount rate.

Interest rates are the result of all the activities mentioned in Table 15.3. By managing the money supply, the Fed impacts interest rates and the cost of borrowing. If the Fed wants to increase economic activity, it can lower interest rates to stimulate the economy by lowering borrowing costs for mortgages, car loans, home equity loans, and all types of loans. If inflation starts moving up too fast or too high, the Fed will raise interest rates to slow down borrowing and the purchase of goods and putting a damper on inflation.

Figure 15.3 shows a 20-year history of interest rates for 1-year U.S. Treasury bills, 10-year Treasury bills, and long-term corporate bonds. The shaded areas are recessions. There are several significant things you can learn from Figure 15.3. First, short-term rates (in red) are more volatile than long-term rates and are almost always lower than long-term rates. Corporate bond rates (in green) are higher risk than U.S. Treasury securities, so they always have a higher interest rate than U.S. Treasuries to compensate for higher risk.

The large shaded area beginning December 2007 and ending June 2009 represents the Great Recession, a very long recession

> " When the Fed wants to expand the money supply, it lowers the discount rate to encourage borrowing. Conversely, when the Fed wants to decrease the money supply, it raises the discount rate. "

to meet reserve requirements. The Fed is the lender of last resort for these banks. When a bank borrows from the Fed, it is said to have borrowed at the "discount window," and the interest rates charged there are often higher than those charged on loans of comparable risk elsewhere in the economy. This added interest expense, when it exists, serves to discourage banks from borrowing from the Fed. When the Fed wants to expand the money supply, it lowers the discount rate to encourage borrowing.

caused by a financial crisis discussed in detail in Chapter 14. Notice that short-term rates began falling before the recession was in full force. Once the Fed realized they had a big problem on their hands, they moved rates lower in dramatic fashion. You can see that short-term rates were less than one percent and long-term rates fell from more than 6 percent in 2000 to less than 1 percent. Rates stayed low as the economic damage from the crisis lingered for many years. The economy was on the

▼ **FIGURE 15.3** History of Interest Rates

Note: Shaded areas indicate U.S. recessions. The end of the recession that began in February 2020 does not yet show up on the graph, but it will once the National Bureau of Economic Research declares the end of the recession.

Source: Federal Reserve Bank of St. Louis, https://fred.stlouisfed.org/graph/?g=rDVw (accessed September 13, 2020).

credit controls the authority to establish and enforce credit rules for financial institutions and some private investors.

upswing by the end of 2015, and the rising interest rates into 2019 showed that the economy was returning to normal.

The increase in rates did not last long as the COVID-19 (coronavirus) pandemic spread across the world in early 2020. To save lives, states closed non-essential businesses (e.g., restaurants, bars, offices, factories), keeping only essential services open (e.g., hospitals, grocery stores, gas stations). The result was massive unemployment that had not been seen since the great depression of the 1930s. At the peak, unemployment was 14.7 percent, with some states reaching upwards of 20 percent.[7] Congress passed more than $3 trillion of aid for unemployment benefits and sent checks to individuals with incomes less than predetermined amounts. The Federal Reserve was doing its part to keep the financial markets liquid. There is an old saying that "markets are driven by fear and greed," and when the pandemic caused businesses to close and workers to be laid off, fear dominated the financial markets. In response, the Fed slashed interest rates to almost zero in the first quarter of 2020 and started a series of asset purchase programs to maintain liquidity in the markets. During the financial crisis of 2007–2009, the Fed entered the market to purchase U.S. Treasury securities, but this time they made the unprecedented move to purchase $2.3 trillion of municipal bonds and corporate bonds, many of them from commercial banks. In times of financial distress, the Federal Reserve uses whatever resources it has to stabilize markets. In times of fear, there are often very few buyers of securities and so the Fed becomes the buyer of last resort. Unfortunately, the Fed could not prevent the recession that began in February of 2020.

One new tool to stimulate economies has been used in Japan for many years and in Europe since 2014 when the European Central Bank approved the implementation of *negative interest rates.* In August of 2019, Charles Schwab reported that there were $13 trillion of negative interest rate bonds in Europe. *Bloomberg* reported that in September of 2019, bond yields in eleven European countries were negative. For example, in Sweden and investor had the choice of earning 4.2 percent in common stock dividends or −0.4 percent on government bonds for a difference of 4.6 percent. What would you do?

One issue in recessions and economic downturns is that people save rather than spend. A perfect example of this was during the pandemic in the United States, Fox Business News reported that the savings rate jumped to 33 percent in April of 2020 from 8 percent in February. Afterall, if you have to stay home, there is a lot of stuff you don't buy, and if you are afraid of a job loss, a reduction in pay, or medical bills, you may just decide to save more. The theory is that if you have negative interest rates, people will spend, investors will invest, and banks will lend. No one will want to hold on to their money since they will not earn any positive return on savings or money market accounts or government securities. Instead, people will spend their money and stimulate the economy, thus keeping the economy from a deflationary spiral. So far, there is no evidence that negative interest rates have had the desired impact in Europe, and the U.S. Federal Reserve Board of Governors said they have no plans to implement a negative interest rate policy even though they are allowed to do so as of 2016.

The final tool in the Fed's arsenal of weapons is **credit controls**—the authority to establish and enforce credit rules for

When the COVID-19 (coronavirus) global pandemic made waves across the globe, nonessential businesses shuttered, events were canceled, travel came to a halt, and companies shifted to working from home and many people lost their jobs. As a result, the general population's banking habits shifted to saving cash and limiting spending. The uncertain economy brought on the highest level of savings since 1981, rising to 33 percent in April of 2020, up from 8 percent just two months prior.

As the personal saving rate increased, disposable income gained $2 trillion and personal savings increased by $4 trillion. Even as government-issued stimulus funds were distributed to Americans through the Coronavirus Aid, Relief, and Economic Security (CARES) Act, people chose to put the majority of their funds toward savings. Fiscal relief from the CARES Act stimulus payments and unemployment benefits, led to an increase in both savings and disposable income. In fact, some unemployed individuals made more than they did working. Between the appeal of unemployment benefits and fear of the rapidly spreading virus, many small businesses had difficulties persuading employees to return to work.

In response to market uncertainty as a result of the pandemic, companies started drawing down credit lines and stockpiling cash with the expectation of a severe recession. This sharp rise in savings by both consumers and corporations led to the continued growth of the largest banks. There were $1.8 trillion in deposits in the first quarter of 2020 alone, with more than 50 percent going to JPMorgan Chase, Bank of America, Wells Fargo, and Citigroup. The Federal Deposit Insurance Corporation assured consumers and companies that banks would be safe, adding more protections. This led to banks acting as a refuge for jittery consumers and companies intending to wait out the shutdown.

Due to solid liquidity levels, banks loaned out more than $500 billion to small businesses while only having to borrow about $50 billion from the Federal Reserve's Paycheck Protection Program (PPP) Liquidity Facility. Though PPP loans had a low interest rate of 0.35 percent, non-interest-bearing accounts made up approximately 30 percent of all deposits at the top four banks, giving the banks an even cheaper alternative for funding. Additionally, executives in the banking industry have suggested that banks would rather not rely on the Fed and risk giving the appearance of financial trouble.[b]

Critical Thinking Questions

1. Why do you think Americans chose to save their stimulus funds rather than spend them?

2. Why did the rise in savings contribute to the growth of the largest banks?

3. What are some of the reasons banks chose not to borrow from the Fed's Paycheck Protection Program?

---

financial institutions and some private investors. For example, the Fed can determine how large a down payment individuals and businesses must make on credit purchases of expensive items such as automobiles, and how much time they have to finish paying for the purchases. By raising and lowering minimum down payment amounts and payment periods, the Fed can stimulate or discourage credit purchases of "big ticket" items. The Fed also has the authority to set the minimum down payment investors must use for the credit purchases of stock. Buying stock with credit—"buying on margin"—is a popular investment strategy among individual speculators. By altering the margin requirement (currently set at 50 percent of the price of the purchased stocks), the Fed can effectively control the total amount of credit borrowing in the stock market.

Regulatory Functions.

The second major responsibility of the Fed is to regulate banking institutions that are members of the Federal Reserve System. Accordingly, the Fed establishes and enforces banking rules that affect monetary policy and the overall level of the competition between different banks. It determines which nonbanking activities, such as brokerage services, leasing, and insurance, are appropriate for banks and which should be prohibited. The Fed also has the authority to approve or disapprove mergers between banks and the formation of bank holding companies. In an effort to ensure that all rules are enforced and that correct accounting procedures are being followed at member banks, surprise bank examinations are conducted by bank examiners each year.

Check Clearing.

The Federal Reserve provides national check processing on a huge scale. Divisions of the Fed known as check clearinghouses handle almost all the checks written against a bank in one city and presented for deposit to a bank in a second city. Any banking institution can present the checks it has received from others around the country to its regional Federal Reserve Bank. The Fed passes the checks to the appropriate regional Federal Reserve Bank, which then sends the checks to the issuing bank for payment. With the advance of electronic payment systems and the passage of the Check Clearing for the 21st Century Act (Check 21 Act), checks can now be processed in a day. The Check 21 Act allows banks to clear checks electronically by presenting an electronic image of the check. This eliminates mail delays and time-consuming paper processing.

Depository Insurance.

The Fed is also responsible for supervising the federal insurance funds that protect the deposits of member institutions. These insurance funds will be discussed in greater detail in the following section.

Citibank is the consumer division of Citigroup, one of the four largest banks in the United States.

Andriy Blokhin/Shutterstock

LO 15-4 Compare and contrast commercial banks, savings and loan associations, credit unions, and mutual savings banks.

Banking Institutions

Banking institutions accept money deposits from and make loans to individual consumers and businesses. Some of the most important banking institutions include commercial banks, savings and loan associations, credit unions, and mutual savings banks. Historically, these have all been separate institutions. However, new hybrid forms of banking institutions that perform two or more of these functions have emerged over the past two decades. They all have one thing in common: They are businesses whose objective is to earn money by managing, safeguarding, and lending money to others. Their sales revenues come from the fees and interest that they charge for providing these financial services.

Since the financial crisis, and during the 2016 political campaign, Wall Street and banks have been the target of politicians as they continue to take out their anger at the banking world for all the economic problems that exist in the United States. However, during President Trump's administration, many of the regulations were relaxed, particularly for regional and community banks. You will see as you go through this section that the financial network is very complex.

Commercial Banks.
The largest and oldest of all financial institutions are **commercial banks**, which perform a variety of financial services. They rely mainly on checking and savings accounts as their major source of funds and use only a portion of these deposits to make loans to businesses and individuals. Because it is unlikely that all the depositors of any one bank will want to withdraw all of their funds at the same time, a bank can safely loan out a large percentage of its deposits.

Today, banks are quite diversified and offer a number of services. Commercial banks make loans for virtually any conceivable legal purpose, from vacations to cars, from homes to college educations. Banks in many states offer *home equity loans*, by which home owners can borrow against the appraised value of their already purchased homes. Banks also issue Visa and Mastercard credit cards and offer CDs and trusts (legal entities set up to hold and manage assets for a beneficiary). Many banks rent safe deposit boxes in bank vaults to customers who want to store jewelry, legal documents, artwork, and other valuables. In 1999, Congress passed the Financial Services Modernization Act, also known as the Gramm-Leach-Bliley Bill. This act repealed the Glass Steagall Act, which was enacted in 1933 after the stock market crash and prohibited commercial banks from being in the insurance and investment banking business. This puts U.S. commercial banks on the same competitive footing as European banks and provides a more level playing field for global banking competition. As commercial banks and investment banks have merged, the financial landscape has changed. Consolidation remains the norm in the U.S. banking industry. The financial crisis and the economic recession that began in 2007 and lasted into 2012 only accelerated the consolidation as large, healthy banks ended up buying weak banks that were in trouble. Most of these purchases were made with financial help from the U.S. Treasury and Federal Reserve. By 2012, the banks had paid back their loans, but the financial meltdown exposed some high-risk activities in the banking industry Congress wanted to curtail. The result was the passage of the Dodd-Frank Act. This act added many new regulations, but the two most important changes raised the required capital banks had to hold on their balance sheet and limited certain types of high-risk trading activities.

Savings and Loan Associations.
Savings and loan associations (S&Ls), often called "thrifts," are financial institutions that primarily offer savings accounts and make long-term loans for residential mortgages. A mortgage is a loan made so that a business or individual can purchase real estate, typically a home; the real estate itself is pledged as a guarantee (called *collateral*) that the buyer will repay the loan. If the loan is not repaid, the savings and loan has the right to repossess the property. Prior to the 1970s, S&Ls focused almost exclusively on real estate lending and accepted only savings accounts. Today, following years of regulatory changes, S&Ls compete directly with commercial banks by offering many types of services.

commercial banks the largest and oldest of all financial institutions, relying mainly on checking and savings accounts as sources of funds for loans to businesses and individuals.

savings and loan associations (S&Ls) financial institutions that primarily offer savings accounts and make long-term loans for residential mortgages; also called "thrifts."

credit union a financial institution owned and controlled by its depositors, who usually have a common employer, profession, trade group, or religion.

mutual savings banks financial institutions that are similar to savings and loan associations but, like credit unions, are owned by their depositors.

Federal Deposit Insurance Corporation (FDIC) an insurance fund established in 1933 that insures individual bank accounts.

National Credit Union Administration (NCUA) an agency that regulates and charters credit unions and insures their deposits through its National Credit Union Insurance Fund.

Savings and loans have gone through a metamorphosis since the early 1990s, after having almost collapsed in the 1980s. Today, many of the largest savings and loans have merged with commercial banks. This segment of the financial services industry plays a diminished role in the mortgage lending market.

Credit Unions.

A **credit union** is a financial institution owned and controlled by its depositors, who usually have a common employer, profession, trade group, or religion. The Aggieland Credit Union in College Station, Texas, for example, provides banking services for faculty, employees, and current and former students of Texas A&M University. A savings account at a credit union is commonly referred to as a share account, while a checking account is termed a share draft account. Because the credit union is tied to a common organization, the members (depositors) are allowed to vote for directors and share in the credit union's profits in the form of higher interest rates on accounts and/or lower loan rates.

While credit unions were originally created to provide depositors with a short-term source of funds for low-interest consumer loans for items such as cars, home appliances, vacations, and college, today they offer a wide range of financial services. Generally, the larger the credit union, the more sophisticated its financial service offerings will be.

Mutual Savings Banks.

Mutual savings banks are similar to savings and loan associations, but, like credit unions, they are owned by their depositors. Among the oldest financial institutions in the United States, they were originally established to provide a safe place for savings of the working classes. Found mostly in New England, they are becoming more popular in the rest of the country as some S&Ls have converted to mutual savings banks to escape the stigma created by the widespread S&L failures in the 1980s.

Insurance for Banking Institutions.

The **Federal Deposit Insurance Corporation (FDIC)**, which insures individual bank accounts, was established in 1933 to help stop bank failures throughout the country during the Great Depression. Today, the FDIC insures personal accounts up to a maximum of $250,000 at nearly 6,000 FDIC member

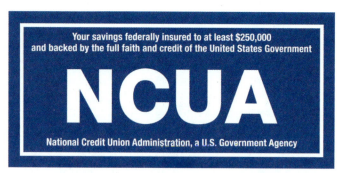

The National Credit Union Administration has the important job of regulating and chartering credit unions and insuring their deposits through its National Credit Union Insurance Fund.

Source: National Credit Union Administration

institutions.[8] While most major banks are insured by the FDIC, small institutions in some states may be insured by state insurance funds or private insurance companies. Should a member bank fail, its depositors can recover all of their funds, up to $250,000. Amounts over $250,000, while not legally covered by the insurance, are, in fact, usually covered because the Fed understands very well the enormous damage that would result to the financial system should these large depositors withdraw their money. When the financial crisis occurred, the FDIC increased the deposit insurance amount from $100,000 to $250,000 on a temporary basis to increase consumer confidence in the banking system. The Dodd-Frank Act passed on July 21, 2010, made the $250,000 insurance per account permanent. The *Federal Savings and Loan Insurance Corporation (FSLIC)* insured thrift deposits prior to its insolvency and failure during the S&L crisis of the 1980s. Now, the insurance functions once overseen by the FSLIC are handled directly by the FDIC through its Savings Association Insurance Fund. The **National Credit Union Administration (NCUA)** regulates and charters credit unions and insures their deposits through its National Credit Union Insurance Fund.

When they were originally established, Congress hoped that these insurance funds would make people feel secure about their savings so they would not panic and withdraw their money when news of a bank failure was announced. The "bank run" scene in the perennial Christmas movie *It's a Wonderful Life,* when dozens of Bailey Building and Loan depositors attempted to withdraw their money (only to have the reassuring figure of Jimmy Stewart calm their fears), was not based on mere fiction. During the Great Depression, hundreds of banks failed and their depositors lost everything. The fact that large numbers of major financial institutions failed in the 1980s and 1990s—without a single major banking panic—underscores the effectiveness of the current insurance system. Large bank failures occurred once again during the Great Recession. According to the FDIC, 52 banks failed between January 2000 and December 31, 2008. Because of the financial crisis and long-lasting recession, 488 failed between January 1, 2009, and December 31, 2014.

Only 21 insured banks failed from 2015 to the end of 2017, so it is clear the crisis is behind us. This reflects an improving economy and a healthier financial system. It is safe to say that most depositors go to sleep every night without worrying about the safety of their savings.

LO 15-5 Distinguish among nonbanking institutions such as insurance companies, pension funds, mutual funds, and finance companies.

Nonbanking Institutions

Nonbank financial institutions offer some financial services, such as short-term loans or investment products, but do not accept deposits. These include insurance companies, pension funds, mutual funds, brokerage firms, nonfinancial firms, and finance companies. Table 15.4 lists the assets of some diversified financial services firms.

Diversified Firms. There are many nonfinancial firms that help finance their customers' purchases of expensive equipment. For example, Caterpillar (construction equipment), Boeing (airplanes), and General Electric (jet engines and locomotives) help their customers finance these large-scale expensive purchases through their finance subsidiaries. At one time, General Electric's credit subsidiary accounted for 40 percent of the company's revenues, but this is slowly falling as the company divests itself of consumer credit operations. Automobile companies such as Ford have also traditionally had credit subsidiaries to help customers finance their cars.

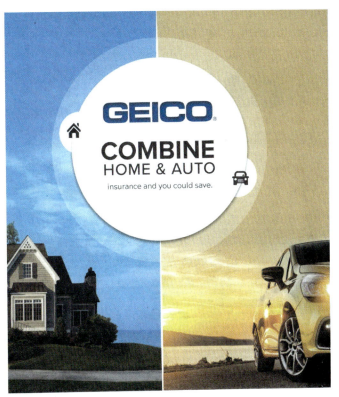

Geico is the second largest auto insurance company behind State Farm. Geico also offers homeowners insurance, renters insurance, and more.

Source: Geico

▼ **TABLE 15.4** Leading Diversified Financial Services Firms

Company Name	Standard and Poor's Financial Industry Subgroup Classification	Stock Symbol	2019 Assets (in millions)	2018 Assets (in millions)	2017 Assets (in millions)
JPMorgan Chase	Diversified Bank	JPM	$2,687,379	$2,622,532	$2,533,600
Citigroup Inc.	Diversified Bank	C	1,951,158	1,917,383	1,842,465
Capital One	Consumer Finance	COF	390,365	372,538	365,693
The Charles Schwab Corp.	Investment Banking and Brokerage	SCHW	294,005	296,482	243,274
American Express	Consumer Finance	AXP	198,321	188,602	181,196
BlackRock Group*	Asset Management & Custody Bank	BLK	168,622	159,573	220,241
Ameriprise Financial	Asset Management & Custody Bank	AMP	151,828	137,216	147,480
Visa	Data Processing & Outsourced Services	V	72,574	69,225	67,977
The Blackstone Group	Asset Management & Custody Bank	BX	32,586	28,925	34,416
Aon	Insurance Brokers	AON	29,405	26,422	26,088
Marsh & McLennan Companies	Insurance Brokers	MMC	31,357	21,578	20,429
Apollo Investment Corp.	Asset Management & Custody Bank	APO	8,542	5,992	6,991

*Adjusted Total Assets

Source: CFRA Stock Reports by S&P Global.

THE FEDERAL RESERVE LEANS ON BLACKROCK

Established in 1988 as a nonbanking financial institution specializing in risk and asset management, BlackRock Financial is the largest asset manager in the world today, with more than $7.4 trillion in assets under management. BlackRock offers funds, products, insights, resources, and professionals to help people invest intelligently and effectively. During the Great Recession, the Federal Reserve looked to BlackRock to dispose of bad mortgage securities from Bear Stearns & Co. and American International Group Inc. The Fed once again looked to BlackRock for help during the COVID-19 (coronavirus) pandemic.

During the global pandemic, the Fed enlisted BlackRock to purchase what would become a $750 billion portfolio of debt in order to support the corporate bond market.

BlackRock's most popular fund is the iShares exchange-traded fund (ETF), marketable securities that trade like common stock and have lower fees than mutual fund shares. The diversified nature of these funds lowers the risk because the investment is not dependent on a single company like a traditional stock. Combined with low fees, ETFs are popular for risk-averse investors. One part of the Fed's plan involved buying bond ETFs.

BlackRock is the largest issuer of ETFs and actively managed upwards of $625 billion in bond funds, so it makes sense that the Fed would look to the financial institution to buy a diverse portfolio quickly. BlackRock also utilizes a complex software called Aladdin to help mitigate risk and determine optimal methods to invest, a software platform that appealed to

the Fed. Though BlackRock's size and ubiquity may be unsettling, the company watches over large sums of money for clients rather than making investments for itself with borrowed money, decreasing the threat to the broader financial system. BlackRock's passion for smart, calculated investing and its global influence have given it an edge in the financial industry.[c]

Critical Thinking Questions

1. What type of nonbanking institution is BlackRock?
2. Is BlackRock a threat to the broader financial system? Why or why not?
3. Why are ETFs attractive to risk-averse investors?

---

insurance companies businesses that protect their clients against financial losses from certain specified risks (e.g., death, accident, and theft).

pension funds managed investment pools set aside by individuals, corporations, unions, and some nonprofit organizations to provide retirement income for members.

Insurance Companies.

Insurance companies are businesses that protect their clients against financial losses from certain specified risks (e.g., death, injury, disability, accident, fire, theft, and natural disasters) in exchange for a fee, called a premium. For example, Geico is one of the largest auto insurers in the United States. In the advertisement, Geico encourages people to combine home and auto insurance to save money. Geico offers insurance coverage for cars, boats, motorcycles and ATVs, RVs, renters, homeowners, and more. Because insurance premiums flow into the companies regularly, but major insurance losses cannot be timed with great accuracy (though expected risks can be assessed with considerable precision), insurance companies generally have large amounts of excess funds. They typically invest these or make long-term loans, particularly to businesses in the form of commercial real estate loans.

Pension Funds. Pension funds are managed investment pools set aside by individuals, corporations, unions, and some nonprofit organizations to provide retirement income for members. One type of pension fund is the *individual retirement*

account (IRA), which is established by individuals to provide for their personal retirement needs. IRAs can be invested in a variety of financial assets, from risky commodities such as oil or cocoa to low-risk financial "staples" such as U.S. Treasury securities. The choice is up to each person and is dictated solely by individual objectives and tolerance for risk. The interest earned by all of these investments may be deferred tax-free until retirement.

In 1997, Congress revised the IRA laws and created a Roth IRA. Although similar to a traditional IRA, the money in a Roth IRA is considered an after-tax contribution. Workers can contribute $6,000 per year, and those over 50 can add an extra $1,000, but in all cases, if you make too much money, you cannot fund a Roth. When the money is withdrawn at retirement, no tax is paid on the distribution. The Roth IRA is beneficial to young people who can allow a long time for their money to compound and who may be able to have their parents or grandparents fund the Roth IRA with gift money.

Most major corporations provide some kind of pension plan for their employees. Many of these are established with bank trust departments or life insurance companies. Money is deposited in a separate account in the name of each individual employee, and when the employee retires, the total amount in the account can be either withdrawn in one lump sum or taken as monthly cash payments over some defined time period (usually for the remaining life of the retiree).

Social Security, the largest pension fund, is publicly financed. The federal government collects Social Security funds from payroll taxes paid by both employers and employees. The Social

Security Administration then takes these monies and makes payments to those eligible to receive Social Security benefits—the retired, the disabled, and the young children of deceased parents.

Mutual Funds.
A **mutual fund** pools individual investor dollars and invests them in large numbers of well-diversified securities. Individual investors buy shares in a mutual fund in the hope of earning a high rate of return and in much the same way as people buy shares of stock. Because of the large numbers of people investing in any one mutual fund, the funds can afford to invest in hundreds (if not thousands) of securities at any one time, minimizing the risks of any single security that does not do well. Mutual funds provide professional financial management for people who lack the time and/or expertise to invest in particular securities, such as government bonds. While there are no hard-and-fast rules, investments in one or more mutual funds are one way for people to plan for financial independence at the time of retirement.

A special type of mutual fund called a *money market fund* invests specifically in short-term debt securities issued by governments and large corporations. Although they offer services such as check-writing privileges and reinvestment of interest income, money market funds differ from the money market accounts offered by banks primarily in that the former represent a pool of funds, while the latter are basically specialized, individual checking accounts. Money market funds usually offer slightly higher rates of interest than bank money market accounts.

Exchange-traded Funds
Exchange-traded funds (ETFs) are similar to mutual funds in that they invest in a pool of assets. The difference is that the assets in the fund duplicate a stock market index such as the Standard and Poor's 500, the Dow Jones Industrials, or the Russell 2000. These funds can also imitate an index tracking an industry such as biotech or banking. One of the benefits of ETFs is that they have very low management fees because they are not actively managed as are mutual funds.

Brokerage Firms and Investment Banks.
Brokerage firms buy and sell stocks, bonds, and other securities for their customers and provide other financial services. Larger brokerage firms like Merrill Lynch, Charles Schwab, and Edward Jones offer financial services unavailable at their smaller competitors. Merrill Lynch, for example, offers the Merrill Lynch Cash Management Account (CMA), which pays interest on deposits and allows clients to write checks, borrow money, and withdraw cash much like a commercial bank. The largest brokerage firms have developed so many specialized services that they may be considered financial networks—organizations capable of offering virtually all of the services traditionally associated with commercial banks. The rise of online brokerage firms has helped investors who want to do it themselves at low costs. Firms like E-Trade and TD Ameritrade offer investors the ability to buy and sell securities. In 2020, major online brokerage firms like

Fidelity, Charles Schwab, E-Trade, and others eliminated commissions on stock trades. The same trade at Morgan Stanley might cost up to 1% on the value of the trade. E-Trade offers banking services, debit cards, wire transfers, and many of the same services that the traditional brokerage firms offer.

Most brokerage firms are really part financial conglomerates that provide many different kinds of services besides buying and selling securities for clients. For example, Merrill Lynch also is an investment banker, as are Morgan Stanley and Goldman Sachs. The **investment banker** underwrites new issues of securities for corporations, states, and municipalities needed to raise money in the capital markets. The new issue market is called a *primary market* because the sale of the securities is for the first time. After the first sale, the securities trade in the *secondary markets* by brokers. The investment banker advises on the price of the new securities and generally guarantees the sale while overseeing the distribution of the securities through the selling brokerage houses. Investment bankers also act as dealers who make markets in securities. They do this by offering to sell the securities at an asked price (which is a higher rate) and buy the securities at a bid price (which is a lower rate)—the difference in the two prices represents the profit for the dealer.

Finance Companies.
Finance companies are businesses that offer short-term loans at substantially higher rates of interest than banks. Commercial finance companies make loans to businesses, requiring their borrowers to pledge assets such as equipment, inventories, or unpaid accounts as collateral for the loans. Consumer finance companies make loans to individuals. Like commercial finance companies, these firms require some sort of personal collateral as security against the borrower's possible inability to repay their loans. Because of the high interest rates they charge and other factors, finance companies typically are the lender of last resort for individuals and businesses whose credit limits have been exhausted and/or those with poor credit ratings.

Electronic Banking
Since the advent of the computer age, a wide range of technological innovations has made it possible to move money all across the world electronically. Such "paperless" transactions have allowed financial institutions to reduce costs in what has been, and continues to be, a virtual competitive battlefield. **Electronic**

mutual fund an investment company that pools individual investor dollars and invests them in large numbers of well-diversified securities.

exchange-traded funds an investment fund made up of a pool of assets that track an underlying index.

brokerage firms firms that buy and sell stocks, bonds, and other securities for their customers and provide other financial services.

investment banker underwrites new issues of securities for corporations, states, and municipalities.

finance companies businesses that offer short-term loans at substantially higher rates of interest than banks.

electronic funds transfer (EFT) any movement of funds by means of an electronic terminal, telephone, computer, or magnetic tape.

automated teller machine (ATM) the most familiar form of electronic banking, which dispenses cash, accepts deposits, and allows balance inquiries and cash transfers from one account to another.

automated clearinghouses (ACHs) a system that permits payments such as deposits or withdrawals to be made to and from a bank account by magnetic computer tape.

funds transfer (EFT) is any movement of funds by means of an electronic terminal, telephone, computer, or magnetic tape. Such transactions order a particular financial institution to subtract money from one account and add it to another. The most commonly used forms of EFT are automated teller machines, automated clearinghouses, and home banking systems.

Automated Teller Machines.

Probably the most familiar form of electronic banking is the **automated teller machine (ATM)**, which dispenses cash, accepts deposits, and allows balance inquiries and cash transfers from one account to another. ATMs provide 24-hour banking services—both at home (through a local bank) and far away (via worldwide ATM networks such as Cirrus and Plus). Rapid growth, driven by both strong consumer acceptance and lower transaction costs for banks (about half the cost of teller transactions), has led to the installation of hundreds of thousands of ATMs worldwide. Table 15.5 presents some interesting statistics about ATMs.

Automated Clearinghouses.

Automated clearinghouses (ACHs) permit payments such as deposits or withdrawals to be made to and from a bank account by magnetic computer tape. Most large U.S. employers, and many others worldwide, use ACHs to deposit their employees' paychecks directly to the employees' bank accounts. While direct deposit is used by only 50 percent of U.S. workers, nearly 100 percent of Japanese workers and more than 90 percent of European workers utilize it. The largest user of automated clearinghouses in the United States is the federal government, with 99 percent of federal government employees and 65 percent of the private workforce receiving their pay via direct deposit. More than 82 percent of all Social Security payments are made through an ACH system. The Social Security Administration is trying to reduce costs and reduce theft and fraud, so if you applied for Social Security benefits on or after May 1, 2011, you must receive your payments electronically.

The advantages of direct deposits to consumers include convenience, safety, and potential interest earnings. It is estimated that more than 4 million paychecks are lost or stolen annually, and FBI studies show that 2,000 fraudulent checks are cashed every day in the United States. Checks can never be lost or stolen with direct deposit. The benefits to businesses include decreased check-processing expenses and increased employee productivity. Research shows that businesses that use direct deposit can save more than $1.25 on each payroll check processed. Productivity could increase by $3 to $5 billion annually if all employees were to use direct deposit rather than taking time away from work to deposit their payroll checks.

Some companies also use ACHs for dividend and interest payments. Consumers can also use ACHs to make periodic (usually monthly) fixed payments to specific creditors without ever having to write a check or buy stamps. The estimated number of bills paid annually by consumers is 20 billion, and the total number paid through ACHs is estimated at only 8.5 billion. The average consumer who writes 10 to 15 checks each month would save $41 to $62 annually in postage alone.[9]

Online Banking.

Many banking activities are now conducted on a computer at home or at work or through wireless devices such as cell phones and tablets anywhere there is a wireless "hot spot." Consumers and small businesses can now make a bewildering array of financial transactions at home or on the go 24 hours a day. Functioning much like a vast network of personal ATMs, companies like Google and Apple provide online banking services through mobile phones, allowing subscribers to make sophisticated banking transactions, buy and sell stocks

▼ **TABLE 15.5** Facts about ATM Use

ATM users spend 20–25 percent more in convenience stores alone.
The average ATM is used 300 times per month.
60 percent of Americans ages 25–34, and 51 percent ages 35–49, withdraw $40.00 8–10 times per month.
Over 10 billion transactions are performed at ATMs in the U.S. every year.
The average 24 hour convenience store ATM performs approximately 3000 transactions per month.

Source: National Cash Systems, "ATM Statistics," http://www.nationalcash.com/statistics/ (accessed June 15, 2020).

Computers and handheld devices have made online banking extremely convenient. However, hackers have stolen millions from banking customers by tricking them into visiting websites and downloading malicious software that gives hackers access to their passwords.

Kite_rin/Shutterstock

A digital wallet is an electronic device, app, or online service that allows electronic financial transfers between two parties. As the world becomes more digitized and mobile, the growth of digital wallets has boomed. Most smartphones are already equipped with phone-specific digital wallets (e.g., Apple Wallet), or consumers can pick from a selection of peer-to-peer payment apps (e.g., Zelle), Bitcoin wallet apps (e.g., Mobi), and credit card or bank wallet apps (e.g. Chase Pay). Users can utilize the apps to make purchases in-store, in-app, or while shopping on the web. Retailers must have the necessary card readers to accept digital payments.

Many wallet apps have the added convenience of storing loyalty cards, plane tickets, event tickets, and more. Digital payments are often faster and more secure than traditional payment methods, and, by not holding cash or physical cards, consumers can protect themselves against theft and fraud. Despite these advantages, more than half of consumers don't trust the technology, according to a survey by Experian. Only 13 percent of Americans use digital wallets on a weekly basis. One way consumers can add an additional layer of protection is to use multi- or two-factor authentication on their mobile device.

Mobile payment adoption in the United States has been slow, however, this has not been the case worldwide. In China, for example, nearly half of all in-store purchases are made with digital wallets. This is due to the Chinese government's active role in creating a digital financial infrastructure. The country is developing a digital currency that is backed by its central bank. Companies such as Alipay and WeChat Pay are growing throughout Asia and stand to be major competitors worldwide as the companies globalize.

While digital wallets have seen great growth, it's too soon to say goodbye to traditional payment methods. One reason is that not all businesses have adopted technology to accept payments from digital wallets. Countries that are deeply invested in legacy payment systems, such as the United States and Europe, will have to play catch up with countries that have quickly developed and adopted digital payment systems such as China and India. However, as more and more consumers adopt the technology, more businesses will follow in order to accept these types of payments.[d]

Critical Thinking Questions

1. Do you think digital wallets will revolutionize electronic banking and in-store transactions?

2. How do you think digital wallets will affect traditional banks?

3. What are some of the risks of digital wallets? What can be done to mitigate these risks?

---

and bonds, and purchase products and airline tickets without ever leaving home or speaking to another human being. Many banks allow customers to log directly into their accounts to check balances, transfer money between accounts, view their account statements, and pay bills via home computer or other Internet-enabled devices. Computer and advanced telecommunications technology have revolutionized world commerce; 62 percent of adults list Internet banking as their preferred banking method, making it the most popular banking method in the United States.[10]

changing, with machines now dispensing more than just cash. Online financial services, ATM technology, and bill presentation are just a few of the areas where rapidly changing technology is causing the banking industry to change as well.

LO 15-6 Analyze the challenges ahead for the banking industry.

Future of Banking

Rapid advances and innovations in technology are challenging the banking industry and requiring it to change. For example, person-to-person (P2P) payment tools like PayPal, Apple Pay, and Venmo have created competition for banks. To compete with third-party P2P apps, Early Warning Services, a financial institution that is owned by seven large banks, introduced Zelle. Eighteen banks in the United States, including Chase and Bank of America, have built-in Zelle to their apps to make cash transfers easy for customers.[11] Additionally, ATM technology is rapidly

> **Rapid advances and innovations in technology are challenging the banking industry and requiring it to change.**

The Fed Response to Crisis.

During the period of both the financial crisis that began in 2007 and again with the crisis brought about by the COVID-19 pandemic in 2020, the Federal Reserve took unprecedented actions. These actions included buying up troubled assets from the banks and lending money at the discount window to nonbanks such as investment banks and brokers. The Fed also entered into the financial markets by making markets in commercial paper and other securities where the markets had ceased to function in an orderly fashion. Additionally, the Fed began to pay interest on reserves banks kept at the Fed, and finally, it kept interest rates low to stimulate the economy and to help the banks regain their health. Because banks make money by the spread between their borrowing and lending rates, the Fed managed the spread between long- and short-term rates to generate a fairly large spread for the banks.

Additionally, to keep interest rates low and stimulate the economy, the Fed bought billions of dollars of mortgages and other financial assets on a monthly basis. By mid-2017, it had accumulated $4.5 trillion of securities on its balance sheet even though it stopped its asset purchases in 2015 as the economy improved. From the end of 2017 to 2019, the Fed was letting the securities in the portfolio mature without reinvesting the proceeds. Unfortunately, the COVID-19 pandemic started the Fed back on the path of purchasing securities for its own portfolio.

In reaction to the financial meltdown and severe recession caused by the financial crisis, Congress passed the Dodd-Frank Wall Street Reform and Consumer Protection Act. The full name implies that the intent of the act is to eliminate the ability of banks to create this type of problem in the future. Fortunately, by the time of the crisis caused by the pandemic, banks and financial institutions were well capitalized, in strong financial condition, and able to handle the financial strain posed by the crisis.

Shadow Banking.
In broad general terms, *shadow banking* refers to companies performing banking functions of some sort that are not regulated by banking regulators. Shadow banking activities are increasing. In a letter to shareholders in its annual report, James Dimon, CEO and chair of JPMorgan Chase, was quoted as saying to his shareholders that the bank will face tough competitors, including shadow banking. He may have said it best in the following quote:

> Many of these institutions are smart and sophisticated and will benefit as banks move out of certain products and services.

Non-bank financial competitors will look at every product we price, and if they can do it cheaper with their set of capital providers, they will. There is nothing inherently wrong with this—it is a natural state of affairs and, in some cases, may benefit the clients who get the better price. But regulators should—and will—be looking at how all financial companies (including non-bank competitors) need to be regulated and will be evaluating what is better to be done by banks vs. non-banks and vice versa.[12]

In addition to shadow banks mentioned by Mr. Dimon, there are the peer-to-peer lenders like Prosper, a company that matches investors and borrowers with loans of between $2,000 and $35,000. There are other sources of funding by Internet websites such as GoFundMe, which helps people enhance their life skills, raise money for health care issues, and more. Another similar website is Kickstarter, which funds creative projects in the worlds of art, film, games, music, publishing, and so on. In many cases, funds provided for these projects replace loans that might have been used to develop the project. These forms of funding are growing rapidly. ■

DO YOU WANT A CAREER // in Finance or Banking? /

You think you might be interested in going into finance or banking, but it is so hard to tell when you are a full-time student. Classes that seem interesting when you take them might not translate into an interesting work experience after graduation. A great way to see if you would excel at a career in finance is to get some experience in the industry. Internships, whether they are paid or unpaid, not only help you figure out what you might really want to do after you graduate, but they are also a great way to build up your résumé, put your learning to use, and start generating connections within the field.

For example, Pennsylvania's Delaware County District Attorney's Office has been accepting business students from Villanova University for a six-month internship. The student works in the economic crime division, analyzing documents of people under investigation for financial crimes ranging from fraud to money laundering. The students get actual experience in forensic accounting and have the chance to see whether this is the right career path. One student who completed the program spent his six months investigating a case in which the owner of a sewage treatment company had embezzled a total of $1 million over the course of nine years. The student noted that the experience helped him gain an understanding about how different companies handle their financial statements, as well as how accounting can be applied in forensics and law enforcement.

Internship opportunities are plentiful all over the country, although you may need to do some research to find them. To start, talk to your program advisor and your professors about opportunities. Also, you can check company websites where you think you might like to work to see if they have any opportunities available. City, state, or federal government offices often provide student internships as well. No matter where you end up interning, the real-life skills you pick up, as well as the résumé boost you get, will be helpful in finding a job after you graduate. When you graduate, commercial banks and other financial institutions offer major employment opportunities. In 2008–2009, a major downturn in the financial industry resulted in mergers, acquisitions, and financial restructuring for many companies. While the immediate result was a decrease in job opportunities, as the industry recovers, there will be many challenging job opportunities available.[13]

sixteen

financial management and securities markets

Rillion Photos/Shutterstock

LEARNING OBJECTIVES

After reading this chapter, you will be able to:

LO 16-1 Describe some common methods of managing current assets.

LO 16-2 Identify some sources of short-term financing (current liabilities).

LO 16-3 Summarize the importance of long-term assets and capital budgeting.

LO 16-4 Specify how companies finance their operations and manage fixed assets with long-term liabilities, particularly bonds.

LO 16-5 Explain how corporations can use equity financing by issuing stock through an investment banker.

LO 16-6 Describe the various securities markets in the United States.

While it's certainly true that money makes the world go around, financial management is the discipline that makes the world turn more smoothly. Indeed, without effective management of assets, liabilities, and owners' equity, all business organizations are doomed to fail—regardless of the quality and innovativeness of their products. Financial management is the field that addresses the issues of obtaining and managing the funds and resources necessary to run a business successfully. It is not limited to business organizations: All organizations, from the corner store to the local nonprofit art museum, from giant corporations to county governments, must manage their resources effectively and efficiently if they are to achieve their objectives.

In this chapter, we look at both short- and long-term financial management. First, we discuss the management of short-term assets, which companies use to generate sales and conduct ordinary day-to-day business operations. Next, we turn our attention to the management of short-term liabilities, the sources of short-term funds used to finance the business. Then, we discuss the management of long-term assets such as plants, equipment, and the use of common stock (equity) and bonds (long-term liability) to finance these long-term corporate assets. Finally, we look at the securities markets, where stocks and bonds are traded. ■

LO 16-1 Describe some common methods of managing current assets.

MANAGING CURRENT ASSETS AND LIABILITIES

Managing short-term assets and liabilities involves managing the current assets and liabilities on the balance sheet (discussed in the "Accounting and Financial Statements" chapter). Current assets are short-term resources such as cash, investments, accounts receivable, and inventory. Current liabilities are short-term debts such as accounts payable, accrued salaries, accrued taxes, and short-term bank loans. We use the terms *current* and *short term* interchangeably because short-term assets and liabilities are usually replaced by new assets and liabilities within three or four months, and always within a year. Managing short-term assets and liabilities is sometimes called **working capital management** because short-term assets and liabilities continually flow through an organization and are thus said to be "working."

Managing Current Assets

The chief goal of financial managers who focus on current assets and liabilities is to maximize the return to the business on cash, temporary investments of idle cash, accounts receivable, and inventory.

Managing Cash. A crucial element facing any financial manager is effectively managing the firm's cash flow. Remember that cash flow is the movement of money through an organization on a daily, weekly, monthly, or yearly basis. Ensuring that sufficient (but not excessive) funds are on hand to meet the company's obligations is one of the single most important facets of financial management.

Idle cash does not make money, and corporate checking accounts typically do not earn interest. As a result, astute money managers try to keep just enough cash on hand, called **transaction balances**, to pay bills—such as employee wages, supplies, and utilities—as they fall due. To manage the firm's cash and ensure that enough cash flows through the organization quickly and efficiently, companies try to speed up cash collections from customers.

To facilitate collection, some companies have customers send their payments to a **lockbox**, which is simply an address for receiving payments, instead of directly to the company's main address. The manager of the lockbox, usually a commercial bank, collects payments directly from the lockbox several times

working capital management the managing of short-term assets and liabilities.

transaction balances cash kept on hand by a firm to pay normal daily expenses, such as employee wages and bills for supplies and utilities.

lockbox an address, usually a commercial bank, at which a company receives payments in order to speed collections from customers.

marketable securities temporary investment of "extra" cash by organizations for up to one year in U.S. Treasury bills, certificates of deposit, commercial paper, or eurodollar loans.

Treasury bills (T-bills) short-term debt obligations the U.S. government sells to raise money.

commercial certificates of deposit (CDs) certificates of deposit issued by commercial banks and brokerage companies, available in minimum amounts of $100,000, which may be traded prior to maturity.

a day and deposits them into the company's bank account. The bank can then start clearing the checks and get the money into the company's checking account much more quickly than if the payments had been submitted directly to the company. However, there is no free lunch: The costs associated with lockbox systems make them worthwhile only for those companies that receive thousands of checks from customers each business day.

For example, State Farm Insurance sends out invoices to their millions of customers for home, auto, and other insurances policies. Their customers send their checks to a lockbox at a post office in Dallas Texas.

More companies are now using electronic funds transfer systems to pay and collect bills online. Companies generally want to collect cash quickly but pay out cash slowly. When companies use electronic funds transfers between buyers and suppliers, the speed of collections and disbursements increases to one day. Only with the use of checks can companies delay the payment of cash by three or four days until the check is presented to their bank and the cash leaves their account.

Investing Idle Cash.

As companies sell products, they generate cash on a daily basis, and sometimes cash comes in faster than it is needed to pay bills. Organizations often invest this "extra" cash, for periods as short as one day (overnight) or for as long as one year, until it is needed. Such temporary investments of cash are known as **marketable securities**. Examples

include U.S. Treasury bills, certificates of deposit, commercial paper, and eurodollar deposits. Table 16.1 summarizes a number of different marketable securities used by businesses and some sample interest rates on these investments as of June 23, 2006, April 18, 2016, January 8, 2019, and May 27, 2020. The safety rankings are relative. While all of the listed securities are very low risk, the U.S. government securities are the safest. You can see from the table that interest rates have had an up and down ride over this time period.

The Fed used monetary policy to lower interest rates to stimulate borrowing and investment during the recession of 2007–2009 and kept rates low into 2016 to stimulate employment and economic growth. The Fed raised interest rates 25 basis points (1/4 of a percent) in December 2015, again in 2016, three times in 2017, and three times in 2018. Rising rates were derailed by the COVID-19 (coronavirus) pandemic as the Fed once again lowered rates close to zero to stimulate an economy in trouble and corporations who needed short-term loans to survive the economic collapse.

Many large companies invest idle cash in U.S. **Treasury bills (T-bills)**, which are short-term debt obligations the U.S. government sells to raise money. Issued weekly by the U.S. Treasury, T-bills carry maturities of between one week and one year. U.S. T-bills are generally considered to be the safest of all investments and are called risk free because the U.S. government will not default on its debt.

Commercial certificates of deposit (CDs) are issued by commercial banks and brokerage companies. They are available in minimum amounts of $100,000 but are typically in units of $1 million for large corporations investing excess cash. Unlike consumer CDs (discussed in the "Money and the Financial System" chapter), which must be held until maturity, commercial CDs may be traded prior to maturity. Should a cash shortage occur, the organization can simply sell the CD on the open market and obtain needed funds.

▼ **TABLE 16.1** Short-Term Investment Possibilities for Idle Cash

Type of Security	Maturity	Seller of Security	Interest Rate				Safety Level
			6/23/2006	4/18/2016	1/9/2019	10/6/2020	
U.S. Treasury bills	90 days	U.S. government	4.80%	0.22%	2.41%	0.10%	Excellent
U.S. Treasury bills	180 days	U.S. government	5.05	0.35	2.48	0.10	Excellent
Commercial paper	30 days	Major corporations	5.14	0.46	2.49	0.09	Very good
Certificates of deposit	90 days	U.S. commercial banks	5.40	0.40	2.25	0.05	Very good
Certificates of deposit	180 days	U.S. commercial banks	5.43	0.45	2.40	0.05	Very good
Eurodollars	90 days	European commercial banks	5.48	0.65	2.87*	0.18**	Very good

* Rate is as of December 31, 2018.
** Rate is as of March 9, 2020.

Sources: Board of Governors of the Federal Reserve System, "Selected Interest Rates (Weekly)—H.15," October 7, 2020, www.federalreserve.gov/releases/H15/current/default.htm (accessed October 7, 2020); Fidelity, "Certificates of Deposit," www.fidelity.com/fixed-income-bonds/cds (accessed October 7, 2020); Eurodollars, Bank of England, bankofengland.co.uk (accessed October 7, 2020).

Companies can invest their idle cash in marketable securities such as U.S. Treasury bills, commercial paper, and eurodollar deposits.

allstars/Shutterstock

commercial paper a written promise from one company to another to pay a specific amount of money.

eurodollar market a market for trading U.S. dollars in foreign countries.

One of the most popular short-term investments for the largest business organizations is **commercial paper**—a written promise from one company to another to pay a specific amount of money. Because commercial paper is backed only by the name and reputation of the issuing company, sales of commercial paper are restricted to only the largest and most financially stable companies. As commercial paper is frequently bought and sold for durations as short as one business day, many "players" in the market find themselves buying commercial paper with excess cash on one day and selling it to gain extra money the following day.

During the Great Recession, which began in 2007, the commercial paper market simply stopped functioning. Investors no longer trusted the IOUs of even the best companies. Companies that had relied on commercial paper to fund short-term cash needs had to turn to the banks for borrowing. Those companies who had existing lines of credit at their bank were able to draw on their line of credit. Others were in a tight spot. Eventually, the Federal Reserve entered the market to buy and sell commercial paper for its own portfolio. The Fed did this again during the COVID-19 pandemic, but this is something the Fed would only do in a crisis situation where markets need liquidity (buyers and sellers) to function. When there are no buyers, the Fed steps into the markets.

Some companies invest idle cash in international markets such as the **eurodollar market**, a market for U.S. dollars held in foreign countries. Because the eurodollar market was originally developed by London banks, any dollar-denominated deposit in a non-U.S. bank is called a eurodollar deposit. For example, if a U.S. or foreign company deposits U.S. dollars in a London bank, it will have "created" a eurodollar deposit. Because the U.S. dollar is an international currency, these dollar deposits can be used by international companies to settle their accounts. The market created for trading such investments offers firms with extra dollars a chance to earn a slightly higher rate of return with just a little more risk than they would face by investing in U.S. Treasury bills.

Managing Accounts Receivable.
After cash and marketable securities, the balance sheet lists accounts receivable and inventory. Remember that accounts receivable is money owed to a business by credit customers. Many businesses make the vast majority of their sales on credit, so managing accounts receivable is an important task.

Each credit sale represents an account receivable for the company, the terms of which typically require customers to pay the full amount due within 30, 60, or even 90 days from the date of the sale. To encourage quick payment, some businesses offer some of their customers discounts of between 1 and 2 percent if they pay off their balance within a specified period of time (usually between 10 and 30 days). On the other hand, late payment charges of between 1 and 1.5 percent serve to discourage slow payers from sitting on their bills forever. The larger the discount for early payment, the faster customers will tend to pay their accounts. Unfortunately, while discounts increase cash flow, they also reduce profitability. Finding the right balance between the added advantages of early cash receipt and the disadvantages of reduced profits is no simple matter. Similarly, determining the optimal balance between the higher sales likely to result from extending credit to customers with less than sterling credit ratings and the higher bad-debt losses likely to result from a more lenient credit policy is also challenging. Information on company credit ratings is provided by local credit bureaus, national credit-rating agencies such as Dun & Bradstreet, and industry trade groups.

Optimizing Inventory.
While the inventory that a firm holds is controlled by both production needs and marketing considerations, the financial manager has to coordinate inventory

From materials management, race timing, or attendee tracking, RFID technology has many practical applications.

nullplus/Getty Images

trade credit credit extended by suppliers for the purchase of their goods and services.

line of credit an arrangement by which a bank agrees to lend a specified amount of money to an organization upon request.

secured loans loans backed by collateral that the bank can claim if the borrowers do not repay them.

unsecured loans loans backed only by the borrower's good reputation and previous credit rating.

purchases to manage cash flows. The object is to minimize the firm's investment in inventory without experiencing production cutbacks as a result of critical materials shortfalls or lost sales due to insufficient finished goods inventories. Every dollar invested in inventory is a dollar not available for investment in some other area of the organization. Optimal inventory levels are determined in large part by the method of production. If a firm attempts to produce its goods just in time to meet sales demand, the level of inventory will be relatively low. If, on the other hand, the firm produces materials in a constant, level pattern, inventory increases when sales decrease and decreases when sales increase. One way companies manage finished goods inventory is through the use of radio frequency identification (RFID) technology. For example, Walmart manages its inventories by using RFID tags. An RFID tag contains a silicon chip and an antenna and allows a company to use radio waves to track and identify the products to which the tags are attached. These tags are primarily used to track inventory shipments from the manufacturer to the buyer's warehouses and then to the individual stores and also cut down on trucking theft because the delivery truck and its contents can be tracked in real time.

The automobile industry is an excellent example of an industry driven almost solely by inventory levels. Because it is inefficient to continually lay off workers in slow times and call them back in better times, Ford, General Motors, and Toyota try to set and stick to quarterly production quotas. Automakers typically try to keep a 60-day supply of unsold cars. During particularly slow periods, however, it is not unusual for inventories to exceed 100 days of sales.

Although less publicized, inventory shortages can be as much of a drag on potential profits as too much inventory. Not having an item on hand may send the customer to a competitor—forever. Complex computer inventory models are frequently employed to determine the optimum level of inventory a firm should hold to support a given level of sales. Such models can indicate how and when parts inventories should be ordered so that they are available exactly when required—and not a day before. Developing and maintaining such an intricate production and inventory system is difficult, but it can often prove to be the difference between experiencing average profits and spectacular ones.

LO 16-2 Identify some sources of short-term financing (current liabilities).

Managing Current Liabilities

While having extra cash on hand is a delightful surprise, the opposite situation—a temporary cash shortfall—can be a crisis. The good news is that there are several potential sources of short-term funds. Suppliers often serve as an important source through credit sales practices. Also, banks, finance companies, and other organizations offer short-term funds through loans and other business operations.

Accounts Payable. Remember from the "Accounting and Financial Statements" chapter that accounts payable is money an organization owes to suppliers for goods and services. Just as accounts receivable must be actively managed to ensure proper cash collections, so too must accounts payable be managed.

The most widely used source of short-term financing, and therefore the most important account payable, is **trade credit**—credit extended by suppliers for the purchase of their goods and services. Most trade credit agreements offer discounts to organizations that pay their bills early. A supplier, for example, may offer trade terms of "1/10 net 30," meaning that the purchasing organization may take a 1 percent discount from the invoice amount if it makes payment by the 10th day after receiving the bill. Otherwise, the entire amount is due within 30 days. For example, pretend that you are the financial manager in charge of payables. You owe Ajax Company $10,000, and it offers trade terms of 2/10 net 30. By paying the amount due within 10 days, you can save 2 percent of $10,000, or $200. Assume you place orders with Ajax once per month and have 12 bills of $10,000 each per year. By taking the discount every time, you will save 12 times $200, or $2,400, per year. Now assume you are the financial manager of Gigantic Corp., and it has monthly payables of $100 million per month. Two percent of $100 million is $2 million per month. Failure to take advantage of such trade discounts can add up to lost cash savings over the span of a year.

Bank Loans. Virtually all organizations—large and small—obtain short-term funds for operations from banks. In most instances, the credit services granted by these firms take the form of a line of credit or fixed dollar loan. A **line of credit** is an arrangement by which a bank agrees to lend a specified amount of money to the organization upon request—provided that the bank has the required funds to make the loan. In general, a business line of credit is very similar to a consumer credit card, with the exception that the preset credit limit can amount to millions of dollars.

In addition to credit lines, banks also make **secured loans**—loans backed by collateral that the bank can claim if the borrowers do not repay the loans—and **unsecured loans**—loans backed only by the borrower's good reputation and previous credit rating. Both individuals and businesses build their credit rating from their history of borrowing and repaying borrowed funds on time and in full. The three national credit-rating services are Equifax, TransUnion, and Experian. A lack of credit history or a poor credit history can make it difficult to get loans from financial institutions. The *principal* is the amount of money borrowed; *interest* is a percentage of the principal that the bank charges for use of its money. As we mentioned in the "Money and the Financial System" chapter, banks also pay depositors interest on savings accounts and some checking accounts. Thus, banks charge borrowers interest for loans and pay interest to depositors for the use of their money. In addition, these loans may include origination fees.

One of the complaints from borrowers during the financial meltdown and recession was that banks weren't willing to lend. There were several causes. Banks were trying to rebuild their capital, and they didn't want to take the extra risk of making loans in an economic recession. They were drowning in bad debts and were not sure how future loan losses would affect their capital. Smaller regional banks did a better job of maintaining small business loans than the major money center banks who suffered most in the recession.

The **prime rate** is the interest rate commercial banks charge their best customers for short-term loans. For many years, loans at the prime rate represented funds at the lowest possible cost. For some companies, other alternatives may be cheaper, such as using commercial paper or borrowing from European banks holding dollar deposits at competitive rates (see Table 16.1).

The interest rates on commercial loans may be either fixed or variable. A variable- or floating-rate loan offers an advantage when interest rates are falling but represents a distinct disadvantage when interest rates are rising. Between 1999 and 2004, interest rates plummeted, and borrowers refinanced their loans with low-cost, fixed-rate loans. Nowhere was this more visible than in the U.S. mortgage markets, where homeowners lined up to refinance their high-percentage home mortgages with lower-cost loans, in some cases as low as 5 percent on a 30-year loan. Mortgage rates rose to 6.5 percent by mid-2006 but fell again after 2012, and in 2020, homeowners could still get a fixed-rate mortgage for less than 4 percent. Individuals and corporations have the same motivation: to minimize their borrowing costs. During this period of historically low interest rates, companies ramped up their borrowing, bought back stock, and locked in large amounts of debt at low rates.

Nonbank Liabilities. Banks are not the only source of short-term funds for businesses. Indeed, virtually all financial institutions—from insurance companies to pension funds, from money market funds to finance companies—make short-term loans to many organizations. The largest U.S. companies also actively engage in borrowing money from the eurodollar and commercial paper markets. As noted earlier, both of these funds' sources are typically slightly less expensive than bank loans.

In some instances, businesses actually sell their accounts receivable to a finance company known as a **factor**, which gives the selling organizations cash and assumes responsibility for collecting the accounts. For example, a factor might pay $80,000 for receivables with a total face value of $100,000 (80 percent of the total). The factor profits if it can collect more than what it paid for the accounts. Because the selling organization's customers send their payments to a lockbox, they may have no idea that a factor has bought their receivables.

Additional nonbank liabilities that must be efficiently managed to ensure maximum profitability are taxes owed to the government and wages owed to employees. Clearly, businesses are responsible for many different types of taxes, including federal, state, and local income taxes, property taxes, mineral rights taxes, unemployment taxes, Social Security taxes, workers' compensation taxes, excise taxes, and more. While the public tends to think that the only relevant taxes are on income and sales, many industries must pay other taxes that far exceed those levied against their income. Taxes and employees' wages represent debt obligations of the firm, which the financial manager must plan to meet as they fall due.

LO 16-3 Summarize the importance of long-term assets and capital budgeting.

MANAGING FIXED ASSETS

Up to this point, we have focused on the short-term aspects of financial management. While most business failures are the result of poor short-term planning, successful ventures must also consider the long-term financial consequences of their actions. Managing the long-term assets and liabilities and the owners' equity portion of the balance sheet is important for the long-term health of the business.

Long-term (fixed) assets are expected to last for many years—production facilities (plants), offices, equipment, heavy machinery, furniture, automobiles, and so on. In today's fast-paced world, companies need the most technologically advanced, modern facilities and equipment they can afford. Automobile, oil refining, utilities, and transportation companies are dependent on fixed assets.

For example, long-term assets for an electric utility can cost hundreds of millions of dollars. There are lots of ways for companies to finance long-term assets, including leasing, selling bonds, selling stock, reinvesting profits, or a combination of these options. Obtaining major long-term financing can be challenging for even

prime rate the interest rate that commercial banks charge their best customers (usually large corporations) for short-term loans.

factor a finance company to which businesses sell their accounts receivable—usually for a percentage of the total face value.

long-term (fixed) assets production facilities (plants), offices, and equipment—all of which are expected to last for many years.

capital budgeting
the process of analyzing the needs of the business and selecting the assets that will maximize its value.

the most profitable organizations. For less successful firms, such challenges can prove nearly impossible, and leasing assets such as equipment, machines, and buildings is often the best option for less-profitable companies. Leasing involves paying a fee for usage rather than owning the asset. We'll take a closer look at long-term financing in a moment, but first let's address some issues associated with fixed assets, including capital budgeting, risk assessment, and the costs of financing fixed assets.

Capital Budgeting and Project Selection

One of the most important jobs performed by the financial manager is to decide what fixed assets, projects, and investments will earn profits for the firm beyond the costs necessary to fund them. The process of analyzing the needs of the business and selecting the fixed assets that will maximize its value is called **capital budgeting**, and the capital budget is the amount of money budgeted for investment in such long-term assets. But capital budgeting does not end with the selection and purchase of a particular piece of land, equipment, or major investment. All assets and projects must be continually reevaluated to ensure their compatibility with the organization's needs. If a particular asset does not live up to expectations, then management must determine why and take necessary corrective action. Budgeting is not an exact process, and managers must be flexible when new information is available.

Assessing Risk

Every investment carries some risk. Figure 16.1 ranks potential investment projects according to estimated risk. When considering investments overseas, risk assessments must include the political climate and economic stability of a region. For example, the decision to introduce a product or build a manufacturing facility in England would be much less risky than a decision to build one in the Middle East.

The longer a project or asset is expected to last, the greater its potential risk because it is hard to predict whether a piece of equipment will wear out or become obsolete in 5 or 10 years. Predicting cash flows one year down the road is difficult, but projecting them over the span of a 10-year project is a gamble.

The level of a project's risk is also affected by the stability and competitive nature of the marketplace and the world economy as a whole. The latest high-technology computer product is far more likely to become obsolete overnight than an electric utility plant. Dramatic changes in world markets are not uncommon. Indeed, uncertainty created by the rapid devaluation of Asian currencies in the late 1990s laid waste to the financial forecasts that hundreds of projects had relied on for their economic feasibility. Financial managers have to consider the probability of changing conditions that could affect their forecast when making long-term decisions about the purchase of fixed assets.

▼**FIGURE 16.1**
Qualitative Assessment of Capital Budgeting Risk

Pricing Long-Term Money

The ultimate success of any project depends not only on accurate assumptions of return on investment, but also on its cost of capital (equity and debt). Because a business must pay interest on money it borrows and generate returns for stockholders, the returns from any project must cover not only the costs of operating the project, but also the cost of capital used to finance the project. Unless an organization can effectively cover all of its costs—both financial and operating—it will eventually fail.

Clearly, only a limited supply of funds is available for investment in any given enterprise. The most efficient and profitable companies can attract the lowest-cost funds because they typically offer reasonable financial returns at very low relative risks. Newer and less prosperous firms must pay higher costs to attract capital because these companies tend to be quite risky. One of the strongest motivations for companies to manage their financial resources wisely is that they will, over time, be able to reduce the costs of their funds and in so doing increase their overall profitability.

In our free-enterprise economy, new firms tend to enter industries that offer the greatest potential rewards for success. However, as

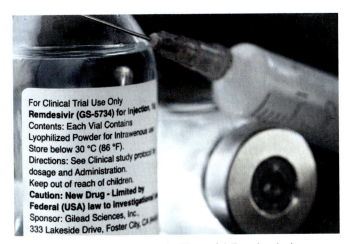

Pharmaceutical companies spend millions of dollars developing drugs without knowing if the drug will pass FDA approval and have a significant profit margin.

Lubo Ivanko/Shutterstock

more and more companies enter an industry, competition intensifies, eventually driving profits down to average levels. The digital music player market of the early 2000s provides an excellent example of the changes in profitability that typically accompany increasing competition. The sign of a successful capital budgeting program is that the new products create higher than normal profits and drive sales, profits, and the stock price up. This has certainly been true for Apple when it made the decision to enter the consumer electronics industry. In 2001, Apple introduced the first iPod, and as the iPod became more popular, it made the iTunes Store possible. The iPhone, introduced in 2007, has now gone through many updates, and over time, iPhones took the place of iPods as music players and have become sophisticated cameras and mini televisions. Apple introduced the iPad in 2010, the Apple Watch in 2015, AirPods in 2016, and the HomePod in 2018. Financial analysts always talk about Apple's ecosystem, which allows all Apple products to be synchronized and be updated on whatever products the user owns. Even with a well-planned capital budgeting program, it may be difficult for Apple to stay ahead of the competition, and many people think Apple has lost its innovation lead to Samsung and Amazon.

On June 9, 2014, Apple split its stock seven for one, meaning that for every share you owned, you would get six more, for a total of seven shares. There is no real gain involved because the stock price is divided by 7, so stockholders still have the same value, just more shares at a lower price. An investor who bought $1,000 of Apple stock in 2003 for $0.91 (price adjusted for stock splits) would have Apple stock worth $389,747 on June 10, 2020. The problem is having the patience to continue to hold such a winner without taking some profits along the way.[1]

Maintaining market dominance is also difficult in the personal computer industry, particularly because tablet computers are taking away market share. With increasing competition, prices have fallen dramatically. Weaker companies have failed, leaving the most efficient producers/marketers scrambling for market share. The expanded market for personal computers dramatically reduced the financial returns generated by each dollar invested in productive assets. The "glory days" of the personal computer industry have long since passed into history. Personal computers have essentially become commodity items, and profit margins for companies in this industry have shrunk as the market matures and sales decline.

long-term liabilities debts that will be repaid over a number of years, such as long-term loans and bond issues.

bonds debt instruments that larger companies sell to raise long-term funds.

LO 16-4 Specify how companies finance their operations and manage fixed assets with long-term liabilities, particularly bonds.

FINANCING WITH LONG-TERM LIABILITIES

As we said earlier, long-term assets do not come cheaply, and few companies have the cash on hand to open a new store across town, build a new manufacturing facility, research and develop a new life-saving drug, or launch a new product worldwide. To develop such fixed assets, companies need to raise low-cost long-term funds to finance them. Two common choices for raising these funds are attracting new owners (*equity financing*), which we'll look at in a moment, and taking on long-term liabilities (*debt financing*), which we'll look at now.

Long-term liabilities are debts that will be repaid over a number of years, such as long-term bank loans and bond issues. These take many different forms, but in the end, the key word is *debt*. Companies may raise money by borrowing it from commercial banks in the form of lines of credit, short-term loans, or long-term loans. Many corporations acquire debt by borrowing from financial institutions such as pension funds, mutual funds, or life insurance funds.

Companies that rely too heavily on debt can get into serious trouble should the economy falter. During recessions, they may not earn enough operating income to make the required interest payments (remember the times interest earned ratio in the "Accounting and Financial Statements" chapter). In severe cases when the problem persists too long, creditors will not restructure loans but will instead sue for the interest and principal owed and force the company into bankruptcy or reorganization.

Bonds: Corporate IOUs

Much long-term debt takes the form of **bonds**, which are debt instruments that larger companies sell to raise long-term funds. In essence, the buyers of bonds (bondholders) loan the issuer of the bonds cash in exchange for regular interest payments until the loan is repaid on or before the specified maturity date. The bond

unsecured bonds
debentures or bonds that are not backed by specific collateral.

secured bonds bonds that are backed by specific collateral that must be forfeited in the event that the issuing firm defaults.

serial bonds a sequence of small bond issues of progressively longer maturity.

floating-rate bonds bonds with interest rates that change with current interest rates otherwise available in the economy.

junk bonds a special type of high interest rate bond that carries higher inherent risks.

itself is a certificate, much like an IOU, that represents the company's debt to the bondholder. Bonds are issued by a wide variety of entities, including corporations; national, state, and local governments; public utilities; and nonprofit corporations. Most bondholders need not hold their bonds until maturity; rather, the existence of active secondary markets of brokers and dealers allows for the transfer of bonds from the owner (seller) to the buyer at an agreed-upon price.

The bond contract, or *indenture*, specifies all of the terms of the agreement between the bondholders and the issuing organization. The indenture, which can run more than 100 pages, specifies the basic terms of the bond, such as its face value, maturity date, and the annual interest rate. Table 16.2 highlights corporate bond information for four companies. The face value of the bond, its initial sales price, is typically $1,000. After this, however, the price of the bond on the open market will fluctuate along with changes in the economy (particularly, changes in interest rates) and in the creditworthiness of the issuer. Bondholders receive the face value of the bond along with the final interest payment on the maturity date. The annual interest rate (often called the *coupon rate*) is the guaranteed percentage of face value that the company will pay to the bond owner every year. For example, the 3M $1,000 bond in Table 16.2 has a coupon rate of 4 percent and would pay $40 per year in interest. In most cases, bond indentures specify that interest payments be made every six months. In the 3M example, the $40 annual payment would be divided into two semi-annual payments of $20.

In addition to the terms of interest payments and maturity date, the bond indenture typically covers other important topics, such as repayment methods, interest payment dates, procedures to be followed in case the organization fails to make the interest payments, conditions for the early repayment of the bonds, and any conditions requiring the pledging of assets as collateral.

Notice that under the Last Price column, seven of the bonds are selling at more than 100 percent of par. For example, the 3M bond sells

at 121.847 percent of par, or $1,218.47. Bonds sell above par when their coupon rate is higher than the current market rate for their risk class. Only Boeing and Dow Chemical sell at discounts to their par value as their coupon rate is less than the current rate for their risk class.

Types of Bonds

Not surprisingly, there are a great many different types of bonds. Most are **unsecured bonds**, meaning that they are not backed by collateral; such bonds are termed *debentures*. **Secured bonds**, on the other hand, are backed by specific collateral that must be forfeited in the event that the issuing firm defaults. Whether secured or unsecured, bonds may be repaid in one lump sum or with many payments spread out over a period of time. **Serial bonds**, which are different from secured bonds, are actually a sequence of small bond issues of progressively longer maturity. The firm pays off each of the serial bonds as they mature. **Floating-rate bonds** do not have fixed interest payments; instead, the interest rate changes with current interest rates otherwise available in the economy and the rate is usually reset every six months.

High-yield bonds, or **junk bonds** as they are popularly known, offer relatively high rates of interest because they have higher inherent risks. Historically, junk bonds have been associated with companies in poor financial health and/or startup firms with limited track records. In the mid-1980s, however, junk bonds became a very attractive method of financing corporate mergers; they remain popular today with many investors as a result of their very high relative interest rates. But higher risks are associated with those higher returns and the average investor would be well-advised to heed those famous words: Look before you leap! The best strategy is to buy a mutual fund specializing in high yield bonds. This provides diversification across lots of risky bonds.

▼ **TABLE 16.2** Corporate Bond Information Listed by Maturity Date

Company	Coupon in %	Maturity	Last Price	Current Yield %	Yield to Maturity %	S&P Rating
Verizon Communications Inc.	3.875	2/8/2029	115.146	3.365%	1.870%	BBB+
Johnson & Johnson	6.950	9/1/2029	145.134	4.789%	1.458%	AAA
Apple Inc.	2.200	9/11/2029	106.497	2.066%	1.418%	AA+
AT&T	4.300	2/15/2030	111.577	3.854%	2.758%	BBB
Dow Chemical Co.	2.450	2/15/2030	93.358	2.624%	3.760%	BBB−
Walmart Inc.	6.200	4/15/2038	152.567	4.064%	2.453%	AA
Boeing Co.	3.500	3/1/2039	82.506	4.242%	4.988%	BBB−
Microsoft Corp.	4.500	10/1/2040	134.688	3.341%	2.390%	AAA
3M	4.000	9/14/2048	121.847	3.283%	2.828%	AA+

Coupon—the percentage in interest payment that the bond pays based on a $1,000 bond.

Maturity—the day on which the issuer will pay off the principal.

Last Price—last price at which the security is traded.

Current Yield—the investment's annual income divided by the current price of the security.

Yield to Maturity—the total return anticipated on a bond if the bond is held until it matures.

S&P Rating—Standard & Poor's rates all bonds from AAA, the best rating, to D for companies in default of interest payments.

Source: https://fixedincome.fidelity.com/ftgw/fi/FIIndividualBondsSearch? (accessed May 27, 2020).

LO 16-5 Explain how corporations can use equity financing by issuing stock through an investment banker.

FINANCING WITH OWNERS' EQUITY

A second means of long-term financing is through equity. Remember from the "Accounting and Financial Statements" chapter that owners' equity refers to the owners' investment in an organization. Sole proprietors and partners own all or a part of their businesses outright, and their equity includes the money and assets they have brought into their ventures. Corporate owners, on the other hand, own stock or shares of their companies, which they hope will provide them with a return on their investment. Stockholders' equity includes common stock, preferred stock, and retained earnings.

Common stock (introduced in the "Options for Organizing Business" chapter) is the single most important source of capital for most new companies. On the balance sheet, the common stock account is separated into two basic parts—common stock at par and capital in excess of par. The *par value* of a stock is simply the stated value of one share of stock and has no relation to actual *market value*—the price at which the common stock is currently trading. The difference between a stock's par value and its offering price is called *capital in excess of par.* Except in the case of some very low-priced stocks, the capital in excess of par account is significantly larger than the par value account. Table 16.3 briefly explains how to gather important information from a stock quote, as it appears on Yahoo's website. You should be familiar with EPS from the "Accounting and Financial Statements" chapter. However, *beta* is a new term, and Nike's beta of 0.58 indicates that its stock price is 58 percent as volatile as the Standard & Poor's 500 Index. The market cap represents the total value of Nike's common stock. The target price of $71.27 is the analysts' consensus of the potential stock price in 12 months.

Preferred stock was defined in the "Accounting and Financial Statements" chapter as corporate ownership that gives the stockholder preference in the distribution of the company's profits but not the voting and control rights accorded to common stockholders. Thus, the primary advantage of owning preferred stock is that it is a safer investment than common stock.

All businesses exist to earn profits for their owners. Without the possibility of profit, there can be no incentive to risk investors' capital and succeed. When a corporation has profits left over after paying all of its expenses and taxes, it has the choice of retaining all or a portion of its earnings and/or paying them out to its shareholders in the form of dividends. **Retained earnings** are reinvested in the assets of the firm and belong to the owners in the form of equity. Retained earnings are an important source of funds and are, in fact, the only long-term funds that the company can generate internally.

When the board of directors distributes some of a corporation's profits to the owners, it issues them as cash dividend payments. But not all firms pay dividends. Many fast-growing firms like Facebook retain all of their earnings because they can earn high rates of return on the earnings they reinvest. Companies with fewer

BIRD SCOOTERS FLY ONTO THE SCENE

Travis VanderZanden, former chief operations officer at Lyft, extended ridesharing to scooters. His company, Bird, allows users to rent scooters by the minute with the company's app. Customers pay a flat fee of $1 plus $0.39 a minute to use scooters in 100 cities. Once finished, they leave the scooter on the sidewalk or near a bike rack.

Each scooter runs on a battery that needs recharging. Users can sign up to be a charger, where they gather uncharged scooters that are marked by the app. Chargers are paid a variable amount depending on how long the scooter has been uncharged. They place the scooters back on the streets to earn commissions.

Bird is one of the most successful startups in recent memory, securing more than $300 million in funding. Now valued at $2.5 billion, Bird secured funding through a number of well-known private equity groups like Sequoia Capital, Index Ventures, and Greycroft. Each scooter costs $500–$600 and is purchased from Segway, another company backed by Sequoia Capital. Because of this funding, Bird has been able to expand rapidly and seems poised for additional growth. However, due to the COVID-19 (coronavirus) pandemic, Bird faced an uphill battle. During the pandemic, Bird laid off about 30 percent of its employees and halted operations in the Middle East. Bird's competitors faced similar difficulties. Bird needs to make a speedy recovery to regain its footing.[a]

Critical Thinking Questions

1. How is Bird financing the business?

2. Name some of Bird's current assets. What liabilities does it have?

3. One challenge Bird has faced involves safety issues because the scooters do not come with helmets. How do you think this issue might affect future funding for Bird?

▼ **TABLE 16.3** A Basic Stock Quote

Nike Inc. (NKE)—NYSE

95.17–6.95 (−6.81%)

Previous Close	102.12	Market cap	147.992B
Open	98.38	Beta	0.81
Bid	95.21 × 800	PE ratio (TTM)	35.13
Ask	95.96 × 800	EPS (TTM)	2.71
Day's range	94.88 − 98.99	Earnings date	June 5, 2020
52-Week range	60 − 105.62	Forward dividend and yield	0.98 (0.96%)
Volume	10,869,181	Ex-dividend date	June 11, 2020
Average volume	9,645,826	1-year target estimate	95.73

1. The **52-week high and low**—the highest and lowest prices, respectively, paid for the stock in the last year; for Nike stock, the highest was $105.62 and the lowest price, $60.00.

2. **Stock**—the name of the issuing company. When followed by the letters "pf," the stock is a preferred stock.

3. **Symbol**—the ticker tape symbol for the stock; NKE.

4. **Dividend**—the annual cash dividend paid to stockholders; Nike paid a dividend of $0.98 per share of stock outstanding.

5. **Dividend yield**—the dividend return on one share of common stock; 0.96 percent.

6. **Volume**—the number of shares traded on this day; for Nike, 69,181 while the average volume over the last three months was 9,645,826 shares.

7. **Net change**—the difference between the previous day's close and the close on the day being reported; Nike was down $6.95 per share.

8. There were 800 shares bid (to buy) and 800 shares asked (for sale) but no prices given for after-hours trading.

Source: Yahoo! Finance, http://finance.yahoo.com/q?s (accessed June 11, 2020); bid/ask from E-Trade after hours.

growth opportunities like Verizon typically pay out large proportions of their earnings in the form of dividends, thereby allowing their stockholders to reinvest their dividend payments in other companies or spend their dividends. Retirees often prefer stocks that pay dividends. Table 16.4 presents a sample of companies and the dividend each paid on a single share of stock. As shown in the table, when the dividend is divided by the price the result is the **dividend yield**. The dividend yield is the cash return as a percentage of the price but does not reflect the total return an investor earns on the individual stock. If the dividend yield is 4.26 percent on Verizon and the stock price increases by 4 percent from $57.74 to $60.04, then the total return would be 8.26 percent. Most large U.S. companies pay their stockholders dividends on a quarterly basis. High-growth companies tend to pay no dividends.

The last column in Table 16.4 is the **payout ratio**, which indicates what percentage of earnings is paid to the stockholders in dividends. Companies like McDonald's and Procter & Gamble with high payout ratios have low expected growth rates. Companies like Amazon, Facebook, and Alphabet have zero payout

DID YOU KNOW?

A single share of Coca-Cola stock purchased during its original 1919 IPO would be worth more than $10 million today.[b]

ratios and are expected to grow fast because they are reinvesting cash flow into investment opportunities.

Disney and Ford both cut their dividends to zero to preserve cash during the COVID-19 pandemic though both are likely to pay dividends again under normal operating conditions. In the case of Procter and Gamble, they paid out more in dividends than they earned, and it is a good lesson to remember that dividends get paid out of cash flow. They could have even borrowed money to pay their dividend rather than cut the dividend.

INVESTMENT BANKING

A company that needs money to expand may be able to obtain financing by issuing stock. The first-time sale of stocks and bonds directly to the public is called a *new issue* or an initial public offering (IPO) and creates a stock that can be traded in the secondary market. Companies that already have stocks or bonds outstanding may offer more stock or a new issue of bonds to raise additional funds for specific projects.

New issues of stocks and bonds are sold directly to the public and to institutions in what is known as the **primary market**—the market where firms raise financial capital. The primary market differs from **secondary markets**, which are stock exchanges and over-the-counter markets where investors can trade their securities with other investors rather than the company that issued the stock or bonds. Primary market transactions actually raise cash for the issuing corporations, while secondary market transactions do not. For example, when Facebook went public on May 18, 2012, its IPO raised $16 billion for the company and stockholders, who were cashing in on their success. Once the investment bankers distributed the stock to retail brokers, the brokers sold it to clients in the secondary market for $38 per share. The stock got off to a rocky start and hit a low of $17.73 in September 2012. However, by March 2014, it was at $71.97, and as you can see from Table 16.4, it was $230.77 on June 5, 2020. You might want to check out its current price for fun, and look at its long-term price chart on Yahoo! Finance.

Investment banking, the sale of stocks and bonds for corporations, helps such companies

Ticker Symbol	Company Name	Price Per Share	Dividend Per Share	Dividend Yield	Earnings Per Share (*)	Price Earnings Ratio	Payout Ratio
AEO	American Eagle	$12.98	$0.14	1.08%	$1.52	8.54	9.21%
AMZN	Amazon	2,483.00	–	0.00%	22.57	110.01	0.00%
AXP	American Express	109.73	1.72	1.57%	6.63	16.55	25.94%
AAPL	Apple	331.50	3.28	0.99%	12.73	26.04	25.77%
DIS	Disney	124.82	–	0.00%	6.64	18.80	0.00%
F	Ford	7.34	–	0.00%	0.40	18.35	0.00%
FB	Facebook	230.77	–	0.00%	6.26	36.86	0.00%
GOOG	Alphabet	1,438.39	–	0.00%	46.60	30.87	0.00%
HOG	Harley-Davidson	25.42	0.08	0.31%	2.33	10.91	3.43%
HD	Home Depot	254.90	6.00	2.35%	10.04	25.39	59.76%
MCD	McDonald's	197.16	5.00	2.54%	7.62	25.87	65.62%
PG	Procter & Gamble	118.33	3.16	2.67%	1.86	63.62	169.89%
LUV	Southwest Airlines	38.18	0.72	1.89%	3.44	11.10	20.93%
VZ	Verizon	57.74	2.46	4.26%	4.43	13.03	55.53%

* Earnings per share are for the latest 12-month period and do not necessarily match year end numbers.

Data for price, dividends, and earning per share are from Yahoo, June 5, 2020. Dividend Yield, Price Earnings Ratio, and Payout Ratio are calculated.

raise funds by matching people and institutions who have money to invest with corporations in need of resources to exploit new opportunities. Corporations usually employ an investment banking firm to help sell their securities in the primary market. An investment banker helps firms establish appropriate offering prices for their securities. In addition, the investment banker takes care of the myriad details and securities regulations involved in any sale of securities to the public.

WILLING TO LOSE: YOUNG INVESTORS DAY TRADE DURING THE COVID-19 LOCKDOWN

Robinhood is a financial services company that processes online stock trades without commissions. It allows fractional share purchases and is designed for the small retail investor. It was started in 2013 to give the "little guy" a chance to build a portfolio. By 2019 E-Trade, Charles Schwab, and Fidelity also went to free trades, perhaps motivated by the success of Robinhood. During the stay-at-home lockdowns of the COVID-19 (coronavirus) pandemic in 2020, day trading—speculating on securities within the same trading day—became popular for many young investors in their 20s and 30s. Robinhood attracted the most registrations during the pandemic with more than 3 million new accounts.

Many young traders experienced short-term success during the pandemic. One report indicated that many day-traders who would normally bet on sports moved to the stock market as sporting events were shut down. Some profited from making smart trades in pharmaceutical companies benefitting from the pandemic.

Interestingly, others invested in companies facing financial struggles and bankruptcy such as Hertz, American Airlines, Luckin Coffee, MGM Resorts, and more. Institutional investors have suggested that while the generation of Robinhood investors might have short-term success, buying these types of companies on the hope that they will survive is not the way to build a portfolio in the long run.

One writer described Robinhood investors as the "New Odd Lot Indicator." There is an old saying by technical analysts following daily trading trends, that when the small investors are buying, it is time to sell and when the small investor is selling it is a time to buy. The Odd Lot Theory goes that small investors are prone to making emotional decisions and they buy at market tops and sell at market bottoms. However, in the pandemic environment, most were buying as the market had already gone down.

One question is whether these types of traders will be taken advantage of by professional, big institutional traders who have access to stock data by the second and build mathematical algorithmic trading models. Academic research points out that it is very difficult to outperform the market on a risk-adjusted basis over the long term. In other words, we expect that risk and reward go hand in hand—the more risk, the higher the probability of gain or loss. In most of the anecdotal stories reported in the media about the success of the Robinhood investors, it is clear they did not play with their retirement funds but were speculating with money they were willing to lose.[c]

💠 Critical Thinking Questions

1. Why do you think that Robinhood is so popular with young investors?

2. What do professional and institutional investors think about Robinhood investors?

3. What is the "Odd Lot Theory" and does it make any sense to you?

Just as large corporations such as IBM and Microsoft have a client relationship with a law firm and an accounting firm, they also have a client relationship with an investment banking firm. An investment banking firm such as Merrill Lynch, Goldman Sachs, or Morgan Stanley can provide advice about financing plans, dividend policy, or stock repurchases, as well as advice on mergers and acquisitions. Many now offer additional banking services, making them "one-stop shopping" banking centers. When Pixar merged with Disney, both companies used investment bankers to help them value the transaction. Each firm wanted an outside opinion about what it was worth to the other. Sometimes mergers fall apart because the companies cannot agree on the price each company is worth or the structure of management after the merger. The advising investment banker, working with management, often irons out these details. Of course, investment bankers do not provide these services for free. They usually charge a fee of between 1 and 1.5 percent of the transaction. A $20 billion merger can generate between $200 and $300 million in investment banking fees. The merger mania of the late 1990s allowed top investment bankers to earn huge sums. Unfortunately, this type of fee income is dependent on healthy stock markets, which seem to stimulate the merger fever among corporate executives.

LO 16-6   Describe the various securities markets in the United States.

THE SECURITIES MARKETS

Securities markets provide a mechanism for buying and selling securities. They make it possible for owners to sell their stocks and bonds to other investors. Thus, in the broadest sense, stocks and bonds markets may be thought of as providers of liquidity—the ability to turn security holdings into cash quickly and at minimal expense and effort. Without liquid securities markets, many potential investors would sit on the sidelines rather than invest their hard-earned savings in securities. Indeed, the ability to sell securities at well-established market prices is one of the very pillars of the capitalistic society that has developed over the years in the United States.

Unlike the primary market, in which corporations sell stocks directly to the public, secondary markets permit the trading of previously issued securities. There are many different secondary markets for both stocks and bonds. If you want to purchase 100 shares of Alphabet (formerly Google) common stock, for example, you must purchase this stock from another investor or institution. It is the active buying and selling by many thousands of investors that establishes the prices of all financial securities. Secondary market trades may take place on organized exchanges or in what is known as the over-the-counter market. Many brokerage houses exist to help investors with financial decisions, and many offer their services through the Internet.

Stock Markets

Stock markets exist around the world in New York, Tokyo, London, Frankfort, Paris, and other world locations. The two biggest stock markets in the United States are the New York Stock Exchange (NYSE) and the Nasdaq market.

Exchanges used to be divided into organized exchanges and over-the-counter markets, but during the past several years, dramatic changes have occurred in the markets. Both the NYSE and Nasdaq became publicly traded companies. They were previously not-for-profit organizations but are now for-profit companies. Additionally, both exchanges bought or merged with electronic exchanges. In an attempt to expand their markets, Nasdaq acquired the OMX, a Nordic stock exchange headquartered in Sweden, and the New York Stock Exchange merged with Euronext, a large European electronic exchange that trades options and futures contracts as well as common stock.

Traditionally, the Nasdaq market has been an electronic market, and many of the large technology companies such as Microsoft, Alphabet Inc., Apple, and Facebook trade on the Nasdaq market. The Nasdaq operates through dealers who buy and sell common stock (inventory) for their own accounts. The NYSE used to be primarily a floor-traded market, where brokers meet at trading posts on the floor of the New York Stock Exchange to buy and sell common stock, but now more than 80 percent of NYSE trading is electronic. The brokers act as agents for their clients and do not own their own inventory. This traditional

The New York Stock Exchange is the world's largest stock exchange by market capitalization.

EdStock/iStockphoto.com

division between the two markets is becoming less significant as the exchanges become electronic.

Electronic markets have grown quickly because of the speed, low cost, and efficiency of trading that they offer over floor trading. One of the fastest-growing electronic markets has been the Intercontinental Exchange (referred to as ICE). ICE, based in Atlanta, Georgia, primarily trades financial and commodity futures products. It started out as an energy futures exchange and has broadened its futures contracts into an array of commodities and derivative products. In December 2012, ICE made an offer to buy the New York Stock Exchange. When the NYSE became a public company and had common stock trading in the secondary market, rather than the hunter, it became the prey. On November 13, 2013, ICE completed its takeover of the NYSE. One condition of the takeover was that ICE had to divest itself of Euronext because international regulators thought the company would have a monopoly on European derivative markets. Also acquired as part of the NYSE family of exchanges was LIFFE, the London International Financial Futures Exchange. Many analysts thought that LIFFE was the major reason ICE bought the NYSE—not for its equity markets trading common stocks. What we are seeing is the globalization of securities markets and the increasing reliance on electronic trading.

The rise of electronic markets has led to the rise of robotic trading, sometimes referred to as "bots" or "algos" because they use algorithmic trading formulas to buy and sell based on market trends. Robotic trading looks for patterns in the market that will trigger a trade to buy or sell. These trading systems rely on programmed instructions that have the advantage of eliminating psychological trading errors. These systems also react to market trends faster than human traders. It is estimated that bots and algo trading accounted for up to 80 percent of the trading volume in 2018, and these systems are mostly responsible for much of the market volatility during 2018. Using artificial intelligence to enhance trading systems is in its infancy but is expected to have an influence on markets over time.

The Over-the-Counter Market

Unlike the organized exchanges, the **over-the-counter (OTC) market** is a network of dealers all over the country linked by computers, telephones, and Teletype machines. It has no central location. Today, the OTC market for common stock consists of small stocks, illiquid bank stocks, penny stocks, and companies whose stocks trade on the "pink sheets." Because most corporate bonds and all U.S. government debt securities are traded over the counter, the OTC market regularly accounts for the largest total dollar value of all of the secondary markets.

over-the-counter (OTC) market a network of dealers all over the country linked by computers, telephones, and Teletype machines.

Measuring Market Performance

Investors, especially professional money managers, want to know how well their investments are performing relative to the market as a whole. Financial managers also need to know how their companies' securities are performing when compared with their competitors'. Thus, performance measures—averages and indexes—are very important to many different people. They not only indicate the performance of a particular securities market, but also provide a measure of the overall health of the economy.

Indexes and averages are used to measure stock prices. An *index* compares current stock prices with those in a specified base period, such as 1944, 1967, or 1977. An *average* is the average of certain stock prices. The averages used are usually not simple calculations, however. Some stock market averages (such as the Standard & Poor's Composite Index) are weighted averages, where the weights employed are the total market values of each stock in the index (in this case 500). The Dow Jones Industrial Average (DJIA) is a price-weighted average. Regardless of how they are constructed, all market averages of stocks move together closely over time. See Figure 16.2, which graphs the Dow Jones Industrial Average. Notice the sharp downturn in the market during the 2008–2009 time period and the recovery that started in 2010. Investors perform better by keeping an eye on the long-term trend line and not the short-term fluctuations. Contrarian investors buy when

▼ **FIGURE 16.2**
Recent Performance of Stock Market and Dow Jones Industrial Average (DJIA)

Dow Jones Industrial Average (DJIA)

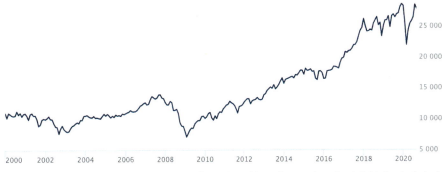

Source: "Dow Jones Industrial Average," *The Wall Street Journal*, https://www.wsj.com/market-data/quotes/index/DJIA/advanced-chart (accessed September 30, 2020).

When most people think of Fidelity Investments Inc., they think of financial services like asset management or mutual funds. Less well-known is the fact that Fidelity has a been a pioneer in technology and finance. The company was the first financial firm to offer electronic funds transfer for money market funds. Its innovation center, the Fidelity Center for Applied Technology, spends $2.5 billion on technology innovation a year.

More recently, Fidelity has been investigating cutting-edge digital technology like virtual reality, cryptocurrency, and blockchain. When Bitcoin—a decentralized peer-to-peer digital currency (a type of cryptocurrency)—first became popular, Fidelity's leadership began investing in Bitcoin and looking for ways it could be used by customers. Bitcoin uses blockchain technology, a digital public transaction ledger that is instantly updated and shared by multiple individuals in a transaction. Fidelity became the first financial services firm to join a blockchain group dedicated to investigating blockchain-based technology. Fidelity launched Blockchain Incubator to further research this new technology's role in finance. According to Fidelity, a third of institutional investors globally have invested in cryptocurrency, though adoption in the United States is slightly lower.

Today's increase in the popularity and value of Bitcoin appears to have made Fidelity's original investment pay off—so much so that it has developed a stand-alone company where it provides institutions with trading, storing, and management of digital assets. The newness of the technology is risky because it is still uncertain how it will affect the financial services industry. However, Fidelity has never been one to shy away from risk. As more customers turn to digital assets, Fidelity is determined to be at the forefront of this new industry.[d]

Critical Thinking Questions

1. In what type of markets does Fidelity operate?

2. Describe how Fidelity has been a pioneer in applying new technology to finance.

3. Do you believe cryptocurrency and blockchain technology will be the next major stage in financial securities trading and investments? Why or why not?

---

everyone else is panicked and prices are low because they play the long-term trends. However, for many, this is psychologically a tough way to play the market.

Many investors follow the activity of the Dow Jones Industrial Average to see whether the stock market has gone up or down. Table 16.5 lists the 30 companies that currently make up the Dow. Although these companies are only a small fraction of the total number of companies listed on the New York Stock Exchange, because of their size, they account for about 25 percent of the total value of the NYSE.

▼ **TABLE 16.5** The 30 Stocks in the Dow Jones Industrial Average

3M Co	Goldman Sachs	Nike
American Express Co	Home Depot	Procter & Gamble
Amgen	Honeywell International	Salesforce.com
Apple	Intel	Travelers Companies Inc.
Boeing	IBM	United Health Group
Caterpillar	Johnson & Johnson	Verizon
Chevron	JPMorgan Chase	Visa
Cisco Systems	McDonald's	Walgreens Boots Alliance Inc.
Coca-Cola	Merck	Walmart
Dow Inc.	Microsoft	Walt Disney

Source: Yahoo! Finance, https://finance.yahoo.com/quote/%5EDJI/components?p=%5EDJI (accessed September 30, 2020).

The numbers listed in an index or average that tracks the performance of a stock market are expressed not as dollars, but as a number on a fixed scale. If you know, for example, that the Dow Jones Industrial Average climbed from 860 in August 1982 to a high of 11,497 at the beginning of 2000, you can see clearly that the value of the Dow Jones Average increased more than 10 times in this 19-year period, making it one of the highest rate of return periods in the history of the stock market.

Unfortunately, prosperity did not last long once the Internet bubble burst. Technology stocks and new Internet companies were responsible for the huge increase in stock prices. Even companies with few sales and no earnings were selling at prices that were totally unreasonable. It is always easier to realize that a bubble existed after it has popped. By September 2002, the Dow Jones Industrial Average hit 7,461. The markets stabilized and the economy kept growing; investors were euphoric when the Dow Jones Industrial Average hit an all-time high of 14,198 in October 2007. However, once the housing bubble burst, the economy and the stock market went into a free fall. The Dow Jones Industrial Average bottomed out at 6,470 in March 2009. The market entered a period of recovery, and by April 2010, it hit a new high for the year of 10,975. By February 12, 2020, the Dow Jones Industrial Average hit an all-time record high of 29,569. Six weeks later, the DJIA bottomed at 18,213 for a 38.4 percent decline, one of the quickest and biggest declines in history. As the country slowly recovered from the COVID-19 pandemic, the market moved up in a quite volatile fashion. Up and down moves in stock prices often scare investors as they focus on the declines and forget to take a long-term view.

However, volatility has always been around as demonstrated in Table 16.6 by using the Standard and Poor's Index of 500 stocks. This index is highly correlated to the DJIA but represents a much broader view of the market of 500 stocks versus 30 for the DJIA. The good news is that even when the market has been rather flat, an investor would have collected dividends, which are not reflected in the index. Perhaps this roller coaster ride indicates why some people are afraid to buy common stocks. If you look at the long-term trend and long-term returns in common stocks, they far outdistance bonds and government securities.

Take a look at the explanation of why the market declined and you will see that anything that might affect both domestic and international economic issues influences the level of the stock market. Also note that if you had bought at the top in 2009 and sold at the top in 2020, you would have an annualized return of almost 12.5 percent not including dividends. Even if you had

During the housing bubble, banks provided loans to riskier subprime borrowers. Although these loans were highly profitable, it was only a matter of time before the bubble burst.

moodboard/Getty Images

▼ **TABLE 16.6** S&P 500 Corrections of >5% since March 2009 Low

Correction Period	S&P High	S&P Low	% Decline	"Stocks Fall On. . ."
2020: Feb 10–Mar 16	3385	2304	−31.9%	COVID-19 (coronavirus) pandemic and economic crisis, collapsing oil prices
2019: Jul 22–Aug 19	3027	2847	−5.9%	Trade tensions with China
2019: Apr 29–May 28	2954	2752	−6.8%	Worries about the recovery
2018: Sep 21–Oct 24	2941	2652	−9.8%	Inflation fears, rising rates, China slowdown, trade war/tariffs, housing
2018: Jan 26–Feb 9	2873	2533	−11.8%	Inflation fears, rising rates
2016: Aug 15–Nov 4	2194	2084	−5.0%	Election fears/concerns/jitters
2016: Jun 8–Jun 27	2121	1992	−6.1%	Brexit concerns, pound crashing, European banks
2015/16: Nov 3–Feb 11	2116	1810	−14.5%	China, EM currencies, falling oil, Middle east, North Korea nukes
2015: May 20–Aug 24	2135	1867	−12.6%	Greece default concerns, China stock crash, EM currency turmoil
2014/15: Dec 29–Feb 2	2094	1981	−5.4%	Falling oil, strong dollar, weak earnings
2014: Dec 5–Dec 16	2079	1973	−5.1%	Falling oil, strong dollar
2014: Sep 19–Oct 15	2019	1821	−9.8%	Ebola, global growth fears, falling oil
2014: Jan 15–Feb 5	1851	1738	−6.1%	Fed taper, European deflation fears, EM currency turmoil
2013: May 22–Jun 24	1687	1560	−7.5%	Fed taper fears
2012: Sep 14–Nov 16	1475	1343	−8.9%	Fiscal cliff concerns, Obama's re-election
2012: Apr 2–Jun 4	1422	1267	−10.9%	Europe's debt crisis
2011: Oct 27–Nov 25	1293	1159	−10.4%	Europe's debt crisis
2011: May 2–Oct 4	1371	1075	−21.6%	Europe's debt crisis, double-dip recession fears, U.S. debt downgrade
2011: Feb 18–Mar 16	1344	1249	−7.1%	Libyan civil war, Japan earthquake/nuclear disaster
2010: Aug 9–Aug 27	1129	1040	−7.9%	Global growth concerns
2010: Apr 26–Jul 1	1220	1011	−17.1%	Europe's debt crisis, stock market flash crash, growth concerns
2010: Jan 19–Feb 5	1150	1045	−9.1%	China's lending curbs, Obama's bank regulation plan
2009: Oct 21–Nov 2	1101	1029	−6.5%	Worries about the economic recovery
2009: Sep 23–Oct 2	1080	1020	−5.6%	Worries about the economic recovery
2009: Jun 11–Jul 7	956	869	−9.1%	World Bank negative growth forecast; fears market is ahead of recovery
2009: May 8–May 15	930	879	−5.5%	Worries that market has gotten ahead of itself
Average			−9.9%	

Source: Adapted from Charlie Bilello, "2018: The Year in Chart," *Pensions Partners,* January 3, 2019, https://pensionpartners.com/2018-the-year-in-charts/ (accessed June 11, 2019).

bought at the top in 2009 and sold at the bottom in 2020, you still would have earned an annualized return of 8.6 percent. Add 2 percent in dividends and you have over a 10 percent total return. Being able to pick the tops and bottoms isn't as important as having patience and a long-term view.

Recognizing financial bubbles can be difficult. It is too easy to get caught up in the enthusiasm that accompanies rising markets. Knowing what something is worth in economic terms is the test of true value. During the housing bubble, banks made loans to subprime borrowers to buy houses. (Remember that the prime rate is the rate for the highest quality borrowers and subprime loans are made to those who have low credit ratings.) As more money poured into the housing market, the obvious supply and demand relationship from economics would indicate that housing prices would rise. As prices rose, speculators entered the real estate market trying to make a fast buck. States such as Florida, Arizona, Nevada, and California were the favorite speculative spots and the states with the largest decline in house prices. To make matters worse, banks had created the home equity loan years ago so that borrowers could take out a second mortgage against their house and deduct the interest payment for tax purposes. Many homeowners no longer thought about paying off their mortgages but, instead, used the increase in the price of their houses to borrow more money. This behavior was unsustainable and created a real estate bubble that burst with dire financial consequences for the whole economy, workers, and investors.

People defaulted on loans when they could no longer afford to pay the mortgage. Many of these subprime borrowers shouldn't have been able to borrow in the first place. The defaults caused housing prices to fall, and some people who had home equity loans no longer had any equity left in their house. Some homeowners owed the bank more than the house was worth, and they walked away from their mortgage. At the same time, investors realized that the mortgage-backed securities they owned were not worth their face value, and prices of these assets plummeted. Banks and other financial service firms that had these assets on their books suffered a double whammy. They had loan losses and losses on mortgage-backed securities that another division of the bank had bought for investment purposes. Soon, many banks were close to violating their capital requirement,

and the U.S. Treasury and Federal Reserve stepped in—with the help of funding from Congress—to make bank loans, buy securities that were illiquid, and invest in the capital of the banks by buying preferred stock.

The consensus of most economists is that through the actions of the U.S. Treasury and the Federal Reserve, the U.S. economy escaped what might have been another depression equal to or worse than the depression of the 1930s. The recession of 2007–2009 lasted 18 months and was the longest recession since the 1930s. Once again, during the COVID-19 pandemic in 2020, the Federal Reserve came to the rescue of the market with some of the same strategies employed in the financial crisis during the Great Recession. These were discussed in Chapter 15.

For investors to make sound financial decisions, it is important that they stay in touch with business news, markets, and indexes. Of course, business and investment magazines, such as *Bloomberg Businessweek*, *Fortune*, and *Money*, offer this type of information. Many Internet sites, including CNN/*Money*, *Business Wire*, *USA Today*, and others offer this information, as well. Many sites offer searchable databases of information by topic, company, or keyword. However, investors choose to receive and review business news, doing so is a necessity in today's market. ■

WHAT IS IT LIKE TO WORK // in Financial Management or Securities? /

Taking classes in financial and securities management can provide many career options, from managing a small firm's accounts receivables to handling charitable giving for a multinational to investment banking to stock brokerage. During the Great Recession, tens of thousands of employees from Wall Street firms lost their jobs. This type of phenomenon is not isolated to the finance sector. In the early 2000s, the tech sector experienced a similar downturn, from which it has subsequently largely recovered. As the markets bounced back, job creation in finance and securities increased again. All firms need financial analysts to determine whether a project should be implemented, when to issue stocks or bonds, or when to initiate loans. These and other forward-looking questions, such as how to invest excess cash, must be addressed by financial managers. During the financial crisis, many job cuts came about as a response to the subprime lending fallout and subsequent bank failures. Thousands of laid off employees flooded the market looking for new jobs, increasing competition.

Economic uncertainty can make it difficult to find a desirable job, especially in the financial and securities market. This was also seen during the COVID-19 (coronavirus) pandemic as many companies laid off employees. Uncertainty results in hiring freezes and layoffs but leaves firms lean and ready to grow when the cycle turns around, resulting in hiring from the bottom up.

Many different industries require people with finance skills. So do not despair if you have a difficult time finding a job in exactly the right firm. Most people switch companies a number of times over the course of their careers. Many organizations require individuals trained in forecasting, statistics, economics, and finance. Even unlikely places like museums, aquariums, and zoos need people who are good at numbers. It may require some creativity, but if you are committed to a career in finance, look to less obvious sources—not just the large financial firms.

notes

Chapter 1

1. Bradley Berman, "GM and Ford plan to make 320K EVs in 2026, less than Tesla's output in 2019," *Electrek*, March 26, 2020, https://electrek.co/2020/03/26/gm-and-ford-plan-to-make-320k-evs-in-2026-less-than-teslas-output-in-2019/ (accessed May 15, 2020).

2. Stuart R. Levin, "Diversity Confirmed to Boost Innovation and Financial Results," *Forbes*, January 15, 2020, https://www.forbes.com/sites/forbesinsights/2020/01/15/diversity-confirmed-to-boost-innovation-and-financial-results/#f2fb48c4a6a5 (accessed May 15, 2020).

3. Esther Fung, "Mall Owners Head for Exits as Retail Tenants Move Out," *The Wall Street Journal,* January 25, 2017, p. A1.

4. "Habitat for Humanity and Home Depot Foundation Partner to Repair Homes for U.S. Military Veterans and Families," Habitat.org, March 16, 2017.

5. Rainer Zitelmann, "China's Economic Success Proves the Power of Capitalism," *Forbes*, July 8, 2019, https://www.forbes.com/sites/rainerzitelmann/2019/07/08/chinas-economic-success-proves-the-power-of-capitalism/#16e952583b9d (accessed May 15, 2020).

6. Bill Chappell, "Electric Cars Hit Record In Norway, Making Up Nearly 60 Percent Of Sales In March," *NPR*, April 2, 2019, https://www.npr.org/2019/04/02/709131281/electric-cars-hit-record-in-norway-making-up-nearly-60-of-sales-in-march (accessed May 15, 2020).

7. "American Politics: In Praise of State-ism," *The Economist,* January 6–12, 2018, p. 10.

8. "Special Report: The Visible Hand," *The Economist,* January 21, 2012, pp. 3–5.

9. "Special Report: The World in Their Hands," *The Economist,* January 21, 2012, pp. 15–17.

10. "The Shark Tank," ABC, http://abc.go.com/shows/shark-tank/bios (accessed May 15, 2020).

11. Jackie Wattles, "How Space Tourism and Rockets to Mars Became 'Crticial' Business During the Pandemic," *CNN*, May 2, 2020, https://www.cnn.com/2020/05/01/business/space-industry-critical-business-blue-origin-spacex-scn/index.html (accessed May 15, 2020).

12. Valentina Sanchez, "Venezuela Hyperinflation Hits 10 Million Percent. 'Shock therapy' May Be Only Chance to Undo the Economic Damage," *CNBC*, August 3, 2020, https://www.cnbc.com/2019/08/02/venezuela-inflation-at-10-million-percent-its-time-for-shock-therapy.html (accessed May 15, 2020).

13. Sarah Chaney and Eric Morath, "April Unemployment Rate Rose to a Record 14.7%," *The Wall Street Journal*, May 8, 2020, https://www.wsj.com/articles/april-jobs-report-coronavirus-2020-11588888089 (accessed May 15, 2020).

14. National Retail Federation, "April Retail Sales Drop Nearly Twice as Much as March During the Coronavirus Pandemic," May 15, 2020, https://nrf.com/media-center/press-releases/april-retail-sales-drop-nearly-twice-much-march-during-coronavirus (accessed May 15, 2020).

15. TreasuryDirect, "The Debt to the Penny and Who Holds It," May 14, 2020, https://treasurydirect.gov/govt/reports/pd/pd_debttothepenny.htm (accessed May 15, 2020).

16. World Trade Organization, "The WTO Can . . . Stimulate Economic Growth and Employment," https://www.wto.org/english/thewto_e/whatis_e/10thi_e/10thi03_e.htm (accessed May 1, 2017).

17. "The Criminalisation of American Business," *The Economist,* August 30–September 5, 2014, pp. 21–24; Tracy Gonzalez-Padron, G. Tomas M. Hult, and O.C. Ferrell, "Stakeholder Marketing Relationships to Social Responsibility and Firm Performance," Working paper, 2015.

18. Ryan C. Fuhrmann, "Okuns Law: Economic Growth and Unemployment," *Investopedia,* 2016, http://www.investopedia.com/articles/economics/12/okuns-law.asp (accessed May 1, 2017); World Trade Organization, "The WTO Can. . . Stimulate Economic Growth and Employment," https://www.wto.org/english/thewto_e/whatis_e/10thi_e/10thi03_e.htm (accessed May 1, 2017).

19. Kelsey Snell, "What's Inside the Senate's $2 Trillion Coronavirus Aid Package," *NPR*, March 26, 2020, https://www.npr.org/2020/03/26/821457551/whats-inside-the-senate-s-2-trillion-coronavirus-aid-package (accessed May 26, 2020).

20. "U.S. Government Current Revenue History," *U.S. Government Revenue,* https://www.usgovernmentrevenue.com/current_revenue (accessed May 15, 2020).

21. Amir El-Sibaie, "2019 Tax Brackets," *Tax Foundation,* November 28, 2018, https://taxfoundation.org/2019-tax-brackets/ (accessed May 15, 2020).

22. Cristina Enache, "Sources of Tax Revenue: U.S. vs. OECD," *Tax Foundation*, March 11, 2020, https://taxfoundation.org/us-tax-revenue-by-tax-type-2020/ (accessed May 15, 2020).

23. "Corporate Tax in America: Let the Games Begin," *The Economist,* December 16–22, 2017, p. 58.

24. "High Tax States: Tax Replanning," *The Economist,* January 6, 2018, p. 17; Elke Asen, "Corporate Tax Rates Around the World, 2019," *Tax Foundation*, December 10, 2019, https://taxfoundation.org/publications/corporate-tax-rates-around-the-world/ (accessed May 15, 2020).

25. U.S. Census Bureau, "State & County Quick Facts," http://quickfacts.census.gov/qfd/states/00000.html (accessed May 1, 2017); Haya El Nasser, Gregory Korte, and Paul Overberg, "308.7 Million," *USA Today,* December 22, 2010, p. 1A.

26. Dana Mattioli and Konrad Putzier, "When It's Time to Go Back to the Office, Will It Still Be There?" *The Wall Street Journal*, May 16, 2020, https://www.wsj.com/articles/when-its-time-to-go-back-to-the-office-will-it-still-be-there-11589601618 (accessed May 18, 2020).

27. Suzanne Kapner and Sarah Nassauer, "Coronavirus Finishes the Retail Reckoning That Amazon Started," *The Wall Street Journal*, May 14, 2020, https://www.wsj.com/articles/coronavirus-finishes-the-retail-reckoning-that-amazon-started-11589459920 (accessed May 15, 2020).

28. Microsoft, "COVID-19 Will Accelerate Digital Adoption, Investments in Cloud, AI and Cybersecurity: Aarthi Subramanian, Group Chief Digital Officer, Tata Sons," May 15, 2020, https://news.microsoft.com/en-in/covid-19-accelerated-digital-transformation-aarthi-subramaniam-tata-sons/ (accessed May 15, 2020).

29. "The Impact of Artificial Intelligence on Unemployment," *Technology Org*, December 17, 2019, https://www.technology.

org/2019/12/17/the-impact-of-artificial-intelligence-on-unemployment/ (accessed May 10, 2020).

30. "How Delta Is Leveraging Apple's Business Chat, AI For Better Customer Service," *PYMNTS*, July 12, 2019, https://www.pymnts.com/call-center-commerce/2019/delta-apple-business-chat-artificial-intelligence-customer-service/ (accessed May 18, 2020).

31. "Here to Help," *The Economist*, March 31, 2018, p. 40–41.

32. "3 Ways Automation and AI Amplify the Role of Firstline Workers," *Forbes*, January 8, 2018, https://www.forbes.com/sites/insights-microsoft/2018/01/08/3-ways-automation-and-ai-amplify-the-role-of-firstline-workers/#2a0411e73b5c (accessed May 18, 2020).

33. Aaron Holmes, "AI Could Be the Key to Ending Discrimination in Hiring, But Experts Warn It Can Be Just as Biased as Humans," *Business Insider*, October 8, 2019, https://www.businessinsider.com/ai-hiring-tools-biased-as-humans-experts-warn-2019-10 (accessed May 11, 2020).

34. Natasha Singer and Cade Metz, "Many Facial-Recognition Systems Are Biased, Says U.S. Study," *The New York Times*, December 19, 2019, https://www.nytimes.com/2019/12/19/technology/facial-recognition-bias.html (accessed May 11, 2020).

35. Bernard Marr, "The Amazing Ways Instagram Uses Big Data and Artificial Intelligence," *Forbes*, March 16, 2018, https://www.forbes.com/sites/bernardmarr/2018/03/16/the-amazing-ways-instagram-uses-big-data-and-artificial-intelligence/#6cb271c5ca63 (accessed June 27, 2019); Mehboob Feelani, "Watson, Come Here. I Want You," *Fortune,* October 27, 2014, 36.

36. Richard Herschel and Virginia M. Miori, "Ethics & Big Data," *Technology in Society*, 49, May 2017, p. 31–36.

37. Jimmy Song, "Why Blockchain is Hard," *Medium*, May 14, 2018, https://medium.com/@jimmysong/why-blockchain-is-hard-60416ea4c5c (accessed May 18, 2020).

38. Merrill Douglas, "Blockchain, Meet Supply Chain," *Inbound Logistics*, April 2020, p. 60–64.

39. Shiraz Jagati, "Walmart's Forway into Blockchain, How Is the Technology Used?" *Cointelegraph*, September 3, 2019, https://cointelegraph.com/news/walmarts-foray-into-blockchain-how-is-the-technology-used (accessed May 18, 2020).

40. Thomas Black, "UPS to Fly Medications by Drone to Florida Retirement Area," *Bloomberg*, April 27, 2020, https://www.bloomberg.com/news/articles/2020-04-27/ups-to-fly-medications-by-drone-to-florida-retirement-community (accessed May 18, 2020).

41. Aaron Mak, "Can You Get Food and Groceries Delivered by Drone Yet?" *Slate*, April 13, 2020, https://slate.com/technology/2020/04/drones-delivery-coronavirus.html (accessed May 10, 2020).

42. UK-RAS Network, "Ethical Issues for Robotics and Autonomous Systems," 2019, https://www.ukras.org/wp-content/uploads/2019/07/UK_RAS_AI_ethics_web_72.pdf (accessed May 11, 2020).

43. Caroline Castrillon, "This CEO Of $100 Million Brand Launched An App To Set Women Up For Success After College," *Forbes*, May 30, 2019, https://www.forbes.com/sites/carolinecastrillon/2019/05/30/this-ceo-is-leading-a-bold-new-movement-to-empower-women-tackling-life-after-college/#71156df431c3 (accessed May 18, 2020).

44. EliLilly, "Heritage," www.lilly.com/about/heritage/Pages/heritage.aspx (accessed May 1, 2017).

45. Joann S. Lublin, "New Report Finds a Diversity Dividend at Work," *The Wall Street Journal,* January 20, 2015, http://blogs.wsj.com/atwork/2015/01/20/new-report-finds-a-diversity-dividend-at-work/ (accessed May 1, 2017).

46. "The 2011 World's Most Ethical Companies," *Ethisphere,* 2011, Q1, pp. 31–43.

47. Isabelle Maignon, Tracy L. Gonzalez-Padron, G. Tomas M. Hult, and O. C. Ferrell, "Stakeholder Orientation: Development and Testing of a Framework for Socially Responsible Marketing," *Journal of Strategic Marketing,* 19, no. 4 (July 2011), pp. 313–338.

a. Dave Brooks, "Taylor Swift's Most Loyal (and Verified) Fans Get First Crack at Reputation Tour Tickets," *Billboard,* December 6, 2017, www.billboard.com/articles/news/8061688/taylor-swift-reputation-tour-presale (accessed September 5, 2018); Shaq Lucas, "Taylor Swift Wants Her Money Back," *Bloomberg Businessweek,* January 31, 2018, https://www.bloomberg.com/news/articles/2018-01-31/taylor-swift-wants-her-money-back (accessed September 5, 2018); Paul Crosby and Jordi McKenzie, "The Economics of Ticket Scalping," *The Conversation,* August 24, 2018, theconversation.com/the-economics-of-ticket-scalping-83434 (accessed September 5, 2018); Anne Steele, "Why Empty Seats at Taylor Swift Concerts Are Good for Business," *The Wall Street Journal,* May 15, 2018, https://www.wsj.com/articles/why-empty-seats-at-taylor-swifts-concerts-are-good-for-business-1526385600 (accessed September 14, 2018); Kaitlyn Tiffany, "How Ticketmaster's Verified Fan Program Toys with the Passions of Fandom," *The Verge,* February 7, 2018, https://www.theverge.com/2018/2/7/16923616/ticketmaster-verified-fan-tumblr-reddit-taylor-swift-harry-styles (accessed September 14, 2018); Richard Smirke, "Ed Sheeran and Taylor Swift Ticket Scalpers Given Six-Plus Years in Prison in 'Major Blow' to Touts," *Billboard*, February 25, 2020, https://www.billboard.com/articles/business/8551862/ticket-scalpers-uk-prison-sentence-peter-hunter-david-smith (accessed May 15, 2020).

b. Dara Moskowitz Grumdahl, "The Future Is Fermented," *Delta Sky,* June 2017, p. 52; Lisa McCoy, "The Facts about Kombucha," *Herald-Mail Media,* August 15, 2018, https://www.heraldmailmedia.com/life/columns/the-facts-about-kombucha/article_992a7c5a-aa2f-5a84-b30d-316507ab0aa2.html (accessed August 24, 2018); Maya McDowell, "Starbucks' Evolution Fresh Brand Came Out with Its Own Kombucha Line," *Delish,* August 13, 2018, https://www.delish.com/food-news/a22717054/starbucks-evolution-brand-kombucha-line/ (accessed August 24, 2018); Jordan Valinsky, "Starbucks Is Getting into the Kombucha Business," *CNN Money,* August 10, 2018, https://money.cnn.com/2018/08/10/news/companies/starbucks-kombucha/index.html (accessed August 24, 2018); "Brew Dr. Kombucha Partners with the Portland Timbers and Portland Thorns FC," *Bevnet,* August 17, 2018, https://www.bevnet.com/news/2018/brew-dr-kombucha-partners-portland-timbers-portland-thorns-fc (accessed August 24, 2018); "Should You Try Kombucha?" *Parade,* August 16, 2018, https://parade.com/690415/clevelandclinic/should-you-try-kombucha/ (accessed August 24, 2018); Royal Kombucha, "Sustainability," http://royalkombucha.com/sustainability-and-kombucha/#.W4mvyJNKi9Y (accessed August 31, 2018).

c. U.S. Department of Labor, "Data & Statistics," http://www.dol.gov/wb/stats/stats_data.htm (accessed May 14, 2020).

d. Andy Pasztor, "Amazon, Google, Others Are Developing Private Air-Traffic Control for Drones," *The Wall Street Journal,* March 9, 2018, https://www.wsj.com/articles/amazon-google-others-are-developing-private-air-traffic-control-for-drones-1520622925 (accessed August 31, 2018); Doug Ross, "Creating Safe Skies as Drones Proliferate," *Standard-Examiner,* July 20, 2018, https://www.standard.net/opinion/national-commentary/creating-safe-skies-as-drones-proliferate/article_bae86a3b-d3ad-5893-8ca2-409f8a08de53.html (accessed August 31, 2018); Samantha Masunaga, "Air Traffic

Control for Drones Is Coming. Here's How It Could Work," *Los Angeles Times,* May 5, 2017, http://www.latimes.com/business/la-fi-drone-traffic-20170501-htmlstory.html (accessed August 31, 2018); Mark Rockwell, "FAA Names Drone Remote ID Tech Contractors," FCW, May 8, 2020, https://fcw.com/articles/2020/05/08/faa-drone-airspace-vendors.aspx?m=1 (accessed May 18, 2020).

e. Kathryn Vasel, "Where Tomorrow's Graduates Want to Work," *CNN,* October 4, 2019, https://www.cnn.com/2019/10/04/success/most-attractive-employers/index.html (accessed May 18, 2020); Deloitte, "Changing the Lens: GDP from the Industry Viewpoint," July 24, 2019, https://www2.deloitte.com/us/en/insights/economy/spotlight/economics-insights-analysis-07-2019.html (accessed May 18, 2020).

Chapter 2

1. Jacquelyn Smith, "The World's Most Ethical Companies," *Forbes,* March 6, 2013, http://www.forbes.com/sites/jacquelynsmith/2013/03/06/the-worlds-most-ethical-companies-in-2013/ (accessed May 3, 2017).

2. Roger Parloff, "How VW Paid $25 Billion for 'Dieselgate'—and Got Off Easy," *Fortune*, February 6, 2018, https://fortune.com/2018/02/06/volkswagen-vw-emissions-scandal-penalties/ (accessed May 21, 2020).

3. Illycaffè, "Illycaffè Named One of the 2020 World's Most Ethical Companies by Ethisphere for the Eighth Consecutive Year," February 26, 2020, https://www.illy.com/en-us/company/store-events/press/press-releases/world-most-ethical-companies-ethisphere-2020 (accessed May 21, 2020).

4. Kimberly Blanton, "Creating a Culture of Compliance," *CFO,* July/August 2011, pp. 19–21.

5. "Walmart Provides $16,000 Grant to 10 Local Organizations," *Shortgo,* October 13, 2019, http://shortgo.co/walmart-provides-16000-grant-to-10-local-organizations/ (accessed May 22, 2020).

6. Kate Pickert, "Medicare Fraud Horror: Cancer Doctor Indicted for Billing Unnecessary Chemo," *Time,* August 15, 2013, http://nation.time.com/2013/08/15/medicare-fraud-horror-cancer-doctor-indicted-for-billing-unnecessary-chemo/(accessed May 3, 2017).

7. Sam Schechner and Emre Peker, "Apple CEO Condemns 'Data-Industrial Complex,'" *The Wall Street Journal,* October 24, 2018, https://www.wsj.com/articles/apple-ceo-tim-cook-calls-for-comprehensive-u-s-privacy-law-1540375675?mod=hp_lead_pos3 (accessed November 15, 2018).

8. O.C. Ferrell, John Fraedrich, and Linda Ferrell, *Business Ethics: Ethical Decision Making and Cases,* 8th ed. (Mason, OH: South-Western Cengage Learning, 2011), p. 7.

9. 3M, "3M Named One of the 2020 World's Most Ethical Companies for the 7th Year in a Row," February 25, 2020, https://news.3m.com/English/3m-stories/3m-details/2020/3M-named-one-of-the-2020-Worlds-Most-Ethical-Companies-for-the-7th-year-in-a-row/default.aspx (accessed May 22, 2020).

10. Patrick Leger, "The Fall of Travis Kalanick," *Bloomberg Businessweek,* January 22, 2018, pp. 46–51.

11. Ferrell, Fraedrich, and Ferrell, *Business Ethics.*

12. Daniels Fund Ethics Initiative, "Compliance Monitoring Challenged by Global Pandemic," April 2020, https://www.danielsfund.org/index.php/Cases (accessed April 22, 2020).

13. "S Korea Ex-Leader Park and Samsung Heir Lee Face Bribery Retrials," *BBC,* August 29, 2019, https://www.bbc.com/news/world-asia-49507401 (accessed May 22, 2020).

14. Ethics Resource Center, *2011 National Business Ethics Survey®: Ethics in Transition* (Arlington, VA: Ethics Resource Center, 2012).

15. Brianna Bradley, "Nearly a Quarter of Staffers Will Shop Online Today," *Biz Women,* November 27, 2017, https://www.bizjournals.com/bizwomen/news/latest-news/2017/11/nearly-a-quarter-of-staffers-will-shop-online.html (accessed April 7, 2018).

16. "Sexual Harassment: #MeToo," *The Economist,* December 23, 2017–January 5, 2018, pp. 81–82.

17. Mengqi Sun and Ezequiel Minaya, "Google Workers' Walkout Signals Crisis of Faith in Company Culture," *The Wall Street Journal,* November 2, 2018, https://www.wsj.com/articles/employee-discontent-threatens-googles-reputation-1541151001?mod=hp_major_pos18 (accessed November 15, 2018).

18. Bryan Robinson, "New Study Says Workplace Bullying On Rise: What You Can Do During National Bullying Prevention Month," *Forbes*, October 11, 2019, https://www.forbes.com/sites/bryanrobinson/2019/10/11/new-study-says-workplace-bullying-on-rise-what-can-you-do-during-national-bullying-prevention-month/#6ae2df932a0d (accessed May 22, 2020).

19. Abigail Hess, "Howard University Employees Fired Following Investigation into Stolen Financial Aid," *CNBC,* March 29, 2018, https://www.cnbc.com/2018/03/29/howard-university-fires-employees-who-allegedly-stole-financial-aid.html (accessed April 7, 2018).

20. Coca-Cola Company, *Code of Business Conduct: Acting Around the Globe,* February 2018, https://www.coca-colacompany.com/content/dam/journey/us/en/policies/pdf/corporate-governance/code-of-business-conduct/coca-cola-coc-external.pdf (accessed May 20, 2020).

21. David Gelles, Michael J. de la Merced, Peter Eavis and Andrew Ross Sorkin, "WeWork C.E.O. Adam Neumann Steps Down Under Pressure," *The New York Times*, September 24, 2019, https://www.nytimes.com/2019/09/24/business/dealbook/wework-ceo-adam-neumann.html (accessed April 1, 2020).

22. Transparency International, "Corruption Perceptions Index," 2019, https://www.transparency.org/en/cpi/2019/results/table (accessed May 22, 2020).

23. "Apple Employee 'Stole Driverless Car Secrets,'" *BBC*, July 11, 2018, https://www.bbc.com/news/technology-44793244 (accessed November 18, 2018).

24. Cecilia Kang, David McCabe and Daisuke Wakabayashi, "U.S. Is Said to Plan to File Antitrust Charges Against Google," *The New York Times*, May 15, 2020, https://www.nytimes.com/2020/05/15/technology/google-antitrust-investigation.html (accessed May 22, 2020).

25. Elaine Watson, "Court Approves $4M Settlement with Health-Ade over Sugar, Alcohol Levels in Kombucha," *Food Navigator*, October 25, 2019, https://www.foodnavigator-usa.com/Article/2019/10/25/Court-approves-4m-settlement-with-Health-Ade-over-sugar-alcohol-levels-in-kombucha# (accessed May 22, 2020).

26. Daniels Fund Ethics Initiative, "You're Out—Baseball Cheating Scandal Follow-Up," January 30, 2020, https://www.danielsfund.org/images/df/Ethics/Mini-Cases/Mini-Case-13-You're-Out-Baseball-Cheating-Scandal-Follow-Up.pdf (accessed May 22, 2020).

27. Jennifer Medina, Katie Benner, and Kate Taylor, "Actresses, Business Leaders and Other Wealthy Parents Charged in U.S. College Entry Fraud," *The New York Times*, March 12, 2019, https://www.nytimes.com/2019/03/12/us/college-admissions-cheating-scandal.html (accessed May 22, 2020).

28. Kyle Stock, "Movers," *Bloomberg Businessweek,* March 6–12, 2017, p. 19.

29. Rachel Abrams, "F.D.A. Warns 3 Tobacco Makers about Language Used on Labels," *The New York Times,* August 27, 2015, http://www.nytimes.com/2015/08/28/business/fda-warns-3-tobacco-makers-about-language-used-on-labels.html (accessed May 3, 2017).

30. Erich Reimer, "The Federal Reserve's Extraordinary Wells Fargo Growth Restriction," *Seeking Alpha,* February 5, 2018, https://seekingalpha.com/article/4143027-federal-reserves-extraordinary-wells-fargo-growth-restriction (accessed March 28, 2018).

31. Thomas M. Jones, "Ethical Decision Making by Individuals in Organizations: An Issue-Contingent Model," *Academy of Management Review* 2 (April 1991), pp. 371–373.

32. Sir Adrian Cadbury, "Ethical Managers Make Their Own Rules," *Harvard Business Review* 65 (September–October 1987), p. 72.

33. Ferrell, Fraedrich, and Ferrell, *Business Ethics,* pp. 174–175.

34. Ethics & Compliance Initiative, "Global Business Ethics Survey: Measuring the Impact of Ethics and Compliance Programs," June 2018, https://43wli92bfqd835mbif2ms9qz-wpengine.netdna-ssl.com/wp-content/uploads/GBES2018-Q2-ProgramImpact-Final.pdf (accessed May 22, 2020).

35. Ethics and Compliance Initiative, "2018 Global Business Ethics Survey™: The State of Ethics and Compliance in the Workplace," (Arlington, VA: Ethics and Compliance Initiative, 2018).

36. Bradley Hope, Drew Hinshaw, and Patricia Kowsmann, "How One Stubborn Banker Exposed a $200 Billion Russian Money-Laundering Scandal*," The Wall Street Journal,* October 23, 2018, https://www.wsj.com/articles/how-one-stubborn-banker-exposed-a-200-billion-russian-money-laundering-scandal-1540307327 (accessed November 15, 2018).

37. Ferrell, Fraedrich, and Ferrell, *Business Ethics,* p. 13.

38. Ethics and Compliance Initiative, "2018 Global Business Ethics Survey™: The State of Ethics and Compliance in the Workplace," (Arlington, VA: Ethics and Compliance Initiative, 2018).

39. Archie B. Carroll, "The Pyramid of Corporate Social Responsibility: Toward the Moral Management of Organizational Stakeholders," *Business Horizons* 34 (July/August 1991), p. 42.

40. Kelly Kennedy, "Pharmacies Look to Snuff Tobacco Sales," *USA Today,* February 6, 2014, p. 1A.

41. Bryan Walsh, "Why Green Is the New Red, White and Blue," *Time,* April 28, 2008, p. 46.

42. Adam Shriver, "Not Grass-Fed, but at Least Pain-Free," *The New York Times,* February 18, 2010, www.nytimes.com/2010/02/19/opinion/19shriver.html (accessed May 3, 2017).

43. "USA Snapshots: Energy Investment Shelton Group's Energy Please Survey," *USA Today,* March 22, 2017, p. A1.

44. Alyssa Danigelis, "Dell Introduces New Laptops in Sustainably-Sourced Packaging," *Environment + Energy Leader,* May 15, 2020, https://www.environmentalleader.com/2020/05/dell-xps-sustainable-packaging/ (accessed May 20, 2020).

45. Suzanne Vranica, "Consumers Believe Brands Can Help Solve Societal Ills," *The Wall Street Journal,* October 2, 2018, https://www.wsj.com/articles/consumers-believe-brands-can-help-solve-societal-ills-1538478000 (accessed November 18, 2018).

46. "2017 World's Most Ethical Companies—Honorees," *Ethisphere,* http://ethisphere.com/worlds-most-ethical/wme-honorees/ (accessed May 3, 2017).

47. Ferrell, Fraedrich, and Ferrell, *Business Ethics,* pp. 13–19.

48. Laura Stevens, "Amazon to Raise Its Minimum U.S. Wage to $15 an Hour," *The Wall Street Journal,* October 2, 2018, https://www.wsj.com/articles/amazon-to-raise-its-minimum-u-s-wage-to-15-an-hour-1538476027 (accessed November 18, 2018).

49. Sarah Nefter, "Closing the Gap," *Delta Sky,* March 2017, p. 78.

50. Charisse Jones, "Here's the Secret to a Successful Company," *USA Today,* March 14, 2017, p. B1.

51. Nina Trentmann, "Lloyds Banking to Pay Equal Pension for Women after Landmark Ruling," *The Wall Street Journal,* October 26, 2018, https://www.wsj.com/articles/lloyds-banking-to-pay-equal-pension-for-women-after-landmark-ruling-1540581084?mod=hp_major_pos15 (accessed November 15, 2018).

52. Kristina Monllos, "Class-Action Lawsuit Alleges Avon Discriminated against Pregnant Women," *Adweek,* November 13, 2018, https://www.adweek.com/brand-marketing/class-action-lawsuit-alleges-avon-discriminated-against-pregnant-women/ (accessed November 18, 2018).

53. Doyle Rice, "Bumblebee Lands Securely on Endangered List," *USA Today,* March 22, 2017, p. A2.

54. Fires in Amazon Forest Rose 30% in 2019," *Reuters,* January 8, 2020, https://www.reuters.com/article/us-brazil-amazon-fires/fires-in-amazon-forest-rose-30-in-2019-idUSKBN1Z804V (accessed February 3, 2020).

55. "WWF: Rainforest Deforestation More than Doubled under Cover of Coronavirus," *DW,* May 21, 2020, https://www.dw.com/en/wwf-rainforest-deforestation-more-than-doubled-under-cover-of-coronavirus/a-53526064 (accessed May 22, 2020).

56. Umair Irfan, "Brazil's Amazon rainforest destruction is at its highest rate in more than a decade," *Vox,* November 18, 2019, https://www.vox.com/science-and-health/2019/11/18/20970604/amazon-rainforest-2019-brazil-burning-deforestation-bolsonaro (accessed February 25, 2020).

57. Melissa Kravitz Hoeffner, "Plastic Bags Feel Integral to Modern Life. But They're a Relatively New Addition We Could Live Without," *NBC News,* August 9, 2019, https://www.nbcnews.com/think/opinion/plastic-bags-feel-integral-modern-life-they-re-relatively-new-ncna1033081 (accessed May 12, 2020).

58. Nancy Luna, "McDonald's Test of Alternative Straws Pushed by Seattle Ban," *Nation's Restaurant News,* July 6, 2018, https://www.nrn.com/quick-service/mcdonald-s-test-alternative-straws-pushed-seattle-ban (accessed November 17, 2018).

59. "Certification," Home Depot, https://corporate.homedepot.com/CorporateResponsibility/Environment/WoodPurchasing/Pages/Certification.aspx (accessed May 3, 2017).

60. GE Foundation, "United Way," www.gefoundation.com/employee-programs/united-way/ (accessed May 3, 2017).

61. Adobe Systems, "Adobe Corporate Responsibility," http://www.adobe.com/corporate-responsibility.html (accessed January 29, 2015).

62. Chad Broughton, "Just Another Factory Closing," *The Atlantic,* September 23, 2015, http://www.theatlantic.com/business/archive/2015/09/factory-closure-privateequity/406264 (accessed May 3, 2017).

63. Peter Cappelli, "The Skills Gap Myth: Why Companies Can't Find Good People," *Time,* June 4, 2012, http://business.time.com/2012/06/04/the-skills-gap-myth-why-companies-cant-find-good-people/ (accessed May 3, 2017).

64. "JPMorgan Chase Commits $7 Million to Remove Barriers to Employment," *Philanthropy News Digest,* October 26, 2019,

https://philanthropynewsdigest.org/news/jpmorgan-chase-commits-7-million-to-remove-barriers-to-employment (accessed May 22, 2020).

a   The NPD Group Inc., "Plant-Based Proteins Are Harvesting Year-over-Year Growth in Foodservice Market and Broader Appeal," *NPD,* June 6, 2018, https://www.npd.com/wps/portal/npd/us/news/press-releases/2018/plant-based-proteins-are-harvesting-year-over-year-growth-in-foodservice-market-and-broader-appeal/ (accessed August 31, 2018); Amanda Little, "Tyson Isn't Chicken," *Bloomberg Businessweek,* August 15, 2018, https://www.bloomberg.com/news/features/2018-08-15/tyson-s-quest-to-be-your-one-stop-protein-shop (accessed August 31, 2018); Alexander C. Kaufman, "The Warped Environmentalism of America's Biggest Industrial Meat Producer," *Huffington Post,* February 28, 2018, https://www.huffingtonpost.com/entry/tyson-foods-environmentalism-regulation-sustainability_us_5a9562d6e4b0699553cc7656 (accessed August 31, 2018); Michael Pellman Rowland, "Tyson Foods Injects More Money into Plant-Based Meat," *Forbes,* December 10, 2017, https://www.forbes.com/sites/michaelpellmanrowland/2017/12/10/tyson-foods-plant-based-meat/#198f0d677efa (accessed August 31, 2018).

b   Adele Peters, "Ikea Is Quickly Shifting to a Zero-Emissions Delivery Fleet," *Fast Company,* September 13, 2018, https://www.fastcompany.com/90236539/ikea-is-quickly-shifting-to-a-zero-emissions-delivery-fleet (accessed September 24, 2018); "New WRI Project to Bring Clean Electricity to 1 Million People in India and East Africa," IKEA Foundation, May 23, 2018, https://www.ikeafoundation.org/pressrelease/new-wri-project-to-bring-clean-electricity-to-1-million-people-in-india-and-east-africa/ (accessed September 24, 2018); "Why CSR Is Becoming a Crucial Part of IKEA's Long-term Recruitment Strategy," Satell Institute, January 31, 2018, https://www.satellinstitute.org/why-csr-is-becoming-a-crucial-part-of-ikeas-long-term-recruitment-strategy/ (accessed September 24, 2018); "IKEA Vision, Culture and Values," IKEA, https://ikea.jobs.cz/en/vision-culture-and-values/ (accessed September 24, 2018); "IKEA Address Ethical and Social Responsibility Challenges," Daniels Funds Ethics Initiative, 2014, https://danielsethics.mgt.unm.edu/pdf/ikea.pdf (accessed September 24, 2018); "History," IKEA Foundation, https://www.ikeafoundation.org/about-us-ikea-foundation/history/ (accessed September 26, 2018).

c   Cody Boteler, "California, Home to Silicon Valley, Considers Controversial Right to Repair," *Waste Dive,* March 19, 2018, https://www.wastedive.com/news/silicon-valley-california-controversial-right-to-repair-legislation/519424/ (accessed March 28, 2018).

d   Alexander Bruell, "Sherwin-Williams Lands in Trouble over 114-Year-Old Paint Ad," *The Wall Street Journal,* September 2, 2018, https://www.wsj.com/articles/sherwin-williams-lands-in-trouble-over-114-year-old-paint-ad-1535886000?mod=searchresults&page=1&pos=1 (accessed September 9, 2018); Jon Bilyk, "Lead Paint Makers Lose Another Round in Long-Running, $1.1 Billion California Lawsuit," November 14, 2017, https://www.forbes.com/sites/legalnewsline/2017/11/14/lead-paint-makers-lose-another-round-in-long-running-1-1-billion-california-lawsuit/#e4d5c343b398 (accessed September 9, 2018); Silicon Valley Newsroom, "$60 Million Settlement Reached in Lead Paint Lawsuit; Companies Fight to Overturn Court Ruling," May 18, 2018, https://www.sanjoseinside.com/2018/05/18/60-million-settlement-reached-in-lead-paint-lawsuit-companies-fight-to-overturn-ruling/ (accessed September 9, 2018); Liam Dillon, "Paint Companies Pull Lead Cleanup Measure from California's November Ballot," *Los Angeles Times,* June 28, 2018, http://www.latimes.com/politics/essential/la-pol-ca-essential-politics-may-2018-paint-companies-pull-lead-cleanup-1530233556-htmlstory.html (accessed September 9, 2018).

e   "Create Jobs for USA Supporters," http://createjobsforusa.org/supporters (accessed February 25, 2016); "Starbucks and Opportunity Finance Network: Taking Action to Reduce Unemployment in America," *Huffington Post,* February 5, 2013, www.huffingtonpost.com/create-jobs-for-usa/starbucks-and-opportunity_b_2622773.html (accessed May 3, 2017); Opportunity Finance Network, "Overview: Create Jobs for USA," 2016, http://ofn.org/create-jobs-usa (accessed May 3, 2017).

Chapter 2A

1. Wilfred Frost, "The Fed's Unprecedented Slap at Wells Fargo May Cost the Bank More than Just $400 Million This Year," *CNBC,* February 4, 2018, https://www.cnbc.com/2018/02/04/the-feds-unprecedented-slap-at-wells-fargo-may-cost-the-bank-more-than-400m-this-year.html (accessed March 30, 2018).

2. Benjamin West Janke, "Hershey's Protects Candy Bar Design," August 6, 2012, http://www.bakerdonelson.com/hersheys-protects-candy-bar-design-08-06-2012/ (accessed June 12, 2017); "Trade Dress," International Trademark Association, November 2015, http://www.inta.org/TrademarkBasics/FactSheets/Pages/Trade-Dress.aspx (accessed June 12, 2017); Danielle Rubano, "Trade Dress: Who Should Bear the Burden of Proving or Disproving Functionality in a Section 43(a) Infringement Claim," *Fordham Intellectual Property, Media and Entertainment Law Journal* 6, no. 1 (1995), pp. 345–367.

3. "Market Down in Markham," *The Economist,* February 24–March 2, 2018, p. 28.

4. "FTC Challenges Proposed Merger of Staples, Inc. and Office Depot, Inc.," Federal Trade Commission, December 7, 2015, https://www.ftc.gov/news-events/press-releases/2015/12/ftc-challenges-proposed-merger-staples-inc-office-depot-inc (accessed February 26, 2016).

5. Maureen Dorney, "Congress Passes Federal Anti-Spam Law: Preempts Most State Anti-Spam Laws," *DLA Piper,* December 3, 2003, http://franchiseagreements.com/global/publications/detail.aspx?pub=622 (accessed April 7, 2014).

6. State of California Department of Justice - Office of the Attorney General, "California Consumer Privacy Act (CCPA)," https://oag.ca.gov/privacy/ccpa (accessed May 26, 2020).

7. Federal Trade Commission, "Google and YouTube Will Pay Record $170 Million for Alleged Violations of Children's Privacy Law," September 4, 2019, https://www.ftc.gov/news-events/press-releases/2019/09/google-youtube-will-pay-record-170-million-alleged-violations (accessed May 22, 2020)

8. "FTC Cracking Down on Social Influencers' Labeling of Paid Promotions," *AdAge,* August 5, 2016, http://adage.com/article/digital/ftc-cracking-social-influencers-labeling-promotions/305345/ (accessed March 30, 2018).

9. Ashby Jones, "Nation's In-House Counsel Are Worried about Ethics, Data and 'Trolls,'" *The Wall Street Journal,* February 2, 2015, http://blogs.wsj.com/law/2015/02/02/nations-in-housecounsel-are-worried-about-ethics-data-and-trolls/ (accessed June 12, 2017).

10. Jean Eaglesham and Ashby Jones, "Whistle-blower Bounties Pose Challenges," *The Wall Street Journal,* December 13, 2010, pp. C1, C3.

11. "Office of Financial Research," U.S. Department of Treasury, www.treasury.gov/initiatives/Pages/ofr.aspx (accessed June 12, 2017); "Initiatives: Financial Stability Oversight Council," U.S.

Department of Treasury, www.treasury.gov/initiatives/Pages/FSOC-index.aspx (accessed June 12, 2017).

a. Tiffany Kary and Emma Orr, "Gibson Files for Bankruptcy with Deal to Renew Guitar Business," *Bloomberg,* May 1, 2018, www.bloomberg.com/news/articles/2018-05-01/gibson-files-for-bankruptcy-with-deal-to-renew-guitar-business (accessed September 7, 2018); Amy X. Wang, "Gibson Drops New Guitars—and Its CEO—amid Financial Mess," *Rolling Stone,* September 6, 2018, www.rollingstone.com/music/music-news/gibson-drops-new-guitars-ceo-amid-financial-mess-719342/ (accessed September 7, 2018); Paul Resnikoff, "Bankrupt Gibson Guitar Introduces a Simplified 2019 Electric Guitar Lineup," *Digital Music News,* September 6, 2018, www.digitalmusicnews.com/2018/09/05/bankrupt-gibson-2019-electric-guitar-lineup/ (accessed September 7, 2018); Anastasia Tsioulcas, "Gibson Guitars Names New Leadership and Exit from Bankruptcy," *NPR,* October 24, 2018, https://www.npr.org/2018/10/24/660185976/gibson-guitars-names-new-leadership-and-exit-from-bankruptcy (accessed November 24, 2018); Matthew Leimkuehler, "Iconic Guitar Brand Gibson Vows to 'Stay True' to Historic Roots after Bankruptcy," *Tennessean,* January 15, 2020, https://www.tennessean.com/story/entertainment/2020/01/15/gibson-guitars-jc-curleigh-interview-ceo-president-casts-vision-post-bankruptcy-les-paul-new-product/2673741001/ (accessed May 22, 2020).

Chapter 3

1. BMW Group, "The BMW Group—A Global Company," https://www.bmwgroup.com/en/company/locations.html (accessed May 26, 2020).

2. Deloitte, "2016 Global Manufacturing Competitiveness Index," 2016, http://www2.deloitte.com/global/en/pages/about-deloitte/articles/global-manufacturing-competitiveness-index.html (accessed May 3, 2017).

3. Jack Nicas, "YouTube Viewership Notches a Global Milestone," *The Wall Street Journal,* February 28, 2017, p. B1.

4. Starbucks, "Starbucks Coffee International," https://www.starbucks.com/business/international-stores (accessed April 1, 2018).

5. Elisabeth Sullivan, "Choose Your Words Wisely," *Marketing News,* February 15, 2008, p. 22.

6. Anne Steele, "Overseas Sales Jump for Indie Records," *The Wall Street Journal,* March 16, 2018, p. B5.

7. Rayna Hollander, "As Apple's Third Largest Market by Sales, China is an Attractive Growth Opportunity," *Business Insider,* December 5, 2017, https://www.businessinsider.com/china-is-apples-third-largest-market-2017-12 (accessed July 25, 2018).

8. Worldometers, "Current World Population," www.worldometers.info/world-population/ (accessed April 1, 2018).

9. Paul Davidson, "We Produce More at Home with New Drilling Methods," *USA Today,* February 11, 2014, p. 1B.

10. U.S. Bureau of the Census, Foreign Trade Division, "U.S. Trade in Goods and Services—Balance of Payments (BOP) Basis," March 27, 2019 www.census.gov/foreign-trade/statistics/historical/gands.pdf (accessed May 11, 2019).

11. Ibid.

12. Ibid.

13. Kimberly Amadeo, "Why the U.S. Dollar Is the Global Currency," *The Balance,* November 24, 2018, https://www.thebalance.com/world-currency-3305931 (November 24, 2018).

14. "Shaken, Not Stirred," *The Economist,* January 24, 2015, p. 48.

15. Thomas Grove, "In Russia, McDonald's Serves Local Fries and a Side of Realpolitik," *The Wall Street Journal,* November 8, 2018, www.wsj.com/articles/in-russia-mcdonalds-serves-local-fries-and-a-side-of-realpolitik-1541678402 (accessed November 26, 2018).

16. Andy Pasztan, "U.S. Drone Deliveries Ready for Takeoff," *The Wall Street Journal,* March 12, 2018, p. B1.

17. Nathaniel Taplin, "Walling off China Won't Help U.S.," *The Wall Street Journal,* March 10–11, 2018, p. B12.

18. BSA, "Security Threats Rank as Top Reason Not to Use Unlicensed Software," http://globalstudy.bsa.org/2013/ (accessed May 3, 2017).

19. Sonja Elmquist, "U.S. Calls for 256% Tariff on Imports of Steel from China," *Bloomberg Business,* December 22, 2015, www.bloomberg.com/news/articles/2015-12-22/u-s-commerce-department-to-put-256-tariff-on-chinese-steel (accessed May 3, 2017).

20. Andrew Tangel, Bob Tita, and Josh Zumbrun, "Metal Users Harden of Levy," *The Wall Street Journal,* March 10–11, 2018, p. B5; Ana Swanson and Peter Eavis, "Trump Expands Steel Tariffs, Saying They Are Short of Aim," *The New York Times,* January 27, 2020, https://www.nytimes.com/2020/01/27/business/economy/trump-steel-tariffs.html (accessed May 26, 2020).

21. Andrea Thomas, Paul Vieira, David Winning, "U.S. Allies Weigh Response to Tariffs," *The Wall Street Journal,* March 13, 2018, pp. 4–7.

22. Simon Goodley and Dan Sabbagh, "China Raises US Trade Tensions with Warning of 'New Cold War'," *The Guardian,* May 24, 2020, https://www.theguardian.com/world/2020/may/24/china-raises-us-trade-tensions-with-warning-of-new-cold-war (accessed May 26, 2020); "Timeline: Key Dates in the U.S.-China Trade War," *Reuters,* January 15, 2020, https://www.reuters.com/article/us-usa-trade-china-timeline/timeline-key-dates-in-the-u-s-china-trade-war-idUSKBN1ZE1AA (accessed May 26, 2020).

23. Kitty Bean Yancey, "Back to Cuba: People-to-People Trips Get the Green Light," *USA Today,* August 4, 2011, p. 4A; Alan Gomez, "Feds Approve First U.S. Factory in Cuba," *USA Today,* February 16, 2016, p. 1B.

24. Kitty Bean Yancey and Laura Bly, "Door May Be Inching Open for Tourism," *USA Today,* February 20, 2008, p. A5; Sue Kirchhoff and Chris Woodyard, "Cuba Trade Gets New Opportunity,'" *USA Today,* February 20, 2008, p. B1; Gardiner Harris, "Trump Tightens Cuba Embargo, Restricting Access to Hotels and Businesses," *The New York Times,* November 8, 2017, https://www.nytimes.com/2017/11/08/us/politics/trump-tightens-cuba-embargo-restricting-access-to-hotels-businesses.html (accessed April 1, 2018).

25. European Commission, "EU Wins a WTO Dispute on Chinese Anti-Dumping Duties," February 13, 2015, http://trade.ec.europa.eu/doclib/press/index.cfm?id=1257 (accessed May 3, 2017).

26. European Commission, "EU Wins a WTO Dispute on Chinese Anti-Dumping Duties."

27. Laurie Burkitt, "Tiffany Finds Sparkle in Overseas Markets," *The Wall Street Journal,* December 26, 2013, p. B4.

28. Julie Jargon, "Starbucks Shifts in Europe," *The Wall Street Journal,* November 30–December 1, 2013, p. B3.

29. Jenna Wang, "Why It Took Starbucks 47 Years to Open a Store in Italy," *Forbes,* September 13, 2018, https://www.forbes.com/sites/jennawang/2018/09/13/why-it-took-starbucks-47-years-to-open-a-store-in-italy/#1aefdfc7fc00 (accessed November 24, 2018).

30. "Slogans Gone Bad," Joe-ks, www.joe-ks.com/archives_apr2004/slogans_gone_bad.htm (accessed May 3, 2017).

31. Steven Dent, "Netflix Has a New Translation Test to Avoid Subtitle Fails," *Engadget,* March 31, 2017, https://www.engadget.com/2017/03/31/netflix-has-a-new-translation-test-to-avoid-subtitle-fails/ (accessed November 26, 2018); Danny Vena, "International Growth Could Triple Netflix Subscribers," *The Motley Fool,* May 22, 2018, https://www.fool.com/investing/2018/05/22/international-growth-could-triple-netflixs-subscri.aspx (accessed November 26, 2018).

32. Danielle Wiener-Bronner, "Why Dolce & Gabbana's China Blunder Could Be Such a Disaster," *CNN,* November 24, 2018, https://www.cnn.com/2018/11/24/business/dolce-gabbana-china/index.html (accessed November 24, 2018).

33. David Millward, "Tesco under Attack for Offering Bacon Flavoured Pringles as Part of Ramadan Promotion," *The Telegraph,* June 25, 2015, https://www.telegraph.co.uk/news/uknews/11697716/Tesco-under-attack-for-offering-bacon-flavoured-Pringles-as-part-of-Ramadan-promotion.html (accessed November 26, 2018).

34. J. Bonasia, "For Web, Global Reach Is Beauty—and Challenge," *Investor's Business Daily,* June 13, 2001, p. A6.

35. Gartner, "Gartner Says Worldwide PC Shipments Declined 9.5 Percent in Second Quarter of 2015," July 9, 2015, www.gartner.com/newsroom/id/3090817 (accessed May 3, 2017).

36. "What Is the WTO," World Trade Organization (n.d.), www.wto.org/english/thewto_e/whatis_e/whatis_e.htm (accessed May 3, 2017).

37. European Commission, "EU Wins a WTO Dispute on Chinese Anti-Dumping Duties."

38. Kimberly Amadeo, "Why NAFTA's Six Advantages Outweigh its Six Disadvantages," *The Balance,* March 6, 2018, https://www.thebalance.com/nafta-pros-and-cons-3970481 (accessed April 1, 2018).

39. "Canada GDP Per Capita," *Trading Economics*, https://tradingeconomics.com/canada/gdp-per-capita (accessed May 26, 2020).

40. U.S. Census Bureau, "Trade in Goods with Canada," https://www.census.gov/foreign-trade/balance/c1220.html (accessed May 26, 2020).

41. Statistics Canada, "Table 1 Merchandise Trade: Canada's Top 10 Principal Trading Partners—Seasonally Adjusted, Current Dollars," December 5, 2014, www.statcan.gc.ca/daily-quotidien/141205/t141205b001-eng.htm (accessed May 3, 2017).

42. "Mexico GDP Per Capita PPP," *Trading Economics*, https://tradingeconomics.com/mexico/gdp-per-capita-ppp (accessed May 26, 2020).

43. U.S. Census Bureau, "Trade in Goods with Mexico," *Foreign Trade,* https://www.census.gov/foreign-trade/balance/c2010.html (accessed May 26, 2020).

44. Jen Wieczner, "Why 2014 Could Be Mexico's Year," *Fortune,* January 13, 2014, pp. 37–38.

45. "A Tale of Two Mexicos: North and South," *The Economist,* April 26, 2008, pp. 53–54.

46. U.S. Census Bureau, "Top Trading Partners—December 2013: Year-to-Date Total Trade," www.census.gov/foreign-trade/statistics/highlights/top/top1312yr.html (accessed May 3, 2017); Heather Long, "U.S., Canada and Mexico Just Reached a Sweeping New NAFTA Deal. Here's What's in It," *The Washington Post,* October 1, 2018, https://www.washingtonpost.com/business/2018/10/01/us-canada-mexico-just-reached-sweeping-new-nafta-deal-heres-whats-it/?noredirect=on&utm_term=.a0f83040eba0 (accessed October 6, 2018).

47. "Crisis Revisited," *The Economist,* December 13, 2014, p. 17; "Euro Area," European Commission, https://ec.europa.eu/info/business-economy-euro/euro-area_en (accessed January 28, 2017).

48. "Euro Area 1999-2015," European Central Bank, https://www.ecb.europa.eu/euro/intro/html/map.en.html (accessed January 28, 2017); "Europe in 12 Lessons," *Europa,* http://europa.eu/abc/12lessons/lesson_2/index_en.htm (accessed January 28, 2017).

49. The World Bank, "European Union," https://data.worldbank.org/region/european-union (acccessed May 26, 2020).

50. Stanley Reed, with Ariane Sains, David Fairlamb, and Carol Matlack, "The Euro: How Damaging a Hit?" *BusinessWeek,* September 29, 2003, p. 63; Irene Chapple, "How the Euro Became a Broken Dream," *CNN,* November 3, 2011, www.cnn.com/2011/09/23/business/europe-euro-creation-maastricht-chapple/ (accessed May 3, 2017).

51. Julia Fioretti, "EU Watchdogs to Apply 'Right to Be Forgotten' Rule on Web Worldwide," *Reuters,* November 26, 2014, www.reuters.com/article/2014/11/26/us-google-eu-privacy-idUSKCN0JA1HU20141126 (accessed May 3, 2017); "Drawing the Line," *The Economist,* October 4, 2014, www.economist.com/news/international/21621804-google-grapples-consequences-controversial-ruling-boundary-between (accessed May 3, 2017); Samuel Gibbs, "European Parliament Votes Yes on Google Breakup Motion," *The Guardian,* November 27, 2014, www.theguardian.com/technology/2014/nov/27/european-parliament-votes-yes-google-breakup-motion (accessed May 3, 2017).

52. Ludwig Siegele, "The Dodd-Frank of Data," *The Economist,* The World in 2018, p. 123.

53. Alex Hunt and Brian Wheeler, "Brexit: All You Need to Know about the UK Leaving the EU," *BBC,* March 26, 2018, www.bbc.com/news/uk-politics-32810887 (accessed April 1, 2018).

54. "Negotiating Post-Brexit Deals: Trading Places," *The Economist,* February 4, 2017, p. 48.

55. Asia-Pacific Economic Cooperation, "About APEC," www.apec.org/About-Us/About-APEC.aspx (accessed May 26, 2020); "U.S.-APEC Trade Facts," Office of the Unites States Trade Representative, https://ustr.gov/trade-agreements/other-initiatives/asia-pacific-economic-cooperation-apec/us-apec-trade-facts (accessed May 26, 2020).

56. Asia-Pacific Economic Cooperation, "About APEC."

57. "China GDP Annual Growth Rate," *Trading Economics,*2017, www.tradingeconomics.com/china/gdp-growth-annual (accessed May 26, 2020).

58. Charles Riley and Feng Ke, "China to Overtake U.S. as World's Top Trader," *CNN,* January 10, 2014, http://money.cnn.com/2014/01/10/news/economy/china-us-trade/ (accessed May 3, 2017).

59. "Retail Sales," *The Economist,* The World in 2018, p. 12.

60. U.S. Environmental Protection Agency, "Global Greenhouse Gas Emissions Data," www.epa.gov/climatechange/ghgemissions/global.html (accessed February 29, 2016); Joshua Keating, "China Passes U.S. as World's Largest Oil Importer," *Slate,* October 11, 2013, www.slate.com/blogs/the_world_/2013/10/11/china_now_world_s_largest_net_oil_importer_surpassing_united_states.html (accessed May 3, 2017).

61. "The Rise of Capitalism," *The Economist,* January 21, 2012, p. 11.

62. Dexter Roberts, "Corporate China's Black Hole of Debt," *Bloomberg Businessweek,* November 19–22, 2012, pp. 15–16.

63. Central Intelligence Agency, "Guide to Country Comparisons."

64. Kathy Chu, "China Loses Edge on Labor Costs," *The Wall Street Journal,* December 3, 2015, p. B1, B4.

65. Association of Southeast Asian Nations, "Overview," www.aseansec.org/64.htm (accessed April 10, 2014).

66. "ASEAN Economic Community: 12 Things to Know," Asian Development Bank, December 29, 2015, www.adb.org/features/asean-economic-community-12-things-know (accessed January 6, 2016).

67. Simon Long, "Safety in Numbers," *The Economist,* The World in 2015 Edition, p. 68.

68. R.C., "No Brussels Sprouts in Bali," *The Economist,* November 18, 2011, www.economist.com/blogs/banyan/2011/11/asean-summits (accessed May 3, 2017).

69. "Thaksin Times," *The Economist,* January 31, 2015, p. 31.

70. Eric Bellman, "Asia Seeks Integration Despite EU's Woes," *The Wall Street Journal,* July 22, 2011, p. A9.

71. David J. Lynch, "The IMF Is . . . Tired Fund Struggles to Reinvent Itself," *USA Today,* April 19, 2006. p. B1.

72. U.S. Energy Information Administration, "Despite the U.S. Becoming a Net Petroleum Exporter, Most Regions Are Still Net Importers," February 6, 2020, https://www.eia.gov/todayinenergy/acdetail.php?id=42735 (accessed May 26, 2020).

73. David Welch and Yon Zhang, "Where Cadillac Is Still Praised," *Bloomberg Businessweek,* February 6–12, 2017, p. 16.

74. WTSC Industrial Group website, http://wtscf.com/associates/index.htm?commerce.htm~index2 (accessed May 26, 2020).

75. Takashi Mochizuki and Eva Don, "TV Snag Blunts FoxConn's Plan for Sharp," *The Wall Street Journal,* January 5, 2017.

76. Walter B. Wriston, "Ever Heard of Insourcing?" Commentary, *The Wall Street Journal,* March 24, 2004, p. A20.

77. James Hagerty and Mark Magnier, "Companies Tiptoe Back toward Made in U.S.A.,'" *The Wall Street Journal,* January 13, 2015, www.wsj.com/articles/companies-tiptoe-back-toward-made-in-the-u-s-a-1421206289 (accessed May 3, 2017).

78. Sobia Khan, "Shell to Open Largest Offshore Delivery Centre Globally in Bengaluru," *Economic Times,* June 5, 2015, http://economictimes.indiatimes.com/jobs/shell-to-open-largest-offshore-delivery-centre-globally-in-bengaluru/articleshow/47548572.cms (accessed May 3, 2017).

79. Kyndal Sowers, "GM Is Cruising from Ohio to Mexico," Alliance for American Manufacturing, July 3, 2018, www.americanmanufacturing.org/blog/entry/GM-Cruising-from-Ohio-to-Mexico (accessed November 26, 2018).

80. Chris Isidore, "Ford, Toyota Team Up to Build Big Hybrids," *CNN Money,* August 22, 2011, https://money.cnn.com/2011/08/22/news/companies/ford_toyota_hybrid/index.htm (accessed November 26, 2018).

81. Calum Fuller, "EY and LinkedIn Announce Strategic Alliance," *Accountancy Age,* October 30, 2015, www.accountancyage.com/aa/news/2432737/ey-and-linkedin-announce-strategic-alliance (accessed May 3, 2017).

82. David Welch and Yon Zhang, "Where Cadillac Is Still Praised," *Bloomberg Businessweek,* February 6–12, 2017, p. 17.

83. Guo Changdong and Ren Ruqin, "Nestle CEO visits Tianjin," *China Daily,* August 12, 2010, www.chinadaily.com.cn/m/tianjin/e/2010-08/12/content_11146560.htm (accessed May 3, 2017); Nestlé, "How Many Factories Do You Have," www.nestle.com/ask-nestle/our-company/answers/how-many-factories-do-you-have (accessed May 3, 2017).

84. O. C. Ferrell, John Fraedrich, and Linda Ferrell, *Business Ethics,* 6th ed. (Boston: Houghton Mifflin, 2005), pp. 227–230.

85. Vu Trong Khanh, "Vietnam Gets Its First McDonald's" *The Wall Street Journal,* February 11, 2014, p. B4.

86. Jack Neff, "Most Engaging Media and Consumer Brands on Social Media," *AdAge,* December 19, 2019, https://adage.com/article/digital/most-engaging-media-and-consumer-brands-social-media/2222471 (accessed May 26, 2020).

87. Export.gov, www.export.gov/about/index.asp (accessed May 3, 2017); CIBER Web, http://CIBERWEB.msu.edu (accessed May 3, 2017).

a. Abby Narishkin and Steve Cameron, "Subway's 42,000 Locations Are the Most of Any Fast-Food Chain on the Planet, But Franchise Owners Are Taking a Hit," *Business Insider*, August 5, 2019, https://www.businessinsider.com/subway-fast-food-chain-locations-franchise-rise-fall-2019-8 (accessed May 26, 2020).

b. Oliver Smith, "Mapped: The World's Most Eco-Friendly Countries—Where Does the UK Rank?" *The Telegraph,* April 22, 2017, https://www.telegraph.co.uk/travel/maps-and-graphics/most-and-least-environmentally-friendly-countries/ (accessed September 22, 2018); Claire Suddath, "Harley-Davidson Needs a New Generation of Riders," *Bloomberg,* August 23, 2018, https://www.bloomberg.com/news/features/2018-08-23/harley-davidson-needs-a-new-generation-of-riders (accessed September 10, 2018); Tim Studt, "Harley-Davidson to Open Electric Motorcycle R&D Center," *R&D Magazine,* September 10, 2018, https://www.rdmag.com/article/2018/09/harley-davidson-open-electric-motorcycle-r-d-center (accessed September 10, 2018); Rich Duprey, "Is Harley-Davidson's Vision for the Future Realistic?" *The Motley Fool,* September 2, 2018, https://www.fool.com/investing/2018/09/02/is-harley-davidsons-vision-for-the-future-realisti.aspx (accessed September 10, 2018); Joe Taschler, "Harley-Davidson Takes Steps to Deal with Sagging Sales as Pandemic Slams Motorcycle Business Worldwide," *USA Today*, April 28, 2020, https://www.usatoday.com/story/money/2020/04/28/harley-davidson-coronavirus-forces-strategy-changes-sales-sag/3042764001/ (accessed May 26, 2020).

c. Tom Nunlist, "Flying High: China's Aviation Industry Is Becoming a Global Force," *CKGSB Knowledge,* July 14, 2017, knowledge.ckgsb.edu.cn/2017/04/17/airline-industry/china-aviation-industry-becoming-global-force/ (accessed September 12, 2018); Hugh Morris, "China Southern, the Airline Poised to Take on the World (and They're Offering Free Upgrades)," *The Telegraph,* May 2, 2018, www.telegraph.co.uk/travel/news/china-southern-london-to-china/ (accessed September 12, 2018); Pamela Parker, "Why Your Next Flight May Go via China," *BBC,* August 16, 2018, www.bbc.co.uk/news/business-45168924 (accessed September 12, 2018); "Chinese Carriers Are the New Disrupters in Air Travel," *The Economist,* April 5, 2018, https://www.economist.com/business/2018/04/05/chinese-carriers-are-the-new-disrupters-in-air-travel (accessed September 28, 2018); Michael Boyd, "Chinese Airlines Not Likely To Rebound For At Least Two Years," *Forbes,* May 19, 2020, https://www.forbes.com/sites/mikeboyd/2020/05/19/a-rebound-at-chinas-airlines-is-not-likely-for-at-least-two-years/#3ee492d1520d (accessed May 26, 2020).

d. Sam Schechner, "Agree to Facebook's Terms or Don't Use It," *The Wall Street Journal,* May 11, 2018, https://www.wsj.com/articles/stage-is-set-for-battle-over-data-privacy-in-europe-1526031104 (accessed August 31, 2018); Adam Santariano, "G.D.P.R., a New Privacy Law, Makes Europe World's Leading Tech Watchdog," *The New York Times,* May 24, 2018, https://www.nytimes.com/2018/05/24/technology/europe-gdpr-privacy.html (accessed August 31, 2018); "GDPR Key Changes," EUGDPR.org, https://www.eugdpr.org/the-regulation.html (accessed August 31, 2018).

Chapter 4

1. Kara Stiles, "Veteran-Turned-Entrepreneur Navigates Young and Evolving Electric Bike Industry," *Forbes,* October 4, 2017, https://www.forbes.com/sites/karastiles/2017/10/04/veteran-turned-entrepreneur-navigates-a-young-and-evolving-electric-bike-industry/#3ef10fbf2e24 (accessed April 11, 2018).

2. Marina Peña, "Why Etsy Loves Women and Women Love Etsy," *Yahoo,* November 23, 2018, https://finance.yahoo.com/news/etsy-loves-women-women-love-etsy-163608149.html (accessed November 25, 2018)

3. Bernardo Martinez, "Three Ways to Close the Business Loan Gender Gap for Good," *Forbes,* January 23, 2020, https://www.forbes.com/sites/forbesfinancecouncil/2020/01/23/three-ways-to-close-the-business-loan-gender-gap-for-good/#6b36d6fb11f3 (accessed May 27, 2020).

4. Caroline Fox, "14 of the Most Successful Companies That Were Started in People's Basements, Garages, and Bedrooms," *Business Insider,* April 17, 2020, https://www.businessinsider.com/successful-companies-started-in-basements-garages-bedrooms-2020-4 (accessed May 27, 2020).

5. Network Solutions LLC, "Hosting Options," http://www.network-solutions.com/hosting (accessed May 4, 2020).

6. Daniela Pierre-Bravo, "How Rebecca Minkoff Went from 'Essentially Homeless' to Fashion Icon," *NBC News,* June 13, 2019, https://www.nbcnews.com/know-your-value/feature/how-rebecca-minkoff-went-essentially-homeless-leading-fashion-icon-ncna1017201 (accessed May 27, 2020).

7. "Master Limited Partnership—MLP," *Investopedia,* http://www.investopedia.com/terms/m/mlp.asp (accessed May 27, 2020).

8. Shobhit Seth, "World's Top 10 Law Firms," *Investopedia,* May 17, 2019, https://www.investopedia.com/articles/personal-finance/010715/worlds-top-10-law-firms.asp (accessed May 27, 2020).

9. Chloe Sorvino, "Cookware Startup Great Jones Has Raised $3.35 Million from the Likes of General Catalyst, David Chang," *Forbes,* November 13, 2018, https://www.forbes.com/sites/chloesorvino/2018/11/13/cookware-startup-great-jones-has-raised-335-million-from-the-likes-of-general-catalyst-david-chang/#3e449aeb65af (accessed November 25, 2018); Hanna Howard, "Great Jones Cofounders Sierra Tishgart and Maddy Moelis Share Their Path to Entrepreneurship," *Teen Vogue,* November 13, 2018, https://www.teenvogue.com/story/great-jones-sierra-tishgart-maddy-moelis-interview (accessed November 25, 2018); Elizabeth Segran, "This Cookware Startup Wants to Take on Le Creuset, All-Clad, and Mauviel," *Fast Company,* November 8, 2018, https://www.fastcompany.com/90262207/this-cookware-startup-wants-to-take-on-le-creuset-all-clad-and-mauviel (accessed November 25, 2018).

10. EY, "EY Reports Record Global Revenues of US$36.4b in 2019," September 5, 2019, https://www.ey.com/en_no/news/2019/09/ey-reports-record-global-revenues-of-us-36-4b-in-2019 (accessed May 27, 2020).

11. Sarah Griffiths, "Snapchat Settles Lengthy Lawsuit with Former University Classmate—and Admit the App WAS His Idea," *Daily Mail,* September 10, 2014, http://www.dailymail.co.uk/sciencetech/article-2750807/Snapchat-founders-settle-lengthy-lawsuit-former-classmate-admit-app-WAS-idea.html (accessed March 1, 2016).

12. "America's Largest Private Companies," *Forbes,* https://www.forbes.com/largest-private-companies/list/ (accessed May 27, 2020).

13. "In Retreat," *The Economist,* January 28, 2017, p. 11.

14. Facebook, "Proxy Statement Pursuant to Section 14(a) of the Securities Exchange Act of 1934," p. 46 (accessed May 27, 2020).

15. Matthew J. Belvedere, "Upwork Shares Rocket More than 50% Higher at the Open on Their First Day of Trading," *CNBC,* October 3, 2018, https://www.cnbc.com/2018/10/03/upwork-ceo-on-ipo-day-we-do-not-incentivize-for-less-pay-for-freelancers.html (accessed November 25, 2018).

16. Brendan Marasco, "3 Reasons Dell Went Private," *The Motley Fool,* November 1, 2013, www.fool.com/investing/general/2013/11/01/3-reasons-dell-went-private.aspx (accessed May 4, 2017); Katherine Noyes, "As a Private Company, Dell-EMC Will Enjoy a Freedom HP Can Only Dream of," *CIO,* October 12, 2015, http://www.cio.com/article/2991551/as-a-private-company-dell-emc-will-enjoy-a-freedom-hp-can-only-dream-of.html (accessed May 4, 2017).

17. "Dell Exploring IPO Option if Tacking Stock Bid Fails," *Reuters,* October 3, 2018, https://www.reuters.com/article/us-dell-tech-ipo/dell-exploring-ipo-option-if-tracking-stock-bid-fails-idUSKCN1MD1GO (accessed November 25, 2018).

18. "The 100 Largest U.S. Charities," *Forbes,* https://www.forbes.com/top-charities/list/ (accessed May 27, 2020).

19. "Habitat for Humanity ReStore," Habitat for Humanity, https://www.habitat.org/restores (accessed April 11, 2018).

20. "Private Operating Foundations," Elko & Associates Limited, February 23, 2011, http://blog.elkocpa.com/nonprofit-tax-exempt/private-operating-foundations (accessed February 23, 2015); Foundation Group, "What Is a 501(c)(3)?" http://www.501c3.org/what-is-a-501c3/ (accessed May 4, 2017).

21. O. C. Ferrell, John Fraedrich, and Linda Ferrell, *Business Ethics: Ethical Decision Making and Cases,* 8th ed. (Mason, OH: South-Western Cengage Learning, 2011), p. 109.

22. Chris Morris, "Pay Raised for Corporate Board Members Far Outpace Average Americans,'" *Fortune,* October 18, 2017, http://fortune.com/2017/10/18/board-of-directors-pay/ (accessed April 8, 2018); Theo Francis and Joann S. Lublin, "Corporate Directors' Pay Ratchets Higher as Risks Grow," *The Wall Street Journal,* February 24, 2015, http://www.wsj.com/articles/corporate-directors-pay-ratchets-higher-as-risks-grow-1456279452 (accessed May 4, 2017).

23. "Board Composition," Procter & Gamble, https://us.pg.com/who-we-are/structure-governance/corporate-governance/board-composition (accessed May 27, 2020).

24. "High Stakes, High Expectations as Earnings Season Heats Up," *Yahoo! Finance,* April 8, 2018, https://finance.yahoo.com/news/high-stakes-high-expectations-earnings-110444292.html (accessed April 8, 2018); Diana Furchtgott-Roth, "Make Domestic Growth Great Again," *U.S. News,* December 20, 2017, https://www.usnews.com/opinion/economic-intelligence/articles/2016-12-20/donald-trump-and-republicans-are-right-to-lower-the-corporate-tax-rate (accessed April 8, 2018).

25. Shi Jing, "Gaming Giants in the Winning Track," *China Daily,* June 21, 2017, http://www.chinadaily.com.cn/business/2017-06/21/content_29825940.htm (accessed April 8, 2018).

26. Robert D. Hisrich and Michael P. Peters, *Entrepreneurship,* 5th ed. (Boston: McGraw-Hill, 2002), pp. 315–316.

27. "The History and Challenges of America's Dominant Business Structure," S-CORP, http://s-corp.org/our-history/ (accessed April 8, 2018).

28. Steve Ranger, "Tired of Your Big Tech Overlords? This Startup Thinks Coding and Build-Your-Own Computer Kits Can Help

You Break Free," *ZDNet,* April 12, 2018, https://www.zdnet.com/article/tired-of-your-big-tech-overlords-how-kanos-computer-kit-can-help-you-break-free/ (accessed December 2, 2018).

29. "Company Overview of Mrs. Fields Famous Brands, LLC," *Bloomberg Business,* February 23, 2015, http://www.bloomberg.com/research/stocks/private/snapshot.asp?privcapId=3553769 (accessed February 23, 2015).

30. "Coop Directory Service Listing," Coop Directory, www.coopdirectory.org/directory.htm#Massachusetts (accessed March 2, 2016).

31. "List of Ford Motor Company's 10 Acquisitions, Including Spin and TransLoc," *Crunchbase,* https://www.crunchbase.com/search/acquisitions/field/organizations/num_acquisitions/ford (accessed November 25, 2018).

32. Jason Lynch, "AT&T CEO Isn't Worried about DOJ Appeal, Details Big Advertising Plans for Turner," *Adweek,* September 12, 2018, https://www.adweek.com/tv-video/att-ceo-isnt-worried-about-doj-appeal-details-big-advertising-plans-for-turner/ (accessed November 25, 2018).

33. Aaron Tilley, "Google Acquires Smart Thermostat Maker Nest for $3.2 Billion," *Forbes,* January 13, 2014, www.forbes.com/sites/aarontilley/2014/01/13/google-acquires-nest-for-3-2-billion/ (accessed May 4, 2017).

34. Eric Savitz, "Did Google Buy a Lemon? Motorola Mobility Whiffs Q4," *Forbes,* January 8, 2012, www.forbes.com/sites/ericsavitz/2012/01/08/did-google-buy-a-lemon-motorola-mobility-whiffs-q4/ (accessed May 4, 2017); Richard Nieva, "Alphabet? Google? Either Way, It's Ready to Rumble," *CNET,* January 29, 2016, http://www.cnet.com/news/larry-page-sergey-brin-google-alphabet/ (accessed May 4, 2017).

35. Bridgett Weaver, "CafePress CEO Departs Company He Founded," *Louisville Business Journal,* November 14, 2018, https://www.bizjournals.com/louisville/news/2018/11/12/cafepress-ceo-out-as-snapfish-completes.html (accessed November 25, 2018).

a. "Cascade Engineering—Corporate Social Responsibility Example," 602 Communications, n.d., http://602communications.com/cascade-engineering-corporate-social-responsibility-example/ (accessed July 27, 2019); Adam Bluestein, "Regulate Me. Please." *Inc.,* May 2011, pp. 72–80; Cascade Engineering, www.cascadeng.com (accessed July 27, 2019); B Corporation, "B Impact Report: Cascade Engineering," https://bcorporation.net/directory/cascade-engineering (accessed July 27, 2019); B Corporation, "About B Corps," https://bcorporation.net/about-b-corps (accessed July 27, 2019); "Cradle-to-Cradle," *Sustainability Dictionary,* https://sustainabilitydictionary.com/2005/12/03/cradle-to-cradle/ (accessed July 27, 2019); Lynn Golodner, "Welfare to Career: Plastics Company Helps People Break Barriers to Success," *Corp Magazine,* December 23, 2015, https://www.corpmagazine.com/industry/human-resources/welfare-career-plastics-company-helps-people-break-barriers-success/ (accessed July 27, 2019); Tim Fernholz, "Best Practices: Cascade Engineering Makes Welfare-to-Career a Reality," *Good,* September 28, 2011, https://www.good.is/articles/best-practices-cascade-engineering-makes-welfare-to-career-a-reality (accessed July 27, 2019); Cascade Engineering, "Welfare to Career," http://www.cascadeng.com/welfare-career (accessed July 27, 2019).

b. Joseph Nathan Kane, *Famous First Facts,* 4th ed. (New York: H.W. Wilson Company, 1981), p. 202.

c. Taylor Soper, "Textile Tech Startup Evrnu Raises $9.1M; Early Partners Include Levi's, Adidas, Target, Others," *GeekWire,* October 4, 2019, https://www.geekwire.com/2019/textile-tech-startup-evrnu-raises-9-1m-early-partners-include-levis-adidas-target-others/ (accessed April 28, 2020); Brett Mathews, "Four Brands on Board as Evernu Closes on Commercialisation," *Apparel Insider,* September 20, 2018, https://apparelinsider.com/four-brands-on-board-as-evrnu-closes-on-commercialisation/ (accessed January 29, 2019); "Evrnu Company Profile," *PitchBook,* https://pitchbook.com/profiles/company/115382-80 (accessed January 29, 2019); Evrnu, "The Problem: Textile Waste," Evrnu, https://www.evrnu.com/ (accessed January 29, 2019); Evrnu, "EvernuTM and Levi Strauss & Co. Create First Jeans. Made from Post-Consumer Cotton Garment Waste," May 11, 2016, https://www.evrnu.com/blog-posts/2016/5/10/evrnu-and-levi-strauss-co-create-first-jeans-made-from-post-consumer-cotton-garment-waste (accessed January 29, 2019); Eliza Jordan, "Stacy Flynn with Evrnu Is Creating New Fabrics from Recycled Ones," *Whitewall,* August 7, 2018, https://www.whitewall.art/fashion/stacy-flynn-evrnu-creating-new-fabrics-recycled-ones (accessed January 30, 2019); PR Newswire, "World Economic Forum Circular Awards Names Closed Loop Partners First Runner Up for Circular Economy Investor in Davos," January 23, 2018, https://www.prnewswire.com/news-releases/world-economic-forum-circular-awards-names-closed-loop-partners-first-runner-up-for-circular-economy-investor-in-davos-300586368.html (accessed January 30, 2019); World Wildlife Fund, "The Impact of a Cotton T-Shirt," WWF, January 16, 2013, www.worldwildlife.org/stories/the-impact-of-a-cotton-t-shirt (accessed January 30, 2019).

d. "Unilever Goes Green with Takeover of Dutch 'Vegetarian Butcher'," *Reuters,* December 19, 2018, https://www.reuters.com/article/us-unilever-m-a-vegetarian-butcher/unilever-goes-green-with-takeover-of-dutch-vegetarian-butcher-idUSKBN1OI19I (accessed May 27, 2020); Mark Ellwood, "Where's the Beef?" *Bloomberg Businessweek,* September 18, 2018, p. 68; Leanna Garfield, "This Vegetarian Butcher Shop Sells Fresh Steaks and Chicken—But It Doesn't Slaughter Any Animals," *Business Insider,* November 1, 2017, https://www.businessinsider.com/vegetarian-butcher-in-the-netherlands-2015-11 (accessed September 25, 2018); Caryn Ginsberg, "The Market for Vegetarian Foods," The Vegetarian Resource Group, http://www.vrg.org/nutshell/market.htm (accessed December 31, 2017); Jaap Korteweg, Founder of De Vegetarische Slager, November 2017 (J. Wienen, Interviewer); "Green Generation: Millennials Say Sustainability Is a Shopping Priority," Nielsen, November 5, 2015, http://www.nielsen.com/us/en/insights/news/2015/green-generation-millennials-say-sustainability-is-a-shopping-priority.html (accessed December 31, 2017); "About Us," The Vegetarian Butcher, 2017, https://www.thevegetarianbutcher.com/about-us/since-1962 (accessed December 31, 2017).

Chapter 5

1. U.S. Small Business Administration Office of Advocacy, "2019 Small Business Profile," https://cdn.advocacy.sba.gov/wp-content/uploads/2019/04/23142719/2019-Small-Business-Profiles-US.pdf (accessed May 29, 2020).

2. "Global Entrepreneurship Index," Global Entrepreneurship Development Institute, http://thegedi.org/global-entrepreneurship-and-development-index/ (accessed May 29, 2020).

3. Marco della Cava, "USA Today Entrepreneur of the Year," *USA Today,* December 11, 2014, pp. 1B–2B.

4. Thrive Causemetics, "How We Give," https://thrivecausemetics.com/pages/how-we-give (accessed December 2, 2018).

5. "Taking Back the Block," *Fast Company*, April 2017, p. 79.

6. U.S. Small Business Administration Office of Advocacy, "Frequently Asked Questions About Small Business," https://www.sba.gov/sites/default/files/advocacy/Frequently-Asked-Questions-Small-Business-2018.pdf (accessed May 29, 2020).

7. "About Us," National Association of Women Business Owners, https://nawbo.org/about (accessed May 29, 2020).

8. U.S. Small Business Administration Office of Advocacy, "Frequently Asked Questions About Small Business," https://www.sba.gov/sites/default/files/advocacy/Frequently-Asked-Questions-Small-Business-2018.pdf (accessed May 29, 2020).

9. Sam Frizell, "Mercado of America," *Time,* April 28, 2015, 42–45; "About Us," The Legaspi Company website, http://www.thelegaspi.com/jos-de-jes-s-legaspi/ (accessed March 3, 2016).

10. "Frequently Asked Questions," Small Business Administration Department of Advocacy.

11. "Bittersweet Synergy: Domestic Outsourcing in India," *The Economist,* October 22, 2009, p. 74.

12. Amy Feldman, "Up, Up, and Away," *Forbes,* November 30, 2018, pp. 43–44.

13. SBE Council, "Facts & Data on Small Business and Entrepreneurship," https://sbecouncil.org/about-us/facts-and-data/ (accessed December 2, 2018).

14. Matthew Diebel, "A Visionary Approach to Selling Eyewear," *USA Today,* December 1, 2014, p. 3B.

15. Christine Lagorio-Chafkin, "How to Use Kickstarter to Launch a Business," *Inc.*, April 24, 2020, https://www.inc.com/guides/2010/04/using-kickstarter-for-business.html (accessed May 29, 2020).

16. Julia Brucculieri, "Here's What It's Really Like to Make a Living Selling on Etsy," *HuffPost,* November 22, 2018, https://www.huffpost.com/entry/how-to-make-money-etsy-secrets_n_5be9f95ee4b0caeec2bc9e91 (accessed December 2, 2018).

17. Joe Keohane, "How One of America's Most Beloved Toy Makers Rebounded from Near Death," *Entrepreneur,* February 20, 2018, https://www.entrepreneur.com/article/308693 (accessed April 21, 2018).

18. Bureau of Labor Statistics, "Employment by Major Industry Sector," September 4, 2019, https://www.bls.gov/emp/tables/employment-by-major-industry-sector.htm (accessed May 29, 2020).

19. Claire Dodson, "Future Forward," *Fast Company,* April 2017, p. 20.

20. "Fight Fire with Foam—and a Resume That Includes the Space Shuttle," *Inc.,* September 2016, p. 51; "Consumer Fire Products," *Inc.,* https://www.inc.com/profile/consumer-fire-products (accessed December 2, 2018).

21. Lev Grossman, "Head Trip," *Time,* April 7, 2014, pp. 36–41.

22. Rachel Botsman presentation, "The Shared Economy Lacks a Shared Definition," *Fast Company,* November 21, 2013, http://www.fastcoexist.com/3022028/the-sharing-economy-lacks-a-shared-definition (accessed May 4, 2017); Natasha Singer, "In the Sharing Economy, Workers Find Both Freedom and Uncertainty," *The New York Times,* August 16, 2014, http://www.nytimes.com/2014/08/17/technology/in-the-sharing-economy-workers-find-both-freedom-and-uncertainty.html?_r=1 (accessed May 4, 2017).

23. Singer, "In the Sharing Economy, Workers Find Both Freedom and Uncertainty."

24. Arun Sundararajan, "The Gig Economy Is Coming. What Will It Mean for Work?" *The Guardian,* July 25, 2015, http://www.theguardian.com/commentisfree/2015/jul/26/will-we-get-by-gig-economy (accessed May 4, 2017).

25. Hal Conick, "How to Make It as a Creative in the Gig Economy," *Marketing News,* April 2018, pp. 53–54.

26. Brian Chesky and Jo Gebbia, "Why Airbnb Is Now Almost Twice as Valuable as Hilton," *Vanity Fair,* March 10, 2017, p. 12.

27. Sadie Williamson, "Blockchain Solutions Are Changing the Sharing Economy," Nasdaq, May 18, 2018, https://www.nasdaq.com/article/blockchain-solutions-are-changing-the-sharing-economy-cm965635 (accessed December 2, 2018).

28. PricewaterhouseCoopers, *The Sharing Economy: Consumer Intelligence Series,* https://www.pwc.com/us/en/industry/entertainment-media/publications/consumer-intelligence-series/assets/pwc-cis-sharing-economy.pdf.

29. "How Dreamers Become Doers," *Inc.* September 2016, p. 44.

30. Ewing Marion Kauffman Foundation, "Access to Capital for Entrepreneurs: Removing Barriers," April 2019, https://www.kauffman.org/wp-content/uploads/2019/12/CapitalReport_042519.pdf (accessed May 29, 2020).

31. "How Dreamers Become Doers," *Inc.*

32. John Ewoldt, "Ever-Profitable, Edina-Based Evereve Bucks Retail Odds by Betting on Moms, Career Woman," *Star Tribune,* June 29, 2019, https://www.startribune.com/ever-profitable-evereve-bucks-retail-odds-by-betting-on-moms-career-women/511952922/ (accessed May 29, 2020).

33. "How Dreamers Become Doers," p. 44.

34. U.S. Small Business Administration Office of Advocacy, "Frequently Asked Questions About Small Business," https://www.sba.gov/sites/default/files/advocacy/Frequently-Asked-Questions-Small-Business-2018.pdf (accessed May 29, 2020).

35. "How Dreamers Become Doers," p. 43.

36. John Clarke, "Necco Wafers, Taste of Childhood and Chalk, Face the Final Crunch," *The Wall Street Journal,* April 9, 2018, p. A1; Spangler Candy, "Necco Wafers," https://www.spanglercandy.com/our-brands/necco-wafers (accessed May 29, 2020).

37. Susan Payton, "Attention, Micropreneurs: You're Not Alone in Small Business," *Forbes,* May 12, 2014, http://www.forbes.com/sites/allbusiness/2014/05/12/attention-micropreneurs-youre-not-alone-in-small-business/ (accessed May 4, 2017).

38. Richard Duncan, "How I Blew It with My Business Plan," *The Wall Street Journal,* May 29, 2015, http://blogs.wsj.com/experts/2015/05/29/how-i-blew-it-with-my-business-plan/ (accessed May 4, 2017).

39. Kate Tracy, "Children's Hair Bow Startup, Born on Etsy, Takes 5K Square Feet in Sunnyside," *BusinessDen,* November 30, 2018, https://businessden.com/2018/11/30/childrens-hair-bow-startup-born-on-etsy-takes-5k-square-feet-in-sunnyside/ (accessed December 2, 2018).

40. "How Dreamers Become Doers," p. 45.

41. Alex Konrad, "Mom and Pop's Best Friend," *Forbes,* October 31, 2018, p. 84.

42. Rolfe Winkler, "Home Reseller Seeks Funds," *The Wall Street Journal,* March 30, 2018, p. B2.

43. Mike Pare, "Chattanooga Firm Plans to Grow to 100 People by Year's End," *Times Free Press,* June 12, 2018, https://www.timesfreepress.com/news/business/aroundregion/story/2018/jun/12/freightwaves-raises-another-13-millionchattan/472901/ (accessed October 18, 2018); FreightWaves, "About FreightWaves," https://www.freightwaves.com/about-1/ (accessed December 2, 2018).

44. "30 Under 30," *Forbes,* November 30, 2018, p. 94.

45. U.S. Small Business Administration, "SBA Administrator Honors Nation's Top Small Businesses," March 12, 2018, https://www.sba.gov/node/1616040 (accessed December 2, 2018).

46. Handshake, "About," https://www.joinhandshake.com/about/ (accessed May 29, 2020); Jeremy Bauer-Wolf, "More Growth for Handshake," *Inside Higher Ed,* April 30, 2018, https://www.insidehighered.com/news/2018/04/30/career-services-platform-handshake-extends-its-reach (accessed December 2, 2018).

47. Jason Feifer, "Turning Rejection into Triumph: How Sarah Michelle Gellar and Her Co-Founders Built a New Baking Brand," *Entrepreneur,* March 27, 2018, https://www.entrepreneur.com/article/310091 (accessed April 21, 2018).

48. Thomas W. Zimmerer and Norman M. Scarborough, *Essentials of Entrepreneurship and Small Business Management,* 6th ed. (Upper Saddle River, NJ: Pearson Prentice Hall, 2005), pp. 118–124.

49. Ibid.

50. "About SCORE," SCORE, https://www.score.org/about-score (accessed December 2, 2018).

51. "Getting Started with Business Incubators," *Entrepreneur,* http://www.entrepreneur.com/article/52802 (accessed May 4, 2017).

52. Adapted from "Tomorrow's Entrepreneur," *Inc. State of Small Business* 23, no. 7 (2001), pp. 80–104.

53. Cheryl Corley, "Millennials Now Out Number Baby Boomers, Census Bureau Says," *NPR,* July 7, 2015, http://www.npr.org/2015/06/25/417349199/millenials-now-out-number-baby-boomers-census-bureau-says (accessed May 4, 2017).

54. Richard Fry, "Millennials Match Baby Boomers as Largest Generation in U.S. Electorate, But Will They Vote?" Pew Research Center, May 16, 2016, http://www.pewresearch.org/fact-tank/2016/05/16/millennials-match-baby-boomers-as-largest-generation-in-u-s-electorate-but-will-they-vote/ (accessed April 20, 2017).

55. Corley, "Millennials Now Out Number Baby Boomers, Census Bureau Says."

56. Chris Morris, "61 Million Gen Zers Are about to Enter the U.S. Workforce and Radically Change It Forever," *CNBC,* May 2, 2018, https://www.cnbc.com/2018/05/01/61-million-gen-zers-about-to-enter-us-workforce-and-change-it.html (accessed December 2, 2018).

57. Molly Smith, "Managing Generation Y as They Change the Workforce," *Reuters,* January 8, 2008, www.reuters.com/article/2008/01/08/idUS129795=08-Jan-2008=BW20080108 (accessed March 4, 2016).

58. Drew Desilver, "Immigrants Don't Make up a Majority of Workers in Any U.S. Industry," Pew Research Center, March 16, 2017, http://www.pewresearch.org/fact-tank/2017/03/16/immigrants-dont-make-up-a-majority-of-workers-in-any-u-s-industry/ (accessed April 6, 2017).

59. Seth Fiegerman, "Slack Is Now Worth More than $20 Billion," *CNN,* June 21, 2019, https://www.cnn.com/2019/06/20/tech/slack-wall-street-debut/index.html (accessed May 29, 2020).

60. "2018 U.S. Home-Based Business Statistics," *Incfile,* April 23, 2018, https://www.incfile.com/blog/post/2018-u-s-home-based-business-statistics/ (accessed December 2, 2018).

61. Jason Nazar, "16 Surprising Statistics about Small Businesses," *Forbes,* September 9, 2013, www.forbes.com/sites/jasonnazar/2013/09/09/16-surprising-statistics-about-small-businesses/ (accessed May 4, 2017); "Home-Based Businesses," U.S. Small Business Administration, www.sba.gov/content/home-based-businesses (accessed February 13, 2015).

62. Henry Blodget, "Walmart Employs 1% of America. Should It Be Forced to Pay Its Employees More?" *Business Insider,* September 20, 2010, http://www.businessinsider.com/walmart-employees-pay (accessed April 6, 2017).

63. Gifford Pinchott III, *Intrapreneuring* (New York: Harper & Row, 1985), p. 34.

64. Paul Brown, "How to Cope with Hard Times," *The New York Times,* June 10, 2008, www.nytimes.com/2008/06/10/business/smallbusiness/10toolkit.html?r%205%201&ref%205%20smallbusiness&orefslogin&gwh=A256B42494736F9E2C604851BF6451DC&gwt=regi (accessed April 22, 2014).

a. "On a Cool October Morning," *Martha Stewart Living,* October 2018, p. 97; Laura Hayes, "Why a Local Chef Bids on Tomatoes alongside Mennonites in Pennsylvania," *Washington City Paper,* September 20, 2017, https://www.washingtoncitypaper.com/food/young-hungry/article/20976132/why-a-local-chef-bids-on-tomatoes-alongside-mennonites-in-pennsylvania (accessed September 19, 2018); Randel A. Agrella, "A Day at the Produce Auction," *Heirloom Gardener,* 2012, https://www.heirloomgardener.com/profiles/destinations/produce-auctions-zmaz12uzfol (accessed September 19, 2018); Christine Des Garennes, "Arthur Auction to Sell Amish Fruits, Veggies," *The News-Gazette,* May 30, 2004, http://www.news-gazette.com/news/local/2004-05-30/arthur-auction-sell-amish-fruits-veggies.html (accessed September 19, 2018); Ad Crable, "Lancaster County Residents Are Picky when It Comes to Pumpkins," *Lancaster Online,* October 10, 2015, https://lancasteronline.com/news/local/lancaster-county-residents-are-picky-when-it-comes-to-pumpkins/article_85b42aaa-6de7-11e5-bf78-6f2192b973a1.html (accessed September 19, 2018).

b. Rob Taylor, "How to Use the World Cup to Build a World-Class Sports Apparel Brand from Scratch," *The Wall Street Journal,* July 7, 2018, https://www.wsj.com/articles/how-to-use-the-world-cup-to-build-a-world-class-sports-apparel-brand-from-scratch-1530961201 (accessed September 14, 2018); Robert Kidd, "This Young Entrepreneur Makes African Soccer Jerseys Affordable," *Forbes,* May 8, 2018, https://www.forbes.com/sites/robertkidd/2018/05/08/the-young-entrepreneur-making-african-soccer-jerseys-affordable/#3ae08ca56f2d (accessed September 14, 2018); Amy Fallon, "The Aussie Student Who Makes Soccer Jerseys for the World's Toughest Market," *The Syndey Morning Herald,* February 15, 2018, https://www.smh.com.au/world/africa/the-aussie-student-who-makes-soccer-jerseys-for-the-world-s-toughest-market-20180216-p4z0l8.html (accessed September 14, 2018); Julian Hettem, "The 23-Year-Old Who Dresses African Soccer Teams," *Racked,* November 20, 2017, https://www.racked.com/2017/11/20/16617568/ams-clothing-soccer-south-sudan (accessed September 14, 2018).

c. U.S. Small Business Administration Office of Advocacy, "Frequently Asked Questions About Small Business," https://www.sba.gov/sites/default/files/advocacy/Frequently-Asked-Questions-Small-Business-2018.pdf (accessed May 29, 2020).

d. Ashley Weatherford, "Nancy Twine Left Finance to Run Her Own Natural Beauty Line," *The Cut,* April 2, 2015, www.thecut.com/2015/03/youngest-black-woman-entrepreneur-at-sephora-nancy-twine.html (accessed at September 27, 2018); Caroline Newman, "How a Former Investment Banker Created a Breakout Hair Care Line," *UVA Today,* March 7, 2018, news.virginia.edu/content/how-former-investment-banker-created-breakout-hair-care-line (accessed September 27, 2018); Chloe Sorvino, "Hair on Fire," *Forbes,* September 30, 2018, pp. 52–54; Chloe Sorvino, "How Haircare Startup Briogeo Went from Zero to $10 Million in Sales in Just Four Years," *Forbes,* October 1, 2018, https://www.forbes.com/sites/chloesorvino/2018/10/01/how-haircare-startup-briogeo-went-from-zero-to-10-million-annual-revenue-in-just-four-years/#730e8289177f (accessed December 2, 2018); Allyson Payer, "The Woman Behind the Fastest-Growing Haircare Brand at Sephora," *Yahoo,* June 24, 2019, https://www.yahoo.com/lifestyle/woman-behind-fastest-growing-haircare-161500748.html (accessed May 29, 2020).

Chapter 6

1. "Waze: For Clearing the Roads," *Fast Company,* March/April 2018, p. 67; Aaron Pressman and Adam Lashinsky, "Why Waze Doesn't Share Traffic Data With Google Maps—Data Sheet," *Fortune,* October 11, 2019, https://fortune.com/2019/10/11/waze-google-maps-how-it-works/ (accessed June 1, 2020).

2. Te-Ping Chen and Eric Morath, "Employers Choose Bonuses over Raises," *The Wall Street Journal,* September 18, 2018, https://www.wsj.com/articles/benefit-gains-exceed-wage-growth-new-labor-data-shows-1537289455 (accessed December 9, 2018).

3. Shawn Donnan and Joe Deaux, "Layoffs Start Turning from Temporary to Permanent Across America," *Bloomberg Businessweek,* May 6, 2020, https://www.bloomberg.com/news/articles/2020-05-06/temporary-coronavirus-layoffs-are-turning-permanent-around-u-s (accessed June 1, 2020).

4. Suzanne Heyn, "Sorting through Options," *Inbound Logistics,* May 2014, pp. 48–52.

5. The Walt Disney Company, "About The Walt Disney Company," https://thewaltdisneycompany.com/about/ (accessed August 27, 2020).

6. Kristina Monllos, "As Soda Sales Suffer, Beverage Marketers Are Shifting to a New Stream of Income: Water," *Adweek,* March 20, 2017, http://www.adweek.com/brand-marketing/as-soda-sales-suffer-beverage-marketers-are-shifting-to-a-new-stream-of-income-water/ (accessed April 7, 2017).

7. "The Dutch Oven, Disrupted," *Bloomberg Businessweek,* March 19, 2018, p. 75.

8. G. Tomas, M. Hult, David W. Cravens, and Jagdish Sheth, "Competitive Advantage in the Global Marketplace: A Focus on Marketing Strategy," *Journal of Business Research* 51 (January 2001), p. 1.

9. "Chevrolet Remains the Industry's Fastest-Growing Full-Line Brand, with 11 Consecutive Months of Growth," General Motors, March 1, 2016, https://www.gm.com/investors/sales/us-sales-production.html (accessed May 4, 2017).

10. "Protecting Your Businesses," Federal Emergency Management Agency, https://www.fema.gov/protecting-your-businesses (accessed June 1, 2020).

11. James E. Ellis, "At KFC, A Bucketful of Trouble," *Bloomberg Businessweek,* March 5, 2018, pp. 20–21.

12. Alexander Coolidge, "P&G Cuts Worldwide Jobs to Lowest in Decades. And There Are More Job Cuts to Come," *Cincinnati Enquirer,* August 8, 2018, https://www.cincinnati.com/story/money/2018/08/07/p-g-cuts-worldwide-jobs-lowest-decades/930154002/ (accessed December 8, 2018).

13. Anna-Greta Nystrom and Mila Mustonen, "The Dynamic Approach to Business Models," *AMS Review,* 2017, p. 123.

14. "AI-Spy," *The Economist,* March 31–April 6, 2018, p. 13.

15. IAPP, "Notes from the Asia-Pacific Rehion, 10 May 2019," May 9, 2019, https://iapp.org/news/a/notes-from-the-asia-pacific-region-10-may-2019/ (accessed June 1, 2020).

16. Ross Kerber, "Growth in Compensation for U.S. CEOs May Have Slowed," *Reuters,* March 17, 2014, www.reuters.com/article/2014/03/17/us-compensation-ceos-2013-insight-idUSBREA2G05520140317 (accessed March 29, 2014).

17. Melissa Behrend, "More Companies Are Reducing CEO Compensation Due to Poor Quarterly Results," *Chief Executive,* March 21, 2016, http://chiefexecutive.net/more-companies-are-reducing-ceo-compensation-due-to-poor-quarterly-results/ (accessed April 7, 2017).

18. "No. 1 Kaiser Permanente, DiversityInc Top 50," *Diversity Inc,* 2017, http://www.diversityinc.com/kaiser-permanente/ (accessed April 7, 2017).

19. Laura Nichols, "Agencies Called to Step Up the Pace on Diversity Efforts," *PRWeek,* February 7, 2014, www.prweekus.com/article/agencies-called-step-pace-diversity-efforts/1283550 (accessed March 29, 2014).

20. Linda Eling Lee, Ric Marshall, Damon Rallis, and Matt Moscardi, "Women on Boards: Global Trends in Gender Diversity on Corporate Boards," *MCSI,* November 2015, p. 3.

21. Del Jones, "Autocratic Leadership Works—Until It Fails," *USA Today,* June 5, 2003, www.usatoday.com/news/nation/2003-06-05-raines-usat_x.htm (accessed May 4, 2017).

22. George Manning and Kent Curtis, *The Art of Leadership* (New York: McGraw-Hill, 2003), p. 125.

23. "Mr. Buffett Has Still Got It," *The Economist,* March 24–30, 2018, p. 16.

24. Richard Gonzales, "Wells Fargo CEO John Stumpf Resigns amid Scandal," *NPR,* October 12, 2016, https://www.npr.org/sections/thetwo-way/2016/10/12/497729371/wells-fargo-ceo-john-stumpf-resigns-amid-scandal (accessed April 12, 2018).

25. Bruce J. Avolio and William L. Gardner, "Authentic Leadership Development: Getting to the Root of Positive Forms of Leadership," *The Leadership Quarterly,* 2005, pp. 315–338.

26. Robert Sation, "A New Model of Leadership," *Fact Company,* April 2017, p. 18.

27. John P. Kotter, "What Leaders Really Do," *Harvard Business Review,* December 2001, http://fs.ncaa.org/Docs/DIII/What%20Leaders%20Really%20Do.pdf (accessed May 4, 2017).

28. "For Building the Next-Gen Clothing Brand," *Fast Company,* March–April 2018, p. 79.

29. C. L. Pearce and C. C. Manz, "The New Silver Bullets of Leadership: The Importance of Self- and Shared Leadership in Knowledge Work," *Organizational Dynamics* 34, no. 2 (2005), pp. 130–140.

30. Michelle Peluseo, "Watson's New Champion," *Fast Company,* April 2017, p. 24.

31. Deborah Harrington-Mackin, *The Team Building Tool Kit* (New York: New Directions Management, 1994); Joseph P. Folger, Marshall Scott Poole, and Randall K. Stutman, *Working through Conflict: Strategies for Relationships, Groups, and Organizations,* 6th ed. (Upper Saddle River, NJ: Pearson Education, 2009).

32. "Sears Secures Court Approval for an Additional $350 Million Loan," *CNBC,* November 28, 2018, https://www.cnbc.com/2018/11/28/sears-secures-court-approval-for-an-additional-350-million-loan.html (accessed December 9, 2018).

33. Kerrie Unsworth, "Unpacking Creativity," *Academy of Management Review,* 26 (April 2001), pp. 289–297.

34. Joann S. Lublin, Leslie Seism, and David Benoit, "AIG's Bound to Weigh Ouster of CEO," *The Wall Street Journal,* February 28, 2017, p. B1.

35. Anna Maria Andriotos and Lara Stevens, "Amazon Voices Payment Strategy," *The Wall Street Journal,* April 7–8, 2018, pp. B1, B2.

36. James E. Ellis, "China Doesn't Want to Go to the Store for Groceries, Either," *Bloomberg Businessweek,* December 4, 2017, pp. 23–24.

37. *Harvard Business Review* 60 (November–December 1982), p. 160.

38. Dan Schwabel, "5 Reasons Why Your Online Presence Will Replace Your Resume in 10 Years," *Forbes,* February 21, 2012, www.forbes.com/sites/danschawbel/2011/02/21/5-reasons-why-your-online-presence-will-replace-your-resume-in-10-years/ (accessed May 4, 2017).

39. U.S. Bureau of Labor Statistics, "Occupational Outlook Handbook: Financial Managers," https://www.bls.gov/OOH/management/financial-managers.htm (accessed June 1, 2020).

40. Ibid.

a. Sarah Frier, "Snap Cuts about 100 Employees in Latest Round of Downsizing," *Bloomberg,* March 29, 2018, https://www.bloomberg.com/news/articles/2018-03-29/snap-cuts-about-100-employees-in-latest-round-of-downsizing (accessed April 16, 2018).

b. Kathryn Kroll, "Rebecca Ray Designs Grew after Owner Let Others into Business," *Cleveland.com,* June 21, 2009, http://www.cleveland.com/business/index.ssf/2009/06/rebecca_ray_designs_grew_after.html (accessed November 11, 2018); Rebecca Ray Designs website, https://rebeccaraydesign.com/ (accessed November 11, 2018); Karen Ammond, "Rebecca Ray Designs," December 13, 2012, http://eliteprofessionals.org/2014/10/05/rebecca-ray-designs/ (accessed November 11, 2018); Holly Phillips, "Horse Love: Rebecca Ray Designs," *The English Room,* September 1, 2015, http://www.theenglishroom.biz/2015/09/01/horse-love-rebecca-ray-designs/ (accessed November 11, 2018); Amy Elbert, "Profile: Rebecca Yuhasz Smith of Rebecca Ray Designs," *Traditional Home,* http://www.traditionalhome.com/design/profile-rebecca-yuhasz-smith-rebecca-ray-designs (accessed November 11, 2018).

c. Claire Zillman, "The Fortune 500 Has More Female CEOs Than Ever Before," *Fortune,* May 16, 2019, https://fortune.com/2019/05/16/fortune-500-female-ceos/ (accessed June 1, 2020).

d. Paul R. La Monica, "Why Lowe's Is Closing Stores and Slashing Inventory," *CNN Money,* August 22, 2018, https://money.cnn.com/2018/08/22/news/companies/lowes-earnings-orchard-supply-hardware/index.html (accessed August 23, 2018); Kimberly Chin and Sarah Nassauer, "Lowe's to Close Orchard Supply Stores, Recruits CVS Finance Officer," *The Wall Street Journal,* August 22, 2018, https://www.wsj.com/articles/lowes-to-close-orchard-supply-stores-recruits-cvs-finance-chief-1534942197 (accessed August 23, 2018); Minda Zetlin, "Lowe's New CEO Eliminates 4 Top Positions, Including COO—Even Though Sales Hit $69 Billion," *Inc.,* July 16, 2018, https://www.inc.com/minda-zetlin/lowes-ceo-marvin-ellison-executive-restructuring-shakeup-new-titles-maltsbarger-mcdermott.html (accessed August 25, 2018); Warren Shoulberg, "In His First Seven Days on the Job, Marvin Ellison Begins the Big Lowe's Remodeling Project," *Forbes,* July 10, 2018, https://www.forbes.com/sites/warrenshoulberg/2018/07/10/seven-days-on-the-job-ellison-begins-the-big-lowes-remodeling-project/#f0162e519b79 (accessed August 25, 2018); "CEO Marvin Ellison Takes Lowe's Back to Basics," *National Retail Federation,* February 8, 2020, https://nrf.com/blog/ceo-marvin-ellison-takes-lowes-back-basics (accessed June 1, 2020).

e. Julie Jargon, "Potbelly CEO's Sandwich Plan," *The Wall Street Journal,* July 2018, p. B5; Potbelly Sandwich Shop, "Our Story," https://www.potbelly.com/our-story (accessed September 9, 2018); Natalie O'Reilly, "Five Fun Things You May Not Know about Potbelly," November 17, 2013, https://www.fool.com/investing/general/2013/11/17/five-fun-things-you-may-not-know-about-potbelly.aspx (accessed September 9, 2018); Joe Cahill, "Potbelly Needs to Stand Apart," *Crain's Chicago Business,* June 3, 2017, http://www.chicagobusiness.com/article/20170603/ISSUE10/170609951/potbelly-needs-to-stand-apart-differentiate-itself (accessed September 9, 2018); Jonathan Maze, "Potbelly Says It Won't Be Sold," *Restaurant Business,* May 9, 2018, https://www.restaurantbusinessonline.com/financing/potbelly-decides-not-sell-itself (accessed September 9, 2018) Ben Coley, "Potbelly Mulling Permanent Closure of up to 100 Locations," *QSR,* May 2020, https://www.qsrmagazine.com/fast-casual/potbelly-mulling-permanent-closure-100-locations (accessed June 1, 2020).

Chapter 7

1. Horace Dediu, "Understanding Apple's Organizational Structure," *Asymco,* July 3, 2013, www.asymco.com/2013/07/03/understanding-apples-organizational-structure/ (accessed May 4, 2017); Sam Grobart, "How Samsung Became the World's No. 1 Smartphone Maker," *Bloomberg Businessweek,* March 28, 2013, www.businessweek.com/articles/2013-03-28/how-samsung-became-the-worlds-no-dot-1-smartphone-maker#p1 (accessed May 4, 2017); Jay Yarow, "Apple's New Organizational Structure Could Help It Move Faster," *Business Insider,* May 1, 2013, www.businessinsider.com/apples-new-organizational-structure-could-help-it-move-faster-2013-5 (accessed May 4, 2017).

2. John D. Still, "Ford Aims to Pivot in Raising CEO's Pay," *The Wall Street Journal,* April 1, 2017, p. B1.

3. Megan McArdle, "'Unlimited Vacation' Is Code for 'No Vacation,'" September 30, 2015, *Bloomberg,* September 30, 2015, http://www.bloombergview.com/articles/2015-09-30/-unlimited-vacation-is-code-for-no-vacation- (accessed May 4, 2017).

4. Micah Solomon, "Take These Two to Rival Nordstrom's Customer Service Experience," *Forbes,* March 15, 2014, http://www.forbes.com/sites/micahsolomon/2014/03/15/the-nordstrom-two-part-customer-experience-formula-lessons-for-your-business/#2ebc60a92335 (accessed May 4, 2017).

5. "Cisco Pulls All Online Ads from YouTube," *Reuters,* May 10, 2018, https://www.reuters.com/article/us-cisco-systems-youtube-advertising/cisco-pulls-all-online-ads-from-youtube-idUSKBN1IB38B (accessed December 15, 2018).

6. Lauren Thomas, "New Ford CEO Promises to Be a 'Cultural Change Agent,' Bill Ford Says," *CNBC,* May 22, 2017, https://www.cnbc.com/2017/05/22/new-ford-ceo-promises-to-be-a-cultural-change-agent-bill-ford-says.html (accessed August 4, 2018).

7. "Holacracy and Self-Organization," *Zappos Insights,* https://www.zapposinsights.com/about/holacracy (accessed April 18, 2018); Aimee Groth, "Zappos Has Quietly Backed Away from Holocracy," *Quartz,* January 29, 2020, https://qz.com/work/1776841/zappos-has-quietly-backed-away-from-holacracy/ (accessed June 1, 2020).

8. Adam Smith, *Wealth of Nations* (New York: Modern Library, 1937; originally published in 1776).

9. Ben Dipietro, "Automakers Face 'Herculean' Task in Implementing Supply Chain Guidelines," *The Wall Street Journal,* May 28, 2014, http://blogs.wsj.com/riskandcompliance/2014/05/28/automakers-face-herculean-task-in-implementing-supply-chain-guidelines/ (accessed May 4, 2017).

10. PopSockets, "Jobs at PopSockets," https://boards.greenhouse.io/popsockets (accessed December 15, 2018).

11. "Brands," Unilever, https://www.unilever.com/brands/ (accessed December 15, 2018).

12. Global Divisions, PepsiCo Inc., http://www.pepsico.com/About/global-divisions (accessed December 15, 2018).

13. "Regions," Diageo, https://www.diageo.com/en/our-business/where-we-operate/global/ (accessed June 1, 2020).

14. Matt Scholz, "The Three-Step Process That's Kept 3M Innovative for Decades," *Fast Company,* July 10, 2017, https://www.fastcompany.com/40437745/the-three-step-process-thats-kept-3m-innovative-for-decades (accessed April 19, 2018).

15. Sarah Whitten, "Fresh Beef Is Coming to a McDonald's Near You," *CNBC,* March 6, 2018, https://www.cnbc.com/2018/03/06/fresh-beef-is-coming-to-a-mcdonalds-near-you.html (accessed April 19, 2018).

16. Sonia Thompson, "How Nike, Disney, and the Ritz Carlton Built Cultures That Always Deliver Great Customer Experiences," *Inc.,* May 18, 2018, https://www.inc.com/sonia-thompson/how-nike-disney-ritz-carlton-built-cultures-that-always-deliver-great-customer-experiences.html (accessed December 15, 2018).

17. United States Postal Service: Office of Inspector General, "Audit Report: Management Structure at the Postal Service," March 18, 2020, https://www.uspsoig.gov/sites/default/files/document-library-files/2020/19SMG011HR000-R20.pdf (accessed June 1, 2020).

18. CVS Health, "Jobs at CVS Health," https://jobs.cvshealth.com (accessed December 15, 2018).

19. "PepsiCo Unveils New Organizational Structure, Names CEOs of Three Principle Operating Units," *PR Newswire,* November 5, 2007, www.prnewswire.com/news-releases/pepsico-unveils-new-organizational-structure-names-ceos-of-three-principal-operating-units-58668152.html (accessed May 4, 2017); "The PepsiCo Family," PepsiCo, www.pepsico.com/Company/The-Pepsico-Family/PepsiCo-Americas-Beverages.html (accessed April 30, 2014).

20. Jon R. Katzenbach and Douglas K. Smith, "The Discipline of Teams," *Harvard Business Review* 71 (March–April 1993), p. 19.

21. Katzenbach and Smith, "The Discipline of Teams."

22. John Baldoni, "The Secret to Team Collaboration: Individuality," *Inc.,* January 18, 2012, www.inc.com/john-baldoni/the-secret-to-team-collaboration-is-individuality.html (accessed May 4, 2017).

23. Courtney Connlet, "Here's How Trello Sets Its Remote Workers Up for Success," *CNBC,* January 26, 2018, https://www.cnbc.com/2018/01/26/heres-how-trello-sets-remote-workers-up-for-success.html (accessed December 15, 2018); Mari Anne Snow, "7 Examples of Virtual Teams Who Broke the Mold and Made It Big," *Sophaya,* November 6, 2018, https://sophaya.com/2016/11/06/examples-of-virtual-teams-who-broke-the-mold-and-made-it-big/ (accessed December 15, 2018).

24. Ari Levy, "Working from Home Is Here to Stay, Even When the Economy Reopens," *CNBC,* May 11, 2020, https://www.cnbc.com/2020/05/11/work-from-home-is-here-to-stay-after-coronavirus.html (accessed June 1, 2020).

25. Anneke Seley, "Outside In: The Rise of the Inside Sales Team," Salesforce.com *Blog,* February 3, 2015, http://blogs.salesforce.com/company/2015/02/outside-in-rise-inside-sales-team-gp.html (accessed May 4, 2017).

26. Patrick Kiger, "Task Force Training Develops New Leaders, Solves Real Business Issues and Helps Cut Costs," *Workforce,* September 7, 2011, www.workforce.com/article/20070521/NEWS02/305219996/task-force-training-develops-new-leaders-solves-real-business-issues-and-helps-cut-costs

(accessed March 10, 2016); Duane D. Stanford, "Coca-Cola Woman Board Nominee Bucks Slowing Diversity Trend," *Bloomberg,* February 22, 2013, www.bloomberg.com/news/2013-02-22/coca-cola-s-woman-director-nominee-bucks-slowing-diversity-trend.html (accessed May 4, 2017).

27. Jerry Useem, "What's That Spell? TEAMWORK," *Fortune,* June 12, 2006, p. 66.

28. Courtney Connley, "Jeff Bezos' 'Two Pizza Rule' Can Help You Hold More Productive Meetings," *CNBC,* April 20, 2018, https://www.cnbc.com/2018/04/30/jeff-bezos-2-pizza-rule-can-help-you-hold-more-productive-meetings.html (accessed August 4, 2018).

29. Natasha Singer, "Intel's Sharp-Eyed Social Scientist," *The New York Times,* February 15, 2014, www.nytimes.com/2014/02/16/technology/intels-sharp-eyed-social-scientist.html?_r=0 (accessed May 4, 2017).

30. Richard S. Wellins, William C. Byham, and Jeanne M. Wilson, *Empowered Teams: Creating Self-Directed Work Groups That Improve Quality, Productivity, and Participation* (San Francisco: Jossey-Bass Publishers, 1991), p. 5.

31. Peter Mell and Timothy Grance, "The NIST Definition of Cloud Computing," National Institute of Standards and Technology, Special Publication 800-145, September 2011, http://csrc.nist.gov/publications/nistpubs/800-145/SP800-145.pdf (accessed April 30, 2014).

32. Michael Christian, "Top 10 Ideas: Making the Most of Your Corporate Intranet," April 2, 2009, www.claromentis.com/blog/top-10-ideas-making-the-most-of-your-corporate-intranet/ (accessed May 4, 2017).

33. Verne Harnish, "Five Ways to Liberate Your Team from Email Overload," *Fortune,* June 16, 2014, p. 52.

34. Sue Shellenbarger, "They're Gossiping About You," *The Wall Street Journal,* October 8, 2014, pp. D1–D2.

35. Kim Komando, "Why You Need a Company Policy on Internet Use," www.microsoft.com/business/en-us/resources/management/employee-relations/why-you-need-a-company-policy-on-internet-use.aspx?fbid=HEChiHWK7CU (accessed April 30, 2014).

36. "Our Values and Standards: The Basis of Our Success," Merck, https://www.merck.com/abo0ut/code_of_conduct.pdf (accessed March 16, 2015).

37. Imani Moise, "New Tools Tell Bosses How You're Feeling," *The Wall Street Journal,* March 29, 2018, p. B6.

38. PBSNewsHour, "Apple Supplier Foxconn Pledges Better Working Conditions, but Will It Deliver?" *YouTube,* www.youtube.com/watch?v=ZduorbCkSBQ (accessed May 4, 2017).

39. Susan M. Heathfield, "Top Ten Employee Complaints," *About.com,* http://humanresources.about.com/od/retention/a/emplo_complaint.htm (accessed March 16, 2015).

40. Gloria Mark, Shamsi T. Iqbal, Mary Czerwinski, Paul Johns, Akane Sano, and Yuliya Lutchyn, "Email Duration, Batching and Self-interruption: Patterns of Email Use on Productivity and Stress," *Proceedings of the 2016 CHI Conference on Human Factors in Computing Systems (CHI '16),* ACM, New York, NY, USA, pp. 1717–1728; Andrew Blackman, "The Smartest Way to Use Email at Work," *The Wall Street Journal,* March 12, 2018, p. R1.

a. Dinah Eng, "The Sweet Taste of Success," *Fortune,* June 1, 2015, pp. 9–20; Sugar Bowl Bakery website, https://sugarbowlbakery.com/ (accessed November 11, 2018); Sugar Bowl Bakery, "Sugar Bowl Bakery Expands Product Line with Launch of Its New Button Cakes at the International Dairy Deli Bakery Association Show," *Globe Newswire,* June 4, 2018, https://globenewswire.com/news-release/2018/06/04/1516474/0/

en/Sugar-Bowl-Bakery-Expands-Product-Line-with-Launch-of-its-New-Button-Cakes-At-The-International-Dairy-Deli-Bakery-Association-Show.html (accessed November 11, 2018); Katie Burke, "Bay Area Bakery Giant Plans East Coast Expansion as It Aims to Double Business in Five Years," *San Francisco Business Times,* June 22, 2018, https://www.bizjournals.com/sanfrancisco/news/2018/06/22/sugar-bowl-bakery-east-coast-production-freight-sf.html (accessed November 11, 2018); "Madeleines, Brownie Bites and Petite Palmiers: Inside the Delicious World of Sugar Bowl Bakery," *NBC,* April 2, 2018, https://www.nbcbayarea.com/news/local/Madeleines-Brownie-Bites-and-Petite-Palmiers-Inside-the-Delicious-World-of-Sugar-Bowl-Bakery-478558873.html (accessed December 15, 2018).

b. Annlee Ellingson, "7 Things We Learned about SpaceX from COO Gwynne Shotwell," *L.A. Biz,* May 24, 2018, www.bizjournals.com/losangeles/news/2018/05/24/7-things-we-learned-about-spacex-from-coo-shotwell.html (accessed September 28, 2018); Ariel Schwartz, "SpaceX's President on Elon Musk: 'When Elon Says Something, You Have to Pause and Not Blurt Out 'Well, That's Impossible'," *Business Insider,* April 11, 2018, www.businessinsider.com/how-spacex-president-and-elon-musk-work-together-2018-4 (accessed September 28, 2018); Max, Chafkin and Dana Hull, "SpaceX's Secret Weapon Is Gwynne Shotwell," *Bloomberg Businessweek,* July 26, 2018, www.bloomberg.com/news/features/2018-07-26/she-launches-spaceships-sells-rockets-and-deals-with-elon-musk (accessed September 28, 2018); Tom Huddleston Jr., "SpaceX President: 'You Don't Learn Anything from Success,' but You Learn from Your Failures," *CNBC,* August 2, 2018, www.cnbc.com/2018/08/02/spacex-president-gwynne-shotwell-you-dont-learn-anything-from-success.html (accessed September 28, 2018); Christian Davenport, "After 2016 Rocket Explosion, Elon Musk's SpaceX Looked Seriously at Sabotage," *The Washington Post,* February 26, 2018, https://www.washingtonpost.com/news/the-switch/wp/2018/02/26/after-2016-rocket-explosion-elon-musks-spacex-looked-seriously-at-sabotage (accessed September 28, 2018); Josh Boehm and Quora, "I Worked at SpaceX, and This Is How Elon Musk Inspired a Culture of Top Performers," *Forbes,* November 8, 2017, https://www.forbes.com/sites/quora/2017/11/08/i-worked-at-spacex-and-this-is-how-elon-musk-inspired-a-culture-of-top-performers (accessed September 28, 2018); Stephen Clark, "NASA Astronaughts Launch from U.S. Soil for First Time in Nine Years," *Space Flight Now,* May 30, 2020, https://spaceflightnow.com/2020/05/30/nasa-astronauts-launch-from-us-soil-for-first-time-in-nine-years/ (accessed June 1, 2020).

c. Michael Feferman, "Company Culture Tips from Netflix, Zappos, Atlassian," *Venture Beat,* January 17, 2016, https://venturebeat.com/2016/01/17/company-culture-tips-from-netflix-zappos-atlassian/ (accessed September 29, 2018); "Cross-Functional Teams," *Inc.,* https://www.inc.com/encyclopedia/cross-functional-teams.html (accessed September 29, 2018); Patty McCord, "How Netflix Reinvented HR," *Harvard Business Review,* January–February 2014, https://hbr.org/2014/01/how-netflix-reinvented-hr (accessed September 29, 2018); Janko Roettgers, "How Netflix Ticks: Five Key Insights from the Company's New Corporate Culture Manifesto," *Variety,* June 21, 2017, https://variety.com/2017/digital/news/netflix-company-culture-document-1202474529/ (accessed September 29, 2018); Jim Schleckser, "Why Netflix Doesn't Tolerate Brilliant Jerks," *Inc.,* February 2, 2016, https://www.inc.com/jim-schleckser/why-netflix-doesn-t-tolerate-brilliant-jerks.html (accessed September 29, 2018); Netflix, "Netflix Culture," https://jobs.netflix.com/culture (accessed September 29, 2018); Patty McCord and Knowledge@Wharton, "Learning from Netflix: How to Build a Culture of Freedom and Responsibility," *Wharton,* May 29, 2018, http://knowledge.wharton.upenn.edu/

article/how-netflix-built-its-company-culture/ (accessed September 29, 2018); Ryan Jenkins, "3 Ways Netflix Created a Culture of High-Performing Employees," *Inc.,* September 5, 2018, https://www.inc.com/ryan-jenkins/this-is-how-netflix-built-a-culture-of-highly-motivated-employees.html (accessed September 29, 2018); Roy Maurer, "Patty McCord: Always Be Recruiting," Society for Human Resource Management, January 19, 2018, https://www.shrm.org/resourcesandtools/hr-topics/talent-acquisition/pages/patty-mccord-always-be-recruiting.aspx (accessed September 29, 2018).

d. "2017 Employee Job Satisfaction and Engagement: The Doors of Opportunity Are Open," Society for Human Resource Management, April 24, 2017, https://www.shrm.org/hr-today/trends-and-forecasting/research-and-surveys/pages/2017-job-satisfaction-and-engagement-doors-of-opportunity-are-open.aspx (accessed April 21, 2018).

Chapter 8

1. "Our Employee First Culture," *Stand For,* 2017, http://standfor.containerstore.com/putting-our-employees-first/ (accessed June 2, 2020).

2. "Personified: 11 Things You Didn't Know about Amazon's CEO Jeff Bezos," *Gadgets Now,* January 12, 2017, http://www.gadgetsnow.com/checklist/personified-11-things-you-didnt-know-about-amazons-ceo-jeff-bezos/checklistshow/56500597.cms (accessed April 11, 2017).

3. Leonard L. Berry, *Discovering the Soul of Service* (New York: The Free Press, 1999), pp. 86–96.

4. Valerie A. Zeithaml and Mary Jo Bitner, *Services Marketing,* 3rd ed. (Boston: McGraw-Hill Irwin, 2003), pp. 3, 22.

5. "SAS Cuts 1,500 Flights," *The Local,* August 27, 2018, https://www.thelocal.se/20180827/sas-cuts-1500-flights (accessed December 15, 2018).

6. Danny Klein, "Why AI is a 'Differentiator for the Future' at Starbucks," *QSR,* November 2019, https://www.qsrmagazine.com/fast-food/why-ai-differentiator-future-starbucks (accessed June 2, 2020).

7. Bernard Wysocki Jr., "To Fix Health Care, Hospitals Take Tips from the Factory Floor," *The Wall Street Journal,* April 9, 2004, via www.chcanys.org/clientuploads/downloads/Clinical_resources/Leadership%20Articles/LeanThinking_ACF28EB.pdf (accessed May 4, 2017).

8. Deborah L. Roberts and Frank T. Piller, "Finding the Right Role for Social Media in Innovation," *MIT Sloan Management Review,* March 15, 2016, http://sloanreview.mit.edu/article/finding-the-right-role-for-social-media-in-innovation/ (accessed April 11, 2017).

9. Debbie Qaqish, "So You Want to Do Experiential Marketing? Consider These 4 Things First," *Marketing News,* April 2018, pp. 4–6.

10. Danielle Muoio, "These 19 Companies Are Racing to Put Driverless Cars on the Road by 2020," *Business Insider,* August 18, 2016, http://www.businessinsider.com/companies-making-driverless-cars-by-2020-2016-8/ (accessed April 11, 2017).

11. Volvo Cars, "Volvo Cars and Uber Present Production Vehicle Ready for Self-Driving," June 12, 2019, https://www.media.volvocars.com/global/en-gb/media/pressreleases/254697/volvo-cars-and-uber-present-production-vehicle-ready-for-self-driving (accessed June 2, 2020).

12. Amber Elliott, "Lancome's Le Teint Particulier Color-Match Technology Lands at the Galleria," *Houston Chronicle,* July 2, 2018, https://www.houstonchronicle.com/life/style/luxe-life/

article/Lancome-s-Le-Teint-Particulier-color-match-13030525. php (accessed December 15, 2018).

13. Charles McLellan, "Blockchain and Business: Looking Beyond the Hype," *ZDNet*, December 2, 2019, https://www.zdnet.com/article/blockchain-and-business-looking-beyond-the-hype/ (accessed June 2, 2020).

14. Laura Shin, "Industries, Looking for Efficiency, Turn to Blockchains," *The New York Times,* June 27, 2018, https://www.nytimes.com/2018/06/27/business/dealbook/industries-blockchains-efficiency.html (accessed December 15, 2018).

15. "Improvements to the Engineering Planning and Development Process," Toyota, 2017, http://www.toyota-global.com/company/history_of_toyota/75years/data/automotive_business/products_technology/research/engineering_planning/details_window.html (accessed April 12, 2017).

16. Ross Toro, "How 3D Printers Work (Infographic)," *Live Science,* June 18, 2013, www.livescience.com/37513-how-3d-printers-work-infographic.html (accessed May 4, 2017).

17. Matt McFarland, "Amazon's Delivery Drones May Drop Packages via Parachute," *CNN Tech,* February 14, 2017, http://money.cnn.com/2017/02/14/technology/amazon-drone-patent/ (accessed April 12, 2017).

18. Stuart Hodge. "SAP—Why Drones Have a Key Role to Play in the Future of Procurement," http://www.supplychaindigital.com/procurement/sap-why-drones-have-key-role-play-future-procurement (accessed April 16, 2018).

19. Claire Cain Miller, "Evidence That Robots Are Winning the Race for American Jobs," *The New York Times,* March 28, 2017, https://www.nytimes.com/2017/03/28/upshot/evidence-that-robots-are-winning-the-race-for-american-jobs.html?_r=1 (accessed April 12, 2017).

20. "Are There Enough Robots?" *Robotics Tomorrow,* February 14, 2017, http://www.roboticstomorrow.com/article/2017/02/are-there-enough-robots/9507 (accessed April 12, 2017).

21. James Henderson, "Hershey Pledges $500mn to Improve Supply Chain Sustainability," *Supply Chain Digital,* http://www.supplychaindigital.com/technology/hershey-pledges-500mn-improve-supply-chain-sustainability (accessed April 5, 2018).

22. "Benefits of Green Building," *USGBE,* http://www.usgbc.org/articles/green-building-facts (accessed June 2, 2020).

23. Katrina Brown Hunt, "Counting Down the 20 Greenest Cities in America," *Travel Leisure,* 2017, http://www.travelandleisure.com/slideshows/americas-greenest-cities/20 (accessed April 12, 2017).

24. O.C. Ferrell and Michael D. Hartline, *Marketing Strategy* (Mason, OH: South Western, 2011), p. 215.

25. "E-Commerce: Cultivating a New Logistics Landscape," *Inbound Logistics,* p. 13.

26. Mike Danby, "Innovation Beyond Drones—Transforming the Supply Chain," *Supply Chain Digital,* http://www.supplychaindigital.com/technology/comment-innovation-beyond-drones-transforming-supply-chain (accessed April 14, 2018).

27. James Henderson, "AI-Driven Procurement Platform, Suplari, Attracts $10.3 Million in Funding," *Supply Chain Digital,* http://www.supplychaindigital.com/technology/ai-driven-procurement-platform-suplari-attracts-103mn-funding (accessed April 6, 2018).

28. William Pride and O.C. Ferrell, *Marketing* (Boston: Cengage Learning, 2018), p. 443.

29. Rich Weissman, "Today's Supply Chains Are Too Lean," *Supply Chain Dive,* March 24, 2020, https://www.supplychaindive.com/news/lean-supply-chain-jit-inventory-covid-19/574693/ (accessed June 2, 2020).

30. Scott McCartney, "The Best and Worst Airlines of 2016," *The Wall Street Journal,* January 11, 2017, https://www.wsj.com/articles/the-best-and-worst-airlines-of-2016-1484149294 (accessed April 11, 2017).

31. National Institute of Standards and Technology, "Six Health Care, Nonprofit and Education Organizations Win Baldrige Awards for Performance Excellence," November 14, 2019, https://www.nist.gov/news-events/news/2019/11/six-health-care-nonprofit-and-education-organizations-win-baldrige-awards (accessed June 2, 2020).

32. Philip B. Crosby, *Quality Is Free: The Art of Making Quality Certain* (New York: McGraw-Hill, 1979), pp. 9–10.

33. Nigel F. Piercy, *Market-Led Strategic Change* (Newton, MA: Butterworth-Heinemann, 1992), pp. 374–385.

34. "ISO Certification and Accreditations," GE Power, 2017, http://www.geinstruments.com/company/iso-certification-and-accreditations.html (accessed April 12, 2017).

35. "Compliance Management Systems—Guidelines," International Organization for Standardization, 2017, https://www.iso.org/standard/62342.html (accessed April 12, 2017).

36. "Monitoring and Auditing Global Supply Chains Is a Must," *Ethisphere,* Q3 2011, pp. 38–45.

37. "Global Supplier Code of Conduct," Kellogg's, 2017, http://www.kelloggcompany.com/en_US/supplier-relations/transparency-in-supply-chain.html (accessed April 12, 2017).

38. Jennifer Smith, "Logistics Spending Jumped 11.4% on Strong Economic Growth," *The Wall Street Journal,* June 18, 2019, https://www.wsj.com/articles/logistics-spending-jumped-11-4-on-strong-economic-growth-11560862800 (accessed June 2, 2020).

39. PayScale, "Quality Assurance Manager Salary," http://www.payscale.com/research/US/Job=Quality_Assurance_Manager/Salary (accessed June 2, 2020).

a. "The Weather Company, an IBM Business, Named Official Weather Partner of NASCAR," NASCAR website, October 6, 2017, https://www.nascar.com/news-media/2017/10/06/the-weather-company-an-ibm-business-named-official-weather-partner-of-nascar/ (accessed September 16, 2018); IBM, "Just Add Weather: How Weather Insights Can Grow Your Bottom Line," IBM Institute for Business Value, https://www-935.ibm.com/services/us/gbs/thoughtleadership/justaddweather/ (accessed September 10, 2018); Ayman Youseff, "How Much Does Weather Affect Your Business?" *LinkedIn,* February 19, 2015, https://www.linkedin.com/pulse/how-much-does-weather-affect-your-business-ayman-youssef (accessed September 16, 2018); Michelle Boockoff-Bajdek, "The Weather Is Good: Harnessing Weather's Power to Drive Revenue," *The Weather Company,* June 19, 2018, https://business.weather.com/blog/the-forecast-is-good-harnessing-weathers-power-to-drive-revenue (accessed September 16, 2018).

b. Michelle Maynard, "Kit Kat Lovers, Listen Up: Hershey Is Betting Big That You'll Break Off More," *Forbes,* March 11, 2018, https://www.forbes.com/sites/michelinemaynard/2018/03/11/kit-kat-lovers-listen-up-hershey-is-betting-big-that-youll-break-off-more/#7c61790d7975 (accessed April 22, 2018).

c. Adobe, "Green Building," https://www.adobe.com/corporate-responsibility/sustainability/green-building.html (accessed June 2, 2020).

d. Angus Loten, "The Morning Download: Walmart Makes Blockchain a Requirement for Veggie Suppliers," *The Wall Street Journal,* September 25, 2018, blogs.wsj.com/cio/2018/09/25/

the-morning-download-walmart-makes-blockchain-a-requirement-for-veggie-suppliers/?mod=hp_minor_pos5 (accessed October 4, 2018); Luzi-Ann Javier, "Yes, These Chickens Are on the Blockchain," *Bloomberg.com,* April 9, 2018, www.bloomberg.com/news/features/2018-04-09/yes-these-chickens-are-on-the-blockchain (accessed October 3, 2018); Steve Banker, "Blockchain Gains Traction in the Food Supply Chain," *Forbes,* July 31 2018, www.forbes.com/sites/stevebanker/2018/07/25/blockchain-gains-traction-in-the-food-supply-chain/#25741cf71cf9 (accessed October 4, 2018); Cisco, "What Is Blockchain?" https://www.cisco.com/c/en/us/solutions/digital-transformation/blockchain/what-is-blockchain.html (accessed October 13, 2018); Arjun Kharpal, "Everything You Need to Know about the Blockchain," *CNBC,* June 18, 2018, https://www.cisco.com/c/en/us/solutions/digital-transformation/blockchain/what-is-blockchain.html (accessed October 13, 2018); Shaan Ray, "Blockchain: The Technology of Transactions," *Towards Data Science,* March 26, 2018, https://www.google.com/search?q=blockchain%2C+append%2C+new+transactions%2C+added+at+end&oq=blockchain%2C+append%2C+new+transactions%2C+added+at+end&aqs=chrome..69i57j33l2.6800j0j7&sourceid=chrome&ie=UTF-8 (accessed October 13, 2018); Billy Bambrough, "U.S. Fed Paper: Central Bank Cryptocurrencies Are Missing the Point," *Forbes,* April 24, 2018, https://www.forbes.com/sites/billybambrough/2018/04/24/us-fed-paper-central-bank-cryptocurrencies-are-missing-the-point/#b1e950c10860 (accessed October 13, 2018).

e. Connie Chen, "Target Is Facing Off Against Amazon with Its Own Super Fast Grocery Delivery Service—Here's How It Works," *Business Insider,* July 19, 2018, https://www.businessinsider.com/target-shipt-same-day-grocery-delivery-how-does-it-work-2018-7 (accessed August 31, 2018); Jennifer Smith, "Target Tests Retail 'Flow Center' for Faster, Nimbler Distribution," *The Wall Street Journal,* May 14, 2018, https://www.wsj.com/articles/target-tests-retail-flow-center-for-faster-nimbler-distribution-1526299200 (accessed August 31, 2018); PYMNTS, "Target Pilots New Distribution Strategy," PYMNTS.com, May 14, 2018, https://www.pymnts.com/news/delivery/2018/target-shipping-distribution-strategy/ (accessed August 31, 2018); Nandita Bose, "Exclusive: Target Gets Tough with Vendors to Speed Up Supply Chain," *Reuters,* May 3, 2016, https://www.reuters.com/article/us-target-suppliers-exclusive-idUSKCN0XV096 (accessed August 31, 2018); "Target Outlines 2020 Strategic Initiatives," *Supply Chain Digital,* March 3, 2020, https://www.supplychaindigital.com/press-release/10639988-0 (accessed June 2, 2020).

Chapter 9

1. Jackie Wattles, Ben Geier, Matt Egan, and Danielle Wiener-Bronner, "Wells Fargo's 20-Month Nightmare," *CNN Money,* April 24, 2018, http://money.cnn.com/2018/04/24/news/companies/wells-fargo-timeline-shareholders/index.html (accessed April 25, 2018).

2. Sue Shellenbarger, "Why Perks No Longer Cut It for Workers," *The Wall Street Journal,* December 3, 2018, https://www.wsj.com/articles/why-perks-no-longer-cut-it-for-workers-1543846157 (accessed December 16, 2018).

3. Dan Heath and Chip Heath, "Business Advice from Van Halen," *Fast Company,* March 1, 2010, www.fastcompany.com/1550881/business-advice-van-halen (accessed April 21, 2018).

4. Áine Cain, "6 Incredible Perks for Apple Employees," *Business Insider,* August 2, 2018, https://www.businessinsider.com/perks-apple-employees-benefits-2017-11 (accessed June 8, 2020).

5. Jeff Beer, "Patagonia: For Growing Its Business Every Time It Amplifies Its Social Mission," *Fast Company,* "The World's 50 Most Innovative Companies," pp. 33–34, March/April 2018.

6. Grant Suneson, "50 Highest Paid CEOs in 2019," *USA Today,* May 19, 2020, https://www.usatoday.com/story/money/2020/05/19/50-highest-paid-ceos-in-2019/111783524/ (accessed June 8, 2020).

7. Frederick Herzberg, Bernard Mausner, and Barbara B. Snyderman, *The Motivation to Work,* 2nd ed. (New York: John Wiley, 1959).

8. "Physician—Gastroenterology Salaries," Salary.com, http://www1.salary.com/gastroenterologist-Salary.html (accessed June 8, 2020).

9. Shelia Eugenio, "4 Innovative Ways to Motivate Your Team," *Entrepreneur,* March 6, 2017, https://www.entrepreneur.com/article/289560 (access April 22, 2018).

10. Douglas McGregor, *The Human Side of Enterprise* (New York: McGraw-Hill, 1960), pp. 33–34.

11. Steven Pearlstein, "A Computer Specialist Reshapes Computer Sciences Corp.," *Washington Post,* August 1, 2015, https://www.washingtonpost.com/business/a-turnaround-specialist-reshapes-computer-sciences-corp/2015/07/30/c2be7c9c-32dd-11e5-97ae-30a30cca95d7_story.html (accessed April 22, 2018).

12. McGregor, *The Human Side of Enterprise.*

13. Scott Koegler, "The Empowered Employee: How 6 Companies Are Arming Their Teams with Data," *IBM Watson,* March 24, 2017, https://www.ibm.com/blogs/watson/2017/03/empowered-employee-6-companies-arming-teams-data/ (access April 22, 2018).

14. William Ouchi, *Theory Z—How American Business Can Meet the Japanese Challenge* (New York: Perseus Group, 1981).

15. Jon L. Pierce, Tatiana Kostova, and Kurt T. Kirks, "Toward a Theory of Psychological Ownership in Organizations," *Academy of Management Review* 26, no. 2 (2001), p. 298.

16. Matt Egan, "Lloyd Blankfein Takes Pay Cut at Goldman Sachs," *CNN Money,* March 17, 2017, http://money.cnn.com/2017/03/17/investing/lloyd-blankfein-goldman-sachs-pay-cut/index.html (accessed April 22, 2018).

17. David Callahan, *The Cheating Culture: Why More Americans Are Doing Wrong to Get Ahead* (Orlando, FL: Harcourt, 2004).

18. Patrick V. Valtin, "How Employees Must Deal with the Source of the Greatest Threat to Their Business Survival," *Tampa Bay Business Journal,* June 24, 2019, https://www.bizjournals.com/tampabay/news/2019/06/24/how-employers-must-deal-with-the-source-of-the.html (accessed June 8, 2020).

19. Katie Reilly, "Shoplifting and Other Fraud Cost Retailers Nearly $50 Billion Last Year," *Time,* June 22, 2017, http://time.com/money/4829684/shoplifting-fraud-retail-survey/ (accessed April 22, 2018).

20. Patrick V. Valtin, "How Employees Must Deal with the Source of the Greatest Threat to Their Business Survival," *Tampa Bay Business Journal,* June 24, 2019, https://www.bizjournals.com/tampabay/news/2019/06/24/how-employers-must-deal-with-the-source-of-the.html (accessed June 8, 2020).

21. Archie Carroll, "Carroll: Do We Live in a Cheating Culture?" *Athens Banner-Herald,* February 21, 2004, www.onlineathens.com/stories/022204/bus_20040222028.shtml (accessed May 4, 2017).

22. Edwin A. Locke, K. M. Shaw, and Gary P. Latham, "Goal Setting and Task Performance: 1969–1980," *Psychological Bulletin* 90 (1981), pp. 125–152.

23. Peter Drucker, *The Practice of Management* (New York: Harper & Row, 1954).

24. "Management by Objectives," *The Economist,* October 21, 2009, http://www.economist.com/node/14299761 (accessed April 22, 2018).

25. Tim Hird, "The Lasting Benefits of Job Rotation," *Treasury & Risk,* January 24, 2017, https://www.treasuryandrisk.com/sites/treasuryandrisk/2017/01/24/the-lasting-benefits-of-job-rotation/ (accessed April 22, 2018).

26. Karsten Strauss, "The 250 Companies Offering the Most Flexible-Time Jobs," *Forbes,* October 11, 2016, www.forbes.com/sites/karstenstrauss/2016/10/11/the-250-companies-offering-the-most-flexible-time-jobs/#5827bead4424 (accessed April 22, 2018).

27. American Sociological Association, "Work Flexibility Benefits Employees, Study Says," *Phys.org,* January 13, 2016, http://abcnews.go.com/Health/Healthday/story?id=4509753 (accessed April 22, 2018).

28. Marco Santana, "Orlando Leaders: Skills Deficiency Poses Challenge as Tech Disrupts Industries," *Orlando Sentinel,* March 22, 2018, https://www.orlandosentinel.com/business/technology/os-bz-digital-workforce-challenges-20180321-story.html (accessed December 16, 2018).

29. Karsten Strauss, "Flextime Jobs: The 10 Best Career Fields For Making Your Own Schedule," *Forbes,* October 12, 2017, https://www.forbes.com/sites/karstenstrauss/2017/10/12/flex-time-jobs-the-10-best-career-fields-for-making-your-own-schedule/#f9bc0e376b9b (accessed April 22, 2018).

30. Dell, "Work Flexibility at Dell," https://jobs.dell.com/work-flexibility (accessed June 8, 2020).

31. Rebecca Wilson, "Work from Home to Increase Productivity," *Recruitment International,* March 31, 2017, https://www.recruitment-international.co.uk/blog/2017/03/work-from-home-to-increase-productivity (accessed April 22, 2018).

32. Dori Meinert, "Make Telecommuting Pay Off," Society for Human Resource Management, June 1, 2011, www.shrm.org/Publications/hrmagazine/EditorialContent/2011/0611/Pages/0611meinert.aspx (accessed April 22, 2018).

33. "The Best Places for Business and Careers," *Forbes,* 2017, https://www.forbes.com/best-places-for-business/list/ (accessed April 22, 2018).

a. BCI Group, "Cooking Up Company Culture with a Side of Happiness," www.bcigroup.com/customer-stories/burgerville (October 16, 2018); Burgerville, "Culture," Burgerville.com, www.burgerville.com/careers/culture/ (October 16, 2018); Leonard Berman, O.C. Ferrell, and Linda Ferrell, *Management: Principles and Applications,* 3rd ed. (Solon, OH: Academic Media Solutions, 2015) pg. 358; Elizabeth Hayes, "Burgerville Serves Up Generous Health Plan, Mandate or Not," *Portland Business Journal,* July 31, 2013, https://www.bizjournals.com/portland/blog/health-care-inc/2013/07/burgerville-serves-up-generous-health.html (accessed October 19, 2018); Moe Godfrey, "Burgerville: Unionization in Restaurants," *Restaurant Nuts,* May 8, 2018, https://www.restaurantnuts.com/unionization-in-restaurants (accessed October 26, 2018); Elise Herron, "Burgerville Workers Union Ends Strike after Management Agrees to Renegotiate Wages," *Willamette Week,* October 27, 2019, https://www.wweek.com/news/2019/10/27/burgerville-workers-union-ends-strike-after-management-agrees-to-renegotiate-wages/ (accessed June 8, 2020).

b. Centers for Disease Control and Prevention, "Worker Productivity Measures," https://www.cdc.gov/workplacehealthpromotion/model/evaluation/productivity.html (accessed June 8, 2020).

c. Patagonia, "Environmental Internship Program," http://www.patagonia.com/us/patagonia.go?assetid=80524 (accessed on November 11, 2018); Giselle Abramovich, "Inside Patagonia's Content Machine," *Digiday,* January 31, 2013, http://digiday.com/brands/inside-patagonias-content-machine/ (accessed November 11, 2018); Leigh Buchanan, "How Patagonia's Roving CEO Stays in the Loop," *Inc.,* March 18, 2013, https://www.inc.com/leigh-buchanan/patagonia-founder-yvon-chouinard-15five.html (accessed November 11, 2018); "Patagonia: A Sustainable Outlook on Business," Daniels Fund Ethics Initiative, http://danielsethics.mgt.unm.edu/pdf/patagonia.pdf (accessed November 11, 2018); Lynda.com, "Patagonia: Case Study," 2013, http://cdn.lynda.com/cms/asset/text/patagonia-case-study--1931751689.pdf (accessed November 11, 2018); Patagonia, "Patagonia's Mission Statement," http://www.patagonia.com/company-info.html (accessed November 11, 2018); Rachel Gillett, "The CEO of Patagonia Makes a Convincing Business Case for This Unorthodox Perk," *Business Insider,* August 17, 2016, https://www.businessinsider.com/patagonia-ceo-makes-a-convincing-business-case-for-this-unorthodox-perk-2016-8 (accessed November 11, 2018).

d. Micah Solomon, "Tony Hsieh Reveals the Secret to Zappos' Customer Service Success in One Word," *Forbes,* December 1, 2017, www.forbes.com/sites/micahsolomon/2017/06/12/tony-hsieh-spills-the-beans-the-one-word-secret-of-zappos-customer-service-success/#6fdd02881acc (accessed October 26, 2018); Zack Guzman, "Zappos CEO Tony Hsieh on Getting Rid of Managers: What I Wish I'd Done Differently," *CNBC,* September 15, 2016, www.cnbc.com/2016/09/13/zappos-ceo-tony-hsieh-the-thing-i-regret-about-getting-rid-of-managers.html (accessed October 26, 2018); Richard Feloni, "A Zappos Employee Had the Company's Longest Customer-Service Call at 10 Hours, 43 Minutes," *Business Insider,* July 26, 2016, https://www.businessinsider.com/zappos-employee-sets-record-for-longest-customer-service-call-2016-7 (accessed October 26, 2018); "Our Common Core: Deliver WOW through Service," Zappos.com, June 1, 2017, https://www.zappos.com/about/core-values-one (accessed October 26, 2018).

Chapter 10

1. Zameena Mejia, "Nearly 9 Out of 10 Millennials Would Consider Taking a Pay Cut to Get This," *CNBC,* June 28, 2018, https://www.cnbc.com/2018/06/27/nearly-9-out-of-10-millennials-would-consider-a-pay-cut-to-get-this.html (accessed January 19, 2019).

2. "Dictionary of Occupational Titles," http://www.occupationalinfo.org/ (accessed April 27, 2018).

3. Alison Doyle, "Best Social Media Sites for Job Searching," *The Balance,* June 7, 2016, https://www.thebalance.com/best-social-media-sites for-job-searching-2062617 (accessed April 18, 2017); Susan P. Joyce, "Guide to Social Media and Job Search," *Job-Hunt,* https://www.job-hunt.org/social-networking/social-media.shtml (accessed April 27, 2018).

4. "Study: Which Companies Offer the Fastest Online Job Application Process?" *Indeed Blog,* August 15, 2016, http://blog.indeed.com/2016/08/15/fastest-job-application-process/ (accessed April 27, 2018).

5. Sachi Barreiro, "Can Potential Employers Check Out Your Facebook Page?" Nolo.com, https://www.nolo.com/legal-encyclopedia/can-potential-employers-check-your-facebook-page.html (accessed April 27, 2018); Diana Coker, "Should the Facebook Password Be Given in a Job Interview?" *HR Digest,* December 29, 2016, https://www.thehrdigest.com/facebook-password-given-job-interview/ (accessed April 27, 2018).

6. "Eight Ways to Leverage Social Media as a Hiring Tool," *Forbes,* February 19, 2018, https://www.forbes.com/sites/forbesagencycouncil/2018/02/19/eight-ways-to-leverage-social-media-as-a-hiring-tool/#785ba1e3750c (accessed April 27, 2018).

7. "70% of Employers Say Prescription Drug Abuse Affects Workplace," *Insurance Journal,* March 10, 2017, http://www.insurancejournal.com/news/national/2017/03/10/444117.htm (accessed April 27, 2018).

8. Alexia Elejalde-Ruiz, "Cost of Substance Abuse Hits Employers Hard, New Tool Shows," *Chicago Tribune,* April 6, 2017, http://www.chicagotribune.com/business/ct-workplace-substance-abuse-0407-biz-20170406-story.html (accessed April 27, 2018).

9. Lauren Weber and Mike Esterl, "E-Cigarette Rise Poses Quandary for Employers," *The Wall Street Journal,* January 16, 2014, p. A2.

10. Roy Maurer, "Know Before You Hire: 2017 Employment Screening Trends," Society for Human Resource Management, January 25, 2017, https://www.shrm.org/resourcesandtools/hr-topics/talent-acquisition/pages/2017-employment-screening-trends.aspx (accessed April 27, 2018).

11. Allison Linn, "Desperate Measures: Why Some People Fake Their Resumes," *CNBC,* February 7, 2014, www.cnbc.com/id/101397212 (accessed April 27, 2018).

12. U.S. Equal Opportunity Commission, "EEOC Releases Fiscal Year 2019 Enforcement and Litigation Data," January 24, 2020, https://www.eeoc.gov/newsroom/eeoc-releases-fiscal-year-2019-enforcement-and-litigation-data (accessed June 9, 2020).

13. Emma Hinchliffe, "The Number of Female CEOs in the Fortune 500 Hits an All-Time Record," *Fortune,* May 18, 2020, https://fortune.com/2020/05/18/women-ceos-fortune-500-2020/ (accessed June 9, 2020); Phil Wahba, "The Number of Black CEOs in the Fortune 500 Remain Very Low," *Fortune,* June 1, 2019, https://fortune.com/2020/06/01/black-ceos-fortune-500-2020-african-american-business-leaders/ (accessed June 9, 2020).

14. Stephen Bastien, "12 Benefits of Hiring Older Workers," *Entrepreneur.com,* September 20, 2006, www.entrepreneur.com/article/167500 (accessed April 27, 2018).

15. Jennifer Calfas, "Women Have Pushed for Equal Pay for Decades. It's Sad How Little Progress We've Made," *Time,* April 10, 2018, http://time.com/money/5225986/equal-pay-day-2018-gender-wage-gap/ (accessed April 27, 2018).

16. Lydia Dishman, "These Jobs Have the Largest and Smallest Gender Pay Gaps," *Fast Company,* September 27, 2017, https://www.fastcompany.com/40474000/these-jobs-have-the-largest-and-smallest-gender-pay-gaps (accessed April 27, 2018).

17. Camaron Santos and Kellye Whitney, "McDonald's Virtual Strategy Aids Big Business Changes," *Chief Learning Officer,* February 8, 2017, http://www.clomedia.com/2017/02/08/restaurants-orders-up-virtual-training/ (accessed April 27, 2018).

18. "Our Employee First Culture," *Stand for,* 2017, http://standfor.containerstore.com/putting-our-employees-first/ (accessed April 27, 2018).

19. Maury A. Peiperl, "Getting 360-Degree Feedback Right," *Harvard Business Review,* January 2001, pp. 142–148.

20. Chris Musselwhite, "Self-Awareness and the Effective Leader," *Inc.com,* www.inc.com/resources/leadership/articles/20071001/musselwhite.html (accessed April 27, 2018).

21. Rachel Feintzeig, "You're Awesome! Firms Scrap Negative Feedback," *The Wall Street Journal,* February 11, 2015, pp. B1, B5.

22. Marcel Schwantes, "Study Says It Comes Down to Any of These 6 Reasons," *Inc.,* October 23, 2017, https://www.inc.com/marcel-schwantes/why-are-your-employees-quitting-a-study-says-it-comes-down-to-any-of-these-6-reasons.html (accessed April 27, 2018).

23. Alison Doyle, "2019 Federal and State Minimum Wage Rates," *The Balance,* January 15, 2019, https://www.thebalancecareers.com/2017-federal-state-minimum-wage-rates-2061043 (accessed January 20, 2019).

24. "Wage and Hour Division (WHD)," U.S. Department of Labor, January 1, 2018, https://www.dol.gov/whd/state/tipped.htm (accessed April 27, 2018).

25. Paycor, "Minimum Wage by State and 2020 Increases," March 13, 2020, https://www.paycor.com/resource-center/minimum-wage-by-state (accessed June 9, 2020).

26. Kevin Dugan, "Wall Street Bonuses Rise for the First Time in Three Years," *New York Post,* March 15, 2017, http://nypost.com/2017/03/15/wall-street-bonuses-rise-for-the-first-time-in-three-years/ (accessed April 27, 2018).

27. Bureau of Labor Statistics, U.S. Department of Labor, "Employer Costs for Employee Compensation—December 2019," March 19, 2020, https://www.bls.gov/news.release/pdf/ecec.pdf (accessed June 9, 2020).

28. Christine Birkner, "Taking Care of Their Own," *Marketing News,* February 2015, pp. 44–49.

29. "Employee Assistance Program," Home Depot, https://secure.livethehealthyorangelife.com/healthy_living/employee_assistance_program (accessed June 9, 2020).

30. Angus Loten and Sarah E. Needleman, "Laws on Paid Sick Leave Divide Businesses," *The Wall Street Journal,* February 6, 2014, p. B5.

31. Georgia Wells, Deepa Seetharaman, and Yoree Koh, "Employees Appear to Be Unfazed by Crisis," *The Wall Street Journal,* April 10, 2018, p. B4.

32. U.S. Bureau of Labor Statistics, "Union Members Summary," Bureau of Labor Statistics, January 18, 2019 https://www.bls.gov/news.release/union2.nr0.htm (accessed January 20, 2019).

33. Tom Walsh, "UAW Needs Stronger Message," *USA Today,* February 17, 2014, p. 1B.

34. "McDonald's Workers in St. Louis Go on Strike over Unsafe Conditions, Lost Hours, Pay Cuts," *KSDK,* April 1, 2020, https://www.ksdk.com/article/news/local/business-journal/mcdonalds-workers-st-louis-strike-unsafe-conditions-lost-hours-pay-cuts/63-223e041f-9843-435e-85ea-5de27cf04b1b (accessed June 9, 2020).

35. "NLRB Says Walmart Retaliated against Workers," *CBS News,* January 15, 2014, https://www.cbsnews.com/news/nlrb-says-walmart-retaliated-against-workers/ (accessed April 27, 2018); Steven Greenhouse and Michael J. De La Merced, "At Judge's Urging, Hostess and Union Agree to Mediation," *The New York Times,* November 19, 2012, https://dealbook.nytimes.com/2012/11/19/hostess-and-bakers-union-agree-to-mediation/ (accessed April 27, 2018).

36. Ted Goodman, "Honeywell Union Workers Agree to New Contract after 10-Month Lockout," *Daily Caller,* February 27, 2017, http://dailycaller.com/2017/02/27/honeywell-union-workers-agree-to-new-contract-after-10-month-lockout/ (accessed April 27, 2018).

37. Evan Horowitz, "When Will Minorities Be the Majority?" *Boston Globe,* February 26, 2016, https://www.bostonglobe.com/news/politics/2016/02/26/when-will-minorities-majority/9v5m1Jj8hdGcXvpXtbQT5I/story.html (accessed April 27, 2018).

38. Ainsley Harris, "Social Capital: For Putting Values into Its Ventures," *Fast Company,* "The World's 50 Most Innovative Companies," March/April 2018, pp. 52–54.

39. Taylor H. Cox Jr., "The Multicultural Organization," *Academy of Management Executives* 5 (May 1991), pp. 34–47; Marilyn Loden and Judy B. Rosener, *Workforce America! Managing Employee Diversity as a Vital Resource* (Homewood, IL: Business One Irwin, 1991).

40. Jeff Green, "At Least 43 California Companies Failed to Add Women to Corporate Boards, Despite New Law," *TIME,* March 3, 2020, https://time.com/5794271/california-women-corporate-boards/ (accessed June 9, 2020).

41. "Facts about Sexual Harassment," U.S. Equal Employment Opportunity Commission, https://www.eeoc.gov/eeoc/publications/fs-sex.cfm (accessed January 15, 2019).

42. Edmund Lee, "CBS Chief Executive Les Moonves Steps Down after Sexual Harassment Claims," *The New York Times,* September 9, 2018, https://www.nytimes.com/2018/09/09/business/les-moonves-longtime-cbs-chief-may-be-gone-by-monday.html (accessed January 14, 2019).

43. Joe Flint, "CBS News Names Susan Zirinsky as Its First Female President," *The Wall Street Journal,* January 6, 2019.

44. Sara Ashley O'Brien, "Former Employee Sues Uber for Sexual Harassment, Discrimination," *CNN,* May 21, 2018, https://money.cnn.com/2018/05/21/technology/uber-sexual-harassment-discrimination-lawsuit/index.html (accessed January 14, 2019).

45. Eric Bachman, "In Response to #MeToo, EEOC Is Filing More Sexual Harassment Lawsuits and Winning," *Forbes,* October 5, 2018, https://www.forbes.com/sites/ericbachman/2018/10/05/how-has-the-eeoc-responded-to-the-metoo-movement/#3ef9189f7475 (accessed January 14, 2019).

46. Rhita Chatterjee, "A New Survey Finds 81 Percent of Women Have Experienced Sexual Harassment," *NPR,* February 21, 2018, www.npr.org/sections/thetwo-way/2018/02/21/587671849/a-new-survey-finds-eighty-percent-of-women-have-experienced-sexual-harassment (accessed January 15, 2019).

47. "Yes, Men Can Be Sexually Harassed in the Workplace," *PLBSH,* https://www.plbsh.com/yes-men-can-be-sexually-harassed-in-the-workplace/ (accessed January 14, 2019).

48. Douglas MacMillan, "Facebook to End Forced Arbitration for Sexual-Harassment Claims," *The Wall Street Journal,* November 9, 2018, https://www.wsj.com/articles/facebook-to-end-forced-arbitration-for-sexual-harassment-claims-1541799129 (accessed January 14, 2019).

49. Joan Farrell, "New California Law Requires Sexual Harassment Training for All Employees," *HR Daily Advisor,* October 4, 2018, https://hrdailyadvisor.blr.com/2018/10/04/new-california-law-requires-sexual-harassment-training-for-all-employees/ (accessed January 15, 2019).

50. Alexandra Bruell, "P&G Challenges Men to Shave Their 'Toxic Masculinity' in Gillette Ad," *The Wall Street Journal,* January 14, 2019, https://www.wsj.com/articles/p-g-challenges-men-to-shave-their-toxic-masculinity-in-gillette-ad-11547467200?mod=hp_lead_pos9 (accessed January 15, 2019).

51. Industrious Office website, https://www.industriousoffice.com/ (accessed April 26, 2018); WeWork website, https://www.wework.com/ (accessed April 26, 2018); BS Interactive Inc., segment narrated by Tony Dokoupil, "Co-Working: The New Way to Work," April 15, 2018, https://www.cbsnews.com/news/co-working-the-new-way-to-work/ (accessed April 21, 2018).

52. Paul Davidson, "Overworked and Underpaid?" *USA Today,* April 16, 2012, pp. 1A–2A.

53. Maurie Backman, "Here's a New Reason to Work Fewer Hours," *CNN,* June 20, 2017, http://money.cnn.com/2017/06/20/pf/work-hours/index.html (accessed April 27, 2018).

54. Alison Doyle, "Difference between an Exempt and a Non-Exempt Employee," *The Balance,* January 17, 2019, https://www.thebalancecareers.com/exempt-and-a-non-exempt-employee-2061988 (accessed January 20, 2019).

55. Parker Poe Adams & Bernstein LLP, "Expletive-Laced Facebook Rant Protected under Federal Law," *Employment Law Alliance,* May 15, 2017, https://www.employmentlawalliance.com/firms/parkerpoe/articles/expletive-laced-facebook-rant-protected-under-federal-labor-law (accessed April 27, 2018); Melanie Trottman, "For Angry Employees, Legal Cover for Rants," *The Wall Street Journal,* December 2, 2011, http://online.wsj.com/article/SB10001424052970203710704577049822809710332.html (accessed April 27, 2018).

56. Jack Kelly, "Thousands of New Jobs Are Being Created in Response to the Coronavirus," *Forbes,* March 27, 2020, https://www.forbes.com/sites/jackkelly/2020/03/27/thousands-of-new-jobs-are-being-created-in-response-to-the-coronavirus/#30508f9f3d3f (accessed June 8, 2020).

a. Antoine Gara, "Generous 401(k) Matches Helped Scott Scherr Build the Ultimate Software Stock," *Forbes,* December 12, 2017, https://www.forbes.com/sites/antoinegara/2017/12/12/generous-401k-matches-helped-scott-scherr-build-the-ultimate-software-stock/#30d1a7cd7b11 (accessed August 31, 2018); Imani Moise, "What's on Your Mind? Bosses Are Using Artificial Intelligence to Find Out," *The Wall Street Journal,* March 28, 2018, https://www.wsj.com/articles/whats-on-your-mind-bosses-are-using-artificial-intelligence-to-find-out-1522251302 (accessed August 31, 2018); "Ultimate Software Hosts Annual 'Connections' Customer Conference with Almost 4,000 HCM Professionals, Partners, and Analysts," *Business Wire,* March 23, 2018, https://www.businesswire.com/news/home/20180323005404/en/Ultimate-Software-Hosts-Annual-%E2%80%9CConnections%E2%80%9D-Customer-Conference (accessed August 31, 2018); Ultimate Software, "Ultimate Software Reveals Xander AI Platform for HCM and Comprehensive Partner Integration Ecosystem at HR Technology Conference," October 17, 2017, https://www.ultimatesoftware.com/PR/Press-Release/Ultimate-Software-Reveals-Xander-AI-Platform-for-HCM-and-Comprehensive-Partner-Integration-Ecosystem-at-HR-Technology-Conference (accessed August 31, 2018).

b. Te-Ping Chen and Eric Morath, "Employers Choose Bonuses over Raises," *The Wall Street Journal,* September 18, 2018, https://www.wsj.com/articles/benefit-gains-exceed-wage-growth-new-labor-data-shows-1537289455 (accessed October 4, 2018); Brendan Greeley, "Employers Know It's Easier to Claw Back a Bonus than a Raise," *Alphaville,* September 28, 2018, https://ftalphaville.ft.com/2018/09/28/1538129627000/Employers-know-it-s-easier-to-claw-back-a-bonus-than-a-raise/ (accessed October 4, 2018); Dami Lee, "Amazon Eliminates Monthly Bonuses and Stock Grants after Minimum Wage Increase," *The Verge,* October 3, 2018, https://www.theverge.com/2018/10/3/17934194/amazon-minimum-wage-raise-stock-options-bonus-warehouse (accessed October 4, 2018); Patricia Cohen, "Where Did Your Pay Raise Go? It May Have Become a Bonus," *The New York Times,* February 10, 2018, https://www.nytimes.com/2018/02/10/business/economy/bonus-pay.html (accessed October 4, 2018).

c. Sarah Elbert, "Modern Super Hero," *Delta Sky,* December 2017, pp. 78–81, 178–179; Henna Inam, "Sheryl Sandberg on Being Human," *Transformational Leadership: Coaching & Leadership Development,* June 21, 2015, http://www.transformleaders.tv/sheryl-sandberg-on-being-human/ (accessed January 14, 2018); Shawn Doyle, "What Every Boss Can Learn about Leadership from Sheryl Sandberg from Facebook," *Inc.,* September 7, 2017, https://www.inc.com/shawn-doyle/what-every-boss-can-learn-about-leadership-from-sh.html (accessed January 14, 2018); Laura Vanderkam, "Women with Big Jobs and Big Families: Balancing Really Isn't That Hard," *Fortune,* June 6, 2015, http://fortune.com/2015/06/06/women-with-big-jobs-and-big-families-balancing-really-isnt-that-hard/ (accessed September 14, 2018); Aparna Alluri, "How the Gender Pay Gap Has Changed (And How It Hasn't)," *NPR,* December 15, 2014, https://www.npr.org/sections/money/2014/12/15/370357880/how-the-gender-pay-gap-has-changed-and-how-it-hasnt (accessed September 14, 2018).

   d.   "The World's 30 Biggest Employers Will Surprise You," *MSN Money,* September 18, 2017, https://www.msn.com/en-us/money/careersandeducation/the-worlds-30-biggest-employers-will-surprise-you/ss-AArVuGH#image=1 (accessed April 27, 2018).

Chapter 11

1. Ashley Halladay, "Classic Trix Shapes Back on Shelves," General Mills, September 30, 2018, https://blog.generalmills.com/2018/09/classic-trix-shapes-back-on-shelves/ (accessed January 27, 2019).

2. "Beauty Queen," *People,* May 10, 2004, p. 187.

3. Michael Treacy and Fred Wiersema, *The Discipline of Market Leaders* (Reading, MA: Addison Wesley, 1995), p. 176.

4. Jefferson Graham, "At Apple Stores, iPads at Your Service," *USA Today,* May 23, 2011, p. 1B; Ana Swanson, "How the Apple Store Took over the World," *Washington Post,* July 21, 2015, https://www.washingtonpost.com/news/wonk/wp/2015/07/21/the-unlikely-success-story-of-the-apple-retail-store/ (accessed May 5, 2017).

5. Kwaku Atuahene-Gima, "Resolving the Capability-Rigidity Paradox in New Product Innovation," *Journal of Marketing* 69, 4 (October 2005), pp. 61–83.

6. Maryalene LaPonsie, "15 Stores with the Best Return Policies," *CBS,* November 22, 2017, https://www.cbsnews.com/news/15-stores-with-the-best-return-policies/ (accessed January 6, 2018).

7. Clare McDonald, "How Birchbox Uses Social Media for Personalisation and Discovery," *Computer Weekly,* November 5, 2018, https://www.computerweekly.com/news/252451955/How-Birchbox-uses-social-media-for-personalisation-and-discovery (accessed January 27, 2019).

8. Jeff Desjardins, "This Is the Lifetime Value of a Starbucks Customer," *Business Insider,* January 28, 2016, www.businessinsider.com/lifetime-value-of-a-starbucks-customer-2016-1 (accessed December 12, 2017).

9. Venky Shankar, "Multiple Touch Point Marketing," American Marketing Association, Faculty Consortium on Electronic Commerce, Texas A&M University, July 14–17, 2001.

10. Catalyst, "Buying Power: Quick Take," April 27, 2020, https://www.catalyst.org/research/buying-power/ (accessed June 9, 2020).

11. Tessa Berenson, "Amazon Is Adding Spanish to Its U.S. Website," *Fortune,* March 10, 2017, http://fortune.com/2017/03/10/amazon-spanish-website/ (accessed December 10, 2017).

12. Chrome Industries website, http://www.chromeindustries.com/our-story.html (accessed December 26, 2016).

13. Craig Giammona, "Hey Mom, Set Another Place at Dinner for Fido," *Bloomberg Businessweek,* November 12, 2015, pp. 26–27.

14. Tim Higgins, "Tesla Steps on the Gas Overtakes Ford in Value," *The Wall Street Journal,* April 4, 2017, p. A1.

15. William Fierman, "This Is Why the SUV Is Here to Stay," *Business Insider,* March 9, 2016, http://www.businessinsider.com/suv-sales-continue-to-grow (accessed May 5, 2017).

16. Laura Stevens, "Amazon's Profit Exceeds Target," *The Wall Street Journal,* February 8, 2017, p. B1.

17. "How Many Users Do Spotify, Apple Music and Other Big Music Streaming Services Have?" *Musically,* February 19, 2020, https://musically.com/2020/02/19/spotify-apple-how-many-users-big-music-streaming-services/ (accessed June 9, 2020).

18. "About Us," Makeup.com, https://www.makeup.com/about (accessed December 10, 2017).

19. "Google AdWords," Google, https://www.google.com/adwords/ (accessed April 4, 2016).

20. Twitter, "What Are Promoted Tweets?" Twitter Help Center, https://support.twitter.com/articles/142101-what-are-promoted-tweets# (accessed April 4, 2016).

21. Christine Birkner, "10 Minutes with . . . Raul Murguia Villegas," *Marketing News,* July 30, 2011, pp. 26–27.

22. "MSPA North America," Mystery Shopping Providers Association, http://mysteryshop.org/ (accessed April 4, 2016).

23. Piet Levy, "10 Minutes with . . . Robert J. Morais," *Marketing News,* May 30, 2011, pp. 22–23.

24. Dave Caldwell, "Where Did All the NASCAR Fans Go?" *Forbes,* November 19, 2019, https://www.forbes.com/sites/davecaldwell/2019/11/19/where-did-all-the-nascar-fans-go/#65b8f3e5710f (accessed June 9, 2020).

25. U.S. Bureau of Labor Statistics, "Beyond the Numbers," May 2019, https://www.bls.gov/opub/btn/volume-8/are-most-americans-cutting-the-cord-on-landlines.htm (accessed June 9, 2020).

26. Steven Kurutz, "On Kickstarter, Designers' Dreams Materialize," *The New York Times,* September 21, 2011, www.nytimes.com/2011/09/22/garden/on-kickstarter-designers-dreams-materialize.html (accessed May 5, 2017).

27. Mya Frazier, "CrowdSourcing," *Delta Sky Mag,* February 2010, p. 73.

28. "LEGO Ideas—How It Works," LEGO, https://ideas.lego.com/howitworks (accessed April 4, 2016).

29. Dan Alaimo, "H&M Turns to Big Data, AI to Tailor Store Assortments," *Retail Dive,* May 9, 2018, https://www.retaildive.com/news/hm-turns-to-big-data-ai-to-tailor-store-assortments/523137/ (accessed January 30, 2019).

30. Robert W. Palmatier, Lisa K. Scheer, and Jan-Benedict E. M. Steenkamp, "Customer Loyalty to Whom? Managing the Benefits and Risks of Salesperson-Owned Loyalty," *Journal of Marketing Research* XLIV (May 2007), pp. 185–199.

31. Ray A. Smith, "Men Shop More Like Women," *The Wall Street Journal,* February 17, 2016, pp. D1–D2.

32. Mike Floyd, "Editor's Letter: What Drives Millennials?" *Automobile Magazine,* May 2015, p. 12.

33. Andrea Petersen, "Secrets of a Hotel Test Lab," *The Wall Street Journal,* October 1, 2015, pp. D1–D2.

34. McKinsey & Company, "Consumer Sentiment Is Evolving as Countries around the World Begin to Reopen," June 5, 2020, https://www.mckinsey.com/business-functions/marketing-and-sales/our-insights/a-global-view-of-how-consumer-behavior-is-changing-amid-covid-19 (accessed June 9, 2020).

35. "Top Green Companies in the U.S. 2016," *Newsweek,* 2016, http://www.newsweek.com/green-2016/top-green-companies-us-2016 (accessed December 27, 2016).

36. "BMW Ultimate Drive for the Cure," National Capital Chapter BMW Car Club of America, http://old.nccbmwcca.org/index .php?cure (accessed December 27, 2016).

37. "Customer Relationship Manager," PayScale Inc., http://www .payscale.com/research/US/Job=Customer_Relationship_ Management_(CRM)_Manager/Salary (accessed June 9, 2020); "Marketing Analyst Salary," PayScale Inc., http://www.payscale. com/research/US/Job=Marketing_Analyst/Salary (accessed June 9, 2020); "Marketing Research Director," PayScale Inc., http://www.payscale.com/research/US/Job=Marketing_ Research_Director/Salary (accessed June 9, 2020).

a. Christopher Mims, "In Apple's Third Act, The iPhone Plays a Supporting Role," *The Wall Street Journal,* September 8–9, 2018, p. B12; The Franklin Institute, "What Is Augmented Reality?" 2018, https://www.fi.edu/what-is-augmented-reality (accessed September 16, 2018); Kevin Bonsor, "How Augmented Reality Works," *How Stuff Works,* https://computer.howstuffworks.com/augmented-reality4.htm (accessed September 16, 2018).

b. Saabira Chaudhuri and Annie Gasparro, "Kraft Heinz Prepares to Take on Hellman's with a New Mayonnaise and 'Mayochup,'" *The Wall Street Journal,* May 20, 2018, https://www.wsj.com/articles/kraft-heinz-prepares-to-take-on-hellmanns-with-a-new-mayonnaise-and-mayochup-1526821200 (accessed August 31, 2018); David Frederick, "How a Social Media Debate Led to Heinz Mayochup's Launch in the US," *PR Week,* June 29, 2018, https://www.prweek.com/article/1486469/social-media-debate-led-heinz-mayochups-launch-us (accessed August 31, 2018); Simon Gwynn, "Heinz Takes the Gloves Off in Mayo Battle with Unilever's Hellmann's," *Campaign Live,* July 20, 2018, https://www.campaignlive.co.uk/article/heinz-takes-gloves-off-mayo-battle-unilevers-hellmanns/1488330 (accessed August 31, 2018).

c. Umair Irfan, "The Ford F-150, America's Most American Pickup Truck, Is Going Electric," *Vox,* January 25, 2019, https://www .vox.com/energy-and-environment/2019/1/24/18195880/ford-f150-ev-electric-pickup-truck (accessed January 27, 2019); Lyndon Bell, "Why the Ford F-150 Is the Best Selling Vehicle in America," *Autobytel,* www.autobytel.com/ford/f-150/car-buying-guides/why-the-ford-f-150-is-the-best-selling-vehicle-in-america-130601/# (accessed September 7, 2018); Krause Ford, "History of the F150," Angela Krause Ford of Alpharetta, www.angelakrauseford.com/history-of-the-f150.htm (accessed September 7, 2018); Keith Naughton, "Can a Blue-Collar Workhorse Go Green?" *Scribd,* December 4, 2017, www .scribd.com/article/365980739/Can-A-Blue-Collar-Workhorse-Go-Green (accessed September 7, 2018).

d. World of Coca-Cola, "About Us: Coca-Cola History," https:// www.worldofcoca-cola.com/about-us/coca-cola-history/ (accessed June 9, 2020).

Chapter 12

1. "The Power of the Jingle," *Advertising Age,* February 8, 2017, http://adage.com/article/iheart-media/power-jingle/307801/ (accessed April 5, 2017).

2. Zac Palmer, "Sonic Doom: GM Reportedly Adds Chevy Sonic to Its Car Kill List," *Auto Blog,* January 18, 2019, https://www .autoblog.com/2019/01/18/chevy-sonic-gm-killing/ (accessed February 2, 2019).

3. Associated Press, "Jobs Says iPad Idea Came before iPhone," *Fox News,* June 2, 2010, www.foxnews.com/tech/jobs-says-ipad-idea-came-before-iphone/ (accessed May 5, 2017).

4. Nike, "A Look Inside Nike's Sport Research Lab," September 8, 2014, http://news.nike.com/news/a-look-inside-nike-s-sport-research-lab (accessed April 11, 2016).

5. John A. Byrne, "Greatest Entrepreneurs of Our Time," *Fortune,* April 9, 2012, pp. 68–86; Google Finance, "Amazon.com, Inc.," April 30, 2014, www.google.com/finance?cid=660463 (accessed April 11, 2016).

6. Dimitra Kessenides and Jeff Muskus, "Delays Ahead for Self-Driving Cars," *Bloomberg Buisinessweek,* January 7, 2019, p 18.

7. Andrew Pollack, "Genetically Engineered Salmon Approved for Consumption," *The New York Times,* November 19, 2015, http://www.nytimes.com/2015/11/20/business/genetically-engineered-salmon-approved-for-consumption.html (accessed May 5, 2017); AquaBounty, "With New CEO, AquaBounty Looks Beyond U.S. for Markets, Partner," January 17, 2019, https:// aquabounty.com/with-new-ceo-aquabounty-looks-beyond-us-for-markets-partner/ (accessed February 2, 2019).

8. Ronn Torossian, "Chipotle's New Marketing Strategy Embraces Current Diet Trends," *Odwyer PR,* January 7, 2019, https:// www.odwyerpr.com/story/public/11838/2019-01-07/chipotles-new-marketing-strategy-embraces-current-diet-trends.html.

9. Divyanshi Tewari, "Smartwatch Market Expected to Reach $96.31 Billion By 2027," *Allied Market Research,* https://www .alliedmarketresearch.com/press-release/smartwatch-market-is-expected-to-reach-32-9-billion-by-2020-allied-market-research.html (accessed June 10, 2020).

10. Peter Hartlaub, "Sweet! America's Top 10 Brands of Soda," *NBC News,* http://www.nbcnews.com/id/42255151/ns/business-us_business/t/sweet-americas-top-brands-soda/#. WHbiQrYrKV4 (accessed December 27, 2016).

11. Nathan Olivarez-Giles, "Nintendo's Switch: Elegant, but Unready," *The Wall Street Journal,* March 2, 2017, p. B1.

12. Burleson, "Vinyl Record Manufacturer in Nashville Is Said to Be Expanding," *The New York Times,* December 25, 2016, https://www.nytimes.com/2016/12/25/arts/music/vinyl-record-manufacturer-in-nashville-is-said-to-be-expanding.html (accessed May 25, 2019).

13. Laura Lorenzetti, "Get Ready for Amazon's New Fashion Line," *Fortune,* February 17, 2016, http://fortune.com/2016/02/17/amazon-fashion-brand/ (accessed May 5, 2017).

14. Christopher Durham, "Private Label Market in the US 2015–2019," *My Private Brand,* March 20, 2016, http://mypbrand .com/2016/03/20/private-label-market-in-the-us-2015-2019/ (accessed April 11, 2016); Lisa Fickenscher, "Retailers Eyeing Private Brand Ownership as Key to Growth," *New York Post,* October 13, 2017, https://nypost.com/2017/10/13/retailers-eyeing-private-brand-ownership-as-key-to-growth/ (accessed April 29, 2018).

15. Nicola Dall'Asen, "Kyle Finally Upgraded Her Makeup Packaging to Feel Less Cheap," *Revelist,* April 19, 2018, http:// www.revelist.com/beauty-news-/kylie-cosmetics-packaging /12476 (accessed April 29, 2018).

16. Mintel, "Beverage Packaging Trends—US—February 2014," February 2014, http://oxygen.mintel.com/sinatra/oxygen/list/ id=680559&type=RCItem#0_1___page_RCItem=0 (accessed May 5, 2014).

17. Saabira Chaudhuri, "IKEA Can't Stop Obsessing about Its Packaging," *The Wall Street Journal,* June 17, 2015, http://www.wsj.com/articles/ikea-cant-stop-obsessing-about-its-packaging-1434533401 (accessed May 5, 2017).

18. Lindsey Beaton, "Packaging as Branding in Pet Food Marketing," Petfoodindustry.com, May 21, 2015, http://www.petfoodindustry.com/articles/5193-packaging-as-branding-in-pet-food-marketing (accessed May 1, 2015).

19. Nathan Bomey, "Volkswagen Will Buy Back 20k More Polluting Diesel Cars," *USA Today,* December 20, 2016, http://www.usatoday.com/story/money/cars/2016/12/20/volkswagen-3-liter-diesel-settlement/95661794/ (accessed April 18, 2016).

20. American Customer Satisfaction Index, "U.S. Overall Customer Satisfaction," https://www.theacsi.org/national-economic-indicator/us-overall-customer-satisfaction (accessed June 10, 2020).

21. "American Demographics 2006 Consumer Perception Survey," *Advertising Age,* January 2, 2006, p. 9. Data by Synovate.

22. "The Top 10 Most Innovative Companies in China," *Fast Company,* 2014, http://www.fastcompany.com/most-innovative-companies/2014/industry/china (accessed May 5, 2017).

23. Rajneesh Suri and Kent B. Monroe, "The Effects of Time Constraints on Consumers' Judgments of Prices and Products," *Journal of Consumer Research* 30 (June 2003), p. 92.

24. Sharon Terlep, "Gillette, in Change Shaves Prices," *The Wall Street Journal,* April 5, 2017, p. B1.

25. Leslie Patton, "Aldi Tries High-End Food and Discounts, Too," *Bloomberg,* August 6, 2015, http://www.bloomberg.com/news/articles/2015-08-06/aldi-grocery-chain-tries-high-end-food-and-discounts-too (accessed May 5, 2017).

26. Rich Duprey, "Amazon Is Expanding Whole Foods, Prime Now in the Suburbs," *The Motley Fool,* January 30, 2019, https://www.fool.com/investing/2019/01/30/amazon-expands-whole-foods-prime-now-suburbs.aspx (accessed February 2, 2019).

27. Ingrid Lunden, "Amazon's Share of the U.S. E-Commerce Market Is Now 49%, or 5% of All Retail Spend," *TechCrunch,* July 13, 2018, https://techcrunch.com/2018/07/13/amazons-share-of-the-us-e-commerce-market-is-now-49-or-5-of-all-retail-spend/ (accessed February 2, 2019).

28. "Primed," *The Economist,* March 25, 2017, pp. 18–19.

29. Amazon, "Amazon Physical Stores Locations," https://www.amazon.com/find-your-store/b/?node=17608448011 (accessed June 10, 2020).

30. Ann Steele, "Sears Creates Stir as It Casts Doubts about Its Future," *The Wall Street Journal,* March 23, 2017, p. B1.

31. Nathan Bomery, "For Sports Retailers Clock Has Run Out," *USA Today,* March 6, 2017, pp. B1–B2.

32. "The Sysco Story," Sysco, www.sysco.com/about-sysco.html# (accessed April 11, 2016).

33. "Top Threats to Revenue," *USA Today,* February 1, 2006, p. A1.

34. Paul Amyerson, "Predictive Analytics Takes Forecasting to a New Level," *Inbound Logistics,* March 2017, p. 46.

35. William Pride and O. C. Ferrell, *Marketing Foundations,* 5th ed. (Mason, OH: Cengage South-Western Learning, 2013), pp. 415–416.

36. Ibid.

37. Next Level Resource Partners, Homepage, https://www.nlrp.com/ (accessed April 29, 2018).

38. ZoomSystems, www.zoomsystems.com/ (accessed June 10, 2020).

39. Pitsinee Jitpleecheep, "Under Armour Set to Cut Back Prices," *Bangkok Post,* February 13, 2018, https://www.bangkokpost.com/business/news/1411475/under-armour-set-to-cut-back-prices (accessed April 29, 2018).

40. Karen M. Kroll, "Retail Logistics Bets on E-Commerce," *Inbound Logistics,* March 2017, p. 73.

41. "Target Reveals Design Elements of Next Generation of Stores," Target, March 20, 2017, https://corporate.target.com/press/releases/2017/03/target-reveals-design-elements-of-next-generation (accessed April 29, 2018).

42. Brian Steinberg, "Super Bowl or Soapbox? Big Game Advertisers Risk All by Trading Silly for Serious," *Variety,* January 28, 2019, https://variety.com/2019/tv/news/super-bowl-commercials-2019-humor-politics-advertising-preview-1203119883/ (accessed February 2, 2019).

43. Peter Loftus, "Ads for Costly Drugs Get Airtime," *The Wall Street Journal,* February 17, 2016, p. B1.

44. Andrew Gould, "Super Bowl Ads 2018: Latest Info on Cost of 2018 Super Bowl Commercials," *Bleacher Report,* February 4, 2018, http://bleacherreport.com/articles/2757119-super-bowl-ads-2018-latest-info-on-cost-of-2018-super-bowl-commercials (accessed April 29, 2018).

45. Natalie Evans, "See PETA 'Vegan Sex' Advert That's So Steamy It's Been Banned from the Super Bowl," *The Mirror,* January 26, 2016, http://www.mirror.co.uk/tv/tv-news/see-peta-vegan-sex-advert-7246273 (accessed May 5, 2017).

46. Jerrid Grimm, "The 10 Best Branded Content Partnerships of 2016," *Advertising Age,* http://adage.com/article/agency-viewpoint/10-branded-content-partnerships-2016/307284/ (accessed January 26, 2017).

47. Jun Hongo and Miho Inada, "To Lure Recruits, Japanese City Tries Gorilla Marketing," *The Wall Street Journal,* February 23, 2016, p. A1, A14.

48. Gerry Khermouch and Jeff Green, "Buzz Marketing," *BusinessWeek,* July 30, 2001, pp. 50–56.

49. Harmeet Signh, "Behind Canadian Tire's (Old) Viral Spot," *Strategy,* February 28, 2017, http://strategyonline.ca/2017/02/28/behind-canadian-tires-old-viral-spot/ (accessed April 29, 2018); "Wheels—The Most Viral Ad of 2017," *YouTube,* August 24, 2017, https://www.youtube.com/watch?v=2GjVG_DguQY&t=89s (accessed April 29, 2018).

50. "70% of Consumers Still Look to Traditional Paper-Based Coupons for Savings," *PR Newswire,* April 16, 2015, http://www.prnewswire.com/news-releases/70-of-consumers-still-look-to-traditional-paper-based-coupons-for-savings-300067097.html (accessed May 5, 2017).

51. Erica Sweeney, "Mountain Dew Shakes Up Baja Blast's Return with Bungalow Stunt," *Marketing Dive,* April 3, 2018, https://www.marketingdive.com/news/mountain-dew-shakes-up-baja-blasts-return-with-bungalow-stunt/520423/ (accessed April 29, 2018).

52. "Blendtec Celebrates 10 Years of Viral Marketing Success," *Nasdaq GlobeNewswire,* November 7, 2016, globenewswire.com/news-release/2016/11/07/887174/10165944/en/Blendtec-Celebrates-10-Years-of-Viral-Marketing-Success.html (accessed February 17, 2017); Blendtec, *YouTube,* https://www.youtube.com/user/Blendtec/about (accessed June 10, 2020).

a. Kurt Schroeder, "Why So Many New Products Fail (and It's Not the Product)," *Business Journals,* March 14, 2017, https://www.bizjournals.com/bizjournals/how-to/marketing/2017/03/why-so-many-new-products-fail-and-it-s-not-the.html (accessed April 24, 2018).

b. Beth Kowitt, "Inside the Secret World of Trader Joe's—Full Version," *Fortune,* August 23, 2010, http://archive.fortune.com/2010/08/20/news/companies/inside_trader_joes_full_version.fortune/index.htm (accessed January 1, 2018); "2010 World's Most Ethical Companies," *Ethisphere,* http://m1.ethisphere.com/wme2013/index.html (accessed October 1, 2013); Lisa Scherzer, "Trader Joe's Tops List of Best Grocery Store Chains," *Yahoo Finance!,* July 24, 2013, https://finance.yahoo.com/blogs/the-exchange/trader-joe-tops-list-best-grocery-store-chains-182739789.html (accessed January 1, 2018); "Trader Joe's: Groceries for the 'Overeducated and Underpaid,'" Technology and Operations Management—A course at Harvard Business School, December 9, 2015, https://rctom.hbs.org/submission/trader-joes-groceries-for-the-overeducated-and-underpaid/ (accessed January 1, 2018); John Boyle, "As Earth Fare Grows, Some Workers Feeling 'Squeezed,'" *Citizen Times,* September 3, 2016, http://www.citizen-times.com/story/news/local/2016/09/03/earth-fare-grows-some-workers-feeling-squeezed/88412772/ (accessed January 1, 2018); Sheiresa Ngo, "15 Secrets Trader Joe's Shoppers Should Know," *Business Insider,* May 8, 2017, http://www.businessinsider.com/15-secrets-trader-joes-shoppers-should-know-2017-5/#3-shoppers-can-win-prizes-3 (accessed January 1, 2018); "Trader Joe's: Food for Thought," Technology and Operations Management—A course at Harvard Business School, December 9, 2015, https://rctom.hbs.org/submission/trader-joes-food-for-thought/ (accessed January 1, 2018); Mark Hamstra, "Trader Joe's, Costco, Amazon Lead Consumer Preference Study," *Supermarket News,* January 16, 2018, https://www.supermarketnews.com/consumer-trends/trader-joe-s-costco-amazon-lead-consumer-preference-study (accessed September 16, 2018); Trader Joe's, "Trader Joe's—Our Story," Trader Joe's website, https://www.traderjoes.com/our-story (accessed September 16, 2018); Troy Chuinard, "How Sustainable Is Trader Joe's Competitive Advantage?" *Investopedia,* May 7, 2016, https://www.investopedia.com/articles/insights/050716/warren-buffetts-moat-how-sustainable-trader-joes-competitive-advantage.asp (accessed September 16, 2018).

c. Esther Fung, "Florida Officials Improve Plan to Build Largest U.S. Mall," *The Wall Street Journal,* June 19, 2018, https://www.wsj.com/articles/florida-officials-approve-plan-to-build-largest-u-s-mall-1529406001 (accessed August 31, 2018); Douglas Hanks, "Nation's Largest Mall Wins Miami-Dade Approval as County Backs American Dream Miami," *Miami Herald,* May 17, 2018, https://www.miamiherald.com/news/local/community/miami-dade/article211306649.html (accessed August 31, 2018); Douglas Hanks, "Largest Mall in the Nation Proposed for Miami-Dade," *Miami Herald,* March 5, 2015, https://www.miamiherald.com/news/local/community/miami-dade/article12605384.html (accessed August 31, 2018); Richard Kestenbaum, "Why So Many Stores Are Closing Now," *Forbes,* April 7, 2017, https://www.forbes.com/sites/richardkestenbaum/2017/04/07/why-so-many-stores-are-closing-now/#6a06f4df4159 (accessed August 31, 2018); Allison Pries, "American Dream Developer Showing Signs of Financial Trouble," *nj.com,* June 3, 2020, https://www.nj.com/news/2020/06/american-dream-developer-showing-signs-of-financial-trouble.html (accessed June 10, 2020).

d. Brad Avery, "PepsiCo Launches Drinkfinity in U.S.," *BevNet,* February 9, 2018, https://www.bevnet.com/news/2018/pepsico-launches-drinkfinity-u-s (accessed October 13, 2018); "Launching Capsule Drink 'Drinkfinity' and Sparkling Water 'Bubly', PepsiCo Is Getting Healthier," *Procool,* August 15, 2018, www.procoolmfg.com/by-launching-capsule-drink-drinkfinity-and-sparkling-water-bubly-pepsico-is-getting-healthier/ (accessed October 4, 2018); Chris Albrecht, "PepsiCo's Drinkfinity: Bad Name, Tasty Beverages," *The Spoon,* March 6, 2018, thespoon.tech/pepsicos-drinkfinity-bad-name-tasty-beverages/ (accessed October 3, 2018); Jenna Blumenfeld, "A Review of Drinkfinity, Pepsi's New Millennial-Luring Beverage," *New Hope Network,* April 11, 2018, www.newhope.com/food-and-beverage/review-drinkfinity-pepsis-new-millennial-luring-beverage. (accessed October 3, 2018); Katharine Schwab, "Pepsi's New Shape of Water Is a Product Called Drinkfinity," *Fast Company,* April 12 2018, www.fastcompany.com/40546330/pepsis-new-shape-of-water-is-a-product-called-drinkfinity (accessed October 4, 2018); "Drinkfinity Announces Brand Relaunch, Release of New Bottle," *BevNet,* November 5, 2019, https://www.bevnet.com/news/2019/drinkfinity-announces-brand-relaunch-release-of-new-bottle (accessed June 10, 2020).

Chapter 13

1. Lauren I. Labrecque, Jonas vor dem Esche, Charla Mathwick, Thomas P. Novak, and Charles F. Hofacker, "Consumer Power: Evolution in the Digital Age," *Journal of Interactive Marketing* 27, no. 4 (November 2013), pp. 257–269.

2. Charisse Jones, "Department Stores Become Endangered," *USA Today,* January 68, 2017, p. 1A.

3. Suzanne Kaper, "Store Closings Accelerating," *The Wall Street Journal,* April 22–23, 2017, p. B1.

4. K.C. Ifeanyi, "How Vimeo Has Armed 1.2 Million Paying Subscribers for the Digital Video Boom," *Fast Company,* March 10, 2020, https://www.fastcompany.com/90457716/vimeo-most-innovative-companies-2020 (accessed June 10, 2020).

5. O.C. Ferrell, "Broadening Marketing's Contribution to Data Privacy," *Journal of Academy of Marketing Science* 23, no. 2 (2017), pp. 160–163.

6. Charisse Jones, "Department Stores Become Endangered," *USA Today,* January 6–8, 2017, p. 1A.

7. Jacob Davidson, "Here's How Many Internet Users There Are (in 2020)," *CNN Money,* May 19, 2020, https://money.com/internet-users-worldwide/ (accessed June 11, 2020).

8. Sam Costello, "How Many Apps Are in the App Store?" *Lifewire,* February 24, 2020, https://www.lifewire.com/how-many-apps-in-app-store-2000252 (accessed June 11, 2020).

9. Emily Orofino, "Can This Genius Beauty Brand Crowdsource the Next Big Thing?" *POPSUGAR,* July 10, 2016, https://www.popsugar.com/beauty/Volition-Beauty-Custom-Made-Beauty-Products-41873521 (accessed March 25, 2017).

10. "Consumers Are Increasingly Researching Purchases Online," *PYMNTS,* January 9, 2018, https://www.pymnts.com/news/retail/2018/omichannel-ecommerce-consumer-habits/ (accessed April 28, 2018); "Number of Digital Shoppers in the United States from 2016 to 2021 (in millions)," *Statista,* 2018, https://www.statista.com/statistics/183755/number-of-us-internet-shoppers-since-2009/ (accessed April 28, 2018).

11. Emma Sopadjieva, Utpal M. Dholakia, and Beth Benjamin, "A Study of 46,000 Shoppers Shows That Omnichannel Retailing Works," *Harvard Business Review,* January 3, 2017, https://hbr.org/2017/01/a-study-of-46000-shoppers-shows-that-omnichannel-retailing-works (accessed June 10, 2020).

12. Kate Rockwood, "Why Spending $1,000 on an Instagram Post Might Actually Be Worth it," *Inc.,* February 2017, http://www.inc.com/magazine/201702/kate-rockwood/tip-sheet-social-media-influencers.html (accessed March 5, 2017).

13. "About Influenster," *Influenster,* https://www.influenster.com/about (accessed June 11, 2020).

14. Melissa S. Barker, Donald I. Barker, Nicholas F. Bormann, Mary Lous Roberts, and Debra Zahay, *Social Media Marketing,* 2nd ed. (Mason, OH: Cengage Learning, 2016).

15. Kerry Flynn, "Cheatsheet: Facebook Now Has 7m Advertisers," *Digiday,* January 2019, https://digiday.com/marketing/facebook-earnings-q4-2018/ (accessed February 9, 2019).

16. Barker et al., *Social Media Marketing.*

17. Darius Fisher, "How to Handle Negative Yelp Reviews," *Huffington Post,* June 7, 2016, http://www.huffingtonpost.com/darius-fisher/how-to-handle-negative-ye_b_10324196.html (accessed March 2, 2017).

18. TikTok, @penguin_teen, https://www.tiktok.com/@penguin_teen (accessed June 11, 2020).

19. Marie-Ennis-O'Connor, "How Much Time Do People Spend on Social Media in 2019? [Infographic]," *Medium,* August 8, 2019, https://medium.com/@JBBC/how-much-time-do-people-spend-on-social-media-in-2019-infographic-cc02c63bede8 (accessed June 11, 2020).

20. Harry McCracken, "Inside Mark Zuckerberg's Bold Plan for the Future of Facebook," *Fast Company,* December 2015/January 2016, pp. 86–100, 136.

21. Wendy Boswell, "Video Websites: The Top Ten," *About Tech,* 2015, http://websearch.about.com/od/imagesearch/tp/popular-videosites.htm (accessed April 18, 2016).

22. "Boost a Post," Facebook for Business, https://www.facebook.com/business/a/boost-a-post (accessed April 18, 2016); Olsy Sorokina, "What Are Facebook Boost Posts and How Can They Help Your Business," *Hootsuite,* October 24, 2014, https://blog.hootsuite.com/how-does-facebook-boost-posts-work/ (accessed April 18, 2016).

23. Nathan Oliverez-Giles, "Facebook Messenger Brings Group Video Calling to Apps and Web," *The Wall Street Journal,* December 19, 2016, www.wsj.com/articles/facebook-messenger-brings-group-video-calling-to-apps-and-web-1482184260 (accessed December 28, 2016).

24. Roberto Garvin, "How Social Networks Influence 74% of Shoppers for their Purchasing Decisions Today," *Awario,* May 11, 2019, https://awario.com/blog/how-social-networks-influence-74-of-shoppers-for-their-purchasing-decisions-today (accessed June 11, 2020).

25. Jeff Elder, "Facing Reality, Companies Alter Social-Media Strategies," *The Wall Street Journal,* June 23, 2014, pp. B1–B2.

26. Jefferson Graham, "Cake Decorator Finds Twitter a Tweet Recipe for Success," *USA Today,* April 1, 2009, p. 5B.

27. Craig Smith, "Twitter Mobile Statistics and Facts," *DMR,* February 17, 2018, https://expandedramblings.com/index.php/twitter-mobile-statistics/ (accessed April 28, 2018).

28. Christine Birkner, "The Goldfish Conundrum," *Marketing News,* April 2015, pp. 18–19.

29. Stephanie Frasco, "100 Facts and Figures about Twitter, and Why They Matter for Your Business," *Social Media Today,* September 26, 2013, http://socialmediatoday.com/stephaniefrasco/1770161/100-facts-figures-about-twitter-business (accessed May 5, 2017).

30. Samantha Grossman, "The 13 Sassiest Brands on Twitter," *Time,* February 7, 2014, http://time.com/5151/sassiest-brands-on-twitter-ranked/ (accessed January 14, 2016); "Taco Bell," Twitter, https://twitter.com/tacobell (accessed January 14, 2016).

31. Belinda Parmar, "50 Companies That Get Twitter—and 50 That Don't," *Harvard Business Review,* April 27, 2015, https://hbr.org/2015/04/the-best-and-worst-corporate-tweeters (accessed May 5, 2017).

32. Nathan McAlone, "Investors Are Going Nuts for Snapchat—Here's How Snap Thinks It Can Turn a $500 Million Loss into Profit," *Business Insider,* March 5, 2017, http://www.businessinsider.com/how-will-snapchat-make-money-2017-3 (accessed March 5, 2017); "Global Annual Net Loss of Snap from 2015 to 2017 (in million U.S. dollars)," *Statista,* https://www.statista.com/statistics/668190/snapchat-annual-net-income-loss/ (accessed April 29, 2018); Garrett Sloane, "Oh Snap! Shares Soar as Snapchat Reports 9 Million More Daily Users and an Ad Surge," *AdAge,* February 6, 2018, http://adage.com/article/digital/snapchat-reports-9-million-daily-users-ad-surge/312286/ (accessed April 29, 2018).

33. Haley Tsukayama, "Snapchat Files for Its Initial Public Offering: Here Are the 10 Most Interesting Things We've Learned So Far," *Washington Post,* February 3, 2017, https://www.washingtonpost.com/news/the-switch/wp/2017/02/03/snapchat-files-for-its-initial-public-offering-here-are-the-10-most-interesting-things-weve-learned-so-far/?utm_term=.591d0ee20f98 (accessed March 5, 2017).

34. Artyom Dogtiev, "Snapchat Revenue and Usage Statistics 2017," *Business of Apps,* April 26, 2018, http://www.businessofapps.com/data/snapchat-statistics/ (accessed April 28, 2018).

35. Douglas A. McIntyre, "YouTube Viewership Hits a Billion Hours of Content a Day," *24/7 Wall St.,* February 27, 2017, http://247wallst.com/apps-software/2017/02/27/youtube-viewership-hits-100-billion-hours-of-content-a-day/ (accessed March 5, 2017).

36. Rachel Strugatz, "Beauty's Battle for Views: Brands vs. Vloggers," *WWD,* February 23, 2017, http://wwd.com/beauty-industry-news/beauty-features/youtube-l2-beautys-battle-for-views-brands-vs-bloggers-10814639/ (access March 5, 2017).

37. Mike Snider, "How YouTube TV Compares to Rivals Sling, PlayStation, DirecTV," *USA Today,* March 5, 2017, http://www.usatoday.com/story/tech/talkingtech/2017/03/05/how-youtube-tv-compares-rivals-sling-playstation-directv/98551276/ (accessed March 5, 2017).

38. Paige Leskin, "Inside the Rise of TikTok, the Viral Video-Sharing App Whose Ties to China Are Raising Concerns in the US," *Business Insider,* January 23, 2020, https://www.businessinsider.com/tiktok-app-online-website-video-sharing-2019-7 (accessed June 11, 2020).

39. Urban Decay, "Legends Never Fade with All Nighter Setting Spray," *TikTok,* https://www.tiktok.com/@urbandecaycosmetics/video/6778148122058067205 (accessed March 5, 2020).

40. Sujan Patel, "How LinkedIn Uses LinkedIn for Marketing," *Forbes,* March 4, 2017, https://www.forbes.com/sites/sujanpatel/2017/03/04/how-linkedin-uses-linkedin-for-marketing/2/#3b96f9d3657f (accessed March 5, 2017).

41. Amanda Walgrove, "5 B2B Brands That Rock LinkedIn Marketing," *Contently,* February 24, 2017, https://contently.com/strategist/2015/02/24/5-b2b-brands-that-rock-linkedin/ (accessed March 5, 2017).

42. Marcelina Hardy, "Statistics on Blogging," *ContentWriters.com,* August 19, 2014, https://contentwriters.com/blog/statistics-blogging/ (accessed April 18, 2016).

43. Niall Harbison and Lauren Fisher, "40 of the Best Corporate Blogs to Inspire You," *Ragan's PR Daily,* September 13,

2012, http://www.prdaily.com/Main/Articles/40_of_the_best_corporate_blogs_to_inspire_you_12645.aspx (accessed May 5, 2017); "Wikipedia," *Wikipedia,* https://en.wikipedia.org/wiki/Wikipedia (accessed April 29, 2018).

44. "Wikipedia:Size Comparisons," *Wikipedia,* https://en.wikipedia.org/wiki/Wikipedia:Size_comparisons (accessed June 11, 2020).

45. Charlene Li and Josh Bernoff, *Groundswell* (Boston: Harvard Business Press, 2008), pp. 25–26.

46. "Percentage of Fortune 500 Companies with Public Blogs from 2010 to 2016," *Statista,* https://www.statista.com/statistics/262466/share-of-fortune-500-companies-with-public-blogs/ (accessed April 29, 2018).

47. "How to Use a Raw Egg to Determine if Your Mattress Is Awful—Purple," *YouTube,* April 26, 2016, https://youtube/4BvwpjaGZCQ (accessed June 11, 2020).

48. Stephanie Hayes, "Michelle Phan, a YouTube Sensation for Her Makeup Tutorials, Has Transformed Her Life," *Tampa Bay Times,* August 22, 2009, http://www.tampabay.com/features/humaninterest/michelle-phan-a-youtube-sensation-for-her-makeup-tutorials-has-transformed/1029747 (accessed May 5, 2017).

49. PR Newswire, "Beyond the Subscription: IPSY Reaches Half a Billion in Revenue," September 26, 2019, https://www.prnewswire.com/news-releases/beyond-the-subscription-ipsy-reaches-half-a-billion-in-revenue-300926103.html (accessed June 11, 2020).

50. "Photoset," Instagram, http://blog.business.instagram.com/post/78694901404/how-yogurt-maker-chobani-uses-instagram-to-open (accessed January 15, 2016).

51. Bryan Clark, "Snapchat Growth Slowed Significantly after Launch of Instagram Stories," *The Next Web,* February 3, 2017, https://thenextweb.com/socialmedia/2017/02/03/snapchat-growth-slowed-significantly-after-the-launch-of-instagram-stories/#.tnw_360bhC9j (accessed March 5, 2017).

52. "4 Key Advantages for Video Marketing on Instagram vs. Vine," *Ad Week,* March 4, 2015, http://www.adweek.com/socialtimes/sumall-dane-atkinson-video-marketing-instagram-vs-vine/616331 (accessed May 5, 2017).

53. Nicole Lee, "Pinterest Uses AI and Your Camera to Recommend Pins," *Engadget,* February 8, 2017, https://www.engadget.com/2017/02/08/pinterest-uses-ai-and-your-camera-to-recommend-pins/ (accessed March 5, 2017).

54. Shannon Liao, "Pinterest Now Lets You Filter Search Results by Skin Tone," *The Verge,* April 26, 2018, https://www.theverge.com/2018/4/26/17286898/pinterest-skin-tone-search-filter-results-feature-update (accessed April 29, 2018).

55. "Marketers' Interest in Pinterest," *Marketing News,* April 30, 2012, pp. 8–9; "PINTEREST INTEREST: Survey: 17 Percent of Marketers Currently Using or Planning to Join Pinterest," The Creative Group, August 22, 2012, http://creativegroup.mediaroom.com/pinterest-for-business (accessed April 18, 2016); Jason Falls, "How Pinterest Is Becoming the Next Big Thing in Social Media for Business," *Entrepreneur,* February 7, 2012, www.entrepreneur.com/article/222740 (accessed April 18, 2016); Pinterest website, http://pinterest.com/ (accessed April 18, 2016).

56. Jeff Bercovici, "Social Media's New Mad Men," *Forbes,* November 2014, pp. 71–82.

57. Zale Jewelers Pinterest page, www.pinterest.com/zalesjewelers (accessed April 18, 2016).

58. Douglas MacMillan and Elizabeth Dwoskin, "Smile! Marketers Are Mining Selfies," *The Wall Street Journal,* October 10, 2014, pp. B1–B2.

59. Natalie Wires, "The Rising Popularity of Podcasts: Why Listeners Are Rediscovering Podcasts," *Tunheim,* March 26, 2014, http://blog.tunheim.com/2014/03/26/rising-popularity-podcasts-listeners-rediscovering-podcasts/1438#.U2pMWYFdVc8 (accessed April 18, 2016).

60. Ann Lukits, "Podcasts Send Shoppers to Omega-3s," *The Wall Street Journal,* December 9, 2014, p. D2.

61. Roger Yu, "Smartphones Help Make Bon Voyages," *USA Today,* March 5, 2010, p. B1.

62. Sean Silverthorpe, "Should Retailers Worry about In-Store Mobile Use?" *Insights from Marketing Science Institute* 1 (2015), pp. 1–2.

63. April Berthene, "Mobile Accounts for Nearly 35% of 2017 E-Commerce Sales," *Digital Commerce 360,* February 19, 2018, https://www.digitalcommerce360.com/2018/02/19/mobile-accounts-for-nearly-35-of-2017-e8209commerce-sales/ (accessed April 29, 2018).

64. Mark Milian, "Why Text Messages Are Limited to 160 Characters," *Los Angeles Times,* May 3, 2009, http://latimesblogs.latimes.com/technology/2009/05/invented-text-messaging.html (accessed May 5, 2017); "Eight Reasons Why Your Business Should Use SMS Marketing," *Mobile Marketing Ratings,* www.mobilemarketingratings.com/eight-reasons-sms-marketing.html (accessed April 18, 2016).

65. "Mobile to Account for More than Half of Digital Ad Spending in 2015," *eMarketer,* September 1, 2015, www.emarketer.com/Article/Mobile-Account-More-than-Half-of-Digital-Ad-Spending-2015/1012930 (accessed January 15, 2016).

66. Jake Jeffries, "10 Incredible Mobile Marketing Stats 2015 [INFOGRAPHIC]," *Social Media Today,* January 13, 2015, www.socialmediatoday.com/content/10-incredible-mobile-marketing-stats-2015-infographic (accessed January 15, 2016).

67. Aaron Pressman and Adam Lashinsky, "Why Waze Doesn't Share Traffic Data With Google Maps—Data Sheet," *Fortune,* October 11, 2019, https://fortune.com/2019/10/11/waze-google-maps-how-it-works/ (accessed June 11, 2020).

68. "Location-Based Services: Definitions and Examples," *Business News Daily,* February 24, 2020, https://www.businessnewsdaily.com/5386-location-based-service.html (accessed June 11, 2020).

69. Anita Campbell, "What the Heck Is an App?" *Small Business Trends,* March 7, 2011, http://smallbiztrends.com/2011/03/what-is-an-app.html (accessed April 18, 2016).

70. Eileen Brown, "Americans Spend Far More Time on their Smartphones than They Think," *ZDNet,* April 28, 2019, https://www.zdnet.com/article/americans-spend-far-more-time-on-their-smartphones-than-they-think/ (accessed June 11, 2020).

71. Pew Research Center, "Mobile Fact Sheet," June 12, 2019, https://www.pewresearch.org/internet/fact-sheet/mobile/ (accessed June 11, 2020).

72. Michelle Yeomans, "Unilever Opts for 'Mobile Marketing Platform' to Reach South-East Asia," *Cosmetics Design,* September 15, 2015, http://www.cosmeticsdesign-asia.com/Business-Financial/Unilever-opts-for-mobile-marketing-platform-to-reach-south-east-Asia (accessed January 19, 2016).

73. Umika Pidaparthy, "Marketers Embracing QR Codes, for Better or Worse," *CNN Tech,* March 28, 2011, http://www.cnn.com/2011/TECH/mobile/03/28/qr.codes.marketing/ (accessed May 5, 2017).

74. Brad Stone and Olga Kharif, "Pay as You Go," *Bloomberg Businessweek,* July 18–24, 2011, pp. 66–71.

75. "Google Wallet," www.google.com/wallet/what-is-google-wallet .html (accessed April 18, 2016).

76. "All about Widgets," *Webopedia,* September 14, 2007, www .webopedia.com/DidYouKnow/Hardware_Software/widgets. asp (accessed April 18, 2016).

77. Rachael King, "Building a Brand with Widgets," *Bloomberg Businessweek,* March 3, 2008, www.businessweek.com/ technology/content/feb2008/tc20080303_000743.htm (accessed May 5, 2017).

78. TripAdvisor, "Welcome to TripAdvisor's Widget Center," www .tripadvisor.com/Widgets (accessed April 18, 2016).

79. Barker et al., *Social Media Marketing.*

80. Matt McGee, "As Google Analytics Turns 10, We Ask: How Many Websites Use It?" *Marketing Land,* November 12, 2015, http://marketingland.com/as-google-analytics-turns-10-we-ask-how-many-websites-use-it-151892 (accessed March 5, 2017).

81. "By Tailoring the Features of Google Analytics, LunaMetrics Helps PBS Increase Both Conversions and Visits by 30%," *Google Analytics,* https://static.googleusercontent.com/media/ www.google.com/en//intl/pt_ALL/analytics/customers/pdfs/ pbs.pdf (accessed March 24, 2017).

82. Quentin Hardy, "Google Introduces Products That Will Sharpen Its Ad Focus," *The New York Times,* March 15, 2016, https:// www.nytimes.com/2016/03/16/technology/google-introduces-products-that-will-sharpen-its-ad-focus.html (accessed March 24, 2017).

83. Nicole Lyn Pesce, "People Are Complete Suckers for Online Reviews," *New York Post,* August 23, 2017, https://nypost .com/2017/08/23/people-are-complete-suckers-for-online-reviews/ (accessed April 29, 2018).

84. GDPR, "What Are the GDPR Fines?" https://gdpr.eu/fines/ (accessed May 6, 2020).

85. Jesse Brody, "Terms and Conditions," *Marketing News,* November 2014, pp. 34–41.

86. "FTC Cracking Down on Social Influencers' Labeling of Paid Promotions," *AdAge,* August 5, 2016, http://adage .com/article/digital/ftc-cracking-social-influencers-labeling-promotions/305345/ (accessed March 5, 2017).

87. Priya Anand, "Cyberthieves Have a New Target: Children," *The Wall Street Journal,* February 1, 2016, p. R8.

88. Elizabeth Weise, "Sony Hack Leaves Intriguing Clues," *USA Today,* December 4, 2014, p. 1B.

89. Elizabeth Weise, "Consumers Have to Protect Themselves Online," *USA Today,* May 22, 2014, p. 1B.

90. Apple, "Apple Card," https://www.apple.com/apple-card/ (accessed June 11, 2020).

91. Kevin Shanahan and Mike Hyman, "Motivators and Enablers of SCOURing," *Journal of Business Research* 63 (September–October 2010), pp. 1095–1102.

92. "The Amazons of the Dark Net," *The Economist,* November 1, 2014, pp. 57–58.

93. Erica E. Phillips, "U.S. Officials Chase Counterfeit Goods Online," *The Wall Street Journal,* November 28, 2014, http:// www.wsj.com/articles/u-s-officials-chase-counterfeit-goods-online-1417217763 (accessed May 5, 2017).

94. Max Chafkin, "The Case, and the Plan, for the Virtual Company," *Inc.,* April 2010, p. 68.

a. "Is It Time to Regulate Social Media Influencer?" *New York Magazine,* January 17, 2019, http://nymag.com/intelligencer/ 2019/01/is-it-time-to-regulate-social-media-influencers.html (accessed February 7, 2019); Suzanne Vranica, "Unilever Demands Influencer Marketing Business Clean Up Its Act," *The Wall Street Journal,* June 17, 2018, https://www.wsj.com/ articles/unilever-demands-influencer-marketing-business-clean-up-its-act-1529272861 (accessed August 29, 2018); Diana Pearl, "Unilever Says No More Fake Followers and Bots. Influencers Cheer, and Question the Future," *AdWeek,* June 26, 2018, https://www.adweek.com/brand-marketing/unilever-says-no-more-fake-followers-and-bots-influencers-cheer-and-question-the-future/ (accessed August 29, 2018); Katie Paulsen, "Let's Keep Influencer Marketing Accountable," *Media Post,* August 23, 2018, https://www.mediapost.com/publications/ article/324027/lets-keep-influencer-marketing-accountable. html (accessed August 29, 2018); "What Is an Influencer? Troubled Times Demand a Fresh Formula," *AdWeek,* August 20, 2018, https://www.adweek.com/digital/what-is-an-influencer-troubled-times-demand-a-fresh-formula/ (accessed August 29, 2018); Neil Waller, "5 Ways to Rethink Influencer Marketing and Make It More Effective," *Adweek,* May 29, 2020, https://www .adweek.com/brand-marketing/5-ways-to-rethink-influencer-marketing-and-make-it-more-effective/ (accessed June 10, 2020).

b. Kristen Herhold, "How Small Businesses Use Social Media in 2018," *Clutch,* March 22, 2018, https://clutch.co/agencies/ social-media-marketing/resources/small-business-social-media-survey-2018 (accessed June 10, 2020).

c. Anne Steele and Douglas MacMillan, "YouTube to Launch New Music-Streaming Service," *The Wall Street Journal,* May 17, 2018, https://www.wsj.com/articles/spotify-amazon-apple-or-youtube-the-streaming-music-showdown-1529845200 (accessed September 14, 2018); "Streaming Helps Music Industry Rebound in 2016 After Years of Decline," *Rolling Stone,* March 31, 2017, https://www.rollingstone.com/music/ music-news/streaming-helps-music-industry-rebound-in-2016-after-years-of-decline-113464/ (accessed September 14, 2018); David Pierce, "Spotify, Amazon, Apple or YouTube? The Streaming-Music Showdown," *The Wall Street Journal,* June 24, 2018, https://www.wsj.com/articles/spotify-amazon-apple-or-youtube-the-streaming-music-showdown-1529845200 (accessed September 14, 2018); "Banding Together," *The Economist,* February 3, 2018, p. 57; Jesse Kirshbaum, "It's 2018 and the Music Business Is Better Than Ever," *AdAge,* January 2, 2018, http://adage.com/article/agencies/2018-music-business/311771/ (accessed September 6, 2018); Andy Bolter, "Collaboration in Music: Nobody Does It Better," *IQ: Live Music Intelligence,* January 27, 2018, https://www.iq-mag .net/2017/01/collaboration-music-nobody-better-andy-bolter/# .W5KGsOhKiUm (accessed September 6, 2018).

d. Daphne Howland, "Amazon's Fakes Problem Hits Lower-Priced Brands Hardest," *Retail Dive,* April 2, 2018, https:// www.retaildive.com/news/amazons-fakes-problem-hits-lower-priced-brands-hardest/530875/ (accessed September 14, 2018); Laura Stevens, "On Amazon, Fake Products Plague Smaller Brands," *The Wall Street Journal,* July 19, 2018, https://www.wsj.com/articles/on-amazon-fake-products-plague-smaller-brands-1532001601 (accessed September 14, 2018); Edgar Alvarez, "Amazon Needs to Get a Handle on Its Counterfeit Problem," *Engadget,* May 31, 2018, https://www .engadget.com/2018/05/31/fulfilled-by-amazon-counterfeit-fake/ (accessed September 14, 2018); Yiling Pan, "Alibaba's Anti-Counterfeiting Efforts Appear to Pay Off," *Jing Daily,* May 21, 2018, https://jingdaily.com/alibaba-anti-counterfeiting/ (accessed September 14, 2018); Ganda Suthivarakom, "Welcome to the Era of Fake Products," *The New York Times,* February 11, 2020, https://www.nytimes.com/wirecutter/blog/ amazon-counterfeit-fake-products/ (accessed June 11, 2020).

Chapter 14

1. "About the ACFE," Association of Certified Fraud Examiners, www.acfe.com/about-the-acfe.aspx (accessed June 14, 2020).

2. Mary Williams Walsh, "State Woes Grow Too Big to Camouflage," *CNBC,* March 30, 2010, www.cnbc.com/id/36096491/ (accessed April 17, 2017).

3. Benjamin Elisha Sawe, "The Largest Banks in the World," *World Atlas,* March 26, 2018, https://www.worldatlas.com/articles/the-largest-banks-in-the-world.html (accessed January 12, 2019).

4. Sarah Johnson, "Averting Revenue-Recognition Angst," *CFO,* April 2012, p. 21.

5. "City Finance Department Receives Distinguished Presentation Award for Its Budget," City of Maricopa, March 25, 2014, www.maricopa-az.gov/web/finance-administrativeservice-home/1029-city-s-finance-department-recieves-distinguished-budget-presentation-award-for-its-budget (accessed May 5, 2017).

6. "Accountants and Auditors: Occupational Outlook Handbook," Bureau of Labor Statistics, April 13, 2018, www.bls.gov/ooh/Business-and-Financial/Accountants-and-auditors.htm (accessed September 2, 2018).

a. Crowe, "The Financial Cost of Fraud 2019: The Latest Data from Around the World," 2019, www.crowe.ie/wp-content/uploads/2019/08/The-Financial-Cost-of-Fraud-2019.pdf (accessed June 14, 2020).

b. Paul Danos, "Back to the Big Eight Again," *Forbes,* April 13, 2007, www.forbes.com/2007/04/12/danos-accounting-bigeight-oped-cx_pd_0413danos.html#2fc36db7b3dc (accessed October 26, 2018); EY, "EY Reports Record Global Revenues of US$36.4b in 2019," September 5, 2019, https://www.ey.com/en_gl/news/2019/09/ey-reports-record-global-revenues-of-us-36-4b-in-2019 (accessed June 14, 2020); "Welcome to EY.com," Ernst & Young, https://www.ey.com/en_gl/who-we-are (accessed June 14, 2020); "Two People. One Vision," Ernst & Young, https://www.ey.com/us/en/about-us/our-people-and-culture/our-history (accessed October 26, 2018); "EY: #52 on 100 Best Companies to Work For in 2017," *Fortune,* 2018, http://fortune.com/best-companies/ey/ (accessed October 26, 2018); "Vault Accounting 50," *Vault.com,* http://www.vault.com/company-rankings/accounting/vault-accounting-50/ (accessed June 14, 2020).

c. Ben Kepes, "Big Four Accounting Firms Delve into Artificial Intelligence," *ComputerWorld,* March 16, 2016, https://www.computerworld.com/article/3042536/big-data/big-four-accounting-firms-delve-into-artificial-intelligence.html (accessed September 14, 2018); Sarah Ovaska-Few, "How Artificial Intelligence Is Changing Accounting," *Journal of Accountancy,* October 10, 2017, https://www.journalofaccountancy.com/newsletters/2017/oct/artificial-intelligence-changing-accounting.html (accessed September 14, 2018); Vipal Monga, "Need an Accountant? Try a Robot Instead," *The Wall Street Journal,* March 7, 2017, https://blogs.wsj.com/cfo/2017/03/07/need-an-accountant-try-a-robot-instead/ (accessed September 16, 2018); Don Reisinger, "A.I. Expert Says Automation Could Replace 40% of Jobs in 15 Years," *Fortune,* January 10, 2019, https://fortune.com/2019/01/10/automation-replace-jobs/ (accessed June 14, 2020).

d. Lillian Cunningham, "Deloitte Is First of 'Big 4' Firms to Name a Female CEO," *The Washington Post,* February 11, 2015, www.washingtonpost.com/news/on-leadership/wp/2015/02/11/deloitte-becomes-first-big-firm-to-name-a-female-ceo/?noredirect=on&utm_term=.7c817b06d460 (accessed September 20, 2018); Anne Fisher, "How Women Can Reach the Top in Accounting," *Fortune,* September 12, 2015, http://www.fortune.com/2015/09/12/women-accounting/ (accessed September 20, 2018); Michael Rapaport, "Women Rarely Run the Biggest Audits at the Big Four Accounting Firms," *The Wall Street Journal,* September 15, 2018, www.wsj.com/articles/women-rarely-run-audits-at-the-big-four-accounting-firms-1537106401 (accessed September 20, 2018); "Women in Accounting," *Catalyst,* January 22, 2018, www.catalyst.org/knowledge/women-accounting. (accessed September 20, 2018); "Women in Industry," Ernst & Young, www.ey.com/gl/en/issues/business-environment/ey-women-in-industry (accessed September 20, 2018).

Chapter 15

1. Paul Krugman, "Why Is Deflation Bad?" *The New York Times,* August 2, 2010, http://krugman.blogs.nytimes.com/2010/08/02/why-is-deflation-bad/ (accessed May 5, 2017).

2. Board of Governors of the Federal Reserve System, "How Much U.S. Currency Is in Circulation?," https://www.federalreserve.gov/faqs/currency_12773.htm (accessed June 10, 2020).

3. "Weird and Wonderful Money Facts and Trivia," *Happy Worker,* www.happyworker.com/magazine/facts/weird-and-wonderful-money-facts (accessed April 25, 2016).

4. "The History of American Currency," *U.S. Currency Education Program,* https://www.uscurrency.gov/history (accessed September 2, 2018).

5. "About the Redesigned Currency," Department of the Treasury, Bureau of Engraving and Printing, www.newmoney.gov/newmoney/currency/aboutnotes.htm (accessed April 2, 2010).

6. Jessica Dickler, "Americans Still Relying on Credit Cards to Get By," *CNN Money,* May 23, 2012, http://money.cnn.com/2012/05/22/pf/credit-card/index.htm (accessed May 5, 2017); Martin Merzer, "Survey: Students Fail the Credit Card Test," *Fox Business,* April 16, 2012, www.creditcards.com/credit-card-news/survey-students-fail-credit-card-test-1279.php (accessed May 5, 2017).

7. Sergei Klebnikov, "These 10 States Have The Highest Record Unemployment Rates," *Forbes,* May 23, 2020, https://www.forbes.com/sites/sergeiklebnikov/2020/05/23/these-10-states-have-the-highest-record-unemployment-rates/#1674efe0568e (accessed June 15, 2020).

8. "Deposit Insurance Simplification Fact Sheet," FDIC website, www.unitedamericanbank.com/pdfs/FDIC-Insurance-Coverage-Fact-Sheet.pdf (accessed June 16, 2014).

9. "NACHA Reports More Than 18 Billion ACH Payments in 2007," *The Free Library,* May 19, 2008, www.thefreelibrary.com/NACHA+Reports+More+Than+18+Billion+ACH+Payments+in+2007.-a0179156311 (accessed May 2, 2016).

10. "Online Banking Far and Away the Preferred Retail Channel, Survey Finds," September 13, 2011, http://www.bankersweb.com/headlines/article/online-banking-far-and-away-preferred-retail-channel (accessed November 19, 2017).

11. Stacy Cowley, "Zell, the Banks' Answer to Venmo, Proves Vulnerable to Fraud," *The New York Times,* April 22, 2018, https://www.nytimes.com/2018/04/22/business/zelle-banks-fraud.html (accessed January 12, 2019).

12. JP Morgan 2013 Annual Report, 10.

13. "CSI Pennsylvania," *CFO Magazine,* March 2008, p. 92; Villanova University, "Delaware County District Attorney's Office Forensic Accounting/Economic Crimes CoOp Program," https://www1.villanova.edu/villanova/business/undergraduate/careerdevelopmentresources/internships/coopopportunities/office-of-DA.html (accessed June 15, 2020).

a. "Like Magic: The Tech That Goes into Making Money Harder to Fake," *NPR,* October 23, 2017, https://www.npr.org/sections/alltechconsidered/2017/10/23/559092168/like-magic-the-tech-that-goes-into-making-money-harder-to-fake (accessed April 24, 2017).

b. "Savings Rate Surges To Highest Level In 39 Years," *PYMNTS,* May 1, 2020, www.pymnts.com/news/banking/2020/savings-rate-surges-to-highest-level-in-39-years/ (accessed June 14, 2020); David Benoit, "Coronavirus Made America's Biggest Banks Even Bigger," *The Wall Street Journal,* April 23, 2020, www.wsj.com/articles/coronavirus-made-america-s-biggest-banks-even-bigger-11587639602 (accessed June 14, 2020); Jurrien Timmer, "Great Expectations in the Stock Market," *Fidelity,* June 1, 2020, https://www.fidelity.com/learning-center/trading-investing/markets-sectors/stock-market-expectations (accessed June 14, 2020); Liz Kiesche, "Banks Pass on PPP Funding as Deposits Pour in, " *Seeking Alpha,* June 1, 2020, https://seekingalpha.com/news/3579049-banks-pass-on-ppp-funding-deposits-pour-in (accessed June 14, 2020); Paycheck Protection Program, https://www.sba.gov/funding-programs/loans/coronavirus-relief-options/paycheck-protection-program (accessed June 14, 2020); U.S. Bureau of Economic Analysis, "Personal Saving Rate," https://www.bea.gov/data/income-saving/personal-saving-rate (accessed June 14, 2020); Yalman Onaran, "Banks Have a Mountain of Deposits So They Don't Need PPP Funding," *Bloomberg,* June 1, 2020, https://www.bloomberg.com/news/articles/2020-06-01/banks-have-a-mountain-of-deposits-so-they-don-t-need-ppp-funding (accessed June 14, 2020).

c. Annie Massa and Caleb Melby, "In Fink We Trust: BlackRock Is Now 'Fourth Branch of Government'," *Bloomberg Quint,* May 21, 2020, https://www.bloombergquint.com/businessweek/how-larry-fink-s-blackrock-is-helping-the-fed-with-bond-buying (accessed June 14, 2020); Dawn Lim, "BlackRock's Assets Blow Past $7 Trillion in Milestone for Investment Giant," *The Wall Street Journal,* January 15, 2020, https://www.wsj.com/articles/blackrocks-assets-blow-past-7-trillion-in-milestone-for-investment-giant-11579089828 (accessed June 14, 2020); BlackRock, "Our History," Blackrock.com, https://www.blackrock.com/corporate/about-us/blackrock-history (accessed June 14, 2020).

d. Deutsche Bank, "The Future of Payments: Part II. Moving to Digital Wallets and the Extinction of Plastic Cards," January 2020, https://www.dbresearch.com/PROD/RPS_EN-PROD/PROD0000000000504508/The_Future_of_Payments_-_Part_II__Moving_to_Digita.pdf (accessed June 14, 2020); J. D. Biersdorfer, "How to Get the Most Out of Your Digital Wallet," *The New York Times,* October 9, 2019, https://www.nytimes.com/2019/10/09/technology/personaltech/how-to-get-the-most-out-of-your-digital-wallet.html (accessed June 14, 2020); Jessica Dickler and Sharon Epperson, "Digital Wallets Are Safe, Yet Americans Remain Wary," *CNBC,* March 3, 2018, https://www.cnbc.com/2018/03/02/digital-wallets-are-safe-yet-americans-remain-wary.html (accessed June 14, 2020).

Chapter 16

1. Calculated by Geoff Hirt from Apple's annual reports and website on June 10, 2020.

a. Sarah Elbert, "The Ultimate Kick-Start," *Delta Sky,* September 2018, p. 44; "Bird CEO Explains Why His Electric-Scooter Startup Needed $300 Million," *AdAge,* June 28, 2018, http://adage.com/article/cmo-strategy/bird-ceo-explains-electric-scooter-startup-needed-300-million/314067/ (accessed September 4, 2018); Nathanael Buckley, "For the Birds," *Slate,* May 22, 2018, https://slate.com/technology/2018/05/charging-bird-scooters-overnight-is-like-a-much-less-fun-version-of-pokemon-go.html (accessed September 4, 2018); Matt McFarland, "Cities Start Giving Scooter Companies a Second Chance," *CNN,* August 29, 2018, https://money.cnn.com/2018/08/29/technology/scooters-cities-bird-santa-monica/index.html (accessed September 4, 2018); Sam Shead, "Bird Is Scrapping Thousands of Electric Scooters in the Middle East," *CNBC,* June 3, 2020, https://www.cnbc.com/2020/06/03/bird-circ-scooters-middle-east.html (accessed June 15, 2020).

b. "Warren Buffet's 1993 Lesson on Coca-Cola Stock," *The Conservative Investor,* October 30, 2018, https://theconservativeincomeinvestor.com/warren-buffetts-1993-lesson-on-coca-cola-stock/ (accessed January 15, 2018).

c. Michael A. Gayed, "The New Odd-Lot Indicator–Robinhood," *Seeking Alpha*, June 15, 2020, https://seekingalpha.com/article/4353865-new-odd-lot-indicator-robinhood (accessed June 22, 2020); Maggie Fitzgerald, "Robinhood Traders Cash in on The Market Comeback That Billionaire Investors Missed," *CNBC,* June 9, 2020, https://www.cnbc.com/2020/06/09/robinhood-traders-cash-in-on-the-market-comeback-that-billionaire-investors-missed.html (accessed June 22, 2020); Avi Salzman, "The Under-40 Set discovers Day Trading," *Barron's,* June 12, 2020, https://www.barrons.com/articles/young-adults-turn-to-stock-trading-in-the-wake-of-the-markets-march-meltdown-51592001988 (accessed June 22, 2020).

d. Kate Rooney, "72-Year-Old Fidelity Bets on the Future of with Blockchain, Virtual Reality and AI," *CNBC,* September 29, 2018, https://www.cnbc.com/2018/09/28/fidelity-the-tech-company.html (accessed November 18, 2018); Michael del Castillo, "Fidelity Launches Institutional Platform for Bitcoin and Ethereum," *Forbes,* October 15, 2018, https://www.forbes.com/sites/michaeldelcastillo/2018/10/15/fidelity-launches-institutional-platform-for-bitcoin-and-ethereum/#6d00576e93c4 (accessed November 18, 2018); Anna Irrera, "Fidelity Becomes First Asset Manager to Join Blockchain Group IC3," *Reuters,* April 9, 2017, https://www.reuters.com/article/us-fidelity-blockchain-idUSKBN17C0AV (accessed November 18, 2018); Dalmas Ngetich, "Blockchain Is the New Cool, Fidelity Channels $2.5 Billion to Research," *Ethereum World News,* October 1, 2018, https://ethereumworldnews.com/fidelity-channels-2-5-billion-blockchain/ (accessed November 18, 2018); "About Digital Fidelity Assets," Fidelity, https://www.fidelitydigitalassets.com/about-us (accessed November 18, 2018); John E. Mulhall, "Blockchain and the Future of Finance," *Forbes,* September 11, 2018, https://www.forbes.com/sites/kpmg/2018/09/11/blockchain-and-the-future-of-finance/#4520f05d620f (accessed November 18, 2018); Samuel Haig, "One-Third of Institutions Have Invested in Crypto Says Fidelity," *Cointelegraph*, June 10, 2020, https://cointelegraph.com/news/one-third-of-institutions-have-invested-in-crypto-says-fidelity (accessed June 15, 2020).

Name Index

Subject Index

Coworking, 205
Crazy Pita Rotisserie & Grill, 105
Creative roles, 247
Creativity, 127
Credit, partnerships and, 81
Credit CARD (Card Accountability Responsibility and Disclosure) Act, 297
Credit card fraud, 264–265, 298
Credit cards, 296–297
Credit controls, monetary policy, 301–302
Credit-rating agencies, 316–317
Credits, 274
Credit unions, 304
Criminal law, 42
Crisis management, 116–117, 128
Critical path, 166
Crowdsourcing, 262
Crowdspring, 262
Crowe LLP, 270
Cruise Planners, 106
Cryptocurrency, 29, 298
C-suite, 203
Cuban, Mark, 9
Cultural barriers to trade, 63–65
Cultural behavioral differences, 64
Cultural differences, 74
Culture
    body language and personal space, 64
    bribery and, 26–27
    buying behavior and, 223
    ethical, 24
    organizational, 131–132
Cummins Inc., 34
Currency, 293
Current assets
    accounts receivable, 315
    balance sheet, 283
    cash, 313–314
    defined, 282
    goals, 313
    investing idle cash, 314–315
    optimizing inventory, 315–316
Current liabilities
    accounts payable, 316–317
    balance sheet, 283
    bank loans, 316–317
    defined, 282
    nonbank liabilities, 317
Current ratio, 287
Current yield, bond, 320

Customer contact, services, 153
Customer departmentalization, 136
Customer relationship management (CRM), 215
Customer satisfaction ratings, 233
Customer service, companies with best, 220
Customization
    products, 156–157
    services, 153
Cutco, 77
CVS, 17, 92, 138
Cybercriminals, 264, 298

D

Daewoo, 68
Dailymotion, 258
Daniels Fund, 86
Danske Bank, 32
Darktrace, 121, 122
Data collection
    marketing analytics, 221–222
    online, 221–222
    primary, 220–221
    secondary, 221
Data protection, 25, 52, 68
David's Bridal, 49
Day traders, 323
Debentures, bonds, 320
Debit card, 297
Debits, 274
Debt, 319
Debt financing
    defined, 319–320
    small business and, 105–106
Debt to total assets ratio, 288
Debt utilization ratios, 287–288
Decentralized organizations, 137–138
Deceptive advertising, online, 263
Decision making
    ethical, 26, 31
    independent, organizational structure and, 141
    partnerships and, 81
    process for, 125–127
Decline stage, product life cycle, 231
Deflation, 12, 294
Dell Computers, 34, 65, 85–86, 95, 96, 103, 157, 184
Deloitte LLP, 84, 269, 270, 271
Delta Airlines, 297

Demand, free-enterprise and, 9–10
Demand curve, 9
Demand deposits, 296
Democratic leaders, 124
Demographics
    market segmentation and, 217
    podcasts and, 259
    social network use, 256
Demographic trends
    diversity recruiting, 121
    small businesses and, 107–108
Denver Broncos, 153
Denver Rescue Mission, 152
Departmentalization, 134–136
    customer, 136
    defined, 134
    functional, 135
    geographical, 135
    product, 135
Department store, 237
Depository insurance, 302
Depreciation, 279
Depression, 12
De Vegetarische Slager (DVS), 90
Development, 195
Diageo beverages, 135
Diagonal formal communication, 145
Dick's Sporting Goods, 236, 237
Digital Advertising Alliance (DAA), 263–264
Digital assistants, 251
Digital catalog, 253
Digital certificates, 264
Digital communications, 249–250
Digital coupons, 245
Digital currency, 309, 326
Digital economy, 15–16
Digital enterprise system, 161–162
Digital marketing
    benefits of, business and, 250
    defined, 249
    false or deceptive claims and, 263
    impact of, 266
    mobile, 259–260
    music industry, 259
    online fraud and, 264–265
    paid advertising on, 254

privacy and, 263–264
    transparency, influencers and, 264
    user-generated content, 254–255
    word-of-mouth posts, 254
Digital marketing mix
    conventional marketing v., 251
    distribution, 253
    pricing, 253–254
    product, 252–253
    social media, 254
Digital media
    consumer behavior and, 262–263
    consumer-generated marketing and, 255–261
    defined, 249
Digital Millennium Copyright Act, 51
Digital signatures, 264
Digital technology, business and, 4
Digital wallet, 309
Diluted earnings per share, 288
Directing, management function, 118
Direct investment, international business, 72
Direct marketing, 237–238
Direct selling, 98, 238
Direct TV, 256
Disabled people in workforce, 203
Discount window, 300
Discover card, 296
Discrimination
    affirmative action v., 204
    legal issues in hiring and, 193–194
    workplace diversity and, 203–204
Disney+, 218
Disney Cruise Lines, 220
Dispute resolution
    alternative methods, 43–44
    arbitration, 43–44
    collective bargaining process, 201
    labor tactics, 200–201
    lawsuits, 42–43
    management tactics, 201–202
    mediation, 43
    mini-trial, 44
    private court system, 44

economy of, 13–19. *See also*
American economy
financial system of, 298–310.
See also American
financial system
gross domestic product,
changes in, 13
largest employer, DOD, 205
minimum wages,
state/federal, 197
organizational unethical
behavior in, 26
recessions and, 12
regulatory administrative
agencies, 44–45
small business role,
economy, 96–97
trade deficits/surpluses,
59–60
trade laws and
regulations, 61
trading partners, top 10, 70
United States-Mexico-Canada
Agreement (USMCA),
66–67
United States Postal Service
(USPS), 137
United Way Worldwide, 86
University of Pennsylvania, 30
University of Phoenix, 19
Unsecured bonds, 320
Unsecured loans, 316
UPS, 17
Upstream supply chain, 160
Upward formal
communication, 145
Upwork, 84
Urban Decay Cosmetics, 257
Urban Outfitters, 104
U.S. Army, 137
U.S. Bureau of Labor
Statistics, 198
U.S. Census Bureau, 12, 203
U.S. Chamber of Commerce, 46
U.S. Department of Commerce,
19, 74, 107
U.S. Department of
Defense, 205
U.S. Department of Labor,
100, 194
U.S. Department of the
Treasury, 13
U.S. Environmental Protection
Agency (EPA), 109
U.S. Federal Reserve, 294
U.S. Food and Drug
Administration, 30, 229

U.S. Food and Drug
Administration (FDA), 45
U.S. Justice Department, 29, 91
U.S. Patent and Trademark
Office, 48, 232
U.S. Postal Service, 86, 153, 216
U.S. Treasury, 328, 295
U.S. Treasury Bills (T-Bills),
300, 314
USAA, 34
USAJobs, 191
USA Today, 25, 105, 328
User-generated content,
254–255

V

Value
calculating, 235
marketing creates, 211
Values, ethical, 23–24
Vault Accounting, 272
Vault.com, 269, 270
Venture capitalists, 105
Verizon Communications,
91, 320, 323
Vertical merger, 91
Victoria's Secret, 74
Video conferencing, 147
Video-sharing sites, 258
Villanova University, 311
Vimeo, 250, 258
Viral marketing, 244, 258, 261
Virgin Galactic, 10
Virgin Group, 96
Virtual reality, marketing
and, 212
Virtual teams, 142–143
Virtual testing, 221
Visa Inc., 34, 296, 303, 305
Vistaprint, 211
VMWare, 183
Vodafone, 91
Voice-over Internet protocol
(VOIP), 78
Volition Beauty, 250, 252–253
Volkswagen, 23, 40
Voluntary agreement, contracts
and, 47
Volvo, 156, 246

W

Wageningen University &
Research, 90
Wages, 197. *See also*
Compensation

Wage and salary survey, 197
Walgreens, 137, 232
Wall Street, 303, 329
Wall Street Journal, 25
Walmart Inc., 10, 17, 18, 40,
109, 127, 161, 162, 205,
232, 236, 250, 251, 257, 280,
316, 320
Walt Disney Company, 78, 323
Walt Disney Production, 96,
322, 324
Wants, assessing consumer,
214–215
Warby Parker, 98, 253
Warehouse club, 237
Warehouse showroom, 237
Warehousing, 240–241
Warner Bros. Home
Entertainment, 52, 264
Warranties, UCC and, 46
Water pollution, 37, 38
W. Atlee Burpee and Co., 102
Waymo LLC, 228
Waze, 113, 260
WD-40, 232
Wealth of Nations, The (Smith),
8, 133
Weather Company, The, 155
Webex, video conferencing, 147
WeChat Pay, 309
Wegmans, 153
Wells Fargo, 23, 115, 124–125,
173, 302
Wendy's, 71
Western Digital, 34
Western Electric Company, 176
Westin Hotels, 153
WeWork, 28–29, 114, 205
Wham-O, 99
WhatsApp, 255
Wheeler-Lea Act, 51
Whistleblower protection,
53–54
Whistleblowing, 32
White knight, 91
Whole Foods, 186, 232, 234
Wholesalers, 238
Wholesaling, small business,
98–99
Wholesaling functions, 238
Wide span of management, 138
Widgets, 261
Wikipedia, 257
Wikis, social network
advertising and, 257–258
Williams & Sonoma, 184
Women. *See* Gender

Word-of-mouth, digital posts, 254
Work-at-home programs, 185
Workforce
diversity and, 19, 202–204
gender and, 15
remote, COVID-19 and, 26
See also Employee(s)
Workforce development
development, 195
mentoring, 195
orientation, 194
training, 194–195
Working capital management,
313. *See also* Current assets;
Current liabilities
Work-in-process inventory,
162–163
Work-life balance, 206
World Bank, 69
Worldcom, 270
World's Most Ethical
Companies, 25
World Trade Organization
(WTO), 66
World Wildlife Fund, 89
Wrigley's gum, 214
Writing, contracts and, 47
Wyndham Hotels & Resorts,
34, 151

X

Xander, software, 191
Xcel Energy, 34
Xerox, 110, 144, 232
Xiaopeng Motors, 29

Y

Yahoo!, 257, 289, 310, 321, 325
Yelp, 234, 255
Yield to maturity, bond, 320
Yoplait, 71
YouTube, 27, 52, 105, 132, 203,
243, 252, 253, 256, 258, 259
YUM! Brands, 70, 85

Z

Zales Jewelers, 259
Zappos, 125, 132, 184, 186, 251
Zelle peer-to-peer payments, 309
Zipline International, 161
Zola, 81
Zoom, 142, 147
ZoomSystems, 241
Zynga Inc., 103

in a nutshell

Goals, activities, and participants make up the fundamentals of business. Understanding the basics of economics and applying them to the United States economy will further your understanding of how business works and provide a framework for learning about business.

The following statements will test your take-away knowledge from this chapter. Do your best to explain each one in the space provided.

LO 1-1 Define basic concepts such as business, product, profit, and economics.

LO 1-2 Identify the main participants and activities of business.

LO 1-3 Explain why studying business is important.

LO 1-4 Compare the four types of economic systems.

LO 1-5 Describe the role of supply, demand, and competition in a free-enterprise system.

LO 1-6 Specify why and how the health of the economy is measured.

LO 1-7 Outline the evolution of the American economy.

LO 1-8 Explain the role of the entrepreneur in the economy.

Did your answers include the following important points?

LO 1-1. Define basic concepts such as business, product, profit, and economics.

- A business is individuals or organizations who try to earn a profit by providing products that satisfy people's needs.
- A product is a good, service, or idea that has both tangible and intangible characteristics that provide satisfaction and benefits.
- Profit, the basic goal of business, is the difference between what it costs to make and sell a product and what a customer pays for it.

LO 1-2. Identify the main participants and activities of business.

- The three main participants in business are owners, employees, and customers, but others—government regulators, suppliers, social groups, and so on—are also important.
- Management involves planning, organizing, and controlling the tasks required to carry out the work of the company.
- Marketing refers to those activities designed to provide goods and services that satisfy customers.
- Finance refers to activities concerned with funding a business and using its funds effectively.

LO 1-3. Explain why studying business is important.

- Studying business can help you develop skills, acquire knowledge to prepare for your future career, and help you better understand the many business activities that are necessary to provide satisfying goods and services.

LO 1-4. Compare the four types of economic systems.

- Communism is an economic system in which the people, without regard to class, own all the nation's resources, whereas in a socialist system, the government owns and operates basic industries, but individuals own most businesses.

- Under capitalism, individuals own and operate the majority of businesses that provide goods and services.
- Mixed economies have elements from more than one economic system; most countries have mixed economies.

LO 1-5. Describe the role of supply, demand, and competition in a free-enterprise system.

- Supply is the number of goods or services that businesses are willing to sell at different prices at a specific time.
- Demand is the number of goods and services that consumers are willing to buy at different prices at a specific time.
- Competition is the rivalry among businesses to persuade consumers to buy goods or services.

LO 1-6. Specify why and how the health of the economy is measured.

- A country measures the state of its economy to determine whether it is expanding or contracting and whether the country needs to take steps to minimize fluctuations.
- One commonly used measure is gross domestic product (GDP), the sum of all goods and services produced in a country during a year.

LO 1-7. Outline the evolution of the American economy.

- The American economy has evolved through the early economy, the Industrial Revolution, the manufacturing economy, the marketing economy, and the service- and Internet-based economy of today.
- New technology associated with artificial intelligence enabled by big data and advanced computing systems are changing the way work is accomplished.

LO 1-8. Explain the role of the entrepreneur in the economy.

- Entrepreneurs risk their time, wealth, and efforts to develop new goods, services, and ideas that fuel the growth of the American economy.

Practical Application

LO 1-1

- When purchasing a product, the consumer is actually buying its anticipated benefits and _____.
- If a business is to be successful in the long run, it must treat its customers, employees, and community with social _____.

LO 1-2

- _____ involves activities designed to provide goods and services that fulfill needs and desires of consumers.
- Advertising, personal selling, coupons, and sweepstakes are forms of _____.

LO 1-3

- Business activities help generate the _____ that are essential to the health of the global economy.

LO 1-4

- Private property, profits, independent business decisions, and choice are rights associated with _____.
- In _____, consumers have a limited choice of goods and services, and prices are usually high.
- Most countries operate as _____, which have elements from more than one economic system.

LO 1-5

- In _____, there are many small businesses selling one standardized product.
- The market structure that exists when there are very few businesses selling a product is called a(n) _____.

LO 1-6

- During a(n) _____ there is a decline in production, employment, and income.
- _____ is the sum of all goods and services produced in a country during a year.
- A(n) _____ occurs when a nation spends more than it takes in from taxes.

LO 1-7

- The Industrial Revolution changed the United States from an agricultural economy to a(n) _____ one.
- _____ relates to machine (computer) learning that is able to perform activities and tasks that usually require human intelligence.

LO 1-8

- A person who risks his or her wealth and time to develop an innovative product or idea for profit is called a(n) _____.

in a
nutshell

You must understand the role of ethics and social responsibility in making good business decisions. Learning to recognize business ethics issues, how businesses can improve their ethical behavior, and the impact of how companies respond to these issues is the basis of social responsibility.

The following statements will test your take-away knowledge from this chapter. Do your best to explain each one in the space provided.

LO 2-1 Describe the importance of business ethics and social responsibility.

LO 2-2 Detect some of the ethical issues that may arise in business.

LO 2-3 Specify how businesses can promote ethical behavior.

LO 2-4 Explain the four dimensions of social responsibility.

LO 2-5 Evaluate an organization's social responsibilities to owners, employees, consumers, the environment, and the community.

Did your answers include the following important points?

LO 2-1. Describe the importance of business ethics and social responsibility.

- The principles and standards that determine acceptable conduct in business organizations are defined as business ethics.
- A business's obligation to maximize its positive impact and minimize its negative impact on society illustrates the concept of social responsibility.
- Business ethics relates to an individual's or a work group's decisions that society evaluates as right or wrong, whereas social responsibility is a broader concept that concerns the impact of the entire business's activities on society.
- Socially responsible businesses win the trust and respect of their employees, customers, and society and increase profits.
- Ethics is important in business because it builds trust and confidence in business relationships.

LO 2-2. Detect some of the ethical issues that may arise in business.

- An ethical issue is an identifiable problem, situation, or opportunity requiring a person or organization to choose from among several actions that must be evaluated as right or wrong.
- Ethical issues can be categorized in the context of their relation with conflicts of interest, fairness and honesty, communications, and business associations.

LO 2-3. Specify how businesses can promote ethical behavior.

- Businesses can promote ethical behavior among employees by limiting their opportunity to engage in misconduct.

- Formal codes of ethics, ethical policies, and ethics training programs reduce the incidence of unethical behavior by informing employees what is expected of them and providing punishments for those who fail to comply.

LO 2-4. Explain the four dimensions of social responsibility.

- The four dimensions of social responsibility are economic (being profitable), legal (obeying the law), ethical (doing what is right, just, and fair), and voluntary (being a good corporate citizen).

LO 2-5. Evaluate an organization's social responsibilities to owners, employees, consumers, the environment, and the community.

- Businesses must maintain proper accounting procedures, provide all relevant information about the performance of the firm to investors, and protect the owners' rights and investments.
- In relations with employees, businesses are expected to provide a safe workplace, pay employees adequately for their work, and treat them fairly.
- Consumerism refers to the activities undertaken by independent individuals, groups, and organizations to protect their rights as consumers.
- Increasingly, society expects businesses to take greater responsibility for the environment, especially with regard to animal rights as well as water, air, land, and noise pollution.
- Many businesses engage in activities to make the communities in which they operate better places for everyone to live and work.

Practical Application

LO 2-1

- If a very successful professional football team has been ignoring the players' use of illegal muscle-building steroids, the owners should begin focusing on improving the organization's _____.
- A company's obligation to increase its positive impact and decrease its negative impact is its _____.
- The _____ criminalized securities fraud and stiffened penalties for corporate fraud.

LO 2-2

- A(n) _____ exists when a person must choose whether to advance his or her own personal interests or those of others.
- Any payment, gift, or special favor intended to influence the outcome of a decision can be considered a(n) _____.
- If a person takes someone's work and presents it as his or her own without mentioning the source, it would be considered an act of _____.

LO 2-3

- _____ occurs when an employee exposes an employer's wrongdoing to outsiders.

- A set of formalized rules and standards that describe what a company expects of its employees is called a(n) _____.
- According to the text, ethical decisions in an organization are influenced by (1) individual moral standards, (2) the influence of managers and co-workers, and (3) _____.

LO 2-4

- Being profitable relates to _____ social responsibility.
- Consumers vote against firms they view as socially irresponsible by not _____.
- Philanthropic contributions made by a business to a charitable organization represent _____ social responsibility.

LO 2-5

- Businesses must first be responsible to their _____.
- Many of the laws regulating safety in the workplace are enforced by _____.
- _____ ensures the fair treatment of consumers who voice complaints about a purchased product.

in a nutshell

To learn about business in a global marketplace, you need to understand the nature of international business, including barriers to and promoters of trade across international boundaries. You must also consider the levels of organizational involvement in international business and the strategies used for trading across national borders.

The following statements will test your take-away knowledge from this chapter. Do your best to explain each one in the space provided.

LO 3-1 Explore some of the factors within the international trade environment that influence business.

LO 3-2 Assess some of the economic, legal, political, social, cultural, and technological barriers to international business.

LO 3-3 Specify some of the agreements, alliances, and organizations that may encourage trade across international boundaries.

LO 3-4 Summarize the different levels of organizational involvement in international trade.

LO 3-5 Contrast two basic strategies used in international business.

Did your answers include the following important points?

LO 3-1. Explore some of the factors within the international trade environment that influence business.

- International business is the buying, selling, and trading of goods and services across national boundaries.
- Importing is the purchase of products and raw materials from another nation; exporting is the sale of domestic goods and materials to another nation.
- A nation's balance of trade is the difference in value between its exports and its imports: a negative balance of trade is a trade deficit.
- An absolute or comparative advantage in trade may determine what products a company from a particular nation will export.

LO 3-2. Assess some of the economic, legal, political, social, cultural, and technological barriers to international business.

- Companies engaged in international trade must consider the effects of economic, legal, political, social, and cultural differences between nations.
- Wide-ranging legal and political barriers include differing laws (and enforcement), tariffs, exchange controls, quotas, embargoes, political instability, and war.
- Ambiguous cultural and social barriers involve differences in spoken and body language, time, holidays, and other observances and customs.

LO 3-3. Specify some of the agreements, alliances, and organizations that may encourage trade across international boundaries.

- Among the most important promoters of international business are the General Agreement on Tariffs and Trade, the World Trade Organization, the United States–Mexico–Canada Agreement, the European Union, the Asia-Pacific Economic Cooperation, the Association of Southeast Asian Nations, the World Bank, and the International Monetary Fund.

LO 3-4. Summarize the different levels of organizational involvement in international trade.

- Countertrade agreements occur at the import–export level and involve bartering products for other products, and a trading company links buyers and sellers in different countries to foster trade.
- Licensing and franchising occurs when one company allows a foreign company to use its name, products, patents, brands, trademarks, raw materials, and production processes in exchange for a flat fee or royalty.
- Contract manufacturing occurs when a company hires a foreign company to produce a specified volume of the firm's product and allows the final product to carry the domestic firm's name. In a joint venture, companies work as a partnership and share the costs and operation of the business. A strategic alliance is a partnership formed to create competitive advantage on a worldwide basis.
- Direct investment involves purchasing overseas production and marketing facilities, whereas outsourcing involves transferring manufacturing to countries where labor and supplies are cheap. A multinational corporation is one that operates on a worldwide scale, without ties to any one nation or region. Offshoring is the relocation of a business process by a company, or a subsidiary, to another country.

LO 3-5. Contrast two basic strategies used in international business.

- A multinational strategy customizes products, promotion, and distribution according to cultural, technological, regional, and national differences, whereas a global strategy (globalization) standardizes products for the whole world as if it were a single entity.

Practical Application

LO 3-1

- South Africa holds a(n) _____ in diamond deposits in the world.
- The difference between the flow of money into and out of a country is called its _____.
- The transfer of manufacturing and other tasks to places where labor and other supplies are less expensive is called _____.

LO 3-2

- The United States' prohibition of imported Cuban cigars is an example of a(n) _____.
- A group of nations or companies that band together to act as a monopoly is known as a(n) _____.
- A country/business that wants to gain a quick entry into a new market sometimes engages in _____ its products.

LO 3-3

- The _____ makes short-term loans to member countries with trade deficits and provides foreign currencies to member nations.
- The _____ is the largest source of advice and assistance with loans for developing countries.

- The North American Free Trade Agreement was replaced by the _____, an agreement that encourages trade among the United States, Mexico, and Canada

LO 3-4

- When a company hires a foreign company to produce a specified volume of the firm's product to specification, it is engaging in _____.
- PepsiCo allows a Canadian firm to use its name, formula, and brands in return for a royalty. This arrangement is known as _____.
- In some industries, _____ allow companies to create competitive advantage on a worldwide basis.

LO 3-5

- Standardizing products for the whole world as if it were a single entity is a characteristic of _____ strategy.
- Most companies doing international business have used the _____ strategy; that is, they have customized their products and distribution to cultural and regional differences.

in a
nutshell

Sole proprietorship, partnership, and corporation are three primary forms of business that are used in traditional business, online-only business, or a combination of both. Other forms of business include S corporations, limited liability companies, and cooperatives. In organizing a business, it is helpful to understand the advantages and disadvantages of these forms of business as well as business trends.

The following statements will test your take-away knowledge from this chapter. Do your best to explain each one in the space provided.

LO 4-1 Describe the advantages and disadvantages of the sole proprietorship form of organization.

LO 4-2 Describe the two types of business partnership and their advantages and disadvantages.

LO 4-3 Describe the corporate form of organization and its advantages and disadvantages.

LO 4-4 Assess the advantages and disadvantages of mergers, acquisitions, and leveraged buyouts.

Did your answers include the following important points?

LO 4-1. Describe the advantages and disadvantages of the sole proprietorship form of organization.

- The most common form of business is the sole proprietorship. The advantages of this form of business include the fact that it is easy and inexpensive to form, it allows for a high level of secrecy, all profits belong to the owner, the owner has complete control over the business, government regulation is minimal, taxes are paid only once, and the business can be closed easily.

- Disadvantages include the fact that the owner may have to use personal assets to borrow money, sources of external funds are difficult to find, the owner must have many diverse skills, the survival of the business is tied to the life of the owner and his or her ability to work, qualified employees are hard to find, and wealthy sole proprietors pay a higher tax rate than they would under the corporate form of business.

LO 4-2. Describe the two types of business partnership and their advantages and disadvantages.

- Partnerships may be general or limited and offer the following advantages: They are easy to organize, they may have higher credit ratings because partners may have more combined wealth, partners can specialize, partnerships can make decisions faster than larger businesses, and government regulations are few.

- Disadvantages include the fact that general partners have unlimited liability for the debts of the partnership, partners are responsible for each other's decisions, the death or termination of one partner requires a new partnership agreement, it is difficult to sell a partnership interest at a fair price, the distribution of profits may not correctly reflect the amount of work done by each partner, and partnerships cannot find external sources of funds as easily as large corporations.

LO 4-3. Describe the corporate form of organization and cite its advantages and disadvantages.

- A corporation, which is owned by stockholders, is a legal entity created by the state, whose assets and liabilities are separate from those of its owners. They are chartered by a state through articles of incorporation and have a board of directors made up of corporate officers or people from outside the company.

- Advantages include the fact that owners have limited liability, ownership (stock) can be easily transferred, corporations are long-lasting, raising money is easier, and expansion into new businesses is simpler.

- Disadvantages include the fact that the company is taxed on its income and owners pay a second tax on any profits received as dividends, forming a corporation can be expensive, keeping trade secrets is difficult because so much information must be made available to the public and to government agencies, and owners and managers are not always the same and can have different goals.

LO 4-4. Assess the advantages and disadvantages of mergers, acquisitions, and leveraged buyouts.

- A merger occurs when two companies (usually corporations) combine to form a new company. An acquisition occurs when one company buys most of another company's stock, whereas in a leveraged buyout, a group of investors borrows money to acquire a company, using the assets of the purchased company to guarantee the loan.

- Advantages include the fact that they can help merging firms gain a larger market share in their industries, acquire valuable assets, and realize lower costs. They can also benefit stockholders by improving companies' market value and stock prices.

- Disadvantages include the fact that they can hurt companies if they force managers to focus on avoiding takeovers at the expense of productivity and profits, they may lead a company to take on too much debt, and they can harm employee morale and productivity.

Practical Application

LO 4-1

- One of the most popular and easiest to establish forms of business in the United States is the _____.

- An individual who is the sole owner of a business faces _____ liability in case of debt.

LO 4-2

- _____ are the least used form of business organization in the United States.

- The decision-making process in a partnership tends to be faster when the partnership is _____.

- As with a sole proprietorship, the sources of funds available to a partnership are _____.

LO 4-3

- Another often-used name for stockholder is _____.

- A(n) _____ is one whose stocks anyone may buy, sell, or trade.

- The organizational form that many consider to be a blend of the best characteristics of corporations, partnerships, and sole proprietorships is the _____.

LO 4-4

- When two companies combine to form a new company, it is called a(n) _____.

- When companies operating at different, but related, levels of an industry merge, it is known as a(n) _____.

- XYZ Inc. is attempting to avoid a hostile takeover by a corporate raider by allowing stockholders to buy more shares of stock at prices lower than current market value; the _____ method is being used here to avoid the takeover.

in a nutshell

A successful entrepreneur or small-business owner understands the advantages and disadvantages of owning a small business, challenges facing small businesses today, and why small businesses succeed or fail.

The following statements will test your take-away knowledge from this chapter. Do your best to explain each one in the space provided.

LO 5-1 Define *entrepreneurship* and *small business.*

LO 5-2 Explain the importance of small business in the U.S. economy and why certain fields attract small business.

LO 5-3 Specify the advantages of small-business ownership.

LO 5-4 Analyze the disadvantages of small-business ownership and the reasons why many small businesses fail.

LO 5-5 Describe how to start a small business and what resources are needed.

LO 5-6 Evaluate the demographic, technological, and economic trends that are affecting the future of small business.

LO 5-7 Explain why many large businesses are trying to "think small."

Did your answers include the following important points?

LO 5-1. Define *entrepreneurship* and *small business*.

- An entrepreneur is a person who creates a business or product and manages his or her resources and takes risks to gain a profit; entrepreneurship is the process of creating and managing a business to achieve desired objectives.
- A small business is one that is not dominant in its competitive area and does not employ more than 500 people.
- Social entrepreneurship is a growing trend among businesses. Social entrepreneurs are individuals who use entrepreneurship to address social problems.

LO 5-2. Explain the importance of small business in the U.S. economy and why certain fields attract small business.

- Small businesses are vital to the American economy because they provide products, jobs, innovation, and opportunities.
- Retailing, wholesaling, services, manufacturing, and high technology attract small businesses because these industries are relatively easy to enter, require relatively low initial financing, and may experience less heavy competition.

LO 5-3. Specify the advantages of small-business ownership.

- Small-business ownership offers some personal advantages, including independence, freedom of choice, and the option of working at home.
- Business advantages include flexibility, the ability to focus on a few key customers, and the chance to develop a reputation for quality and service.

LO 5-4. Analyze the disadvantages of small-business ownership and the reasons why many small businesses fail.

- Small businesses have many disadvantages for their owners, such as expense, physical and psychological stress, and a high failure rate.
- Small businesses fail for many reasons: undercapitalization, management inexperience or incompetence, neglect, disproportionate burdens imposed by government regulation, and vulnerability to competition from larger companies.

LO 5-5. Describe how to start a small business and what resources are needed.

- Have an idea for developing a small business and devise a business plan to guide the development of the business. Then you must decide what form of business ownership to use and provide funds, either your own or funds provided by friends, families, banks, investors, or other organizations.
- You must also decide whether to start a new business from scratch, buy an existing one, or buy a franchise operation.

LO 5-6. Evaluate the demographic, technological, and economic trends that are affecting the future of small business.

- Changing demographic trends include more older adults as baby boomers age; a large gain in individuals born between the early 1980s and early 2000s known as echo boomers, millennials, or Generation Y; and an increasing number of immigrants to the United States.
- Technological advances and an increase in service exports have created new opportunities for small companies to expand their operations abroad, whereas trade agreements and alliances have created an environment in which small business has fewer regulatory and legal barriers.
- Economic turbulence presents both opportunities for and threats to the survival of small businesses.

LO 5-7. Explain why many large businesses are trying to "think small."

- Large companies are copying small businesses in an effort to make their firms more flexible, resourceful, and innovative, and improve the bottom line.
- This involves downsizing and intrapreneurship, by which an employee takes responsibility for developing innovations within the larger organization.

Practical Application

LO 5-1

- _____ operate by the same principles as other entrepreneurs but view their organizations as vehicles to create social change.
- The Small Business Administration was established to provide _____ assistance to small businesses.
- Small business refers to an owner-managed business that employs not more than _____ people.

LO 5-2

- The _____ is an economic model involving the sharing of underutilized resources.
- _____ attracts entrepreneurs because gaining experience and exposure is relatively easy.
- The fastest growing sector of the U.S. economy is represented by _____.

LO 5-3

- When market conditions change rapidly, a small business usually has fewer layers of management to work through in making decisions; this advantage of a small business is called _____.
- _____ is one of the leading reasons that entrepreneurs choose to go into business for themselves.
- Unlike many large corporations, small businesses can focus on developing products for a defined _____, that is, specific customers.

LO 5-4

- Many people turn a hobby into a business without identifying a(n) _____ for that product; this leads to failure.

- _____ is one of the leading reasons for business failure because most businesses suffer from seasonal variations in sales.
- Initially, the factor that probably affects a company's reputation more than anything else is poorly managed _____.

LO 5-5

- Since Rachel Hollings decided to purchase the rights to own and operate a McDonald's fast-food restaurant rather than start her own operation, she is probably a(n) _____.
- A mortgage is an example of _____.
- _____ are persons or organizations that agree to provide some funds for a new business in exchange for an ownership interest or stock.

LO 5-6

- The _____ segment of the population is probably the wealthiest in the United States.
- Deregulation of the _____ market and an interest in fuel conservation has spawned many small businesses.

LO 5-7

- Reducing management layers, corporate staff, and work tasks to make a firm more flexible, resourceful, and innovative is known as _____.
- Individuals who take responsibility for the development of innovations of any kind within larger organizations are called _____.

in a nutshell

A successful manager needs to possess certain skills and follow steps for effective decision making. In doing so, managers accomplish various functions and participate in differing levels and areas of management.

The following statements will test your take-away knowledge from this chapter. Do your best to explain each one in the space provided.

LO 6-1 Explain management's role in the achievement of organizational objectives.

LO 6-2 Describe the major functions of management.

LO 6-3 Distinguish among three levels of management and the concerns of managers at each level.

LO 6-4 Specify the skills managers need in order to be successful.

LO 6-5 Summarize the systematic approach to decision making used by many business managers.

Did your answers include the following important points?

LO 6-1. Explain management's role in the achievement of organizational objectives.

- Management is a process designed to achieve an organization's objectives by using its resources effectively and efficiently in a changing environment.
- Managers make decisions about the use of the organization's resources and are concerned with planning, organizing, staffing, directing, and controlling the organization's activities to reach its objectives.

LO 6-2. Describe the major functions of management.

- Planning is the process of determining the organization's objectives and deciding how to accomplish them. Organizing is the structuring of resources and activities to accomplish those objectives efficiently and effectively.
- Staffing is the hiring of people with the necessary skills to carry out the work of the company.
- Directing is motivating and leading employees to achieve organizational objectives, and controlling is the process of evaluating and correcting activities to keep the organization on course.

LO 6-3. Distinguish among three levels of management and the concerns of managers at each level.

- Top management is responsible for the whole organization and focuses primarily on strategic planning. Middle management develops plans for specific operating areas and carries out the general guidelines set by top management.
- First-line, or supervisory, management supervises the workers and day-to-day operations.
- Managers can also be categorized according to their area of responsibility: finance, production and operations, human resources, marketing, or administration.

LO 6-4. Specify the skills managers need in order to be successful.

- Managers need technical expertise, conceptual skills, analytical skills, human relations skills, and leadership skills.
- Leadership is the ability to influence employees to work toward organizational goals.
- Managers can be classified into three types based on their leadership style. *Autocratic leaders* make all the decisions and then tell employees what must be done and how to do it. *Democratic leaders* involve their employees in decisions. *Free-rein leaders* let their employees work without much interference.
- Another type of leadership gaining in popularity is authentic leadership. Authentic leaders are passionate about the goals and mission of the company, display corporate values in the workplace, and form long-term stakeholder relationships.
- Employee empowerment occurs when employees are provided with the ability to take on responsibilities and make decisions about their jobs. To empower employees, leaders should adopt systems that support their ability to provide input and feedback on company decisions, encourage them to participate in decision making, and train them in leadership skills.

LO 6-5. Summarize the systematic approach to decision making used by many business managers.

- A systematic approach to decision making follows these steps: recognizing and defining the situation, developing options, analyzing options, selecting the best option, implementing the decision, and monitoring the consequences.

Practical Application

LO 6-1

- If a manager is concerned about doing work with the least cost and waste, her primary managerial concern is _____.
- _____ make decisions about the use of an organization's resources and are concerned with planning, organizing, leading, and controlling the organization's activities.
- Managers need to make efficient use of the company's _____ to reach organizational objectives.

LO 6-2

- The type of planning conducted on a long-range basis by top managers is usually called _____.
- Dividing work into small units and assigning it to individuals are tasks related to _____.
- Hiring people to carry out the work of the organization is known as _____.

LO 6-3

- _____ are responsible for tactical planning that will implement the general guidelines established by the top management.
- Decisions regarding adding new products, acquiring companies, and moving into foreign markets would most typically be made by the _____.
- Most people get their first managerial experience as _____ supervising workers and daily operations.

LO 6-4

- Joe met with department heads to listen to their opinions about buying a new machine. Although they all thought it was a good idea, Joe did not buy the machine. Joe's leadership style is _____.
- Those managers who can communicate well, understand the needs of others, and deal effectively with people inside and outside the organization are said to have good _____ skills.
- _____ leaders let their employees work without much interference.
- Authentic leaders are passionate about the goals and mission of the company, display _____ in the workplace, and form long-term _____.
- _____ occurs when employees are provided with the ability to take on responsibilities and make decisions about their jobs.

LO 6-5

- When analyzing options in the decision-making process, managers must consider the appropriateness and _____ of each option.
- Effective implementation of a major decision requires _____.
- Managers need to spend a lot of time in _____ with those who can help in the realization of organizational objectives.

in a nutshell

An organization's culture affects its operations. It is important in organizing a business to understand the development of structure, including how tasks and responsibilities are organized through specialization and departmentalization, as well as the different forms organizational structure may take.

The following statements will test your take-away knowledge from this chapter. Do your best to explain each one in the space provided.

LO 7-1 Explain the importance of organizational culture.

LO 7-2 Describe how organizational structures develop.

LO 7-3 Describe how specialization and departmentalization help an organization achieve its goals.

LO 7-4 Determine how organizations assign responsibility for tasks and delegate authority.

LO 7-5 Compare and contrast some common forms of organizational structure.

LO 7-6 Distinguish between groups and teams.

LO 7-7 Identify the types of groups that exist in organizations.

LO 7-8 Describe how communication occurs in organizations.

Did your answers include the following important points?

LO 7-1. Explain the importance of organizational culture.

- Organizational culture is the firm's shared values, beliefs, traditions, philosophies, and role models for behavior.
- Organizational culture helps ensure that all members of a company share values and suggests rules for how to behave and deal with problems within the organization.

LO 7-2. Describe how organizational structures develop.

- Structure develops when managers assign work activities to work groups and specific individuals and coordinate the diverse activities required to attain organizational objectives.
- Organizational structure evolves to accommodate growth, which requires people with specialized skills.

LO 7-3. Describe how specialization and departmentalization help an organization achieve its goals.

- Structuring an organization requires that management assign work tasks to specific individuals and groups. Under specialization, managers break labor into small, specialized tasks and assign employees to do a single task, fostering efficiency.
- Departmentalization is the grouping of jobs into working units.
- Businesses may departmentalize by function, product, geographic region, or customer, or they may combine two or more of these.

LO 7-4. Determine how organizations assign responsibility for tasks and delegate authority.

- Delegation of authority means assigning tasks to employees and giving them the power to make commitments, use resources, and take whatever actions are necessary to accomplish the tasks.
- The extent to which authority is delegated throughout an organization determines its degree of centralization.

LO 7-5. Compare and contrast some common forms of organizational structure.

- Line structures have direct lines of authority that extend from the top manager to employees at the lowest level of the organization.
- A multidivisional structure gathers departments into larger groups called divisions. A matrix or project-management structure sets up teams from different departments, thereby creating two or more intersecting lines of authority.

LO 7-6. Distinguish between groups and teams.

- A group is two or more persons who communicate, have a common identity, and have a common goal. A team is a small group whose members have complementary skills; a common purpose, goals, and approach; and who hold themselves mutually accountable.
- The major distinction is that individual performance is most important in groups, while collective work group performance counts most in teams.

LO 7-7. Identify the types of groups that exist in organizations.

- Special kinds of groups include task forces, committees, project teams, product-development teams, quality-assurance teams, and self-directed work teams.

LO 7-8. Describe how communication occurs in organizations.

- Communication occurs both formally and informally in organizations. Formal communication may be downward, upward, horizontal, and even diagonal.
- Informal communication takes place through friendships and the grapevine.

Practical Application

LO 7-1

- Work philosophies, values, dress codes, work habits, extracurricular activities, and stories make up _____.

LO 7-2

- The arrangement or relationship of positions within an organization is called _____.

LO 7-3

- _____ departmentalization arranges jobs around the needs of various types of customers.
- General Motors is organized into these groups: GMC Trucks, Chevrolet, Buick, and Cadillac. This is called _____ departmentalization.
- Adam Smith illustrated improvements in efficiency through the application of _____.

LO 7-4

- An organization with many layers of managers is considered to be _____.
- An organization operating in a complex and unpredictable environment is likely to be _____.
- When the decisions of a company are very risky and low-level managers lack decision-making skills, the company will tend to _____.

LO 7-5

- The _____ of organization allows managers to specialize in their area of expertise.
- The _____ organizational form is likely to be complex and expensive.
- _____ permit delegation of decision-making authority, and ensure that better decisions are made faster.

LO 7-6

- It is important for _____ to retain their individuality.

LO 7-7

- A temporary group of employees responsible for bringing about a particular change is a(n) _____.
- A special type of project team formed to devise, design, and implement a new product is a(n) _____.
- A(n) _____ is a group of employees responsible for an entire work process or segment that delivers a product to an internal or external customer.

LO 7-8

- When managers recognize that a(n) _____ exists, they should use it to their advantage.
- Progress reports and complaints are part of _____ communication.
- When individuals from different organizational units and levels communicate with each other, it is called _____ communication.

in a
nutshell

Production and operations management involves planning and designing the processes that will transform resources into finished products, managing the movement of resources through the transformation process, and ensuring that the products are of the quality expected by customers.

The following statements will test your take-away knowledge from this chapter. Do your best to explain each one in the space provided.

LO 8-1 Define *operations management*.

LO 8-2 Differentiate between operations and manufacturing.

LO 8-3 Explain how operations management differs in manufacturing and service firms.

LO 8-4 Describe the elements involved in planning and designing an operations system.

LO 8-5 Specify some techniques managers may use to manage the logistics of transforming inputs into finished products.

LO 8-6 Assess the importance of quality in operations management.

Did your answers include the following important points?

LO 8-1. Define *operations management*.

- Operations management (OM) is the development and administration of the activities involved in transforming resources into goods and services.

LO 8-2. Differentiate between operations and manufacturing.

- The terms *manufacturing* and *production* are used interchangeably to describe the activities and processes used in making tangible products, whereas operations is a broader term used to describe the process of making both tangible and intangible products.

LO 8-3. Explain how operations management differs in manufacturing and service firms.

- Manufacturers and service firms both transform inputs and outputs, but service providers differ from manufacturers in several ways: They have greater customer contact because the service occurs at the point of consumption; their inputs and outputs are more variable than those of manufacturers; because of the human element, service providers are generally more labor intensive; and their productivity measurement is more complex.

LO 8-4. Describe the elements involved in planning and designing an operations system.

- Operations planning relates to decisions about what products to make and for whom and what processes and facilities are needed to produce them.
- Common facility layouts include fixed-position layouts, process layouts, and product layouts.
- Where to locate operations facilities is a crucial decision that depends on proximity to market, availability of raw materials, availability of

transportation, availability of power, climatic influences, availability of labor, and community characteristics.
- Technology is also vital to operations, particularly computer-assisted design, computer-assisted manufacturing, flexible manufacturing, robotics, and computer-integrated manufacturing.

LO 8-5. Specify some techniques managers may use to manage the logistics of transforming inputs into finished products.

- Logistics, or supply chain management, includes all the activities involved in obtaining and managing raw materials and component parts, managing finished products, packaging them, and getting them to customers.
- Common approaches to inventory control include the economic order quantity (EOQ) model, the just-in-time (JIT) inventory concept, and material-requirements planning (MRP).
- Logistics also includes routing and scheduling processes and activities to complete products.

LO 8-6. Assess the importance of quality in operations management.

- Quality is a critical element of operations management because low-quality products can hurt people and harm business.
- Quality control refers to the processes an organization uses to maintain its established quality standards.
- To control quality, a company must establish what standard of quality is desired and determine whether its products meet that standard through inspection.

Practical Application

LO 8-1

- Viewed from the perspective of operations, the money used to purchase a carpenter's tools and the electricity used to run his power saw are _____.
- If an employee is involved with transforming resources into goods and services, then she is in _____.
- From an operations perspective, food sold at a restaurant and services provided by a plumbing company are _____.

LO 8-2

- Operations management is the "core" of most organizations because it is responsible for the creation of the organization's _____ and _____.

LO 8-3

- Due to the high degree of automation, products in the manufacturing industry are more _____ than those in the service industry.
- Most goods are manufactured _____ purchase, whereas most services are performed _____ purchase.
- The service industry is _____ intensive, whereas the manufacturing industry is _____ intensive.

LO 8-4

- Television sets, ballpoint pens, and tortilla chips are _____ products because they are produced on an assembly line.
- _____ involves building an item in self-contained units that can be combined or interchanged to create different products.
- When a customer goes to a print shop to order business cards, the manufacturing process used would most likely be _____.

LO 8-5

- A company that requires all its resources to be brought to a central location is using a(n) _____.
- Materials that have been purchased to be used as inputs in making other products are included in _____.
- _____ helps engineers design components, products, and processes on the computer instead of on paper.

LO 8-6

- Determining how many items are to be inspected is called _____.
- The degree to which a good or service meets the demands and requirements of customers is called _____ .
- _____ is a philosophy that a uniform commitment to quality in all areas of an organization will promote a culture that meets customers' perceptions of quality.

in a nutshell

Managers who understand the needs and motivations of workers and strategies for motivating them can help workers reach higher levels of productivity, subsequently contributing to the achievement of organizational goals.

The following statements will test your take-away knowledge from this chapter. Do your best to explain each one in the space provided.

LO 9-1 Explain why the study of *human relations* is important.

LO 9-2 Summarize early studies that laid the groundwork for understanding employee motivation.

LO 9-3 Compare and contrast the human relations theories of Abraham Maslow and Frederick Herzberg.

LO 9-4 Investigate various theories of motivation, including Theories X, Y, and Z; equity theory; expectancy theory; and goal-setting theory.

LO 9-5 Describe some of the strategies that managers use to motivate employees.

Did your answers include the following important points?

LO 9-1. Explain why the study of *human relations* is important.

- Human relations focuses on what motivates employees to perform on the job.
- Human relations is important because businesses need to understand how to motivate their employees to be more effective, boost workplace morale, and maximize employees' productivity and creativity.

LO 9-2. Summarize early studies that laid the groundwork for understanding employee motivation.

- Time and motion studies by Frederick Taylor and others helped them analyze how employees perform specific work tasks in an effort to improve their productivity.
- Taylor and the early practitioners of the classical theory of motivation felt that money and job security were the primary motivations of employees; however, the Hawthorne studies revealed that human factors also influence workers' behavior.

LO 9-3. Compare and contrast the human relations theories of Abraham Maslow and Frederick Herzberg.

- Abraham Maslow defined five basic needs of all people and arranged them in the order in which they must be satisfied: physiological, security, social, esteem, and self-actualization.
- Frederick Herzberg divided the characteristics of jobs into hygiene factors and motivational factors.

- Herzberg's hygiene factors can be compared to Maslow's physiological and security needs; motivational factors may include Maslow's social, esteem, and self-actualization needs.

LO 9-4. Investigate various theories of motivation, including Theories X, Y, and Z; equity theory; expectancy theory; and goal-setting theory.

- Douglas McGregor contrasted two views of management: Theory X suggests workers dislike work, whereas Theory Y suggests that workers not only like work but seek out responsibility to satisfy their higher-order needs.
- Theory Z stresses employee participation in all aspects of company decision making, whereas the equity theory indicates that how much people are willing to contribute to an organization depends on their assessment of the fairness, or equity, of the rewards they will receive in exchange.
- The expectancy theory states that motivation depends not only on how much a person wants something but also on the person's perception of how likely he or she is to get it.
- Goal-setting theory refers to the impact that setting goals has on performance.

LO 9-5. Describe some of the strategies that managers use to motivate employees.

- Strategies for motivating workers include behavior modification and job design. Among the job design strategies businesses use are job rotations, job enlargement, job enrichment, and flexible scheduling strategies.

Practical Application

LO 9-1

- An inner drive that directs behavior toward objectives is called _____.
- Good morale in an employee is likely to result in _____.
- A(n) _____ is the personal satisfaction that we feel from achieving a goal.

LO 9-2

- Prior to the Hawthorne studies, management theorists believed that the primary motivators of employees were job security and _____.
- The birth of the study of human relations can be traced to _____ and _____ studies.

LO 9-3

- According to Maslow, living life to the fullest is most closely associated with fulfilling one's _____ need.
- According to Frederick Herzberg, the aspects that relate to the work setting form the _____ factors.

LO 9-4

- Jim has learned that his company is offering a Hawaiian vacation to its best salesperson. He almost won last year and really wants the trip. He is working very hard because he thinks he has a good chance to win. This exemplifies the _____ theory.
- Jack believes that he can get some extra work completed before the deadline by withholding his workers' vacation schedules until the job is completed. Jack is a manager who follows _____.
- The approach that suggests that imagination, ingenuity, and creativity can help solve organizational problems is _____.

LO 9-5

- A work system that allows employees to choose their starting and ending times as long as they are at work during a specified core period is called _____.
- _____ adds tasks to a job instead of treating each task as a separate job.
- When Kelly reprimands Sarah each time Sarah is late for work, Kelly is applying _____.

chapter 10

in a nutshell

Human resource managers need to plan for, recruit, and select qualified employees. Yet another aspect of the human resource manager's job is to train, appraise, compensate, and retain valued employees, which can present an added challenge among unionized and diverse employees.

The following statements will test your take-away knowledge from this chapter. Do your best to explain each one in the space provided.

LO 10-1 Explain the significance of human resource management.

LO 10-2 Summarize the processes of recruiting and selecting human resources for a company.

LO 10-3 Describe how workers are trained and their performance appraised.

LO 10-4 Identify the types of turnover companies may experience.

LO 10-5 Explain why turnover is an important issue.

LO 10-6 Specify the various ways a worker may be compensated.

LO 10-7 Discuss some of the issues associated with unionized employees, including collective bargaining and dispute resolution.

LO 10-8 Describe the importance of diversity in the workforce.

Did your answers include the following important points?

LO 10-1. Explain the significance of human resource management.

- Human resource management is concerned with maximizing the satisfaction of employees and improving their efficiency to meet organizational objectives.

LO 10-2. Summarize the processes of recruiting and selecting human resources for a company.

- Human resource managers must determine the firm's human resource needs, develop a strategy to meet those needs, and recruit qualified applicants from whom management will select the employees.
- Selection is the process of collecting information about applicants, using that information to decide which to hire, and putting potential hires through the process of application, interview, testing, and reference checking.

LO 10-3. Describe how workers are trained and their performance appraised.

- Training teaches employees how to do their job tasks, whereas development is training that augments the skills and knowledge of managers and professionals as well as current employees.
- Appraising performance involves identifying an employee's strengths and weaknesses on the job. Performance appraisals may be subjective or objective.

LO 10-4. Identify the types of turnover companies may experience.

- A promotion is an advancement to a higher-level job with increased authority, responsibility, and pay. A transfer is a move to another job within the company, typically at the same level and wage.
- Separations occur when employees resign, retire, are terminated, or are laid off.

LO 10-5. Explain why turnover is an important issue.

- Turnovers due to separation are expensive because of the time, money, and effort required to select, train, and manage new employees.

LO 10-6. Specify the various ways a worker may be compensated.

- Wages are financial compensation based on the number of hours worked or the number of units produced, whereas commissions are a fixed amount or percentage of a sale paid as compensation.
- Salaries are compensation calculated on a weekly, monthly, or annual basis, regardless of the number of hours worked or the number of items produced.
- Bonuses and profit sharing are types of financial incentives; benefits are nonfinancial forms of compensation such as vacation, insurance, and sick leave.

LO 10-7. Discuss some of the issues associated with unionized employees, including collective bargaining and dispute resolution.

- Collective bargaining is the negotiation process through which management and unions reach an agreement on a labor contract.
- If labor and management cannot agree on a contract, labor union members may picket, strike, or boycott the firm; management may lock out striking employees, hire strikebreakers, or form employers' associations.
- In a deadlock, labor disputes may be resolved by a third party.

LO 10-8. Describe the importance of diversity in the workforce.

- Companies with diverse workforces experience more productive use of human resources, reduced conflict, better work relationships among workers, increased commitment to and sharing of organizational goals, increased innovation and creativity, and enhanced ability to serve diverse customers.

Practical Application

LO 10-1

- In some companies, the department that handles the human resource management function is still called _____.
- The observation and study of information about a job is called _____.
- The qualifications required for a job are spelled out in a job _____.

LO 10-2

- _____ tests are restricted to specific government jobs and those involving security or access to drugs.
- Professionals who specialize in luring qualified people away from other companies are known as _____.
- Recruiting for entry-level managerial and professional positions is often carried out on _____.

LO 10-3

- The _____ includes a panel consisting of the employee's peers, superiors, and subordinates.
- If Greta received training by watching videotapes and discussing case studies, she received _____ training.
- Joseph has worked at his position for years. He is currently participating in management seminars at company expense. This is an example of _____.

LO 10-4

- Sandy Smith moved to a new job that involved more responsibility and an increase in compensation. She received a(n) _____.

- Susan was terminated from her job by her employer because she was repeatedly late to work. She was _____.

LO 10-5

- A(n) _____ rate signifies problems with the selection and training program.

LO 10-6

- To motivate employees such as car salespersons to sell as much as they can, they are paid _____.
- June works at McDonald's part-time as a grill operator. She will probably be paid with the _____ compensation method.
- An employee stock ownership plan is an example of _____.

LO 10-7

- Workers seeking to improve pay and working conditions may join together to form a(n) _____.
- _____ make carrying out normal business operations difficult, if not impossible.
- A(n) _____ might be brought in as a neutral third party to keep union and management representatives talking.

LO 10-8

- Age, gender, and race are _____ characteristics of diversity.
- Secondary characteristics _____.
- Having a diverse workforce has many benefits. One benefit is the _____ use of a company's human resources.

nutshell

Marketers develop marketing strategies to satisfy the needs and wants of their customers; they also need to consider buying behavior and use research to determine what consumers want to buy and why. Marketers also need to consider the impact of the environment on marketing activities.

The following statements will test your take-away knowledge from this chapter. Do your best to explain each one in the space provided.

LO 11-1 Define *marketing.*

LO 11-2 Describe the exchange process.

LO 11-3 Specify the functions of marketing.

LO 11-4 Explain the marketing concept and its implications for developing marketing strategies.

LO 11-5 Examine the development of a marketing strategy, including market segmentation and marketing mix.

LO 11-6 Investigate how marketers conduct marketing research and study buying behavior.

LO 11-7 Summarize the environmental forces that influence marketing decisions.

Did your answers include the following important points?

LO 11-1. Define *marketing*.

- Marketing is a group of activities designed to expedite transactions by creating, distributing, pricing, and promoting goods, services, and ideas.

LO 11-2. Describe the exchange process.

- Marketing facilitates exchange, the act of giving up one thing in return for something else. The central focus is to satisfy needs.

LO 11-3. Specify the functions of marketing.

- Marketing includes many varied and interrelated activities: buying, selling, transporting, storing, grading, financing, marketing research, and risk taking.

LO 11-4. Explain the marketing concept and its implications for developing marketing strategies.

- The marketing concept is the idea that an organization should try to satisfy customers' needs through coordinated activities that also allow it to achieve its goals.
- If a company does not implement the marketing concept by providing products that consumers need and want while achieving its own objectives, it will not survive.

LO 11-5. Examine the development of a marketing strategy, including market segmentation and marketing mix.

- A marketing strategy is a plan of action for creating a marketing mix for a specific target market. Some firms use a total-market approach, designating everyone as the target market.

- Most firms divide the total market into segments of people who have relatively similar product needs.
- A company using a concentration approach develops one marketing strategy for a single market segment, whereas a multisegment approach aims marketing efforts at two or more segments, developing a different marketing strategy for each segment.

LO 11-6. Investigate how marketers conduct marketing research and study buying behavior.

- Carrying out the marketing concept is impossible unless marketers know what, where, when, and how consumers buy; marketing research into the factors that influence buying behavior helps marketers develop effective marketing strategies.
- Marketing research is a systematic, objective process of getting information about potential customers to guide marketing decisions.
- Buying behavior is the decision processes and actions of people who purchase and use products.

LO 11-7. Summarize the environmental forces that influence marketing decisions.

- Several forces influence marketing activities: political, legal, regulatory, social, competitive, economic, and technological.

Practical Application

LO 11-1

- James Johnson has developed a new product, found a store willing to sell it, and agreed to help promote the product's sale. He is engaging in _____.

LO 11-2

- When a customer hands the cashier $3 and receives a loaf of bread, a(n) _____ has occurred.

LO 11-3

- When a storeowner spends a lot of money for new products that have yet to be proven as successful sales items, the owner is engaging in the marketing function of _____.
- Richard has acquired a supply of canned fruits and vegetables. He does not yet have a buyer for them, but he's using promotion and other activities to find a buyer. He is performing the marketing function of _____.

LO 11-4

- The goal of the marketing concept is _____.
- _____ remains a major element of any strategy to develop and manage long-term customer relationships.
- During the Industrial Revolution, new technologies fueled strong _____.

LO 11-5

- A plan of action for developing, pricing, distributing, and promoting products that meets the needs of a specific customer is a(n) _____.
- People visiting a ski resort would be viewed by a ski equipment storeowner as the business's _____.
- The aim of _____ is to communicate directly or indirectly with individuals, groups, and organizations to facilitate exchanges.

LO 11-6

- _____ is a systematic and objective process of getting information on potential customers.
- _____ is a psychological variable of buyer behavior.
- _____ are the least expensive data to collect.
- _____ involves large data sets that can provide the opportunity for advanced analysis to provide information for marketing decisions.

LO 11-7

- Purchasing power, recession, and inflation are associated with _____ forces.
- The public's opinions and attitudes toward living standards, ethics, and the environment are considered _____ forces.

in a nutshell

There are four dimensions of marketing—product, price, distribution, and promotion. These elements are used to develop a marketing strategy that builds customer relationships and satisfaction.

The following statements will test your take-away knowledge from this chapter. Do your best to explain each one in the space provided.

LO 12-1 Describe the role of product in the marketing mix, including how products are developed, classified, and identified.

LO 12-2 Explain the importance of price in the marketing mix, including various pricing strategies a firm might employ.

LO 12-3 Identify factors affecting distribution decisions, such as marketing channels and intensity of market coverage.

LO 12-4 Specify the activities involved in promotion, as well as promotional strategies and promotional positioning.

Did your answers include the following important points?

LO 12-1. Describe the role of product in the marketing mix, including how products are developed, classified, and identified.

- Products are among a firm's most visible contacts with consumers and must meet consumers' needs to be successful. New-product development is a multistep process including idea development, the screening of new ideas, business analysis, product development, test marketing, and commercialization.
- Products are classified as either consumer or business products. Consumer products can be further classified as convenience, shopping, or specialty products.
- The business product classifications are raw materials, major equipment, component parts, processed materials, supplies, and industrial services.
- Products can also be classified by the stage of the product life cycle. Identifying products includes branding, packaging, and labeling.

LO 12-2. Explain the importance of price in the marketing mix, including various pricing strategies a firm might employ.

- Pricing objectives include survival, maximization of profits and sales volume, and maintenance of the status quo.
- A firm may use price skimming or penetration pricing when introducing a new product. Psychological pricing, reference pricing, and price discounting are other strategies.

LO 12-3. Identify factors affecting distribution decisions, such as marketing channels and intensity of market coverage.

- Making products available to customers is facilitated by middlemen or intermediaries, who bridge the gap between the producer of the product and its ultimate user.
- A marketing channel is a group of marketing organizations that directs the flow of products from producers to consumers.
- Market coverage relates to the number and variety of outlets that make products available to customers; it may be intensive, selective, or exclusive.

LO 12-4. Specify the activities involved in promotion, as well as promotional strategies and promotional positioning.

- Promotion encourages marketing exchanges by persuading individuals, groups, and organizations to accept goods, services, and ideas. The promotion mix includes advertising, personal selling, publicity, and sales promotion.
- A push strategy attempts to motivate intermediaries to push the product down to the customers, whereas a pull strategy tries to create consumer demand for a product so that the consumers exert pressure on marketing channel members to make the product available.
- Typical promotion objectives are to stimulate demand; stabilize sales; and inform and remind customers. Promotional positioning is the use of promotion to create and maintain an image of the product in the mind of the buyer.

Practical Application

LO 12-1

- _____ allows a company to discover the strengths and weaknesses of a product before it is fully launched in the market.
- _____ are less expensive than manufacturer brands and are owned and controlled by a wholesaler or retailer.
- _____ generally appeal to those consumers who are willing to sacrifice quality and product consistency for the sake of lower prices.

LO 12-2

- The pricing policy that allows a company to cover the product's development cost most quickly is _____.
- _____ enables a product to enter the market and rapidly gain market share.
- A cosmetics company believes that it makes more sense to sell its eye shadow at $11.99 rather than $12.00; it is using _____.

LO 12-3

- _____ buy products from manufacturers and sell them to consumers for home and household use.
- When a product is to be made available in as many outlets as possible, wholesalers and retailers engage in _____.
- When a firm is _____ in a supply chain relationship, it receives goods from suppliers further up the stream.

LO 12-4

- When Ford pays a television network to air its commercial, it is using _____.
- When Chiquita uses newspaper ads to introduce its new fruit drink to consumers before introducing it to supermarkets, it is using the _____.
- The mass media willingly carry _____ for a company or product, when believing it has general public interest.

in a nutshell

You must understand the concepts of digital media and digital marketing and how they have become extremely important in strategic planning. The Internet and social media are becoming increasingly important in people's lives, so you need to understand their impact on business today.

The following statements will test your take-away knowledge from this chapter. Do your best to explain each one in the space provided.

LO 13-1 Recognize the increasing value of digital media and digital marketing in strategic planning.

LO 13-2 Demonstrate the role of digital marketing in today's business environment.

LO 13-3 Show how digital media affect the marketing mix.

LO 13-4 Illustrate how businesses can use different types of social networking media.

LO 13-5 Explain online monitoring and analytics for social media.

LO 13-6 Identify legal and ethical considerations in digital media.

Did your answers include the following important points?

LO 13-1. Recognize the increasing value of digital media and digital marketing in strategic planning.

- Digital marketing uses digital media to create communications and exchanges with customers.

LO 13-2. Demonstrate the role of digital marketing in today's business environment.

- Firms can use real-time exchanges to stimulate interactive communication, forge closer relationships, and learn more accurately about consumer and supplier needs.
- Digital communication is making it easier for businesses to conduct marketing research, provide price and product information, and advertise.
- A social network is a web-based meeting place for friends, family, co-workers, and peers that lets users create a profile and connect with other users for different purposes.

LO 13-3. Show how digital media affect the marketing mix.

- The Internet is a new distribution channel making products available at the right time, at the right place, and in the right quantities.
- Online promotions are creating well-informed consumers.
- Digital media enhance the value of products by providing extra benefits such as service, information, and convenience.
- The Internet gives consumers access to more information about products and prices.

LO 13-4. Illustrate how businesses can use different types of social networking media.

- Internet users participate in blogs, wikis, social networks, media-sharing sites, mobile marketing, and applications and widgets.

- Marketers have begun investigating and experimenting with promotion on social networks, including Facebook, Twitter, Snapchat, YouTube, TikTok, and LinkedIn.
- Blogs answer consumer concerns and obtain free publicity, whereas wikis give marketers a better understanding of how consumers feel about their companies.
- Photo-sharing sites enable companies to share images of their businesses or products with consumers and often have links that connect users to company-sponsored blogs.
- Video sharing is allowing many businesses to engage in viral marketing.
- Podcasts are audio or video files that can be downloaded from the Internet with a subscription that automatically delivers new content to listening devices or personal computers.
- Mobile phones are also being used for communicating with consumers and conducting business, especially in the service industry.
- Apps can help consumers perform services and make purchases more easily; widgets can be used to inform consumers about company updates and can easily go viral.

LO 13-5. Explain online monitoring and analytics for social media.

- Social media monitoring involves activities to track, measure, and evaluate a firm's digital marketing initiatives.
- Marketing analytics uses tools and methods to measure and interpret the effectiveness of marketing activities.

LO 13-6. Identify legal and ethical considerations in digital media.

- The Internet and e-business have raised concerns such as privacy concerns, the risk of identity theft, online fraud, and intellectual property rights.

Practical Application

LO 13-1

- _____ are electronic media that function using digital codes and are available via computers, cell phones, smartphones, and other digital devices.
- _____ uses digital media to develop communication and exchanges with customers.
- _____ means carrying out the goals of business through the use of the Internet.

LO 13-2

- The Internet _____ the cost of communication and is therefore significant in industries such as entertainment, health care, and education.
- Digital media can be a(n) _____ backbone that helps store knowledge, information, and records in management information systems for the employees of a company.

LO 13-3

- The Internet has become a new _____ to make products available for people.
- Nielsen Marketing Research reveals that people today spend more time on _____ than they do on _____.
- The aspect of marketing that still remains unchanged by the digital media is the importance of achieving the _____.

LO 13-4

- Some companies have started using _____ as internal tools for projects that require a lot of documentation.
- Marketers generally engage in _____ of their products on social networking sites.
- _____ is the most popular social networking site in the world.

LO 13-5

- _____ should be embedded at the onset of a social media strategy and can allow almost real-time measurement and evaluation.
- The Google Analytics dashboard is broken down into five sections: _____, audience, acquisition, behavior, and conversions.

LO 13-6

- _____ occurs when criminals obtain personal information that allows them to impersonate someone else in order to use the person's credit to access financial accounts and make purchases.
- _____ is a method of initiating identity theft fraud that is growing rapidly.
- _____ of content is a major intellectual property problem especially in the areas of software, music, movies, and videogames.

in a
nutshell

The use of accounting information and the accounting process is important in making business decisions. Understanding simple financial statements and accounting tools is useful in analyzing organizations worldwide.

The following statements will test your take-away knowledge from this chapter. Do your best to explain each one in the space provided.

LO 14-1 Describe the different uses of accounting information.

LO 14-2 Demonstrate the accounting process.

LO 14-3 Examine the various components of an income statement in order to evaluate a firm's "bottom line."

LO 14-4 Interpret a company's balance sheet to determine its current financial position.

LO 14-5 Analyze financial statements, using ratio analysis, to evaluate a company's performance.

Did your answers include the following important points?

LO 14-1. Describe the different uses of accounting information.

- Accounting is the language businesses and other organizations use to record, measure, and interpret financial transactions.
- Financial statements are used internally to judge and control an organization's performance and to plan and direct its future activities and measure goal attainment.
- External organizations such as lenders, governments, customers, suppliers, and the Internal Revenue Service are major consumers of the information generated by the accounting process.

LO 14-2. Demonstrate the accounting process.

- Assets are an organization's economic resources; liabilities are debts the organization owes to others; owners' equity is the difference between the value of an organization's assets and liabilities.
- This principle can be expressed as the accounting equation: Assets = Liabilities + Owners' equity.
- The double-entry bookkeeping system is a system of recording and classifying business transactions in accounts that maintain the balance of the accounting equation.
- The accounting cycle involves recording transactions in a journal, posting transactions, and preparing financial statements on a continuous basis throughout the life of the organization.

LO 14-3. Examine the various components of an income statement in order to evaluate a firm's "bottom line."

- The income statement indicates a company's profitability over a specific period of time. It shows the bottom line, the total profit (or loss) after all expenses have been deducted from revenue.
- Major components of the income statement include revenue, expenses, and net income.

LO 14-4. Interpret a company's balance sheet to determine its current financial position.

- The balance sheet, which summarizes the firm's assets, liabilities, and owners' equity since its inception, portrays its financial position as of a particular point in time.
- Major classifications included in the balance sheet are current assets, fixed assets, current liabilities, long-term liabilities, and owners' equity.
- The statement of cash flows explains how the company's cash changed from the beginning of the accounting period to the end.

LO 14-5. Analyze financial statements, using ratio analysis, to evaluate a company's performance.

- Ratio analysis, calculations that measure an organization's financial health, brings the information from the income statement and balance sheet into focus so that people can measure and compare the organization's productivity, profitability, and financing mix with other entities.

Practical Application

LO 14-1

- A(n) _____ is an individual who has been state-certified to provide accounting services ranging from the preparation of financial records and the filing of tax returns to complex audits of corporate financial records.
- An internal financial plan that forecasts expenses and income over a set period of time is known as an organization's _____.
- A(n) _____ is a summary of the firm's financial information, products, and growth plans for owners and potential investors.

LO 14-2

- Trendy, an organization that specializes in hand-stitched clothes, owes money to its suppliers and to the Small Business Administration. The money owed is an example of Trendy's _____ .
- The system of recording and classifying business transactions in separate accounts to maintain the balance of the accounting equation is called _____.
- A(n) _____ is a book or computer file with separate sections for each account.

LO 14-3

- The _____ is the amount of money the firm spent to buy and/or produce the products it sold during the accounting period.

- _____ is the process of spreading the costs of long-lived assets such as buildings and equipment over the total number of accounting periods in which they are expected to be used.
- The _____ shows the profit or loss once all taxes and expenses have been deducted from the revenue.

LO 14-4

- Short-term assets that are used or converted into cash within the course of a calendar year are also known as _____.
- _____ represents amounts owed to suppliers for goods and services purchased with credit.
- All unpaid financial obligations of a company are kept in the _____ account.

LO 14-5

- _____ measure how much operating income or net income an organization is able to generate relative to its assets, owners' equity, and sales.
- _____ measure how well a firm uses its assets to generate each $1 of sales.
- _____ compare current (short-term) assets to current liabilities to indicate the speed with which a company can turn its assets into cash to meet debts as they fall due.

 in a
nutshell

The Federal Reserve Board and other major financial institutions play significant roles in the financial system. In understanding finance, you need to consider the definition of money and the forms money may take. You also need to consider the future of the finance industry and the changes likely to occur over the course of the next several years.

The following statements will test your take-away knowledge from this chapter. Do your best to explain each one in the space provided.

LO 15-1 Define *money*, its functions, and its characteristics.

LO 15-2 Describe various types of money.

LO 15-3 Specify how the Federal Reserve Board manages the money supply and regulates the American banking system.

LO 15-4 Compare and contrast commercial banks, savings and loan associations, credit unions, and mutual savings banks.

LO 15-5 Distinguish among nonbanking institutions such as insurance companies, pension funds, mutual funds, and finance companies.

LO 15-6 Analyze the challenges ahead for the banking industry.

Did your answers include the following important points?

LO 15-1. Define *money*, its functions, and its characteristics.

- Money is anything generally accepted as a means of payment for goods and services. Money serves as a medium of exchange, a measure of value, and a store of wealth.
- To serve effectively in these functions, money must be acceptable, divisible, portable, durable, stable in value, and difficult to counterfeit.

LO 15-2. Describe various types of money.

- Money may take the form of currency, checking accounts, or other accounts.
- Checking accounts are funds left in an account in a financial institution that can be withdrawn without advance notice.
- Other types of accounts include savings accounts, money market accounts, certificates of deposit, credit cards, and debit cards as well as traveler's checks, money orders, and cashier's checks.

LO 15-3. Specify how the Federal Reserve Board manages the money supply and regulates the American banking system.

- The Federal Reserve Board manages the U.S. money supply by buying and selling government securities, raising or lowering the discount rate, raising or lowering bank reserve requirements, and adjusting down payment and repayment terms for credit purchases.
- It also regulates banking practices, processes checks, and oversees federal depository insurance for institutions.

LO 15-4. Compare and contrast commercial banks, savings and loan associations, credit unions, and mutual savings banks.

- Commercial banks are financial institutions that take and hold deposits in accounts for and make loans to individuals and businesses.

- Savings and loan associations are financial institutions that primarily specialize in offering savings accounts and mortgage loans. Mutual savings banks are similar to S&Ls, except that they are owned by their depositors.
- Credit unions are financial institutions owned and controlled by their depositors.

LO 15-5. Distinguish among nonbanking institutions such as insurance companies, pension funds, mutual funds, and finance companies.

- Insurance companies are businesses that protect their clients against financial losses due to certain circumstances, in exchange for a fee.
- Pension funds are investments set aside by organizations or individuals to meet retirement needs.
- Mutual funds pool investors' money and invest in large numbers of different types of securities, brokerage firms buy and sell stocks and bonds for investors, and finance companies make short-term loans at higher interest rates than banks.
- Exchange traded funds (ETFs) are investment funds made up of a pool of assets that track an underlying index.

LO 15-6. Analyze the challenges ahead for the banking industry.

- Future changes in financial regulations are likely to result in fewer but larger banks and other financial institutions.
- A growing trend is shadow banking, which refers to companies performing banking functions of some sort that are not regulated by banking regulators.

Practical Application

LO 15-1

- Trading one good or service for another of similar value is known as _____.
- When a dollar bill is handled hundreds of times and is still being used, it has _____.
- When inflation is very high, people no longer believe that money is _____.

LO 15-2

- Another name for a savings account is a(n) _____.
- In general, the longer the term of a certificate of deposit, the higher its _____.
- The acronym NOW, when used in financial circles, stands for _____.

LO 15-3

- To carry out its functions of controlling the supply of money, the Federal Reserve Board uses its _____.
- When the Federal Reserve buys securities, it _____.

LO 15-4

- If employees of a local school district conduct their financial business through the same financial institution that they own and only they are allowed to join, the institution is probably a(n) _____.
- _____ are the oldest and largest of all financial institutions.
- The _____ was established in 1933 to help stop bank failures throughout the country during the Great Depression and has nearly 8,000 member institutions at present.

LO 15-5

- Insurance companies invest premiums from insured individuals and businesses or make short-term loans, particularly to businesses in the form of _____.
- _____ permits home computer users to conduct banking activities through their personal computers.

LO 15-6

- _____ is an increasing trend that may be concerning because it is not regulated by banking regulators.
- The future of the structure of the American banking system is largely in the hands of the _____.

ANSWERS LO15-1 • bartering • durability • stable LO15-2 • time deposit • interest rate • negotiable order of withdrawal LO15-3 • monetary policy • increases the money supply LO15-4 • credit union • Commercial banks • Federal Deposit Insurance Corporation (FDIC) LO15-5 • commercial real estate loans • Online banking LO15-6 • Shadow banking • U.S. Congress

in a nutshell

Companies use short-term assets to generate sales and conduct ordinary day-to-day business operations and short-term liabilities to finance business. They also use long-term assets such as plant and equipment and long-term liabilities such as stocks and bonds to finance corporate assets. Financial management depends on the management of these assets and liabilities as well as the trade of stocks and bonds.

The following statements will test your take-away knowledge from this chapter. Do your best to explain each one in the space provided.

LO 16-1 Describe some common methods of managing current assets.

LO 16-2 Identify some sources of short-term financing (current liabilities).

LO 16-3 Summarize the importance of long-term assets and capital budgeting.

LO 16-4 Specify how companies finance their operations and manage fixed assets with long-term liabilities, particularly bonds.

LO 16-5 Explain how corporations can use equity financing by issuing stock through an investment banker.

LO 16-6 Describe the various securities markets in the United States.

Did your answers include the following important points?

LO 16-1. Describe some common methods of managing current assets.

- Current assets are short-term resources such as cash, investments, accounts receivable, and inventory.
- Financial managers focus on minimizing the amount of cash kept on hand and increasing the speed of collections through lockboxes and electronic funds transfer and by investing in marketable securities.
- Marketable securities include U.S. Treasury bills, certificates of deposit, commercial paper, and money market funds.
- Managing accounts receivable requires judging customer creditworthiness and creating credit terms that encourage prompt payment.
- Inventory management focuses on determining optimum inventory levels that minimize the cost of storing the ordering inventory without sacrificing too many lost sales due to stockout.

LO 16-2. Identify some sources of short-term financing (current liabilities).

- Current liabilities are short-term debt obligations that must be repaid within one year, such as accounts payable, taxes payable, and notes payable.
- Trade credit is extended by suppliers for the purchase of their goods and services, whereas a line of credit is an arrangement by which a bank agrees to lend a specified amount of money to a business whenever the business needs it.
- Secured loans are backed by collateral; unsecured loans are backed only by the borrower's good reputation.

LO 16-3. Summarize the importance of long-term assets and capital budgeting.

- Long-term or fixed assets are expected to last for many years, such as production facilities, offices, and equipment. Businesses need up-to-date equipment to succeed in today's competitive environment.

- Capital budgeting is the process of analyzing company needs and selecting the assets that will maximize its value; a capital budget is the amount of money budgeted for the purchase of fixed assets.

LO 16-4. Specify how companies finance their operations and manage fixed assets with long-term liabilities, particularly bonds.

- Two common choices for financing are equity financing and debt financing. Long-term liabilities are debts that will be repaid over a number of years, such as long-term bank loans and bond issues.
- A bond is a long-term debt security that an organization sells to raise money. The bond indenture specifies the provisions of the bond contract—maturity date, coupon rate, repayment methods, and others.

LO 16-5. Explain how corporations can use equity financing by issuing stock through an investment banker.

- Owners' equity represents what owners have contributed to the company and includes common stock, preferred stock, and retained earnings.
- To finance operations, companies can issue new common and preferred stock through an investment banker that sells stocks and bonds to corporations.

LO 16-6. Describe the various securities markets in the United States.

- Securities markets provide the mechanism for buying and selling stocks and bonds. Primary markets allow companies to raise capital by selling new stock directly to investors through investment bankers.
- Secondary markets allow the buyers of previously issued shares of stock to sell them to other owners. Major secondary markets are the New York Stock Exchange, the American Stock Exchange, and the over-the-counter market.
- Investors measure stock market performance by watching stock market averages and indexes.

Practical Application

LO 16-1

- A(n) _____ is an address for receiving payments from customers.
- _____ are short-term debt obligations that the U.S. government sells to raise money.
- Good financial managers minimize the amount of cash available to pay bills in _____.

LO 16-2

- A finance company to which businesses sell their accounts receivable, usually for a percentage of the total face value, is a(n) _____.
- The most widely used source of short-term financing is _____.

LO 16-3

- Plants, offices, and equipment are considered _____ assets.
- The process of analyzing the needs of the business and selecting the assets that will maximize its value is called _____.
- In general, the longer the expected life of a project or asset, the _____ the potential risk.

LO 16-4

- _____ are a sequence of small bond issues of progressively longer maturity.
- Items such as a bond's value, date, and rate are specified in the _____.
- A method of long-term financing that requires repaying funds with interest is _____.

LO 16-5

- The first-time sale of stocks and bonds to the public directly is called _____.
- If a company retains all of its earnings, it will not pay _____.
- Corporations usually employ an investment banking firm to help sell their securities in the _____.

LO 16-6

- A(n) _____ is a network of dealers rather than an organized exchange.
- A(n) _____ compares current stock prices with those in a specified base period.

ANSWERS LO16-1 • lockbox • Treasury bills (T-bills) • transaction balances LO16-2 • factor • trade credit LO16-3 • long-term • capital budgeting • greater LO16-4 • Serial bonds • indenture • issuing bonds LO16-5 • new issue • dividends • primary market LO16-6 • over-the-counter (OTC) market • index